Leadership

Leadership

Practice and Perspectives

Kevin Roe

OXFORD
UNIVERSITY PRESS

UNIVERSITY PRESS

Great Clarendon Street, Oxford, OX2 6DP,
United Kingdom

Oxford University Press is a department of the University of Oxford.
It furthers the University's objective of excellence in research, scholarship,
and education by publishing worldwide. Oxford is a registered trade mark of
Oxford University Press in the UK and in certain other countries

Impression: 1

Published in the United States of America by Oxford University Press
198 Madison Avenue, New York, NY 10016, United States of America

British Library Cataloguing in Publication Data
Data available

Library of Congress Control Number: 2013947196

ISBN 978-0-19-964233-5

Printed in Great Britain by
Ashford Colour Press Ltd, Gosport, Hampshire

Outline contents

Detailed contents

PART TWO **Related Themes**

Guide to key learning features

Leadership: Practice and Perspectives **offers a number of learning features, designed to help you develop and strengthen your understanding of key topics.**

After reading this chapter you will:

- Understand the evolution of trait theory trait theory has changed over the past h

- Be able to appraise the theory critically- why this view developed, and what criti

Learning objectives

Short bullet-point lists clearly identify what you will learn from every chapter. This feature can also be used to effectively plan and organize your revision.

 Pause for thought

1. What do you think are the implication

2. Why do you think the theorists used t

Pause for thought boxes

Reflect on key issues throughout the text and formulate your own perspectives on the material presented.

 Case study   Ed Miliban

On 25 September 2010, Ed Miliband ups
He beat his older brother, David, in a tigh
members voting for him, found himself a
trade unions GMB, Unison, and Unite. Ed

Case study boxes

Plenty of case studies with accompanying discussion questions feature throughout every chapter, offering real-world context to illustrate leadership theory in practice.

Summary

Behavioural models began to evolve
theories of leadership which ascribed
hope, was that, with the right kind of

End-of-chapter summaries

Check your progress and recap on key points with summary sections at the end of every chapter.

Assignment questions

Apply your knowledge with end-of-chapter assignment questions that test your learning and allow you to practise your exam skills.

Assignment—2,000 words

- Consider a current 'leader'—you can cho
- Drawing on the frameworks outlined in impact on their leadership.

Self-test questionnaires

Investigate your own approach to leadership and learn more about your preferred leadership styles.

Big five trait questionnaire

You can either complete this yourself them to consider how they see you.

Further reading

Take your learning further with relevant and reliable sources of further reading found at the end of chapters.

Further reading

Stephen Zaccaro's paper 'Trait-based perspec issue: Leadership): 6–16), is a useful overview different themes to aid understanding of the s

Guide to the Online Resource Centre

There are a range of accompanying online resources available for students and registered lecturers. Visit the Online Resource Centre at www.oxfordtextbooks.co.uk/orc/roe/ to access all of the supporting content.

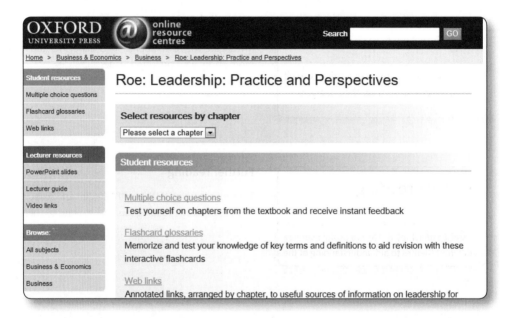

For students:

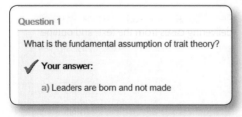

Multiple-choice questions

Apply your learning and test your knowledge with multiple-choice questions organized by chapter. The instant feedback ensures you can easily check your progress.

Flashcards

Memorize key leadership terms with this useful revision tool. Click through the definitions and see if you can identify which key term they are describing.

> **Roe: Leadership Flashcards**
>
> **Instructions:** Click on the card to flip it, use the buttons to view the previous/next cards, and the additional functionality.

Web links

Links to relevant and reliable online content will simplify your Internet research and allow you to widen your reading from a selection of authoritative sources.

> This is a link to the BBC's online 'personality test' based a
> http://www.bbc.co.uk/science/humanbody/mind/surveys/p
> 2013)
>
> Dr Jan Freed's view on why 'good' leaders go 'bad'. Sligh
> some useful research material. You can compare her vie
> railers'.
> http://www.youtube.com/watch?v=8olHsj04LLs (accessed

For registered lecturers

PowerPoint slides

A suite of PowerPoint slides can be fully customized to suit your own presentation style, for use in lectures or as class hand-outs.

> **The Big '5' Model**
>
> - Extraversion   through to Introversion
> - Agreeableness   ⟹ Tough Minded
> - Conscientiousness ⟹ Unstructured
> - Neuroticism   ⟹ Confident

Lecturer guide

The lecturer guide provides additional discussion points, suggestions for using and delivering cases from the text, and outline answers to the end of chapter case studies to support your teaching.

> **Case Study – The Occupy Movement**
>
> Question 1
>
> What do you make of the claim of the organization to b
>
> Themes to be explored here:
>
> How have you defined leadership?

Links to video clips

Links to a selection of relevant video clips can be used in class to encourage further discussion of material from the book.

> **Video Clips for C1 - Introduction**
>
> Chapter 1
>
> This first clip links to a talk that asks the listener to cons
> terms rather than as a grand event only displayed by 't
> www.ted.com/talks/drew_dudley_everyday_leadership

Acknowledgements

I would like to express my thanks to the following people who have contributed to this book. First my parents who, despite leaving school with few formal qualifications, somehow managed to pass on their love of learning to me; secondly, to my wife, Linda whose drive and dedication to our family has inspired me to write and study; and thirdly to my children, Abigail and Harry—their commitment to becoming the best person they can possibly be has been another reason for me to keep going with the book. Professor John Burgoyne, my PhD supervisor, was another who I need to thank for his wise council and quiet encouragement. I must not forget Steve, my brother; I wish I could draw as well as he can! Finally to those who feature in the book and my editors at Oxford University Press—your example and belief has crucial in getting me to sit down and write.

Part 1

The Basic Frameworks

Introduction

After reading this chapter you will:

- Understand how to 'use' this book.
- Begin to formulate your own thoughts about 'leadership'.
- Have a grasp of the breadth and depth of the literature and practice surrounding 'leadership'.

Overview

First the bad news; this book does not tell you what leadership either 'is' or 'is not', so if you were expecting this that may come as a disappointment. Now for the better news, the book will help set you on your journey towards finding out what you think leadership is. However, you may never arrive at a conclusion and even if you do, it is likely you will change your mind many times throughout your career. Why is this the case? Well, just pause for thought (*a regular feature of this text*) and finish this sentence: 'Leadership is ...' . Now go to either a friend or the World Wide Web and ask the same question. If you asked a friend what response did you get? If you asked a well-known search engine did you get anything less than about 1,730,000,000 results in 0.21 seconds? Leadership is rather like a UFO or the Loch Ness monster—many people claim to have seen it and yet the evidence for it remains illusory and elusive. The problem this causes becomes apparent immediately, for if we have this myriad of definitions how can we explain what leadership is about, study it, write about and speculate on it, and, ultimately, become 'leaders' ourselves? Most of the current texts, such as Yukl (2010), Northouse (2010), and Grint (2010), come up against the same problem with Grint putting it thus: 'despite three thousand years of ponderings and over a century of "academic" research into leadership, we appear to be no nearer a consensus as to its basic meaning' (2010:1).

   To show how and why learned writers have struggled to agree, this book presents a number of 'classical' approaches to leadership that have emerged over the past hundred years. The models are presented as discrete theories with some authors featuring in one section but not others. However, the reader should be aware that these very authors may disagree with this taxonomy and their place within certain chapters simply because many of their models and ideas do not fit into a simple classification but span different concepts. As Yukl (2010:30) points out, 'attempts to organize the literature according to major approaches or perspectives show only partial success'. However, for the reader trying to grasp the complexity of the topic, the 'chunks' of knowledge should assist with getting to grips with the subject matter before moving into some of the recommended reading. Following on from the principal models, the book explores some of the related ideas that have emerged, which add richness to the basic outlines in Part 1. Some of these concepts were not originally seen as 'leadership' issues—such as emotional intelligence—but have since been adapted to this area of study. The idea is to allow individuals a straightforward introduction to leadership and to help understand the 'vast and bewildering literature' (Yukl 2010:30) that has grown up around the subject. In addition, the related themes gather some of the topics the prospective leader will need to consider when formulating their own ideas on what it means to be called a 'leader', thus adding depth to the breadth of the study.

The models presented try to follow a rough timeline from the early part of the twentieth century through to more current models. What is certain is that this book will need updating within the next five years, as new ideas constantly emerge when different sociological dimensions exert their influence on how leadership is regarded. For example, one of the early approaches was Thomas Carlyle's 'Great Man' theory (see: Chapter 2, Evolution of the idea) which was concerned with trying to understand what personality traits were necessary for a man to emerge as a leader. What is curious, of course, is the notion that it was *men* that became leaders and not women. Gender issues were not generally the hot topic of conversation when the Great Man theory was being formulated, but as broader society became concerned with diversity in all aspects of our daily lives, so the role and success of women changed and the Great Man theory became unfashionable and consigned to history. Similarly, with the failure of many institutions, such as banks, governments, and businesses previously trusted by the populous, newer ideas such as authentic leadership (see: Chapter 8) have emerged with the further suggestion that this is the 'right' way to lead and, by implication, other ways are 'wrong' or bad. The point here is that leadership is a complex and complicated theme, it is being studied and updated almost daily with new ideas emerging from researchers, the media, and self-styled leadership coaches. This means that trying to capture the essence of what leadership 'is' or 'is not' requires constant thought, reflection, adaptation, and action.

In addition, we can see leaders and leadership all around us and it is these different situations and contexts that provide a rich platform to demonstrate the varying manifestations of leadership. Television shows such as *The Apprentice* and *Dragons' Den* amplify our exposure to business leaders; there are at any one time many wars and battles going on around the world featuring heroism; the global obsession with football has daily coverage of the managers of Premiership teams featuring in the newspapers. Leaders we adore one minute are pilloried the next—consider any football manager who fails to win a few games, or a president elected one year and voted out at the next election. However, it is a mistake to think that only these public figures can 'lead'. Consider yourself for a moment, you have made life changing decisions throughout your life—you may have decided to go to university (or not), to get married (or not), to buy a house or a car. All of these decisions require thought, reflection, and action on your part and will have had profound implications for your future. You will have effectively led yourself to this point in your life. Of course getting others to follow you may be slightly more difficult—or is it? The point being made here is that leadership exists in many forms, which is why it is such an interesting and fascinating area to study. However, leadership and leaders should not be viewed as 'gods' or celebrity figures, for leadership occurs in our daily lives and is carried out by any mature individual throughout their lives. They may not recognize it as such but by reading and reflecting on the theories and case studies in this book, perhaps each person can become surer of their own merits in this area.

> ⏸ **Pause for thought**
>
> Complete this sentence, 'Leadership means .... '
>
> Complete this line, 'This means a leader ....'
>
> Important decisions I have made in my life include:
>
> 1. ....
>
> 2. ....
>
> 3. ....

One thing we can perhaps agree on though is the phenomenal interest in the topic, for leadership is seen as a highly desirable commodity with organizations, nation-states, sports teams, and just about any other field of human endeavour clamouring for 'leaders'. Individuals invest heavily in their own development in this field, spending millions on books, courses, and seminars all alluding to the 'magic bullet' that will transform them into this revered figure. Professional bodies, such as the Chartered Management Institute and the Institute for Leadership & Management, as well as research bodies, such as the Leadership Trust, focus almost their entire energies into further populating the topic. Business schools abound and leadership 'qualifications' have proliferated along with workshops and courses that often involve outdoor pursuits designed to 'build your character and test your inner leader'. All of this energy is often accompanied by studying ancient writers such as Sun Tzu's (400–320 BC) *The Art of War* (see: Sawyer 2005), which details some of the 'rules' for fighting a successful war and is still studied by many military training schools. Alternatively, the book shelves are loaded with autobiographies from leaders such as Tony Blair (2010), stories about 'how I did it my way', for example Lord Sugar's (2011) *The Way I See It: Rants, Revelations And Rules For Life*, and 'recipe' books such as Covey's (2004) *The 7 Habits of Highly Effective People* (now available as a workbook, minibook, and a version by his son). The underlying paradigm being that by studying 'leadership' (remember no one is sure exactly what this is) and 'successful' leaders, individuals can become the perfect leader themselves.

Different perspectives

Consider, for a moment, the various terms we use to describe a leader. We have a Prime Minister who leads a country, a Chief Executive who leads a company, a Manager who leads a sport team, a Conductor who leads an orchestra, a Director who leads the production of a film or play, and a Prophet who leads a religion. All of these titles relate to the activity of an individual placed at the head of the organization—they are a label attached to a job. So even here we have a myriad of descriptions that are concerned with outlining the activities required of the prospective leader. Each of these people is expected to lead the organization to 'success', however that is defined. Failure to succeed usually results in dismissal regardless of any other circumstance, whereas success often results in near deification for the individual—think about Sir Alf Ramsey, who managed England to their only success at football's World

Cup in 1966, or Nelson Mandela, who led South Africa out of the international wilderness as Apartheid crumbled, or Richard Branson, who created the Virgin brand. In each of these cases success was put down to the individual leader rather than any supporting structure or condition. But Bones (2011) regards this as, at best, dangerous and, at worse, a disaster. He points out that the leaders of banks, governments, and business have conspired to create a future that, far from being rosy for the vast majority of citizens, is likely to have them working longer, paying more, experiencing more natural disasters, and generally having a worse time than their parents. It is the 'cult of leadership' as he terms it that has led to a real confusion over exactly what leadership is concerned with, as over the past decade it seems to him that leaders have simply sought to benefit themselves rather than their 'followers', whoever they are. He says the 'modern leader is egotistic, blind to their own faults, surrounded by people created in their own image and committed to actions driven more by the need to enhance self-image than anything else' (Bones 2011:7). This interpretation, as Grint (2005) suggests, locates or has leadership existing 'as a person' (Bass 2008:15), which means leadership is an act carried out by an individual—until recently, usually a man. This in turn means leadership equates to *leading*—an act carried out by leaders. For many individuals yet to explore the multi-faceted world surrounding these ideas, this may seem an obvious point. Certainly many of the early writers such as Bingham (1927) and Bowden (1926) would have sympathy for this leader-centric view which has the character and personality of the individual at the heart of the matter. Leadership was for them, and probably most individuals looking at leadership from a purely lay perspective, about a man or woman sitting at the head of an organization issuing instructions to a spellbound group of followers. This book gives an insight into these views and many other ideas from a broad cross section of academics and more practice-driven writers. Both perspectives, that of the researcher and of the consultant, are examined to give a rounded picture of how leadership has changed and evolved over the past hundred or so years.

To begin to shed light on how complex a topic this area is, consider for a moment the views of writers such as Arnott (1995) and theorists who support **'Attribution' theory** (see: Chapter 9). They go so far as to suggest that leadership is only a product of followers assigning positive (or negative) outcomes to a person sitting at the top of a hierarchy, when these results are simply a set of conspiring circumstances that have led to the phenomenon and nothing to do with any decisions made by the leader. This view suggests that leadership does not really exist at all, it is just an invention to explain a certain outcome. For example, consider the degree of influence and control Gordon Brown or Barack Obama (both elected leaders) had on the global economic crisis originating in 2008 and stretching through to beyond 2013. Is it simply a case of being in the right (or wrong) place at the right (or wrong) time? People rarely blame themselves when something goes wrong and often look for a 'reason' that can be manipulated to be someone's fault. This can happen even if the original judgement was to laud the person as some kind of gifted alchemist. Sir Fred Goodwin (see: Chapter 3) is one such example where he was, for a while, a knight of the English realm and feted as a banking god. Not long afterwards, as he became blamed for the disaster surrounding his organization, the Royal Bank of Scotland (RBS), he was driven from his home, had his children taunted at school, and was stripped by the establishment of his honour. Perhaps as Tolstoy (1993) suggested, a leader is the wave pushed ahead by the ship, and when the ship stops, there is no wave and so no leader.

Part 1—Overview of different approaches to leadership

As pointed out, this book offers an insight into various different ideas that have emerged to help understand the leadership phenomenon. Each of these approaches have merits and drawbacks, and by examining each of them the reader is encouraged to use these ideas to reflect and shape their own personal approach to a highly individualized subject. However, what is certain is that simply thinking about leadership does not help an individual become a leader. There needs to be action, and the text certainly tries to encourage the reader to think but also to take action after the thought. Go back to your original definitions of leadership and leaders. Look again at how you have defined these two areas and examine the following outlines so you can begin to grasp some of the implications for your starting point.

Traits and characteristics

Did your definitions have any words or phrases like 'ability to', 'values', and 'character'? Do you view leadership as something 'done' by someone who is born with some abilities or attributes that mean they have a natural propensity to lead? For this reason some people can just lead, they are 'naturals'. Just as David Beckham is a 'natural' footballer, Winston Churchill was born to lead his country during the Second World War and Joan of Arc to lead the French against the English invaders. It is who you are that enables you to lead. If so, it is likely your starting point is to have some empathy with one of the earliest approaches to studying leadership, which is known as the Trait Approach. This approach attributes success in any field of endeavour to the characteristics of the person in charge of, at the head of, or somehow responsible for the outcomes of the organization. It does not matter if that 'organization' is a company, an army, a nation-state, a football team, or a primary school, the reason things go well is down to the personality of the guy or woman at the top. Intervening environmental variables or circumstance is either incidental or ignored, and it is the personality of the leader which persuades people to bend to their will and perform acts they would not have done otherwise. The leader is directly responsible for success or for steering 'the ship straight onto the rocks of catastrophe' (Grint 2011:5). The leader has been born to lead—this is a case of 'nature' being more powerful than 'nurture'. A typical supporter of this approach would be someone like the decorated American, Admiral Arleigh Burke, who said, 'leadership is understanding people and involving them to help you do a job. That takes all of the good characteristics, like integrity, dedication of purpose, selflessness, knowledge, skill, implacability, as well as determination not to accept failure' (Montor 1998:18). Here we have a typical list of traits that Burke thinks are necessary to become a leader. This approach of trying to identify the golden traits of leadership occupied the minds of researchers for around 50 years. The search proved ultimately fruitless and the academic community turned its attention to other ideas that moved away from leadership being about who you were, to more about what you did and how you did it.

The reason for this starts to become clearer if you consider, for a moment, the traits that you consider necessary to become a good leader or even how individuals gain such labels and become associated with success. If, for example, you were asked to name the individuals responsible for leading the experiments that discovered DNA, the building block of life itself, most people would name Crick and Watson, who studied at Cambridge and are widely accredited with uncovering the double helix shape of the molecule. Few, though, will know the name of Rosalind Franklin who formed part of the loose confederation of scientists investigating the subject in the early 1950s and worked with Crick and Watson at Cambridge. Franklin was capable of producing brilliant X-Rays, which were the key to uncovering the structure of the molecule, and she had initiated a series of experiments designed to uncover the shape of DNA. She wrote up her experiments and thoughts in non-confidential papers which were read by Crick and Watson and gave them the raw material from which they eventually drew their conclusion. Crick and Watson rather be-grudgingly acknowledged her work, and others in the team, in a letter to *Nature* magazine in 1953: 'We have also been stimulated by a knowledge of the general nature of the un-published results and ideas of Dr. M. H. F. Wilkins, Dr. R. E. Franklin, and their co-workers at King's College, London' (Judson 1986:57). In speculating why the two men gained the Nobel Prize and yet she remains barely remembered outside specialist circles, perhaps it is instructive to note Watson's remarks about her being rather standoffish, a woman who took little interest in her personal appearance and did not, to use a more modern term, 'network' well (*note that, although Franklin was jointly awarded the prize with Crick and Watson, she had already died by the time the award was made and Nobel rules prevent posthumous awards*). Franklin's personality and sex made it unlikely that she was going to receive the same accolades as the two men despite it being her pictures and experiments that led to the ultimate discovery. The point of this story is to illustrate that individuals can become labelled as 'leaders' when their success is down to other circumstances and not their personality traits. Likewise, a person with intelligence, knowledge, skill, integrity, selflessness, and purpose (i.e. all of Burke's list) can somehow be missed by history's Award Board. Leadership is something more than a collection of traits—however virtuous those traits are or noble the person is who holds them. Leaders are more than a set of ingredients in a recipe for a cake.

Behavioural models, leadership, and management

Chapter 3 examines not who a leader is, but how a leader behaves. As researchers became more and more exasperated by the search for a set of traits, attention was turned towards how leaders spend their time resolving some of the organizational dilemmas that face them (Rickards 2012). For example, how do they make sure resources are allocated to the right areas? How do they resolve conflict between followers? How do they ensure the organization is doing the right things and following the right strategy? These researchers looked at different contexts and began to come up against another problem—that of management and leader-ship. The concern and continuing debate is to understand the relationship between these two organizational functions and to what extent they are different or the same.

The etymology (root) of the word 'lead' can be traced back to a number of old languages that have phrases such as 'showing the way', 'guiding to safety', and 'the person at the front', whereas 'manager' has its origin in the Latin word for hand (*manus*). It became associated with the task of moving, controlling, and training horses (the Italian word is *maneggiare*) and slowly worked its way into the general lexicon of business. The early writers studying successful organizations, such as Fayol (1916) and Taylor (1911), brought to the mainstream thought the notion of management and organization as the key and the 'right' way to build a successful business. Leadership and management began to mean different things and many writers maintain that they are fundamentally different activities. Kotter (1990) was quite clear that management was about administering the status quo and bringing order to the chaos that can exist within organizations. Leadership, on the other hand, was about change and innovation. He did feel that both were necessary within an organization in order for it to flourish and survive. Management kept things going along a given path and leadership defined the path. Leadership seems to be about creativity and has an organic feel to it—it relates to growth and change. Management, on the other hand, is much more mechanistic, with any number of metaphors being about seeing the organization as a machine that needs to be maintained by process (Terry 1995).

Yet the academic literature does not seem to reflect this clear blue water between the two disciplines. A quick glance at the plethora of available journals seems to suggest something else—the *Journal of Management*, the *Leadership & Organization Development Journal*, *Leadership*—as well as magazines such as *Professional Manager*, *Management Today*, and the *Journal of Leadership and Management in Engineering* all seem to conflate the terms, or at least make less of a distinction between them. Consider also terms such as Managing Director (why not Leading Director?) or the fictional aliens who land and demand 'Take me to your leader!', why don't they ask to be taken to your manager? Why, when you are angry with a lack of service or product at a shop, don't you ask to 'see the leader'? What exactly is the difference between these two terms, and does it matter that we define them as somehow competing or mutually exclusive terms? It would seem not only are the academics confused but the organizations and the popular press also seem undecided about what exactly a manager is and what a leader does.

Grove (1986:22) and Gardner (1986) both attacked this need to classify management and leadership as different activities. Gardner (1986:7) said, 'every time I encounter an utterly first class manager, he turns out to have quite a lot of leader in him'. Indeed, if a group of individuals offered the choice between being seen and described as either a leader or a manager, they would probably choose leader as this is often seen as the creative driving force whereas 'manager' has the association with greyness and a rather staid approach. Henry Mintzberg (2009) suggests this is wrong and that management and managers have been side-lined by the style over substance attraction provided by leadership and leaders. He feels it is time to get a grip on the prosaic basics of managing rather than being dazzled by the romance of leadership. In most organizations, individuals will find themselves operating in both disciplines with some of their time spent managing and other times leading. The behavioural group of ideas tries to explore this dichotomy and offers several different approaches that essentially aim to show that a leader can learn how to act like a leader by displaying certain behaviours.

If your definition contained any themes such as 'a leader acts ...' or 'leadership is a set of skills', then your thinking is more closely aligned with this approach.

Style approach

If your thinking goes along the lines of 'a leader gets the job done' or 'a leader likes working with people' then the style approach may have resonance for you. The style approach still has leadership located in an individual but, whereas the previous models seemed to consider the leader almost in isolation, the style approach begins to consider the relationship between a leader and followers. As with many of the early theory and theorists, this set of ideas is based around North American ideology and institutions such as the Universities of Michigan and Iowa. The early models were based on research done on US aircrews and concluded that leaders could be either *task* orientated—that is, they focused their leadership on getting the job done with the implied suggestion that people's feeling did not matter—or they could be *people* orientated, with the implication being the leader cared more about relationships than the job in hand. Various different interpretations have been developed, which add a degree of sophistication to the dichotomous approach, but essentially the view that leadership is about tasks and people has prevailed from the original experiments in the mid-1960s to today's organizations.

The development of this approach by Rensis Likert, Robert Tannenbaum, and Warren Schmidt added some subtlety to the model. Their approaches outlined a number of different leadership styles such as 'Directive', 'Consultative', and 'Delegative' as well as allowing a blend of approaches that moved away from an 'either, or' model to one where the ideals were not seen as mutually exclusive. The main theme underpinning this approach is to consider the focus of the leader's decision making. If the leader's decisions are crafted towards the delivery of an end result, and has a touch of 'the ends justify the means', it is likely that the leader has a stronger *task* orientation. However, if the leader's decisions are centred on group harmony as a mechanism for task achievement, then the leader is likely to be orientated towards *people* and relationships. As you may suspect, the opinion as to which approach produces the optimum outcome varies depending on the researcher. Likert (1979) has the view that leaders with a people orientation were more successful than those with a task focus. Kurt Lewin, on the other hand, felt the most productive (if rather unhappy) workers were those with an autocratic leader (Lewin et al. 1939).

Situational theories

The next set of ideas presents the reader with a further set of challenges because, on the face of it, situational theories seem intuitively to make sense. A leader's approach, claim supporters such as Ken Blanchard and Paul Hersey, depends on the situation facing the leader, and successful leaders can adapt their approach to suit the circumstances. So, if your earlier thoughts about leadership went along the lines of 'well it depends what is going on at the time', then you may have some sympathy for this perspective. However, the horns of the dilemma come when faced with academics who demand a more heuristic approach—just because the statement that a leader should *adapt* their approach sounds feasible does not necessarily make it true. The academics point towards a distinct lack of empirically derived evidence to support the claims made by situational theories. So those beginning an exploration of leaders are now faced with a further complication—in analysing the significance of the division between researchers who demand 'proof' and practitioners who have developed courses, books, and other material to support their perspective.

Some other attractions of this approach include being able to explain the emergence of leaders as a state of affairs unfolds, because it may be the case that a certain individual can match their style to the situation—especially if that situation is unfamiliar or has an air of crisis about it. For example, Strom and Eyerman (2008) point to the relatively ordinary women and men who performed heroic acts of leadership in the aftermath of the London Underground bombings of 2005.

Contingency theory

Some of the earlier ideas have hinted that the efficacy of leadership depends upon certain factors external to the individual leader. Contingency theory develops this theme by outlining a number of interacting dynamics that combine to show the prospective leader the 'correct' approach to take in any number of different scenarios. This means that if you consider leadership to be a highly complex set of judgements that relate to the nature of the task being faced, the type of people working with you, and the degree of authority you have to make decisions, this type of model may intrigue you. The ideas put forward suggest that a leader needs to take into account a plethora of environmental considerations before deciding on an appropriate approach. However, furthering the debate that rages between researchers and practitioners is the controversial claim made by Fiedler et al. (1976) that it is unlikely a leader would be successful unless they could 'match' their own traits to the demands of the situation. His organization has subsequently developed a highly successful commercial product designed to help train prospective leaders to recognize the demands of the situation and so lead 'correctly'. Unsurprisingly, this view has its critics who point out the conflicting data said to support this view and the implications for individual leaders.

What these models and those from the Style and Situational groups have in common is the belief that leadership as an act can, and needs to be, placed in a broader context for the full implications of the act to be accurately judged. They also suggest a 'right' way and, by implication, there must be a 'wrong' way. However, critics of these approaches suggest the models fail to show *how* a leader may change style to meet different situations. In addition, the approaches, if taken literally, can produce a bewildering array of options for a leader who may be facing an urgent decision without the luxury of reflection or consideration about the 'right' approach.

Charisma and Transformational theory

These ideas are interesting in that they purport to take a different tack, whilst simultaneously harking back to the earlier work around traits. Transformational leadership suggests that leadership is related to an almost messianic approach, changing workers and followers into avid disciples whose hearts and minds have been inspired by an internalized belief in the veracity of the leader's decisions. This contrasts sharply with the *transactional* approaches taken earlier whereby a leader exchanges something (e.g. money or 'favour') for the obedience and compliance of the followers. In order to achieve this transformation from a sullen, acquiescent crowd to an enthusiastic, fervent team, a leader may need to possess the rarest of traits—that of charisma.

So, if your definition of leadership brought to mind some strong, powerful images of a person such as Nelson Mandela, Mahatma Ghandi, or Barack Obama, then you should read Chapter 7 carefully, for this approach has a darker side. Consider, for a moment, other 'charismatic' figures, such as Adolf Hitler, Jimmy Jones, or Josef Stalin, and you begin to encounter some concerns about wanting leaders to be charismatic, for these individuals were able to persuade many ordinary men, women, and children to commit acts of brutality that still shock today. The ability to convince others they are following a higher morality and therefore have 'god' on their side, has powered many a despotic crusade. Bass and Avolio (1997) call this 'pseudo charisma', as the leader controls the followers and guides them to their own ends rather than a broader social benefit.

It is with this set of ideas that many, such as Bones (2011) discussed earlier, have the most difficulty as they claim that the pursuit and deification of the charismatic leader has led many societies and organizations to ruin. However, the subtlety introduced by the concept of Trans-formational leadership is said to satisfy this concern by ensuring that such leaders address the broader demands of society when identifying their vision for the future. More recently, Bass and various colleagues (e.g. Bass and Riggio 2006; Kirkbride 2006) have outlined a further model where the leader can range from transactional through to transformational with the added dimension of a passive-avoidant/non-leadership mode. This is called the full-range leadership model and has been further developed by examining how female leaders operate. Research by Vinkenburg et al. (2011) and Barbuto et al. (2007) suggests that successful female leaders are adept at displaying both transactional and transformational styles—a theme ex-plored later in Part 2 when diversity and leadership are considered.

Authentic leadership

The massive shake up in the world's economy fuelled by the banking crisis, further erosion of trust between politicians and the electorate, the ripples caused by the Arab Spring in 2011, and concern over global warming have all contributed to a sense of uncertainty over the future for many people. This, in turn, has led to a reappraisal of what is meant by a 'right' and 'wrong' way to lead, with many observers suggesting that leadership (or lack of) has contrib-uted significantly to many of the ills facing the world today and tomorrow. As a reaction to this disillusion with existing leaders, a newer concept has been discussed, which has various labels including authentic and ethical leadership. As with many nascent concepts, scholars are divided as to what this concept actually is, or is not, but if there is a consensus it lies in the thought that leaders should first know their own 'true' self and, secondly, act in accordance with that true self. This means that a leader should be open and honest in their interactions with others and value truth when considering how to communicate with followers. Consider your own exposure to leaders here—how have you felt towards a person (let alone a 'leader') whom you trusted, but was subsequently found to be 'economical with the truth'? Tony Blair, the British Prime Minister for ten years from 1997 to 2007, had his reputation for openness and honesty somewhat muddied by lingering doubts as to his portrayal of Saddam Hussein's Iraq as a state armed with 'weapons of mass destruction' (WMD). He supported the invasion of Iraq in 2003 partly based on the assertion that Iraq was poised to unleash these weapons on its neighbours and the West. He stated, on the eve of war, 'we are asked to accept Saddam decided to destroy those weapons. I say that such a claim is palpably absurd' (Blair 2003). Subsequent enquiries found that no such weapons existed.

To many, this approach may sound eminently reasonable and sensible and, if asked, most would say that they act in this way consistently across all of their interactions with other peo-ple. This has led to some, such as Avolio and Gardner (2005), putting forward the view that au-thentic leadership is not a new construct at all but something that should underpin any form of effective leadership. The empirical research in this area is still evolving, with themes developing around the definition of authentic leadership as well as some questioning the very nature of the 'true' self. This complication arises partly because of the interdisciplinary nature of these studies, with individuals attracted to the idea having different areas of professional expertise. Some are psychologists; others have a professional interest in 'leadership'; whilst yet more have a background in organizational behaviour. This can mean that it is difficult to agree on a starting point, let alone an agreed definition that would allow for meaningful empirical studies.

What is probably certain is that the constant evolution and development of studies surrounding leadership will continue to expand. The concern, as Grint (2010) worries, is that we may actually end up knowing more but understanding less about the phenomenon. This does not mean that we should cease to examine the topic, because, through this endeavour, we may begin to shed some light and help those engaged with the task.

Followership

The final chapter in Part 1 covers the theme of 'followership'. This term is relatively new in the lexicon of leadership studies and yet it probably resonates more in most modern organizations than ideas about the heroic leader. The thinking is that organizational success depends on a much wider group of people than one person at the head. This is not about denigrating that role but more about emphasizing the need for leadership to be considered a shared activity rather than being located in a single role. Chapter 9 considers the delicate nature of the relationship between the leader and followers. However, the chapter is not directly about team work—this is covered in later chapters. Teamwork is a special and difficult activity that involves subtly different processes, such as mutual sense making. Followership is more about the relationship between the leader and those who contribute towards the achievement of the organization's goals. If anything, the chapter has more links to Chapter 6, Contingency theory than Chapter 14, Leadership and teams, as the nature of followers is an essential part of the situation facing any leader. Finally, if the importance of followership resonates with you, consider why top flight footballers demand astronomical transfer fees and weekly wages beyond many people's annual earnings. Managers of football clubs know they are powerless without good players. Pep Guardiola, the manager of Barcelona FC, won the Champion's League and five other trophies in two years at the club. However, his team included half of Spain's World Cup winning side and the World Player of the Year, Lionel Messi.

Part 2—Related themes

The second half of this book supports Part 1 by drawing in a number of different themes to add depth to the theoretical ideas discussed. Some of these ideas were not originally designed to be directly employed in leadership teaching, but have evolved or been adapted to this purpose. Again, the reader will be encouraged to reflect on the ideas rather than to accept them as 'truth'. There will also be opportunities to question your own practice and be able to see how the ideas work by reference to a number of discrete case studies. Each of the chapters can 'stand alone' so the reader can choose to read in whatever order they wish and to move back to Part 1 if appropriate.

Psychodynamic approaches to leadership

Psychometric assessment and testing has been part of the human resource development industry for many years. It forms the basis of most assessment centres, team development sessions, and coaching interventions. The number of different tools available is huge and the industry itself generates over £1 billion worth of sales worldwide. In the UK there are a number of different organizations, such as OPP, who market the Myers–Briggs tool and SHL–the OPQ32, whose entire business revolves around these tools. It is fair to say the use of these tools and their fundamental ontological status is, at least, contested. However, regardless of this controversy, many organizations do use these forms of assessment in their leadership development strategy so it would seem legitimate to examine the basis for the tools and their place in understanding leaders and leadership.

If trait theory suggested it was the character of the person that decided their likely success as a leader, the styles approach that suggested leaders need to consider the demands of the task and followers, and contingency theory that suggested a match between a leader's approach and their broader environment was necessary, the psychodynamic approach suggests that personality is the key to being a successful leader. Supporters of this approach, such as Zaleznik (1977), expand on this by suggesting that psychometric assessment helps a person to understand their own motives and drivers *and* those of other people. They claim this helps leaders because they can predict what response a decision is likely to create. Having this insight can guide a leader to the 'correct' way of managing an individual. For example, it can cast light on why some team members prefer a quiet work environment whilst others need more attention, and so on.

Chapter 10 reviews two different approaches to psychodynamics to give an indication of the breadth of this field. The two perspectives occupy different positions, with one (MBTI) having a 'scientific' basis in that it has been used for over 30 years, has a bank of statistical evidence to support it, and is in use across hundreds of reputable companies. The other (NLP) has a more recent history, generates huge income from followers, and yet attracts disparaging reviews from those unconvinced by its veracity. There are many other models, theories, and tools, such as Transactional Analysis, in this area but, by reviewing these two, the reader is given an insight into its breadth.

One important idea that underpins this approach, and perhaps links back to the idea of authentic leadership discussed in Chapter 8, is the extent to which an individual is aware of their own strengths, preferences, and dislikes. Supporters claim there are real benefits to raising the level of consciousness associated with deep, hidden emotions and urges. In addition, if one accepts that personality is largely fixed (another controversial claim), then the key to being 'successful' means coming to terms with your 'true' self and understanding your reaction to certain events, people, and decisions. Psychodynamics in terms of leadership is said to aid this understanding and, hence, can assist leaders to become more effective by placing knowledge about the outcome of forthcoming events within their grasp.

Emotional intelligence

If ever a subject divided opinion so sharply, it is the topic of emotional intelligence (EI). The concept, popularized by Dan Goleman in the later part of the twentieth century, purports to hold the key to a long, happy, and contented life. It has since metamorphosed into a multi-facetted methodology of Hydra-like proportion worth millions of pounds worldwide. The concept claims that EI is a more effective predictor of success in life than how intelligent a person is. The basic idea being that by understanding your own emotions you can alter your perceptions of the world and also begin to manipulate the emotions of others to your advantage. The idea was not originally designed to be used in leadership development but now forms part of many courses, books, and workshops linked to this theme. The link to themes such as Transformational leadership is clear with this concept being associated with follower's emotions and the battle to win over their hearts as well as their minds.

Chapter 11 takes the reader through the development of the idea from the earlier work by Howard Gardner on multiple intelligences, through Goleman's popularized version, and some criticism of the concept. The point of this is to present the reader with a rounded view of the topic so they are able to make a more informed decision as whether to adopt some of the ideas or to look for other ways to develop their leadership approach.

Diversity

Chapter 12 opens by worrying if it should be a separate chapter at all. This is because 'diversity' can be an antagonistic theme with some authors considering it to be a defeat if diversity is mentioned as a 'special' theme, whilst others champion the need to keep enthusing about the need to incorporate different perspectives. The chapter looks at some of the reasons behind discrimination and how this affects our perception of 'good' and 'bad' leadership. The idea of social identity theory is also discussed, in particular how this shapes a leader's perception of 'followers'. As a separate theme then, we can see how these ideas in Part 2 start to play across the earlier, more formalized themes associated with leadership. The chapter moves on to discuss specifically the impact women have made and are making on leadership—almost as a counter-weight to the first idea in the book, the Great Man. The chapter concludes with a brief report on the GLOBE project which is an on-going attempt to consider how culture affects leadership.

Power

Do leaders have power? Chapter 13 explores this question and identifies a number of ideas associated with the use of power by those in a position of authority. The notion of power being a corrupting and 'dark' force is discussed as is the mechanism through which leaders seek to wield their power. Readers are encouraged by this stage in the book to consider how these 'related themes' start to relate back to their earlier reading. For example, how does power and the use of it by a leader relate to 'followership' discussed in Chapter 9?

Teams

Many individuals will have had an exposure to teams but not necessarily in a work setting. Sports teams, project teams, or even presentations can require individuals to collaborate and to work towards a common goal. Chapter 14 examines some different ideas about how teams 'work'. The purpose being to give the prospective leader some insight into the complexities and challenges faced when either leading a team or working as part of a broader group. For example, there may be a project team being led by a programme manager who requires different sub-units to complete different tasks. Each of these sub-units will need 'leading' as will activities within the broader network. How this is carried out can affect the outcome of the sub-tasks and the overall goal being attempted, and it is a role almost every manager will experience during their career. After asking the reader to think about what they understand a 'team' to be, and thinking about differences between a team and a group, the chapter looks at three different approaches to teams. First, teams are viewed as a collection of individuals with different psychological attributes which enable them to carry out different 'roles' within the team. This means that individuals with a meticulous eye for detail have as vital a role as the person who drives the team towards its goal. The next model views teams as evolving through a series of phases which require different techniques to ensure a smooth transition to the next period. Each period has different interpersonal behaviours associated with the interactions occurring in the team. Supporters of this type of approach point out the changes over time as an initially disparate group of individuals form into a tightly knit team. You might like to think about the first time you started work or walked into university. How did you feel about the situation and people around you? And how do you feel now?

The final set of ideas in this chapter examines the concept of teams creating and sharing a common view of the world. This is known as a shared mental model. This means that individuals within the team will all have a similar view of their environment, what they have to achieve, and their part in this bigger activity. This, in turn, makes communication much easier, builds trust and empathy between team members as they all work towards the same end. Whilst this coherence may produce a tightly knit team, there are dangers with this concept. The main one being the phenomenon of Groupthink (Janis 1972) whereby the team may make utterly disastrous decisions as their view of 'reality' becomes distorted. Advocates of this idea have examined a number of decisions by various American organizations, including NASA and the Bush Administration, to attempt to explain why poorly evaluated ideas make it into policy and action. For example, in 1987 the space shuttle, Challenger, exploded shortly after take-off, killing all its occupants. The launch was authorized by NASA and their associated engineers despite concerns about a relatively small component. This component, a small rubber 'O' ring, failed and destroyed the shuttle. It was actually discussed by the NASA team, but no one was sufficiently robust in their objections so the matter was swept under the table. The shuttle was passed as fit to fly—a decision that ultimately cost seven people their lives (Forrest 2005). The main message here is be very afraid if no one disagrees with you.

Change

Chapter 15 begins by acknowledging that change and the study of how organizations cope with this is a discipline in its own right. What the chapter seeks to do is to ensure readers are conscious of the role leaders play in change processes. The chapter positions 'change' as an activity—it is about the 'what' of leadership rather than the 'how'. During the chapter, the reader is introduced to the concept of Soft Systems Methodology and different change models. At the heart of the chapter lies the declaration that change requires a clear understanding of where the organization is moving to for the leadership to be clear on what the organization will look like and feel like for its stakeholders. Resistance to change is also considered, for change does make many feel threatened and uncomfortable. A leader will have a choice to make (as is often the case) between the task and relationship—getting the job done and managing people's feelings. Again, think back to earlier chapters on style to see how this influences leadership.

Leadership development

Chapter 16 moves from looking at individual themes surrounding leadership to a broader organizational setting. The development of leaders within organizations is a key theme in terms of ensuring the organization thrives. It is a specialist theme in its own right with practitioners having their own professional body, the Chartered Institute of Personnel and Development (CIPD). There are several case studies of different organizational approaches to this theme. In addition, there is a critique of how organizations manage development. The question asked by the chapter is, broadly, how does your own understanding of leadership shape how you would approach the development of leaders in your own company? So, if you thought leadership was essentially about 'the person', how would you recruit this type of person? Or, if you thought leadership was largely concerned with 'following and giving orders', what would your organization feel like to an employee? Consider your responses as you read the final chapter.

Strategic leadership

The final chapter in this book looks at the world as experienced by those that run organizations. So it is more role specific than the earlier chapters. The very need for a strategic leader is discussed, and you might want to think about your reaction to the very first case study, at the end of this chapter—that of the 'Occupy' movement. The nature of the external environment is also considered and how this has evolved and changed over time. Implicitly, the final chapter tries to address the concern expressed by Bones (2011) that, somehow, leadership either does not matter or that leaders have lost their way. Leadership does matter, probably more now as the world faces a number of serious challenges. However, this may be a daunting thought and hopefully the chapters will give the reader a perspective on their own leadership, self-identity, and confidence so that they are able to answer some of the questions that emerge when facing their own existence.

Conclusion

Having stated at the beginning that this book does not 'define' leadership, and risked it being put back on the shelf, the hope is that the introduction will encourage the reader to give it a chance. The chapters are illustrated by some diverse case studies to give the reader an idea of the range of people and situations in which leadership can be 'experienced'. The main hope is that it will inspire thought and reflection in a reader who will continue then to explore ideas and notions linked to their own leadership approach. Use the Pause for Thought boxes to do exactly that!

Case study   The 'Occupy' movement

On the face of it, Kalle Lasn (b.1942) and Micah White (b.1982) appear to be unlikely bedfellows. Lasn is a 70-year-old Estonian filmmaker now living in Canada, whilst White is of mixed race and edits a magazine called *Adbusters*, based in California. However, they are the drivers behind a global movement that has activities in over 80 countries worldwide and has countless hours of newsreel coverage. Their organization is called the 'Occupy' movement and it has, at various times, shut down areas of New York, London, and Madrid. The purpose of the group is to protest against what they see as an unsustainable economic system that disadvantages everyone but a very few rich and powerful people. Their motto of 'we are the 99%' is a reflection of their cause, which sees them trying to create publicity for their mission by staging sit-ins and camps in major financial districts such as Wall Street and Paternoster Square in London. The group states that it is 'leaderless ... by the people and for the people'.

In terms of decision making and leadership, the movement has an unusual model that attempts to allow as many people as possible to participate in the group's processes. At the heart of it is the General Assembly which, according to their website,

> is a gathering of people committed to discussing issues and making decisions based upon a collective agreement or 'consensus'. Anyone is free to propose an idea or express an opinion as part of the General Assembly. There is no single leader—everyone's voice is equal.

This devolved type of decision making takes the form of a large debating circle where a proposer outlines a particular issue and invites comment from the audience. After a debate there is a vote decided on by a show of hands. To add some subtlety to the process, the group uses a number of different hand signals to communicate their thoughts to the collective. To ensure everyone can hear what a particular speaker is saying, the group employs a technique known as the 'People's Mic' (as in 'microphone'; see: http://youtube.com/watch?v=becF8cn09pU (accessed 24 July 2013)). To use this technique, the main speaker speaks half of a sentence which is repeated loudly by the first few rows of the audience. This can be repeated if necessary to create a ripple effect ensuring the information reaches the very back of the audience. If there is no physical gathering, the group uses the internet and local websites to communicate with its supporters

If there is a particularly important decision to be debated, the group splits into smaller working parties and reports their thoughts back to the main group. It is proposed by the group that this leads to consensus decision making and involves many more people in the activities of the group. An added layer of sophistication comes with the concept of the 'progressive stack'. Normally, those who wish to speak are added to a list and called to speak in the chronological order they were added to the speaker's list. In a progressive stack, the order of speakers is determined by a different criteria—that of belonging to 'under represented groups'. So-called 'stack keepers' keep order and it is alleged that this process encourages women, gay, and coloured people to speak by allowing them priority over young white males.

Critics of the group suggest that the group is run by a hard core of anarchists who turned the movement into a version of *Animal Farm*, a novel by George Orwell that satirizes revolutionary leaders. There are also reports of fall-outs between members over the allocation of funds donated by well-wishers, and some disagree over who actually founded the movement in the first place. The progressive stack is attacked for being a 'forced' process that imposes a new form of discrimination on the group. Campaigners against the group also point out the cost of cleaning up sites after the protests. One such site in London is said to have cost £100,000 to return it to its pre-camp state, with nearly eight months of human detritus spread over the ground needing to be removed.

Sources

Allen, E. (2011) 'They've turned Occupy London into Animal Farm'. *The Daily Mail*, 2 December 2011. London. http://dailymail.co.uk/news/article-2069061/Animal-Farm-St-Pauls-protesters-accused-equal-others.html (accessed 16 August 2013).

Gardner, T. and McDermott, N. (2012) 'Occupied Territory: Protesters Move on From Camp in Finsbury Square … But Look What They Left Behind'. *The Daily Mail*, 14 June 2012. London. http://dailymail.co.uk/news/article-2159353/Occupy-London-protesters-evicted-Finsbury-Square-Shoreditch-Park-east-London.html (accessed 16 August 2013).

Lasn, K. (2012) *Occupy Econ 101*. New York: Seven Stories Press.

Lazar, S. (2011) 'Occupy Wall Street: Interview with Micah White from *Adbusters*'. *Huffington Post*, 7 October 2011 http:/huffingtonpost.com/shira-lazar/micah-white-adbusters-_b_996931.html (accessed 16 August 2013).

Orwell, G. (1945) *Animal Farm: A Fairy Story*. London, Secker & Warburg.

http://adbusters.org (accessed 24 July 2013).

http://occupylondon.org.uk (accessed 24 July 2013).

Questions

1. What do you make of the claim of the organization to be 'leaderless'?

2. What do you make of the 'progressive stack' and the notion of 'stack keepers'?

3. What does this case study suggest to you about leadership?

Trait theory: description, analysis, and use

After reading this chapter you will:

- Understand the evolution of trait theory and how the relative importance of trait theory has changed over the past hundred years.
- Be able to appraise the theory critically—that is, to understand what it proposes, why this view developed, and what critics consider to be its weaknesses.
- Begin to formulate your own perspective on your leadership approach and the implications of adopting this as a framework for understanding 'leaders'.

Overview

Napoleon declared that an army of rabbits commanded by a lion could do better than an army of lions commanded by a rabbit. Trait theory could be summed up by Napoleon's view—in that leadership is about the characteristics of the person at the top of the organization—whether that organization is an army, a country, or an organization. Whilst leadership remains, as Grint (2005:17) reminds us, 'an essentially contested concept', trait theory remains a popular framework when considering and studying leadership simply because its basic premise of a leader being born rather than created or trained offers us an attractive and spontaneous solution to this incorrigible challenge of trying to find a universal leadership theory. In addition, trait theory asks us to focus on the *person* occupying a leadership role when considering the efficacy of that individual as a 'leader', rather than the support structures, circumstances, followers, or wider environment that surround that person. Again, this is a relatively easy task given the media's preoccupation with the theme and the frequency of 'leadership battles' that make such attractive television. One has only to consider programmes, such as *The Apprentice*, the coverage given to political battles, such as the leadership election for the Pope in 2013, and sporting events, such as golf's bi-annual Ryder Cup, to begin to grasp the somewhat obsessive preoccupation we have with this peculiar theme.

Most people, when asked to think about leadership, will immediately have a mental image of what they consider to be a 'leader' in their mind's eye. The choice of this 'chosen one' will often be influenced by factors such as their own cultural heritage, life experiences, and current media opinion. However, what is likely to be consistent is that this mental image will be of a real person, such as Margaret Thatcher, Winston Churchill, or perhaps even Steven Gerard, the Liverpool FC and England football captain. The person will have been chosen because, for the interviewee, this person displays behaviours that are admired by the interviewee and which have become associated with 'leadership' in their mind. It is assumed by the interviewee that these behaviours are the result of the subject's personality. Trait theory is an attempt to link an individual's personality with leadership behaviour and suggests that leaders are born rather than 'made'. This chapter examines the historical evolution of this theory, its strengths and weaknesses, and asks if it still has a place in the development of leadership studies.

Evolution of the idea

In its most reduced state, leadership **trait** theory is essentially the idea that people are born with certain character traits (such as self-confidence or extroversion) or qualities and these particular traits offer those that possess them innate abilities. Since certain traits are associated with proficient leadership, it also assumes that if you could identify people with the 'correct' traits, you would be able to identify leaders and people with leadership potential. Researchers in the twentieth century, such as Munson (1921) and Bingham (1927), tried to examine political, military, and other 'leaders' to see if they could distil the essence of these individuals to create what had become known as a 'Great Man' (Carlyle 1849). The thinking at the time was that there could be a common link between such individuals as Attila the Hun, Joan of Arc, George Washington, and the like. If this common link could be established, then both the identification of potential new leaders could be nurtured and the development of leaders would be much more effective.

> A **trait** is defined by Saul Kassin (2003) as habitual patterns of behaviour, thought, and emotion. According to this perspective, traits are relatively stable over time, differ among individuals (e.g. some people are outgoing whereas others are shy), and influence behaviour.

Typical of this work is Gardner's approach outlined in Table 2.1. He studied a large number of North American organizations and leaders and came to the conclusion that there were some qualities or attributes that did appear to mean that a leader in one situation could lead in another. The list seems at first glance to be quite reasonable—it would be difficult to conceive of a leader who did not display self-confidence, for example. In addition, when considering those individuals such as Ghandi, Mandela, and Mother Theresa of Calcutta, it is relatively easy to observe their behaviour and hence draw a conclusion that their personality traits must include the fulsome list as given in Table 2.1.

Table 2.1 Gardner's meta-survey of traits

Physical vitality and stamina
Intelligence and action-oriented judgement
Eagerness to accept responsibility
Task competence
Understanding of followers and their needs
Skill in dealing with people
Need for achievement
Capacity to motivate people
Courage and resolution
Trustworthiness
Decisiveness
Self-confidence
Assertiveness
Adaptability/flexibility

Source: Adapted from Gardner (1989).

However, this search for a common set of attributes with which individuals could be identified has had, as Zaccaro (2007) remarks, a somewhat chequered history. The search for unique properties displayed by the unique and idiosyncratic individuals outlined above proved to be a difficult and frustrating one, probably because, as Lord et al. (2001) suggest, the traits associated with leadership vary enormously depending on whether the leader is a sportsman, politician, military officer, or businesswoman.

 Pause for thought

Let us consider why this search was difficult.

Think about three of your favourite leaders—perhaps think about a sporting leader, such as David Beckham, or a politician, such as Angela Merkel, or a businessman, like Ratan Tata. Try to remember their good and bad points.

Write down the five traits of these people that, in your opinion, make them stand out as a leader. Now compare the lists.

In what ways are they similar? What are the differences? Why?

How much does your current perspective influence what traits you chose to focus on? For example, would a Manchester City Football Club supporter choose David Beckham? Would a Greek choose Angela Merkel?

Why do some people think certain individuals are 'leaders' whilst others completely disagree?

 Case study   Lord Alan Sugar

Alan Sugar was born in 1947 in east London. His family came from a humble background and he left school at age 16 with few formal qualifications. However, he is now a well-known media celebrity, successful businessman, and has been knighted. Lord Sugar's first success was with his electronics company Amstrad which he founded in 1968, the name being an acronym of his initials—**A**lan **M**ichael **S**ugar **Trad**ing.

By 1970, his first manufacturing venture was underway. He achieved lower production prices by using injection-moulding plastics for hi-fi turntable covers, severely undercutting competitors who used vacuum-forming processes. Manufacturing capacity was soon expanded to include the production of audio amplifiers and tuners. On 31 July 2007, it was announced that broadcaster BSkyB had agreed to buy Amstrad for about £125 million. At the time of the takeover, Sugar commented that he wished to move aside from playing a part in the business, saying: 'I turn 60 this year and I have had 40 years of hustling in the business, but now I have to start thinking about my team of loyal staff, many of whom have been with me for many years.' On 2 July 2008, it was announced that Sugar was standing down from Amstrad as chairman, to focus solely on his other business interests.

Sugar became the star of the BBC reality show *The Apprentice*, which has had eight series broadcast in each year between 2005 and 2012. In the programme, the candidates are set tasks to achieve. After being appraised on their performance and questioned on their success or failure, Sugar fires a candidate each week until one candidate is left. Although the format changes, the winner receives financial and mentoring support from Lord Sugar. The firing is done in a mocked-up boardroom and delivered by Sugar via a pointed finger and the iconic phrase 'you're fired!'

Critics have described Sugar as 'out-of-touch' and his work ethic as 'a model of bad management in the UK. Negative, bullying and narrow-minded ... [Sugar] rules by fear' (Behan 2007). Concerns have been raised by anti-bullying charity, Kidscape, that 'publicly humiliating' contestants on *The Apprentice* may give credibility to bullying.

Further links

Behan, R. (2007) 'Why on Earth Would Anyone Want to Work for Sir Alan Sugar?'. *The Daily Mail*, 13 June 2007 http://dailymail.co.uk/news/article-461607/Why-earth-want-work-Sir-Alan-Sugar.html. (accessed 16 August 2013).

Sugar, Sir A. (2010) *What You See Is What You Get: My Autobiography*. London: Pan Books.

http:// youtube.com/watch?v=vvMhv1nOvME&feature=channel.

http://kidscape.org.uk

Questions

1. What traits do you think Lord Sugar displayed in his early career that made him successful?

2. What traits have enabled him to move from being a successful businessman to a television celebrity? Are these different or similar to those above?

3. To what extent do you feel Lord Sugar's success supports or undermines the basic premise of trait theory?

Traits: a brief outline

Before continuing, it is probably worth pausing to reflect on the supposed nature of a 'trait' as this is fundamental to understanding this model, its implications, and how it can be used or commented upon. It is probably fair to say that psychologists are still in some disagreement over the nature of 'personality' and are likely to remain so for some time. This disagreement has led to many different interpretations of exactly what 'personality' is and how this evolves in different individuals. Whilst the exact nature of this debate lies outside the scope of this book, readers may wish to refer to writers such as Allport (1937), Cattel (1965), or Eysenck (1991) if a more in-depth analysis is deemed necessary. Trait theorists such as Allport believe that an individual's behaviour can be explained by an understanding of their *traits*—which can be defined as habitual patterns of behaviour, thought, and emotion. According to this perspective, traits are relatively stable over time, differ among individuals (e.g. some people are outgoing whereas others are shy), and hence these attributes influence behaviour.

However this is by no means a universally accepted view of human characteristics and there are many different alternative explanations put forward to explicate the unique nature of human beings. For example, Jung's (1971) work taken forward by Katherine Briggs and her daughter, Isabel Myers, suggested humans are characterized by personality *types* (see: Chapter 10: Myers–Briggs Type Indicator—MBTI). In essence, the difference between these two views is that, generally speaking, type theorists have a much more dichotomous view of personality with an individual being attributed with being *either* an introvert (for example) *or* an extrovert (see: Figure 2.1). Whereas trait theorists would suggest there is a continuum at work (see: Figure 2.2) and an individual can as such be *more* or *less* than another person in terms of these, and multiple other, descriptors.

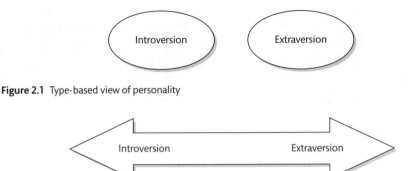

Figure 2.1 Type-based view of personality

Figure 2.2 Trait-based view of personality

Type theory enables researchers to classify individuals using an appropriate model such as the 16 types made available in the Myers–Briggs approach. Type theory means we can post individuals into certain categories and make assumptions about their likely response to a given stimulus. Each of the 16 Myers–Briggs types have certain characteristics that are said by proponents to be common and shared by others within the same type 'box'. The trait approach does not use this type of taxonomy and, as such, does not 'allocate' individuals to a predetermined descriptive classification.

Even more confusing is the debate that rages over what are the traits that make up the 'core' of human personality as there is disagreement between the advocates of trait theory as to what the key traits could be. However, more recently there has been the emergence of a model now called the 'Big Five Model' (see: Table 2.2) which tries to distil the various ideas into one useable framework. Whilst the origin of this model is contested, Digman (1990) suggests it should be attributed to the early work of two US Air Force researchers, Ernest Tupes and Raymond Cristal (1961). It is important to remember the central theme of trait theory—the continuum. This means that for each of these five traits, there exists a hypothetical scale with 'High' at one extreme and 'Low' at the other. Psychologists also use more descriptive phrases where appropriate, such as 'introvert' and 'extrovert' to describe individuals at the opposite ends of the dimension. There is a popular (and free) assessment tool available for individuals to assess their position on these scales—it is called the International Personality Item Pool (IPIP) (see: http://www.personal.psu.edu/j5j/IPIP/).

This approach suggests that an individual's core attributes can be complex and multifaceted. However, if consideration is given to these five traits then a prediction can be made as to the likely personality of any given individual and, hence, their suitability to take on a particular role.

Having distilled the essence of the human personality into five components, researchers such as Judge et al. (2002) could begin to try to see if there was any link between these characteristics and leadership. This work continues with psychologists (for example, see Boyce et al. 2010; Digman 1990) rather than management researchers examining personality and leadership or group dynamics. The model has now also extended to the investigation of the behaviour of 'followers' (see: Mushonga and Torrance 2008) which is a topic covered in Chapter 9.

Table 2.2 The 'Big Five Model', also known as OCEAN or CANOE

Factor	Possible behavioural characteristics
Openness	This trait relates to an individual's tendency to be open to new experiences and appreciative of a range of different likes and dislikes, more inclined to explore ideas and concepts. Someone with a low tendency might be described as rather narrow minded, perhaps someone who avoids new situations preferring to stick with experiences they know and trust.
Conscientiousness	This describes the tendency to show self-discipline, act dutifully, and aim for achievement; often displaying planned rather than spontaneous behaviour. A high preference would have behaviour that might be described as scrupulous, meticulous, principled behaviour that conforms to one's own conscience.
Extraversion	A person with a high preference would have the tendency to display outward, visible signs of energy and positive emotions, and the tendency to seek stimulation in the company of others. Whilst a character with a lower tendency, described by psychologists as introverted, would generally prefer to think things through and would appear to be quieter and possibly consumed by their own thoughts.
Agreeableness	A person with a high preference would have a tendency to be compassionate and cooperative rather than suspicious and antagonistic towards others. An individual with a high tendency towards this might be described as having a compliant, trusting, empathic, sympathetic, friendly, and cooperative nature.
Neuroticism	This trait describes the individual's tendency to experience unpleasant emotions easily, such as anger, anxiety, depression, or vulnerability. So, a person with a high preference could be seen as a worrier, emotional, and often upset or 'down'.

Note: OCEAN and CANOE are acronyms for the five trait factors—O = Openness and so on.

Traits and leaders

Running in parallel with the psychologist's view of exactly what was meant by 'personality', were the researchers investigating the nature of leadership and an increasingly frustrating attempt to link the achievements of 'Great Men' vide supra. Many researchers working in this area had run out of steam by the 1940s simply because they could not agree on, or find a consistent set of, traits that differentiated leaders from 'non-leaders'. However, it is worth examining two well-known studies from this period to understand what their research concluded and how this work has been updated for modern organizations and leaders. Galton (1869) and Carlyle (1849) both paint a similar picture of the Great Man, 'all things that we see standing accomplished in the world are properly the outer material result, the practical realization and embodiment, of Thoughts that dwelt in the Great Men sent into the world' (Carlyle 1849:1). In other words, the view was that these 'Great Men' were responsible through their own actions for creating and shaping the world. These individuals were considered to be endowed with a genetic makeup that predisposed them to 'leadership'. These innate, inherited qualities marked them out as 'natural' leaders that were truly born to lead. The implication of this view, as Zaccaro (2007:1) puts it, 'is that leadership quality is immutable and therefore not amenable to developmental interventions'. In other words, you were either born a leader or you were not and no amount of training or development was going to change that inheritance.

It was this view that leaders were effectively born with the requirements of leadership that held sway in both the academic and popular press for most of the early and mid-twentieth century.

 Pause for thought

1. What do you think are the implications for organizations if they accept this view?
2. Why do you think the theorists used the phrase 'Great Man'? What if you are a female leader?

Decline

Stogdill (1948) and Mann (1959) cast doubt on this view by examining more than 120 different studies on traits carried out from the turn of the twentieth century to just after the Second World War. Stogdill continued with this meta-survey and analysed over 160 different papers published between 1948 and the early 1970s. In this analysis, he claimed to have identified a number of different traits that were present in leaders that were not apparent in non-leaders. However, he also suggested that the presence of these traits did not necessarily mean the possessor would become a leader but that circumstance and situation were also a factor in determining whether an individual would become a leader. More popul05arist books, such as Gladwell's *Outliers* (2008), also connect with this sentiment by suggesting that circumstance and institutional structures contribute as much to success as any inherited personality condition. Gladwell cites the statistical anomaly whereby a higher proportion of elite Canadian ice hockey players are born in the early months of the calendar year. He attributes this to the fact that in Canada school and college level ice hockey is organized into calendar year age groups. This means that a young player born in January is competing against his younger compatriots born in December. Given the opportunity to develop physically, especially at the crucial point of puberty, these older players, being bigger and stronger, are singled out for extra attention and coaching, thus having a greater chance of success. The environment, not the personality, has 'created' the elite athlete, which of course challenges the view that Great Men will rise regardless on account of their personality.

Whilst Stogdill's stance was fairly strident in terms of denouncing trait theory in favour of situational factors, he did modify his position slightly in his later work by suggesting that traits and situation working in combination was a better indicator of leadership success. Northouse (2010) goes so far as to suggest that in fact Stogdill validated the underpinning premise of trait theory in supporting the view that personality impacts on an individual's leadership competence. However, what is certain is that trait theory as an approach to leadership began to wane as an influential framework after this critique.

By examining some of the major studies carried out by researchers keen to identify these key qualities, it is possible to begin to understand why Stogdill became so disillusioned with trait theory. Many studies—Stogdill and, more recently, Zaccaro (2007)—have carried out investigations into a whole range of different occupational areas and contextual frames. Leadership has been examined in military settings, in hospital emergency rooms, in sporting events, and in numerous organizations. These investigations used a whole number of different research methods from direct ethnographical observations (e.g. Chapple and Donald 1946) through to various rating or scoring mechanisms designed to associate numerical values with particular

Table 2.3 Summary of six studies examining leadership traits

Bird (1940)	Stogdill (1948)	Stogdill (1974)	Flemming (1933)	Bennis (1997)	Yukl (2006)
Accuracy in work	Intelligence	Achievement	Sociability	Self-Knowledge	Intelligence
High moral habits	Alertness	Persistence	Diplomacy	Open	Creative
Knowledge of human nature	Insight	Insight	Tact	Able to learn	Adaptable
	Responsibility	Initiative	Courtesy	Risk Taker	Extrovert
	Initiative	Self-confidence		Focused	Risk taker
	Persistence	Responsibility		Balanced	Openness
	Self-confidence	Cooperativeness		Role model	
	Sociability	Tolerance		Understand systems	
		Influence			
		Sociability			

attributes. These studies, carried out over a number of years, cover just about every conceivable location for leadership activities and attempt to codify the traits displayed by individuals operating in leadership roles. Table 2.3 illustrates the results of a limited sample of these studies.

What is clear from the sample in Table 2.3 is that there appears to be very little correlation or agreement across the studies. Grint (2005:34) supports this view when he remarks: 'No two lists constructed ... ever seem to be the same and no consensus exists as to which traits or characteristics or competencies are essential or optional.' It is here the foundations of trait theory start to crumble and the decline of this approach really emerges after Stogdill's (1948) review. Stogdill remarks, 'that persons who are leaders in one situation may not necessarily be leaders in other situations' (1948:65). This, of course, runs counter to the view that if you have leadership traits then you are 'a leader'—it is really as straightforward as that. With Stogdill and a growing band of other researchers, such as Jenkins (1947), now challenging that view, trait theory has slowly lost its hold as the universal leadership theory.

In addition to this theme, one of the other questions raised—and this is hardly surprising given the historical context when the approach had its heyday—concerns their apparent 'maleness' (e.g. Rosener 1990; Ayman and Korabik 2010). Remember the very name of the theory—Great Men. When men and women are asked about each other's characteristics and leadership qualities, some significant patterns emerge. One of these is that both sexes tend to have difficulties in seeing women as leaders despite women occupying some high profile roles in recent history. Leaders such as Margaret Thatcher, the British Prime Minister who served for more than 10 years from 1979, and Angela Merkel, the current (2013) Chancellor of Germany, are two individuals that have occupied positions of worldwide significance. The attributes associated with leadership on these lists are often viewed as male. However, whether the characteristics of leaders can be gendered is questionable. If it is next to impossible to make a list of leadership traits that stands up to questioning, then the same certainly applies to lists of gender specific leadership traits. In addition to this lack of universally agreed traits, complexity started to become an issue with various writers (e.g. Fielder 1964) now claiming that the situation or broader circumstance was the overriding factor that 'created' a leader—that is, a particular situation required a particular leader to solve or manage it. So, for example, a house fire needs a fireman whilst a successful company requires a competent managing director.

'Derailing'

Not every researcher dismissed trait theory, and investigations continued by individuals such as McClelland and Boyatzis (1982). Taking a slightly different perspective were McCall and Lombardo (1983) who, instead of looking for those traits that ear-marked possessors for a life of leadership, searched for traits that would prevent or 'derail' those with a predisposition or ambition to become 'leaders'. In other words, they looked for the 'dark side'—for personality traits that, instead of *enabling* leadership, would *disable* this activity. Their study identified five contenders, which included emotional instability, defensiveness, a lack of integrity, an over reliance on technical skills, and, finally, an absence of social skills. Their conclusion was that individuals displaying these traits would have great difficulty in performing well in leadership roles because these traits would hinder their ability to influence others. However, whilst many of these types of studies did use a number of strong empirically-based methodologies to generate their conclusions, Zaccaro (2007) felt there was little by way of a robust theoretical framework that linked the absence or presence of attributes to prescribed leadership criteria. Nevertheless, it is worth considering the 'derailers' to see if they offer a way forward in terms of helping leadership students to understand more about the concept.

1. **Emotional instability**. Here, those individuals struggling to develop effectively as a 'leader' were seen to be unpredictable in their response to environmental disturbances. This means that individuals could, on any given occasion, when reacting to an event, display strong coping behaviour one day and the next be prone to mood swings, anger, and bewilderment. This, in turn, means that 'followers' and colleagues find it difficult to form intimate relationships because this type of behaviour puts strains on personal networks. Followers become very wary of the leader, unsure as to how they will react to good or bad news, simple requests, or more complicated scenarios. The leader may fly into a rage or appear depressed or excited—it is this lack of certainty that undermines the relationship with colleagues to the extent that they are fearful of communicating directly with the leader, resorting to third party or indirect modes.

2. **Defensiveness**. Essentially what is meant here is that unsuccessful leaders were less likely to accept responsibility for failure than successful candidates. Observed behaviour included a tendency to blame others or circumstance for the failure rather than an acknowledgement of an error of judgement. Mea Culpa, and the ability to learn and change from mistakes, was missing from the makeup of the unsuccessful leader. Whilst a certain confidence in their ability is seen as a sign of strength, the research found that, should this become a barrier to learning, then failure often followed.

3. **Lack of integrity**. In terms of leadership, this is likely to manifest itself in an individual more concerned with their own personal aggrandizement than that of followers or even the task they have been asked to achieve. Broken promises, a failure to back up words with deeds, and a lack of trust can also be symptoms of this trait. The leader's focus is on ensuring their own success rather than that of the organization or the supporting team. Taking the credit for others' work and success is likely to be another sign that this particular individual may not be able to sustain a high-level leadership role over a significant period of time.

4. **Interpersonal skills**. Regardless of definition, most agree that leaders need followers. In derailed leaders there appeared to be a higher tendency to alienate colleagues and follow-ers. This seemed to be caused by the individual concerned lacking in empathy, often being

rude and inconsiderate, or displaying bullying behaviour. There was evidence that this type of behaviour was actually tolerated at lower managerial functions, where the leader's strong technical skills were valued more than the ability to generate a successful team. However, as the task complexity increased as the leader moved towards more difficult and challenging problems, the ability to generate a network focused on these unique and unconventional tasks became more important than tactical problem solving skills.

5. **Technical skills**. It is largely true that leaders were promoted based on their performance at lower levels within the organization. An ability to grasp and solve relatively simple tactical challenges is rewarded by advancement. The unsuccessful managers rely on this proven ability and grasp of the technicalities of their profession rather than developing the different and unique techniques required to be a successful leader. As a leader moved further upward within an organization, it was more likely that the problems they faced had very different attributes from those they solved regularly when at a lower or less strategic position. Unfortunately, unsuccessful leaders were seen to be arrogant and lacked the humility to accept advice and guidance, preferring to rely on their understanding of 'how things used to be' rather than accepting the complexity of problems that require unique, untried solutions.

There have been several attempts to expand this approach. For example, the Hogan Development Survey (see: Table 2.4) is a psychometric tool that aims to 'measure' individuals against a set of scales with the aim of predicting future leadership performance—or a lack of performance in this case (see: http://hoganassessments.com/assessments-hogan-development-survey).

Whilst this approach to uncover 'negative' traits—or at least traits that may be counterproductive in terms of accessing leadership—may have merit, there is still the fundamental question of coherence and consistency across related investigations. Just by reading the two examples from McCall and Lombardo and Hogan, it is difficult to see any agreement or similarity between their two taxonomies.

Table 2.4 Hogan Development Survey indicators

Excitable	moody, easily annoyed, hard to please, and emotionally volatile.
Sceptical	distrustful, cynical, sensitive to criticism, and focused on the negative.
Cautious	unassertive, resistant to change, risk-averse, and slow to make decisions.
Reserved	aloof, indifferent to the feelings of others, and uncommunicative.
Leisurely	overtly cooperative but privately irritable, stubborn, and uncooperative.
Bold	overly self-confident, arrogant, with inflated feelings of self-worth.
Mischievous	charming, risk-taking, limit-testing, and excitement-seeking.
Colourful	dramatic, attention-seeking, interruptive, and poor listening skills.
Imaginative	creative, but thinking and acting in unusual or eccentric ways.
Diligent	meticulous, precise, hard to please, and tends to micromanage.
Dutiful	eager to please and reluctant to act independently or against popular opinion.

Other writers, such as Roberts-McCabe (2010), attempting to explain leadership 'failure', hint at a broader set of concerns that may include changing circumstance and external environment. There has been much written (see for example: Blake and William Roger 1992) about Winston Churchill's rise and fall in terms of his political career and his removal as British Prime Minister in the 1945 election. This rejection staggered both him and political commentators at the time, coming as it did in the aftermath of his greatest triumph—the winning of the Second World War. However, it was clear that the electorate were tired of war and associated Churchill with this period. A change was required and, although Churchill returned to power in the 1951 election, he was forever associated with the 1940–1945 period. The question remains as to whether Churchill's traits led him to be elected in one particular set of circumstances but 'derailed' him in another. This theme is discussed further in Chapter 7.

 Pause for thought

Let us think about these 'derailers' for a moment.

1. Can you think about a manager or leader that you have come across that you have not admired?
2. Why do you think that was? Did the leader display any of these 'traits'? How did they manifest themselves? What did the manager or leader do to make you think they possessed these traits?

 Case study   Lance Armstrong

Armstrong (*nee* Gunderson) was born in Texas, USA, in 1971. He started swimming and cycling from an early age and, in 1989, he won his first race as a professional triathlete aged just 16. However, it soon became apparent that his greatest strength lay with cycling and, after finishing fourteenth in the 1992 Olympic Games, he joined the Motorola professional cycling team. His career followed a successful if unspectacular course over the next four years but his performances began to decline. Then, in 1996, he was diagnosed with third-stage testicular cancer, which had spread to his brain and lungs. Armstrong was given a 40 per cent chance of survival but, after chemotherapy and surgery on his brain, the cancer went into complete remission. Armstrong resumed his cycling career and married Kristin Richard in 1998.

From this point on, Armstrong's career remains highly controversial. He joined the US Postal team and, after a period of intensive training, he entered and won the Tour de France, thought by many to be the toughest sporting event in the world. The tour, which typically lasts around 21 days, covers 2,000 miles across France and travels through the mountains of the Alps and Pyrenees before finishing on the Champs Elysées in Paris. Armstrong won his first tour from Alex Zülle, by 7 minutes 37 seconds but, because several 'big name' riders were missing from the tour, Armstrong's win was not thought to be particularly significant. However, this view changed when he went on to win the tour every year for the next six years, meaning he became the only person to win the tour seven times. His work ethic and will to win was legendary, some of his oft quoted lines are 'losing and dying, it's the same thing' and 'pain is temporary, quitting is forever'. This focus alongside his physical attributes—his resting heartbeat is around half that of a 'normal' person—made him unbeatable during his time on the tour. In addition to his wins, Armstrong founded The Lance Armstrong Foundation, which raises money for cancer awareness—current estimates suggest he has raised in the region of US$ 500 million.

However, in 2012, Armstrong declared he would no longer contest long-standing drug abuse allegations made against him by the US Anti-Doping Agency (USADA). As a result, he was banned for life from professional cycling by the USADA and critics such as the *Sunday Times* journalist, David Walsh, were vindicated. Armstrong has been accused of doping and cheating ever since he won his first tour but he has never failed any of more than 500 drug tests. Stories of blood doping, frozen urine samples, and other nefarious practices have swirled around him for most of his professional career. But, whilst his competitors such as the British rider, David Millar, and the German rider, Jan Ullrich, were caught and banned, he always passed tests. He maintained there was a witch-hunt against him led by the French who could not stomach an American winning 'their' race. Whilst drug abuse and doping were largely endemic during the dark years of the late 1990s, with whole teams such as Festina being caught up in police raids, Armstrong always strongly denied any wrongdoing. His 2005 triumph was marked by his winning speech in which he said, 'to the cynics and sceptics, I'm sorry for you'.

In January 2013, Armstrong admitted to the chat show host, Oprah Winfrey, that he had taken performance-enhancing drugs. The evidence against Armstrong has continued to build with several ex-team mates prepared to testify that Armstrong not only took drugs but was also the ringleader in the team helping everyone else to dope. His supporters and sponsors are in two camps, with some wringing their hands over the affair as an all-American hero follows many other athletes into purgatory; whilst others take a different view, preferring to focus on his charitable work and suggesting his cheating does not matter when balanced against the money raised and the lives saved. Typical of this view is *Forbes* Magazine: 'The Foundation has helped 2.5 million cancer survivors with free patient navigation services. There are more than 1,000 grassroots Livestrong Day events held in 65 countries annually to support the cancer battle. Was it all a lie? Who cares. Cheater or not, has any athlete done more with their fame than Lance Armstrong to benefit people?'

Sources

Badenhausen, K. 2012 'Why Lance Armstrong Still Matters'. *Forbes*, 24 August 2012.

Pavia, W. (2012) 'Punctured Illusions as a Fallen Hero Rides Off into the Sunset'. *The Times*. 25 August 2012.

Voet, W. (1999) *Massacre à la Chaîne* (Translated as 'Breaking the Chain'). Paris: Calmann-Lévy.

Walsh, D. and Ballester, P. (2004) *LA Confidentiel: Les Secrets de Lance Armstrong*. London: Points Publisher.

Whittle, J. (2012) '"I'm Finished with all this Nonsense" – Armstrong Gives Up Fight to Clear Name'. *The Times*, 25 August 2012.

Questions

1. What traits do you think drove Armstrong to become the world's leading road cyclist?

2. Why do you think he is viewed as a hero to some and a villain to others?

3. Do you think he has 'derailed' or is he the victim of his environment?

So where does this leave trait theory and organizations?

Before completely discarding trait theory as an approach that can help organizations and human resources professionals to plan, execute, and monitor their leadership development and recruitment strategies, it is worth reviewing the strengths of the approach. First, the approach is consistent with a philosophy that defines leadership as being, in a sense, a 'person' rather than a 'role' or a hierarchical position. Both Grint (2005) and Northouse (2010) make the point that leadership can be conceived in many different ways, but usually involving a combination of situation, followers, and leaders. Trait theory asks us to focus on only one of these—the leader—and in particular the *personality* of that leader. This enables organizations to seek out individuals they feel will be able to perform leadership tasks by developing pre-existing attributes *regardless* of circumstance. The justification here is that modern organizations are in an almost constant state of flux and change. Therefore, trying to predict what circumstances, environment, and regulatory frameworks will be emergent in two or three years' time is difficult if not impossible. For example, despite modern forecasting techniques almost every commentator missed the implications of the failing sub-prime mortgage market in the USA prior to the 2008 crash. This piece of financial mismanagement began the avalanche that became the 'credit crunch' and the threatened meltdown of world's financial markets in 2008/09. This means organizations can try to recruit a certain type of person who displays a set of traits defined by the organization as likely predictors of future leadership success. It is likely that these traits will vary from organization to organization as a result of the different cultures prevalent within differing institutions—and as such this undermines the 'universality' of trait theory. However, it could be argued that, from a purely pragmatic position of helping organizations to recruit to a template, the approach has merit. Organizations develop 'competency frameworks' (see: Chapter 16) that try to describe the personality and characteristics associated with a 'model' recruit whether that individual is at a managerial grade, technician, or administrator. The hope is that, by making explicit their expectations, this will predict good future performance. This approach is heavily based on trait theory as it is ascribing traits to overt displays of behaviour and via a causal chain outlined by Yukl (2010:31) to organizational performance (see: Figure 2.3).

Figure 2.3 Causal link from performance to trait

Source: Adapted from Yukl (2010).

Second, using the 'derailer' approach discussed above, organizations have implemented ideas generated by the research at the Centre for Creative Leadership (CCL) (see McCall and Lombardo 1983; Van Velsor and Leslie 1995) which has given a different perspective. The concept asks questions about traits that are likely to stop an individual becoming a leader, and some organizations use these as 'negative indicators' that may harm an individual's progression through to senior managerial levels. Val Velsor and Leslie quote a situation: 'He was a bad people manager... A manipulator of people. He started creating a poor climate in the office, making the work life not productive. After several warnings, he was fired' (1995:63). So trait theory could help this organization by identifying those individuals with poor interpersonal skills and, if necessary, by developing an intervention strategy designed to help them develop behaviours that are more in keeping with the organization's value set.

Third, researchers, such as Judge et al. (2002), found that the presence of extraversion, conscientiousness, and openness to new ideas, i.e. three of the Big Five traits, did have a significant positive correlation with leadership effectiveness. There is still debate in this area as to whether these findings are significant, but there does seem to be a renewed interest among researchers to link certain traits with behaviours associated with leadership. Interestingly, this includes the field of gender, with Ayman and Korabik (2010) in the vanguard. This research emerged as a result of a meta-analysis that suggested 'masculinity' and 'dominance' were characteristic of those people who emerged as leaders (Lord et al. 1986). This may have an impact on the evolution of female leaders and is discussed in more depth in Chapter 12.

Finally, trait theory may offer organizations and individuals a chance to operate on a level playing field in terms of recruitment and promotion because leadership traits are not exclusive to either sex, race, social class, or educational achievement. This means that individuals can be selected and moved through the organization based on their innate abilities rather than for other, less diverse, reasons, such as being from a particular caste.

▣ Case study

The NHS uses a broadly trait-based model for their leadership framework. It is called the Leadership Qualities Framework (LQF) and has been used by over 180,000 employees since its launch in 2002 by Lord Nigel Crisp (then Chief Executive of the NHS and Permanent Secretary of the Department of Health).

Figure 2.4 illustrates the model and the format that is displayed to users. It is often referred to as the 'doughnut' and comprises a core and outer layer. It comprises 15 leadership qualities arranged in three clusters—personal qualities, setting direction, and delivering the service. Each quality is broken down into a number of levels which help to identify the key characteristics, attitudes, and behaviours required of effective leaders at any level of the service. In particular, the 'personal qualities' inner core contains five different traits that may be familiar to students from the discussion above; self-belief, self-awareness, self-management, drive for improvement, and personal integrity are the key themes. Whilst there may be debate over whether certain terms are indeed 'personal qualities'—for example, drive for improvement is a rather nebulous term—the NHS is committed to the use of the model across its 10 strategic health authorities.

The model is used to help individuals analyse their own position and it is linked into a development agenda whereby users can opt for coaching or mentoring, for example to help them improve in

Figure 2.4 NHS leadership framework

Source: NHS Institute for Innovation and Improvement (2005) *NHS Leadership Qualities Framework*: www.nhsleadershipqualities.nhs.uk.

(Continued...)

terms of organizational performance. There is also widespread explicit recognition within the NHS now of the direct link between leadership capability and sustained high performance. The NHS make such statements as: 'Management and Leadership talent is one of the most important assets of an organization.' This theme continues with a sentiment expressed by the organization that, whilst there may be environmental and situational factors, such as financial investment and technical knowledge, contributing to organizational success, these factors are irrelevant 'unless their leaders can utilize these resources creatively and effectively'. The NHS strongly believes that it is necessary for organizations to not only understand what leadership is, but also that it actively seeks to link this ability to organizational development.

Questions

1. How accurately do you think the model reflects 'modern' leadership?
2. How do you think a formalized model such as this contributes to leadership development in organizations?
3. What does trait theory contribute to such models and does trait theory hinder or assist the NHS in their leadership development agenda?

Further work

1. Can you find any other similar models in organizations?
2. Are these models different or similar to the NHS version?
3. Can you uncover any themes? If so, what are these constructs?

 Pause for thought

Before reading the summary, stop to think about trait theory and what you now think about both the theory *and* your position. Do you support the theory or have doubts? Why?
    Has your position changed? Why?

Summary

Trait theory was the first leadership approach to be studied rigorously and it held sway as the universal leadership theory until after the Second World War. Its basic premise is that leadership as observed in 'Great Men' arose as a result of these extraordinary people possessing innate and immutable personal qualities that preordained them for positions of high influence. Researchers used many different methods to collect their data and each researcher generated a slightly different set of conclusions that contained the 'key traits' needed to succeed as a leader. The consistent theme was that leadership was concerned with the study and understanding of personality.

This view was challenged and disputed as it failed to either generate an agreed list of attributes or to consider the effect of circumstance and situation in terms of identifying leaders from non-leaders. For example, Pedler et al. (2007:1) put it thus: 'Leadership is a doing thing;

a performance art. It is not defined by any set of personal qualities or competencies, but by what we actually do when faced with challenging situations.' As a result of this challenge, further research dwindled until recently when investigations, from a more psychologically driven perspective, have made claims to have linked some of the Big Five (CANOE) traits to successful leaders. Judge and Bono (2000), for example, suggested that Extraversion and Agreeableness positively predicted Transformational leadership capability (see: Chapter 7). Others, such as McCall and Lombardo (1983), focused on 'derailers', which looked at traits that would be likely to prevent an individual becoming a successful leader.

From an organizational perspective, trait theory is still an attractive option as it is often used by organizations to describe the type of individuals that could be marked for further development and aspiration for senior management. From an academic perspective, the work continues in terms of trying to establish a relationship between personality and leadership.

 Case study   Ed Miliband

On 25 September 2010, Ed Miliband upset the odds by becoming the Leader of the Labour Party. He beat his older brother, David, in a tight election and, despite having fewer MPs and Labour Party members voting for him, found himself as the winner thanks to backing from powerful block votes from trade unions GMB, Unison, and Unite. Ed has spent much of the first 40 years of his life in the shadow of his older, better-known brother, David, who was the former Foreign Secretary. He did the same course—Philosophy, Politics, and Economic—at Oxford University, at the same college (Corpus Christi) and followed David into a similar backroom role in the Labour Party, albeit on different sides of the Tony Blair/Gordon Brown divide. They both sat in Gordon Brown's cabinet, with Ed filling the less high profile role of Climate Change and Energy Secretary. Ed often used to introduce himself at meetings as 'the other Miliband'.

Given this, it is worth considering his situation and how he managed to become leader. His supporters insisted during the leadership campaign that Ed was more 'human' and less aloof than David. He is a self-confessed maths 'geek'. He was a secret *Dallas* fan as a boy. They are hardly Bobby and JR, but Ed had enough of a ruthless streak to challenge his brother for the job long thought of by David to be his inheritance; a move that both fascinated the media—the *Financial Times* called it a 'Wagnerian drama of a fratricidal contest'—and appalled parts of the Labour Party still bruised by the Brown vs Blair in-fighting.

During the leadership contest, both Miliband brothers made much of the fact that they went to an ordinary North London comprehensive school. Whilst this is true, their childhood will have been a little more colourful, and possibly more intellectually stimulating, than that of the average North London schoolboy. Their father, Ralph, a Polish Jew who fled the Nazi invasion of Belgium in 1940, was one of the leading Marxist theorists of his generation and a fierce critic of the Labour Party. Their mother, Marion Kozak, is also a well-known figure on the British Left. Their Primrose Hill home apparently played host to the leading intellectuals and Labour Party politicians of the age, with dinner guests including Ken Livingstone and Tariq Ali. The family's basement dining room was the scene of high-minded and often heated debates between major figures on the Left. The young brothers were always encouraged to contribute to the debate with their own opinions, and Tony Benn was even said to have given the brothers a few pointers with their homework.

Friends say the contest between the brothers was a huge 'strain' for their mother. It has been suggested that she told people it would have been much easier had they simply become academics rather than politicians.

(Continued...)

David and Ed's background helped speed their way into Labour politics—Ed spent the summer after finishing school doing work experience for Tony Benn, then a senior Labour Left-winger. Mr Benn would reward him years later by backing his leadership campaign. By their teenage years, both brothers were fully-fledged campaigners for Labour. Ed says he was never part of the 'cool' set at school, although he has joked that he did not get beaten-up too often.

Both brothers have said that the experience of seeing equally bright pupils, from less privileged backgrounds, failing to reach their potential had a profound impact on their politics and outlook. The more academically gifted of the two, Ed, did better than David in his A-levels, following his brother to in Oxford, where he became involved in student activism. 'My best four weeks at university were when we had a rent dispute with the college,' he told *The Guardian* (2008) in an interview. At the time, Ed was described as being less opinionated than his brother, who had a reputation for being fiercely bright but rather socially inept.

After briefly working as a television journalist, Ed was taken on by current deputy Labour leader, Harriet Harman, then a shadow minister, as a speech writer and researcher. He gained a reputation as something of a diplomat, whose skill at defusing rows was reportedly much in demand in the escalating battle between Brownites and Blairites. It is said that Ed would often be despatched from the Brown camp to make peace with Downing Street, where David worked as head of Blair's policy unit.

In 2003, Ed spent a year on sabbatical at Harvard University, to study and lecture at Harvard's Centre for European Studies, before becoming an MP for the safe seat of Doncaster North in 2005. Like his brother, he belongs to the generation of Labour politicians who, until recently, had known nothing but power.

The brothers have disagreed on Britain's war with Iraq—with Ed calling the 2003 invasion a; 'tragic error' and saying he would have voted to give weapons inspectors more time had he been an MP at the time.

There were no public rows with David during the seemingly never-ending series of leadership hustings around the country, but, as the election contest for leader reached its climax, and it became increasingly clear that it was a straight fight between the two Milibands, tensions began to surface. In one particularly telling exchange, David warned Labour against retreating into its Left wing 'comfort zone'. Within minutes, Ed had responded by warning the party not to retreat into its New Labour 'comfort zone'.

Ed is more adept at working the Commons tearoom as well as dealing with ordinary voters, his relaxed demeanour is said by some commentators to mask a true killer instinct. Some worry that he was schooled in the dark arts of negative briefing during his years in the Treasury. He insists that the main attribute he learned from Gordon Brown was 'toughness'.

Sources

For more information see: http://bbc.co.uk/news/uk-politics-11316855. There is an abbreviated version of Ed's first speech to the Labour Party Conference at: http://youtube.com/watch?v=i0fYWp8DS50&feature=related.

Aitkenhead, D. (2008) 'Band of Brothers'. *The Guardian*, 12 July 2008.

Asthana, A. (2010) 'Ed Miliband: Profile of the New Labour Leader'. *The Observer*, 25 September 2010.

Packer, P. (2012) 'Ed Miliband Sets Out His Leadership Vision in Keynote Labour Conference Speech'. *Professional Manager*, 2 October 2012.

Questions

1. What traits do you think Ed possesses that David does not? Do not forget to consider the 'derailers'.

2. What significance do you think these traits made to his victory and David's defeat?

3. Could David have done anything differently?

Assignment—2,000 words

- Consider a current 'leader'—you can choose from any field such as politics, sport, or business.
- Drawing on the frameworks outlined in Chapter 2, analyse their key 'traits' and assess how these impact on their leadership.
- Conclude with your thoughts on whether leaders are *born* or *made*.

Big five trait questionnaire

You can either complete this yourself or ask individuals you know well to complete it. Ask them to consider how they see you.

1	Talkative—you speak freely with anyone you meet	1	2	3	4	5
2	Thorough—you finish a task before moving on	1	2	3	4	5
3	You get upset easily	1	2	3	4	5
4	You are easily distracted	1	2	3	4	5
5	You have an active imagination	1	2	3	4	5
6	Reliable—people can rely completely on you	1	2	3	4	5
7	You think you are considerate and kind	1	2	3	4	5
8	You are sociable and outgoing	1	2	3	4	5
9	Lazy—sometimes you just run out of energy	1	2	3	4	5
10	You are inventive—full of ideas	1	2	3	4	5
11	You get nervous easily	1	2	3	4	5
12	Trusting—you trust other people	1	2	3	4	5
13	Rude—you can be rude to other people	1	2	3	4	5
14	You value artistic and aesthetic experiences	1	2	3	4	5
15	Worry—you worry a great deal about life	1	2	3	4	5

Scoring

Add your score for questions 1, 4, and 8 together. This gives you your Extroversion score...

Add your score for questions 2, 6, and 9 together. This gives your Conscientious score...

Add your score for questions 3, 11, and 15 together. This gives your Neuroticism score...

Add your score for questions 5, 10, and 14 together. This gives your Openness score...

Add your score for 7, 12, *reverse* score for 13 (5 becomes 1, 1 becomes 5, etc.) together. This gives your Agreeableness score...

1–5 is LOW

6–10 is MEDIUM

11–15 is HIGH

Further reading

Stephen Zaccaro's paper 'Trait-based perspectives of leadership' (in *American Psychologist*, 62(1) (Special issue: Leadership): 6–16), is a useful overview of the subject, and he proposes a model that integrates several different themes to aid understanding of the subject.

Jack Welch 'Bosses Who Get It All Wrong. Blowhards. Jerks. Wimps. How inept leaders can derail a thriving enterprise', in *Business Week* 23 July 2007 (4043): 88) is an entertaining and easy-to-read commentary on how poor leaders can hamper or even destroy a solid organization.

Nan Langowitz carried out a study in which he looked at more than 150 small companies in Canada to see if he could link their success or failure in terms of entrepreneurial 'traits'. It is a useful read for any student in an SME-sized organization (see: 'Small business Leadership: Does Being the Founder Matter?' in *Journal of Small Business and Entrepreneurship* Winter 2010, 23(1): 53–64).

Behavioural models

After reading this chapter you will:

- Be able to understand how behaviours and skills became important in the study of leadership.
- Grasp the challenges using this approach to analyse leaders.
- Begin to formulate your own thoughts by using the case studies and questionnaire.

With the concerted attacks on trait theory resulting in doubts as to the wisdom of seeking an answer to the Great Man conundrum, attention turned to trying to find a new approach to the universal leadership theory. The Second World War provided an impetus, as a large number of leaders (officers and non-commissioned officers) were needed by the respective armies. Leadership schools based at British officer training bases such as Cranfield, Sandhurst, and Dartmouth began to consider how best to address the demands being placed on them by their respective services. They needed to train men quickly from a wide range of different backgrounds to lead soldiers, sailors, and airmen into battle. Their quest, reflecting work being done by academic researchers, evolved into the behavioural and skill theories examined in this chapter. To some extent, the behavioural models of leadership are similar to trait-based approaches and yet they offer a completely different perspective. Behavioural models are still very much focused on the person. This means that the approach places the individual at the centre of any study and has a premise that leadership is about understanding the person rather than the situation or context within which individuals finds themselves. So in this respect it is similar to the underpinning philosophy of trait theory discussed in Chapter 2. However, whereas trait theory could be summarized by a view that states leaders are born and not made, behavioural models suggest that leaders can be made and they are not necessarily born. This is because the focus of this set of theories is around the knowledge, skills, and associated behaviours needed for leadership rather than any innate characteristics of the person being observed. If trait theory sided with 'nature' in the 'nature vs nurture' debate so often discussed, then behavioural approaches take the 'nurture' route.

Another issue to bear in mind when considering this particular model is that most of the researchers (e.g. Mintzberg 1973; Katz 1955; Adair 1973) who support this view do so from a perspective that places an organizational context at the heart of their studies. Individual leaders were studied using a variety of different methods but these studies were carried out within large organizations—albeit varied ones such as the US Army and the Swedish airline, SAS. This means that this approach also becomes embroiled in the 'management versus leadership' debate explored earlier, in the Introduction. The efficacy of a leader, it is argued by protagonists of behavioural theory (e.g. Mumford et al. 2000), comes from their ability to resolve organizational challenges by deploying a set of skills, demonstrating behaviours, and acting according to a predetermined set of competencies, such as 'leading change' (see: Chapter 15). The effective leader, it is argued, can learn these behaviours by appropriate developmental programmes such as training courses, role modelling, or executive coaching. Furthermore, organizations can define what they consider to be the required behaviours for their leaders and, by codifying these into a framework, can generate a 'competency framework' against which leaders, both current and future, can be measured and assessed.

This model soon became popular, especially with organizations and management development specialists because, unlike trait theory, it, in a sense, offers hope. The hope being that anyone can learn new skills or improve existing ones—for example, learning to drive or reducing your golf handicap. The approach suggests that, by first identifying a set of skills and behaviours that reflect 'leadership', a prospective leader could study these and, with practice, develop behaviours to match. Therefore, anyone could become a 'leader' simply by attending a course, being mentored, and role modelling an existing leader. This approach is fashionable, with many books being written that purport to aid the reader with their 'skills', for example Covey's (1989) popular *The Seven Habits of Highly Effective People* or Kouzes and Posner (2007) *The Leadership Challenge*, all adopt a similar stance—follow this recipe and you will improve. Pollitt's article (2010) is a further example of how training and development can develop leadership skills and hence behaviour in managers—in this case, a warehouseman trained to take on the role of a senior director.

 Pause for thought

1. Consider your idea of a 'leader'—what behaviours does he/she demonstrate? What do you think a CEO of a modern organization needs to be skilled at? Running meetings perhaps or deciding on the corporate strategy. Write these thoughts down.

2. Now consider how you would learn these skills. Could you read about them or develop a training course? Would a management development programme such as a Master of Business Administration (MBA) achieve the development?

3. Consider an organization you are familiar with. How do they define 'leadership'? Do they have a skills framework or a set of 'competencies'? How are individuals assessed against this framework and how does the organization develop its leaders?

Foundation principles

Whilst it is probably unnecessary to fully explore the world of 'behaviourists' or behavioural psychologists in order to grasp the underpinning philosophy of this approach, it is worth identifying the fundamental premise so that the relative strengths and weaknesses of the model can be explored. Typical of supporters of behaviourism is John Watson, who made the now oft-quoted statement;

> Give me a dozen healthy infants, well-formed, and my own specified world to bring them up in and I'll guarantee to take any one at random and train him to become any type of specialist I might select—doctor, lawyer, artist, merchant-chief and, yes, even beggar-man and thief, regardless of his talents, penchants, tendencies, abilities, vocations, and race of his ancestors.
>
> Watson (1930:82)

Here he is suggesting that, given a relatively young individual, he could develop that person into an expert in any given field. The subject could be trained and coached to act, think, and behave according to a prescribed model of behaviour regardless of their individual propensities. Essentially, behavioural psychology is a theory of learning based upon the idea that all behaviours are acquired through conditioning. This conditioning occurs via the subject interacting with their environment.

There are two major types of conditioning: Classical conditioning is a technique used in behavioural training in which a naturally occurring stimulus is paired with a response. Next, a previously neutral stimulus is paired with the naturally occurring stimulus. Eventually, the previously neutral stimulus comes to evoke the response without the presence of the naturally occurring stimulus. The two elements are then known as the conditioned stimulus and the conditioned response. Pavlov's (1960) experiment with dogs is perhaps the best known of this particular approach (see: Figure 3.1). In this experiment, a dog was taught to salivate at the sound of a bell. The sound of the bell had been previously associated with the reward of food.

Operant conditioning (sometimes referred to as instrumental conditioning) is a method of learning that occurs through rewards and punishments for behaviour. Through operant conditioning, an association is made between behaviour and a consequence for that behaviour. It was first extensively studied by Edward L. Thorndike (1874–1949), who observed the behaviour of cats trying to escape from homemade puzzle boxes. When first constrained in the boxes, the cats took a long time to escape. However, as the cats became more experienced, their struggles to escape occurred less frequently and

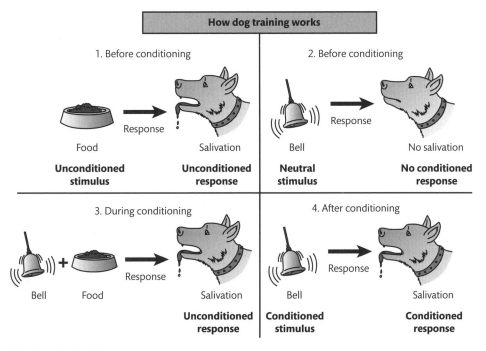

Figure 3.1 Pavlov's dogs

successful attempts to release themselves occurred more frequently. In his law of effect, Thorndike theorized that successful responses, those producing satisfying consequences, were 'stamped in' by the experience and thus occurred more frequently. Unsuccessful responses, those producing annoying consequences, were stamped out and subsequently occurred less frequently. In short, some consequences strengthened behaviour and some consequences weakened behaviour (Thorndike 1901). B. F. Skinner (1904–1990) formulated a more detailed analysis of operant conditioning based on reinforcement, punishment, and extinction (Skinner 1953).

This view of 'learning' is widely contested but that debate lies outside this book. What is useful is to understand is where the basis for the approach originated from—namely, a view that individuals are able to acquire knowledge about their surroundings by exposure to that environment. This means that individuals could evolve and begin to adapt to local circumstances (Domjan 2003). Extending this postulation to leadership generated the behaviourist school which has, broadly, two different themes—that of skills needed, and another that examines the roles carried out by effective leaders.

 Pause for thought

1. How do you 'learn'? By reading, listening, 'doing something', or perhaps by just thinking?

2. Do you think Watson could have moulded those children?

3. What impact has your experiences of leaders had upon you? Have you a 'role model'?

What are 'leadership behaviours'?

The first step to be considered is, of course, what activities, functions, roles, and jobs do organizations need their leaders to be effective at? Robert Katz was one of the first academics to consider the question of identifying what a manager needs to accomplish as opposed to a more senior executive. In his ground breaking article, 'Skills of an Effective Administrator'(Katz 1955), he proposed a model that had three basic developable skills—technical, human, and conceptual. These skill areas related to the ability of the leader to grasp the technical knowledge of their specialism (e.g. accountancy or surgeon); to be able to work with people both superiors and subordinates; and, finally, to understand in a broad sense how the organization works together, both internally and externally.

In addition, Katz proposed that at different levels within an organization, managers needed a different emphasis in terms of their skills. The overall balance of the three skills altered as an individual moved higher or lower within the bureaucracy with relatively more conceptual skill needed at senior levels than at junior levels. Figure 3.2 shows this changing situation.

Henry Mintzberg also considered this question of what managers actually did in his book, *The Nature of Managerial Work* (1973). Mintzberg mapped out the activities undertaken by managers. His findings contrasted starkly with the assumptions about the nature of a manager's world, in place since Fayol (1916 (trans. 1949)) described the world of management as a combination of planning, organization, command/motivate, communicating, review, and

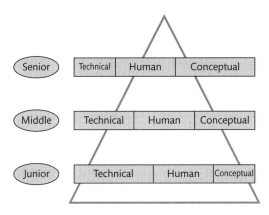

Figure 3.2 Skills at different organizational levels

Source: Adapted from 'Skills of an Effective Administrator', R. L. Katz, 1955, *Harvard Business Review*, 33(1), pp 33–42.

 Case study

Peter is a young graduate engineer working for a large defence contractor. He has a first class degree in aeronautical engineering from Durham University and has been managing relatively small projects as part of the European Eurofighter programme. He has been with his employer for three years now and has always had 'good' to 'excellent' reviews from his line manager at his annual appraisal. Earlier this year, Peter was promoted and he began to run a small team of engineers and commercial specialists. The new project was to design and sell a new component for the Typhoon aircraft. The project team had to negotiate with the Ministry of Defence (MoD) who had commissioned the project as well as manage a network of external suppliers who would be supplying the highly specialized electronics for the new piece of equipment.

Initially, the project went smoothly but before long divisions became apparent in the team with the engineers disagreeing with the commercial group about how best to proceed. The commercial group were under pressure from their customer, the MoD, who wanted to bring forward the launch date of the new product. The engineers did not want to agree as they were worried they would not have enough time to test the product, refine it, and iron out any 'bugs'. Peter went back and forth between the two groups, listening to each group and getting more and more exasperated by their inability to sort this out between themselves. Eventually, he called a team meeting where he laid out his frustrations clearly. He could not see why everyone was arguing and he told the engineers to deliver what he said was needed and he instructed the commercial team to tell the MoD to wait until he was ready.

This resulted in mayhem with both groups now effectively at war with Peter as well as each other. Eventually, a senior director had to intervene. After the project had been completed, the senior director asked Peter what had gone wrong. Peter's response was that no one could see the bigger picture, each group focused on their technical specialism and could not appreciate the overall purpose of the project.

(Note: Names have been changed to preserve anonymity.)

Questions

1. Using your current understanding of the behavioural model, suggest why Peter struggled with this project.

2. Consider what he needed to understand at his level of responsibility and what skills his director possessed.

3. What would you suggest as an appropriate developmental route for Peter?

control. This view of managerial activities had been taken forward by Luther Gulick (1937) who developed the acronym 'POSDCORB' to describe the activities of a chief executive:

1. Planning: working out in broad outline the things that need to be done and the methods for doing them to accomplish the purpose set for the organization.

2. Organizing: establishing the formal structure of authority through which work subdivisions are arranged, defined, and coordinated for the defined objective set via planning.

3. Staffing: designing and running the human resource functions of bringing in and training staff, and maintaining favourable conditions of work.

4. Directing: the continuous task of making decisions and embodying them in specific and general orders and instructions, and serving as the leader of the enterprise.

5. Coordinating: the important duty of relating the various parts of the work.

6. Reporting: keeping those to whom the executive is responsible informed as to what is going on, which includes keeping self and subordinates informed through records, research, and inspection.

7. Budgeting: budgeting in the form of planning, accounting, and control.

Mintzberg wanted to explore this and he used an empirically-based methodology to test out the view and to see if 'modern' executives still carried out their role in this manner. He employed a combination of observation and personal diaries to establish exactly what executives spent their time on when at work. From the collected data, he developed a taxonomy of managerial roles that divided the manager's activities into 10 main activities within three broad roles: interpersonal, information processing, and decision making.

Interpersonal roles

1. Figurehead—this is a largely symbolic role where the leader must perform largely ceremonial duties, such as signing documents for contracts, giving speeches at dinners, or receiving formal visitors. Often, the organization can become associated with the leader via this role; for example, think of Amstrad and Virgin associated with Lord Sugar and Sir Richard Branson, respectively.

2. Leader—here the role is to define the culture of the organization as well as providing guidance and role modelling for subordinates. The leader will be responsible for creating the conditions for work, integrating the various functions of the organization, and motivating the workforce.

3. Liaison—this is the networking role whereby the manager's job is to develop and maintain a web of contacts outside the enterprise. The purpose of this is to find and secure new opportunities for the organization to increase its sphere of influence.

Information processing role

4. Monitor—in this function the manager is seeking to understand what is going on within the organization and its immediate environment. He will be able to access information and data from a wide variety of sources such as the internet, subordinates, meetings, reports, and emails.

5. Disseminator—the manager will pass the gathered information down to subordinates. Some of this information will be concerned with 'facts' whilst other views will be more opinion based developed as a result of influence being exerted on the leader from superiors or others seeking to gain position.

6. Spokesperson—Mintzberg describes this role thus: 'to gain respect of outsiders, the manager must demonstrate an up-to-the minute knowledge of his organisation and its environment' (1973:81). Here the manager is transmitting information about the organization to its external stakeholders but this may also manifest itself internally where a manager has to report to a board.

Decision-making role

7. Entrepreneur—the essence of this role is to control and manage change within the organization in order to take advantage of the opportunities identified via the monitoring and networking role. These changes may be new product development, new equipment, or a new structure. Of course, these may result in expansion (e.g. purchase of competitor) or contraction (e.g. de-layering) depending on the circumstance.

8. Disturbance handler—this is a 'fire fighting' role where the manager will seek to resolve unforeseen disturbances in the organization. These disturbances could be a strike, accident, or other localized disaster. This role can occupy a significant proportion of the manager's workload.

9. Resource allocator—using legitimate authority, the manager will oversee three essential elements of resource allocation within the enterprise. He will seek to schedule individual employees' time, programme work, and authorize expenditure. By doing this he can maintain control over the strategic decision made within his leader role.

10. Negotiator—as a result of the decisions made above, there may be conflict between subordinates and other stakeholders, such as formal trade unions or other functional departments. Mintzberg sees the leader as having to work between these individuals to produce the best outcome for the organization.

 Pause for thought

What do you think about Mintzberg's list?

1. Is it still accurate or are there activities that he has not identified correctly?

2. What roles do you see your superiors carrying out?

3. What roles do you think they do not perform?

If you have a supervisory role, think about:

1. What do you spend your time on?

2. What does the model say about an individual's ability to perform these tasks?

As this approach gathered support, further researchers, such as Robert Blake and Jane Mouton, set out to apply the ideas of behavioural scientists, such as Rensis Likert, to the practice of management. They built on studies conducted at Ohio State University and the University of Michigan in the 1940s, which attempted to identify the behavioural character-istics of successful leaders. Blake and Mouton identified two fundamental drivers of mana-gerial behaviour as: a) concern for getting the job done—in other words, a task-focused approach; and, b), concern for the people doing the work, or a relationship approach. They argued that, on the one hand, an exclusive concern for production (task) at the expense of the needs of those engaged in production (people) leads to dissatisfaction and conflict, thus adversely affecting performance; but that, on the other hand, an excessive concern to avoid conflict and maintain good relationships is also detrimental to the achievement of goals and objectives.

In order to provide a framework for describing management behaviours, the two variables of 'concern for production' and 'concern for people' were plotted on a grid showing nine degrees of concern for each, from 1, indicating a low level of concern, to 9, indicating a high level of concern. Five positions on the grid represent five differing managerial behaviour pat-terns with the grid becoming known as the Managerial Grid® or, more latterly, the Leadership Grid® (see: Figure 3.3)

The model in Figure 3.3 is represented as a grid with Concern for Production as the hori-zontal X-axis and Concern for People as the vertical Y-axis; each axis ranges from 1 (Low) to 9 (High). The resulting leadership styles are:

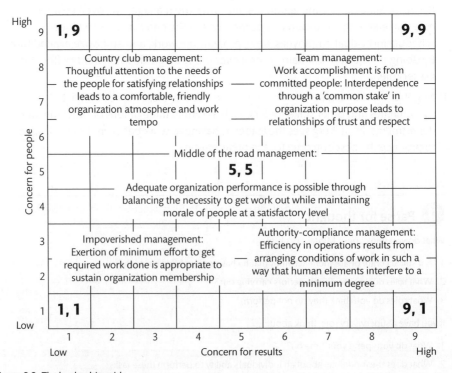

Figure 3.3 The leadership grid

Source: Adapted from Blake and Mouton (1964).

Impoverished style

The indifferent (previously called impoverished) style (1,1): evade and elude. In this style, managers have low concern for both people and production. Managers use this style to preserve job and job seniority; they may also be seeking to protect themselves by avoiding decisions. The main concern for the manager is not to be held responsible for any mistakes, which may result in less innovative decisions but certainly has a low risk threshold for managers. Colloquially, this is a 'keep your head down in case it gets knocked off' approach with the manager seen as unengaged with the workforce and apathetic to the demands of the organization.

Country club approach

The accommodating (previously, country club) style (1,9): yield and comply. This style has a high concern for people and a low concern for production. Managers using this style pay attention to the security, well-being, and harmony of the employees. Their belief here is that being accommodating to employee needs will increase performance, as everybody will be happy and contented. The resulting atmosphere is usually friendly and easy-going but not necessarily very productive as the development of relationships takes priority over the delivery of production targets. More task-focused individuals may also find this approach cloying and frustrating as chat, gossip, and social activity take centre stage.

Authority-comply style

The dictatorial (previously, produce or perish) style (9,1): control and dominate. With a high concern for production, and a low concern for people, managers using this style have decided that employee needs are relatively unimportant. Their approach is likely to be caricatured as, 'my way or the highway'. They provide their employees with direct rewards, such as money, and expect compliance and performance in return. Managers using this style may also coerce their employees through rules and punishments to achieve the company goals. This dictatorial style has echoes of Theory X developed by Douglas McGregor (1960). Often derided, this style may be appropriate in times of crisis or when a quick decision is required.

Middle of the road

The status quo (previously, middle of the road) style (5,5): balance and compromise. Managers using this style try to balance between company goals and workers' needs. This is essentially a compromising approach with the manager trying to avoid conflict whilst pushing for moderate production or task delivery. The manager's aim here is that by giving some concern to both people and production both outcomes are delivered. Of course, the downside is the danger that neither aspect is delivered satisfactorily, so both production and relationships suffer. The manager may also be seen as lacking integrity and confused as to where priorities really lie.

Team management

The sound (previously, team) style (9,9): contribute and commit. In this style, high concern is paid to both people and production with managers choosing to use this style to encourage teamwork and commitment among employees. This method relies heavily on making employees feel they are constructive parts of the company. The manager will consult with individuals, share decision making, and delegate tasks to the team. There will be an atmosphere of mutual trust and dependency within the business. Individuals are likely to be committed to the organization and recognize their part in the overall business process. Naturally, Blake and Mouton, in their initial development of the model (1964), indicated that this was the preferred position.

However, in subsequent developments of the grid, Blake and Mouton (1982) asserted that effective leadership was not as simple as choosing and using a particular blend of relationship management and task-focused behaviour, and that a more complex approach was needed. This led them to suggest two different approaches that they identified as 'Paternalism/Maternalism' and 'Opportunism'. The former approach refers to a leader who oscillates between the 1,9 and 9,1 positions. Here, the leader is seen as a kind of caring dictator who, as long as you do as you are instructed, will treat you well. However, failure to comply is likely to lead to punishment and ostracization from the group. The opportunistic style, which can be described as 'exploit and manipulate', seeks to ensure that the leader gains maximum advantage by using a different grid position depending on their interpretation of what is likely to result in the maximum benefit. This means that individuals using this style do not have a fixed location on the grid, preferring to adopt whichever behaviour offers the greatest personal benefit.

 Case study   Carlos Ghosn

In the early 1980s, Nissan was a highly profitable Japanese car maker and had four of the top 10 cars in the world. However, during the mid-1990s the company teetered on the edge of bankruptcy with seven years of heavy losses between 1993 and 1999. The Asian financial crisis contributed to their troubles and credit rating agencies were threatening to lower their credit rating status from 'investment grade' to 'junk'. The incumbent CEO, Yoshikazu Hanawa, gained an alliance with the partly nationalized French car maker, Renault, who took a 36.8 per cent equity stake in Nissan. In the agreement Hanawa negotiated, Nissan retained its own name, the Nissan CEO would be selected by Nissan Board of Directors, and Nissan would be responsible for its own revival plan. In addition, Hanawa asked for Carlos Ghosn to join Nissan as chief operating officer.

Carlos Ghosn was born of Lebanese parents, in Brazil, and educated in Paris. He spent 18 years with Michelin in Brazil and North America and, whilst CEO of Michelin North America, he led the merger with Uniroyal Goodrich. He joined Renault in 1996 as Vice President of Advanced R&D and arrived in Japan with the brief to save Nissan. He began with a savage cost-cutting strategy, closing plants and taking heavy criticism for slashing more than 20,000 jobs. His nickname became 'Le Cost Killer'.

Nevertheless, his plan to revive Nissan began to bear fruit and the manufacturer was saved from bankruptcy. This achievement sealed Ghosn's reputation and he is feted wherever he is seen in public. This fame even includes a manga style comic called 'The True Story of Carlos Ghosn' in which he is portrayed as a superhero—the comic reportedly sold more than 500,000 copies!

He has attracted controversy for his candour and for his demanding and sometimes confrontational style. He has also drawn criticism for investing heavily in developing economies, including Brazil, Russia, Korea, India, and, in particular, China, where Nissan is now the number one foreign car maker. By contrast, more traditional car makers focus on wealthy markets, such as North America and Western Europe, which are seen as less risky bets. His strategy for penetrating emerging markets includes selling cars with prices under US$3,000 and successfully commercializing affordable zero-emission vehicles:

'If you're going to let developing countries have as many cars as they want—and they're going to have as many cars as they want one way or another—there is no absolutely alternative but to go for zero emissions. And the only zero-emissions vehicle available today is electric ... so we decided to go for it,' he told the University of Pennsylvania's Wharton School of Business.

Ghosn stars in the 2011 CNN documentary *Revenge of the Electric Car*, which follows four men in their quest to build electric cars. Ghosn, who is responsible for the zero-emission Nissan Leaf, is the only protagonist whose company successfully launched a mass-produced electric vehicle (EV).

Sources

Berfield, S. (2008) 'Career Advice from a Comic Book'. Businessweek.com. Available at: http://businessweek.com/stories/2008-02-20/career-advice-from-a-comic-book (accessed 16 August 2013).

CNN (2008) *The Tue Story of Carlos Ghosn*. CNN international.com. Available at: http://edition.cnn.com/2008/BUSINESS/06/11/ghosn.profile/#cnnSTCText (accessed August 30 2013).

CNN video link (n.d.) *Carlos Ghosn Revealed*. CNN international.com. Available at: http://edition.cnn.com/CNNI/Programs/revealed/ghosn/ (accessed 28 August 2013).

Fonda, D. (2003) 'Motor Trends: Le CostKiller'. *Time Magazine*. Available at: http://time.com/time/magazine/article/0,9171,1004877,00.html (accessed 16 August 2013).

Madslien, J. (2005) 'Renault-Nissan emerges as global giant'. BBC News. Available at: http://news.bbc.co.uk/1/hi/business/4291105.stm (accessed 16 August 2013).

Questions

1. Where would you place Ghosn on the Blake and Mouton Grid? Why?

2. Why is he so revered in Japan? What behaviours do you think appeal to the Japanese media and public?

3. Do you think his template for success would work everywhere?

Another influential writer, John Adair, approached this theme slightly differently. Adair has had a varied career and used his experiences in the British armed forces, on a fishing boat based in Hull, and as an academic researcher to develop a functional model of leadership still in use with military forces. His approach divides the leadership 'function' as he calls it, into three distinct, but crucially interrelated, areas. These roles, achieving the task, building and maintaining the team, and developing the individual form an integrated web as seen in Figure 3.4.

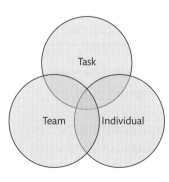

Figure 3.4 Action centred leadership

Source: Adapted from *The Handbook of Management and Leadership*, by J Adair, 2004, Thorogood Publishing.

Table 3.1 Action centred leadership

Headline function	Sub-tasks
TASK	Identify aims and vision for the group, purpose, and direction; identify resources, people, processes, systems. Create the plan and establish responsibilities, set standards, quality, time, and reporting parameters.
TEAM	Establish, agree, and communicate standards of performance and behaviour. Anticipate and resolve group conflict, struggles, or disagreements.
INDIVIDUAL	Understand the team members as individuals—personality, skills, strengths, needs, aims, and fears. Give recognition and praise to individuals—acknowledge effort and good work. Develop individual team members.

In his book, *Action Centred Leadership*, first published in 1973, Adair proposes three principal considerations a leader needs to address if they are to be successful—or effective. What is important here is to recognize that Adair firmly believed that leadership was a transferrable skill, which means it can be both taught and learnt. He listed out a number of activities that underpinned each of the functions with a view to providing a practical, usable workbook style for practicing managers. In the model, he identifies sub-tasks that need to be achieved to secure the integrity of the task (see: Table 3.1). A useful metaphor to explain Adair's approach may be that of a circus juggler who is balancing spinning plates. The performer has to ensure he attends to each plate to ensure his act is successful. Failure to keep working around his spinning plates will result in one or more falling. Adair suggests something similar, with the leader needing to attend to the three domains and failure to focus on one area threatening to undermine the whole model. However, he also adds a degree of sophistication by suggesting that the relative size of the circles may be larger or smaller than each other depending on the circumstance facing the leader. For example, using his military background, he would argue that when under imminent and unexpected attack from an enemy, the leader's focus is likely to be on the *task* function of defending his position. Whereas, when developing a new team, he would suggest spending time on getting to know the *individuals* within the team and working out how the *team* would best work together.

As well as identifying the model, Adair sets out core functions of leadership and suggests they are vital to the action centred leadership model:

- Planning: seeking information, defining tasks, setting aims
- Initiating: briefing, task allocation, setting standards
- Controlling: maintaining standards, ensuring progress, on-going decision making
- Supporting: individuals' contributions, encouraging, team spirit, reconciling, morale
- Informing: clarifying tasks and plans, updating, receiving feedback and interpreting
- Evaluating: feasibility of ideas, performance, enabling self-assessment.

Bringing the 'skills debate' forward is the Mumford et al. (2000) skills-based model outlined in Figure 3.5. Again, they set the context for leadership at the forefront of their analysis—the organization is held to be the focal point for their studies. In this context, their argument is

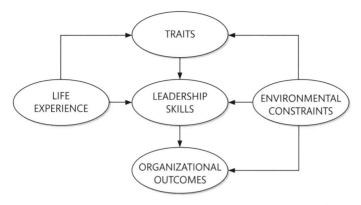

Figure 3.5 Skills model of leadership

Source: Adapted from 'Leadership Skills for a Changing World: Solving Complex Social Problems', by Mumford, M., Zaccaro, S., Harding, F., Jacobs, T.O., Fleishman, E. (2000) Leadership Quarterly, 11(1), 11–35.

 Pause for thought

1. What are the potential uses of Adair's practical model?

2. What are the similarities and differences between Adair's 'core functions' and Mintzberg's taxonomy?

3. Which approach more closely resembles your current experience of leadership?

that leadership is about solving complex social problems. The difficulty as they interpret the situation is, first, defining what exactly the problem is, second, dealing with the mass of information available for the analysis of the problem, and, finally, trying to use 'experience' to solve novel and unique problems. With echoes of Adair's model, effective leadership is seen as the product of three separate but related skills: problem solving skills, social judgement skills, and social skills. However, they go further by setting these skills or competencies in a broader framework, which includes environmental constraints and career or life experiences of the leader. They make the point that leadership is 'not viewed as the province of a few gifted individuals', but that effective leadership 'is held to be a potential in many individuals' (2000:21). This means that, on account of so many factors influencing the organizational outcome of any decision made by the leader, 'leaders are not born, nor are they made; instead their inherent potentials are shaped by experiences enabling them to develop the capabilities needed to solve significant social problems' (2000:24).

Organizational implications–strengths and weakness

As we first discussed, behavioural and skills models place the focus on the individual and are largely an attempt to analyse and create a similar profile, albeit one based on externally observable phenomena rather than hidden personality traits. It is also a largely descriptive approach in that each model describes a method that can be followed by a leader to deliver an organizational solution. It is not the leader's personality that makes the ultimate difference between success and failure—rather their skills in resolving the tensions inherent in developing an organization. This means that individual workers can learn problem solving techniques, such as 'Ishikawa (Fishbone) Analysis', and creative thinking techniques, such as brainstorming. They can attend courses or be 'coached' to develop certain organizationally desired behaviours. So, in a sense, regardless of the different theoretical approaches to 'learning' adopted, it is taken as read that individuals can, and do, learn. This basic human ability can be exploited, and leadership is seen as a set of trainable skills. These skills may vary across organizations, from culture to culture, and within different hierarchical layers, but the basic assumption still remains constant.

This underpinning set of assumptions make this approach very appealing for individuals and organizations alike as it gives them both a structure and methodology for developing leaders and leadership within their context. If an organization can define what it means by 'leadership' in skills terms (a significant assumption) then individuals within the business have a template against which they can be mapped and measured. As a result of this, other organizational activities, such as performance appraisal, objective setting, and leadership development, become inherently easier as there is a model available against which both the organization and the individual leader can mirror themselves.

If this model is combined with the latest, broader view that incorporates some environmental conditions and the experiences of the individual leader, it creates a view of leadership that is complex, rich, and subtle, which contrasts with the earlier prescription of leadership as a simple function of personality. It means that leadership is not the domain of a few singular individuals but that leadership is now accessible to a much wider number of candidates if they have the motivation.

However, before concluding that now we have uncovered the 'truth'—that leadership can be boiled down to a number of 'competencies'—it is necessary to examine the potential weaknesses within the approach. It is the final point made above that can first be questioned, in that behavioural approaches sought to explain leadership by looking at the external actions of leaders rather than the internal traits. However, by expanding the notion of leadership to include other domains, such as 'experience' and 'environmental constraints', a degree of complexity has been added that could make it very difficult for organizations and individuals to grasp the concept as a developmental tool. What, for example, would be the implication for an individual who does not have the 'experience' deemed appropriate and necessary? What are the implications for an organization, when presented with a solution to a problem deemed too difficult because of 'environmental constraints'? Has this rendered any previous analysis, in terms of behaviour, redundant and superfluous?

The motivation of the leader is also key, for, as Mumford et al. (2000) observe, there are three characteristics that need to be present within an individual in order for them to make the often painful and lonely journey that is leadership. Initially, the individual must be 'willing to tackle difficult, challenging organizational problems' (Mumford et al. 2000:22). Second, whilst there may be disagreements over the definition of leadership, most would agree that leaders exercise influence over followers and so the potential leader must be willing to exercise influence.[1] Finally, in terms of this influence, the leader should be motivated to demonstrate social commitment. This means doing the right thing for society's long-term interest (see: Case study Fred Goodwin at the end of this chapter). Again, Chapter 8 examines this theme in greater detail but there is evidence (for example, O'Connor et al. 1995) to suggest

---

[1] Note: Chapter 9 'Followership' has a slightly different perspective here.

that leaders who lack this foresight often delivered negative long-term outcomes for their particular stakeholder community. What is clear here is that we are now discussing a characteristic or trait that behavioural models sought to move away from.

Finally, the causal link between skill and effective outcomes for the leader is not made particularly explicit. This means that the model does not explain how an improvement in skill will lead to a corresponding improvement in performance. This means also that it is often difficult to evaluate fully the link between training, development, and other activity designed to affect behaviour and any changes in organizational efficacy. To a degree, though, this is the holy grail of any training intervention and the criticism could be levelled at almost any complex training and development programme. Therefore, the same return on investment (ROI) model borrowed from a more industrial heritage is likely to be difficult to implement in these types of instances. It is relatively easy to grasp the ROI for a new machine that is producing widgets twice as fast as an older version, but it is harder to make the same link between sending a manager on an expensive MBA and an increase in shareholder value.

 Pause for thought

Before reading the summary, stop and think about your position now.

1. Why are you reading this book?

2. How will you know if anything is different about your behaviour?

3. How will you know if reading the book caused this change?

Summary

Behavioural models began to evolve as a result of dissatisfaction with the Great Man type theories of leadership which ascribed successful leadership to inherited traits. The belief, and hope, was that, with the right kind of developmental procedures and processes in place, individuals could be trained to become leaders. This belief was supported by the growing science and theories investigating how humans learn. Whilst there was (and is) disagreement over this process, leadership writers and academics have used the underpinning philosophy—that humans could learn—to develop the behavioural and skills model. Effective leadership became about what you did and not about who you were.

This approach gathered support from many different writers, some of whom we have reviewed, who all proposed differing but ultimately similar models based on the belief that leadership was a skill and therefore could be learnt by students. This gave rise to leadership development programmes, courses, and a plethora of books all purporting to hold the elusive magic key to unlocking leadership. The model also appealed to organizations that used the philosophy to develop checklists, guides, and competency frameworks to recruit, develop, and evaluate their leadership cohort.[2] Adair's model, for example, was used by the British military as a model for officer training and development.

---

[2] See examples at http://www.managers.org.uk/practical-support (accessed 27 September 2013).

However, despite the intuitive appeal of the approach, the model is not without its drawbacks. It is largely descriptive rather than prescriptive, and it does not make the link between an improvement against a particular predetermined metric and performance gain explicit. Additionally, even supporters of the approach, such as Mumford and Katz, do not completely remove themselves from the trait perspective citing 'characteristics' or 'individual attributes', respectively, as elements that contribute to a leader's potential effectiveness.

Despite these issues, behavioural model can help both organizations and individuals define what they mean by 'leadership'. However, this may not result in a universal definition as the behaviours and skills required in one situation may vary from one circumstance to the next. This is a theme explored in the next chapter.

 Case study   Fred Goodwin

Frederick Anderson Goodwin CA FCIBS (born 17 August 1958) is a chartered accountant and banker who was formerly chief executive of the Royal Bank of Scotland Group (RBS). He gained notoriety by presiding over the bank's fall and gained the nickname 'Fred the Shred' as a caustic comment on his leadership approach gained at the Clydesdale Bank. From 2000 until 2008 when he was known as Sir Fred Goodwin, he presided over RBS's rapid rise to global prominence as the world's largest company (by assets of £1.9 trillion), and fifth-largest bank by stock market value, and its even more rapid fall as RBS was forced into effective nationalization in 2008. Fred Goodwin took over as chief executive of RBS in 2000, and proceeded to make 26 acquisitions, topped by the €71 billion (£55 billion) takeover of the Dutch bank, ABN Amro, in the summer of 2007, just as the foundations of the world's banking system were starting to creak audibly. Though RBS put up only some of the money paid by a consortium bidding for ABN, it proved to be a deal too far for RBS's over-stretched finances and the man once feted as the most talented banker of his generation said that he now had no plans more specific than 'a good long rest'. 'If you've got any ideas let me know,' he added.

The son of an electrician, Goodwin was raised on a council estate in Paisley, Scotland, and he went to grammar school before studying law at Glasgow University. He then trained as an accountant and was a partner at Touche Ross by the age of 30. He made his name overseeing the liquidators recovering assets from the collapse of the Bank of Credit and Commerce International in the early 1990s. By 1995, he was deputy chief executive of the Glasgow-based Clydesdale Bank, only to be poached by Sir George Mathewson, then the chief executive of RBS, in 1998 to become his deputy.

Nicknamed 'Fred the Shred' whilst at the Clydesdale for his ruthless cost-cutting, and aggressive task focus, Goodwin came into his own in 2000 with RBS's £23.6 billion hostile takeover of NatWest, a rival three times its size, which resulted in 18,000 job cuts. A courteous, quiet man, he won huge credit for his efficiency and attention to detail in the integration of the two businesses. But detractors accuse him of micro-management and the flurry of deals that followed, such as the US$1.6 billion minority stake in the Bank of China, saw him accused of megalomania. 'The vision for an ambitious bank built by acquisition was originally George Mathewson's; what he found in Fred Goodwin was the executor par excellence,' Simon Maughan, an analyst at MF Global Securities, said. 'He was exactly the right person because he would not suffer fools or listen to detractors, but just pursue the grand aim to take RBS to the top table.'

On 11 October 2008, Goodwin officially announced his resignation as chief executive and his early retirement, effective from 31 January 2009—one month before RBS announced that its 2008 loss totalled £24.1 billion, the largest annual loss in UK corporate history. Following this, in February 2009, the disclosure of his, approximately, £700,000 per year pension award from RBS led to him becoming the subject of widespread public, political, and media criticism. But true to his reputation, Goodwin defended to the last the takeover, now widely characterized by Robert Peston at the BBC as the deal junkie's fatal overdose. 'ABN is not the cause of all this—we would be having a lot of these difficulties whether we had bought ABN or we hadn't,' Goodwin said.

During the heady years following his promotion to chief executive, the ABN deal was the one that he will be remembered for—in that its disastrous outcome came to symbolize the 'fat cat' culture blamed by many members of the public and media as the real reason behind the recession of 2008 to 2010. One of Fred's acquisitions, Charter One, had prompted questions about the bank's capital reserves and Fred publicly ruled out any more big deals. But then along came the opportunity at ABN Amro. Just as the world financial system was beginning to seize up, Goodwin's consortium of RBS, Fortis, and Santander were ramping up their bidding war with rival suitor, Barclays. In his desire to win, it now looks as if he went too far, creating an internally-funded cash offer that Barclays' share bid did not stand a chance of beating but that left RBS dangerously leveraged. 'The ABN deal totally stretched a balance sheet that was already stretched,' Mr Maughan said.

Unfortunately for Goodwin, the ABN deal was not the only problem for RBS. Alongside the eight-year acquisition spree, RBS also massively expanded its investment banking business, building upon both the City-leading conventional products inherited with NatWest, and also upon the small Greenwich Capital operation concentrating on the then-novel field of mortgage-backed securities in the US. 'It was the combination of acquisition and the aggressive push into the area of investment banking, many of which subsequently soured, that caused the problem,' Mr Maughan said.

But it was ABN that pushed RBS over the edge and into the abyss. After repeated protestations of his bank's financial health, Goodwin surprised shareholders in April with one of the biggest rights issues in British corporate history, aimed at raising more than £12 billion to shore-up a balance sheet that was suffering under £6 billion worth of write-downs, a third of which were from the Dutch bank. But it was too late and between then and the start of January 2009 RBS lost more than 80 per cent of its market capitalization.

Ultimately, ABN was simply a risk too great. As Goodwin said himself, shortly after RBS announced its plan to bid for the Dutch bank: 'The key to good deal-making is being prepared to walk away.' If only he had listened; as a consequence he went from being one of the most revered figures in the City to one of the most reviled.

The former RBS boss disappeared from public view shortly after being hauled before the Treasury select committee along with his chairman and their counterparts at the equally-stricken HBOS. All four men publicly apologized for their bank's downfall, and Goodwin said he 'could not be more sorry'. He admitted he had made a 'bad mistake' buying ABN Amro at the top of the market, but Tory MP, Michael Fallon, told him: 'You've destroyed a great British bank.'

As a result of the losses, there were calls for him to be stripped of his knighthood with around 70 MPs signing a Commons motion calling for Goodwin to lose the right to call himself 'Sir' and, in April 2009, Labour MP, Gordon Prentice, wrote to the cabinet secretary, Sir Gus O'Donnell, who chairs the forfeiture committee, to ask him to take action. Prentice wrote:

> I am told that cancellation is considered in cases where retention of the appointment or award would bring the honours system into disrepute. Sir Fred's role in the collapse of the RBS, and his refusal to countenance any reduction in his grotesquely extravagant £700,000-a-year pension, convinces me it would be wholly inappropriate for him to retain the high honour of a knighthood.

On 1 February 2012, the Queen formally stripped Goodwin of his knighthood. In March 2009, Goodwin's Edinburgh home was attacked by vandals, who left three windows shattered, and they smashed the rear window of his black Mercedes. Goodwin, who was not inside the house, was said to have been 'shaken' by the incident. An anonymous email was sent to media organizations shortly after the attack threatening further action against 'criminal' bank bosses. The email said:

> We are angry that rich people, like him, are paying themselves a huge amount of money, and living in luxury, while ordinary people are made unemployed, destitute and homeless. This is a crime. Bank bosses should be jailed. This is just the beginning.'

(Continued...)

Eighteen police officers, including five detectives and forensic specialists, investigated the attack but failed to identify those behind it.

Sources

http://bbc.co.uk/1/hi/scotland/7962825.stm 'Vandals Attack Sir Fred Goodwin's Home' BBC, 25 March 2009.

Bloomberg Business Week 'Executive Profile'. Available at: http://investing.businessweek.com/research/stocks/private/person.asp?personId=1001741&privcapId=2031367&previousCapId=312897&previousTitle=WASHINGTON%20TRUST%20BANCORP (accessed 16 August 2013).

Finch, J. (2009) 'Pay Gap Widens Between Executives and Their Staff'. *The Guardian*, 18 June 2009.

Low, V. (2009) 'World's Worst Banker: Sir Fred Goodwin Ousted by the Prince's Trust'. *The Times*, 26 January 2009.

Peston, R. (2009) 'BBC – Robert Peston Blog'. BBC, 25th February 2009.

Wintour, P. (2012) 'Fred Goodwin stripped of knighthood.' *The Guardian*, 31 January 2012.

Video Link: http://news.sky.com/skynews/Home/Business/Sir-Fred-Goodwins-Edinburgh-Home-Is-Attacked-Windows-Are-Smashed-And-A-Car-Is-Vandalised/Article/200903415248540?f=rss 'Sir Fred Attack: "This Is Just The Start"'. Sky News, 25 March 2009.

Questions

1. What behaviours do you think Fred Goodwin displayed that led him to being successful and recruited by Mathewson?

2. Given the various behavioural models outlined how can you explain Goodwin's collapse? What, for example, do you think Adair would have recommended?

3. What lessons can you draw from this example of a very successful individual becoming virtually unemployable almost overnight?

Assignment—2,000 words

- Choose an organization with which you are familiar.
- Observe the behaviour of the senior management team. You can either watch at first hand, if you can access the organization, watch them on television, or choose to read about their exploits.
- Use one of the models reviewed to analyse their performance. Do they cover all of the themes or is there a weakness in their approach? What are the implications for the organization when considering the leader's behaviour patterns?

Behaviour questionnaire

Read each item and decide how much you agree with each statement or how much it reflects your normal behaviour as a leader. Circle your response and proceed smoothly and quickly through the questions.

Scoring Key: 1 = Not True/Never; 2 = Rarely; 3 = Sometimes; 4 = Often/Agree; 5 = Definitely/Always.

1	I enjoy getting into the details of the task in hand	1	2	3	4	5
2	I can 'read' people's faces	1	2	3	4	5
3	How things work excites me	1	2	3	4	5
4	Working together with friends is important to me	1	2	3	4	5
5	People should come first in an organization	1	2	3	4	5
6	I can usually get things working	1	2	3	4	5
7	Being in a team is fun, exciting, and powerful	1	2	3	4	5
8	I care about my work colleagues	1	2	3	4	5
9	Paperwork is necessary	1	2	3	4	5
10	I listen to other people's ideas	1	2	3	4	5
11	Harmony at work is important to me	1	2	3	4	5
12	Open communication is the key to success	1	2	3	4	5
13	Once I start something I finish it	1	2	3	4	5
14	You must get the basics right in any job	1	2	3	4	5
15	I have many friends at work	1	2	3	4	5
16	More hands make light work!	1	2	3	4	5
17	I find people interesting	1	2	3	4	5
18	I work best on my own	1	2	3	4	5

This short questionnaire is designed to measure your affinity with three broad skill areas: your task focus, your social skills, and your closeness to other people. Add together your responses to questions 1, 3, 6, 9, 13, and 14—this is your task score. Next, add together 2, 5, 8, 10, 15, and 17—this is your people score. Finally, add together 4, 7, 11, 12, 16 and 18. But reverse the score for item 18 so that 1 becomes 5, 2 becomes 4, 4 becomes 2, and 5 becomes 1. This is your social score.

Interpretation

By identifying the different preferences you have in these three areas you can begin to consider where your relative strengths lie. You can also begin to consider if this is a reflection of your current role or if there are other factors that influence your choices. You can ask colleagues about their perspective and look at how your organization reflects these different skills

Further reading

John Adair's material is plentiful and easily accessible. His more recent book, *How to Grow Leaders: The Seven Key Principles of Effective Leadership Development* (2009, London: Kogan Page) looks at leadership development programmes and how these have proliferated. He is sceptical about the effectiveness of these programmes and attempts to identify seven key principles of leadership development, and he provides some thought provoking insights into the key questions on how to select, train, and educate leaders at the level of team, operational, and strategic leadership.

A Manager's Guide to Self Development (Pedler, M., Burgoyne, J., Boydell, T. (2007)) is now in its fifth edition. The book details a self-development programme aimed at helping readers to improve their managerial performance and to advance their careers. It is written in a self-help format with questionnaires and more than 50 different activities designed to help the inexperienced manager with practical advice.

In *Managing the Innovative Process: The Dynamic Role of Leaders* (2011), Stenmark, Shipman, and Mumford look at what they consider to be a key 'skill' in organizations. They suggest a template or process for managing innovation and go on to identify cognitive skills and social behaviours that a leader should follow at each stage in order for the process to be successful. They also point towards the external environment and recommend that the leader scans for environmental disturbances.

The style approach to leadership

4

After reading this chapter you will:

- Understand how leadership theories evolved to include the style of the leader as a model for a universal theory of leadership.
- Explore the pressures on leaders that emerge from their environment.
- Be able to review different perspectives on the style approach critically, and be further able to consider your approach and thinking using this model.

Introduction

Whilst the 'styles approach' does represent a further evolution of how leadership is viewed, discussed, and researched, it also remains rooted in the same territory as the previous models; namely, trait and behavioural. This approach is still focused on the individual leader—it is person centric and Gordon (2011) certainly considers this to be one of the classical or 'traditional' approaches to leadership. However, it does involve a more sophisticated view of leadership in that, almost for the first time, the role of, and relationship between, followers and the leader is now considered, as is the nature of task being attempted. Lussier and Achua (2004:75) put it thus: 'leadership style is the combination of traits, skills and behaviours leaders use as they interact with followers'. This approach suggests that in order to be 'successful' the leader should adopt a leadership style that is appropriate to the nature of the followers and circumstance the leader inhabits. That leaders have followers is now acknowledged and there is a nod towards the abilities, competences, and motivation of those followers. So, the styles approach places the leader into a much more dynamic and complex world with certain assumptions made about the nature of this environment. This chapter explores this environment and the impact these added complexities make on the function of leadership.

Essentially, this set of models largely focus on the decision-making process that surrounds the leader. As Yukl (2006:81) suggests, 'making decisions is one of the most important functions performed by leaders'. This could involve and impact on a whole plethora of other actions such as planning the workload of different departments, hiring and firing team members, choosing different strategies, and allocating resources to different managers (see: Chapter 3). Such decisions can be made using different processes and starting points. The early work in this area followed the research of three different American universities, at Iowa, Ohio, and Michigan, who examined the impact of these themes on leaders. This work was refined by Tannenbaum and Schmidt (1958) and Vroom and Yetton (1973), further analysed by Arvonen and Ekvall (1991), and has expanded to include a cultural dimension (e.g. Mills 2005). To a degree, the early work reviewed here is similar in its content and outcomes to some of the literature reviewed in the previous chapter. However, the differences with these ideas are the recognition of the significance of the environment occupied by the leader and the underpinning ideology being linked—not to behaviourism—but much more about focusing on leadership actions and how these affect followers. Finally, it is significant and important to understand how the research evolved into a much more sophisticated approach than the simple two-dimensional models reviewed in Chapter 3.

Evolution of the approach

As already seen, Ralph Stogdill (1948) found little or no positive relationship between a manager's traits and success. Frustrated by the lack of success in this area, Stogdill changed tack and led a team at Ohio State University that studied how managers behaved and acted in their role as leader. Stogdill and his team used a lengthy questionnaire of 150 different questions derived from more than 1,790 statements relating to a leader's behaviour. The questionnaire was directed at subordinates who were asked to assess their superior's behaviour. The questionnaire, called the Leadership Behaviour Description Questionnaire (LBDQ),[1] has gone through several different versions, and has evolved into the LBDQ XII. It is still in use today across the USA, and can be accessed free for research purposes and non-commercial use. There is also a version at the end of this chapter that you can use to develop your own thoughts in this area.

From the results, Stogdill's team developed a two-dimensional model of leadership behaviour. The model purported to have uncovered two distinct and independent behaviours that evolve as a consequence of the leader's interactions with followers. These two approaches were labelled Consideration and Initiating structures (Stogdill and Coons 1957). The team suggested that Consideration was the extent to which a leader exhibits concern for the welfare of the members of the group. This factor is oriented towards interpersonal relationships, mutual trust, and friendship, and has echoes of Blake and Mouton's model discussed in Chapter 3. The other dimension was found to be a set of behaviours that involved the leader defining leader and group member roles, initiating actions, organizing group activities, and defining how tasks are to be accomplished by the group. This leadership style was felt to be more task oriented.

Meanwhile, Rensis Likert and the University of Michigan team were pursuing a different strategy—albeit with a similar methodology. His team again developed a model focusing on two different leadership approaches—these were labelled employee orientation and production orientation. The former approach was associated with a leader who focused on developing strong human relationships, whereas the latter was about delivering results for the organization. Both of these findings were very similar to the Ohio studies but there was a fundamental difference in how these two institutions initially conceptualized their findings. Whereas Stogdill and the Ohio team used a two-dimensional model which meant that, like Blake and Mouton, a leader could demonstrate both (or no) human and task orientation, Likert and Michigan placed their dimensions at either end of a continuum (see: Figure 4.1). This meant that a leader could be either human oriented or task oriented but not both. This

---

[1] http://fisher.osu.edu/research/lbdq the LBDQ is available free of charge via this site (accessed 29 July 2013).

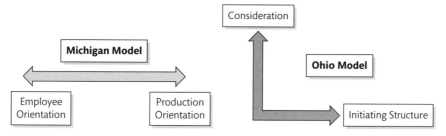

Figure 4.1 Iowa and Michigan models

idea of a continuum is something explored later in the chapter. Likert (1961:7) also concluded thus: 'supervisors with the best records of performance focus their primary attention on the human aspects of their subordinates' problems and on endeavouring to build effective work groups with high performance goals'. Whilst there has been additional research into these ideas in terms of trying to ascertain which more accurately reflect the experiences of leadership, the results have been 'inconclusive' (Northouse 2010:72).

 Pause for thought

Consider the different models suggested by Iowa (Stogdill) and Michigan (Likert):

1. In what ways are they similar?

2. How do they differ?

3. Can you see any similarities or challenges to Blake and Mouton or Adair's ideas seen in Chapter 3?

 Case study   Bob Quarta

Roberto Quarta is an Italian born, American raised manager who has just taken over as chairman at IMI, a West Midlands engineering company. His previous jobs include work for BBA—a large conglomerate with pre-tax profits of £118 million. Now in his sixties, Mr Quarta has earned the sobriquet of 'Give no'. He acquired this dubious title as a result of his decisions at BBA, which, when he joined, was losing £11 million per year. Whilst at the company he consolidated the company's extensive and diverse portfolio of interests, closing two dozen businesses and making more than 2,000 workers redundant. Lea (2011) says he has 'a reputation as a formidable knife-wielder'. Whereas Sir Owen Green, former chairman of BTR, says: 'He'd already made up his mind after three months what to keep and what to divest at BBA. Some people had their doubts but he has been proved to be right. I don't know who else could have done it.' Another comment coming from one of his colleagues is: 'His biggest plus point is his sheer energy level, and the fact that he knows how to motivate people. He's a very challenging manager but he likes to have fun too. He enjoys a good laugh.'

Sources

Davidson, A. (1996) 'UK: The Davisdson Interview: Roberto Quarta'. *Management Today*. Teddington: Haymarket Media Group Ltd. Available from: http://www.managementtoday.co.uk/news/410666/ UK-DAVIDSON-INTERVIEW---ROBERTO-QUARTA/?DCMP=ILC-SEARCH (accessed 30 August 2013).

(Continued...)

Lea, R. (2011) '"Give No" Quarta returns'. *The Times Newspaper*, 7 May 2011. London: The Times Newspaper Group. Available from: http://www.thetimes.co.uk/tto/business/industries/engineering/article3011132.ece (accessed 30 August 2013).

White, G. (2011) 'Sir Terry Leahy joins US buyout firm Clayton, Dubilier & Rice'. *The Daily Telegraph Newspaper*. London: The Telegraph Media Group. Available from: http://www.telegraph.co.uk/finance/newsbysector/banksandfinance/8520045/Sir-Terry-Leahy-joins-US-buyout-firm-Clayton-Dubilier-and-Rice.html (accessed 30 August 2013).

Questions

1. What style do you think Mr Quarta has? Is he employee or production oriented?
2. In what kind of company do you think Mr Quarta would be successful as a chairman?
3. Where do you think Mr Quarta would be unsuccessful?

Organizational culture

Likert went on from his early work to develop what he called a 'Management System'. This was a more complex model that tried to define the relationship, involvement, and roles of managers and subordinates in industrial settings. He conducted his study in a large insurance company, and, along with his wife, Jane, attempted to extrapolate the study to educational settings. They initially intended to define the roles of head teachers, students, and teachers; eventually others such as school inspectors, administrative staff, and parents were included in the model. It is clear to see how the idea of a continuum plays out in his mind with these different roles moving further away from each other in terms of authority and power. Likert thought it would be difficult to conceive of an organization that could combine both task and people orientation and he leaves us with a sense that he sees leadership and the culture of organizations as mutually dependent. Leaders have a considerable effect on the predominant culture within the organization, (see Chapter 17) and the resulting relationships between the various stakeholders suggested above and the leadership generate very different experiences for those stakeholders.

A. Exploitative authoritative system

In this system decisions are made exclusively by the management. The role of the subordinate or follower is simply to obey those instructions and there is no consultation by the management with those affected by or implementing the decisions. There is often coercive use of power with punishment the consequence of not following orders from superiors. The organization's focus is exclusively focused on task achievement and the pursuit of profit where the means is justified by the end result. The leader's style is likely to be task or production focused.

B. Benevolent authoritative system

This is similar to exploitive systems because decisions are still made by the organization's leaders and strict hierarchies are in place to ensure compliance. However, the difference is that incentives and rewards are offered to employees for their compliance and effort. There may also be a 'flow' of information from the bottom to the top of the organization but this information is likely to be focused on passing information believed to 'please' the leadership. The leadership style is interesting here because it may appear to the outside observer to be focused on the human side of the organization. However, the reality is likely to be different, with task delivery still the main concern for the business.

C. Consultative system

Here there is a limited degree of involvement by subordinates in the decision-making process. Leaders will be seen to be asking, listening, and using some of the ideas proposed by subordinates. However, it is still clear that, ultimately, decisions will be made by senior organizational figures and information collected may not be used by the leadership. As a consequence, there is a flow up, down, and across the business, but this flow is likely to be limited in terms of both quality and quantity. Rewards are available to the workforce and are distributed by managers as recognition of the effort of the subordinates.

D. Participative (group) system

In this 'ultimate' organizational type, which Likert suggests is the preferred model, the leadership of the organization have complete confidence in their subordinates. There is a clear and plentiful flow of communication and subordinates are fully involved in the decision-making process. Because of the atmosphere of trust and mutual support, subordinates feel comfortable in expressing opinions. The preferred method of working is via teamwork. A unique attribute of these workplace teams is the presence of what Likert calls 'linking pins'. These are individuals who belong to more than one team and can exercise a degree of coordination across the organization by identifying and informing teams of the activities of other areas of the business. Individual employees throughout the organization feel responsible for achieving the organization's objectives and this acts as motivation for the employees who will be in receipt of financial and other inducements as a result of delivering the organization's goals. When combined with good management and achievable goals, this system has been shown to result in more loyalty, better production, higher motivation, and more profit than the other systems (Effrat 1968).

The four alternative approaches have a very different 'feel' to them and the leader's style in each case is different—especially when decision making is considered. The decision-making approach of the leader is implicit in the model, and the result of this on the overall culture of the organization is fundamental to Likert's thinking. However, limited by his 'either–or' model, he could only offer a limited range of alternative styles. Other researchers returned to the central theme of decision making as the focus for their investigations on leadership styles and it is this work that is considered next.

Widening the choice

Robert Tannenbaum was an American psychologist, who, with his writing partner, Warren Schmidt, wrote an influential article called 'How to Choose a Leadership Pattern' (1958). In

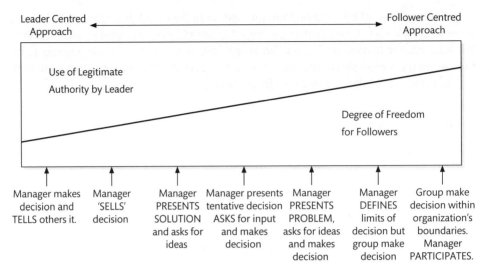

Figure 4.2 The continuum of leadership behaviour

Source: Adapted from Tannenbaum and Schmidt (1958).

this ground-breaking paper, they identified not just two possible alternatives for leaders but seven different styles. These styles arise as a function of the degree of legitimate authority wielded by the leader in pursuit of the organizational goal and the amount of freedom accorded to followers. Figure 4.2 graphically illustrates their findings. It is important to note that the diagonal line in the model does not run from corner to corner. This is because, as Tannenbaum and Schmidt note, 'neither extreme is absolute; authority and freedom are never without their limitations' (1958:96).

Examining each of their behaviour and style points, the subtle differences can be explored which show how the leader can change styles as he moves along the continuum.

1. The manager makes the decision and announces it (*tells*). At this extreme, the manager has all of the information he believes necessary to make a decision. Indeed, he will have identified what he believes to be the 'problem'; he has considered a number of possible solutions himself and will report both the problem and solution to his subordinates. He may or may not consider what his subordinates think about the decision and may or may not have factored in any impact the decision will have on the followers. Even if these constraints have been considered, the followers will not be given any opportunity to participate in either the problem definition stage or the decision on how to resolve the problem so defined. The use of legitimate authority by the leader is exercised to the full limit of organization's constraints. There may also be the explicit or at least implied use of coercive threat should instructions not be followed by the followers.

2. The manager makes the decision but attempts to persuade others (*sells*). Moving to the right implies a reduction in the degree of legitimate authority exercised by the manager. So here we see the manager using a slightly different approach from the extreme position identified above. The leader is still making the decision himself. He has both identified the problem and the solution as above, so he still believes he has the correct information and is best placed

because of his position within the organization to make the optimum decision for the organization. He will, though, attempt to 'sell' his position to his followers. He will present his analysis and how he wishes to solve the problem given the constraints he has identified. Almost explicit in this approach is the assumption that he is now considering the impact on his followers and that they may react to his decision. This reaction may not be entirely favourable so he will have to use a number of conflict resolution techniques or be prepared to influence his followers. He could also use rewards and be prepared to incentivize his followers to follow his instructions.

3. The manager makes the decision and invites comments (*presents situation*). Again, the manager has already made the decision but he is prepared to outline his thinking by explaining his solution to the followers. The sub-text here is that he believes his decision is correct but he knows that for his followers to perform his instructions they must, to a degree, buy into his thinking and understand more fully the implications of their actions. It may also be that, by this discursive process, both the manager and subordinates understand more about each other and how the decision will affect their own positions. His followers will be encouraged to ask questions of clarity rather than challenging the fundamental soundness of the decision. They will not be able to change any essential element of the decision but can ask why certain choices have been made.

4. The manager presents a tentative decision that could be subject to changes (*asks*). If the previous approaches were heavily weighted towards the manager making a decision, this option, for the first time, allows the subordinates some limited input to this process. This style still asks the manager to identify the initial problem and diagnose the possible solutions. He will also have sorted through in his own mind a preference for a solution but this will be tentative and he will be prepared to accept comment and criticism from his followers. At the initial meeting with his followers he will present his analysis of the problem and offer his preferred solution. But, crucially, he will invite and accept reaction from his followers. He will encourage feedback and be open to new ideas but he will still reserve the right to attempt his solution despite the input from subordinates.

5. The manager has identified a problem but not the solution (*presents problem*). Note the difference here between options 3 and 4. Using this style, the manager has crucially not made the decision on what to do about a problem. However, he has made the initial diagnosis and has identified the challenge to be overcome by the organization. His approach to his team will be one of presenting the analysis and asking the group to come up with a number of possible solutions. From these options generated using the combined experience, skill, and know-how of the group, the manager will select what he considers to be the solution most likely to produce a positive outcome for the organization (or generate the least negative outcome). As Tannenbaum and Schmidt put it, the purpose of the team is to increase 'the manager's repertoire of possible solutions to the problem' (1958:97). So although the team has a role to play in the formulation of the decision, in that they have generated the options, they still do not have any role in making the ultimate decision as to which choice is to be taken.

6. The manager states the limits and the group is allowed to make the decision (*defines*). This is a crucial point in the choice of styles available in that decision making is passed from the manager to the group—albeit the manager may still form part of the group. The manager still will have defined the problem but will not have considered any possible solutions. All

the manager will have done will be to set boundaries within which the proposed solution must fit. These constraints may be financial or have other resource implications—for example, time or labour. So, a manager may say to his team that their solution must be within a fixed budget, be delivered by a certain point in time, or be achieved by a set number of work-hours. The group will investigate a number of options and will be able to choose one of the solutions. They may also, depending on the context, have the capacity to implement the solution.

7.   The group makes the decision (*participates*). At the extreme end of the continuum lies this rare style whereby decision making lies exclusively within the control of the team. The only constraints here are those imposed by the organization's wider limitations—maybe in terms of cash, risk, and strategy. Tannenbaum and Schmidt identify the possibility of this approach being located within a university or organizational research team. Here the team will explore their field identifying ideas, challenges, and new innovative solutions to existing or future problems. The manager will be seen as an equal participant with no more formal authority than other team members. There will be an explicit understanding that decisions reached by the group will be carried forward by the manager who will act on behalf of the team.

 Pause for thought

1. What do you think your current 'preferred' style is?

2. Why have you come to this decision?

3. Have you ever tried an alternative approach? What happened? Did you feel uncomfortable or threatened?

4. What style do you respond best to when thinking about how you want to be managed? Why? Is this style similar to or different from your preferred style?

 Case study

Lee joined the Royal Navy, aged 20, as a junior rating. He worked at sea aboard various ships where his job was to ensure the ship was able to respond to enemy threats. However, he also had a ceremonial role when the ship was overseas. This secondary role saw him become part of the ship's Guard of Honour whereby, when the ship was in a foreign harbour, Lee would be part of a squad of sailors that would formally announce visiting foreign dignitaries as they boarded the ship on official visits. This is considered to be an important task as it helps to maintain British influence abroad, but it is often seen by sailors as a distraction from their main duties. Far from being disgruntled at this additional task, Lee enjoyed the pomp and ceremony associated with the role and he slowly worked his way into a position of influence in the Guard of Honour. His naval career continued and Lee was promoted, slowly at first, but ultimately he gained the rating of Chief Petty Officer, which is the highest rank a non-commissioned officer can attain in the navy—the army equivalent is Sergeant Major, or Warrant Officer in the Royal Air Force.

In this role Lee was able to command his own Guard of Honour and was involved in preparations for various royal events as well as instructing both army and air force personnel on how to conduct these highly regulated and high profile events. He became an expert in marching, inspecting uniforms, and the tight ritualized formations used in these occasions.

 He left the navy after 25 years' service and became a health and safety inspector. He worked at large public events where he advised the organizers on ensuring their events were compliant with the law in this area. His remit was to ensure that spectators and participants were following the law and that legal obligations were being observed. He used checklists to ensure he followed a logical system and that there was a verifiable backup to any decision he made. He has enjoyed this work too and has become a successful inspector working at high profile events, such as the Goodwood Festival.

Questions

1. What style do you think Lee would be using in the Royal Navy?

2. How would this approach need to be modified in his civilian role? Why?

3. What would be the implication for Lee of using only one approach in these different situations?

Factors affecting style

The key question for the leader is to be able to identify which style is both practical and desirable in order to achieve whatever organizational goal has been set. According to Tannenbaum and Schmidt, different 'forces' will come to bear which will affect this decision. It is important to recognize here that Tannenbaum and Schmidt explicitly believe that the manager does have a choice. The manager should, according to this approach, have the wherewithal and understanding to make a decision on the style he is going to employ. They strengthen this position by suggesting that, 'the manager who is sensitive to them [the forces] can better assess the problems which face him and determine which mode of leadership behaviour is most appropriate for him' (1958:98).

 These forces (see: Figure 4.3) are split into three areas:

- Forces in the manager.
- Forces in the subordinates.
- Forces in the situation.

Figure 4.3 Tannenbaum and Schmidt's Forces

Forces in the manager

There is recognition that personality influences decisions and that life experiences will affect the decision of the manager in terms of which style is appropriate.

1. **Value system.** Here the manager will be assessing his own perspective on the role of leaders and followers. He will consider the 'right' he has to make decisions and his own perceptions of the expectations of the organization for him to exert legitimate authority. His own upbringing and exposure to authority figures will add further complexity to this area. He will be making a judgement on the needs of individuals, organizational task achievement, and personal gain. Unfortunately, as Chris Argyris (2001) points out, our own perceptions and beliefs can become confused and misleading and this may lead us to inappropriate decisions.

2. **Confidence in subordinates.** Again, perception is key here for in this area the manager is making a judgement call on what he believes the skill, knowledge, and competence his team have in order to complete the assignment. From this judgement he will decide on how much he can trust subordinates to deliver the task as directed by the organization. He will be considering their experiences, past track record, and his own history when delegating tasks. He may eventually decide that he is best qualified to deliver the task and opt not to involve his team in any significant decision making.

3. **Personal leadership tendency.** Tannenbaum and Schmidt are a little vague here, but in essence they seem to suggest that certain 'traits' may enable a leader to be more or less directive in decision making. Some individuals, they suggest, are inclined to a directive authoritative stance, whereas others are more inclined to delegate and cooperate with team members. They do not identify why this may be the case but clearly the themes raised in point 1 above will have a bearing here.

4. **Manager's attitude to risk.** Here, the manager will be considering the issue of control—in that by releasing the decision-making process, he will be losing control over both the process and the outcome. This means he will not be able to predict the outcome of the decision and the associated ambiguity and uncertainty this will generate. In turn, this will represent a degree of risk on behalf of the manager. For example, what if the decision made is either of poor quality or has implications for the manager and the organization that may not be 'politically' sensitive? A manager who is more comfortable with possible vagueness and regards this as an exciting and innovative process is more likely to adopt a style to the right hand side of the continuum.

Forces in the subordinate

In this arena, the manager has to make a number of assumptions about the nature of the subordinate and his expectations of him. A junior member of a team may have certain beliefs about what kind of support and direction a more senior manager will offer.

1. **Need for independence.** Some professions, for example, often display a need for freedom in terms of their approach to a problem. Highly specialized, highly skilled workers may feel they 'know best' when asked a technical question and may resent a generalist making decisions about their specialism.

2. **Need for responsibility.** Some individuals are more confident in their abilities and readily accept the responsibility for their actions. Others may, because of individual beliefs

or organizational pressures, not accept such demands. Many people will have experienced a 'jobs-worth'—an individual, as Kent (2010:36) describes thus: 'clipboard and pencil in hand, sucking their teeth at each indiscretion before delivering a doom-laden verdict at the end of the morning'. The manager will need to make a judgement on the amount of responsibility individuals within his team are able and willing to accept.

3. **Need for boundaries.** Myers (1980) points out that individual traits may drive some individuals to require a degree of clarity to any instruction, with firm guidance and boundaries to their task; whereas others will reject such input and will relish, and possibly demand, freedom to make these choices themselves.

4. **Competence, experience, motivation.** Contributing to the manager's decision will be his determination of the follower's abilities in terms of technical skills and track record in relation to delivery of similar tasks. He will also be interested in their motivation to deliver the task and their identification with the wider organizational goals. He may be unlikely to give as much freedom to a recent recruit as an experienced technician with many years of high quality service.

5. **Subordinate expectations.** Individual employees will have a set of assumptions about their role and position in terms of the formal and informal hierarchy that exists in the business. One of these assumptions may be related to the degree to which they are involved in the decision-making process. In terms of the psychological contract this establishes between the organization and the individual, this may mean an individual expects to be involved or excluded from decision making. A manager will risk breaking this contract if he changes the method without explanation. Finally, there is also the reciprocal nature of trust to be considered—namely, the degree to which followers have confidence in their boss. If the subordinates feel their superior is competent and have trust in his decision-making abilities, they are more likely to accept his decisions about how much responsibility is devolved to a group level. They could, if they feel they have no confidence, view an attempt to involve them as 'buck passing'; alternatively, if they do have confidence, they may welcome the opportunity to share thoughts and ideas.

Forces in the situation

There will be pressures that affect the manager's decision that arise from the situation—and the recognition of this marks the real difference between these particular models and the two-dimensional behavioural models outlined in Chapter 3. The culture of the organization, the coherence of the team, the distinct nature of the problem, and the pressure to deliver results will be just some of the external factors weighing on the mind of the manager.

1. **Organizational type and culture.** Organizations are, to a degree, like people—in that they have 'personalities' and a 'way of doing things', to paraphrase Deal and Kennedy (1982). These characteristics are usually labelled as organizational culture. This culture will manifest itself in many different forms. Johnson and Scholes' 'Cultural Web' (2001) suggests a number of domains that will illustrate how an organization's culture may emerge—artefacts, myths and stories, job descriptions, and job titles will all combine to create a unique atmosphere. Included in this diverse and complex pattern will be an implicit instruction on how, when, and to what degree decision making is to be devolved to different layers within

the organization's hierarchy. Some organizations will view the role of the executive very differently from others. For example, the chief executive may be viewed as having a forceful, dynamic, and decisive nature whereas in another organization the role will be filled by an individual with the ability to engage individual hearts and minds in solving the organization's challenges. A newcomer to the organization will quickly establish the degree to which compliance with or deviance from the established ways of working will be tolerated. This will lead to him adopting a leadership style aligned with the broader organizational value set. Tannenbaum and Schmidt also comment on the geographic proximity and structure of the organization. They suggest that a wide dispersal of an organization may preclude participative decision making. However, given the relatively recent evolution of collaborative work systems involving asynchronous and real time video and voice software tools, it could be that this concern is no longer as restrictive as it would have seemed to a manager operating in the 1950s.

2. **Team coherence.** Whilst this theme is reviewed in more depth in Chapter 14, it is sufficient to note here the manager's need to understand the coherence and effectiveness of his team. The extent to which they are capable and motivated to work together will be a major influence on his decision to use group work as a problem solving method. A manager may feel it is more appropriate to test out a group's abilities in this area with a relatively simple, low risk job before asking them to embark on a more complex, high risk task.

3. **Task complexity.** A manager may feel that, for a certain type of task, he is best suited to its resolution. For example, he may feel that for the highly complex, strategically important tasks he was recruited to resolve, he has the knowledge and experience to go it alone in terms of solving. However, as many problems facing businesses are now unique and without precedent, he may feel the power of multiple minds make it necessary to involve other individuals in a quest for a solution. It is a question of 'horses for courses'.

4. **Time pressure.** A manager may feel this pressure most keenly and it is likely to result in a different approach as a deadline approaches. When there is less time pressure in terms of decision, a delegative process may allow the manager to gather ideas before reaching a solution. However, when time pressures mount, managers often feel there is little opportunity to ask for input and to listen to different thoughts and opinions. It may also be inappropriate to ask for input as crisis situations often demand an immediate response because of the pressing nature of the circumstance being faced. However, it is important to understand this should not been seen as an excuse for not choosing a more involved decision-making process, especially post event.

Whilst Tannenbaum and Schmidt's approach created a degree of academic debate, there was a concern among other researchers, such as Norman Maier (1968), that an important issue was missing from these models—that of the quality of the eventual decision reached using whatever style thought appropriate by the leader. Vroom and Yetton (1973), and later Vroom and Jago (1988), explored these ideas and developed a quasi-mathematical approach using a decision tree type model (see: Figure 4.4) to aid and improve the quality of decisions made by managers. This 'normative' model was developed trying to use rational logic rather than a more subjective approach based on human intuition to reach a decision on leadership style.

Vroom and Yetton (1973:13) defined five different decision procedures or styles. Two are autocratic (A1 and A2), two are consultative (C1 and C2), and one is group-based (G2).

- A1: Leader takes known information and then decides alone. Follower role is to implement decision.
- A2: Leader gets information from followers, and then decides alone. Follower role is to provide information and to implement leader's decision.
- C1: Leader shares problem with followers individually, listens to ideas, and then decides alone. The leader's decision may or may not reflect the thoughts of the followers.
- C2: Leader shares problems with followers as a group, listens to ideas, and then decides alone. Again, the leader may or may use the ideas generated by the group.
- G2: Leader shares problems with followers as a group and then seeks and accepts consensus agreement. The leader, to a degree, acts as a chairperson guiding the group but not trying to influence the group towards his preferred option.

Given these five different options, their model provides two additional factors the manager needs to consider before embarking on the decision-making process.

Decision quality is the selection of the 'best' alternative, and is particularly important when there are many alternatives. It is also important when there are serious implications for selecting (or failing to select) the best alternative. However, if the alternative options all deliver roughly the same outcome for the organization, then decision quality may not be of such importance.

Decision acceptance is the degree to which a follower accepts a decision made by a leader. Vroom suggests that leaders should focus more on decision acceptance when decision quality is more important. There is a basic assumption behind the model that the more influence subordinates have over the decision, the more committed they are likely to be in terms of delivering the outcomes. However, the manager may not be overly concerned about this theme and may decide to use legitimate authority in order for his wishes to be implemented.

From their analysis, Vroom and Yetton (1973) formulated seven questions a leader should ask in order to arrive at the most appropriate style given the variables outlined above. They require the leader to answer with a simple 'Yes' or 'No' to these questions and ask each question in strict sequential order.

1. Is there a quality requirement? Is the nature of the solution critical? Are there technical or rational grounds for selecting among possible solutions?
2. Do I have sufficient information to make a high quality decision?
3. Is the problem structured? Are the alternative courses of action and methods for their evaluation known?
4. Is acceptance of the decision by subordinates critical to its implementation?
5. If I were to make the decision by myself, is it reasonably certain that it would be accepted by my subordinates?
6. Do subordinates share the organizational goals to be obtained in solving this problem?
7. Is conflict among subordinates likely in obtaining the preferred solution?

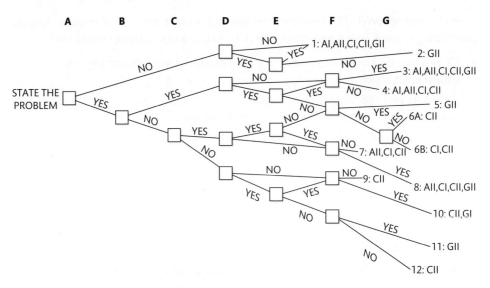

Figure 4.4 Vroom and Jago's normative model

Source: Vroom and Jago (1988). Reproduced with kind permission of the publisher.

By using the process and answering the questions, the model leads you down a path to a given style—with some outcomes offering a choice whereas other routes direct the leader to only one style. Vroom and Jago (1988) reviewed a series of studies that sought to validate this approach and by conducting a meta-analysis they found the mean success rate for decisions made using this approach was at 62 per cent whereas decisions made not using the model scored 37 per cent. However, empirical research is weak and Yukl (2006) points out that more studies are needed if a definitive answer is to be obtained.

 Pause for thought

Try using the Vroom and Jago/Yetton model on a recent decision you have made.

1. Did the outcome match the style you actually chose?
2. What are the implications of this for you?
3. Were you able to answer all of the questions?
4. Was it difficult or easy to use?

 Case study   The Chinese government

China is governed by the largest political party in the world, the Communist Party of China (CPC), which has around 80 million members. The CPC was founded in 1921 and, after winning a protracted civil war, assumed control in 1949 and has ruled China ever since. The party operates in a hierarchical manner with the National Party Congress electing nine members of the Politburo who nominally run the executive, legal system, and military within China.

The 'election' system is interesting in that it is based on what appears to be a bottom up model. The National Party Congress meets every five years and brings together upwards of 3,000 party officials from across China. Their role is to elect a Standing Committee of 200 individuals who, in turn, will elect the nine member of the Politburo—the de facto cabinet. At the head of the Politburo sits the General Secretary, currently Hu Jintao, who has a similar role to a president or prime minister. However, as many observers point out, the Chinese elections do not have the same underpinning philosophy experienced in a Western democracy. The allegiance of a party member is to the party itself and there is only one significant party in China—the CPC. This means that 'elections' are carried out on the basis of grace and favour of mentors, patrons, and power blocks. Generating influence and cultivating favour is a key part of any Chinese politician but open disagreement is rare.

The Politburo operates on a consensus decision-making basis, where different ideas are discussed but after a decision is reached the whole group must abide by it. This system has enabled China to become one of the world's most powerful nations and, with a huge population, ample resources, and a hard working ethos, this looks set to continue into the future. Western business people often comment on the ability of the Chinese government to get things done. Decisions made in the Politburo are quickly implemented and new infrastructure projects are rapidly constructed. The Beijing Olympic Games of 2008 was an example of the state creating a spectacular set of buildings and associated structures unparalleled in modern sport.

However, there are signs that the grip on China's middle and working classes may be slipping from the grasp of the rulers. Whilst it is true that the wages of many Chinese have risen, and new Western products are sought-after goods, society as a whole is becoming increasingly fragmented, with some suspecting that China is guilty of erecting a 'Potemkin Village' system to convince the West and their own people that all is well. The rise in corruption within the CPC is a constant source of embarrassment to the Chinese; for example, in September 2012 Wang Guoqiang became the latest official to flee China, with £20 million stolen from CPC funds. Another case in 2012, where the murder of a British businessman, Neil Haywood, was unsuccessfully covered up by the wife of a powerful politician, further exposed the Chinese to international condemnation. Furthermore, dissatisfaction with the poor standard of public services is also on the increase, with many questioning the basic communist ethos of equality. For a system that relies on patronage, it is easier for a minor government official to defer a decision upwards and to kow-tow to a superior than to dissent or risk making an unpopular choice. This means that, despite attempts to decentralize some of the powers of the Politburo, China remains a secretive and difficult place to be a citizen with a different political view or a grievance against an official.

Sources

http://gov.cn the Official Chinese Government website.

The Economist, March 2011.

The Daily Telegraph, 15 April 2012.

BBC, August 2012.

Questions

1. What challenges face the General Secretary in the next five years?

2. What style do you think the General Secretary will take?

3. How would you describe the leadership role of the General Secretary?

Style approach–strengths and weaknesses

Whilst the approach, in many ways, reflects the Western paradigm of leadership being about a person, in that the studies in this area have been about understanding how a 'leader' leads, 'style' is a very different template as the model offers the would-be leader a whole raft of options and possibilities. These possibilities arise because the focus is not on the attributes of the leader or even their behaviour in a rather narrow, two-dimensional sense, but on a much richer and dynamic world more familiar to those who inhabit organizations. This approach asks the leader to consider and choose from a plethora of different approaches depending on a number of contingent factors, such as their relationship with their followers and the nature of the task in hand. This complexity has evolved to incorporate subordinates capable of decision making and is very much a 'modern' leadership approach.

Secondly, despite the relative modernity of the approach, there is a rich seam of research, both historic and current, said to support the ideas contained in this model. The American universities previously mentioned, Ohio, Michigan, and the like, are still active in this area. This means that the style approach is 'live' and evolving as more insight is gained into leadership behaviours.

Finally, because the approach is not limited by the very essence of a person, the approach can be 'learned'. This means a leader can use the ideas to develop their style and they may become more effective as a result. So, in this sense, it is similar to the behaviour approach but also more complex and complicated because of the recognition of significant external pressures and influences on the leader. It can help organizations identify an approach that may suit their organizational culture and may also assist a manager to identify why an approach that is successful in one context is not working in another.

However, in terms of being the universal leadership theory its supporters had hoped for, there are some significant issues with the model. First, despite the research, it is still not clear how the leader's style actually influences the outcomes of a given task. Consider the underpinning assumption behind this model for a moment; the style of the leader should match the situation. However, this approach only considers a limited number of factors in terms of 'the situation'—there is no mention of the role of technology, for example. It tries to provide a simple answer to a complex and dynamic situation but, it could be argued, over simplifies to the point of being useless.

There would also appear to be a clear preference for the leader to show a degree of 'human', 'relationship', or 'collaborative' behaviour. These approaches, supported by organizations with the mantra 'our people are our most important asset', are at odds with the experiences of many individuals and managers. Yukl (2006) does support this view but there is little empirical evidence to back this approach up and a need to expand this area of research.

However, using the approach is not difficult and it has a 'common-sense' feel to it. By looking at their own natural style and developing the skills, language, and behaviour associated with a number of others, leaders can seek to stretch and develop their influencing skills. Many training courses using psychometrics tools such as the Myers–Briggs Type Indicator (MBTI) (see Chapter 10) try to illustrate a leader's style preference and assist with the development of other approaches. 360-degree feedback is another popular tool in this area, where individuals are rated anonymously on their style by peers, superiors, and subordinates. Again, the desire here is for a manager to be able to develop different approaches or to change their style according to the people and tasks upon which they are working.

Summary

The style approach moved on from the behavioural approach in that it sought to introduce a nod towards the complexity of the situation facing the leader. The early studies in this area instigated by Likert and Stogdill developed a simple two-dimensional approach that had similarities to the behavioural grid approach favoured by Blake and Mouton, discussed in Chapter 3. However, other researchers, such as Tannenbaum and Schmidt, saw the opportunity to develop a unique approach that offered a wider range of options to the prospective leader. Vroom and Yetton, and later Vroom and Jago added yet more complexity with a decision tree style that gave the leader a logic-driven approach to making his decision on which consultative approach he was going to deploy.

 Case study   Sir Alex Ferguson

'Managers seeking outstanding success would do well to look at the style of football giants like Bill Shankly and Alex Ferguson' (Professor Tom Cannon, Chief Executive of the Management and Enterprise National Training Council in *The Guardian*, 12 June 1999: 22).

Sir Alex Ferguson was, until May 2013, an eminent football manager. Born on 31 December 1941 in Glasgow, Scotland, he married Cathy and they had three sons. He was a talented striker with Ayr United, scoring 167 goals in 327 appearances for his Scottish team. From there he entered the challenging world of football management and he managed the Scotland national football team for a brief period before he moved to Aberdeen Football Club. However, it is being manager of Manchester United, which he joined in November 1986, making him, at the time, the longest serving football manager in the English Premiership that makes him one of the most iconic figures in world sport. He is also the most successful manager, winning (as of May 2013), among many other trophies, 13 Premier League titles, the FA Cup five times, and the UEFA Champions League twice.

Sir Alex Ferguson is, nevertheless, a controversial figure in a sport where passions run high, but his achievements have drawn leaders in many other areas of business to study his leadership approach. Football management is a notoriously unstable profession, dominated by fickle fans, domineering chairmen, and a voracious media. Ferguson is often particularly recognized for his commitment to long-term planning in a short-term industry, and for his motivational skills and emphasis on teamwork in an environment where team members are wealthy, much-feted stars. Whilst able to draw on enviable financial resources, and benefiting from an established, historical club reputation, these advantageous factors also create high expectations and place pressure on the manager.

An illuminating insight into Ferguson's leadership can be found through his involvement with the Collyhurst and Moston Lads Club, an inner-city boxing club. This Mancunian institution attempts to turn young people into champions, a practice that struck a chord with such a 'dressing room alchemist' (Taylor 2011) as Ferguson. The boxers Robbie Reid and Michael Jennings emerged from this club, whose alumni also include Manchester United's Brian Kidd and Nobby Stiles. Such places remind Ferguson of his formative years in Glasgow, where he attended the Harmony Row Club with its ambitious football teams. When Damien Hughes, son of Collyhurst and Moston's boxing coach, Brian Hughes, asked Ferguson to support the club, the United manager invited him to Carrington (the Manchester United training ground). Here he outlined his views on management and he has now written the foreword to Hughes' book (2009), *Liquid Leadership*, helping to raise funds for the club. A further clue to Ferguson's approach is his oft-quoted reference to Napoleon's thoughts that a 'leader is a dealer in hope'.

(Continued...)

Sir Richard Greenbury, former chairman of Marks and Spencer, has referred to Alex Ferguson as the 'best man-manager' in Britain today, and Ferguson certainly has the ability to motivate talented, highly paid young men who have found success at an early age. 'At some clubs you get players who think they have made it. Not here. The manager and other players don't stand for that' (Steve McLaren in *The Times*, 20 May 1999). Ferguson also seems able to motivate players when they are under great pressure. Two good examples of his success in this have been with Eric Cantona and David Beckham. After Cantona was banned for kicking an opposition fan and Beckham was sent off whilst playing for England in a World Cup match, both these well-known players were subjected to strong public criticism. Nevertheless, under Ferguson's management, they went on to make influential contributions to their team and to redeem themselves. 'He amazes me, day in, day out with his man-management, the way he treats people with the utmost respect ... He has tremendous influence over the way the players play, behave and train ... Anybody who comes in immediately knows what the standards are' (Steve McLaren in *The Independent on Sunday*, 23 May 1999).

In the past, Ferguson managed and motivated partly through making his players fear him, which is hardly a good example of modern, textbook management. He is known to be aggressive sometimes, and is often criticized for his short temper, particularly when he attacks referees and the media rather than admitting to failings in himself or in his players. 'I've got a temper if I need it. Nothing wrong with losing your temper if it's for the right reasons' he points out. However intimidating he may sometimes be, Ferguson's explosive personality has become part and parcel of his approach to motivation. It may be part of the driving force behind the team's success and seems to be accepted by most players as his unique style.

Some argue that Ferguson has now mellowed, and that his motivational force depends more than it used to on the mutual trust and respect between players and manager. This could be particularly true of those players, such as Paul Scholes and Ryan Giggs, who have come up through the youth team and have grown up under Ferguson's care. Trust is certainly important to Ferguson, and he sets an example of loyalty that players can rely on. For example, they can be sure that he will not criticize them in public (although he might do so before the rest of the team) or gossip about them. 'The players are well aware that if they need anything, if they're in trouble in any shape or form, they know they can knock on my door, they all know that and they all do', says Ferguson in his autobiography.

Whilst loyal to individual players, Ferguson values the team over the individual, and emphasizes teamwork even though the team includes multi-million pound stars. He operates a squad system to allow young players to gain experience, to rest senior players, and to ensure that one player can replace another without disturbing the balance of the team. However, it has taken years to convince the players, the football authorities, and the press of the merits of this system.

Drawing parallels between different industries can be fraught with danger; nevertheless, it could be suggested that Ferguson is capable of demonstrating the following attributes:

- Vision: he is clear how he wants the side to play and the competitions he wants the club to win.
- Passion: to be the very best in England, Europe, and probably the world.
- Commitment: to the club through hard work and discipline.
- People management: through motivation, loyalty, teamwork, and leading-edge training methods.
- Knowledge and understanding: of the organization's culture and corporate history, of the industry; awareness of the strengths and limitations of available skills within the club and intelligence about the competition.
- Corporate strategy: a recognition of the need for short-term success balanced against the importance of a long-term perspective.

- Positive attitude to change: to keep the organization moving forward, even when it involves an element of risk, such as selling influential players.
- Business awareness: a focus on the core competency of the business (although he is interested in all aspects of the organization's business, Ferguson concentrates on winning matches).
- Business ethics: he believes that managers should act with probity and expects the same standard of behaviour from his players—it is important to him how they conduct themselves both on and off the field. It is perhaps here that Ferguson attracts most negative comment.

Sources

http://manutd.com (accessed 29 July 2013).

http://siralexferguson.net/ (accessed 29 July 2013).

The Alex Ferguson Story, Granada Television, 1998.

Anonymous (2001) *The Official Manchester United Illustrated Encyclopaedia* (3rd edn). Manchester: Manchester United Books.

Hughes, D. (2009) *Liquid Leadership*. Chichester, UK: Capstone.

McIvanney, H. (1999) *Managing my life: My Autobiography*. London: Hodder Headline.

Taylor, D. Blog http://guardian.co.uk/football/blog/2011/may/08/sir-alex-ferguson-manchester-united-league-title (accessed 29 July 2013).

White, J. (1999) 'A Manager for all Seasons'. *The Guardian*, Saturday Review 22 May 1999: 6–7.

Questions

1. How would you assess Ferguson's leadership style? Has it changed at all?

2. What do you consider to be the strengths and weaknesses of his style?

3. How do you think he would cope in a 'normal' organization which had managers, subordinates, workers, and possibly trade unions involved?

Assignment—2,000 words

Consider a leadership or managerial decision that you have made recently. Think about the style you used to try to convince others as to the wisdom of your decision. Identify this style and the evidence you have used to come to this conclusion.

Now identify two other possible alternative styles you could have used. Explore the process, language, advantages, and disadvantages these different approaches may have had. What conclusions do you make on the efficacy of your original style? Would you make the same decision in a similar situation?

Style questionnaire

Read each item and decide how much you agree with each statement or how much it reflects your normal approach to leadership. Circle your response and proceed smoothly and quickly through the questions. If you are completing the form to rate another person, answer as you see them being *most* of the time.

Scoring Key: 1 = Not True/Never; 2 = Rarely; 3 = Sometimes; 4 = Often/Agree; 5 = Definitely/Always.

1	The more the merrier is better when making decisions	1	2	3	4	5
2	The leader is paid to make a decision	1	2	3	4	5
3	I am flexible when it comes to decisions	1	2	3	4	5
4	Everyone knows their place in my team	1	2	3	4	5
5	I listen to every idea made by my colleagues	1	2	3	4	5
6	I am clear on what needs to be done	1	2	3	4	5
7	Everybody is equal in my team	1	2	3	4	5
8	Teams slow things down	1	2	3	4	5
9	Sharing ideas is more productive and fun	1	2	3	4	5
10	Leading is about drive, energy, and decision making	1	2	3	4	5
11	'Listen and learn' is a positive mantra	1	2	3	4	5
12	I set the standard and expect everyone to meet it	1	2	3	4	5
13	Changing your mind takes strength	1	2	3	4	5
14	It's my way or the highway	1	2	3	4	5
15	My team like me	1	2	3	4	5
16	I communicate clearly what I want done	1	2	3	4	5
17	Leading is not about ego, it is about cooperation	1	2	3	4	5
18	Changing your mind shows weakness	1	2	3	4	5
19	Sharing decisions results in a motivated team	1	2	3	4	5
20	Discipline and order makes for effective decision making	1	2	3	4	5

This short questionnaire is designed to measure your affinity with the two extremes of Tannenbaum and Schmidt's model. The odd numbers represent your Follower (democratic) score and the even numbers your Leader Centred (autocratic) score. Subtract the two scores to give your overall rating.

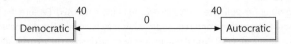

Interpretation

By identifying the different preferences you have towards these extremes you can begin to consider where your relative strengths lie. You can also begin to consider if this is a reflection of your current role or if there are other factors which influence your choices. You can ask colleagues about their perspective and look at how your organization reflects these different tendencies.

Further reading

Leadership Styles by Tony Kippenberger (2002, Oxford: Capstone) is a relatively easy read with an overview of the styles approach and a number of different case studies drawn from the world of international business. It has a limited theoretical discussion but offers a 'fast track' to grasping your leadership style.

Conclusions on Leadership Style by Dr Robert Clinton (1986, Abingdon: Barnabas Publishers) is a short, unusual book. It does examine leadership style theories and presents the major theorists reviewed above. However, he then attempts to merge these basic notions into a set of concepts he suggests can develop a 'Christian leader'. He suggests that leadership styles are one of the major causes of conflict in modern organizations and draws on parallels from the Scriptures.

Finally, a biography, *John F. Kennedy on Leadership: the Lessons and Legacy of a President* by John A. Barnes (2005, New York: AMACOM). Here there's an outline of the 'Kennedy' approach to leadership and some reflective questions to help you find your inner 'Kennedy'. An entertaining read with some interesting hypotheses about how modern politicians adapt their style to meet different situations.

5 Situational leadership

After reading this chapter you will:

- Understand how situational leadership theories evolved.
- Have gained an insight into the applications, strengths, and weaknesses of the model.
- Be able to see how your own approach is influenced by situational theory.

Introduction

Hopefully, what should be becoming clear is the explosion of different ideas and models relating to leadership that have begun to emerge. After years spent in the frustrating search for the Great Man and his traits, new ideas, and research into the nature of leadership have begun to surface and are still doing so—as we shall see later. In this chapter, we review the early contingency theories that are based on understanding how the circumstance the leader finds themselves in affects his influence on his subordinates and followers. The models reviewed are still based on the assumption there is a 'right' and 'wrong' way to lead, whilst there is additional focus on the followers and the organizational context. In particular, we shall examine Reddin's (1967) 3-D management style theory, Hersey and Blanchard's (1977) situational leadership theory, and Kerr and Jermier's (1978) substitutes for leadership approach so the evolution of this approach can be gauged. Although different in their construction, these ideas have some similarities in that they focus on aspects of the situation facing the leader (hence *situational* leadership) and they have all provoked a degree of controversy for being populist but having questionable empirical support. In essence, what these theories suggest is a leader's ability to lead depends (is **contingent**) upon certain factors and by understanding, recognizing, and adapting to these factors, the leader will be able to influence their surroundings and followers much more successfully than if these issues are ignored. Another theme explored here is the beginnings of a split between the academics and pragmatists, such as those concerned with leadership development and corporate trainers. Some of the ideas presented here are very popular both with organizations and with leadership development specialists because they offer a simple, easily grasped cognitive map that helps inexperienced leaders to feel they have a 'scientific' approach to leadership and, by using the tools, can become better at their job. Academic researchers, on the other hand, have been rather dismissive of these models, suggesting they are intellectually bankrupt and empirically untested. The chapter will explore why this divergence occurred and some of its implications.

> **Contingent:** contingent on/upon occurring or existing only if (certain circumstances) are the case. Dependent on: 'his fees were contingent on the success of his search'. *Oxford English Dictionary* 2011.

We saw in the previous chapter the focus on the style of the leader which, to a large degree, meant altering the decision-making process as a result of the leader's attitude to either people or task accomplishment. We also saw the various terms that have been used for these two domains; autocratic vs democratic, authoritarian vs equalitarian, employee vs production orientation, leader centred vs follower centred. This next approach differs in that the situational variables are largely focused on external factors rather than on the leader, which contrasts with some of the previous ideas that had the leader at the centre of the study. However, what is still postulated is that, by understanding these situational factors, any person can become 'better' in their leadership function.

 Pause for thought

1. What are your initial thoughts—does the situation matter or should a good manager be able to lead in any given situation?
2. Should you try to 'fit in' or should people take you how you are?
3. Can you spot any managers who struggle because *'their'* way is not *'our'* way?

Early developments

Reddin (1967) felt a degree of frustration with the two-dimensional approach proposed by supporters of Ohio and Michigan. He pointed out that, 'attempts to consider "the manager" as a single, internally undifferentiated job function have proven consistently fruitless' (1967:11). He felt the idea there was a 'best' approach was inaccurate and did not reflect reality because, for him, management was a varied and complex role that covered a diverse number of activities. So, for example, the suggestion by Blake and Mouton that a '9,9' manager was the ultimate aim, or that the 'Y' approach of McGregor (1960) was in some way preferable to the 'X' approach, did not sit well with Reddin's experiences of the industrial settings inhabited by many post-war American managers. He was convinced there was a third dimension to be considered in addition to the attitude the manager held towards his followers and their task. As well as his own observations he cites the work of Fleishman and Peters (1962) who struggled to find a high degree of correlation between effective managers and their orientation either towards 'consideration' or towards 'structure'. He concluded that effectiveness is an independent variable. What, in effect, he is suggesting, is that a different approach is needed in different organizations— for example, what works in the armed forces may not work in an Indian foundry or in a Cambridge University college. For him, these different situations required a different approach, so he suggested a three-dimensional model based around effectiveness and the task/relationship orientation of the manager. The model proposes 12 different options split into four less effective types, four latent types, and four more effective types (see: Table 5.1) to which he gave metaphorically inspired names to evoke a certain set of attributes.

Table 5.1 Reddin's 12 3-D styles

	No orientation	Relationship orientation	Task orientation	Task and relationship orientation
Latent	Separated	Relationships	Task	Integrated
Ineffective	Deserter	Missionary	Autocrat	Compromiser
Effective	Bureaucrat	Developer	Benevolent autocrat	Executive

Source: Adapted from Reddin (1967).

Outlined below is a brief character profile for each type.

The four basic types

1. Separated: an individual largely removed from both people and tasks, who is mainly concerned with maintaining the system and status quo. They are likely to be competent administrators, content with managing paperwork and communicating by email.

2. Relations: A friendly, open, and chatty person concerned about a pleasant environment. Communication is possibly typified by long conversations about personal matters but with little focus on driving the business forward.

3. Task: A hard driving, ambitious individual who wants to get the job done. Probably self-reliant and often sets individual's goals rather than thinking about a broader agenda.

4. Integrated: This individual wants and supports teamwork and prefers a shared set of objectives.

Four 'less effective' type descriptors

1. Deserter (low task/low relationship): A manager who seems to be both ineffective and destructive with no interest in delivering the outcomes required or the people involved in the task. Reddin considers this type dangerous because not only may they 'desert' but they may also destroy the morale and hence performance of those in the immediate vicinity unlucky enough to be managed by this person.

2. Missionary (high relationship/low task): Although this person is oriented towards the people in his team, he is classified as ineffective because he is more concerned about maintaining relationships and harmony. This may mean that production could be disrupted by their need to be seen as popular and friendly rather than making hard decisions that could meet with disapproval from subordinates.

3. Autocrat (high task/low relationship): This person uses legitimate authority and possibly strong-arming tactics to ensure the task is delivered regardless of the human cost. They are ineffective because they achieve this by fear and individuals will only respond when coercion can be used. Team members will not respond willingly and may exhibit resistance to the broader organizational objectives.

4. Compromiser (high task/high relationship): This individual is of a type that knows what should be done but is either inept or unable to make the right decisions. They may

vacillate and procrastinate, usually reacting to the loudest demand first. This means they aim to resolve immediate crises but not the longer term issues that require strategic decisions to be made. Another attribute suggested by Reddin is that they may selfishly choose to focus their energy on satisfying individuals able to assist with their own career development.

Four 'more effective' type descriptors

1. Bureaucrat (low task/low relationship): Whilst this person can be efficient and effective it is via a strict adherence to a formulaic set of instructions. They may not make this rigorous application of 'the rules' obvious but they do not have any significant interest in people or the effect the 'rules' will have on the people affected. Indeed, they do not really care about the process either and will make little attempt to improve or modify it.

2. Developer (high relationship/low task): Essentially this person sees their managerial function as a coach. Their strength lies in growing and developing the skills, talents, and knowledge of others in their team. By motivating and creating an atmosphere of trust, this manager will been seen as effective as his team deliver the required results.

3. Benevolent autocrat (high task/low relationship): Here we have an individual who is seen as effective in delivering the required organizational goals. This is done by creating a culture where task achievement is rewarded with either tangible benefits or praise from the manager. Thus, individual follower behaviour is modified towards the broader organizational goals and away from relationships within the group.

4. Executive (high task/high relationship): This manager recognizes the importance and primacy of delivering the organization's requirements but, in order to achieve this, the coordinated effort of every member of his team will be needed. This kind of manager understands people and how to switch them on using motivational techniques. They are committed to doing 'right' by their team and are committed to their individual development in so far as this development leads to a more effective organization.

Reading through the model, the similarities with some of the previously discussed ideas should begin to surface. However, the key observation that Reddin makes is that the difference between more or less effective managerial types is often a trait-based analysis—in other words, what creates and drives these 'types' is a direct function of their personality. This could mean an effective leader with the requisite traits would be successful in any given situation. However, Reddin believes a better explanation of the efficacy of the leader would be to ascertain how closely the manager's style is congruent with the demands of the situations in which he finds himself. Figure 5.1 outlines his model and summarizes the 'forces' that can influence the approach of the prospective leader.

He does not elaborate on why he considers these elements to be significant or what they may actually mean but he does explain what he believes to be the implications of considering these domains. For example, a style that is effective in one situation would not necessarily be so in an alternative culture. A Bureaucrat with an affinity towards rules, regulations, and process who is treasured within an organization with hierarchy, strict norms, and a product or service that demands a certain indifference to 'people' would provoke a very different

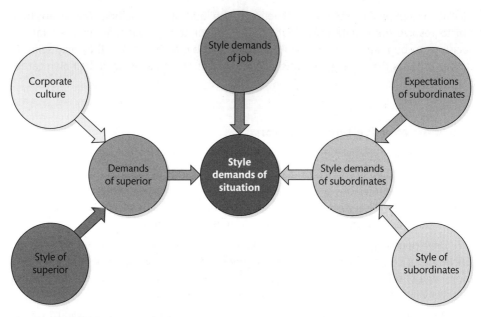

Figure 5.1 Reddin's Style Demands of Situation

reaction in a company which needed its managers to motivate staff, be 'customer focused', and flexible in their approach to red tape.

Drawing on Reddin's ideas as an inspiration for his work, in 1969 Dr Paul Hersey (1931–2012) and his invited collaborator, Ken Blanchard, developed a theory that has become one of

> ### ⊙ Case study   Karen Callaghan—People Director, Innocent Drinks
>
> Innocent Drinks, founded in 1999, currently has a majority share (around 70 per cent) of the £170 million UK smoothie market. Karen joined Innocent Drinks in 2006 from Standard Chartered Bank. She has worked with its board to create an innovative and unusual working environment where you are likely to see clutter and chaos everywhere. The walls in Fruit Towers—the company's current office in London—are covered in hand written notes, bunting hangs from the ceilings, and stuffed toy animals and teddy bears sit side by side with the workforce. Karen believes the noise, décor, and branding all create a unique atmosphere that adds to the creativity the company is renowned for. However, she makes the point that she has a very sophisticated and 'live' handle on every employee's progress towards their performance targets. She can track and measure individual compliance of workforce objectives at any point from her computer terminal. She says the image of Innocent being an easy-going organization is misplaced. 'Our values are not that soft, fluffy or ephemeral but they capture the things we are,' she says. This commercial edge was controversially demonstrated in 2010 when the directors sold 58 per cent of the company to Coca-Cola for £68 million. This prompted social networking sites to propose a boycott of their products, with customers suggesting they had 'sold out'. Callaghan denies this and says the product is still identical

to when it was first sold at music festivals in the late 1990s. She feels her mission is to maintain this creative and fun atmosphere as the company goes through significant changes, such as their new owners and the fact they are about to leave Fruit Towers and relocate to Portobello Dock later in 2011. Karen wants to take all of the 'fun' items to make sure the employees remain happy and committed. She points out the high satisfaction ratings employees give to working at Innocent and what she feels is more than mere lip service to their values—such as giving 10 per cent of their profits to charity via the Innocent Foundation.

Sources:

Professional Manager, June 2011.

Steele, Francesca (2010) 'Coca-Cola takes a bigger slice of Innocent'. *The Times* (London), 9 March 2010.

http://innocentdrinks.co.uk.

http://innocentfoundation.org.

http://linkedin.com/company/innocent-drinks.

Questions

1. What pressures and forces do you think will affect Karen's leadership approach?

2. Do you think the recent changes will affect her style?

3. Do you think she is being naïve or over-optimistic if she thinks things can stay the same?

the most well used (Rollinson 2002) and popular leadership models employed in industry (Hersey et al. 1982). However, the subsequent model has also been criticized for its lack of 'logical and internal inconsistencies, conceptual ambiguity, incompleteness and confusion associated with multiple versions of the model' (Graeff 1983:285). The model, and how Hersey originally intended it to be used, is outlined in the following section—and it must be noted that, despite these disparaging comments, the framework developed by Hersey remains well respected and research into his ideas continues to this day.

Hersey and Blanchard's life cycle theory of leadership

We have examined in previous chapters the tensions that often emerge between academic and more 'practitioner' focused researchers. Perhaps this strain is no better illustrated than by examining Hersey's work. Hersey remained, until his recent death, a staunch advocate of education whilst Blanchard, his collaborator, pursued a more economic agenda. Paul Hersey and Ken Blanchard worked collaboratively at first on the theory that a leader's approach should be dependent on the 'maturity' of the followers. However, as Van Maurik puts it, 'Ken Blanchard is one of those writers who best illustrate the thin line between academic and popular approaches to writing on leadership' (2001:21) because, in subsequent years, Blanchard has promoted 'The Situational Leadership Model II®' (SLII®) and his subsequent range of books, such as *The One Minute Manager* (Blanchard and Johnson 1982) which has sold more than 13 million copies. Until 1977, Hersey and Blanchard worked together on the theory there was no one 'best' leadership style, then they agreed to part company and to focus on their own agendas. However, their early work remains a benchmark for moving the debate surrounding leadership away from 'one size fits' all to a more dynamic approach which can be mastered by applying a few simple checks. Their original theory was called the Life Cycle Theory of Leadership (Hersey and Blanchard 1969) and it evolved into Situational Leadership Theory (Hersey and Blanchard 1977). The theory now has two different models associated with it; The Situational Leadership Model® and Situational Leadership® II.

The current version of The Situational Leadership Model can be viewed directly at http://situational.com (accessed 30 July 2013). For further information on Situational Leadership II®, see: http://kenblanchard.com (accessed 30 July 2013).

Essentially, their original proposal was that leaders should adjust their approach to their subordinates according to certain conditions existing in the wider environment (the *situation*). In particular, they ask the leader to consider their follower's 'maturity'. In their view, if a leader were to remain effective, then they would have to modify their approach as their followers and subordinates changed in terms of their ability and readiness to direct their own actions. They based this view on their research (Hersey and Blanchard 1969) which suggested that a leader's relationship with followers went through different stages or phases. This evolution was largely driven by the *maturing* of a follower as they became more confident and able to take on responsibility for their own task related decisions and subsequent actions. The maturity of the follower to assume more responsibility for their actions is a term that encompasses two aspects of the subordinate's characteristics:

1. Psychological readiness: The degree to which an employee is willing to take on responsibility for their actions in relation to task achievement. This aspect encompasses themes such as motivation and confidence in their own ability.

2. Task readiness: This covers their ability to deliver what has been asked of them. Their skills, knowledge, and ability will affect their delivery of a task independently of a leader offering structure and direction to their task.

One of the major implications of this idea was that 'leadership' was closely associated with 'development'—in that a leader should be concerned with developing the followers so they could move forward in terms of their own 'maturity'.

 Pause for thought

1. What do you think could be some of the implications for judging individuals against these criteria?

2. Do you think individuals 'mature' or could they stay 'immature'?

3. Why do you think this? What examples from your own experiences do you have that support your thoughts?

By assessing and reviewing these two themes, a leader should, according to them, make a judgement on the follower's maturity. (It is important to note here that this term has no chronological overtones, but simply refers to the follower's condition when assessed against these two criteria.) Then, by drawing on the Ohio State leadership model reviewed in Chapter 4, the leader could adjust their own behaviour to ensure that the individual followers received the 'correct' support to deliver the task. This creates a more dynamic relationship between leader and subordinate that supporters of this approach feel more accurately reflects 'real life'. The manager has to make a shift between the two types of leadership behaviour explored earlier; namely, directive/task or relationship/supportive. This 'either/or' approach generates a relatively simple two by two matrix format of the model, which in turn suggests four different behaviour patterns a leader could deploy when seeking to maximize his influence on a given subordinate. These styles, originally known as Telling, Selling, Participating, and Delegating (Hersey and Blanchard 1969), have, like other aspects of the model, gone through some changes and are likely to have been encountered in recent books (e.g. Hersey et al. 2001) as Directing, Coaching, Supporting, and Delegating. This development is a theme returned to in the next section when the challenges to this approach are considered in more detail.

How the model operates

The Situational Leadership Model® begins with two assumptions: that there is a task to be achieved, and that there are a set of followers available to deliver the required outcomes. The first stage for the prospective leader is to consider the maturity of his followers when judged against the *current* task requirements. This is a vital step because it may be there could be an instance whereby the leader encounters a follower with a great deal of experience in one particular skill, environment, or situation but relatively none in the current situation. For example, a highly trained soldier who is now in a civilian role, or a highly skilled scientist now faced with man-management challenges. The leader needs to consider a number of factors to help him correctly assess the state of his followers. For example, the task complexity, the skills in relation to the task, their drive and energy to start and complete the task, how well they have functioned previously, and other historical data. This analysis of the subordinates by the leader generates four different categories of follower.

1. R1: This follower is unable to complete the task requirement because they do not possess the necessary skills. In addition they may also be either unwilling to deliver the required performance or be insecure in their belief they can complete the task as requested. This could for a number of different reasons, such as low self-esteem.

2. R2: In this category, the follower is unable to comply with the task requirements but, in contrast to R1, is willing to try. So they may lack the ability, knowledge, or skill but are motivated to attempt the task. An example of the type of worker in this category could be new employees who are keen to impress but have little grasp of the complexities of the task, or perhaps older, experienced workers who come across a new process or product.

3. R3: Here the follower is likely to be able to carry out the task demands—in that they will have the necessary technical knowledge. However, they will be unwilling to do so. This

could be for two different reasons, they could be unmotivated to comply with the leader's request or be nervous about doing so without support and encouragement from the leader. An example might be a highly skilled worker who has simply lost their enthusiasm for the task or organization and is just going through the motions doing enough to get the job done, or, perhaps, a newly qualified accountant reviewing her first set of corporate accounts.

4. R4: Ready, willing, and able is probably the best way to summarize the state of this follower. The subordinate is motivated to carry out the task and has the necessary intellectual skills, personal attributes, and confidence to carry out the job.

As the model has evolved, it is interesting to note the changing language used by Hersey and the implications of the decision by the pair to go their separate ways. In their initial drafts, the term 'maturity' was used to describe the followers but this gained a certain 'ageist' connotation and was replaced (Hersey et al. 2001) by 'readiness' (hence R1 to R4). This was more than a semantic change and really tried to reflect the accelerating business environment. Readiness is a function of the amount of 'willingness' and 'ability' the follower or group demonstrates whilst attempting to perform the required task. However, versions by Blanchard (Blanchard et al. 1985) have the term 'development' incorporated, and the eponymous diagram is relabelled D1 to D4—meaning 'directing', 'coaching', 'supporting', and 'delegating', respectively.

The next stage is for the leader to consider their own style or behavioural pattern. Hersey and Blanchard believed managers had a preferred or natural style and developed an instrument to enable individuals to assess their position on their model. Hersey's legacy lives on within his own organization (see: http://situational.com) where clients can be assessed using a variety of tools developed to assist with leadership development. However, according to this approach, effective leaders need to do more than recognize their own style because at the heart of this model is the belief that *followers* determine the appropriate leader behaviour.

The leader has access to four different styles, labelled S1, 2, 3, and 4, to enable him to achieve his goals via influence over his followers.

1. S1: Telling. This is a *high* task but *low* supportive style. Here, the leader is primarily concerned with task delivery and little concerned with developing the individuals completing the task. Typical behaviours would be offering step-by-step instructions, close supervision, and a clear explanation of the consequences of non-performance. The leader will clearly define the task and be very clear on the stages and process to follow. This is necessary because the leader believes the follower either does not know what to do, and hence needs clear instructions, or they are unwilling and require a degree of coercive power to be used to ensure they comply with instructions. Of course, there will be a subtle difference in the leader's manner in each of these different scenarios but the essential elements are a close supervision coupled with firm instructions. There is likely to be a certain remoteness in terms of the relationship between the leader and follower with little by way of interpersonal interaction between the leader and follower over and above that necessary to complete the task.

2. S2: Selling. Following the curve upwards from right to left brings the next approach into focus, which lies in the *high* task and *high* support quadrant. The judgement made by the leader is that his followers are willing but not able (R2 types) to complete the task. So,

although the leader is still making the vast majority of the decisions about what is delivered and how the task is to be achieved, the relationship is also concerned with developing the confidence and skills of the follower so that ultimately they can take on more responsibility for their actions. The leader will allow questions and take time to explain why actions have to be taken. There is likely to be a degree of closer personal interaction as the leader seeks to develop the subordinate's self-belief. He will encourage, reinforce and reward 'good' behaviour, and demonstrate patience when something does not go quite to plan.

3. S3: Supporting. The next quadrant gives the *high* support and *low* task style option for the leader. The leader's approach is one of support when required by the subordinate but relatively less directive instruction. This may involve listening, praise, and a high level of interaction between the two parties. The leader trusts the follower to achieve the day-to-day tasks with the leader resisting any temptation to tell the follower what to do, when, or even how. The leader will encourage and offer feedback but this is designed to motivate and develop the employee rather than act as a comment on the task achievement, unless it is felt this will act as a motivator for the follower. What underpins this approach is the assumption made by the leader that the follower is capable of achieving the task but needs a supportive environment in which to do this.

4. S4: Delegating. The final quadrant offers a *low* support and *low* task perspective. The leader here is providing a strategic overview of the activities by observing and monitoring the progress of the subordinate but this is a very much hands-off approach. The employee will have the skills, know-how, and motivation to deliver what is required and can be left mostly unsupervised to deliver the required outcomes. The leader can further encourage autonomy and focus their energy on providing the necessary support and resources required by the follower. However, the leader should guard against either overloading the willing employee or withdrawing completely from their proximity.

According to the model, the leader should be able to identify the maturity/readiness of his followers and match his style to their demands. 'What a marvellous thing we now have available to use at home, at the office, in any kind of interpersonal situation,' states Hersey (Hersey et al. 2001:188). One implication is that a leader's *preferred* style (assessed using an appropriate tool) may not be the most *effective* style. This means that a leader needs

---

 Pause for thought

Think of phrases a leader might say to his subordinates that would typify each of the four leadership styles:

S1–Directing

S2–Coaching

S3–Supporting

S4–Delegating.

1. Which ones can you 'hear' yourself using?

2. Which ones do you feel most uncomfortable saying? Why?

to be proficient in using a number of different styles depending on the state of the followers. In addition, a leader needs to recognize the dynamic nature of the model, which suggests that individuals may move back and forth along the curve as the task requirements change. This could mean that she will need to employ a different style with the same individual as that person's attributes change over time and as different tasks emerge. For example, a very experienced car mechanic asked to work on a new model or engine may move from being classified as a R4 type, willing and able employee, to a R1 type because they do not have the necessary skills.

Hersey et al. (2001) expand on the attributes for the model by claiming it cannot only suggest the most appropriate approach a prospective leader should use when confronted by a given situation, but it can also predict the likely success of other styles if a leader, for whatever reason, is unable to use the 'correct' approach. Table 5.2 illustrates the suggested priority order and rating for each different approach in each different situation.

This means, for example, if a leader encounters a R1 type employee (remember this is a person who is unable is carry out the task requirements because they either do not have the ability or the confidence to do so unaided) then the S1 (telling) approach is likely to give the 'best' outcome, with the S4 (delegating) approach likely to fail.

So, what does this approach offer the end user? As remarked on earlier, it is widely used and has stood the test of the market place for over 30 years. Organizations and

---

 Case study

Abigail is a recent graduate and has just completed her year-long training programme to become a qualified primary school teacher. She has been on three different placements at primary schools in London. In each placement, she has been under the direct supervision of a classroom teacher and a mentor based at her teacher training college. As each placement has progressed, she has taken on more and more teaching. So, in her first placement she was listening to her classroom teacher and helping her to deliver the lessons to a class of eight-year-old children. In the next, she was responsible for teaching four lessons per week with a class of ten-year-old children, and in her final school she taught and planned six lessons per week to a class of six-year-old students. At each stage, she was observed and offered feedback on her performance by the class teacher and mentor. Abigail has a new job that begins in September where she will be responsible for the entire planning, teaching, and assessment of her own class. During this year, she will again be observed by her school head and will need to be assessed as making satisfactory progress in order to be given Qualified Teacher Status. The possible consequences of her not passing this final hurdle is that she could be refused a licence to teach, the school will need a another new teacher, and the state will have wasted thousands on her training, so it is vitally important this first year is handled correctly.

Questions

1. What leadership approach should her head adopt to maximize Abigail's chance of achieving Qualified Teacher Status?

2. What assumptions have you made to reach your decision?

3. What would happen if any of your assumptions are incorrect?

Table 5.2 Predicted style success

Follower classification	Leader style			
	S1	S2	S3	S4
R1	High	Medium/High	Medium/Low	Low
R2	Medium/High	High	Medium/Low	Low
R3	Low	Medium/High	High	Medium/Low
R4	Low	Medium/Low	Medium/High	High

Source: Adapted from Hersey et al. (2001).

supporters point to this as almost a badge of honour, remarking that if it was not useful then either the market would have stopped using it or something else would have replaced it. Dr Paul Hersey runs a highly successful organization dedicated to developing commercial opportunities for the model whilst Dr Ken Blanchard has a string of books and website promoting his expertise. It is this practical nature that tends to appeal to end-users and trainers alike. The model can be applied to a range of different situations from organizational settings, organizational roles (e.g. see: Hersey 1984), through to parenting situations (see Hersey et al. 2001:188).

It is also different from some previously explored approaches in that it is relatively simple and intuitive to grasp with only four styles available to the leader. It does not require the leader to go through a complex path (similar to, for example, Vroom's model reviewed in Chapter 4) before ending at a decision as to what to do next. Also worthy of note is the prescriptive nature of the model and perhaps it is this feature that lies at the heart of its appeal to new leaders or those unsure of their response to a given scenario. The model effectively tells a manager how to behave and what language and style to deploy in a given situation. If the perception is that a leader's team is highly skilled but demotivated, then a leadership style that is supportive would, it is suggested, give the highest chance of success, whereas a directive/telling style is most likely to further exasperate the situation (see: Table 5.2). By using this approach, a leader can direct their energy towards behaving in a manner most likely to produce the desired end result.

Using the model offers the leader a degree of flexibility in their approach. As an individual gains skills and confidence, they will require different degrees of support from their manager. This support may wax and wane as different tasks are attempted. The model allows for this movement and, rather than dictating a fixed position, encourages the manager to treat people differently and to recognize the dynamic nature of leadership.

However, despite these attractive characteristics, there are some issues that need to be considered when reviewing this approach. First, it is worth reviewing the three basic assumptions upon which the model is built:

1. As individuals develop their skills and confidence they will follow the development path as described. It would be difficult to move, for example, straight from S1 to S4. It is also assumed that individuals with a certain degree of maturity or readiness will all require the same input from the leader. So every well qualified, highly motivated individual needs a delegative style.

2. The manager needs the skill and insight to be able to correctly assess the state of readiness of his followers. He needs to have sufficient abilities and background data to be able to judge accurately the status of followers in terms of their maturity/readiness based on the two criteria outlined above. For example, the number one error in diagnosing a follower's 'willingness' is to view someone as unmotivated when they are in fact insecure or apprehensive about a task. The leader must be sufficiently skilled to be able to notice the subtleties associated with these differences.

3. The manager must have the skills and emotional tools to be able to carry off the four different styles sufficiently well to convince his followers these are genuine behaviours. Failure to do this is likely to result in suspicion and the perception of a lack of sincerity on the part of the manager, which, in turn, is likely to lead to resentment and ridicule.

Despite this excellent pedigree and user support, some criticisms began to emerge. The first of these has been hinted at and is related to the evolution of the model as it has gone through several iterations since being introduced in the late 1970s. As the model has been developed, and the original authors have turned to different collaborators for inspiration, the terminology used in the model has also changed. For example, the labels attached to the curvilinear contour at the heart of the model changed significantly, as both Hersey and Blanchard's work diverged. The claim by detractors (e.g. Byrne 1986; Kilmann 1984) is that this leads to pedagogic confusion by those unfamiliar with the tool. Their view is that the model is a reactive attempt to exploit the desire of managers and organizations to look for the 'magic bullet' that will solve their organizational woes. Changing the terms of the model, they argue, points to a degree of intellectual expediency in the face of commercial gain, something vehemently denied by Dr Hersey, who makes quite clear the model is based on empirically derived data. Vecchio (1987) supports this response as does 'the market' where Hersey's Situational Leadership Model® is in high demand. For example, Kris Sakowicz, the Global Learning Operations Manager at Motorola, said, 'After attending the Situational Leadership® workshop, our managers are better equipped to lead their employees in taking on projects and/or responsibilities' ('What Clients Are Saying', http://situational.com (accessed 16 August 2013)).

Several criticisms relate to how the authors originally reached their conclusions about the 'maturity' of the follower based on the two original criteria of psychological and task readiness. Graeff (1997:156) is particularly worried about this, and other, ambiguities within the model, because 'the model lacks theoretical or logical justification for the way the components of maturity combine'. This concern over the meaning of words can also be illustrated by the comments surrounding the confidence of the followers which, according to the model, ebb and flow between the different maturity phases but it is not always clear why. In addition, it could be argued that other factors affect this aspect of a subordinate such as age, education level, culture (see: GLOBE in Chapter 12), or even gender.

Although the model proudly boasts about its practical nature, there are several concerns relating to this attribute. Consider, for example, the allusion towards the skills of the manager. The manager has to make a judgement call on the 'maturity' of his followers using the aforementioned criteria. The question remains whether this is a skill that managers possess and, if they do not, how it can be taught or otherwise obtained. Second, an explicit part of the model is that managers should change their behaviour given the situation. Again, this is refuted by some (e.g. Fiedler (1967) see: Chapter 6) who sees little evidence to suggest that

Case study Angela Merkel

Angela Merkel, born in 1954, is the current German Chancellor, winning a third term in office in the elections held in September 2013. As well as being the first female German head of state, she is a Protestant from the former East Germany. By becoming first head of her party and then Chancellor in 2005, she broke the leadership mould of the Christian Democrats Party (CDU), which was traditionally dominated by Catholic West German men. Over the past four years she has had to steer Germany and Europe through some difficult times, but she remains very popular both within her country and abroad. After first being elected in 2005, she entered into coalition with her rivals in the Social Democrats (SPD), including her 2009 election challenger, and foreign minister, Frank-Walter Steinmeier. This meant ditching some of her planned free market reforms, and agreeing to more Left-leaning measures like a minimum wage in some sectors and a huge fiscal stimulus. Many thought the coalition would break apart, but Mrs Merkel managed to hold it together, and took the credit for Germany's emergence from recession, and the deal that kept Opel, a huge vehicle manufacturer, a going concern. From 2006 to 2009, *Forbes* magazine has named her the most powerful woman in the world and the *New Statesman* named her in 'The World's 50 Most Influential Figures' in 2010. The dowdy image that supporters feared would stymie her progress to the top is long forgotten, she has modernized her appearance, wearing bright colours and sporting more stylish hairstyles. 'Some people said Angela Merkel was boring and provincial, but they underestimated her,' says Detmar Doering, the head of the Liberal Institute in Potsdam. In June 2011, following the near nuclear catastrophe in Japan, she announced that Germany will be the first industrialized country in the world to renounce nuclear power. This reversed an earlier decision to continue to operate nuclear power stations until 2035. She is widely recognized as being both a pragmatist and a leader capable of winning compromises from her allies and opponents. Her detractors suggest that she is shifting to the Left, whereas her supports claim this is good leadership which keeps everyone on-board.

Sources

http://bundeskanzlerin.de/Webs/BK/EN/ (accessed 30 July 2013). This is the official website for the German Chancellor.

Mills, Clifford (2007) *Angela Merkel* (Modern World Leaders). New York: Chelsea House Publishers.

Questions

1. What do think Mrs Merkel's preferred style would be?

2. What evidence do you have that she changes her approach?

3. How does she encourage her followers?

managers can and do change their interpersonal approach. Regardless of Fiedler's perspective, this is another skill the manager will have to develop in order to become effective as a leader.

Finally, the model does little to help a manager leading a team of different personalities. Chapter 14 explores the theme of teams in more depth but in this case the model does not specify whether the leader should adopt a different approach for each individual or take a decision based on the majority state of 'readiness' present within the team. Different approaches to different people may lead to accusations of bias and unfair discrimination. Yet, despite the challenges, the Situational Leadership Model® has been used extensively in leadership train-ing worldwide for several decades, and has acquired considerable face validity.

Leadership substitutes theory

Over 30 years ago, Kerr and Jermier (1978) were puzzled by the lack of success in link-ing individual leaders to successful outcomes for organizations. They could not understand why, despite the investigations into trait theory—that had been superseded by the style and behavioural schools already reviewed—that still there was no clear answer as to why some leaders succeeded in some situations but failed in others. One has only to look at historical and sporting examples to see this is true; for example, Walt Disney was fired from his first few jobs for allegedly lacking in ideas and imagination. In the original version of the model, Kerr and Jermier were interested in exploring alternatives for what they called 'supportive' and 'in-strumental' leadership—further terms for 'relationships focus' or 'task focus' behaviour. They turned their attention to aspects of the organization, followers, and task that could either act as a *substitute* for leaders or *negate* the effect of leadership. In a sense, they rejected the leader-centric view of the earlier theories that suggest leadership emanates from a single person and without this person making decisions about their style, or altering their approach based on the nature of their followers, then no positive outcomes were likely. Their view widened situational theory to suggest that factors within the task, organization, and followers themselves have just as much significant impact on the outcomes of a task as that of any leader—and, they argued, sometimes more so. This view ran counter to the prevailing view that leadership was the key to organizational success, and, they suggested, helped to 'explain both the occasional successes and frequent failures of the various theories and model of leadership' (1978:377).

They sought to identify factors present within the 'situation' that could reduce the impact of formal leaders. For example, Gordon (1994) cites an example of a hospital emergency ward where, upon the arrival of an ambulance containing a patient, each nurse, doctor, and orderly went about their tasks without instruction from an overseeing manager (see also: Kunzle 2010). Leadership Substitute Theory seeks to explain these kinds of situations by proffering the view that, under certain circumstances, leadership in a formal sense is neither needed nor wanted and may actually have a demotivating and negative impact on the achievement of a task.

They used two different terms; namely, substitutes for leadership and neutralizers. Sub-stitutes describe the characteristics of the task, organization, or followers that make leader-ship behaviours either irrelevant or unnecessary. These are factors 'which render relationship and/or task oriented leadership not only impossible but also unnecessary' (Kerr and Jermier 1978:396); whereas neutralizers are characteristics that either prevent effective leadership or nullify the effects of leadership. An example of a substitute would be a leader operating with a highly skilled team of technicians who do not need any guidance in how to complete their specialized task; a neutralizer could be a leader operating in an organization where strong performance is not rewarded appropriately.

Their model describes three different aspects of the situation that may mitigate against ef-fective leadership and they maintained that without considering these aspects a leader may be doomed to fail even if they attempt to develop the behavioural flexibility outlined by Situational Leadership Theory. They felt substitutes and neutralizers had their origin in a com-bination of three possible sources.

Characteristics of followers

Ability and experience. Subordinates with the requisite depth of task knowledge and experience may not need a supervisor to tell them what to do or how to do it. In short, they can act competently without interference from a third party. Indeed, it may be counterproductive for a leader to interfere in this way as this may undermine the worker or trigger a defensive reaction in the individual.

Emotional needs. Some individuals simply prefer to work unsupervised. They reject external influence and demand autonomy. This allows them to control their workload and, to an extent, how they complete their task. Close monitoring or micro management will serve to act as a demotivator with this type of individual.

Professional orientation. Accountants, doctors, university lecturers, and the like often give more credence to comment from their peer group than that from their own organization. This may mean they either reject or ignore organizational influence where this does not tie in with this external validation.

Reward orientation. The degree to which an individual responds to external rewards offered by the organization can neutralize any leadership behaviour. For example, if a follower values time with his family, he will not respond particularly well to an offer of overtime payments for working late.

Characteristics of tasks

Task structure. If a task is straightforward and simple, a follower may not want or even need a leader's input. An undemanding task that has very little scope for creativity, such as data input, may only have one process to be completed. This type of work, although often treating the worker as part of the machine, does not need a leader to oversee how it is completed, merely that a task has been achieved.

Nature of feedback. A quote, attributed to Ken Blanchard, suggests that 'feedback is the breakfast of champions'. What he means here is that obtaining feedback on performance is likely to lead to an increase in satisfaction and understanding on the part of the recipient; so the role of a leader is to provide that feedback to his followers. However, where this feedback is provided by the task outcome, effectively the leadership has been substituted. A worker building a wall can see if the wall is straight and true and hence has feedback on his performance.

Intrinsic satisfaction. Some tasks can generate reward simply because they are either difficult to achieve or by their very nature, 'good'—for example, a charitable act. These interesting and enjoyable tasks do not need a leader to motivate others to complete them. They offer a substitute for a leader offering extrinsic rewards such as praise or pay.

Characteristics of the organization

Bureaucracy. An organization with rigid rules and control structure may also have strict procedures and policies that mitigate against creativity or discretion when attempting to try new ideas. This may rule against innovation and change, as the workforce will know what the outcome of any discussion is likely to be. This may neutralize a leader who wants to investigate new processes or working methods. Civil services or other public sector organizations, such as councils, are often accused of this malfunction.

Formalization. An associated theme is the degree to which an organization formalizes its expectations of behaviour and performance outcome. During the task definition stage, where each individual sub-task is defined and ascribed to a given individual, there is little room for negotiation or misunderstanding about what is required from a given work. In this case, with clear written contracts, letters of understanding, and a codified performance system, there may be no need for further leadership intervention.

Group coherence. A group with a high degree of coherence may gain all necessary guidance and support from its own internal resources without the need to refer to an outside authority. The team will manage its own expectations and performance without the need for reference to external individuals. There may also be a neutralizing effect if the relationships within the team are stronger and override the input from the leadership. Peer pressure in this case will be the lead factor when an individual considers his actions.

Limited positional power. There may be cases where a leader has little or no scope for rewarding or punishing followers. This will mean desire on the part of the leader to recognize or reprimand an employee is neutralized. For example, a predetermined pay and bonus structure can limit a leader's ability to reward a hard working employee. This may also be true if the employee is subject to trade union membership that could be sufficiently powerful to diminish any organizational influence.

Geographic proximity. Where structures exist that preclude regular meetings between a leader and subordinate, it can be notoriously difficult to influence and manage behaviour (for example see: Duarte and Snyder 2006). Supportive behaviour from a leader is neutralized as it becomes difficult to maintain a degree of consistency in terms of contact between, say, a remote sales manager and his team of sales representative dispersed across Europe. Whilst it is true that modern synchronous and asynchronous communication systems, such as email and video conferencing, make this less of an issue than when originally proposed, it is still certainly true that virtual teams are more difficult to maintain than static, conventional units.

Kerr and Jermier's view was that, by considering each of these items, their effect on both supportive (relationships) or instrumental (task) leadership could be calculated. They also went as far as to suggest that, where substitutes were sufficiently well developed, leadership—in the formal sense—could be completely discounted. Their findings suggested that formal leadership was shared out amongst group members or by other informal mechanisms rather than being located in any one point or person.

When this challenging perspective became available—that leaders may not be either needed in some circumstances or be stymied by various situational factors—other research-ers started to investigate this idea. Podsakoff et al. (1983) found a lack of leaders' expertise to be an important neutralizer of instrumental leader behaviour so an inexperienced, ill-informed leader could neutralize the best laid organizational plans. Howell et al. (1986) built on this work and added 'enhancers' and 'supplements' to the mix. 'Enhancers are moderators which augment relationships between leader behaviours and criteria' (1986:89). The example they cite is the experience of subordinates, which enables more knowledgeable employees to grasp quickly what their leadership require of them in ambiguous situations. So, enhancers act as a kind of spice to the recipe helping the relationship between leader and follower to develop. Supplements, on the other hand, act to support the work of the leader, with task feedback and peer support thought to add to a leader's consideration and task related behaviour. This suggests that followers getting job satisfaction and feeling supported by their colleagues were more receptive of leader task oriented behaviour than those feeling unloved and bored by their jobs.

Academic support for the hypothesis is currently rather mixed. Howell et al. (1990) and Manz and Simms (1987) have both generated studies that seem to support the view that, in some circumstances, leadership is indeed redundant. More recently, though, Wu (2010) challenges some of the findings through examining the basis for the original study by contesting the research methodology used to generate the statistical data underpinning their conclusions. Nevertheless, with organizations ever more concerned about 'de-layering', and self-reliance a common theme as workers are expected to be capable of making decisions, then the concept of a leaderless organization has some profound implications.

 Pause for thought

1. What do you intuitively think about this idea—that leadership can be influenced both positively and negatively by external situational variables?

2. What about the idea that leadership in some circumstances actually exacerbates situations and makes matters worse?

3. What could be the implications for organizations seeking to restructure their management teams?

Summary

Situational leadership models are a set of prescriptive leadership models that can act as a useful practical guide both for organizations and for leaders. The approach, being leader-centric, describes a number of approaches to help a leader maximize their impact in a number of different situations. The models try to take into account different circumstances, and can be implemented at different levels within an organization. They also try to capture the dynamic nature of leadership by showing how different styles need to be deployed over time even if the followers remain the same individuals.

However, the approach has been criticized for its lack of detailed research and weaknesses in some of its conceptualizations. For example, how individuals move from one state of 'readiness' to another, how a manager is to gain the necessary skills and deploy them, and how subordinates' commitment changes over time. The popularity of the model has been interpreted by some critics as a 'dumbing down' approach.

Later work on situational models has taken a different tack with the suggestion that leadership can be stymied, enhanced, or negated by some organizational factors and, if delivered inappropriately, 'leadership' can make situations worse (Howell 1997).

Case study   Hugo Chávez

At time of his death in 2013, Hugo Chávez was the elected President of Venezuela, the oil rich state in South America. During his life he inspired devotion and drew adoration from his supporters but was also criticized by some overseas governments and internal opponents who considered him to be nothing short of a dictator. Chávez was born into a middle class family in rural Venezuela in 1954. His parents were schoolteachers and, although he described his childhood as happy, he did experience times of hardship. From these humble beginnings he rose to become President of his country and was elected three times, serving from 1999 through to his death in March 2013.

His early career was shaped by his experiences in the army, where he served as an officer. During his service, he fought against a Left wing insurgency called The Red Flag. This exposure to Left wing politics, coupled with his growing disillusionment with the corruption and brutality in the army, led him to conclude: 'The Hugo Chávez who entered there [the army] was a kid from the hills, a "llanero" [cowboy] with aspirations of playing professional baseball. Four years later, a second-lieutenant came out who had taken the revolutionary path' (cited in Jones 2007). After forming a secretive cabal of likeminded individuals, and meeting surreptitiously with leading South American Marxists, Chávez made his first attempt at seizing political power. He led an attempted coup d'état in 1992 against the incumbent president, Carlos Andrés Pérez, who was seen to be a puppet of The United States of America. This clumsy attempt was foiled and he was jailed for two years before being pardoned by Rafael Caldera, the new president.

However, this time in prison had not dampened his revolutionary fires, which were still fed by his perception that the government was corrupt and operated as a method to enable those at the top to garner the riches of Venezuela's oil wealth. He changed strategy and moved away from a military approach to a political one. His charismatic oratory and appeal to the poor of his country won him instant appeal and he won the general election in 1999 with nearly 60 per cent of the votes cast. His message clearly resonated with the public at large who had seen their circumstances worsen during the 1990s despite the country sitting on a huge reservoir of natural resources. He appointed new people with similar political leanings to his own to key government posts and he implemented a programme of social change. His vision was to turn Venezuela into a socialist republic in the mould favoured by one of his heroes, the revolutionary Simon Bolivar. In one of his later speeches, he said: 'After many readings, debates, discussions, travels around the world, I am convinced, and I believe this conviction will be for the rest of my life, that the path to a new, better and possible world is not capitalism. The path is socialism.' His thoughts on privatization can be seen when he said, 'privatisation is a neoliberal and imperial plan. Health cannot be privatised because it is a fundamental human right, nor can water, electricity or education. These cannot be surrendered to private capital that divides the people from their rights.'

However, this popularist appeal was also marked by criticism from within his own country and from the majority of the world. He openly supported some other leaders with, at best, questionable records on human rights including Robert Mugabe of Zimbabwe, Muammar Gaddafi of Libya, and Bashar al-Assad of Syria. In addition, he delighted in attacking the United States at every opportunity, once calling President Bush a 'devil and mass murderer', Tony Blair 'an imperialist pawn', and President Obama 'a clown'. He was accused of being anti-enterprise and, as a result of his decision to nationalize the oil industry, of scaring off international investment.

His supporters would counter these criticisms with reference to his increase in government spending on health care, education, and significant increases in staple foods, such as milk and soybeans, making these basic goods accessible to many more of his citizens. He also passed decrees that guaranteed protection for indigenous peoples and women. He granted community access to media, and a right to participate in acts of civil disobedience. Despite these moves in his later years as president, he did make controversial moves to quell opposition to his rule and he targeted opposition broadcasters, passing laws and decrees that forced at least one major broadcaster and dozens of smaller radio and television stations off the air. Through decrees and a judiciary sympathetic to him, many political opponents found themselves barred from running in elections against the ruling party. Even former allies, like Chávez's onetime defence minister, General Raul Baduel, faced corruption charges that some suspect were fabricated.

Even in death he remains an enigmatic figure with supporters claiming he had been infected with cancer by the United States. His supporters thronged in their millions to the capital, Caracas, to see his coffin and to declare the revolution would continue in his memory. However, detractors sighed with relief and they hope now that the country's oil wealth can be used to develop the country's infrastructure and to broaden the economy which is heavily dependent on oil.

Sources

AP (5 March 2013) 'Hugo Chávez, 58, dies after battle with cancer'. *New York Post*.

Bellos, Alex (17 December 1999) 'New Venezuela hands Chávez wide powers'. *The Guardian*.

Hawkins, Kirk A. (2010) *Venezuela's Chavismo and Populism in Comparative Perspective*. New York: Cambridge University Press.

Jones, Bart (2007) 'Hugo! The Hugo Chávez Story from Mud Hut to Perpetual Revolution'. Hanover, New Hampshire: Steerforth Press.

Questions

1. What insight to Chávez can you gain by considering his life through Leadership Substitute Theory?
2. What approach would Reddin's model suggest that Chávez preferred?
3. Why do you think he was so opposed to American foreign policy and drawn to other controversial leaders?

What ties these different approaches together is still the assumption there is a 'right' and 'wrong' way to lead with the leader very much at the heart of the process—albeit a process that the leader alone cannot control. Situational models move leadership theories towards the assumption there are 'other forces' at work that could affect how a leader approaches tasks.

Assignment—3,000 words

Consider three different circumstances where you have experienced or observed 'leadership'. This may be at work, at play—for example, in a sports team or a musical group—or even on television in programmes like *The Apprentice*.

Part 1: Using Hersey and Blanchard's model, identify the styles of the leader. What evidence do you have for these observations? How do you see the styles changing as the followers 'evolve'?

Part 2: Identify a set of substitutes in an organization you are familiar with that have affected how leadership was either delivered or experienced by followers.

Situational leadership questionnaire

Examine the following four different scenarios and indicate your thoughts on the most appropriate response.

Situation A

You are the head of human resources and you have a recruitment campaign to organize. You decide to delegate responsibility to a senior member of the team whom you know has done this kind of exercise successfully in the past. However, when you ask them, they appear to be reluctant to take on the job.

1. Hand over the campaign and allow them to work out what needs to be done.
2. Work out milestones for the task but listen to their ideas and, where possible, allow these ideas to be incorporated into the final plan.
3. Ask why they feel reluctant and make sure they know you are there to help out.
4. Hand them a detailed plan with instructions on what, when, and how to complete the task. Ensure you check the milestones are being achieved regularly.

Situation B

You are heading up the engineering department in a large national defence contractor. Your department brought in three new graduates last year and they are engaged on a number of different projects. One of them seems to be rushing around with arms full of paperwork but you have had others grumble that he never signs off on anything before starting something else.

1. Sit him down and explain your concerns—that he does not complete tasks. Try to find out what you both can do to make things better.
2. Ask for his thoughts but leave him in no doubt what needs to be done and when.
3. Tell him that until things improve you are going to ask for daily updates on his tasks. Set him a schedule and check he is doing what is expected.
4. Just let him know you are worried and ask him to try to improve.

Situation C

You're the chairperson of a national bank. The company has gone through some tough times and, rather reluctantly, you need to trim the workforce. You decide to ask your managing director to carry out this task. She is well respected in the business and the workforce know she will treat them with dignity. She also knows the state of the company and understands that in order for the business to survive, cuts are needed.

1. You ask her to make the necessary plans and turn your attention to other pressing matters.
2. Hand her a detailed plan of who, where, and when redundancies are to be made. Ensure she reports back to you after each day.
3. Offer your support and any necessary resources but let her know she is responsible for delivering the plan.

4. Tell her you want to trim the workforce by 10 per cent, ask for her thoughts, and incorporate these ideas into the main plan.

Situation D

Roughly six months ago, you took on the responsibility for building a new marketing function for a national charity. You recruited the team and laid out the new team's objectives, making sure everyone understood what was expected and how things were to be done in the new team. You watched people closely and were initially very pleased with the outcomes. However, recently there have been instances of people missing meetings, deadlines being ignored, and a general air of apathy around the place.

1. Crack down on slack attitudes, make sure you track people, and find out exactly what is going on.
2. Check individual progress but generally allow individuals time and space to sort things out.
3. Keep the overall aim of the department the same but ask the team for ideas; perhaps have an 'away day' to see if different ways of achieving the aim can be developed.
4. Try to physically and mentally get alongside the employees. Join in on their discussions and support their efforts to overcome the various challenges facing the team.

Scoring

Task A
The director should use a *Supportive* style (C). The person is obviously experienced and can do the job but they need some reassurance that they are capable.

Task B
You should use a *Directing* approach (Option C). The graduate is enthusiastic but really does need direct supervision until he can finish tasks he has started.

Task C
The approach should be *Delegating* (Option A). Your managing director is experienced, motivated, and ready to take on the task.

Task D
A slightly more ambiguous situation but situational leadership suggests Option C—a *Coaching* style. This is because the individuals have developed confidence and abilities but have lost motivation.

 Pause for thought

Think about what your responses were.

1. Why did you make the choices you did?
2. Did you make consistent choices regardless of the situation—all 'Directive' for example?
3. Did your experience of organizations affect your choice?
4. What would happen if you made these choices in an organization you are familiar with? Would they work or would leadership 'substitutes' or 'neutralizers' come into play?

Further reading

Blanchard, K., Zigarmi,P., and Zigarmi, D. (2010) *Leadership and the One Minute Manager* London: HarperCollins. This is an easy, quick read that gives a number of 'leadership lessons' in the form of a dialogue between an entrepreneur and the reader. As usual with Blanchard's material, it is littered with snappy statements and finishes with a Buddhist quote: 'To know and not to use is not yet to know!' It is not, strictly speaking, a particularly academic text but it does give an insight into the mind of Blanchard, and how he sees situational leadership as a practical, straightforward toolkit.

Goffee, Rob and Jones, Gareth (2007) 'Leading Clever People'. *Harvard Business Review*, 85(3): 72–79. A relatively short article that deals with the challenges facing organizations who employ relatively intelligent people. The authors suggest that clever people do not actually want to be led and a successful leader needs to take a different approach if they are to be successful in ensuring organizational goals can be delivered.

A slightly more esoteric read is Roger Brun's biography of Cesar Chavez who is a celebrated (in Latin communities) labour leader who used a series of non-violent methods, such as hunger strikes, to campaign for and win better rights for migrant farm workers. He formed the National Farm Workers Association and was posthumously awarded the presidential Medal of Freedom by President Clinton. After his death, he became a major historical icon for Latino communities and for liberals generally, symbolizing militant support for workers. His slogan, 'sí, se puede' (Spanish for 'yes, it is possible' or, more roughly, 'yes, it can be done'), was reflected in President Barack Obama's 'Yes we can' mantra. Bruns, R. (2005) *Cesar Chaves: A Biography*. Westport, CT: Greenwood Press.

Contingency theory

By reading this chapter you will:

- Begin to understand how contingency theory evolved.
- Be able to appraise critically the various forms this approach describes.
- Be able to apply these ideas to your own practice.

Introduction

Contingency theory suggests that a leader's ability to influence followers is affected by external environmental factors. In other words, effective leadership is dependent (contingent) upon circumstance. Proponents of this theoretical approach believe that, to succeed, a leader needs to adapt their behaviour to take into account the demands of the situation they face.

To a degree, the previous chapter was also concerned with contingency theories because one of the underpinning assumptions made was that there is no one 'best' way of leading. The efficacy of a leader depended on making a series of judgements about certain factors, such as the readiness of the subordinates to take on responsibility for their own actions. This means that the ability to lead well depends on something else—it is contingent on something. This is actually true for most of the previous chapters, including trait theory, because, as Yukl (in Bryman et al. 2011:287) points out, 'even when a leadership theory is initially proposed as a universal theory, limiting and facilitating conditions are usually found in later research'. The reason for identifying a series of models separately from the situational theories reviewed in Chapter 5 is to demonstrate the growing complexity of both theoretical and empirical research in the field of leadership. These sets of conceptual frames draw on a much wider set of theoretical perspectives from organizational behaviour to psychodynamics and, as such, challenge the view that leadership can be considered a stable, self-contained area of research. It is no longer sufficient to consider just the nature of the leader or the followers, it is also necessary to think about more global issues such as attributes of the task, the followers, the leader's relationship with the followers, and the nature of the organization. So, contingency theory suggests that aspects of a leader's environment influence and have a direct bearing on the impact a leader has on the subordinates. This chapter will explore the building blocks of contingency theory in terms of leadership that emerged from broader organizational studies carried out in the late 1950s and 1960s. From here, the chapter explores three different approaches to contingency from Fiedler (1967), House (1971), and Yukl (1981); each one takes a slightly different approach and focuses on different aspects of the environment. By studying these three different models, the reader will be able to understand how this set of ideas evolved, the broader implications of contingency theory, as well as some of the more specific leadership theories that have emerged.

Development of the theory

Early contingency theories took their inspiration from Joan Woodward, who was a researcher based at Imperial College, London. Professor Woodward was not an expert in leadership but, in 1958, she wrote a book, *Management and Technology* (Woodward 1958), which examined the relationship between organizational structure and technology. She argued that alternative technologies, and the associated production methods generated by different systems, directly affected the host organization's structure. This was possible because different socio-technological systems required different procedures to control them, different operating processes, and different hierarchies to ensure correct integration with the overall organizational goals. This view ran counter to the prevailing Weberian ethos and Taylor's **scientific management** approaches (1911) because, almost for the first time, she suggested that organizations should be structured according to different operational factors, rather than having one idealized form. In other words, organizational form and its associated management and leadership were shaped by external forces. The associated style of leadership was therefore dependent (contingent) on a number of different factors.

Scientific management, also called Taylorism, is a theory of management that proposed increasing efficiency by analysing workflows inside organizations. Its main objective is improving economic efficiency, especially labour productivity, and it was one of the earliest attempts to apply science to the engineering of processes and management. Its development began with Frederick Winslow Taylor (1856–1915) in the late nineteenth century within the emerging manufacturing industries, such as Henry Ford's car plant. Its main features include such themes as analysis, logic and rationality, empiricism, efficiency, and the elimination of waste. It aims for the standardization of best practices and the transformation of craft production into mass production via the knowledge transfer between workers and from workers into machines, processes, and documentation.

This theme, whereby organizations could be affected by external influences, was picked up by two other British researchers, Tom Burns and G. M. Stalker. In *The Management of Innovation* (Burns and Stalker 1961), they examined the progress made by Scottish electronic companies. By and large, these organizations were moving from a relatively stable, albeit diminishing, environment to a much more fluid and dynamic environment. They coined two forms of organization structure that they suggested could be found within organizations: 'organic' or 'mechanistic'. They also suggested that the form of organization is 'dependent on the situation the concern is trying to meet' (1961:103). Mechanistic organizations had a great deal in common with bureaucracies, whilst organic companies had a more fluid structure with little of the formality associated with a traditional hierarchical firm. Moreover, they suggested that a mechanistic management system 'is appropriate to stable conditions' (1961:104). Table 6.1 shows some of the features ascribed to such an entity.

In summary, a mechanistic organization would have the following features:

- It is likely to be highly structured, members have well defined, formal job descriptions/roles, and precise positions in terms of relationships with other co-workers and managers.

Table 6.1 Features of a mechanistic organization

Stable environment	This organizational structure works best when the environment is relatively stable.
Low differentiation of tasks	Tasks will not be differentiated significantly and each subtask is relatively stable and easy to control.
Low integration of departments and functional areas	On account of the stability of tasks, there will be low integration between departments and functional areas. Tasks stay relatively stable and, because the functional areas are not heavily dependent on each other for their success, there is little need for mutual cooperation.
Centralized decision making	Decision making is centralized at the top of the organization because there is no need for a complex, inclusive, innovative set of decisions.
Standardization and formalization	Tasks are stable, therefore processes and procedures to ensure tasks are achieved are also standardized and formalized. This means that operations are designed to run in a machine-like manner, which may include humans.

- Strategic direction is from the top proceeding downwards through the hierarchy. Communication is similarly vertical in nature with instructions being delivered from those higher in the hierarchy to those lower down.

- The organization insists on loyalty and conformity from members to each other, to managers, and to the organization itself in relation to policies and methods. This means the culture is likely to reflect this with formal job titles and other artefacts, such as bigger company cars for those further up the hierarchy.

- The organization will also tend to recognize those with functional ability who can operate within organizational constraints rather than those with different ideas or alternative views.

In contrast with this, they described a polar extreme called the organic organization. Table 6.2 shows the features of such an outfit.

In summary, an organic organization is likely to have some of the following features:

- Rather than a rigid, highly specialized structure, a fluid organizational design is adopted which facilitates flexibility, adaptation, and job redefinition as the organization tries to cope with an unpredictable environment.

- Departments, sections, and teams are continuously formed and reformed. Communication is lateral as well as vertical, with emphasis on a network or matrix rather than a hierarchy.

- Organizational members are personally and actively committed to delivering outcomes beyond what is basically operationally or functionally necessary.

Burns and Stalker did not present their models as a dichotomy (either one *or* the other) but rather as a polarity sitting at opposite ends of a scale (see: Figure 6.1). This means a 'pure' form of the two types is unlikely to be encountered.

Table 6.2 Features of an organic organization

Dynamic and uncertain environment	This organizational structure works best when the environment is relatively dynamic and uncertain.
High differentiation of tasks	On account of the environment, tasks are unpredictable and probably unique in their solution. This means specialists will be involved in the development of responses. These specialists are likely to be able to respond to a limited number of different scenarios but will be 'experts' in their field.
High integration of departments and functional areas	As the external environment is ever changing and shifting constantly in terms of its requirements, a differentiated response is needed from the organization. This will mean that each department will be changing its demands on its members and those adjoining or dependent functions.
Decentralized decision making	Those closer to the environment are best placed to ensure an appropriate organization response. This generates two features: a diffused decision-making function, with individuals empowered to make decisions based on their judgement.
Few normative processes	Because of the nature of the tasks and the changing, innovative solutions, it is unlikely there will be a simple, straightforward approach to the successful completion of such tasks. This means that there is a need to be reactive and quick in terms of response to an environmental disturbance rather than relying on a well tried and trusted approach.

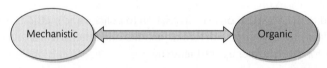

Figure 6.1 Polar scale for mechanistic and organic organizations

 Pause for thought

1. What type of organization are you most familiar with? Think about a school, college, university, or company.
2. Where does it 'fit' on the scale?
3. Would the workforce and the management agree with each other on where it fits?

Gareth Morgan took up this theme in his book, *Images of Organisation* (Morgan 1986) where he describes the main ideas underlying contingency theory. The book is concerned with analysing different metaphorical approaches to how organizations are conceived. For example, in the book he reviews, among other themes, the implications for viewing an organization as a machine, an organism, a brain, a 'culture', and even as a 'psychic prison'. He states that understanding how an organization achieves the balance between strategy, structure technology, the needs of people, and their external environment is key to understanding how organizations operate. He says this is 'the essence of modern contingency theory' (1986:54).

He offers, in summary, four ideas that he believes are true regardless of the metaphorical stance used to analyse the organization

- Organizations are open systems that need careful management to satisfy and balance, often competing, internal needs and they have to adapt to complex environmental circumstances.
- There is no one idealized form of organizational structure. The appropriate form depends on the kind of task or environment one is dealing with.
- Management must be concerned, above all else, with achieving alignment and good fit between their environment and internal pressures.
- Different types or species of organizations are needed in different types of environments.

It would seem logical to suggest that, if organizations need to 'match' their environment to flourish, then the leadership within these organizations should also seek to take advantage of situational variables.

 Case study

Brian has recently been appointed as head of centre for The Den, which is an art centre based in a rural county town. The centre has a long history of success and has been supported by both the city council and the county council in terms of cash grants to pay for a diverse range of shows and exhibitions. However, recent budget cuts have reduced cash support from the public sector to around half of its previous levels. This threatens staff numbers, the range of shows, and perhaps even the centre itself. However, Brian has a number of good contacts in the West End and he has persuaded several large stage shows to go on a tour which will include a short residency at The Den. These shows are not cheap to put on, though, and the free or discounted tickets made available by the previous administration will no longer be sold to the general public. Brian has also been concerned about the general structure of The Den, especially in terms of the staffing. The Den has a complex mix of full time and part time employees plus a number of volunteers that assist with stage decorations, bar sales, ticket enquiries, and usher duties when performances are held. There does not appear to be any routine to the centre and people seem very relaxed about when they work. This does not seem to affect the centre adversely—it is popular with the local community and everyone seems to get along with each other.

Note: Names have been changed to preserve anonymity.

Questions

1. What kind of environment do you think The Den inhabits?
2. What steps do you think Brian should consider taking?
3. Where would you place The Den on Burns and Stalker's model? Why?

Fiedler's contingency theory

Most approaches in this field take the view that there are dependent and independent variables when it comes to leadership. In this case, the dependent variable is the degree to which a leader can be construed as 'effective'. This can be measured by such methods as follower satisfaction or task achievement. The independent variables are aspects of the situation the leader cannot change in the short term. This may be areas already reviewed, such as the follower's psychological makeup, or aspects of the leader's position in the team, or even parts of the leader's own character or belief set. The external environment can also be considered part of this set of independent variables outside the immediate control of the leader. The theme postulated upon by the early organizational theorists was that a leader needed to shift their behavioural patterns between a task and relational focus to take into account this complex web of variables. Fiedler's (1967) approach to this complex web of uncertainty and change was to suggest that the effectiveness of a leader was contingent upon three distinct factors or situational dependent variables. Basing his work on a series of empirical studies on American military cadets and officers, he proposed that 'the leader's effectiveness depends on personality as well as the degree to which the leadership situation provides control and influence' (1967:61). What is interesting about Fiedler's approach is that he implies that certain types of leaders, because of their personality, will be more successful than others in some situations. He expands on this theme, and one of the ramifications of his stance is that some leaders will fail in some circumstances and, he feels, it may be better to change the leader rather than try to employ the 'wrong' type of leader. However, in his later work Fiedler (Fiedler and Mahar 1979) softens his position somewhat and suggests a methodology whereby a leader can change the situation to suit their personality. He, along with some colleagues, (Fiedler et al. 1976) have developed a leadership development tool called 'Leader Match' which aims to show how leaders with a 'given' personality can alter the situation to better suit their own beliefs. He claims that, by doing this, the leader will achieve better outcomes. However, his claims are disputed by some (e.g. Kabanoff 1981) but exploring the model will give some insight into the original ideas.

The first stage of Fiedler's approach was to develop the Least Preferred Co-Worker (LPC) scale. The purpose of this short self-completed questionnaire was to establish the leader's preferred style, which was, according to Fiedler, either task motivated or relationship motivated (see: Chapter 4). The questionnaire asks a leader to consider all of the individuals they have ever worked with and then to think about the person with whom they have found it most difficult to achieve the desired task outcomes. Once they have this person in mind, they rate this person against a set of 18 bi-polar scale questions (see: Figure 6.2)

The questionnaire does not ask a manager to think about the type of people they like least or find unpleasant but to consider whom they find it most demanding to work alongside. Fiedler makes an assumption here that the average manager's least preferred type of person is roughly as unpleasant as the next manager's. So everyone dislikes an arrogant, selfish bully equally. However, he feels that a task-oriented manager will rate this person lower on the scale and hence score lower on the LPC. In contrast, a relationship-oriented person will value the relationship more highly, score the person higher, and receive a higher LPC score.

	1	2	3	4	5	6	7	8	
Uncooperative									Cooperative
Unfriendly									Friendly
Hostile									Supportive

Figure 6.2 Sample dimensions from the LPC scale

Source: Adapted from Fiedler & Chemers (1984).

This is because the LPC seeks to test out a person's emotional reaction to, perhaps, missing a deadline or spoiling a task. He feels a task-oriented manager would be more upset with a person who does not deliver a task than a relationship-oriented person who would tend to value the relationship, even if it is strained, more than missing a deadline. There is a LPC style questionnaire at the end of the chapter for you to try. Once a manager had completed the test and received the LPC score, the next phase could be tackled, which involved analysis of certain situational variables looking for 'situational favourableness'.

Broader situational factors

Situational favourableness is established by examining a complex set of interacting variables: leader–member relations, task structure, and positional power.

1. Leader–Member relations. This is a qualitative judgement that incorporates the atmosphere within the group, the degree of trust and confidence each party (leader and follower) has in each other, and how attracted the group members feel towards each other. To determine leader–member relations, the manager responds to such items as: 'The people I supervise have trouble getting along with each other'; 'My subordinates are reliable and trustworthy.' In a situation where the group members cooperate, feel positively towards each other, and try to support each other towards a mutually accepted task, then the atmosphere can be defined as positive or good. It is suggested that, where leader–member relationships are good, the leader will have more chance of success in terms of influencing followers' opinions and behaviour.

2. Task structure. The next situational variable to be considered is the nature of the task being attempted by the group. The task can be defined as either high or low structure. Shaw (1963) gives four dimensions to be considered: (1) goal clarity, (2) goal-path multiplicity, (3) decision verification, and (4) solution specificity. A high structure type task is typified by a clear set of stages or a well tried and tested process, an unambiguous desired outcome, and a lack of options in terms of how the task is to be completed. In these cases, the follower has little room for creative input and the leader will have a great deal of control. An example would be a worker on a production line where he is fitting a component to an engine. There will be only one way of fitting the part to the engine, it will be clear if he has or has not done the task, and there will be no room for manoeuvre in terms of deciding which way up to fit the part. At the other extreme a task could be seen as having a low structure where there is no unique given solution. This could be because of the task being unclear or perhaps a situation never having been encountered before. In these cases, Fiedler argues that the leader will have less influence because he is more reliant on the group coming up with ideas and solutions to the problem facing the group. There is probably no 'correct' solution and the group will have to work through a number of options before coming up with a 'best fit' proposition.

3. Leader position power. Examining Fiedler's questionnaire here gives a real clue as to what he is seeking to establish. Two items he asks of the leader are: 'Can you directly or by recommendation administer rewards and punishments to subordinates?' and 'Is it your job to evaluate the performance of subordinates?' What he is attempting to ascertain is the level of formal, legitimate authority the leader has over his followers. Those with high levels of authority are judged to have strong power relationships, whereas, in contrast, those with little authority are judged to have weak power relationships.

Pause for thought

1. What do you make of these three criteria for assessing a situation?

2. Do you think they are comprehensive enough to cover most circumstances?

3. Could there be any other factors you think should be considered? What about the risk associated with 'getting it wrong' for example?

In combination, these three environmental variables combine to produce a 'favourable' or 'unfavourable' situation. A favourable situation would typically be found where leader–member relationships are good, the task is clear, and the leader has a legitimate authority. Whereas, an unfavourable situation is one with poor team relationships, a poorly defined task, and a weak leader.

The final stage is to now combine these four situational variables into one model with a view to predicting a leader's chance of success. Table 6.3 shows how the model is designed to operate.

Although the model looks complicated, it is relatively straightforward to use. The leader should begin by working down from the top row, 'Leader–member relationship', to assess a good or poor response, next consider the 'Task structure'—high or low—and then consider the 'Position power' held (strong or weak). This will identify the favourableness of the situation and, ultimately, a behavioural style that Fiedler suggests will have the greatest chance of success. He posits that those leaders with low LPC scores, i.e. with a task orientation, are likely to succeed in circumstances such as those with a good group atmosphere, a highly structured task, and clear, legitimate authority. Whereas, a leader with a high LPC score, i.e. relationship-oriented, is more likely to succeed in a task with a poor group atmosphere, a high task structure, and a weak positional power.

The controversial step made by Fiedler is to suggest that, as leaders' LPC scores are driven by their traits, which are fixed, there is little chance of success if a leader does not 'match' the situation. This leaves two options: change the leader or change the situation. In his view, the most appropriate is the latter and he advocates a reengineering of the situation to suit the leader (Fiedler et al. 1976).

Table 6.3 Fiedler's contingency theory

Contextual circumstance	Leader–member relationship	Good				Poor			
	Task structure	High		Low		High		Low	
	Position power	Strong	Weak	Strong	Weak	Strong	Weak	Strong	Weak
Favourableness of situation		High				Medium		Low	
Behavioural style		Task				Relationship		Task	
LPC score		Low				High		Low	

Source: Adapted from Fiedler (1967).

Table 6.4 Leader Match suggestions to change a situation

Contingency variable		
Leader–member relations	Improve relations Transfer people in and out of group. Raise feeling of satisfaction by helping group members to achieve their goals. Develop positive group dynamics by spending time with the group.	
Task structure	Increase task structure Only select straightforward tasks for the group. Break tasks down into smaller parts.	Lower task structure Gather tasks that are unique and need innovative approaches. Disseminate information and ask for group input.
Leader position and power	Enhance position power Use legitimate power demonstrably and with clarity. Draw information and authority to self. Become the sole channel for information into and out of the group.	Weaken position power Encourage group members to share in decision making. Delegate jobs and roles. Create an atmosphere of shared responsibility.

Source: Adapted from Fiedler and Garcia (1987:49–93).

Fiedler and Garcia (1987) suggest a method by which a leader can allegedly change their environment to suit their LPC score. They have developed an innovative training programme called Leader Match, which forms the basis of a leadership development programme. Most development programmes seek to affect change in a person's outward behaviour—for example, Hersey and Blanchard's Situational Leadership Approach reviewed in Chapter 5. However, Leader Match is different in that it suggests ways of changing the situation to suit the leader (see: Table 6.4).

Despite Rollinson stating that 'Fiedler's model is a huge advance on style theories' (2002:379), the approach is not without its conceptual faults and critics. The studies to support or challenge Fiedler's original findings have proliferated. Support comes from Strube and Garcia (1981) as well as Mockler (1971) among others, whereas critics include Kabanoff (1981) and Grean et al. (1971). Both sets of theorists point to statistical data that either supports or challenges the model. However, there are also some further questions posed by some of the assumptions built into the model.

Fiedler skirts around one problem by referring to it as a 'black box', i.e. a problem too difficult to understand but for which a solution is apparent. He does not entirely answer why a certain style of leader would work in one situation and not another. It is not clear why certain task/team/power combinations result in certain LPC scores being favoured over others, and whilst some options feel intuitively correct, it is this lack of clarity that unsettles some critics.

Comment (Hunt 1991) is also directed towards the LPC instrument which some, as mentioned, consider to be a difficult and misleading instrument. For example, does it actually measure a person's task/relationship orientation or is it a measure of individual motivation? A highly task focused leader, striving to deliver a project on-time and to budget, is likely to drive very hard towards delivery of the required outputs, especially if pressure and stress are building in that person. Anyone who frustrates that goal is likely to be resented and scored lower on the LPC scale, so the instrument measures a leader's view of those who get in their way for delivering outcomes, and could be influenced by recent events as opposed to personality. Also within this area of critique lies a degree of confusion about how to complete the questionnaire. There could be a degree of misunderstanding between a least preferred colleague and someone the manager simply dislikes. Fiedler and his supporters would probably argue that it is not necessary to like someone in order to work with that person. However, for some this subtlety may be lost and the LPC will reflect who they like and do not like.

Although the Leader Match programme does make an attempt to explain what an organization could do if a leader's style does not match a situation, it is a rather clumsy approach, fraught with difficulties. For example, what should a leader do when promoted from one team to another? The new team may have different characteristics that make the leader's style inappropriate and yet it may be impossible to alter the task set to suit the preferred style. Could there—according to the model—be a case for making team relationships worse to take advantage of a low LPC leader?

Debate continues around the model, with Fiedler (1996) responding vigorously to claims that discredit the approach. It is also true to say that interest in the approach has waned in recent years but it remains a significant event in terms of leadership studies because it recognizes the complex web a leader inhabits and the forces within the environment that may not

---

 Pause for thought

1. What do you think about Fiedler's claims that a leader can change the environment to suit their approach?
2. Should a leader try to control their environment in this way?
3. What expectations does this model place on managers as they move through jobs and different organizations?

 Case study

Julie is an academic lecturer based in Cambridge. As part of her role, she has overall responsibility for a post-graduate Diploma in Management Studies. The course attracts part time students who are typically experienced managers employed at local companies. Julie's role is to ensure the course runs smoothly and she is assisted by a member of the support team. However, Julie has no formal authority with regard to the teaching team that deliver the various modules on the course so she cannot reward or punish teaching practice. Similarly, she does not line manage the administrator. On several occasions, students have complained to her about the quality of teaching on one particular module. This module, which has always proved unpopular with students, covers a range of different 'skills for business' such as interpreting financial data, manipulating statistics, and using proprietary IT software. Julie has real doubts as to whether one person can teach such a broad range of subjects to post-graduate level. In addition, the lecturer in this case is a relatively inexperienced colleague who has recently completed a doctorate. On a more positive note, the administrator is excellent and she receives really positive feedback from all those with whom she has dealings.

Questions

1. What should Julie do about the comments made as far as the teaching is concerned?
2. How should Julie approach the administrator?
3. Would the responses to the above questions change if Julie were a senior manager with line management responsibility for administrators and academics? Why?

be controllable. This more holistic, systemic view challenges the more reductionist perspectives previously held by theorists and practitioners alike.

Path-Goal theory

Continuing the theme of drawing on other fields of research for inspiration, House (1971), following Evans (1970), developed a leadership model that draws on Vroom's (1964) ideas on motivation called Expectancy theory. Essentially Path-Goal theory suggests a leader should aim to improve follower performance by enhancing their motivation.

Vroom suggests motivation is an 'explanation of choices made by organisms among different voluntary responses' (1964:9). In other words, when individuals are free to make a choice over what they do, they are driven towards a particular end by a force he called motivation. To understand this force and the choices made, he defines three concepts of Valence, Expectancy, and Force and describes how these work in conjunction to determine how people will decide to act, given possible routes of behaviour leading to potential outcomes.

1. Valence: This covers the extent to which the individual considers the outcome of the task worthwhile. For example, a manager wanting a promotion will work hard to achieve a task linked to that outcome.
2. Expectancy: This is the extent to which a person thinks that their efforts will lead to the task being achieved. Vroom says 'a momentary belief concerning the likelihood that a particular act will be followed by a particular outcome' (1964:17). This can have a value of zero (no likelihood) through to one (definitely).
3. Force: A quasi-mathematical equation (see: Figure 6.3) that links these two ideas, which suggests the outcome with the greatest value will be the path followed by the individual.

Where F is the motivational force resulting from the sum of expectancy and valence, E is the expectancy measure reflecting the probability of an outcome, and V represents the valence for the individual of a particular outcome:

$$F = \Sigma\,(E \times V)$$

Figure 6.3 Vroom's Expectancy theory

The implication of motivation being a function of expectancy *times* valence is that if expectancy is zero, then motivation is also zero. This is because any number multiplied by zero is zero. Try it out on your calculator if you doubt this!

So, by achieving a given task, an individual receives 'satisfaction' and by helping a follower to achieve a task, the leader will increase the 'satisfaction', and hence motivation. House felt there were three main determinants of how effective a leader would be in increasing this motivational force. First, consider their leadership style. In contrast to Fiedler, who, of course, did not think a leader could alter their style, House offered the prospective leader a choice of styles. Whereas previous approaches have suggested a bi-polar approach, Task or Relationship—or variants on those themes—House originally offered a leader four options:

1. Participative: Consulting with subordinates and producing a shared decision.

2. Directive: Telling individuals what to do, when, and how to carry out actions.

3. Supportive: Creating a warm and friendly group atmosphere—looking after the feelings of the team.

4. Achievement orientation: Role modelling behaviour by the leader that seeks to set standards and improve performance by non-directive methods.

House (1996) went on to develop his model and produced a further six behaviours (see: Table 6.5) so the model now offers the leader a choice of 10 approaches.

Table 6.5 House's additional leadership styles

Leader behaviour	Characteristics
Work facilitation	Planning and scheduling tasks so the follower can focus energy on task achievement rather than peripheral activities.
Interaction facilitation	Ensuring collaborative and positive interaction, resolving disputes, and facilitating communication.
Group oriented decision process	Posing problems, not solutions, to the group, searching for and identifying mutual interests of group members with respect to solving problems, and encouraging all members of the group to participate in discussion.
Representation and networking	Presentation of the group in a favourable manner, and communicating the importance of its work to other members of the organization.
Value-based leader behaviour	Engaging the follower by appealing to a set of internal values, hopes, and fears.
Shared leadership	Establishing collaborative shared responsibility for task delivery across members of the team.

Next, the leader should consider the follower's characteristics in a similar manner to Hersey and Blanchard's approach in Chapter 5. These characteristics will determine how a follower views the leader in terms of assisting the follower achieve their goals.

Follower characteristics

1. Need for achievement: How much does task achievement motivate a person? An individual who welcomes a challenge will need a different approach from a person who is not task focused.

2. Desire for control: House suggests individuals with an internal **locus of control** will respond better to a participative style. For those with an external locus of control a more directive style is appropriate. This is because these approaches mirror their own internal value set.

A person with an:

Internal **locus of control** believes they are in control of events and their lives.

External **locus of control** believes that external factors they cannot control drive their lives.

3. Ability to achieve task: This is the follower's own view of their ability to achieve the task. Confident individuals are less likely to welcome a directive style than those who feel unsure of their ability.

4. Desire for clarity: Those individuals with a greater tolerance for ambiguity within the team and task function are likely to tolerate a more 'hands-off' approach from the management than those who need a more directive style with clarity over what is expected from them.

5. Need for affiliation: Just as leaders can have task or relationship preferences, so can followers. Directive leadership behaviours suit those have little need for relationship or affection from their superiors, whereas a more relationship focused approach is needed for followers with more affection requirements.

Environmental and task concerns

The final contingent factor considered by House examined the task characteristics.

1. Task: Is the task routine and straightforward or is it complex and unique? House maintains that routine tasks require a leader to offer support to workers in order to maintain their motivation. An ambiguous task needs a leader to supply structure and shape to the task.

2. Authority system: This asks about the culture in the organization. A situation with a strong, formal hierarchy will demand a different approach from an organization with a less well defined bureaucracy.

3. Group norms: A coherent, mutually supportive team with individual members looking out for each other is likely to have a different requirement from a leader when contrasted with a group of diverse individuals, concerned only with their immediate survival or task achievement.

Figure 6.4 shows how the various components operate together to produce a complex yet practical map to show how a leader needs to adapt their style to take into account the environmental pressures that will affect the follower group in terms of their satisfaction and motivation.

So, the Path-Goal theory offers a degree of additional sophistication over Fiedler's approach in that it offers the leader a much wider range of behaviours. The two-dimensional approach of task and relationship has been replaced by initially four and subsequently up to ten different alternatives. Supporters claim that the complexity of now having to consider

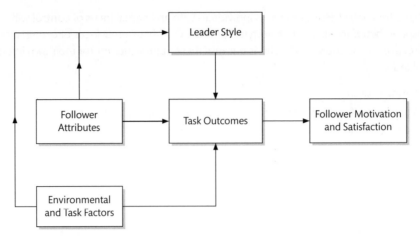

Figure 6.4 Path-Goal process

the follower and task adds subtlety and offers a richer set of options that make it possible to choose an approach that will result in the desired outcomes.

It is also a unique approach in that House tries to integrate motivational theory into a leadership approach. Although it could be argued that the question of motivation is at the heart of any leadership study—how can I get people to do what I want?—this model is different in that it makes this question explicit and tries to answer it from a theoretically informed perspective.

Finally, in a similar vein to Fiedler, House offers a predictive model that suggests which approach a leader should adopt in any given combination of circumstances. This means that a leader who can analyse the situation facing him correctly has a greater chance of success—in terms of motivating the followers—than a leader who approaches a situation blind or with little forethought.

However, despite these attractions, the model is not without its faults. Its complexity may make it difficult for a manager to apply to a 'real' situation. The increasing number of behaviours a leader needs to master has grown from two to four and now ten. There is also little empirical data to support its validity. Both Evans (1996) and Jermier (1996) point out this challenge but there is little by way of clear, validated studies that categorically support House.

Consider the underpinning theory—Expectancy theory—this model is also open to criticism as it deals with a controversial and complex aspect of human behaviour. Motivational approaches abound and Vroom's model is one of many in a hotly disputed field. For House

 Pause for thought

1. Can you summarize the key differences between the House and Fiedler approaches?

2. What do you make of their stance on how flexible a leader needs to be when operating in a leadership role?

3. Which model, in your opinion, better reflects your experiences of leadership? You could consider your own direct experience or perhaps any exposure you have had via television shows showing leaders in action.

to take a theory from one field and apply it to another domain shows creativity certainly, but does he really explain how a leadership style can motivate individuals—for example, he claims that a directive style in an ambiguous task will motivate, and a supportive leader in a routine task likewise.

Multiple linkages model

The final set of ideas to be examined here come from Gary Yukl, an American academic. Yukl's approach is still based on the assumption that leaders can influence their surroundings, but he tries to incorporate a wide number of contingent factors into his 'multiple linkage model' (1981, 1989). He proposes a yet more complex mix of linkages, factors, and the additional complication of a time-based strategy to show how a leader should address their situation. Figure 6.5 illustrates the relationships between Yukl's various components.

His model has four different variables, which he calls leader behaviour, situational variables, criterion variables, and intervening variables. Yukl uses ideas from other sources— Kerr and Jermier's concept of substitutes and neutralizers reviewed in Chapter 5 is incorporated into the model and acts directly on the 'intervening variables' irrespective of actions taken by the leader.

Intervening variables

This set of variables are factors that determine the effectiveness of the work group. Yukl draws on the research of others, such as McGrath (1984), to help establish these factors but, in contrast with the earlier models, he positions the variables at group, not individual, level. This helps to negate some of the criticisms of earlier approaches, which do not adequately answer the challenge of what a leader should do when faced with different personalities within a wider group setting. Each of these variables can have higher or lower relative importance

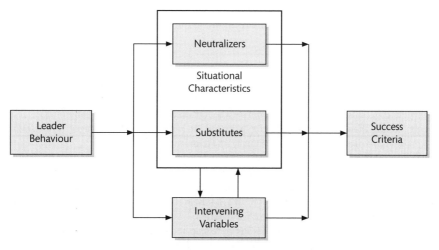

Figure 6.5 Causal relationships in the multiple linkages model.

Source: Adapted from Yukl (2006).

depending on the situation. A deficiency in one area may be able to be overcome by another, but, likewise, a serious deficiency may result in the group's effectiveness being compromised.

1. Task commitment: How motivated are the group to achieve a high level of performance?
2. Ability and role clarity: How well do the group members understand their individual roles and the extent of their ability to carry out that role?
3. Work organization: Is the task organized in such a way to maximize resources?
4. Trust and cooperation: Do the group members trust each other sufficiently to achieve their mutual goals?
5. Resources and support: Does the group have the right amount of requisite resources to deliver the outcomes?
6. External coordination: Are the activities of the group in line with the wider organization?

Yukl states 'the basic proposition of the theory is that leader actions to correct any deficiencies in the intervening variables will improve group performance' (2006:232). This suggests a short-term action plan designed to correct deficiencies within the immediate tactical control of the leader; for example, organizing the work differently or perhaps trying to develop a 'team ethos' by taking the group on an outdoor activity. However, Yukl suggests leaders can make a more sustainable and significant impact by addressing the situational factors; for example, by affecting the culture of the organization or by establishing new customers, markets, and opportunities for the services of the team. He believes that 'effective leaders act to reduce constraints, increase substitutes and reduce the importance of intervening variables that are not amendable to improvement' (2006:234). Whilst this may indeed be true, it is much harder to evaluate the impact of these changes and make certain the causal link between improvements in group performance and leader behaviour. This complex mix of variables, a systemic view of the broader landscape, and the nature of the relationship between the variables do make this a difficult model for a leader to operate. It does not have the same predictive elements of the earlier contingency models and may remain a conceptual framework rather than a specific 'theory'. Nevertheless, it does show how contingency models have evolved, with current thinking drawing on a whole range of ideas and the broader organizational environment featuring in these frameworks.

 Case study   Horatio Nelson

Horatio Nelson is regarded by many as one of the greatest of Britain's admirals and was rated by the BBC, in 2002, as the ninth greatest Briton. He was born on 29 September 1758 in Burnham Thorpe, Norfolk, the sixth of 11 children of a clergyman. He joined the Royal Navy aged 12, on a ship commanded by a maternal uncle, and eventually rose to the rank of Admiral.

As a commander he was known for taking bold and decisive action in the battlefield. He also had an occasional disregard of orders from his seniors. This defiance brought him victories against the Spanish off Cape Vincent in 1797, and at the Battle of Copenhagen four years later, where he ignored orders to cease action by putting his telescope to his blind eye—lost in an earlier battle—and claiming, 'I really do not see the signal!'; not 'I see no ships' as is often reported.

Over the period 1794 to 1805, under Nelson's leadership, the Royal Navy proved its supremacy over the French. His most famous engagement, at Cape Trafalgar on 21 October 1805, saved Britain from threat of invasion by Napoleon. Before the battle, Nelson sent out the famous signal to his fleet: 'England expects that every man will do his duty.' Sadly, he was killed by a French sniper a few hours later whilst leading the attack on the combined French and Spanish fleet. His body was preserved in brandy and transported back to England where he was given a state funeral.

Nelson was regarded as a highly effective leader, and, unusually for someone of his social standing, he was able to sympathize with the needs of his men. He based his command on inspiring love rather than authority, motivating both his superiors and his subordinates with his considerable personal courage, commitment, and charisma, which has been dubbed 'the Nelson touch'. Nelson combined this talent with an adept grasp of strategy and politics, making him a highly successful naval commander. For example, he is credited with transforming naval battles from drawn out affairs to short, destructive engagements focused on quickly destroying the enemy.

However, Nelson's personality was complex, often characterized by a desire to be noticed by his superiors and the general public. He was easily flattered by praise and upset when he felt he was not given sufficient credit for his actions. It is said this narcissistic tendency led him to take unnecessary risks with his and others' lives. He has also been accused of being a blatant self-publicist, enthusiastically broadcasting his resultant successes. Nelson was highly confident in his abilities, very determined, and able to make important decisions. His key strategy was creating trust among his officers and men, which allowed him to rely on simple strategies rather than complicated battle plans. This meant that his subordinates would support one another in achieving the overall objective and be confident enough to use their own initiative when required—another unique attribute in a time of 'top down' command.

Sources

Adkins, Roy and Adkins, Lesley (2006) *The War For All The World's Oceans*. Lancaster Place, London: Little Brown Book Group.

Sugden, John (2004) *Nelson: A Dream of Glory*. London: Jonathan Cape.

White, Colin (2002) *The Nelson Encyclopaedia. Park House, Russell Gardens*, London: Chatham Publishing, Lionel Leventhal Limited.

http://bbc.co.uk/history/historic_figures/nelson_admiral_horatio_lord.shtml (accessed 31 July 2013).

http://navynews.co.uk/trafalgar/nelson.asp (accessed 31 July 2013).

Questions

1. What were the defining characteristics of the environment surrounding Nelson?

2. What were the 'leader–member relations', the 'task structure', and the 'position power' that enabled Nelson to lead in the way he did?

3. What are the ideas and lessons you could take from studying historical leaders—or do you think the situations faced by modern leaders are totally different? Justify your answer by reference to theoretical frameworks.

Summary

In this chapter we have reviewed a set of ideas that contribute to the study of leadership by beginning to consider the impact of the wider organizational environment. Collectively, these models propose that a leader needs to be aware of this environment and suggest how political, human, and technical sub-systems relate to each other in a complex system. Emerging from studies concerned with analysing organizational responses to environmental change, they lead further away from the focus being on the leader alone and towards a more integrated approach with the leader seen as a 'player' in a much more dynamic setting.

To assist the leader in managing this increased complexity lies the view that the leader can and should employ a number of different techniques to influence his followers and local environment. However, within the models there is significant difference in opinions as to the ability of the leader to enact a change in their behavioural style. Fiedler (1965) is not convinced individual leaders can change their 'natural' style and advocates changing the situation to match the leader, whereas later studies, such as those by House, offer a whole range of behavioural options to the leader. Yukl attempts to draw a conceptual map that offers the additional option of a leader being held prisoner by a combination of substitutes and neutralizers making any influence difficult. In addition, he introduces a strategic and tactical dimension by suggesting the leader attempts a long and short term change strategy.

There are also significant differences in the factors that are considered to be key to determining the likelihood of a leader being successful. The LPC approach asks the leader to consider their own stance in terms of style alongside three situational variables: leader–member relationships, task structure, and position power. Whereas House draws his inspiration from the world of motivational theory and suggests attributes of the followers, tasks, and environment contribute to a leader being successful or not.

However, more often than not these models break down because of a lack of empirical research emphatically and unequivocally supporting the ideas proposed (Utecht and Heier 1976), or they do not make explicit the link between a change in style and desired task outcome. Fiedler (1993) skirts around one problem by referring to it a 'black box', i.e. a problem too difficult to understand but for which a solution is apparent. This 'black box' approach is sometimes ignored or left as a mystery—in either case, a stance that opens the model to criticism from users and academics alike.

Nevertheless, contingency theories do represent a further move away from seeing the leader as a 'Great Man' in charge of all he surveys. The conditions in which the leader operates, the group being managed, and wider environmental concerns are all recognized as having an impact on the effectiveness of the leader in addition to a set of personal characteristics.

Case study   Margaret Thatcher

Margaret Thatcher was Britain's first female prime minister and won three consecutive terms in office, serving for more than 11 years between 1979 and 1990. She was one of the dominant political figures of twentieth-century Britain, and Thatcherism continues to have a huge influence on modern Britain (Marr 2007). However, as the reaction to her death in April 2013 illustrated, she remains a highly controversial figure, 20 years after she left office (see, for example, http://isthatcherdeadyet.co.uk).

Margaret Hilda Roberts was born on 13 October 1925 in Grantham, Lincolnshire. She was the daughter of a grocer who held strong moral and religious beliefs. His influence on her was profound and she eventually left home for Oxford University where she trained to become a research chemist, retraining to become a barrister in 1954, and entering politics in 1959. In 1951, she married a wealthy businessman, Denis Thatcher, with whom she had two children. After the Conservatives were defeated by Harold Wilson's Labour Party in 1974, Mrs Thatcher challenged Ted Heath for the leadership of the Conservative Party and, to the surprise of many, she won. In the 1979 general election, the Conservatives came to power with a 44-seat majority and Margaret Thatcher became prime minister—the first female to lead a major Western democracy.

If her early political career had been controversial—she was, for example, known as 'Thatcher The Milk Snatcher' after her decision to remove free milk for school children—her subsequent time as prime minister divided the nation. She came to power at a time of great social unrest. Racial tension was rising, union power was at an all-time high, British influence abroad was in decline, and the economy was in recession. In her opening remarks to the Conservative Party, Mrs Thatcher wrote of 'a feeling of helplessness, that a once great nation has somehow fallen behind'. After winning the election, she embarked on a radical overall of the economy, largely based on the ideals of monetarism expounded by the American economist, Milton Freidman. This doctrine, largely untested in modern economies, meant cutting direct taxation and reducing the influence of the state. Her own philosophy is probably best summed up by her (in)famous remarks to the journalist, Douglas Keay, in which she argued 'there was no such thing as society'; she went on to say '[i]t is our duty to look after ourselves and then also to help look after our neighbour and life is a reciprocal business and people have got the entitlements too much in mind without the obligations'. With this in mind, she set about reforming just about every aspect of life in Britain.

Her vision was of a self-sustaining and independent Britain with a population freed from the shackles of the state. She believed in self-sufficiency and wanted to pare back the state, freeing up businesses and individuals to act as they saw fit. She believed market forces should drive the economy, not the state. This resulted in mass privatization of state owned organizations, such as the steel industry, British Gas, the telecoms giant British Telecom, and the airline British Airways. It is almost unthinkable in twenty-first-century Britain that these industries were ever state owned but they were and the Thatcher administration sold them to the private sector. Harold Macmillan, a former Conservative prime minister, is alleged to have said that this process was 'selling off the family silver'. Her most far-reaching change was probably the removal of many restrictions on the London Stock Exchange, called the Big Bang, in 1986, which almost overnight changed the way in which the financial sector operated on a global basis.

On 2 April 1982 the ruling military junta in Argentina ordered the invasion of the Falkland Islands and South Georgia, which belonged to the United Kingdom, thereby triggering the Falklands War. The subsequent crisis was held to be 'a defining moment of her [Thatcher's] premiership' (Jackling 2005:21). She authorized and despatched a naval task force to retake the islands, and they were recaptured on 14 June 1982 with the operation hailed a success by the British public. However, the war cost the deaths of 255 British servicemen and three Falkland Islanders as well as 649 Argentinean soldiers and sailors, half of them after the nuclear-powered submarine, HMS *Conqueror*, controversially torpedoed and sank the cruiser, *General Belgrano*, on 2 May 1982. The 'Falklands factor', coupled with an economic recovery and a bitterly divided Labour Party, contributed to Margaret Thatcher's second election victory in 1983.

In foreign affairs, Mrs Thatcher cultivated a close political and personal relationship with US President Ronald Reagan, based on a common mistrust of communism and a free-market economic ideology. She was nicknamed the 'Iron Lady' by the Soviet Leader, Mikhail Gorbachev, and they formed an unlikely triumvirate that contributed to the fall of the Berlin Wall.

In the 1987 general election, Mrs Thatcher won an unprecedented third term in office. But controversial policies, including the poll tax and opposition to closer integration with Europe, produced divisions within the Conservative Party. This led to a leadership challenge—something unthinkable a few years beforehand. On 1 November 1990, Geoffrey Howe, the last remaining member of Mrs Thatcher's original 1979 cabinet, resigned from his position as deputy prime minister over her refusal to agree to a timetable for Britain to join the European single currency. In his resignation speech, on 13 November, Howe commented on Mrs Thatcher's European stance: 'It is rather like sending your opening batsmen to the crease only for them to find the moment that the first balls are bowled that their bats have been broken before the game by the team captain'. The next day, Michael Heseltine mounted a challenge

(Continued...)

for the leadership of the Conservative Party. Although Thatcher won the first ballot, Heseltine attracted sufficient support (152 votes) to force a second ballot. Mrs Thatcher initially remarked to a waiting media scrum that she intended to 'fight on and fight to win' the second ballot, but pressure from her cabinet persuaded her to withdraw. After seeing the Queen, calling other world leaders, and making one final speech, she left Downing Street in tears. Her final comments were, 'we leave Downing Street for the very last time, leaving Britain in a much better state than when we first arrived eleven years ago'.

Thatcher was replaced as prime minister and party leader by her Chancellor, John Major, who oversaw an upturn in Conservative fortunes and led the Conservatives to their fourth successive election victory in 1992. Later that year, Mrs Thatcher left the House of Commons for the House of Lords, as Baroness Thatcher of Kesteven.

She wrote two best-selling volumes of memoirs—*The Downing Street Years* (1993, London: Harper Collins) and *The Path to Power* (1995, London, Harper Collins)—whilst continuing to tour the world as a lecturer for a full decade. A book of reflections on international politics—*Statecraft*—was published in 2002 (London, Harper Collins). During this period, she made some important interventions in domestic British politics, notably over Bosnia and the Maastricht Treaty. In March 2002, following several small strokes, she announced the end of her career in public speaking. Denis Thatcher, her husband of more than 50 years, died in June 2003, receiving warm tributes from all political parties.

During her term of office she reshaped almost every aspect of British politics, reviving the economy, reforming outdated institutions, and reinvigorating the nation's foreign policy. She challenged, and did much to overturn, the psychology of decline that had become rooted in Britain since the Second World War, pursuing national recovery with striking energy and determination.

Margaret Thatcher remains an intensely controversial figure in Britain. Her critics claim that her economic policies were socially divisive and that she was a harsh, uncaring person. She was, they suggest, hostile to the institutions of the British welfare state. Defenders point to a transformation in Britain's economic performance over the course of her governments. Trade union reforms, privatization, deregulation, a strong anti-inflationary stance, and control of tax and spending created better economic prospects for Britain than seemed possible when she became prime minister in 1979. Most people, whether critics or supporters, recognize the Thatcher premiership as a period of fundamental importance in British history. As Andrew Marr puts it in his *History of Modern Britain* (2007), we are all 'children of Thatcher'.

Sources

http://margaretthatcher.org (accessed 31 July 2013).

http://www.bbc.co.uk/history/historic_figures/thatcher_margaret.shtml (accessed 31 July 2013).

Jackling, Roger (2005) 'The Impact of the Falklands Conflict on Defence Policy'. In Badsey, Stephen, Grove, Mark, and Havers, Rob. *The Falklands Conflict Twenty Years On: Lessons for the Future* (Sandhurst Conference Series). Abingdon, UK: Routledge.

Keay, Douglas (1987) 'An Interview with Margaret Thatcher'. *Woman's Own* Magazine, 23 September 1987.

Marr, A. (2007) *A History of Modern Britain*. London: Macmillan Publishers,.

Thatcher, Margaret (1979). 'Foreword'. *Conservative Party Manifesto 1979*. Available at: http://conservativemanifesto.com (accessed 31 July 2013).

Questions

Use one of the contingency theory models to explain how Margaret Thatcher first came to power and why she was forced from power in 1990.

1. Do your findings alter if you use a different model?

2. What conclusions can you draw for both a) leaders and b) contingency theory?

Assignment—3,000 words

Identify a situation where a leader has moved from one organization or situation to another:
a) Successfully.
b) Unsuccessfully.
   You could look to the world of sport, political office, business, or fiction. Use the knowledge you have from examining contingency theories to explain why this happened.

Least preferred co-worker (LPC) measure

Instructions

Think of all the different people with whom you have ever worked; for example in a job, in social clubs, in student projects, or wherever. Next, think of the one person with whom you could work least well; that is, the person with whom you had the most difficulty getting a job done. This is the one person (a peer, boss, or subordinate) with whom you would least want to work. Describe this person by circling numbers at the appropriate points on each of the following pairs of bi-polar adjectives. Remember you are NOT describing someone you do not like but someone you just find it difficult to work with. Work rapidly and do not think too long over each question.

Pleasant	8	7	6	5	4	3	2	1	Unpleasant
Friendly	8	7	6	5	4	3	2	1	Unfriendly
Rejecting	1	2	3	4	5	6	7	8	Accepting
Tense	1	2	3	4	5	6	7	8	Relaxed
Distant	1	2	3	4	5	6	7	8	Close
Cold	1	2	3	4	5	6	7	8	Warm
Supportive	8	7	6	5	4	3	2	1	Hostile
Boring	1	2	3	4	5	6	7	8	Interesting
Quarrelsome	1	2	3	4	5	6	7	8	Harmonious
Gloomy	1	2	3	4	5	6	7	8	Cheerful
Open	8	7	6	5	4	3	2	1	Guarded
Backbiting	1	2	3	4	5	6	7	8	Loyal
Untrustworthy	1	2	3	4	5	6	7	8	Trustworthy
Considerate	8	7	6	5	4	3	2	1	Inconsiderate
Nasty	1	2	3	4	5	6	7	8	Nice

Agreeable	8	7	6	5	4	3	2	1	Disagreeable
Insincere	1	2	3	4	5	6	7	8	Sincere
Kind	8	7	6	5	4	3	2	1	Unkind

My LPC score

Scoring Instructions: Add up the numbers you have ringed. This is your LPC score.

A score of 57 or below = TASK MOTIVATION.

A score of 58 to 63 = INDEPENDENT.

A score of 64 or above = RELATIONSHIP MOTIVATION.

Further reading

Lex Donaldson's book *American Anti-Management Theories of Organization: A Critique of Paradigm Proliferation* (1995, Cambridge: Cambridge University Press) whilst not directly concerned with 'leadership', does present an interesting angle on the debate surrounding organizational structure. He is highly critical of the manner in which management is presented, which he believes is in a negative light. He further attacks academic researchers who, he suggests, have not helped in clarifying some of the issues facing modern American organizations. The proliferation of new models, each subtly different, but based on a contingency approach, is clouding rather than clarifying decision making for organizational leaders.

Systems thinking—a view that involves considering a holistic, as opposed to a reductionist, view of organizations and other socio-technical groups—is a field that may interest readers who want to read around contingency theory. A good start would be Peter Checkland's book (1997, Chichester: J. Wiley & Sons) *Systems Thinking, Systems Practice*, or Peter Senge's (1990, New York: Doubleday) *The Fifth Discipline*, which focuses on how organizations may be considered biological entities and, hence, be able to learn. This topic is covered in more detail in Chapter 15.

Finally, Ron Heifetz, Marty Linsky, and Alexander Grashow in their book, *The Practice of Adaptive Leadership: Tools and Tactics for Changing Your Organization and the World* (2009, Boston: Harvard Business Press), try to make the case for dealing with change. They draw on ideas from evolutionary biology and refer to the process that organisms follow if they are going to survive and thrive. The three components of this process that they apply to organizations are to: (1) preserve the organizational elements necessary for survival, (2) remove (or modify) the elements that are no longer necessary or useful, and (3) create new arrangements that enable the organization to thrive.

7 Charisma and Transformational leadership

After reading this chapter you will:

- Understand the development of charisma as a leadership theme.
- Be able to evaluate charisma and Transformational leadership critically as conceptual frames.
- Be able to consider your own practice in the light of this discussion.

This chapter deals with two popular and current themes that are sometimes conflated and often confused: charismatic leadership and Transformational leadership. Transformational leadership is a different notion from the models studied to date. It is probably fair to suggest the previous chapters have largely been concerned with theories collectively known as *transactional* theories. Transactional leadership focuses on the social exchange process that occurs between leader and follower when the leader attempts to exercise influence. The term implies an exchange or transaction between the two parties—for example, a leader may offer promotion or reward or punishment in exchange for compliance with an instruction. In a different sphere, a politician will promise tax cuts or policy changes in exchange for your votes. It is this transaction that gives the leader the ability to influence followers—consider House's Path-Goal theory in Chapter 6. Transformational leadership, on the other hand, implies that something very different occurs within the influencing process. Transformational leadership suggests a successful leader changes or transforms followers into avid disciples who internalize the broader organizational aims and, by fulfilling these aims, become self-actualized.

However, before examining this concept it is necessary to work through an earlier construct—that of charisma. This is because charisma and Transformational leadership can be linked together and by understanding charisma, Transformational leadership should become an easier topic to grasp. This chapter explores these differences and overlaps before drawing attention to the latest research into this intuitive and interesting idea

Charisma

As Potts (2009) suggests, charisma is a word used throughout modern society but, nevertheless, it remains an elusive target. Consider those individuals thought of as 'charismatic' by some—for instance, Mahatma Gandhi, Nelson Mandela, Adolf Hitler (albeit in a negative context), Fidel Castro, or Bill Clinton—and the challenge starts to emerge. Who decides on whether a person is or is not 'charismatic' and what exactly is this quality, which for Potts 'retains a mysterious, elusive quality' (2009:3)?

Pause for thought

Write down the names of three individuals you consider to be charismatic.

1. What do they have in common?
2. What differences do they have?
3. What do you think 'charisma' is?

The etymology of the English word 'charisma' can be traced back to the ancient Hellenistic word, Χαρισμα (kharisma) which means 'divine favour' or 'gift' (Conger 2011:86). The expression has a long history, and has been associated through biblical times with some kind of characteristic that marks out an individual as being different from the norm. In his epistles, Paul used it to describe 'the gift of God's Grace'. This strong religious element explains why it continued to be used to explain God's influence on man. God (or gods) transferred power to mortals and they became charismatic or touched by a higher power. There are many examples from biblical texts that point towards such individuals; consider, for example, Moses or the prophet, Muhammad, both of whom were able to speak directly with God.

The first writer accredited with expanding this meaning into a secular sense was the German sociologist, Max Weber (1864–1920), who came across the word used by Rudolph Sohm (1841–1917) writing in a series of polemic debates about the position of the Protestant church (Sohm 1892). Weber took the word and applied it to leaders occupying roles outside the church but still associated the biblical theme of supernatural power to individual men.

> Charisma is a certain quality of an individual personality by virtue of which he is set apart from ordinary men and treated as endowed with supernatural, superhuman, or at least specifically exceptional powers or qualities. These are such as are not accessible to the ordinary person, but are regarded as of divine origin or as exemplary, and on the basis of them the individual concerned is treated as a leader.
>
> (Weber 1947:358)

'Charismatic' became for him one of three different types of political authority apparent in society. His typology featured three idealized forms of authority—charismatic, traditional, and rational-legal. Charismatic authority stemmed from an individual seen as exceptional, in contrast to authority based on rules, bureaucracy, and tradition. However, it was another generation before House (1976) and Burns (1978) led the expansion of studies into the application, definition, and measurement of charisma in a leadership context.

Whilst there were some who were arguing for charisma to remain linked to its religious origins (see for example: Loewenstein 1966: Friedrich 1961; Perinbanayagam 1971), the word entered the modern lexicon with the meaning broadly understood by many lay people as 'star quality'. Friedrich is somewhat scathing about these attempts to bring into modern debate such ancient terms, whilst Loewenstein argues that the term cannot be applied to modern leaders because the only source of reference was from history and therefore no modern records or testable evidence is available. Nevertheless, the ideal of the charismatic, visionary leader is a powerful one and pervades many aspects of business, politics, and sport.

Case study

Richard is the ebullient host of Colliters Brook Farm (see: http://collitersbrookfarm.com) which is a bed and breakfast just outside Bristol. He runs the place on a mixture of adrenaline and enthusiasm, greeting visitors with a hearty 'Hello Buddy!' As well as a bed and breakfast outlet, he organizes drop off and pick up at the nearby Bristol Airport so there are numerous cars parked at the farm. He has a camping field and workshops to contend with along with ducks, chickens, and dogs. His energy is amazing to witness as he is up late settling visitors into their rooms and then rising at the crack of dawn to ferry people to the airport before returning to the kitchen to cook breakfast for more guests. After this, he has to strip rooms, finish the laundry, and prepare for the evening rush. His mission statement published on the web site states:

To create the most user friendly local bed and breakfast, to cater for airport travellers and southwest visitors alike. To promote our service levels beyond all others and leave all our guests satisfied, content and happy with our efforts. To make each stay a great stay.

Typical of comments made about Richard are these two remarks from recent visitors:

Thank you so much for making the start and end of our holiday memorable, Outstanding accommodation, the best full English breakfast in the UK. It's been a pleasure meeting you. Thanks for your hospitality and kindness. We wish you all the best for the future, hope to see you again soon.

We had a great time in your house, it is really great experience for us as Tibetan monks with our friends from Africa. Thanks for your warm welcome and we really enjoyed your environment. We hope to come again. See you and bye.'

Richard can be seen late in the evening trying to relax with a tin of local beer and a cigarette in hand.

Questions

1. Is this an example of 'charisma' as you understand the term now?
2. Can you see any dangers for Richard?
3. Do you think you are charismatic?

House and Shamir self-concept theory

To further complicate matters, there are different theoretical approaches to charisma, each with a slightly different interpretation of what charisma 'is', where 'it' originates from, and how 'it' works. Examining two of these ideas will demonstrate the difficulty this concept presents for those who would seek to use the notion or, perhaps, would like to consider themselves to be 'charismatic'. The first to be considered is 'self-concept theory', which was developed by Shamir et al. (1993) from House's (1976) earlier work. The idea rests on the presumption that humans create mental images of themselves and seek ways of affirming and reinforcing this self-identity. Psychologists are familiar with this idea and it is known as the 'self-concept'. Shamir's theory tries to link this notion with the motivational power wielded by individuals who have been labelled 'charismatic' by followers. The model tries to explain why charismatic leaders are able to exert influence and, hence, motivate followers. Their argument is that charismatic leaders create a vision whereby the self-concept of an individual is tied to task

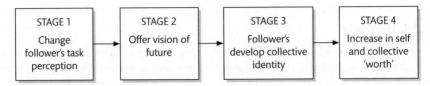

Figure 7.1 Self-concept process map

achievement. By achieving the mission in whatever context is set by the leader, the followers will reinforce their sense of worth and build their sense of 'self'. Figure 7.1 shows the process map through which Shamir and colleagues argued how charismatic leadership operated.

Stage 1

The leader needs to change how 'work' is seen by the followers. This could mean emphasizing the morality of the task or the heroic nature of the activity whilst downplaying the technical or operational element. Essentially, as Conger (2011) points out, the leader is focusing on the intrinsic values as opposed to the extrinsic rewards. This moves the work from being a matter of simple reward and punishment to a matter of possible life and death—or at least something that matters more than a pay packet at the end of the week.

Stage 2

To achieve a change in follower perception, the leader should use strong and expressive language to create a shared vision of the future. There is a degree of caution required here, as this vision needs to be appealing and inspirational but not so radical as to attract ridicule or be seen as unobtainable. The leader should try to emphasize the attractiveness of the future and the integral part that achieving the mission goals have to arriving in this new future. As important is the need to create a shared mental model of this future, which is necessary to create a collective identity.

Stage 3

Pursuing this shared mental model, the leader needs to ensure the followers identify with the collective. The dominant belief needs to be that by working together—and only by working together—can the vision be achieved. Conger et al. (2000) make the point that followers need to identify with the group and understand their role within this larger group— much like a worker bee within a hive. This creation of a social 'whole' can be further aided by the use of symbols, clothing, marks—such as tattoos—and other rituals designed to differentiate the group and mark them as an identifiable body. This helps to create a group history whereby stories can be told of heroic acts and deeds by past members. Consider, for example, stories told by any follower of a famous football club—past victories are routinely discussed, as are the memories of old players who are inevitably better than the current crop of players. Groups may also share a lexis of slang or in-phrases that reinforce this view of identity.

Stage 4

The ultimate stage is for the leader to generate higher levels of self-esteem and self-worth amongst the followers. This is done by expressing confidence in the followers and maintaining the belief they can collectively achieve great things. Bandura's research (1977) and theories (1986) support this perspective as do other much older motivational theories, such as Maslow's (1943) ideas around self-actualization. Bandura established the position that individuals were proactive and self-organizing beings not just reactive organisms driven by environmental forces or inner impulses based on evolutionary 'fight/flight' type urges. He established that those with strong sense of self-worth are likely to drive harder towards a goal than those with lower or weaker self-images. In a similar vein, a collective with a higher sense of belonging and collective esteem will be more willing to cooperate towards a mutually shared and agreed goal.

This approach moves House's original ideas of charisma operating on a individualistic level, based on a dyadic relationship between a leader and follower, to more of a collective basis operating across groups.

 Pause for thought

Consider one of the leaders you identified as 'charismatic' earlier.

1. Can you identify these four stages?
2. What language did the leader use to move between each stage?
3. What were the symbols and artefacts that identified 'the collective'?

Attribution theory

Conger and Kanunga (1987, 1998) presented a theory of charismatic leadership based on a psychological theory called **attribution theory**. Attribution theory, in this context, can be applied because it suggests that individuals, when faced with an action or behaviour, attribute a reason for this observed phenomenon. For example, a manager, when observing a worker, may make inferences as to the character of that person based on the perceived quality of work. The manager will claim the quality of the work can be explained by a characteristic of the individual. In a similar manner, a sports fan will associate a player with a characteristic based on the player's on-field performance not on any intimate knowledge of the player; armchair critics abound and a whole industry exists to try to mitigate against unfavourable press that may exacerbate character assassination via tabloid.

Attribution theory is a model developed by Austrian psychologist, Fritz Heider (1958). His view was that 'man' as he passes through life observes events and makes causal inferences to explicate occurrences. These inferences may, or may not be true, but they help individuals understand their world. Eventually these inferences become embedded within a person's psyche and form part of their values and beliefs. A person then uses these to predict future events and to make judgements about the world they inhabit.

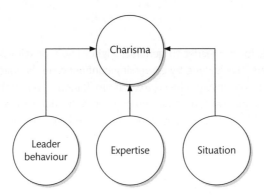

Figure 7.2 Factors influencing charismatic leaders

Of course, within organizations, sport, politics, and indeed every field of human endeavour there is the need to explain and to understand why events occur. Pfeffer (1977) and Meindl et al. (1987) both make the point that leadership can be used to explain both success and failure in organizations. However, their research shows that later analysis of situations and outcomes attributed to 'leadership' indicate that other factors have in fact been the cause of the events rather than a dynamic leader. **Reich**'s rather emotively titled piece, *The Executive's New Clothes* (1985) is an example where the success of the organization was found to be attributable to environmental factors, such as economic cycles, rather than 'leadership'. Nevertheless, according to Conger and his supporters, followers are apt to attribute success to a person identified as the 'leader' as a result of the interaction between three dependent variables (see: Figure 7.2). For Conger and Kanungo, charismatic leadership is 'considered an observable behavioural process that can be described and analysed in terms of a formal model' (1998:47). The first point to make here is the explicit role of followers in defining what and who is charismatic. It is not sufficient for a person to merely stand up and state 'I am charismatic', for it is the followers who have decide this based on a combination of factors. This model suggests that followers attribute 'charisma' to a person whose behaviour appeals to them on an emotional basis rather than a rational-logical level. In addition, this behaviour is likely to be unconventional or at least at odds with the current status quo. Bear in mind, too, that if this theory holds true, followers will also attribute non-charismatic qualities to other people along with a whole host of previously studied leadership attributes, such as autocratic or democratic.

> **Reich** makes a play on the fable by Hans Christian Andersen *The Emperor's New Clothes*. This tale tells the story of a vain king who is swindled by two tailors who say they can make clothes visible to all except those who are 'hopelessly stupid'. The king decides to parade his 'new' clothes but the sham is revealed when a child points out that the king is actually naked.

For Conger a combination of leader behaviour, a perception of a leader's given expertise in a field and the situation facing the followers drives the attribution of charisma onto an individual via the process outlined in the three stages below. A position supported by Warren Bennis when he commented, 'more leaders have been made by accidental circumstances, sheer grit or will, than have been made by all the leadership courses put together' (2003:34).

Conger and Kanungo see a process emerging whereby the leader moves the followers psychologically from one existing state to another future state via three stages.

Stage 1. Sees the leader making a critical evaluation of the current situation, examining environmental constraints and, crucially, the needs of the followers. What distinguishes charismatic from non-charismatic behaviour in this initial stage is the ability to recognize deficiencies and short-comings in the status quo. An unexploited opportunity or latent desires within a target audience are examples a charismatic leader may look towards. Essentially, the charismatic leader opposes the status quo and seeks to change the situation fundamentally.

Stage 2. Has the leader creating a vision for the future that exploits the opportunities. Crucially though, the leader can articulate this vision into terms that are understandable to the followers. The leader is extremely sensitive to followers' wants and desires as well as their abilities, which means the vision becomes a shared vision 'wanted' by the followers. The use of impression management using articulate and powerful oratory is another useful attribute of charismatic leaders. They can make the achievement of the vision seem inevitable given sufficient sacrifice and effort on the part of the collective. Having said that, this concept, whilst initially easy to envisage, presents problems when trying to define and pin down. What exactly is a 'vision' beyond the biblical implications? Is it sufficient for a leader to 'have a dream' after Martin Luther King's example? And yet it is a word that appears consistently in the leadership literature (for example see Handy (1989) or Mintzberg (1983)) albeit in a rather vague manner. Despite the title, Selznick's book, *Leadership in Administration: A Sociological Interpretation* (1957), is focused on leadership and he tries to capture the flavour of what a vision is with his definition as being 'sensitive to changes in an organization's environment, together with an accurate perception of the direction in which the organization must move if it is to take advantage of environmental changes' (1957:137).

Stage 3. Sees the leader illustrating how these goals and visions can be achieved by the group. The leader may resort to personal risk taking by taking the first steps—going 'over the top' first—and is more likely to empower the followers to achieve the goals. What marks the charismatic from non-charismatic in this final stage is the use of unconventional methods to deliver the end goal. This is tied into their expertise in the field, which encourages followers to see the leader as trustworthy—they see the leader as someone who knows what they are doing.

Whilst their approach is discussed and presented in three discrete stages, in a similar fashion to Figure 7.1, they do recognize that, in practice, this linear flow is seldom seen in such an explicit form. The changing environmental context, shifting follower base, and organizational constraints make this a much more fluid and iterative process with the leader having to move from one stage to another frequently.

Case study   Aung San Suu Kyi

Aung San Suu Kyi is the general secretary of the National League for Democracy (NLD) and a Burmese opposition politician. She has become an international symbol of peaceful resistance in the face of political oppression. Suu Kyi is the daughter of the country's independence hero, General Aung San. He was assassinated during the transition period between military and civilian rule in July 1947, just six months before independence. She was only two years old at the time and did not get to know her father well.

She left Burma and was educated in England but soon felt she had to return to carry on her father's mission. 'I could not, as my father's daughter, remain indifferent to all that was going on', she said in a speech in Rangoon on 26 August 1988, and with this she was soon propelled into leading the revolt against the then-dictator, General Ne Win. Inspired by the charismatic non-violent campaigns of US civil rights leader, Martin Luther King, and India's Mahatma Gandhi, she organized rallies and travelled around the country, calling for peaceful democratic reform and free elections. However, the demonstrations were brutally suppressed by the Burmese army, who seized power in a coup on 18 September 1988.

In the 1990 general election, Suu Kyi's party won 59 per cent of the national votes and 81 per cent (392 of 485) of the seats in the Burmese parliament. However, she had already been detained under house arrest by the ruling military before the elections, and she remained there for almost 15 of the 21 years from 20 July 1989 until her release on 13 November 2010. Despite this, she was awarded the Nobel Peace Prize in 1991 with the Nobel Committee stating: 'Suu Kyi's struggle is one of the most extraordinary examples of civil courage in Asia in recent decades. She has become an important symbol in the struggle against oppression.'

Since her release she has had to tread carefully in terms of her political activity but on 28 July 2011 she wrote an open letter to the country's new president, army, and ethnic insurgents calling for an end to the decades-long civil conflict. In her first talks with a minister in the new government, she said reconciliation between state forces and armed ethnic minority rebel groups could not be achieved by 'military means'.

'I would like to earnestly call for an immediate ceasefire and the peaceful resolution of the conflicts for the benefit of all ethnicities in the Union of Myanmar,' she said in the letter, which she also addressed to ethnic groups. On 1 April 2012, the NLD announced that Suu Kyi had won the vote for a seat in parliament, and she was popularly expected to take up this seat. However, she has been criticized for her comparative silence over the 2012 Rakhine State riots when Burmese Muslims were killed by ethnic Rakhine—some say this is a politically motivated move by her.

Sources

http://bbc.co.uk (accessed 1 August 2013).

http://burmacampaign.org.uk

http://guardian.co.uk (accessed 1 August 2013).

http://nobelprize.org (accessed 1 August 2013).

Questions

1. Would you consider Suu Kyi to be 'charismatic'? Why have you made this judgement?

2. What influence, if any, do you think her heritage had on her?

3. How can you use attribution theory to explain Suu Kyi's performance?

Characteristics of charismatic leaders

One aspect not yet discussed in any depth amongst these 'process maps' is, perhaps, the most intuitive aspect of charisma—that of an individual leader's characteristics or traits. Both of the models reviewed so far make little mention of this aspect, preferring to focus on the process *through* which influence occurs. Whilst either approach explicitly avoids the question of what makes a person charismatic, they prefer to look for the mechanism through which said charismatic person exercises their influential power. However, it is clear that followers do not ascribe charisma to just anyone and everyone. As Bass (2008:582) remarks, 'the person who is so endowed must have abilities that are relevant to the situation'. The challenge faced by researchers here is, of course, the same as those encountered in Chapter 2 when trying to define the 'Great Man'. What do these words such as 'charisma' really mean? However, one advantage that Conger's model provides is maybe to suggest that it does not really matter how these words are defined as long as a follower *attributes* them to a leader.

House (1976) has the charismatic leader being dominant, having a desire to influence, self-confident, and possessing strong moral values. The Conger and Kanungo (1998) approach, whilst not ignoring these characteristics, focuses more on the attributional and relational aspects of leadership, with the leader fulfilling a role for the followers. However, Bass (1985) is fairly confident in ascribing a set of characteristics to illustrate a charismatic as opposed to a non-charismatic leader. Bass and Avolio (1995) went further with the development of the Multifactor Leadership Questionnaire (MLQ), which tried to measure elements their research suggested were central to a charismatic approach. The MLQ exists in different forms since it was first developed by Bass (1985) from his studies in South Africa and is designed to 'measure, explain and demonstrate to individuals the key factors that set truly exceptional leaders apart from marginal ones' (Bass and Avolio 1995). There is a short questionnaire you can try at the end of this chapter.

Emotional expressiveness

This characteristic relates to the use of verbal and non-verbal signals 'to move inspire or captivate others' (Friedman et al. 1980:133). Typical examples of this type of behaviour are direct eye contact, reaching out and touching friends when talking, and an engaging tone of voice. Users of the Myers–Briggs Type Indicator (see Chapter 10) may notice a similarity with 'extroversion', whilst poker players would hope for much the opposite when trying to bluff an opponent. Open body language and a smiling, relaxed visage are also said to be indicators of this attribute.

Self-confidence

Bass (2008:585) makes the point that charismatic individuals 'display complete confidence in the correctness of their position'. This means they have an almost unshakeable belief that their method and vision is the correct solution to the inherited situation. This conviction—their way is the right way—will be constantly projected by the leader with no sense of defensiveness. An example of this may be Tony Blair's position when prime minister towards his decision to take the United Kingdom to war in Iraq in 2003. His statement to the House of Commons included:

> This is not the time to falter. This is the time for this House, not just this Government or indeed this Prime Minister, but for this House to give a lead, to show that we will stand up for what we know to be right, to show that we will confront the tyrannies and dictatorships and terrorists who put our way of life at risk, to show at the moment of decision that we have the courage to do the right thing.
>
> (Blair 2003)

Despite several inquiries being held that cast doubt on the central justification for the war being the existence of weapons of mass destruction (WMD), Blair has never wavered from his belief that he did the right thing.

Self-determination

This term seems to suggest an individual who does not conform to pressure from those in power but are driven to follow a 'calling'. To reach this, they are likely to give up almost everything material in exchange for achieving their goals. Mahatma Ghandi illustrates this element in that he was an Indian trained in England to be a lawyer, he returned to India via South Africa, and he advocated non-violence and truth in all situations. Whilst he could have commanded a comfortable, middle class lifestyle, he lived modestly in a self-sufficient residential community and wore the traditional Indian dhoti and shawl, woven with yarn he had hand spun on a charkha.

Insight

Of particular note is the ability to first spot and then articulate a particular hidden or ill-formed desire in followers. Not only are they able to do this but they are able to offer innovative solutions to followers' perceived problems. An example of this might be to examine one of the reasons why President Obama won his largely unexpected victory in 2008. Commentators such as Deborah White (2011) suggest he was able to connect with middle class Americans, clearly articulating their concerns about housing, jobs, and the state of the American economy.

Freedom from internal conflict

Because charismatic leaders have this in-built confidence and belief in their chosen path, they rarely experience periods of self-doubt or inner conflict. The moral superiority of their vision overrides any concerns about the veracity of how this is to be achieved. Subordinates, or those not seen as competent, are likely to be replaced quickly and without remorse. Lord Sugar's 'you're fired!' exhortation at the end of an episode of *The Apprentice*, as another hapless candidate is removed from the boardroom, could be a good illustration to consider here.

Eloquence

This aspect is one often seized upon as evidence of charisma in a particular person—indeed, it is this skill that seems to resonate with many observers. Two aspects of oratory are worth examining: the content and the delivery. The content is straightforward and direct, with a focus on the collective identity and the moral justification of the cause, and it generates an emotional response from the audience. The delivery is also important with metaphors, alliteration, and a rhythmical rousing lilt featuring in many famous speeches. Consider Winston Churchill's 'we will fight them on the beaches' speech or his accolade to the Battle of Britain fighter pilots, 'never has so much been owed, by so many, to so few', as examples of the genre.

Energy

Crant and Batemans's study (2000) and Seibert et al.'s (2001) subsequent work makes the link between activity and judgements made by others as to the success of that person. Anecdotal evidence supports their research—for example, consider the mental images that spring to mind when words such as lazy, tardy, or sloth are mentioned as opposed to sprightly, proactive, or enthusiastic. Other psychologists have begun to examine this link between elements of personality and behaviour to see if and how these are linked to success—for example, see Brown and O'Donnell's (2011) examination of the link between a proactive personality and the ability to learn. Whilst not suggesting that it is necessary to continually demonstrate a tendency to hop from one foot to another, appearing excitable and enthusiastic, being seen to be interested, and being able to work for long hours and maintain a level of performance over a sustained period, is seen as a charismatic trait by some researchers.

Self-sacrificial

Considering some of the world leaders judged by history to have charisma, the theme of voluntarily giving away power, prestige, and the trappings of success is apparent. Ghandi's desire to give up his middle class existence, Jesus giving up his life, the Second World War American general, George Patton, riding into battle at the head of his army are just three examples whereby a leader makes a sacrifice in order to build trust and loyalty amongst followers. The aim of the leader is to encourage followers to share their example and to make similar sacrifice if called upon by the organization. Mansour Javidan (2004) has done some interesting work in this area and has drawn in a number of cross-cultural themes which adds another complexity to this dimension.

Context and crisis

One aspect that has intrigued observers of charismatic leaders is the impact that environmental conditions have on the emergence and influence of charismatic leaders. There are some writers, studying political and religious situations, who contend that the emergence of a social crisis (such as mass unemployment or civil unrest) is a fundamental precondition for a charismatic leader who emerges to 'save' society from impending disaster. Bryman (1992) feels that, in times of uncertainty and change, when individuals and society in general are looking for a 'solution' to their problems, a charismatic individual with a radical and visionary approach can seem to be the only option out of a crisis. Weber (1947) supports this

Pause for thought

Complete this table for the three characters you identified as charismatic earlier

Characteristic	Person		
Expressive			
Confident			
Self-determined			
Insight			
Free from Internal conflict			
Eloquent			
Energetic			
Self-sacrificial			

1. Is the entire table filled in? Why?
2. What real examples came to mind as you thought about the behaviour patterns?
3. Are you any of these?

view, with followers becoming attracted to the leader as a result of their need for meaning and hope. Again, anecdotal evidence may seem to support this view with Thatcher, Hitler, Muhammad Ali Jinnah, and Martin Luther King responding in kind to different social crises. Their visions were either a new way of living, for example King's 'dream', or a return to a golden age, for example Thatcher's Victorian values. However, it would be fair to say that this field is currently under-researched with little depth in terms of empirical studies into this aspect, so it is difficult to state categorically that out of a crisis a leader emerges. Conger (1989), for example, looked at entrepreneurs thought of as charismatic—such as the chairman and inspiration behind Virgin, Richard Branson—and found they thrived in times of optimism and opportunity and were able to capture the enthusiastic mood of the times. He also explored the notion that the prevailing environment did not so much create the circumstance for the leader to emerge but that there was a symbiotic relationship between the leader and the environment, which meant that each influenced the other and created mutually supportive feedback.

The negative aspects of charisma

As in George Lucas's epic series of films, *Star Wars*, there is a dark side to charisma, with any number of writers (for example see: Conger 1989: Conger and Kanungo 1998; Kets de

Vries 2001) exploring the negative aspects of this powerful attractive force. There are also many examples from history of political, religious, and business leaders misleading their followers or exploiting their positions to their own advantage. For example, Hitler's vision of a Thousand Year Reich led his people and the world to the edge of destruction. In commerce, Tourish and Vatcha (2005) examine the leadership at Enron, the US energy company that collapsed in 2001 with billions of dollars of debt, and they lay fault at the feet of the leadership who lied about the company's debt and who convinced others the organization was sound. Other, more tragic, examples of leaders convincing their followers to follow their lead include James 'Jim' Jones who was the founder and leader of the People's Temple, an American religious cult. In 1978, more than 900 Temple members in Jonestown, Guyana, committed mass suicide in response to Jones's instructions. Both Bass and Avolio (1997) and House and Howell (1992) point to the 'pseudo' or false nature of some charismatic leaders as they encourage an 'us vs them' mind set, which can result in followers taking extreme action. Howell's approach was to produce a dichotomous model that has charismatic leaders divided into one of two camps—socialized or personalized—the former being individual leaders who lead for the betterment of the collective, whereas the latter lead for their own self-interest. However, as Conger (2011) suggests, even this may be a false distinction with perhaps a scalar approach being more appropriate, as individuals change as their power evolves. The Arab Spring of 2011 has highlighted many leaders originally feted by their supporters—such as Colonel Gaddafi of Libya—but who became despotic and corrupted by the power assigned to them.

The question of why this ability can have disastrous consequences is explored by Yukl (2006) who points towards a number of different factors that may operate as a process whereby the awe in which a charismatic leader is held by followers leads to followers accepting everything the leader espouses as 'fact'. This, in turn, leads to a dependence on the leader, which drives down the competence of the followers, which, in turn, leads to a leadership crisis when the leader eventually departs or dies. Again, historical examples abound whereby organizations fail after a period of control by a charismatic leader. England's win at the Rugby World Cup in 2003 was followed by relative failure following the departure of head coach, Clive Woodward; the Conservative Party struggled for years to replace Margaret Thatcher; Pope Benedict XVI often suffers in comparisons with his more outgoing predecessor, John Paul II, even though he wrote most of John Paul's speeches.

Ultimately, charisma presents a real challenge of organizations and leaders alike. The highly risky nature of this volatile attribute may offer short-term benefits but, unless controlled and institutionalized, can result in the destruction or, at least, damage to the organization. Bryman (1992) and Conger (1989) point out the pitfalls of the obsession with the search for charismatic leaders. The radical changes driven by a charismatic leader may not be the solution to organizational woes and may result in internal conflict. Trice and Beyer (1993) make the point that, as Weber originally suggested, charisma is a rare phenomenon that can be difficult to manage. Current research into this field is wide and varied, and covers aspects of show business (Big Brother and celebrity see: James Bennett 2008), sport (coaches and captains see: Grix and Parker 2011), and politics (Sarah Palin and the Tea Party see: Whisker 2012).

Case study   Simon Cowell

Simon Cowell is a music producer, and television and media star, who was voted by the British magazine, *New Statesman*, number 41 in their list *The World's 50 Most Influential Figures 2010*. He is estimated to be worth more than £200 million.

He was born on 7 October 1959 in London, England. His father, Eric Cowell, was an estate agent developer and music industry executive, whilst his mother, Julie Brett, was a former ballet dancer and socialite. He is a polarizing character with some viewing him as a brash, rude person who exploits a celebrity-obsessed public. Others see him as an entrepreneur who has captured the zeitgeist of the times to become an internationally recognized businessman.

Cowell attended school at Dover College, England, but dropped out when he was 16 years old. From there he held various short-term jobs without showing much by way of enthusiasm for learning a trade. In time, he was promoted to accounts receivable assistant and eventually to a spot in the music publishing department of EMI. Having learnt what it took to make a hit record, he left EMI to form E&S Music with Ellis Rich, a former colleague. Unfortunately, the company collapsed and went under a few years later, forcing Simon to return to EMI. A short time later, he set up his own label, Fanfare, with fellow EMI executive, Iain Burton; this also folded.

However, from these early setbacks, he went on to discover various pop artists, such as Westlife, who have has achieved sales of more than 25 million albums, 70 Top 30 records, and 17 Number 1 singles.

Over the past 10 years or so, Simon has been involved with many television talent show competitions. The first major hit was *Popstars*, which paved the way for *Pop Idol* and the spin off *American Idol*, which is now one of the biggest talent competitions in the world. After those, he moved on to *The X Factor* and *Britain's Got Talent*.

He is now well-known for his acerbic and cutting remarks to contestants on his talent shows. In his autobiography, *I don't mean to be rude but...*, he says:

> since the birth of Pop Idol and its explosive success ... people have expected nothing less of me. You see I have become famous for being rude. At first I was the record executive but in no time I became the nasty one, the obnoxious one or the brutal one. Well in my mind I'm the honest one. That's all.
>
> Cowell (2004)

Cowell has been involved in charity work for many years and he supports children from The Association Of Children's Hospices. He also supports animal rights and has appeared in a video for People for the Ethical Treatment of Animals (PETA) in which he reminds drivers of the cruelty to animals that can occur when their pets are locked in cars in the summer. He also produced the charity single, *Everybody Hurts*, in aid of victims of the earthquake in Haiti in 2010.

Sources

Cowell, S. (2004) *I don't want to be rude but....* London: Ebury Press. *New Statesman* Magazine, 27 September 2010.

'The Sunday Times Rich List 2010'. *The Sunday Times*, 25 April 2010.

http://peta.org.uk (accessed 1 August 2013).

http://entrepreneurs.about.com (accessed 1 August 2013).

Questions

1. Is Cowell charismatic according to your understanding of the word?

2. How would self-concept theory deal with Cowell's success?

3. Would you consider Cowell to be 'socialized' or 'personalized'?

Transformational leadership

At the beginning of this chapter, the concept of transactional and transformational approaches to leadership was introduced with the idea being these were somehow different methodologies. James (Jim) Downton, in his 1973 book, *Rebel Leadership*, is accredited with using the term first, but James MacGregor Burns (1978) really drew attention to the idea of 'transforming leadership' to describe a different approach from those we have studied in previous chapters. Subsequent writers, such as Bass and Riggio (2006), developed the theme and say transformational leaders 'are those who stimulate and inspire followers to both achieve extraordinary outcomes and, in the process, develop their own leadership capacity' (2006:3). Transformational leadership suggests a process which involves changing the hearts and minds of followers by something more than straightforward gifts, promises, or threats. It is suggested (for example see: Bass 1998) that to achieve this change an individual needs to have certain attributes and charisma may help or enable this process but, as Conger and Kanungo (1987) make clear, they are different concepts.

Burns (1978) placed transactional and transformational leaders on a continuum, with transformational at one end and transactional at the other, whilst Bass (1985) originally had these concepts as separate dimensions—you could be either a transactional leader or a transformational leader. However, in subsequent models, Bass and his collaborators, such as Avolio, have developed the Full Range Leadership model (FRL) (see: Figure 7.3), which has nine different factors that contribute towards a leader's approach. This means an effective

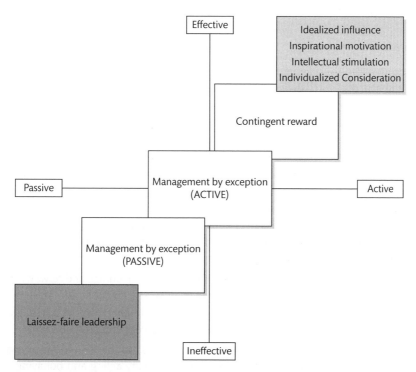

Figure 7.3 The full range leadership model

leader may employ transformational, transactional, and a laissez-faire approach depending on the requirements of the followers.

Clearly, there is overlap between the transactional approach and the charismatic leader. The distinction between the two approaches is subtle and there is significant overlap, as Conger and Kanungo (1998:11) acknowledge 'there is far more overlap between the two than there are differences'. Some researchers (Bass 1985; Weber 1947) placed charisma as an important personal attribute for change agents, whereas others suggested transformational leaders should aspire to charismatic leadership (Conger 1989; Conger and Kanungo 1987). Perhaps one way of considering if these two ideas are different is to look on charismatic leadership as focusing on the attributes of the leader, whereas transactional leadership considerers how the leader intrinsically motivates the followers. Diaz-Saenz (2011:299) states: 'transformational leadership is the process by which a leader fosters group or organizational performance beyond expectation by virtue of the strong emotional attachment with his or her followers combined with the collective commitment to a higher moral cause.' So, as Yammarino (1993) suggests, whilst being charismatic may assist in this process, it is not sufficient merely to be charismatic. A leader needs to understand more fully the needs of the followers and the demands of the situation so that an appropriate approach is employed.

So, we can now explore exactly what transformational leaders do if, as Bass and Riggio (2006:5) suggest, they 'do more with colleagues and followers than set up simple exchanges or agreements'. The FRL model offers a leader a range of options in terms of behaviour that range from passive to active and effective to ineffective. By examining each of these factors, the depth of the model becomes clearer, as do the similarities and subtleties between the charismatic approach and the transactional approach.

Transformational leadership

1. Individualized consideration: here the leader focuses on the individual and treats each team member according to their specific needs. The leader coaches each individual to higher performance by creating a supportive environment based on what the individual needs to flourish. Personal conversations are remembered and the employee is seen as a 'whole person' rather than as a piece of a larger machine. An example would be a managing director who personally hands an employee a card on the occasion of their birthday.

2. Inspirational motivation: this factor requires the leader to inspire their followers by communicating a compelling vision of the future and getting the team involved in its creation and delivery. This has real echoes of the charismatic leader with the vision forming an essential part of the leader's message. Team spirit is also key here, with the leader arousing this and convincing the team they can achieve more by working together as one coherent unit.

3. Intellectual stimulation: in this element, the leader will encourage and reward followers to be creative and innovative. If a mistake is made, there will be no public admonishment and followers will be asked to challenge the status quo. An example would be a manager who states and delivers a 'no blame policy' and encourages his team to try out new ideas.

4. Idealized influence: this factor is probably the closest to the definitions of charisma examined earlier in the chapter, with leaders with this ability acting and behaving as role

models for their followers. They are admired and respected as individuals with high moral code and can be relied upon to 'do the right thing'. Because of these characteristics, followers attribute other positive capabilities to the leader and the leader gains further trust from the group as a result.Collectively, these four factors are known as the 'Four Is' and form the basis for transformational leaders. The FRL model is also closely associated with the MLQ, which, when a sufficient sample is available, is suggested to be a validated indication of leadership performance (Humphreys 2001). The FRL model extends to cover aspects of transactional leadership which, according to the model, are still legitimate approaches capable of achieving results because it is in the best interests of followers to acquiesce to the leader's demands.

Transactional leadership

5. Contingent reward: here the leader negotiates with the followers a suitable reward for delivery of a set objective. The exchange can be physical in terms of cash or promotion; however, it can be psychological as well—for example, praise or recognition. The basic formula is that by achieving X the follower will receive Y.

6. Management by exception: there are two forms to this leadership pattern, active and passive. In the active version, a leader will monitor deviations from a selected path or objective. If there is any deviation detected, then corrective action will be taken to return the individual or team to the correct point. For example, a production manager may monitor the quality of units produced by his workforce to ensure they are of the right standard. With the passive version, the manager will simply wait for an exception to be flagged up—perhaps a customer complaint, for example—before taking any action. It is usual in both of these variants to use punitive or negative measures to reinforce the required behaviour or task outcome. So it is likely that any deviation from the desired path will result in punishment rather than reward.

Avoidance leadership

7. Laissez-fare: Laissez-faire is French for 'allow to do'. In this sense, it means a leadership approach that passes responsibility for action to the followers. However, far from being an empowering device, the leader makes no attempt to support or engage with the followers so this can be a rather dangerous option. Followers can feel disengaged, ignored, and frustrated by a leader who, although having the title, has abdicated responsibility for their role.

Bass and Riggio (2006:9) make the point that 'every leader displays each style to some amount'. An optimal profile sees the transformational factors (1–4) being seen more frequently than the transactional (5 and 6) or laissez-faire (7) factors.

 Pause for thought

Recall your thoughts on 'styles' in Chapter 4. Can you see any congruence or divergence between these two ideas?

Summary

Charismatic leadership and Transformational leadership are both subjects that have attracted a degree of attention recently. Most of the empirical research supports 'the notion that transformational leadership has a favourable influence upon follower's performance' (Diaz-Saenz 2011:307). Indeed, there is a powerful anecdotal pull towards this notion of a heroic leader, with many historical examples available to support the idea of a singular person striding through the haze to lead a bedraggled and confused group towards safety. Hollywood and popular fiction too supports this idealized image; however, there are some concerns that need to be considered.

Yukl (1999) feels this heroic leadership focuses too much on the leader and how the leader manipulates followers towards a goal. As we will see in Chapter 9, followers can influence leaders too, and perhaps this approach glosses over the dynamics of this relationship. Tied to this is the view that such a model is elitist, with the transformational leader creating change and directing effort regardless of the needs of the followers. Certainly, the 'pseudo' transformational leaders who see self-aggrandizement as the end rather than a broader social benefit do conform to this perspective. However, Bass and Avolio (1993), in responding to criticism, suggested a transformational leader can be directive as well as participative, which may undermine some of the characteristics highlighted in their FRL model around factors (1) to (4).

An additional concern focuses on the lack of conceptual clarity—is Transformational leadership different from charismatic leadership, or is one an extension of the other? Bryman (1992) feels they are synonymous whereas Bass (1985) argues they are different, with charisma forming part of a broader transformational approach. This leads to the concern as to whether charisma is a trait because, if it is, one of the implications, as we have already discussed in Chapter 2, is that it cannot be learnt. Indeed, some may argue this is true—where are the credible 'Learn to be Charismatic' courses they ask?

 Case study   Lord Sebastian Coe

Sebastian Coe (born 29 September 1956) is an English athlete and double Olympic Gold Medal winner. Following his retirement from the sport, he served as the Conservative Member of Parliament for Falmouth from 1992 to 1997. He was awarded a life peerage in 2000 and became Lord Coe. However, it is in his role as head of the 2005 Olympic Games bid team that many people will remember him.

In May 2004, Coe took over from the American businesswoman, Barbara Cassani, as head of the bid team. At the time, the bid was faltering and both Paris, the favourite, and Madrid, a dark horse outsider, were threatening to overwhelm another British attempt at securing the Games. As soon as news of Coe's elevation became public, the International Olympic Committee (IOC) chief, Jacques Rogge, hailed the appointment, calling Coe 'a very capable man who has all the credentials'. Coe set about meeting and greeting the IOC delegates, identifying their concerns, and finding out more about their aspirations for a modern, twenty-first-century Games. Coe pointed out the passion the English have for sport, and reminded them about the successful staging of the Commonwealth Games in Manchester in 2002.

'The British, they explained their love of the sport,' said Dutch IOC member, Anton Geesink, after meeting with Coe, 'Love, you can explain, but you can't sell it.'

Despite this glad-handing, at the final presentation ceremony in Singapore, Paris was felt by many to be the favourite, with most French commentators suggesting the deal was already struck. However, Coe was not finished quite yet. As the team gathered one evening to talk about their prospects, the conversation turned to why they had bothered with all of this in the first place; most of the team had 'day jobs' and this additional workload was an enormous strain on their resources. Lord Coe began to explain how, as a 12-year-old boy growing up in Sheffield, he had watched the Olympics on a black and white television and was so overcome with emotion as the British runner won he vowed that, one day, that would be him. Other team members followed with their stories, and eventually the comment was made as to why, if this story was so powerful and compelling, did they not tell it to the IOC. The story of youth being inspired by the Olympics reflects back on the original dream Baron Pierre de Coubertin had when he established the modern games in 1896—that of inspiring the youth of the world.

Paris began with a slick presentation coordinated by the Hollywood director, Luc Besson. With the decision on a knife-edge, Coe took to the stage and related his dream to a hushed conference. London was allowed 100 representatives in the voting hall, and, in a bold move, bid leaders made sure 30 of them were young people from the capital. Coe appealed 'on behalf of the youth of today'. He then went on: 'Choose London today and you send a clear message to the youth of the world—that the Olympic Games are for you.' Coe coupled his speech with a video presentation showing young children from around the world watching athletes and reacting as their home nation won.

'Some might say your decision is between five similar bids but that would undervalue the opportunity before us. In the past you have made bold decisions which have taken the movement forward in powerful and exciting ways.' He added: 'It's a decision about which city will help us show a new generation their sport matters, that in a world of many distractions that Olympic sport matters, in the 21st century why the Olympic ideal matters so much. On behalf of the youth of today and the Olympics of the future we humbly submit the bid of London 2012.' As a final master stroke, Coe introduced Amber Charles, a 14-year-old basketball player from Newham, East London. The message was clear—vote for London and vote for youth.

At the conclusion, there was uproar as chants of 'Paris, Paris' began to be heard but soon the crowd settled into a state of nervous tension. It was clear something extraordinary was about to happen. Rogge tore open the envelope and uttered the magic word, 'London'. The bid was narrowly won, by 54 votes to 50, triggering disbelief in both London and Paris, but for contrasting reasons. The French, led by President Chirac, had felt they were destined to win—London was the rank outsider, but won.

After the vote, Rogge remarked of Coe: 'He really is a "Lord of the Rings".' Coe stayed on to head the organizing committee for 2012. He not only won over the IOC, he also helped convince London's 7.3 million citizens of the benefits the Olympics would bring to their city. Even the British media, initially sceptical about the possibilities of staging an Olympics in their crowded city, were won over, with newspapers uniting to wish London good luck. The Queen, in a message to Coe, said: 'I send my warmest congratulations to you and every member of the London 2012 team for winning the bid for the UK. It's a really outstanding achievement to beat such a highly competitive field.'

However, Former IOC Athletes Commission member, Ken Read, says the IOC may have simply felt that because Britain had not hosted the Games since 1948, it was their turn. 'The UK has bid several times,' Read told Canada AM, referring to three recent unsuccessful bids: Birmingham in 1992, and Manchester in 1996 and 2000. 'But they haven't held the Games since 1948, whereas if you look at France... they have organized a number of Winter Games.' Read went on to say, 'tradition, technical skill, and some of the people behind the scenes also played a huge role in putting London in front'. It is certainly true that the incumbent prime minister, Tony Blair, and iconic figures, such as the footballer David Beckham, were engaged in the bid team.

Sources

Kay, A. 2012 London had blown it! Coe saved Olympic bid from disappearing without a trace. London, *Daily Mail Newspaper*. 27th July 2012. Available online at: http://www.dailymail.co.uk/sport/olympics/article-2179761/London-2012-Olympics-Sebastian-Coe-saved-bid--Michael-Payne.html#ixzz2i4raetfN (accessed 18 November 2013).   *(Continued...)*

Oxford Brookes University (2010) *Case Study LONDON 2012: How We Won The Bid*. Oxford, Oxford Brookes University 2010. oxb:060111:009cs. Available online at: http://www.heacademy.ac.uk/assets/hlst/documents/olympic_sig/case_studies/CS10-How-we-won-the-Bid.pdf (accessed 18 October 2013).

Campbell, D. (2005) 'The day Coe won gold'. London, *The Guardian Newspaper*. Available online at: http://www.theguardian.com/uk/2005/jul/10/olympics2012.olympicgames6 (accessed 18 October 2013).

Keogh F., Fraser, A. (2005) 'Why London won the Olympics'. BBC online. Wednesday, 6 July, 2005. Available online at: http://news.bbc.co.uk/sport1/hi/other_sports/olympics_2012/4618507.stm (accessed 18 October 2013).

Questions

1. To what extent do you think Sebastian Coe is a charismatic leader?
2. Would you consider Coe to have used any Transformational leadership techniques?
3. Could there be an alternative explanation as to why London was selected?

Nevertheless, transformational leaders remain attractive and appealing to most. Nelson Mandela is an iconic figure in the world's history who has transformed South Africa and held the world transfixed. Historical figures such as President Kennedy, Muhammad Ali Jinnah, and Mahatma Ghandi have made lasting impressions on the world with each of them displaying elements of Transformational leadership. In organizational terms, the FRL model and the associated MLQ (Bass and Avolio 1995) have been used for some time and Bass and Avolio (1990) have established training programmes to teach Transformational leadership to executives. Whilst Bones (2011) may decry the heroic leader, for many this vision remains compelling and attractive.

Assignment—300 words

Identify two leaders you consider to be 'good' in terms of their charisma, and another you consider to be bad. Analyse their behaviour patterns using the models in the textbook to justify your original proposition. Go on to argue whether you consider yourself to be 'transformational'.

Transformational leadership—develop your charisma

1. Listening to music makes me want to move in time to the beat.

   Never   sometimes   often   always

2. My laugh makes others smile.

   Never   sometimes   often   always

3. People always know what mood I am in.

   Never   sometimes   often   always

4. I am fashionably dressed for the occasion.

   Never   sometimes   often   always

5. People confide in me.

   Never   sometimes   often   always

6. I should really be on the stage.

   Never   sometimes   often   always

7. People say I look younger than I am.

   Never   sometimes   often   always

8. I make a plan and stick to it.

   Never   sometimes   often   always

9. I like to hug and shake hands.

   Never   sometimes   often   always

10. I do not mind being the centre of attention.

    Never   sometimes   often   always

Scores

Mostly never

You are probably more of a shy character and whilst your friends may know you well, others could take longer to get to know you. This may mean they lose interest and move on to a person who is easier to get to know quickly. To develop your charisma try to smile more and learn to ask open questions when you next meet someone you do not know well.

Mostly sometimes

In your own circle of friends and acquaintances you appear to be comfortable. However, in more public settings you can feel exposed and wary. This may mean when you need to make a quick positive impression you feel tongue tied and nervous. To develop your charisma make sure you stand up straight when in social settings, take a deep breath before you start speaking and don't doubt what you have to say has real value to your audience.

Often

Most people view you as friendly and positive. You probably have a large circle of acquaintances and don't usually have any problems making new contacts. To develop your charisma create firm boundaries between you and your audience. Let them know you are focusing on them and let your natural warmth show through.

Always

You probably like to feel you can impress with your positive energy and enthusiasm for life. You will be seen and heard in most social settings. However, some may view you as over bearing and arrogant unless they know this is your 'normal' self. To develop your charisma try to develop a range of styles that suit your audience rather than having one 'full on' approach. Be careful of burning yourself out and remember to take time for yourself occasionally.

Reproduced by special permission of the publisher: Mind Garden, Inc., http://mindgarden. com. These questions are taken from Bass, B. M. and Avolio, B. J. (1995) *Multifactor Leadership Questionnaire*. Menlo Park, CA: Mind Garden, Inc. Further reproduction is prohibited without the publisher's written consent.

Further reading

Don Shula, the legendary American Football coach, co-authored a booked called *Everyone's a Coach* with Ken Blanchard (Blanchard, K. and Shula, D. (1996) *Everyone's a Coach: Five Business Secrets for High Performance Coaching*. New York: HarperCollins). Using a conversational style, they alternately outline steps to help aspiring managers using a mnemonic COACH (conviction-driven, over-learning, audible ready, consistency, and honesty). Shula also relates his experiences to his faith, and discusses how his belief in God has influenced his approach to leadership. It is a practical rather than theoretical approach but Shula won more games in his chosen profession than anyone else, so he speaks from experience about small things that make a big difference.

Leadership Charisma (Haney, B., Sirbasku, J., and McCann, D. (2010) *Leadership Charisma*. Waco, TX: S & H Publishing Company LLC) puts the case for charisma being a learnt skill rather than an inherited trait—so anyone can become 'charismatic'. It is written in a self-help manner and is heavily influenced by American thinking and anecdotes. A four-part Leadership Charisma Model is constructed to guide the reader to becoming charismatic. Again, it is not a difficult academic read and can be picked up and put down easily. As long as the starting points for the underlying assumptions being made are kept clear, it is an entertaining book.

Finally, there are many books by politicians, celebrities, and sports people that can provide an insight into the world of transformational leaders. However, one that stands out and has received many plaudits is Nelson Mandela's autobiography (Mandela, N. (1995) *Long Walk to Freedom: The Autobiography of Nelson Mandela*. Austin, TX: Holt, Rinehart and Winston). The book, although long, has a hook in every chapter and goes some way to exploring his relationship with his followers and the South African authorities. From an academic perspective, the challenge of identifying his charismatic attributes is also of interest.

Authentic leadership

In this chapter we will examine:

- The nature of authentic leadership.
- The split between academics and practitioners in this field.
- Your reflections on the nature of your 'true self'.

Introduction

It is probably fair to suggest that the themes of authentic, spiritual, and ethical leadership have come to the fore in recent times as a reaction to economic conditions surrounding the recession that began in 2008 (Burgoyne et al. 2013). The turmoil in the world's economy, coupled with the failure of large organizations such as Enron, Lehman Brothers, Northern Rock, and RBS, and the growing distrust of corporations has led some to question the underpinning paradigms that govern our economic system. Events such as the Occupy London movement, disquiet in relation to high bonus payments to bankers worldwide, and various European protests linked to austerity measures are all said to be evidence of a growing dissatisfaction with the leadership of key social organizations, including governments and commercial enterprises. In this chapter, we will examine the concept in terms of its evolution and how, in practical terms, researchers are trying to use the idea of '**authenticity**' to develop leaders.

> **Authentic:** of undisputed origin; genuine: 'authentic fourteenth-century furniture'. Made or done in the traditional or original way: 'authentic Italian meals'. **Synonyms:** genuine, real, original.

Authentic leadership has its roots in psychology where the concept of the 'true self' (Winnicott 1965) contrasted with a 'false self'. These two terms were used to describe the psychological state of an individual who could use the 'false self' to hide the 'true self' for reasons of defence or protection from discovery by others. The true self enables a person to be 'real' and spontaneous, whereas the false self, instead of reacting to its environment in a way that is connected to true feelings, merely complies with expectations of significant other individuals (such as a parent). However, in a leadership sense, this concept was not discussed with any real vigour until around 2003 when George (2003) published his work, accompanied by Luthans and Avolio 's (2003) contribution. This sparked a whole series of debates and further research. However, the field remains fragmented and the concept ill-defined.

The challenge facing individuals with an interest in this field is the relative novelty of the idea. This means there is still an evolving view of exactly what authentic leadership 'is', how it can be defined, and, indeed, if it exists at all. Empirical research is rather sparse and tends not to follow an accepted definition. However, what is more certain, as the slow development of the concept emerges and more research is carried out, is a conviction among supporters that a new leadership paradigm is called for in the twenty-first century.

The background

A brief exploration of the underpinning assumptions surrounding the nature of authenticity and a 'true' self will assist with understanding the development of the idea and how it may evolve in the future.

Donald Winnicott (1896–1971) was born in Plymouth, England, where his father, a prominent local citizen, was mayor twice. However, Winnicott's mother had a tendency towards depression and his relationship with her shaped much of his later theorizing. He studied medicine at Cambridge and eventually found his calling as a paediatrician and psychoanalyst by way of St Bartholomew's Hospital in London. During his career, he wrote more than 200 articles and books as well as formulating a number of new ideas about the relationship between an infant child and its mother. However, here we are concerned with his concept of the 'true' and 'false' self. According to him, these two different, but related, states emerge in childhood as a result of the interaction between child and carer (which he called 'the mother'). The true self was a reaction to a baby being nurtured and encouraged when young. The baby develops an authentic sense of self when it is supported and given positive feedback when interacting with the 'mother'. He says the implication of this nurturing is that only the true self can be creative and only the true self can feel real' (Winnicott 1965:141). This creates a feeling of well-being in the child and the ability to experience and express feelings that are spontaneous and unforced. The behaviours mean that the child is able to form close emotional bonds with others.

The false self emerges, in Winnicott's writing, as a defence, a kind of mask of behaviour that complies with others' expectations of the individual. Winnicott thought a false self was what allowed one to present a 'polite and mannered attitude' in public (1965:145). Using the false self enabled the individual to predict and anticipate what was expected by others of the individual. The parallels with Freud's concept of the id, ego, and super-ego are apparent although Winnicott merges the concept of the ego and super-ego (see: Chapter 10). These two states exist in every person; however, in healthy people the balance between the two states is clear to the individual. In unhealthy people, the false state comes to dominate with the result of the individual becoming empty, unreal, and a copy of those people the individual has chosen to imitate.

Winnicott's ideas have been criticized (Philips 1994) as a reflection of his own relationship with his mother. However, he made his work accessible to others by using everyday language

 Pause for thought

1. What do you think of this idea of a person having a 'true' and 'false' persona?
2. Can you identify any examples where you:
   a) were true to yourself?
   b) did what was expected?
3. Did either of these positions cause you any emotional discomfort?

and regular television appearances. The notion of a true self that is open and honest springs from these ideas and forms the basis for the later models of the authentic leader.

Defining authentic leadership

The ills facing many established economies has been partly attributed to a selfish and morally bankrupt style of leadership which emphasizes short-term profit over long-term investment, self-aggrandizement over collective appreciation, and personal greed over shared returns (for example see: Rayment and Smith 2011). This theme, coupled with the slightly unfinished themes of pseudo-transformational leadership, explored in Chapter 7, where both Nelson Mandela and Adolf Hitler could be described as 'charismatic', has led scholars to seek a more 'positive' approach to leadership. Advocates of this approach suggest existing models of leadership are no longer sufficient for developing leaders facing an uncertain future (Avolio and Gardner 2005: May et al. 2003). They seek to establish a new set of norms for leaders that produce leadership behaviour that is ethical in nature and delivers 'results' in a socially responsible manner. The view being that the current ideological approach to leadership is socially irresponsible and unsustainable in the long term. Whilst this view may resonate with many observers, Cooper et al. (2005) are right to caution against a headlong rush into embracing this new future without first addressing four key issues.

1. First, they suggest, is the need to define the construct adequately and form a set of measures so researchers can agree on what it is they are attempting to investigate.

2. It is then necessary to determine the validity of the construct—in other words, is the idea different from previous notions of leadership and, if so, how?

3. Then identification is required of how the construct delivers the desired outcomes. This should accompany an understanding of how authentic leadership connects together the various parts of the system the leader operates within. In effect, how does authentic leadership produce results?

4. Finally an investigation is needed of whether authentic leadership is a trait or state. This will enable researchers to cultivate leadership development programmes to effect the necessary changes to existing and inexperienced leaders wishing to improve their performance.

Whilst it may be relatively straightforward to define authentic leadership as 'do the right thing', suggesting a somewhat deontological approach to decision making, there is little agreement among academics as to what authentic leadership means beyond this ethos. Some of the problems with the approach are evident when writers such as Shamir and Eilam (2005:395) say: 'all definitions are arbitrary. They reflect choices that cannot be proved or validated.' However, this does not mean the concept cannot be investigated or should not be a subject for research. For, in the genesis of the idea, comes the hint that leaders, by acting authentically, can improve the lives of their followers, their organization, and their broader stakeholder network—and surely this is something to be welcomed.

The underpinning philosophy behind the theoretical stance is that leaders should 'be true to themselves'. However, this concept has been around for some time—for example, consider the leadership of Sir Adrian Cadbury, who continued the Quaker tradition of leadership, and

Joseph Rowntree, who founded the Joseph Rowntree Foundation. Alternatively, Barnard (1938) introduces some themes surrounding ethical considerations in his examination of the moral stance of administrators who had to work with people who had differing ideas of right and wrong.

 Case study   Cadbury and Rowntree

Joseph Rowntree (1836–1925) was a Quaker, successful businessman, and philanthropist, who, together with his brother, developed the Rowntree confectionary company from its modest beginnings as a cocoa works in York. He wanted his money to be used to tackle the root causes of social problems, rather than treating their symptoms. In 1904, he established what was to become the Joseph Rowntree Foundation (JRF). Then known as the Joseph Rowntree Village Trust, its original purpose was to build and manage the garden village of New Earswick, York.

In a similar fashion, in 1893 the Cadbury family, headed by George Cadbury, bought 120 acres of land close to their factory in Bourneville, Birmingham, and planned, at their own expense, a model village which, they claimed, would 'alleviate the evils of modern more cramped living conditions'. However, in line with their firm religious beliefs as Quakers, there were no pubs in the village. By 1900, the estate had expanded to include more than 300 dwellings, built on 330 acres of land, including almshouses for retired workers. This attractive quadrangle of 35 houses still stands, and is administered by an independent trust. This theme of inclusivity continued into the twentieth century with the introduction of elected workers' councils including both men and women. Today, the area is still heavily influenced by the Cadbury Foundation and its charitable work continues with many employees volunteering. The Cadbury website declares that Cadbury recognizes 'it does not operate in isolation but has responsibilities to its employees and society in general'. Today, the trust is independent from the brand and now manages more than 1,000 acres, in excess of 7,000 homes, and shares the village with 25,000 people.

However, in 2010, Kraft launched a takeover bid for Cadbury. The move, heavily criticized by unions, workers, and the general public, was successful and the organization has been de-listed from the London Stock Exchange. Following the merger, Kraft announced the closure of a factory near Bristol with the loss of more than 400 jobs. In another twist, RBS, a bank 84 per cent owned by the United Kingdom Government, funded the Kraft takeover.

Sources

The main charity website for the Rowntree Foundation can be found at http://www.jrf.org.uk/about-us/our-heritage (accessed 18 October 2013).

The Rowntree Society which covers both Sir Joseph Rowntree and the broader family can be found at http://www.rowntreesociety.org.uk/ (accessed 18 October 2013).

de la Merced, M., Nicholson, C. (2010) 'Kraft to Acquire Cadbury in Deal Worth $19 Billion'. New York, *New York Times*. January 19, 2010. Available online at: http://www.nytimes.com/2010/01/20/business/global/20kraft.html?_r=0 (accessed 18 October 2013).

Questions

1. Would you consider the actions of Joseph Rowntree and George Cadbury to be 'authentic'?

2. How did their religious beliefs shape their leadership?

3. Is authentic leadership really an anachronistic throwback that is unsustainable in modern economies?

Figure 8.1 Authentic leadership

In theoretical terms, the model suggested by Shamir and Eilam (2005) and Yammarino et al. (2008) is worth examining as it places context at the heart of the problem. They suggest a hierarchy whereby the individual's authenticity, the leader's authenticity, and the phenomenon of authentic leadership operate as a mutually inclusive social network (see: Figure 8.1). This means that authentic leadership depends initially on an individual being 'authentic'. This translates into the leader being seen as authentic which, in turn, creates authentic leadership.

Clearly, advocates support the philosophical basis of the word 'authentic'. For example, Harter (2002) refers back to the etymological root in ancient Greek with Socrates' assertion, that 'the unexamined life is not worth living for a human being' (Adam 1916), being an early indication of how this term would evolve. This suggests a person should first know their true self and then act in accordance with this true self.

However, the further difficulty in identifying and codifying this concept comes when studying the different approaches taken by practitioners such as George (2003) and academics such as Luthens and Avolio (2003).

The academic approach

Cooper et al. (2005:477) begin by pointing out the requirement to establish 'the key dimensions of authentic leadership and then create a theoretically based definition of the construct'. But they then point to the current lack of clarity and multiple conceptual frames created by authors such as Bass (1990) and Lowe et al. (1996). However, since these early musings others have entered the fray and a broad consensus seems to be appearing which combines the psychological view with a more phenomenological approach. For example, both Avolio and Gardner (2005) and Harter (2002) make the point that authenticity is very much in the mind of the individual leader so that if a person honestly believes they are being authentic and true to themselves then, in a sense, they are. Still, the obvious difficulty here is actually testing if this assertion is true—a point that Terry (1993) makes when describing his Action Wheel. Caza and Jackson (2011:354) combine these two different views with the opinion that authentic leadership is 'having clear and certain knowledge about oneself in all regards (e.g. beliefs, preferences, strengths, weaknesses) and behaving consistently with that knowledge'.

This leads to the position whereby authentic leaders, according to Walumbwa et al. (2008), exhibit a mastery of four components:

1. Self-awareness,
2. Internalized moral perspective,
3. Balanced processing,
4. Relational transparency.

This view, which evolved from a meta-analysis of the literature surrounding the theme, is close to Kernis's (2003) opinions expressed earlier which define the various components thus:

Self-awareness: this refers to the degree to which an individual understands their 'true self'. Benjamin Franklin's words (1740), although rather dated, may still have a certain resonance here: 'observe all men, thyself most'. It examines the knowledge a person has about their own strengths and weaknesses and how they impact on their behaviour—especially when in the company of others. There is also the need to understand one's own feelings when confronted with a particular event or person. Implicit in this is the requirement to grasp the implications of their own values, what these mean for a person, and the impact these have on their decision making. Gardner et al. (2005a) make the point that individuals with this enhanced sense of self-awareness have a greater credibility in terms of their authenticity than those with a lower understanding of what they stand for.

Internalized moral perspective: this aspect is concerned with the degree to which a person follows their own heart rather than being swayed by others or the demands of the situation. It is a self-regulatory process as each individual can choose the degree to which they make their own minds up or the extent they allow others to influence their actions. This means that followers and others will see the leader acting in a way which is consistent with their espoused values. Saying one thing and doing another, on the other hand, is usually seen as being inconsistent and, hence, inauthentic. A leader who stands up for what they believe to be right in the face of determined group or situational pressure, it is argued, are more likely to be seen as authentic than those leaders who act according to short-term external demands.

Balanced processing: this is another self-regulatory ability which acts as a counter balance to the above theme which, if not equalized, could lead to an entrenched mind-set and dogmatic behaviour. The leader should listen to and take into account views from those surrounding the context or decision. The leader should do this prior to coming to a conclusion and decision themselves, retaining an independent mind about what should or should not be done. This includes actively seeking views that may run counter to the leader's own beliefs and those that challenge the leader's perspective. This is to ensure that the leader ensures there is a balanced input to the final decision, that individuals feel engaged with the decision-making process, and the final decision has the best possible chance of success. The consideration of relevant, objective information from a multitude of perspectives gives the leader a chance to analyse the situation impartially and without bias.

Relational transparency: this means showing and sharing honest feelings and thoughts with others rather than hiding 'true' emotions. **Lewis Carroll**, the English author, has some thoughts here. In his most famous book, *Alice's Adventures in Wonderland* (1865), the character of the March Hare implores the heroine, Alice, thus:

'Then you should say what you mean!,' 'I do,' Alice hastily replied; 'at least—at least I mean what I say—that's the same thing, you know.'

Whereas the rather more unsavoury character of Humpty Dumpty says in *Through the Looking Glass* (1872):

'When I use a word,' Humpty Dumpty said in rather a scornful tone, 'it means just what I choose it to mean—neither more nor less.'

> **Lewis Carroll** (1832–1898) was born Charles Lutwidge Dodgson and was an English author. His most famous writings are *Alice's Adventures in Wonderland* and its sequel, *Through the Looking Glass*, as well as the poems *The Hunting of the Snark* and *Jabberwocky*. For an academic appraisal of his work, consider Collingwood (1898) and Leach (1999).

Essentially, the leader should be comfortable with showing their strengths, weaknesses, positive and negative emotions to followers. The risk here, for the leader, is that they will be seen to be weak, especially in cultures where the open expression of true feelings is anathema. However, Gardner et al. (2005a) are convinced it is worth the risk. Sharing insights into the leader's true core values, their hopes and dreams as well as their doubts, helps to establish a strong bond of trust between followers and leader.

Most researchers are also convinced of the need for the authentic leader to display all four of these attributes (Gardner et al. 2005a; Ilies et al. 2005). Their argument is that, even if a leader is self-aware, they may choose to neither display this self-awareness nor act in accordance with their own belief system. If this is the case, then authenticity will be doubted and hence authentic leadership cannot be established. What becomes clearer from these types of assertions is the nature and current positioning of authentic leadership. Supporters such as Avolio, Walumbwa and colleagues are reluctant to claim authentic leadership is in some way 'new' or a relabelling of existing practice such as the Quaker businesses explored earlier. Their opinion is that authentic leadership is rather the 'root construct of all positive, effective forms of leadership' (Avolio and Gardner 2005:xxii), in other words for leadership to be effective and sustainable, the authentic approach should underpin and be fundamental to the leader's approach.

This leaves the definition of authentic leadership favoured by Walumbwa et al. (2008:94) as being:

A pattern of leadership behaviour that draws upon and promotes both positive psychological capacities and a positive ethical climate, to foster greater self-awareness, an internalised moral perspective, balanced processing of information, and relational transparency on the part of leaders working with followers, fostering positive self-development.

Whereas, Avolio et al. (2004:4) explain authentic leaders as:

those who are deeply aware of how they think and behave and are perceived by others as being aware of their own and others' values/moral perspectives, knowledge and strengths; aware of the context in which they operate; and who are confident, hopeful, optimistic, resilient, and of high moral character.

This definition offers a number of different insights for it includes aspects not mentioned by Walumbwa, such as interpretation of the leader by others—in this case, the followers. Other themes include a set of traits, behaviours, and personal attributes assigned to the authentic leader as well as a nod towards the situation inhabited by the leader.

The challenge these diverse opinions present to the field is ensuring that researchers focus their investigations into the same phenomenon.

 Pause for thought

1. What are you thinking now you have seen the demands made of an 'authentic' leader?

2. Are these ideals 'real' and achievable?

3. Or, are they just a set of fantasy ideals that no one person can hope to display?

 Case study   Larry Page and Google

Used by many millions of people as their primary web search engine, Google has risen to become one of the most powerful, richest, and influential organizations in the modern world. The organization is the brainchild of two men, Sergey Brin and Larry Page, who met whilst studying at Stanford University in California. In 1998, they were researching a project for their PhDs and they began to experiment with an idea that would rate how closely web pages satisfied search requests. The organization is now worth something in excess of £100 billion with the personal wealth of the founders said to run into several billions. However, of more interest is the style and approach taken to leadership by Brin and Page. Google's declared code of conduct is 'Don't be evil', a phrase which they went so far as to include in their 2004 corporate prospectus (aka 'S-1'), noting: 'We believe strongly that in the long term, we will be better served—as shareholders and in all other ways—by a company that does good things for the world even if we forgo some short term gains.' Supporting this statement is the declared aim of the organization, which is 'to organize the world's information and make it universally accessible and useful'.

In 2004, Google formed a non-profit philanthropic wing, Google.org, giving it a starting fund of roughly £800 million. This not-for-profit organization (run by Dr Brilliant!) has the express mission of helping with the issues of climate change, global public health, and global poverty. Among its first projects is a viable plug-in hybrid electric vehicle that can attain 100 mpg and runs on ethanol, electricity, and petrol. Their approach mirrors their roots as student entrepreneurs and they are known to be informal and laid back with their teams. In his rare interviews, Page's approach to leadership slowly starts to emerge. His main points appear to be:

Pay attention to your ideas and cultivate the best of them. By this, he means ensuring that creativity and innovation remain at the heart of the business. The original idea behind Google was at the time beyond the scope of any known solution but Page and Brin were inspired enough to think innovatively about how they could solve a problem. Likewise, Tim Berners-Lee, who is credited with founding the Internet, said he created the net because, 'he needed it'. His boss, responding to his original paper, wrote 'Interesting but vague' on his copy.

Build your team and avoid bureaucracy. It is reported that not only are the senior team at Google among the original group recruited by Page but that he still has an interest in the recruitment process. Individual teams are given the responsibility for their project area and are allowed to try new ideas to see if they work. If these projects turn into a commercial success, they are allowed to share in the profits by way of bonus schemes. Failure is also not frowned upon, which means the engineers can try out new untested ideas.

Be quick and concise. This approach means that communication and decision making are designed to be faster because plans are not delayed by endless meetings or committee hearings. Although Google is a technologically driven organization, meetings are still held but they are infrequent and the use of email, video conferencing, and such measures speed up the decision process. This mirrors the approach taken at Innocent Drinks where their ethos is to say 'yes' to a project if there is a 70 per cent chance it will work.

Recognize the significance of minor achievements. In a reflection back to well-established manufacturing techniques, such as **kaizen**, Google's evolution is clear. The number of incremental steps taken from the early days has slowly built a hugely valuable portfolio that includes the video sharing site, YouTube, and the Android phone operating system. This approach has slowly but surely diversified Google's product range, influence, and income.

Perseverance. In common with many entrepreneurs, both Page and Brin have stamina which is born from a belief in their ideas. They know what they want to achieve and have created an organization that mirrors their own set of beliefs.

Sources

Elmer, Vicky, (2011) 'What would Larry Page do?'. *Fortune* Magazine, 18 April 2011.

Ovide, Shira (2011) 'What Would Google Say About Antitrust Probe?'. *The Wall Street Journal*, 23 June 2011.

Stross, Randall (2008) *Planet Google: One Company's Audacious Plan to Organize Everything We Know.* New York: Free Press, September 2008.

http://bbc.co.uk/news/business-15300838 (accessed 2 August 2013).

Questions

1. Do you consider Larry Page to be an 'authentic' leader?

2. What impact do you think his early experiences as a student have had on his leadership?

3. Can you see any dangers for this approach as the company matures?

Kaizen: a Japanese word that means improvement or change for the better. It can be applied to any number of businesses such as manufacturing, operations, or engineering. The ethos is that every day a small change or improvement is made in the process so that over a period of time the organization continuously improves.

The practitioner approach

Individual managers and organizations attracted to this 'better' way of leading have increased steadily since the introduction of the term in 2003. The number of books and organizations attaching the notion of authenticity to their practice has accelerated as the commercial value of authentic leadership increases. This has led commentators such as Cooper et al. (2005) and Luthens and Avolio (2009) to point out the difference between authentic leadership development and authentically developing leadership. They suggest the two affairs are not synonymous with the former, relating quite clearly to the themes explored above and the need to inculcate leaders in this ethos. The latter, they point out, relates to ensuring leadership development programmes focusing on developing skills or attributes, such as charisma, should aim to deliver against the declared aims of the particular programme. Early texts, such as Handy's *The Empty Raincoat* (1994), or more modern books, such as The Arbinger Institute's (2010) *Leadership and Self Deception: Getting Out of the Box* or Bennis and Thomas's (2002) *Geeks and Geezers*, are some examples of how this field has transmogrified into a range of directions.

When Handy wrote *The Empty Raincoat*, the term 'authentic leadership' had not been discussed and yet the text makes for interesting reading as it identifies nine paradoxes that he claims contribute to a dysfunctional society. These paradoxes include the paradox of the organization and the paradox of justice, which he claims means that organizations are now fundamentally different from those that we have experience of running. This, in turn, means there is no blueprint for how to operate a modern business. Coupled with this is the demand from individuals to be treated fairly and as a discrete unit, but this is beyond most organizations as they depend on routine and consistency rather than innovation and diversity.

To cope with this new world, Handy offers three strategies, including what he calls the 'doughnut principle'. Using this metaphorical model, he asks the reader to consider their life as an inside-out American style doughnut, i.e. a ring of dough with a hole in the middle. 'The doughnut principle, however, requires an inside-out doughnut, one with the hole on the outside and the dough in the middle. It can only, therefore, be an imaginary doughnut, one for thinking with, not eating' (Handy 1994:65). Explaining further, he asserts that life is like this doughnut but at its core should be the essential elements of 'self' (the dough) surrounded by our potential (the empty ring). As individuals we can expand the potential to whatever we want but need to know and understand what lies at the core of our world. Without knowing this, our potential is limited and there is will a mismatch between our core and eventual destiny.

On a less esoteric level, George (2003) and George and Sims (2007) offer a practical 'how to be authentic' guide. Their formula is based on interviewing leaders they feel are 'authentic'. From this, they distil a number of characteristics or traits they feel are representative of authentic leaders. In his first book, George, the ex-CEO of a large American conglomerate, identified five facets that when combined formed the essential core of the authentic leader.

1. Purpose: authentic leaders have a clear idea about their own destiny and are highly motivated to achieve these goals.

2. Values: the leader not only understands their own values but their behaviour and action towards others is exclusively directed by these values.

3. Relationships: rather than being the inaccessible and distant head of the organization, an authentic leader is accessible physically and emotionally. This means being open and honest with their followers when discussing their feelings and thoughts.

4. Self-discipline: this means the leader keeps going when times get tough. They have the persistence and motivation to remain calm but resolute when others may doubt their ability to reach their self-declared goals.

5. Compassion: an understanding of how others are feeling, and being empathetic to their needs, is an essential element for the authentic leader. This attribute enables the leader to connect with others, and for others to see the leader sharing their hopes, dreams, and fears.

Pause for thought

1. How does this list compare to the academic community's ideals?

2. What do you think of the claim that this list is just about 'charisma'?

3. Can you identify any person in your life that exhibits some or all of these? Do you?

From this beginning George and Sims went further with their next text, *True North* (2007), which expands on these themes. The book is split into three parts which combine together to provide a thoughtful route map for the prospective authentic leader.

Pursuing the metaphorical 'journey' favoured by many lifestyle writers, in Part One, the anecdotal stories from more than 100 different leaders are described. Although a criticism may be that many of these leaders are the usual suspects, what emerges is the impact that critical events and key episodes had on these leaders—a theme echoed earlier by Bennis and Thomas (2002). The stories are told in an open and honest manner with failure, doubt, and anxiety figuring as frequently as success. The point being that authentic leaders share their failures as well as their success. They are not afraid to discuss what motivates them and the lessons they have taken from setbacks and defeats as well as celebrations. It is this honesty, openness, and vulnerability that enables such individuals to appear 'authentic'—they have the same faults as many of their followers and yet manage to come through these difficult times stronger and more able to cope with adversity.

Part Two looks at five facets of authentic leaders each designed to build authenticity in the prospective leader. Again the similarities with work outlined earlier are worthy of note. The first attribute is 'knowing' your authentic self through self-awareness. This can be built using feedback from trusted others or by reflective practice or perhaps using one of the many psychometric tests such as, 'Authentic Leadership—the competencies senior women need in order to be successful' marketed by Tracey Carr (see: http://.eve-olution.net). Having established the bedrock for the leader, the second stage is to understand clearly the values and principles on which your belief set is built. In this stage, the leader is encouraged to consider at what point their own moral compass points in a direction which may be at odds with that of the organization or wider context. Third, is to be clear on your own motives and drivers. The text makes the point that it is rare to find a highly successful leader who is motivated by personal success. In the case of international statesmen like Ghandi and Mandela, quite the opposite is true with both men suffering for a cause they strongly believed was a right and just one. A strong network or support group is their next step, which is designed to ensure access to advice, guidance, and moral support as the context of the situation unfolds. The leader can ensure tasks are delegated appropriately and that she can have access to information from a variety of sources. The final part lies in creating a balance between work and play, or an 'integrated life' as George and Sims refer to it. They suggest this is necessary so that neither part of a leader's existence dominates to the detriment of the other. A leader with a wider perspective on life is more likely, they argue, to make decisions that reflect a responsibility towards a wider set of stakeholders than simply those benefiting within an organizational context.

The final sections in the book deals with how to motivate and empower the workforce. Again, a series of anecdotes are used to offer practical insights into the steps successful leaders have taken to develop their own skills in this area. The leaders are asked to focus on their intrinsic motivations and how these have been shaped by powerful personal experiences, including familial bereavement. The purpose of this activity is to demonstrate to the reader that individuals perceived as strong and commanding often have very significant failures in their curriculum vitae. It is this vulnerability that marks out such individuals, if they are prepared to share their experiences, as authentic. Followers can more easily relate to leaders who have shared some of their own emotions, such as disappointment and fear. By overcoming these setbacks and coping with negative emotions, the authentic leader is able to show that success is possible after failure and the implication for the follower is that the leader will achieve this success again.

 Case study   Richard Reed and Innocent Drinks

Richard Reed is the co-founder of Innocent Drinks, the brand of smoothies and vegetable pots that has grown its turnover from £400,000 to £16.5 million in 12 years. After reading geography at St John's College, Cambridge, Reed worked for four years as an account manager in an advertising agency. In the summer of 1998, he and two of his closest friends, Jon Wright and Adam Balon, took some fruit-based drinks they had made to a local jazz festival to try and sell them.

They put up a big sign above their stall asking: 'Do you think we should give up our jobs to make these smoothies?' After trying the smoothie, drinkers were asked to vote by putting their empty bottle into a bin saying 'YES' or a bin saying 'NO'. At the end of the weekend, the 'YES' bin was full, so the three men all went to work the next day and resigned. The team has now expanded from the three original founders to 250 people, who are based across the organization in London, Paris, Dublin, Amsterdam, Copenhagen, Stockholm, Hamburg, and Salzburg.

Visitors to the London headquarters—called Fruit Towers—will immediately be struck by the appearance of the office. It is covered in bunting, pictures, and balloons. There is artificial grass on the floor, table tennis tables, and a general air of chaos. The staff can be seen walking around the office in casual clothing—some even in their dressing gowns! On the left-hand-side of the office is a 'wheel of fortune' used to make some decisions. The options are stuck onto the wheel and it is spun around with the outcome decided on where the wheel stops. Reed says that if the organization is 70 per cent sure of a positive outcome he will encourage his team to make a decision rather than wait for further evidence or authorization.

The organization has a philosophy that by encouraging people to 'be themselves', they will work harder and be more committed to the business. This means offering breakfasts, allowing people to wear whatever they wish, and encouraging an open dialogue. Reed and his fellow directors are usually casually dressed, do not have their own offices, and are well known for their love of life. All employees receive an equity share in the business and there is a profit sharing scheme. When questioned, Reed says that Innocent want to leave things a little better than they found them. He believes there is a consistency between his espoused values and their actions, which include the use of green electricity at Fruit Towers and only sourcing their fruit from farms that look after both their workers and the environment. Since 2006, all bananas used in Innocent's drinks have come from Rainforest Alliance accredited farms, and every year 10 per cent of all profits are donated to the Innocent Foundation. This charity operates separately to the commercial arm and invests in projects overseas with the aim of improving the lives of indigenous workers.

However, in 2008 the business crashed and lost all of the profit accumulated since its inception. Reed and his friends faced an uncomfortable dilemma— either lose a significant part of the business or look for external investment. They took the controversial decision to sell an initial 18 per cent of the business to Coca-Cola for £30 million. This share has now risen to 58 per cent. Reed maintains this was the right thing to do as it guaranteed the future of the organization and secured the majority of jobs in the company. He says Coca-Cola do not interfere with the day-to-day decision making of the business, neither does the business compromise its values. However, Terry McAllister, writing for *The Guardian* says: 'Innocent, which markets itself as Europe's favourite smoothie company, is the latest in a long line of UK firms falling into the hands of foreign ownership but is also another example of a business set up with high-minded goals that has been taken over by a very large and conservatively-run predator.'

In response, Reed has said he was aware that some Innocent enthusiasts did not like the idea of a large outside group becoming involved. 'I respect different opinions. But for me it's not about whether it's a large or a small company, it's about whether it is good or bad one. And we think Coke is good.'

Sources

http://innocentdrinks.co.uk (accessed 2 August 2013).

Graham, Natalie, 'My First Million: Richard Reed of Innocent Drinks'. *The Financial Times*, 1 July 2011.

Jones,Peter (2011) *How We Made Our Millions*. UK: BBC TV.

Macalister, Terry and Teather, David 'Innocent Smoothie Denies Sell-Out After Coca-Cola Gets Majority Stake'. *The Guardian*, Friday 9 April 2010.

Northedge, Richard 'Slaughter of the Innocent? Or is Coke the real deal?'. *The Independent*, 12 April 2009.

Questions

1. Do you consider Reed to be an 'authentic' leader?

2. What do you make of the decision to sell to Coca-Cola?

3. What do you think Reed said to his employees about the Coke takeover?

Perhaps one attribute that George hints at, but does not make particularly explicit, is the need for humility in authentic leaders. It is this quality which can assist the leader to recognize their own shortcomings and to reach out for help when needed from their followers. Jim Collins (2001a, 2001b) wrote about a hierarchy of leadership culminating in what he called 'level 5' leadership. The model proposed five different stages individuals could inhabit in terms of their contribution to an organization:

Level 1. At this level, you are competent in your role and are capable of high quality contributions. You possess useful levels of knowledge along with the talent and skills needed to do a good job.

Level 2. Contributing team member: Here you are a proactive member of the team and help others to achieve the overall team goal.

Level 3. Competent manager: Now you are capable of organizing the group to achieve your aims, which are consistent with the overall organization's mission.

Level 4. Effective leader: Collins suggests that it is this domain that most leaders inhabit and here their abilities are focused on making sure the organization reaches its goal and delivers its mission.

Level 5. Great leader: Here the leader needs all of the qualities outlined for the preceding four stages but to achieve 'greatness' needs a combination of humility, self-awareness, and professional will.

Pseudo-authenticity

Another interesting approach is that of Criswell and Campbell whose short book, *Building an Authentic Leadership Image*, is aimed at enabling leaders to 'recognize genuine aspects of themselves that should be coming across to people—but aren't' (2008:1). The book, divided into sections, attempts to take the reader through a series of diagnostic steps aimed at developing their image in terms of their body language, verbal and non-verbal gestures, and other visual signals. Although the authors make the point that this development is not about projecting a false image, it does prompt the challenge as to exactly what is authenticity and what is pseudo-authenticity (Chan et al. 2005), if it can be 'created' or managed in this manner.

Just as Bass and Avolio (1997) and Howell and House (1992) point towards a form of negative charisma and use the term 'pseudo' charisma, there is a debate surrounding the possibility of a leader acting 'pseudo' authentically or displaying authentic behaviours but holding inauthentic 'values'. Chan et al. (2005:31) suggest this is indeed possible and it occurs when there is a disconnection between self-awareness and self-regulation. Using Winnicott's ideas explored earlier, the false self dominates and takes over with the result the leader is unable or unwilling to carry out a true analysis of their own motives and values. This means it can be almost impossible for followers to detect this lack of authenticity because the leader may personally be unaware of their deception. However Chan et al. (2005) suggests this duplicity is only sustainable in the short term and only in certain circumstances where there is limited interaction between the followers and leader, where there is limited transparency within the host organization, and where there is a relatively large psychological 'gap' between followers and leader. In these cases, it may be both more difficult for the followers to determine the 'true' nature of their leader and also for the leader to hide their 'true' self, thus making it easier to practise a pseudo-authentic approach. However, what happens when followers discover this deception can have cataclysmic consequences for both the leader and the organization. In what Gilbert and Jones (1986) referred to as the 'boomerang effect', but more colloquially as 'what goes around comes around', or 'you reap what you sow', individual leaders found out to be acting in this rather **Machiavellian** manner are often vilified and hounded from office, with their reputation suffering permanently. The reason for this swift turnaround is put down by Gardner (1992, 2003) to the process through which authentic leadership manifests itself in terms of follower influence and compliance. He refers to this as 'exemplification', which refers to a type of impression management by the individual leader. The authentic leader may be perceived by the followers as having high moral standards and an ethical stance towards the followers. This elevated stance, whereby the followers look up to, admire, and perhaps even worship their leader, can also elicit feelings of inadequacy and guilt among the followers who may feel they are not worthy of being led by such an esteemed leader. They may strive to live up to the example set by this paragon of virtue but feel unable to match their leader. When any deception is detected by the followers, this guilt can turn to anger as the realization that

---

Machiavellian is a word taken from the Italian writer, Niccolò di Bernardo dei Machiavelli. His most famous book, *The Prince* (1532), deals with the political manoeuvrings in the Florentine Court of the sixteenth century. The text explains how 'the Prince' gains power by sly, devious manoeuvring of opponents. Today a person described as 'Machiavellian' is seen to be immoral, underhand, and not to be trusted.

they were duped by the leader sets in. This, in turn, may lead to vilification and a disparagement of the leader.

A second reason has to do with the fragile nature of trust that exists between a leader and follower. As the authentic leader is viewed in a certain context, and their abilities as an authentic leader are assumed by followers to be an indicator of their whole personality, followers make the assumption that the leader applies these same standards throughout their lives. This means that any deviation from these in any aspect of their existence can puncture the perception of this 'great man'. For example, political leaders are expected by their electorate to behave in a statesmanlike manner in every aspect of their private and public lives, similarly sportsmen and women, and so there is public outrage when the latest dalliance with affairs, drink, or drugs is uncovered by the media.

Summary

The attraction of authentic leadership in these uncertain times is clear. It offers hope in that there may be an alternative to the institutionalized greed and narrow mindedness that, it is alleged, has resulted in many of the social, economic, and political woes facing the world. Authentic leadership has been seen as the 'magic bullet' to solve the systemic issues within the socio-economic systems surrounding the lives of most individuals, organizations, and governments. Its simple message of 'being yourself' appears to be relatively easy to grasp and moves away from trait-based or charismatic models. It can be applied in different contexts and situations too, negating the need to consider a host of different elements and demands.

It is also attractive in that the model prescribes a set of behaviours for leaders—it tells leaders what to do. Usually, this manifests itself in actions that Immanuel Kant would recognize as being 'good'. 'Doing the right thing' is a sentiment often expressed by supporters who adopt a stance that has a person's intensions at its heart—their goodwill or desire to see the situation made better is what matters. Furthermore, there appears to be any number of practical approaches that champion a methodology and process through which this set of intentions can be accomplished. The link between the authentic 'self', the authentic leader, and authentic leadership has been made clear with the building blocks based around the need for the individual to act true to themselves before trying to become an authentic leader.

Finally, as the process appears defined, so too is the implication that authentic leadership can be developed and learnt. The first step towards becoming an authentic leader is the need to understand one's own values, motives, and passions. This is a skill that can be taught by way of self-reflective activities, feedback from peers, and psychometric assessments—as discussed in Chapter 11.

However, despite the attractions of the concept, the warnings given by Garger (2008) are clear. The concept is still evolving conceptually and, despite the recent increase in academic research into the idea, it remains elusive in terms of an agreed definition or rigorous empirical research. Tests for the existence and development of the phenomenon are available but their validity is disputed because there is only partial agreement on exactly what is being measured. In addition, the exact natures of the moral and ethical dimensions are only slowly emerging. There is also a degree of confusion, especially among the practitioners, as to the significant difference between the ideas of authentic leaders, ethical leaders, and spiritual leadership. Each of these areas has a body of knowledge and the overlap between the ideas is creating an ill-defined conceptual space.

Finally, sceptics would point towards the lack of evidence to show how authentic leadership 'works' in an organizational context. It is not clear how this approach can make a contribution to the outcomes required by the organization. Supporters would counter this by suggesting that organizations need to change their definitions of success and begin to consider the wider impact of their activities.

Nevertheless, despite these misgivings it is likely that authentic leadership will continue to be an attractive area for academic research and practical 'how to' guides for the immediate future. It offers attractive benefits to researchers, practitioners, and prospective leaders alike. As the concept becomes steadily more 'mainstream', so too is the body of evidence likely to increase as more research is carried out into the link between values and behaviour in a leadership context.

 Case study   News International

In 2011 a mobile phone hacking controversy in the UK claimed many victims, including the reputation of senior police officers, freelance journalists, managers and employees, as well as a notable and vibrant newspaper. The tabloid newspaper, the *News of the World*, owned by Rupert Murdock's News International Group, paid its employees, third party private investigators, and serving police officers for information. It has since emerged that some of this information was obtained illegally by hacking into private mobile phones owned by prominent people. Several investigations into the scandal have been held, with the first, in 2005, concluding that hacking was limited to high profile celebrities such as Sienna Miller, Hugh Grant, and J.K. Rowling. However, in July 2011 it emerged that other members of the public were also targeted, with the phones of the murdered schoolgirl, Milly Dowler, victims of the July 2005 London bombings, and relatives of deceased British soldiers were also accessed. This resulted in a public outcry against News International Corporation, its owners, and its key management figures such as Rebekah Brooks. The media storm that quickly developed, along with boycotts by prominent advertisers such as Virgin and Vodafone, contributed to the closure of the *News of the World* on 10 July 2011, ending 168 years of publication.

Criminal proceedings were instigated against various *News of the World* employees and contractors, which resulted in the convictions, in 2007, of the *News of the World* royal editor, Clive Goodman, and the private investigator, Glenn Mulcaire. However, others besides these two individuals have since been implicated, including Ian Edmondson and the *News of the World*'s chief reporter, Neville Thurlbeck. A third journalist at the newspaper, James Weatherup, was arrested on 14 April 2011, and a further five executives were arrested in August 2011. The total number of individuals who were targeted by the reporters is still unclear, with some reports suggesting that notebooks containing the names and numbers of more than 3,000 people have been retrieved.

In charge of the newspaper during the period when the phone hacking was in progress, were two different chief executives, Andy Coulson and Rebekah Brooks, whilst Rupert Murdock's son, James, was the chairman of News International. In the fallout, amid parliamentary enquiries, both Coulson and Brooks resigned from their jobs in the government and the newspaper, respectively. The case against them is that, although they did not willingly sanction rogue reporters, their leadership tacitly endorsed the gathering of information from any source, legal or illegal. At one of the first enquiries, held in 2006, Coulson said: 'I apologise unreservedly on behalf of the *News of the World*. As the editor of the newspaper, I take ultimate responsibility for the conduct of my reporters. Clive Goodman's actions were entirely wrong and I have put in place measures to ensure that they will not be repeated by any members of my staff' (Coulson, 29 September 2006).

A parliamentary panel called both Rupert and James Murdoch to explain their roles. Rupert Murdoch argued that he ran a global business of 53,000 employees and that the *News of the World* was 'just 1 per cent' of this; therefore, he was not ultimately responsible for what went on at the tabloid. His son described the 'illegal voicemail interceptions' as a 'matter of great regret' but that the company was 'determined to put things right and make sure they do not happen again'. The company issued an apology on 16 July 2011 in the form of an open letter from Rupert Murdoch. As the enquiry progressed, the role of James Murdoch was questioned further, with one member of the panel describing him as a 'Mafia boss'. Geoffrey Robertson, writing for *The Guardian*, made the point that Murdoch has had a difficult path to tread in that he needed to convince the inquiry that he managed at sufficient arm's length to ensure he did not know about the activities of his senior team but that he was not incompetent in his leadership.

Karl Grossman, writing in the online magazine, *The Huffington Post*, attacks the ethical stance of News International:

The scandal shaking Rupert Murdoch's media holdings in Britain could be expected of a global media empire intoxicated with power and lacking any ethical base. What is unfolding—revelations of bribery and massive phone hacking—could go down as the greatest press scandal in the English-speaking world. Overarching it is a media machine built by Murdoch that is the most dishonest, unprincipled and corrupt of any media empire in the history of the English-speaking world (against stiff competition).

Carl Bernstein, the reporter who exposed the Watergate scandal, reports that he was told by a senior unnamed executive that, 'this scandal and all its implications could not have happened anywhere else. Only in Murdoch's orbit. The hacking at *News of the World* was done on an industrial scale. More than anyone, Murdoch invented and established this culture in the newsroom, where you do whatever it takes to get the story, take no prisoners, destroy the competition, and the end will justify the means.'

For more information search for 'The Leveson Enquiry'.

Sources

BBC News (21 July 2011) 'James Murdoch Evidence Questioned By Former Executives'.

The Guardian (2011) *Phone Hacking: How the Guardian Broke the Story* (1st edition: ebook). Guardian Shorts, 4 August 2011.

The Huffington Post (13 July 2011) 'Murdoch Media Empire: A Journalistic Travesty'.

Newsweek (11 July 2011) 'Is Phone-Hacking Scandal Murdoch's Watergate?'.

Questions

1. What is your reaction to this story?
2. How would you describe the leadership of News International?
3. What grounds are there for accepting James Murdock's protestations?
4. How can the concept of authentic leadership address this issue?

Assignment—3,000 words

1. Examine the arguments for and against authentic leadership and evaluate the robustness of the construct as a genuine leadership model.
2. Examine a leader you are familiar with and assess their performance against the criteria demanded of authentic leaders. Conclude as to whether you believe they are or are not 'authentic'.

Authentic leadership self-assessment questionnaire

The questionnaire below is based on the four building blocks identified by Walumbwa et al. (2008). It is intended to be used a personal guide alongside other evidence, such as feedback from friends, psychometric assessment, and such like.

1.	I know what my greatest strength is	1	2	3	4	5
2.	I act according to my own beliefs	1	2	3	4	5
3.	Before making up my mind I ask around for thoughts	1	2	3	4	5
4.	People know how I am feeling	1	2	3	4	5
5.	I can tell you what my weaknesses are	1	2	3	4	5
6.	In a team I stand up for what I think is right regardless	1	2	3	4	5
7.	Opposing views to my own interest me	1	2	3	4	5
8.	Others would say they do know the 'real' me	1	2	3	4	5
9.	I ask my friends what they think of me	1	2	3	4	5
10.	My colleagues know where I stand on things	1	2	3	4	5
11.	In discussions I allow everyone to have their say	1	2	3	4	5
12.	I am consistent in my behaviour to everyone	1	2	3	4	5
13.	I like myself	1	2	3	4	5
14.	My values are important to me and influence my behaviour	1	2	3	4	5
15.	I gather ideas from those around me to help my decisions	1	2	3	4	5
16.	If I am wrong I admit it	1	2	3	4	5

Key: 1 = Certainly NOT   2 = Not really   3 = No strong opinion   4 = Sort of   5 = Definitely

Scoring

A.   Self-Awareness: Add up your response to Questions 1, 5, 9, 13 =

B.   Moral Perspective: Add up your responses to Questions 2, 6, 10, 14 =

C.   Balanced Processing: Add up your responses to Questions 3, 7, 11, 15 =

D.   Relational Transparency: Add up your responses to Questions 4, 8, 12, 16 =

Authentic Leadership TOTAL =

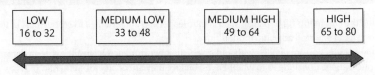

| LOW 16 to 32 | MEDIUM LOW 33 to 48 | MEDIUM HIGH 49 to 64 | HIGH 65 to 80 |

Further reading

Goffee, R. and Jones, G. (2006) *Why Should Anyone Be Led by You?* Boston, MA: Harvard Business School Press.

The strap line for this book is 'great leadership requires being yourself—with skill'. Written by an academic and an ex-human resources director, the book is of a practical nature and describes a process that begins by stating that great leaders are 'authentic chameleons'. By this, the authors mean that, despite the changes in context and individuals encountered, great leaders display a consistent set of behaviours. This is despite them being required to inhabit different roles depending on the situation. They are able to do this because they 'know themselves well' and, hence, are able to act in accordance with their known values.

Terry, R. W. (2001) *Seven Zones for Leadership: Acting Authentically in Stability and Chaos*. London: Nicholas Brealey Publishing.

This book, along with the accompanying manual, builds on his earlier work, *Authentic Leadership: Courage in Action* (1993). In this book, he attempts to link spirituality, authenticity, and leadership together. He encourages the reader to ask the question: What is really going on? By this he means an individual should ask themselves profound questions about their own motivation as well as try to understand the world when all around is in a state of constant flux and change. He identifies a number of activities, such as 'Building Core Competencies' and 'Designing Sustainable Systems', to 'Affirming Shared Identity' and 'Creating Ownership', and he tries to demonstrate the power of each zone's core ideas in practice, whilst exploring the provocative themes of spirituality and authenticity.

Although not directly concerned with authentic leadership, any text that deals with whistleblowing as a theme is worth delving into. The classic story of the rise and fall of Enron by Bethany McLean and Peter Elkind (McLean, B. and Elkind, P. (2004) *The Smartest Guys in the Room: The Amazing Rise and Scandalous Fall of Enron*. New York: Portfolio Trade) is insightful and frightening at the same time—especially as it happened before the 2008 crash. For UK-based readers the text *Whistleblowing* (Bowers, J., Fodder, M., Lewis, J., and Mitchell, J. (2007) *Whistleblowing: Law and Practice*. Oxford: Oxford University Press) gives some guidance to this area and it will be interesting to see how the law changes in the light of recent scandals in the NHS and News International.

9 Followership

After reading this chapter you will:

- Understand the evolution of the term 'followership'.
- Be able to evaluate critically the idea and some of the associated themes, such as leader-member exchange theory.
- Be better placed to consider your own position when either leading or supporting in a group setting.

Introduction

With the frustration surrounding the lack of progress, and ideological challenges that surrounded the search for the heroic leader, attention started to turn in the late 1990s towards a broader view of what leadership 'meant'. James Meindl (1990) was conscious of the pendulum that swings from viewing leaders as 'Great Men' to regarding a distributed form of leadership as the Holy Grail, and he was a major contributor to an idea of leadership that included followers (1998). Grint likes to use the term 'having followers' (2010:2) as a definition of leadership. This implies that without followers, leaders do not exist. This seems a reasonable assertion and various follower-centric theories have begun to emerge that have suggested leadership is better understood as a theme that includes followers as well as leaders. Although Follett (1949) felt this was an area deserving more attention, Robert Kelley is largely credited with 'formalizing' this approach after his article, 'In Praise of Followers', was published in 1988. In it, he suggested that success in modern, lean organizations was as much down to the work of staff in lower hierarchical positions as it was to a 'heroic' manager.

However, the roots of the idea do go back much further than Kelley and, when examined, many other ideas, such as Transformational leadership, situational leadership, and attribution theory, all have some of their substance associated with the dyadic relationship between the leader and the flock that follow. Chaleff's (1995) book followed Kelley's work and both contributed to the study of followers as the next focus for leadership researchers and writers. The basic premise is that effective and successful leadership depends as much on attributes of the followers as it does on the corresponding set associated with the leader.

This chapter will examine two different approaches to the field; that of the attributes of followers, and the relationship between leaders and followers.

Pause for thought

Before reading further, what do you make of this statement attributed to Fred Manske?

> The ultimate leader is one who is willing to develop people to the point that they eventually surpass him or her in knowledge and ability.

> He was the former CEO of Purolator Courier, and senior vice-president of sales and operations at FedEx. He is also the author of the book, *Secrets of Effective Leadership—a Practical Guide to Success* (1988).

1. Do you think this is true and if so, can you think of any leader that has done this?
2. Could this be risky for a leader?

Background

Commentators, such as Hannah et al. (2008), are openly speculating if the current crises facing the human race mark the death knell of leadership. Hall (2012) and Bones (2012) both point to the challenges that seem to have been partly caused by either poor leadership or bad leaders. Global warming, the economic recession, the unrest in many Arab states, and other social crises in the Eurozone have been attributed to a lack of decisive leadership. However, despite this lack of faith in our leaders, the vast majority of research continues to focus on leaders and leadership—search for titles on 'leadership' and then search for 'follower' if you have any doubt about this. The reason for this, suggest Bjugstad et al. (2006:304) is 'that there is a stigma associated with the term "follower"'. They point out that 'follower' has a number of rather derogatory word associations, such as being conformist, weak, and passive. The mental picture of a leader inspires an upstanding person whereas the follower is often either seen as cowed or scheming. The claim of Nazi prison camp guards of simply 'following orders' was rightly seen as an abhorrent assertion but does little to enhance this image. The term 'yes men' conjures up a scene of a dominant leader surrounded by fawning acolytes keen to please their master.

 Case study   Mutiny on HMS *Bounty*

The infamous mutiny in 1789 aboard HMS *Bounty* has entered legend and Hollywood, with five films being made to date. The facts are reasonably clear; however, the motives behind the events are open to conjecture. In 1787, HMS *Bounty* departed from Portsmouth on a voyage to acquire breadfruits from Tahiti with a view to introducing them to other British colonies. The ship was commanded by Captain William Bligh, who had acquitted himself well when accompanying Captain Cook on his final voyage. Bligh made some structural alterations to the ship and appointed his second in command, Mr Fletcher Christian, another experienced sailor hailing from an aristocratic family based on the Isle of Man. Christian and Bligh had sailed together before, and Bligh now promoted him to Acting Lieutenant. This promotion caused resentment among some of the crew more loyal to the ship's master, John Fryer, who had effectively been demoted.

It is reported that Bligh was concerned for the welfare of his men and made positive changes to the watch routine as well as ensuring the crew stayed healthy—even to the extent of taking over from the ship's doctor who had turned out to be an alcoholic! However, he did insist on a harsh system of discipline and often punished miscreants with the lash. After a long 10-month voyage, the ship arrived in Tahiti where the crew loaded the breadfruit saplings. This part of the operation took only six weeks, but after five months the ship still had not sailed. During this lull, the crew enjoyed the hospitality of the island relaxing in the sunshine and partaking in various hedonistic activities—Christian even married a local woman, Maimiti.

Eventually, in April 1789, the *Bounty* set sail but soon tensions arose between Bligh and Christian. Bligh is alleged to have frequently found fault with Christian; Hough (2000:132) cites a crew member saying: 'Whatever fault was found, Mr Christian was sure to bear the brunt.' Conditions aboard were not good and the crew, after the paradise of Tahiti, were not looking forward to the arduous return journey through uncharted waters. Hough puts it thus, 'he [Bligh] failed to anticipate how his company would react to the severity and austerity of life at sea' (2000:128). After three further weeks at sea, the tension erupted and Bligh accused Christian of stealing some coconuts. Christian, feeling humiliated, planned to jump ship himself but on hearing other crew members were also disgruntled, decided that Bligh should be the one to leave. He gathered the crew loyal to him and on 28 April 1789, after a brief struggle, put Bligh, along with 19 other crew still loyal to Bligh, into a boat and cast them adrift. Bligh, through an act of supreme seamanship, managed to navigate 3,618 nautical miles to safety eventually landing in Timor. He ultimately returned to Britain on 15 March 1790, 2 years and 11 weeks after leaving England, and reported the mutiny.

The mutineers in the meantime sailed to the Pitcairn Islands (where their descendants still live). Later, some of the mutineers were captured by the Royal Navy and hanged for their crime; however, some were acquitted and they published their own accounts of the events. These accounts painted Bligh as a bullying commander who made the lives of the crew a misery. Christian's brother, Edward, who was a noted professor of law at Cambridge, wrote a highly pejorative version of events, which made a significant impact on the subsequent reputation of Bligh and the events aboard the *Bounty*.

Sources

The Bounty (1984), starring Anthony Hopkins as William Bligh and Mel Gibson as Fletcher Christian, is regarded as the most historically accurate film portrayal as it uses historical records from Bligh as part of the screenplay.

Bligh, W. (1792) *A Voyage to the South Sea, undertaken by command of His Majesty, for the purpose of conveying the bread-fruit tree to the West Indies, in His Majesty's Ship the Bounty, commanded by Lieutenant William Bligh*. This is Bligh's own account of the mutiny and is freely available through various sources including The Project Gutenberg.

Hough, R. (2000) *Captain Bligh and Mr Christian: The Men and the Mutiny*. London: Chatham Publishing.

http://royalnavalmuseum.org/info_sheets_bounty.htm (accessed 5 August 2013).

Questions

1. What do you think about the characters of Bligh and Fletcher—who was the leader and who was the follower?

2. Do you consider the mutiny to have been inevitable?

3. Why do you think Bligh and Christian's relationship changed so much?

This view is at odds with realities of life and most modern organizations, where almost all operate in some form of hierarchy with even the board answering to shareholders. Public organizations answer to the public through an increasingly open network. As Bob Dylan puts it in his song, *Gotta Serve Somebody*, 'it may be the Devil or it may be the Lord but you're gonna have to serve somebody'. Coupled with these perceptions comes the engrained Western belief that it is leadership that really matters and followers do as instructed by the leader.

Consider how many modules or courses are targeted at the 'follower' market, or whether you have come across anyone proudly declaring they are a great follower. Many organizations have a set of codified 'leadership indicators' against which new management trainees and existing managers will be graded annually as part of their appraisal—very few will have corresponding 'follower indicators'. However, this situation has some interesting inconsistencies that are prompting some to examine the role of followers in organizational success.

The attributes of followers

Empowerment and the associated theme of devolved decision making is one of the themes Ralph Stacey (2012) discusses in the context of change management. His grid for mapping decision making points towards organizations seeking more involvement in this process from all levels of the organization. This puts greater emphasis on the knowledge, skills, and motivation of employees as they are becoming more informed about the organization as well as being expected to contribute to decisions. Senge's *Learning Organization* (1990) predates this theme but suggests a 'system view' of the organization which has all the components linked together to form a whole—which, by implication, includes the managers, employees, and anyone else connected with the organization. Senge felt this holistic approach was a better way of understanding the complexities of organizational life rather than the more reductionist approach where 'leadership' was in some way disconnected from the context (which, by implication, includes the followers) of the organization. So we can see that this move towards followership, or at least the engagement of workers at all levels in the organization, has been a consistent, albeit muted, theme in many different management fields for some time.

Robert Kelley's article sought to crystallize this view of 'modern' leadership being as much about the condition of followers as it was about the person at the very top of the hierarchy. Kelley is an American academic who is largely accredited with reinvigorating the debate surrounding followers and he has authored several books on the subject (see: Further reading at the end of this chapter). His article for the *Harvard Business Review* in 1988 contained a series of instructions for organizations that were designed to enable firms to harness and cultivate effective followers. The paper also proposed a recipe of four qualities that contribute towards a person being an 'effective follower' (1988:144).

1. Self-management: This is different from 'self-motivated' in that Kelley sees a good follower as a person who can think and make decisions for themselves rather than waiting for instructions from above. Clearly, there are implications for both the organization and the individual here, as it may be easy for the follower to go 'off message'. Yet, for Kelley, followers should see themselves as part of a hierarchy but not be cowed by it. They should feel confident to challenge their superior but recognize that their line manager also has pressures 'from above'. Effective followers can manage these various paradoxes and offer the organization significant advantages—especially when it comes to designing structures, as such followers do not need a huge amount of monitoring and control. There are risks here for such a follower, for some managers may view this kind of person with fear and may prefer a more subservient individual. Kelley rather glibly suggests that followers in this kind of situation should 'protect themselves with a little career self-management' (1988:144). In other words, look for another job—something that may just not be possible for the individual concerned.

2. Commitment: This means being devoted to a cause that is something other than their own advancement but should still be aligned to the broad aim of the organization. This association with a goal is not the same as being loyal to a person and transcends hierarchies. Themes associated with Transformational leadership start to emerge here and this aspect can be very powerful in terms of maintaining motivation and focus. However, it can also lead to problems, for example, where a school teacher who is committed to teaching her children may become frustrated by a head teacher who is more concerned with exam results and league tables.

3. Self-development and continuous professional development: As Kelley puts it, 'committed incompetence is still incompetence' (1988:145). This suggests that good followers seek to improve their skills at both a core level and peripheral range. They will seek out development opportunities rather than waiting for the human resource department to send them on a course. They understand their own strengths and weaknesses and, having pointed out the risks, will take on assignments that stretch them into new areas. This requires both them and the organization to be capable of managing the associated risks to ensure the organization is not damaged by any resultant failure. It is interesting to note how many professional managerial bodies, such as the Chartered Management Institute (see: http://managers.org.uk) and the Chartered Institute for Personnel and Development (see: http://cipd.co.uk), have explicit requirements for members to demonstrate their own continuous professional development (CPD) annually as a requirement of continued membership.

4. Personal properties: Kelley lists a whole series of personality characteristics that make followers effective. Credibility, honesty, courage, and insightfulness coupled with a strong ethical stance are some of the traits suggested, which on reflection look very similar to those of a leader reviewed in Chapter 2. As well as identifying the benefits to the organization of having this kind of individual present, Kelley identifies the potential for whistleblowing (or disloyalty) if an individual does not agree with the principles of their leader or feels their own ethics are being compromised by being required to 'follow orders'.

Reading through the list above, you may come to same conclusion as Kelley when he points out that the items read the same for a leader as they do a follower. Kelley suggests that this apparent contradiction—how can a follower be the same as a leader?—is on account of the labels attached to leadership and followership. He feels that 'followership is not a person but a role' (1988:146). This is consistent with the earlier themes of all individuals having to follow someone at some point and allows them to move between these two different roles whilst occupying the same position in a hierarchy.

Kelley went on to develop a typology of followers that depended on the degree to which the individual follower was capable of independent, critical thinking and their general attitude towards work. He gave these five types the following labels:

1. Alienated followers: Individuals who think for themselves but have become disillusioned with the organization. They are negative in their outlook and can frustrate the efforts of the leader.

2. Effective followers: These individuals are capable of independent thought and are active in the organization. If they agree with the leader's decisions, they will back them with their mind and body. They will also challenge the leader if they think a decision is wrong.

3. Survivors: Followers who tend to play a waiting game to see what the leader is like. They do enough to get by and keep out of the limelight.

4. Sheep: This type follows orders but waits for these to be issued. They do not exercise any critical thinking nor are they motivated by allegiance to an organizational goal.

5. Yes-people: These individuals, whilst enthusiastic about their work, do not exercise any critical appraisal of their job. They will follow the leader's instructions with gusto but do not consider the effectiveness or efficiency of these instructions.

Ira Chaleff's (1995) approach has similar antecedents with five different 'tests' that underpin his question as to why followers often stand up when their leader enters their presence. Consider, for example, the courtroom when the judge enters or a Catholic church when the priest and his entourage begin their walk to the altar. Chaleff asserts that organizations need followers who will both stand up *for* leaders and stand up *to* their leaders. By this, he means feeling able and willing to challenge, participate, and take on the responsibility for decisions and change management.

He classifies followers according to a model, which, like Kelley's, has followers classified according to two broad concepts. He considers: a) the degree to which an individual supports

 Pause for thought

Consider yourself against Kelley's criteria. How would you rate yourself? If you have work experience, you could consider some of the people you have worked with too.

1. Self-management

My boss should tell me what to do		Occasionally I will suggest something		Consistently prompting
1	2	3	4	5

2. Commitment to a cause

My cause is me		If it suits me		I believe!
1	2	3	4	5

3. CPD

I know it all anyway		When I'm told to		Learning is for life
1	2	3	4	5

4. Courage

If the company wants to do it so what?		As long as I don't get implicated		I would 'do the right thing'
1	2	3	4	5

    a. How does this make you feel about your role as a 'follower'?

    b. Which one of the Kelley's types do you feel you fit?

    c. What are the implications for your role as a leader?

the leadership, and b) the level of willingness to challenge authority. Using a two by two matrix, he places followers into one of four quadrants:

1. Resource: This person turns up for work, takes their instructions, and delivers the outcome. They are not proactive and do not take on additional tasks. They fit the low challenge/low support quadrant.

2. Individualist: These followers can be both a challenge and a benefit to the leader. They tend not to follow the mainstream and can be highly creative with their ideas. However, they can be extremely challenging to the leader if they do not agree with a decision. These are low support/high challenge.

3. Implementer: This group sits in the low challenge/high support area. They are similar to the Yes-people in Kelley's model as they have a 'can do' approach but this comes with little critical thinking.

4. Partner: High support/high challenge individuals correlate to Chaleff's eponymous 'courageous followers'. These individuals support the organization's goals with their hearts and minds. However, they are not blind and they will speak when they feel something is not right or challenges their own moral code. Again, other themes, such as those from authentic leadership, appear to be relevant here, further reinforcing this notion of a certain duality between followership and leadership.

There are distinct similarities between the models and there are also similar concerns about the concept. For example, the linkage between these models and Hersey and Blanchard's situational leadership model (1993), discussed in Chapter 5, is fairly clear—as the follower's competence develops so does the relationship with the leader. However, it is not clear how an individual can move between these 'boxes'—is it a matter of training, or is it matter for the follower, or the leader or the organization? Both Chaleff and Kelley feel it is the duty of an individual not in a leadership position to support those that are in such roles. What is certain, is this field is open to more research and study as the role of followers in organizations is under much more scrutiny. The easy access to information about organizational performance and political leaders, and increasing pressure to get more from a firm's assets will further increase the demands on followers and strengthen the need for followers who are capable of delivering an operational response to a strategic vision.

Leader–member exchange theory (LMX)

One of the more theoretical approaches that incorporates the notion of followers, and has a slightly different approach from the previous models reviewed, is leader–member exchange theory (LMX). The approach, also known as vertical dyad linkage (VDL) theory, was developed over 35 years ago by Dansereau et al. (1975) and it still attracts research interest (for example see: Subramaniam et al. 2010). It is predicated on the belief that the relationship between a leader and followers is not a simple, stable one but one composed of multiple interactions between the leader and individual followers (see: Figure 9.1).

Most of the other approaches discussed in this book tend to view followers as a 'powerless mass' (Burns 1978:3) or at least as a collective whole (see: Figure 9.1 A. traditional view).

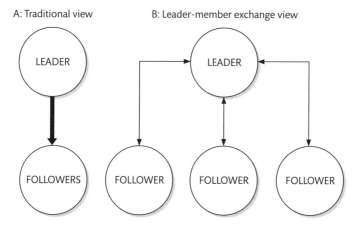

Figure 9.1 Leader–member exchange theory

The leader (an individual) is hypothesized to make leadership decisions based partly on a judgement about the commitment and competence of the 'followers'—but viewing them as a homogeneous unit. LMX disputes this and places the relationship between an individual follower and the leader as the important factor to be considered. LMX views this as a series of single, dyadic links (see: Figure 9.1 B. leader member exchange view). This view runs counter to some of the themes present in, say, contingency theory, which had the leader's approach influenced by an assessment of the overall competency of 'the subordinates'. The implications of this approach are that, as a leader deals with followers on a one-to-one basis, these interactions will vary in quality and quantity and are unique to each follower. The reason for this has been put down to the difference in relationship between individuals, who will form different opinions about each other, have multiple likes and dislikes, and generate different degrees of trust as a result. It may also be down to the simple issue of time—the leader may not have sufficient time available to develop relationships with all of the team members. It has a more 'transactional' feel to it than transformational models as its title, 'exchange', explicitly suggests a movement of intellectual resources between follower and leader.

In this model, a leader and follower form individual relationships and the nature of these relationships influences the behaviour of the leader and follower. As this relationship matures, it can make a fundamental difference to the quality of the follower's future career, the achievement of the task, and a whole host of other organizational matters. Sparrowe and Liden (1997) made further enquiries into the nature of these relations because it was felt that if these links were individual in nature, it may also be true that they varied in their quality. Their study and subsequent investigations by Liden and Maslyn (1998) found there were two different sets of followers associated with different types of link between the leader and follower. One group, characterized by high quality interaction and mutual respect, was called the 'in-group', whilst another group displaying a more formal, distant, and transactional nature, were known as the 'out-group'. This is a controversial view because it suggests that, in an age of equality and anti-discrimination laws, that some individuals are treated less favourably than others—however, more of that later.

Researchers examining this phenomenon suggested that those individuals experiencing high quality LMX interactions were in receipt of higher tangible rewards, such as pay, bonuses, and more challenging assignments, as well as intangible items, such as the leader's

Pause for thought

1. Do you have different relationships with some people than others when you are working as a group? Think about any group work you have done or when you have been in a team.

2. Why is this?

3. How do you feel about the individuals you consider close to you?

4. Who would you trust to carry out a job for you that required a little discretion and tact?

'favour'. This contrasted sharply with those in the 'out-group' who were treated in accordance with their employment contracts, had less discretionary activity, and were regarded by the leader as less competent. As Greenberg (1982) points out, this will not go unobserved by the respective group members who are likely to react accordingly—especially if in the out-group. This, in turn, will affect the whole group's morale, work effectiveness, and overall coherence.

Graen and Schandura (1987) and Grean and Uhl-Bien (1991) tried to map the evolution of this relationship between a leader and follower over time. They proposed a model that had three distinct phases based on a life cycle. This cycle begins with each character in 'Stranger' phase. This period is characterized by rather strained relationships, low quality exchanges, and with a focus on self-interest. Each member is testing the other out and both are largely exploring the limits of the formal contract between themselves and the hierarchy. The relationship may stay at this level or it may mature and move to the next phase, known as 'Acquaintance'. In this stage, the roles between the two have been tested out and the beginning of a mutual bond is beginning to emerge. There may well be an invitation from either the leader or follower for an exchange of personal, social details. This invites a degree of trust between the two as both are taking a risk by offering this to the other. The leader may also, at this point, test to see to what extent the follower is capable and willing in terms of workload. Now their exchanges are likely to be of higher quality and their mutual interest turns away from their individual wants to, at least considering, the broader goals of the team. Finally, the relationship may enter its final stage, that of 'Partnership'. In this stage, which not all relationships will reach, the parties will have tested out each other and found they can rely and trust one another. In a sense, they have taken psychological steps towards each other and will have uncovered elements about each other that have drawn them closer emotionally. This will mean they move outside the narrow scripted confines of an employment contract and begin to do favours for each other, possibly engaging in social activities and banter. The relationship is mutually dependant as the leader requires the follower to carry on completing additional tasks and the follower needs the favour and support of the leader. In this way, the relationship moves from a formal hierarchical position to one where influence and control are more evenly partitioned between the partners.

As Wayne et al. (1997) and Harris et al. (2009) propose, those followers who move to the third stage find they have easier access to organizational 'benefits', such as more challenging assignments, higher pay, better promotion prospects, and an increased flow of ideas. These individuals form the leader's in-group. Those who remain at phase 1 find the converse true and remain in the out-group. Those in the in-group work hard for the leader and the leader reciprocates, thus a mutually supportive, positive feedback loop is established between the dyad. However, those in the out-group feel more distant from the leader, deliver what is contractually obliged of them, and have little commitment to the future of the leader or the in-group.

Implications of LMX

The initial studies linked to LMX aimed to describe leadership behaviour. In later observations, the approach has been used as a prescription for helping a leader to generate a more transformational approach to their leadership. The theory explicitly states that different relationships exist within an organization and those that are the most productive are to be found within an in-group. This suggests a leader should aim to develop in-group relationships with as many individuals as possible. By extending the range of the in-group, the leader can attempt to draw in individuals into the in-group and have more followers willing to go the extra mile for the sake of the group task. Because of the different personalities, likes, dislikes, and idiosyncrasies of the group membership, this may mean acting differently with different people to ensure the relationships stay at the 'partnership' level.

However, it is also clear, not least from a legal perspective, that this behaviour cannot overstep the boundaries of fairness and equality. It is here that dangers lie for any prospective manager attempting to create a large in-group and for a follower seeking to curry favour with their leader. Many individuals have conscious and unconscious biases and prejudices that may, if not recognized, contribute to decision making. LMX can serve as a warning by bringing to the explicit attention of the leader that in-groups can form which may be illegal and discriminatory. It may also feel morally corrupt as it suggests there is inherent unfairness at work here, with some people potentially receiving more benefits for no other reason than being part of some arbitrary clique.

The theory has a common-sense feel to it as almost any individual who has worked for or experienced an organization, such as a school, a college, or a company, 'feels' the presence of those 'in' with the teachers, lecturers, or boss. This may feel unfair but as long as it not discriminatory, it remains a reality for most. On the other hand, it also has an element of moral justice about it because it suggests that those who put in the most will get back more than those who just turn up and do the minimum amount of work. The counter view to this is that those who are skilled or able to become emotionally close to and friendly with the boss are likely to get on in the organization, regardless of their ability. Again, many individuals will recognize a person they regard as incompetent occupying a more senior position than their expertise would suggest—could this be attributed to the effects of LMX? LMX is also unclear on the development of the in and out-groups. For example, how does an individual move between these two camps—either voluntarily or via the leader's discretion? Chapter 13 discusses the use of social power, among other themes, and it is clear the threat and promise of inclusion is a weapon used by humans in many different social settings, not least in the workplace, whilst Chapter 11 looks at the darker side of emotional intelligence. This could suggest a Machiavellian leader may use the suggestion of annexation from an inner cabal as a way of influencing followers.

LMX is considered unique in that at its heart is this two-way connection between manager and follower—the dyadic relationship. It says nothing about the character of the leader or the situation they find themselves managing. What it does say is that, for a leader to succeed, effective relationships between leader and follower are necessary. Communication between the leader and follower forms an integral part of the model and it suggests that a leader needs to ensure they actively listen to their followers. This 'individualized consideration', explored in Chapter 7, forms part of Transformational leadership and Deluga (1992) explored this particular link, uncovering a correlation between the two ideas.

Case study *The Godfather*

The Godfather is a multi-award winning film made in 1972, directed by Francis Ford Coppola and starring Marlon Brando as the head of a fictional Mafia family living in post-war New York. The epic portrays the violence that underpins the power and prestige that surrounds Brando as he manages his crime empire during 1945 to 1955. In the film, Brando plays the titular role of Vito Corleone who is the Don, or head, of one of five powerful crime families who, although competitive, are, at the beginning of the film, in a state of truce with each other.

As the film progresses, it plots the slow moral degeneration of Michael Corleone who is Vito's youngest son, played by Al Pacino. In the opening scene, Michael is seen attending his sister's wedding and he introduces his girlfriend to his father. At this stage, Michael is said to be unaware of his family's 'business'. He is college educated and has been away serving in the army during the Second World War. During the wedding, the viewer is left in no doubt as to the power of his father. A popular entertainer, Jonny Fontane, asks The Godfather for a favour to boost his flagging career by persuading a movie director to cast him in a film. Corleone agrees to this but ensures Fontane knows this will result in a debt to him that could be reclaimed at any point. When Fontane asks Vito how he will convince the studio head to acquiesce to his request, Vito replies with the oft-quoted line, 'I'll make him an offer he can't refuse'. This turns out to be uncovering the severed head of his favourite racehorse in his bed.

The plot darkens further as open warfare breaks out between the rival criminal families, with each group exacting revenge upon the other for real and perceived slights against their respective familial groups. Michael, having been made aware of the various plots to assassinate his father, faces a choice over whether to continue with his upstanding life or to defend his family's honour. He decides for the latter and exacts a murderous toll on his family's enemies. Eventually, his father dies of natural causes and his older brother is murdered. This propels Michael into the role of head of the family from which there is no escape and he eventually becomes a ruthless, embittered recluse resorting to fratricide.

One of the more compelling aspects of the film is the examination of the crime gang from the sympathetic angle of a family. This contrasts with previous perspectives which tended to focus more upon the actual criminality. During the film, violence against people features but this is justified on the grounds that these people were disloyal or from another 'group' and hence deserved to die. There is little exposure to crimes, such as enforcement, prostitution, or illegal scams, which are the source of the family's wealth. *The Godfather* attempts to paint Vito as an honourable, incorruptible man who cares passionately about his family. Indeed one of the reasons for the internecine war is Vito's objection to drugs. He will do almost anything to protect those he considers loyal and close to him whilst ensuring death and destruction of anyone outside his clan.

Sources

De Stefano, George (2007) *An Offer We Can't Refuse: The Mafia in the Mind of America*. New York: Faber & Faber.

Patterson, J. (2006) 'Mob Mentality'. *The Guardian*, 22 April 2006.

The Godfather DVD Collection (2001).

Questions

1. Could LMX help to explore the development of the relationships between Vito and his entourage?

2. How would Michael's passage from 'outsider' to the eventual head of the family be described in LMX terms?

3. In your experience, do you think individuals outside the inner cabal want to become part of the inner group?

Attributes of followers and leaders

It is worth considering an idea developed outside mainstream leadership studies which can shed some light on the complex nature of the relationship between leaders and followers. Although it is not a 'core' theory, it can help to understand how relationships and impressions of others develop. By understanding this process—or at least thinking about it—a prospective leader can begin to grasp some of the implications of leader–follower relationships.

Attribution theory is an idea developed by Green and Mitchell (1979) and based on a theory expounded by the Austrian psychologist, Fritz Heider (1896–1988). It was discussed briefly in Chapter 7 but applied to leaders not followers. The basic premise of the theory suggests that social perception is similar in process to our perception of physical objects. So, if we see an object we make assumptions about the object based on our experiences of life; we attribute characteristics to the object without much direct contact with it. For example, if we hear a ticking noise we attribute the noise to the clock in the corner of the room and that we can use the clock to tell the time. However, our senses can be misled, either deliberately, by a magician for example, or by accident in the form of an optical illusion—say, how the light is bent by a glass of water.

Heider (1958) suggested this distortion could also happen in social situations so a circumstance or set of behaviours can be seen by an observer to have an effect—say, a person shouting at another. The cause of this incident can be explained by attributing characteristics to a person—one person was angry with another. Another example might be if a student hands in their assignment late the tutor may consider the cause to be because the student is lazy, disorganized, or stupid. However, the real reason may be down to external environmental factors, such as a serious illness. Behaviour, in this example a late assignment, is directly attributed to a person's disposition. Heider thought that 'we' overemphasize the contribution personality makes towards a circumstance downplaying any external factors—our perception of the person is distorted like the bent light in a glass of water.

In terms of leadership, this has several implications. The first, reviewed in Chapter 7, is to assign organizational success to a leader rather than anything to do with the marketplace occupied by the organization. In terms of followership, the same process may influence the decision made by the leader about the competence of the follower. In a situation where a worker performs a task poorly, the leader may assume the worker to be incompetent rather than examining the situation surrounding the task. Green and Mitchell (1979) and Mitchell (1979) investigated a manager's response to a follower who does not complete a task outlined a two-part process; first identifying the cause and then deciding what to do to solve the problem. The manager could choose to focus on the environment, the follower, or a combination of both. Their research, and subsequent studies by Crant and Bateman (1993) in which they studied accountants, uncovered an inherent bias in managers that affected how they attributed effect to cause. They suggest that a manager is more likely to attribute the reason for poor performance to external factors (such as a lack of resources, no support from partners, or the inherent nature of the task) when:

1. The subordinate has a track record of success.

2. Similar individuals achieve similar results with such tasks.

3. The subordinate is considered to be useful to the team or organization.

4. The leader has a stake in the success of the project so the subordinate's failure directly affects the leader.

5. The subordinate has a credible excuse or apologizes.

6. Task failure does not have major organizational implications.

7. Data supports external issues as the root cause of failure.

Further research by Lord and Maher (1991) into this phenomenon has validated the findings.

In 1981 Green et al. extended this by suggesting that individuals with low LMX relationships—i.e. in the 'out-group'—are more likely to be on the receiving end of critical interpretation of their behaviour than those in the 'in-group'. The leader will attribute task failure to incompetence or other less desirable personal characteristics, such as being lazy, rather than the points made above.

For those in the in-group the opposite was true—circumstance was the reason for task failure rather than personal traits. This has major implications for the out-group, as it means they are more likely to remain in this group because any task failure is likely to be seen as 'their fault' and reinforce the judgement of the leader that they are untrustworthy and do not merit closer attention. For the in-group, it is the external environment that will be blamed for task failure and possibly put down to an 'Act of God' or some other spurious reason, rather than a lack of competence on the part of the follower. This phenomenon may of course be true—it may be someone else's fault or it may indeed be that a certain person is just not up to the task. However, another process may be at work, which is known as impression management.

 Pause for thought

Consider the list below. When you were last working with someone and things did not go exactly to plan which of the factors did you consider to be the reason for task failure?

Reason	Yes	No
Track record of success		
Everyone else achieving the same result		
Subordinate is useful		
Success directly affects me		
Subordinate has excuse		
Task is relatively unimportant		
Facts suggest outside forces		

1. Why did you make these judgements?

2. What was the outcome of your decisions?

Impression management is a conscious and unconscious effort by one person to attempt to influence how others view them. The theory emerges from the world of psychology (for example see: Leary and Kowalski 1990) but it does have an impact on the study of followership as both leaders and followers may use tactics to suggest a certain image of themselves to the other. Followers may seek to ingratiate themselves with a leader by presenting themselves as friendly and on their wavelength. Observers may notice a follower nodding profusely as the leader suggests an idea, or laughing at the boss's jokes. Another tactic may be to ensure those achievements and awards won are obvious and talked about. This is done to ensure the follower is seen as competent and an 'achiever'. Leaders, on the other hand, may use intimidation as a tool, which is designed to show the follower they are powerful and will punish behaviour outside the desired description. This may produce a demotivating effect, as discussed in Chapter 13, but is still deployed by many individuals. Impression management could be seen as Machiavellian or simply trying to make a good impression. A leader's task is to ensure they understand the implications of this concept.

Summary

The study of followers and their role in organizational success has developed in academic circles (Baker 2007; Bligh 2011) but has not made a significant impact to date on how those organizations rate, develop, and recognize followers. The ideas outlined above are worth considering as they present an alternative view of leadership that differs significantly from the concept of a lone person standing proudly atop the organization's hierarchy like a modern day Moses. Kelley (2008) and Chaleff (1995) suggest organizations should examine their employees for good followership potential as well as their leadership potential. Both of these are roles rather than positions and as such need to be viewed with the same level of interest. However, Rost (2008:54) is not entirely satisfied with the lack of clarity surrounding the concept of followers and followership, and examines 'what followers do when they follow'.

Leader–member exchange theory gives a map for examining the individual relationship between two people in two different roles. It goes on to suggest that different quality relationships emerge between a leader and followers. This quality, in turn, affects the perception of the leader who may view some individuals as trustworthy and competent and others as lazy and unreliable. This judgement may be affected by a leader's past experiences as well as impression management on the part of the follower. However, as Miller et al. (2004) point out, trying to predict the likely outcome of any follower/leader interaction may be challenging.

It is almost inevitable, given the nature of the human spirit, that different relationships will emerge between colleagues. However, the dangers for the manager are both legal and moral. In legal terms, there are well established laws that defend employees from direct and indirect discrimination with punitive measures available if an organization or individual manager transgresses these rules. On a moral front, treating some people more favourably than others may be counterproductive. The 'out-group' may become resentful and seek to undermine the manager further, and the original judgement on who was competent may be flawed. Leaders may wish to remember they are also followers and it may serve their own long-term interests to ensure their relations, judgement, and treatment of their followers is based on fairness, equity, and honesty. Finally, Shamier et al. (2007) do bring these themes together and they urge leadership to be existing at the interface of situation, followers, and leaders.

Case study   Sun Myung Moon

Sun Myung Moon, who died on 2 September 2012, was a Korean religious leader and a controversial character who inspired loyalty from followers and hostility from critics alike. He was the leader of the Holy Spirit Association for the Unification of World Christianity, also called the Unification Church, but perhaps best known as the Moonies. Moon was born in modern day North Korea in 1920. When he was 16, he claimed that Jesus appeared and implored him to finish his work on Earth. Jesus had been unable to do this as he had been crucified. From this point on, Moon dedicated his life to this mission and established, at its peak in the 1970s and 1980s, an organization worth billions of pounds with several hundred thousands, possibly millions, of members.

Moon's main teaching focused on the importance of 'the family' and the belief that man was born with sin. This made passage to heaven impossible without 'proper' values, forming families, and uniting all Christian churches. He also suggested there would be a new messiah to take humanity forward, and many of his followers believed he was this new saviour. Moon codified his beliefs in a book, *The Divine Principle*, which first saw light in 1946. Arrested and jailed by North Korean troops in 1948 for alleged spying, he spent five years in a prisoner of war camp before escaping as UN troops approached the camp in 1950. He rarely spoke in public for the next 20 years, but in the 1970s this changed and he began to address increasingly large gatherings of young people, particularly in the USA.

His right wing views and opposition to communism made him popular with the Nixon presidency, and in 1974 he was thanked by Nixon for standing by him during the infamous Watergate scandal. Moon's exhortation that sinless marriage and a life without sin was the passage to heaven struck a chord with many individuals seeking meaning in their lives during the 'hippy' period of American culture. This message and influence spread across the Christian world and his church was soon operating out of huge buildings, with business interests that included the *Washington Post* and private jets for Moon and his entourage.

His followers considered him to be the embodiment of God on Earth and continue to dedicate their lives to spreading his message. They often shunned their families, preferring to find companionship with other members. Mass weddings, where Moon would pair off members, were a feature of the church with upwards of 2,000 individuals being married at one time—most of whom only met immediately before the wedding.

However, it is this devotion to the church's cause that has proved controversial as the church has been accused of being a 'sect' that brainwashes suggestible young people into disavowing their parents and signing over their income to the church. Young people who wanted to join the church were encouraged to see Moon and his wife, Hak Ja Han, as their 'true' parents. This is because their biological parents were born into sin, whereas Moon was 'sinless'. Passage to heaven could only be through the new messiah who, acting as a new Adam, could replace the original parents.

Church leaders refute the charges of indoctrination, pointing out that isolation, a feature of their induction period, is no different to the period of contemplation and reflection advocated by most religions. Similarly, the accusations of 'love bombing' where new members are welcomed enthusiastically by church members is no more sinister than the handshakes practiced by congregations at Sunday worship. However, parents alarmed by the sudden and total lack of contact with their children employed 'de-programming' (or kidnap as the church states), which became a regular feature in the media during the late 1970s and 1980s. Several ex-members have testified to the grip of the church and how they felt towards their messiah during their time as members, which bordered on complete idolatry.

The main blow to the church, though, came with Moon being convicted of tax evasion by the US authorities in 1982 and a failed libel action against the *Daily Mail* newspaper in 1978 which, on hearing of his death, said, 'the fact is that any tears shed in Moon's memory will be but a drop compared with the river of misery inflicted by his twisted cult'.

Moon's death has prompted a power struggle for leadership of the church. Moon had 14 children of whom 11 survive. His eldest son died after a life marked by drug and alcohol abuse and Moon appointed his youngest son, Hyung Jin (aka Sean), as his successor. Hyung is Western educated with an MBA from Harvard, is erudite, and speaks English fluently. His rival is his elder brother, Hyun Jin (aka Preston). Currently, they are locked in an increasingly acrimonious legal dispute that seeks to establish ownership of the vast business empire inherited from their father.

In terms of the legacy inherited by whoever wins the battle, some things are still unclear. Moon advocated a unified Christian church which is nowhere nearer being achieved. The membership is in decline, and has been for some time, and the controversies surrounding the church's views on both homosexual relationships and the Jewish religion remain. Nevertheless, the business empire is still in place, which stretches around the globe and includes a car manufacturer, sports teams, and hotels employing thousands of people. Followers now await Moon's next communication, expected to be via a medium, and continue to promote his beliefs.

Sources

Chryssides, G. (2012) 'Can the Moonies Keep on Shining?'. *The Telegraph*. 6 September 2012. London.

Introvigne, M. (2000) *The Unification Church*. Salt Lake City, UT: Signature Books.

Moon, S. M. (1973) *Divine Principle* (2nd edn). Washington, DC: Holy Spirit Association for the Unification of World Christianity.

Rawstorne, T. (2012). Messiah of Misery'. *Daily Mail*. 4 September 2012.

Urquhart, C. (2012) 'Sun Myung Moon, Founder of the Moonies, Dies in South Korea'. *The Guardian*, 3 September 2012

http://unification.net (accessed 5 August 2013).

Questions

1. Why do you think Moon inspires such polarized views?

2. What does 'follower' mean in this sense?

3. Can you make any links between followership and charisma?

Assignment—3,000 words

Choose one of these questions and draft a 3,000 word essay around the central theme:

1. To what extent is the image of the heroic leader at odds with the realities of organizational life?

2. How could an organization use 'follower competencies' as opposed to 'leadership competencies'?

3. Do you agree or disagree with this statement: 'Ultimately it is still about leadership. A good leader creates good followers NOT the other way around.' Why?

Discussion themes

a. Think about your relationship with people around you. If they let you down—say you agree to meet at a certain time—who or what gets the blame?

b. How could a company reward and recognize 'good' followership?

Follower quiz

Think about your attitude at work or if you have no direct experience of work then consider your school teachers, college lecturers, or another setting where you have experienced 'authority' figures—perhaps even your parents.

1. I think my boss is right.

Yes Always	Often	Rarely	Never
0	2	3	5

2. I can decide what needs to be done.

Never	Rarely	Most of the time	Always
0	2	3	5

3. If I think my boss is wrong I will say something immediately.

Never	Rarely	Most of the time	Always
0	2	3	5

4. If I disagree I will still carry out the instructions.

Yes Always	Often	Rarely	Never
0	2	3	5

5. I know what my development needs are and actively manage these.

Never	Rarely	Most of the time	Always
0	2	3	5

6. If I thought my work was unethical I would stop it.

Never	Rarely	Most of the time	Always
0	2	3	5

7. In my view my boss is paid to think. I am paid to 'do'.

Strongly agree	Agree	Disagree	Strongly Disagree
0	2	3	5

8. If I say anything negative I will get labelled as 'lacking commitment'.

Strongly agree	Agree	Disagree	Strongly Disagree
0	2	3	5

9. It is not my role to do the management's thinking for them.

Strongly agree	Agree	Disagree	Strongly Disagree
0	2	3	5

10. I get paid therefore I am basically a tool for the organization to use.

Strongly agree	Agree	Disagree	Strongly Disagree
0	2	3	5

Follower type

0–10 You feel you are simply a cog in a machine and as such you should perform your duties as instructed with unquestioning obedience. You may wish to think about why this is the case and if you feel this approach meets the demands of modern organizations.

Many companies increasingly want employees to think for themselves and to be confident about taking on additional responsibility.

11–25 Most of the time you comply with the organization but you may not feel completely comfortable with this. You may wish to explore the boundaries of what the organization actually expect of you and how your direct superior reacts to constructive comments.

26–40 You actively challenge your organization when you consider it appropriate. You may want to think about when you make this decision and how far you would go if the organization continued to ignore your comments.

41–50 You may feel the organization and you are continually at loggerheads and you are surrounded by poor, unethical workers. You may wish to think why this is the case and what is the best option to help you achieve greater satisfaction in your work.

Further reading

Kelley, Robert Earl (1985) *The Gold-Collar Worker: Harnessing the Brainpower of the New Work Force*. Reading, MA: Addison-Wesley. In this book, Kelley uses, for the first time, this nomenclature to describe a group of workers he thought of as vital to a successful organization. These employees were characterized as having 'brainpower' and were seen by Kelley as being highly motivated by success and progression. Because of this, and the value they added to the organization, he suggested companies needed to change the way in which they managed this group. Failure to make the necessary changes would result in them leaving the company. Interestingly enough, the term 'Gold-Collar Worker' has not entered the lexicon of business terms in this sense but has metamorphosed to mean several different themes, such as young, relatively under qualified individuals who have a high level of disposable income but few job prospects.

Rodger Adair's chapter titled 'Developing Great Leaders One Follower at a Time' in Riggio, R. E., Chaleff, I., and Lipman-Blumen, J. (2008) *The Art of Followership: How Great Followers Create Great Leaders and Organizations* (San Francisco: Jossey-Bass), is worth a read as he presents an alternative two by two model of followers based on three broad concepts: (a) turnover or likelihood to stay; (b) job satisfaction; and (c) productivity. His four quadrants are labelled: Disciple, Doer, Disengaged, and Disgruntled. The first two are 'positive' employees who are likely to be productive. The second two are negative and stressful for the individual concerned.

If you want to delve further into impression management, Erving Goffman's (1959) original work is still available (*The Presentation of Self in Everyday Life*. New York: Doubleday). Although there are more up-to-date texts, such as Sinha, J. B. (2009) *Culture and Organization National Behaviour* (Thousand Oaks, CA: SAGE Publications), or Newman, D. M. (2009) *Sociology: Exploring the Architecture of Everyday Life* (Thousand Oaks, CA: Pine Forge Press). The problem with these texts is that they are written for a different audience and specialism rather than students of leadership studies. A better approach may be DuBrin, A. J. (2011) *Impression Management in the Workplace: Research, Theory, and Practice* (Abingdon: Routledge). This has a chapter on impression management for leaders which outlines the practical steps taken by managers to influence others, including acting skills. DuBrin also makes some interesting links to charismatic leadership and emotional intelligence.

Barbara Kellerman's (2008) book *Followership: How Followers Are Creating Change and Changing Leaders* (Cambridge, MA: Center for Public Leadership) takes a more discursive approach to followership by relating stories that illustrate the impact followers have made on recent events. She does this to try to challenge the view that suggests following is somehow 'weak' and has no part in a modern, capitalist society.

If you want something not 'business' orientated, then try Tracey Armstrong's (2010) *Followership* (Shippensburg, PA: Destri) which takes a more spiritual approach and cites a more 'moral' approach to leadership. The text incorporates religious examples and suggests followership has a rich history that makes it relevant for social leaders today.

Finally, a controversial approach is taken by Mark van Vugt and Anjana Ahuja in their book *Selected* (2010 London: Profile Books). They attempt to link evolution and leadership to explain why some people lead and others choose to follow. Given both of these themes are theories, and contentious ones at that, this is an ambitious step. However, it is worth a glance if only to broaden out further the range leadership studies can stretch into.

Part 2

Related themes

Part 2

Related themes

10 Psychodynamic approaches to leadership

After reading this chapter you will be able to:

- Understand what is meant by a psychodynamic approach to leadership.
- Critically analyse different methods within this broad framework.
- Examine your own practice and understanding of leadership using this approach.

Introduction

The psychodynamic approach to leadership is different from many of the previously explored ideas in that it is not a singular 'theory' but more a collection of approaches connected by a broad philosophy. The approach is centred on understanding personality and the psychological make-up of both the leader and followers. The argument being presented is that by understanding more about your own personality as the leader, and that of your followers, you can make more informed decisions about what behaviour may, or may not, influence a given group of individuals. Part of this approach is helping followers to understand their own personality profile, their own motivation, wants, and needs so that they can respond to these needs and those of their colleagues. Team members can also identify emotional patterns, the emotional reaction of others to stimuli, and how individuals relate to each other. This approach is also different in that it does not seek to affect personality directly, neither does it claim that certain characteristics (traits) make a person more or less effective as a leader. Rather it seeks to direct the leader towards understanding their own preferred method of operating, how others operate, and how to take advantage of these various combinations.

There is a huge industry that has grown up around this approach with any number of different personality questionnaires being developed that purport to categorize and classify an individual's personality. These include the OPQ32®, FIRO-B®, 16PF®, DiSC®, and the Myers–Briggs Type Indicator (MBTI®). These tools seek to uncover the consistent, natural pattern of behaviour, thought processes, and associated emotions a person experiences as they go about their daily lives. Each model is usually based on a series of empirical studies performed under laboratory conditions by a psychologist. Each model suggests a different focus and measurement, as far as 'rating' or classifying a person, and this classification is usually accompanied by some predictive text whereby the subject is offered insights into their likely behaviour in a given situation.

The approach is underpinned by the work of Sigmund Freud (1938) and his collaborators, such as Jung (1923). It remains a controversial approach because of some of the underpinning assumptions about the nature of the human 'condition'—for example, that a person's adult life is driven by childhood experiences. By exploring these foundations, the relative merits of the approach can be critically assessed. In this chapter, we will explore two different models—the Myers Briggs Type Inventory (MBTI) and neuro-linguistic programming (NLP).

Freud, Jung, and personality

Sigmund Freud was born Sigismund (later changed to Sigmund) Freud on 6 May 1856 in Freiberg, Moravia, which is now Pribor in the Czech Republic. He developed a completely new way of considering human personality. The approach remains controversial as it suggests the human condition is one of perpetual conflict between primitive urges and moral responsibility. He believed that many 'conditions' could be explained by understanding the causes and roots of this conflict.

Freud proposed that the adult personality, or psyche, has three parts: the id, the ego, and the superego. The id is the combination of pleasure seeking desires, and we are born with it—this controls most of our basic biological drivers such as sex, eating, drinking, and aggression. The superego is the moralistic part of personality which develops as a child interacts with significant others, such as its parents. The superego uses anxiety and guilt to stop us acting on the urges from the id. The superego can be seen as the conscience of a person. Sitting between the two is the ego, which develops later in life and tries to maintain a balance between the id and the superego. The ego attempts to satisfy the id but also attempts to make sure these urges are satisfied in a socially acceptable way. The ego, it is said, may use psychological 'tricks' to ensure this happens. For example, if a person becomes angry with a parent or close friend, this may be displaced onto a more acceptable target, such as the person driving their car too close to you. A process called sublimation may also be used which replaces socially unacceptable behaviour; for example, overt public sexual displays with something more conventional such as performing on stage with a pop group.

 Pause for thought

1. What is your immediate reaction to this view of a human being in a state of inner turmoil?

2. Have you ever become cross with someone at work or college because of an argument at home?

3. Does this idea explain performers' provocative stage acts, such as Elvis Presley or Michael Jackson?

According to Freud, the mind can be seen as being similar to an iceberg with only the very tip being exposed and the bulk of the iceberg being unseen (see: Figure 10.1). The id is completely in the unconscious (beneath the sea) and the ego and superego operate at conscious, pre-conscious, and unconscious levels. Our consciousness is what is currently in our minds but we react to motives that are hidden from our immediate awareness. These hidden urges come from previous experiences and may lead us to behaviours and actions we cannot

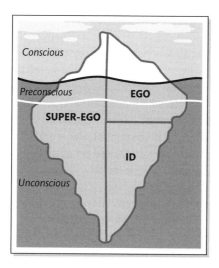

Figure 10.1 Freud's concept of personality

Source: McLeod, S. A. (2008). *Id Ego Superego—Simply Psychology* www.simplypsychology.org

immediately explain. It is claimed that by using one of the tools mentioned earlier, such as the MBTI®, we can become aware of these hidden aspects of ourselves, and be better placed to understand and manage these urges.

One of Freud's contemporaries was Carl Jung (1875–1961). Jung exchanged many letters with Freud and they frequently spoke about matters of the mind—although Freud was well into his fifties by the time they met face to face. Jung had a slightly different approach from Freud, and it is Jung's perspective that has remained fashionable whilst the Freudian approach is often dismissed by psychologists today.

Jung developed the idea of archetypes of personality. He believed that individuals were not born as blank templates upon which the experiences a person encountered in life formed and shaped personality—the tabula rasa approach as it is known—but had inbuilt, unconscious predispositions that immediately shaped their perceptions of the world. He sought to explain why individuals with similar backgrounds evolved differently and had different understanding of the world, but also why people from different backgrounds could share ideas with individuals from completely different social settings. He identified five main archetypes, which he claimed helped to explain a number of human conditions. From this idea, and his relationship with Freud and other psychologists, he went on and developed the idea of psychological 'types'. He claimed, 'it is one's psychological type which from the outset determines and limits a person's judgment' (Jung 1961:207). Essentially, he did not believe that each person was unique—a product of their own heredity and environment. He thought there were *types* of individuals that meant people could be classified into different groups. The approach he took was to describe people as '*either*' type X '*or*' type Y. This is different from a trait approach which places personality on a scale. This dichotomous approach means individuals can be grouped and predictions made about their likely response in any given situation. In his book, *Psychological Types* (1923) he describes theoretically pure types of individual who fit into an ordered taxonomy.

The Myers–Briggs Type Indicator

During the Second World War, an America psychologist, Katharine Cook Briggs, (1875–1968) used some of Jung's ideas to help women find work that suited their personality. She recommended Jung's work to her daughter, Isabel Briggs Myers. Isabel, horrified by the suffering and destruction during the war, wondered if these ideas about different personalities could help people understand each other more and hence avoid conflict.

After many years of research and development, Isabel and Katherine produced a piece of work that has evolved into 'the most widely used personality measure' (Myers 1980:xii), the MTBI. Their questionnaire seeks to determine an individual's preferences in terms of their psychological type (Myers and McCaulley 1985). This, in turn, gives predictive clues to their likely behaviour in given situations, and how they are likely to react to other people. They believed there were basic differences that drive people and by understanding these differences, people could deal with each other constructively. Their theory is 'that much seemingly chance variation in human behaviour is not due to chance; it is in fact the logical result of a few basic, observable differences in mental functioning' (1980:1). By combining their own insights and Jung's observations that differences in behaviour can be explained by an individual's inborn tendencies to use their minds in different ways, they created a model of human behaviour based on four key components. Each of these components is described by two different words that are a reflection of Myers' background as a psychologist. It is important to grasp the meaning of these words as used by both Jung and Myers–Briggs—rather than the more common 'lay' use—as this can lead to incorrect understanding of how the type preferences manifest themselves.

A. Extroversion–introversion dichotomy (E or I)

This first set of preferences are based quite heavily on Jung's ideas in his book, *Psychological Types* (1923). Here, the concern is with understanding where an individual gains their ideas, inspiration, and energy from. With an extravert (note: Jung's original spelling is extravert, although the extrovert version is equally valid), their attention and energy is drawn from their local environment. They seek to actively interact with their surroundings and are energized by events that happen within their locale. In a sense, we can see energy flowing out of an extravert into people, events, and objects that surround them. They may seek to describe themselves as talkative, learning best by doing something or discussing ideas with others. They may be seen as sociable and outgoing with a wide range of interests. Often, they are expressive and may be described as 'wearing their hearts on their sleeve'. They can also be frank with others and become bored if not able to find inspiration from their surroundings.

The other type on this first dichotomy is that of the introvert which contrasts with the extravert by drawing energy and inspiration from their own inner world of ideas. They direct their energy inwards and gain energy from reflecting on thoughts and concepts. Their preference is likely to be communicating with others in writing and working on ideas by reflecting before expressing a view. This can make them seem to be quieter and more reserved. They usually enjoy solitude and can have an air of detachment making them seem unapproachable.

Myers–Briggs are keen to stress these are 'preferences' and not behaviours that are fixed in stone, so an extravert can display introvert behaviours and vice versa. They go on to explain the implications of such behaviour. In this case, an introvert faced with, say, a large social gathering with many unfamiliar people is likely to feel exhausted by the extended period of social contact because they will be acting outside of their natural preference, i.e. a reserved, thinking approach. In a similar way, an extravert faced with a solitary and focused task, such as data input, will relish an interrupting phone call and the chance to build energy by interacting with others.

B. Sensing–intuition dichotomy (S or N)

Here, the instrument is trying to establish how an individual prefers to acquire information about their environment. As with the first function, the individual is classified into one of two possible types. The types are poles, which can both be used by the individual but not at the same time or with the same degree of confidence. The 'Introduction to Type' workbook (Myers: 2000) likens this lack of confidence to attempting to write with your non-preferred hand. Whilst the preferred hand feels natural and effortless, the non-preferred hand feels clumsy and needs a high degree of concentration to perform.

Those with a sensing preference unsurprisingly use their senses to take in information about their surroundings. So they will use their sight, hearing, taste, smell, and touch to gather data. Because of this, they tend to focus on things they feel are real and tangible. They observe what is going on around them and focus on the here and now. They appreciate facts and remember detail about events. Experience and proven methodologies will resonate with them and they will want to know the practical implications and applications for any idea.

Intuitive people, on the other hand, prefer to gather information by an intuitive fantasy about possibilities and options, which contrasts with the sensing approach of fact seeking. They immediately seek to grasp the connection and relationship between ideas and have a feel for 'the big picture'. They are apt to move swiftly to conclusion and follow their hunches for no better reason than 'it feels the right thing to do'. Collections of raw data or statistics may bore them until they can see patterns and meaning.

If asked to describe an everyday object, such as a house brick, a sensing person would want to describe its weight, dimensions, and colour and practical data such as how strong it is. A person with an intuition bias may seek to outline its possible uses such as a counterweight on a balance, a piece of art, a weapon, or a door stop.

C. Thinking–feeling dichotomy (T or F)

Having acquired data through one of the two routes outlined, it is time to make a decision based on that information. However, the model offers two distinct alternatives—both of which will appear rational to the individual because they will be using what they see as reason to reach this decision. In each case, the starting point for the decision is different and, as a consequence, may have different outcomes given the same 'facts'. It is important to remember, as with the other types, neither preference is 'better' or 'worse' than its opposite and no claim is made to the quality of the decision. This merely examines the mental process through which a person goes in order to reach a conclusion.

A thinking preference person would feel they examine the logical consequences of the choice. Individuals are driven by logical connections so cause and effect tend to be their driver. Mentally they will step outside the immediacy of the situation and try to view the scenario impersonally, considering all of the pros and cons objectively. They seek what they consider to be the objective truth that will be seen as 'fair' and 'reasonable' by everyone concerned. This may cause them to be seen as impersonal and 'tough-minded', unconcerned with the emotions of the situation.

Alternatively, a person with a feeling preference will mentally step inside the situation to try to appreciate the various perspectives of the people involved with the decision being made. The feeling preference seeks to reach subjective judgements based on achieving harmony and personal values. They would claim to have an innate ability to understand people, to get under the skin of others, and to be able to treat everyone individually. They may be described as 'tender hearted' and compassionate.

As with the other dimensions, it is dangerous to make rash generalizations based on pre-existing prejudices or preconceptions. With this domain, for example, it is dangerous to jump to the conclusion that men are 'thinkers' whilst women are 'feelers'. Hirsh and Kummerow (1998) make this point and, additionally, how many organizations and business schools have focused on 'T' type behaviour to the exclusion of an 'F' approach, thus reinforcing the view that an objective, task-based decision-making process is in some way preferential to a broader perspective that considers the relational consequences of any decision. However, it may be that recent events, such as the world banking crisis and continuing tensions within the world's communities, mean such distinctions become more erroneous and difficult to justify.

D. Judging–perceiving dichotomy (J or P)

This section tries to uncover how an individual relates or deals with the outer world or life in general. It seeks to understand their overall attitude to life and this function is acknowledged as being fundamental to understanding how the various components outlined above operate together. However, whilst most of the labels given by Myers to the constructs have some direct link to their meaning, these two words used in the final section can cause a degree of confusion, as their common use does not play easily across the behavioural MBTI descriptions. 'Judging' in this sense does not mean 'judgemental', neither does 'perceiving' mean 'perceptive'.

A person who prefers to use a judging process in terms of living their daily lives can be described as having a structured life style. They like to have everything settled and planned out. In terms of energy, they will approach new tasks with a burst of enthusiasm, planning out what needs to be done and by when. They may create schedules and charts to ensure events happen, and how these can be monitored or 'ticked off' when completed. Once this has been done, they relax and allow the plan to proceed towards the closure of the project or event. They will seek to use planning and forethought to avoid any unforeseen hitches, and may become distressed should the plan start to unravel on account of circumstances they cannot control or did not predict. Because they are driven to seek closure, they will often rush to make a plan immediately they feel they have enough information to reach a conclusion as to what needs to be done. They would consider themselves to be ordered and may enthuse about the benefits of inventories—such as a shopping list.

On the other hand, a person with the perceiving preference can be considered to have a flexible, more laid-back approach to life. In energy terms, whereas the judging preference has a burst of input at the beginning of a task, the perceiving preference has an increase towards the end of the task. So last-minute deadlines are likely to energize rather than distract such a person. An example might be a student faced with an end of term assignment—the 'J' character would seek to quickly plan out what needs to be done, rush to carry out their reading, write and review their paper thereby meeting the deadline accordingly. The 'P' character is likely to read a little, write a little, going back and forth with little apparent plan, until the deadline approaches when the midnight oil is likely to be burnt so the deadline is achieved. Remember, there is no suggestion here as to which approach is likely to produce the higher quality result—the two approaches are merely suggested to be dissimilar in behaviour rather than qualitatively differentiated.

So, we can see that rather than seeking the closure preferred by the 'J' type, the 'P' likes to leave open the decision as they will feel more information is needed or may emerge as the process unfolds. Changing tack, altering deadlines and decisions may often occur and their resourcefulness will carry them through the demands of the situation.

As with all of these dimensions, there is scope for positive as well as negative outcomes when two or more different types encounter each other. It was Isabel's hope that, by exploring and making explicit the differences in type, this would lead to greater understanding and harmony. For example, a 'J' type who likes to operate a 'clear desk policy' may get irritated by a 'P' at work who leaves their desk untidy with files strewn everywhere. Similarly, a 'P' may find a 'J' rushing to a decision before properly considering the latest data or report foolhardy and unnecessarily rigid. Whereas the truth of the matter, according to Myers, is that both approaches have their merits as well as shortcomings.

 Case study

Linda is a school teacher with six years' experience, although relatively late entering into her teaching career (she is now in her mid-forties), she has performed well as a Year 6 teacher (her students are roughly 10 to 11 years old). Her children perform well in their end of school examinations (known as SATs), achieving results that are above the national average. She puts her success down to hard work and planning. Her week is structured and ordered with each lesson having a clear set of objectives, resources, and outcomes detailed in a written plan. Her children have to comply with the school's disciplinary code, which requires them to be in correct uniform and to follow a code of conduct. Each of her pupils has a detailed personal learning plan, which identifies their focused learning objectives term by term. Colleagues describe Linda as gregarious and outgoing—she plans the Christmas party, for example. At the end of the summer term she decided she needed a change and left her school, which was her first teaching post—she had been there since qualifying—and she joined a new school. Here she was initially very confused by the laissez-faire approach of the head teacher who left her to teach and did not require much detail in the plans she did have to submit. The display boards in the school were also different from her previous school. Yes, they were covered with the children's work but there was little organization about which class's work was displayed, the displays themselves were higgledy-piggledy with different fonts, colours, and pictures. Linda was taken aback and did not know how to cope with this, and she has struggled to come to terms with her new colleagues and environment.

Questions

Thinking about the MBTI, can you suggest any 'type' letters for Linda? (E or I; S or N; T or F; J or P).

1. Why do you think she has struggled in her new school?

2. What recommendations would you offer to Linda if you were her new head teacher?

How the model operates

This system allows for 16 different combinations or types with the type being classified using a unique four letter code—for example, a person could be a 'ESTJ'. This means they prefer extraversion, sensing, thinking, and judging. Alternatively, another individual could be a 'INFP'—preferring introversion, intuition, feeling, and perceiving. Each of the combinations produces significantly different behavioural patterns, which may affect how a person develops their leadership. Table 10.1 shows the 16 different types and how they interact with each other to produce the different behavioural attributes that manifest themselves as a different leadership style.

This suggests that each type has leadership potential but there will be dangers and limitations to each type as well. It may also be true that different situations (see: Chapter 5) may

Table 10.1 Type and leadership approach

ISTJ	ISFJ	INFJ	INTJ
Uses experience to make decisions. Rewards rule observation. Pays attention to immediate and practical needs.	Complies with rules and structure. Uses personal influence behind the scenes. Uses head for detail to reach practical results.	Quiet yet persistent. Inspires with their ideals. Leads via vision of what is best for others.	Drives themselves and others forward. Can be tough-minded. Conceptual and may seek to reorganize entire system when necessary.
ISTP	**ISFP**	**INFP**	**INTP**
Leads by setting example. Cooperative approach. Manages loosely preferring minimal supervision.	Prefers cooperative team approach. Gently persuades others. Apt to praise rather than criticize.	Takes a facilitative approach. Praises rather than criticizes. Prefers unique situation rather than conventional.	Applies logical thinking. Relates to others expertise. Seeks to interact on intellectual level with others.
ESTP	**ESFP**	**ENFP**	**ENTP**
Takes charge in a crisis. Direct and assertive style. Seeks action and results.	Promotes goodwill. Manages crises well. Makes things happen by focusing on immediate problem.	Leads with energy and enthusiasm. Likes to be in at the start. Works to include and support others.	Acts as a catalyst between people and system. Encourages independent thought. Uses logical approach.
ESTJ	**ESFJ**	**ENFJ**	**ENTJ**
Seeks leadership opportunities. Crisp and direct. Applies experience and respects hierarchy.	Gains goodwill by focusing on people. Keeps team informed. Sets good example.	Leads through personal enthusiasm. Responsive to followers. Inspires change.	Action orientated. Enjoys complex problems. Attempts to run everything. Has long-term view.

Source: Adapted from Hirsh and Kummerow (1998).

require a different style. For example, a crisis situation may need a person more comfortable with making instant decisions rather than taking a reflective approach. However, it is dangerous to assume that a particular type is incapable of using another style or that one's preferred approach is necessarily the best or the one that will produce the highest quality outcome.

Case study   Mark Zuckerberg

Mark Zuckerberg is an American computer scientist probably best known for co-creating the social networking site, Facebook, which, as of October 2011, had more than 800 million users worldwide. Mark was born in 1984 in White Plains, New York, into a Jewish, middle class family. At school, he excelled at the Classics, Latin, Greek, and Hebrew, before focusing on science-based subjects, such as mathematics and physics. He was also a good sportsman and captained the school fencing team.

Introduced to computers by his father, it quickly became apparent that Mark had a real affinity for programming—his tutor has remarked that it was difficult to stay ahead of his ability. His friendship group during his school days included artistic individuals and Mark would look at their work and create computer games based on the ideas he saw in their drawings.

Mark won a place at Harvard, a prestigious American university, where he began to pull together ideas drawn from comments, observations, and existing ideas into a website called 'Facemash'. This site allowed college students to select the best-looking person on their course from a choice of photos. According to Zuckerberg's roommate at the time, Arie Hasit, 'he built the site for fun'. Hasit explains:

> We had books called Face Books, which included the names and pictures of everyone who lived in the student dorms. At first, he built a site and placed two pictures, or pictures of two males and two females. Visitors to the site had to choose who was 'hotter' and according to the votes there would be a ranking.

However, the site was quickly removed after it overwhelmed the college server. But the seeds had been sown and Zuckerberg went on to develop the largest social networking site in the world and, despite never graduating from Harvard, is estimated to have a personal fortune of more than US$17.5 billion.

It is true that Zuckerberg has been dogged by controversy, after several of his college friends disputed his ownership of the Facebook idea. The film based on his life, *The Social Network*, also paints him in a less than flattering light. The court cases that followed Mark's success have all been settled out of court with rumours of over US$20 million being paid to three former roommates. It is also true that in 2010 Zuckerberg donated US$100 million to a New York school charity and has agreed to work towards donating half of his wealth to philanthropy.

Sources

http://facebook.com. This is the main site with various options to explore.

The Social Network (2010) DVD available.

Rohrer, F. (2012) 'Facebook's Mark Zuckerberg: Does it matter that he wears a hoodie?' http://bbc.co.uk (accessed 9 May 2013).

Questions

1. What type do you think Mark is?

2. Why? Are there any conflicting statements that make it difficult to assess?

3. What do you think his leadership approach is likely to consist of?

This is because the instrument is not a 'test' or measuring ability. It is worth remembering that Myers' and Briggs' original purpose in developing the MBTI was to help individuals gain access to their own preferences and from this to develop self-understanding. It certainly was not originally meant to be a leadership instrument or aid to recruitment as there are many other factors that can affect both of these areas—indeed, it could be argued this is unethical. Nevertheless, the MBTI remains a popular instrument in both Europe and the USA (it is available in 20 different languages) and as long as these various caveats are born in mind, it can assist organizations and individuals in terms of their communication style and how they deal with conflict and stress management.

 Case study

Jasmin is the manager of the finance department for a family-owned regional chain of clothing shops. She has a well-deserved reputation within the organization for her accounting excellence, and she has a strong academic track record to support her with a first class degree from a London-based university. She has recently passed her accountancy exams and, without doubt, is well positioned to advance her career.

She is so good that she was promoted to department manager in her previous company after only two years on the job. She moved to her current company six months ago and has implemented two changes in as many months. She has implemented a change in the accounting system that has reduced the time taken to chase debtors and saved the company around £5,000 in bank charges.

Jasmin now reports directly to the managing director of the business. Rodney is the great-grandson of the founder and is rightly proud of the family feel the stores have and the longevity of the employees. He is concerned about Jasmin who, despite her technical excellence, seems to be upsetting more and more people with her leadership style.

Jasmin can be aloof and distant, sitting in her office poring over data and statistics. When she has one of her insights, she emails her instructions and issues direct orders as to her wishes. At the weekly team meetings, she outlines the progress made towards the department's targets, gives her forecast for the coming week, and closes the meeting.

Her managing director has noticed this approach and has asked her why she feels this is the right approach. Jasmin's response is that work is work and people need to know what is expected of them. She can clearly identify issues and problems and by directing people to the right areas, time, money, and effort can be saved. (Names changed to preserve anonymity.)

....

Questions

1. Do you agree or disagree with Jasmin's view of work?

2. Why?

3. What do you think the danger is for Jasmin and Rodney?

4. Could an understanding of 'type' help either Jasmin or Rodney?

Neuro-linguistic programming

Neuro-linguistic programming (NLP), is both a controversial and a popular approach to personal development, coaching, and management development. It was co-created in the 1970s by the unlikely pairing of a computer scientist, Richard Bandler, and a linguistics professor,

John Grinder. For its supporters, NLP is a psychotherapeutic approach to numerous mental disorders, such as phobias, obsessions, and learning disorders. In the field of management development, it has been used to develop self-confidence, communication skills, and influencing techniques (for example see: O'Connor and Seymour 1993). However, for critics such as Corballis (1999:41) 'NLP is a thoroughly fake title, designed to give the impression of scientific respectability'. NLP has been criticized for a lack of empirical studies and intellectual rigour. Nevertheless, there remains a 'professional' body, formed in 2003 (The Professional Guild of NLP), and a set of over 100,000 practitioners who can obtain 'Master Practitioner' status from this body.

> **Neuro** relates to the way in which a person makes sense of their environment. This is the balance between their senses, and how they are used to inform the thinking processes that occur inside the brain to create an understandable 'map' of the world.
>
> Linguistic: the nature of the words and associated language used by individuals to influence both themselves and others around them.
>
> Programming: how an individual acts and reacts as a result of internally developed ideas and actions. These actions can produce expected as well as unexpected outcomes.

It is this breadth of usage that makes defining 'NLP' so problematic. However, an examination of the early work of the founders gives a degree of insight into their original aims, and, from there, the approach's metamorphosis into a wider personal development toolkit can be mapped.

Early days

Shapiro (2007) suggests NLP was developed to answer two specific questions;

- How do individuals who are 'outstanding' achieve the results that make them 'outstanding'?
- What is it that makes the difference between a person who is competent in any field and somebody who is excellent in the same field?

Bandler, as a student, studied three therapists whom he believed achieved outstanding results in terms of helping individuals achieve success. He examined the work of Virginia Satir, Fritz Peris, and Milton Erickson as role models of excellence in their respective fields, which ranged from hypnotherapy to gestalt therapy. Bandler, using Grinder's linguistic insights, sought to identify why these three scientists could achieve the results they did—he felt there must be a common theme or pattern (he was a computer scientist) that was hidden in their language. By studying their techniques, Bandler and Grinder hoped to be able to produce a model that would enable anyone to replicate the outcomes of the aforementioned therapists.

Working together, the two men analysed the taped conversations between a therapist and client, and Bandler worked out how he believed the therapist was able to challenge a client's thinking. Grinder applied his specialism and composed an approach using words, phrases, images, and self-reflective questioning to offer individuals a way of accessing 'excellent' performance in whatever field was pertinent to their own life and career goals. The two quickly produced books, such as *The Structure of Magic* (1975) and *Frogs into Princes* (1979), as well as endorsing a highly lucrative series of lectures and courses. These courses captured the self-help zeitgeist of the times and returned healthy profits for both men. Unfortunately, more recent history between them features court cases and a litigious struggle for rights to their product. In 2000, they settled their case with an agreement to be jointly recognized as co-founders of the movement.

The approach is largely based on the thinking of Alfred Korzybski (1879–1950), who was a Polish-American philosopher. He suggested individuals respond to 'reality' via a series of internal models or maps generated via information brought in by their senses. In particular, he considered that language played a key role in shaping a person's map. These maps were considered to be largely unconscious and affected a person's behaviour and language. Their progress through 'life' was largely a matter of reinforcing these maps unless there was a large discrepancy or difference between the map and a particularly powerful or unique experience. Again, this is a highly contentious perspective but nevertheless gives a clue into how NLP is said to be effective. Bandler and Grinder believed that, by affecting these internal maps (neuro) using appropriate language and images (linguistic), they could change (programme) a person to view their 'reality' differently, thus helping them to achieve goals and outcomes previously considered beyond the capability of that person.

What are the basic NLP techniques?

NLP is based on a series of presuppositions about the nature of the human 'condition'. The first is that a person is considered to be a connected system with the mind and body operating in a manner that connects them both and hence they are capable of affecting each other. (Dilts et al. 1980). More than this, there is a complex system that operates between these internal sub-systems, language, behaviour, and the external environment. The implication being that, by affecting, changing, and stimulating one part, the other parts will be affected too.

Next comes, via a quote attributed to Korzybski (1933:58): 'A map is not the territory it represents, but if correct, it has a similar structure to the territory, which accounts for its usefulness.' What this statement is taken to mean is that each person has a 'map' representing their interpretation of reality (the territory). As each of these maps is likely to be an interpretation, hence all maps and all individuals are likely to be unique because all will interpret the territory differently on account of the filtering mechanism of their senses. This, according to NLP practitioners, is why different people viewing the same 'event' can interpret the situation differently.

 Pause for thought

1. Consider this perspective: If you saw a shaven headed man running towards you holding a handbag with another man chasing him, what would you think?

2. But who has stolen a bag? Is it the first man or perhaps the second man with the first man snatching it back? Are the two events actually connected? Perhaps they are just running for the bus or it is a coincidence that they are in the same place? What personal experiences or deep-seated beliefs could influence your interpretation of the event?

Linked to this is the supposition that a person's own 'map' eventually becomes 'reality'. So a person will look for evidence, facts, and likeminded individuals that reinforce their perspective. Predictions about events and outcomes—including those that relate to their own destiny—become self-fulfilling. Henry Ford's maxim of, 'if you think you can or you think you can't, you are right', is an example of this approach.

Third, comes the view that knowing what an individual actually wants out of life is key to success. Alongside this lies the implicit assumption that each person has the capability to achieve whatever their aims or desires are. This remains one of the most controversial aspects of this approach, as it would seem to suggest that any human is capable of achieving anything another human has achieved.

Fourth, communication between humans takes place on a conscious and unconscious level, and consists of verbal and non-verbal signals. So body language, along with the tone and pace of voice, are of equal of importance with the spoken word. Linked to this assumption is the view that the meaning of any communication is the response received back by the 'sender'. This means that an intended message may be misinterpreted by the recipient, which in turn could lead to misunderstanding and confusion between the two parties.

Using these underlying principles, NLP has developed numerous threads and advocates. Some of these ideas have been roundly criticized for lacking any rigour or displaying uncontested evidence as to their efficacy. However, two techniques are regularly taught at leadership training courses with a view to improving the degree of 'influence' or empathy between two people. The first approach uses the view expressed above—that individuals construct a 'map' of reality based on information coming via their senses. In NLP terms, this process of accessing, processing, and storing information is known as the VAKOG model. This stands for visual (what we see), auditory (what we hear), kinaesthetic (what we feel and touch), olfactory (what we smell), and gustatory (what we taste). With this mind, NLP practitioners believe that, by understanding an individual's predisposition towards a particular approach, a skilled communicator can ensure the message they wish to communicate is received and processed by their chosen target in the manner intended. Individuals, it is claimed, give various verbal and non-verbal clues as to their preference for a particular sensory message. By observing these signals and adapting a message to meet with the target's preference, it is possible to gain influence as the message is couched in such a manner as to be powerful and meaningful for the target audience. For example, it is suggested by Shapiro (2007) that a visual person (i.e. an individual who prefers messages they can see) may wish to see the minutes of a meeting emailed so she could read them—hence using their preferred learning mechanism. Alternatively a person with an auditory preference may want to talk through the results using their hearing as the major input to their internal map.

Detecting the clues as to an individual's preferences, according to Shapiro, is a matter of listening and observing various verbal and non-verbal signals from the target. For example, it is claimed that a person with a kinaesthetic preference would use phrases such as 'let's touch base', or 'can I run this idea past you?' Table 10.2 gives some further illustrations said to betray a preference for a particular sensory stimuli. Shapiro says, 'you are more likely to gain rapport with a person who thinks in the same way as you and you discover this by listening to the words they use' (2007:63).

The second method of identifying an individual's preferences is by observing their eye movement as they relate an incident. It is claimed that an individual using a visual

Table 10.2 Examples of phrases

Examples of Phrases			
Visual	**Auditory**	**Kinaesthetic**	**Ol/Gus**
Show me what you mean	I hear what you say	Grab the bull by the horns	I smell a rat
I can't really see that	Singing from the same hymn sheet	That is a solid idea	You look as fresh as a daisy
That looks good to me	I can't hear myself think!	We're in a sticky situation	I like the smell of that!

representation system tends to look upwards, those with a kinaesthetic disposition look downwards, and those with an auditory preference look sideways. As an added refinement, it is suggested that a right-handed person looks to the left when recalling past events, i.e. a pre-existing memory, whilst they will look up to the right (when observed from the front) when imagining something for the first time. In a similar way, those with an auditory and kinaesthetic preference are said to look in different directions depending on what their mind is attempting to achieve (see: Figure 10.2).

Another technique that is claimed to aid the rapport building process is that of mirroring or matching another person's body language, voice patterns, and language. Ellerton (2005) claims this is the key to establishing trust between two people because, he claims, people tend to like people who share their perspective and approach to life. Mirroring behaviours suggests to another person that you share their mindset and probably have similar views. He goes further and suggests that, by convincing another that you are like them, even if you are not, you can seek to influence that person. Some may suggest this is either Machiavellian or even immoral but nevertheless NLP disciples consider this to be an appropriate tactic.

In summary, NLP is a broad church that aims to assist individuals achieve their life goals. In leadership terms, this means using a number of different techniques to quickly establish rapport, empathy, and influence over others. The approach is controversial because, as Tosey

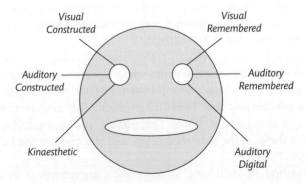

Figure 10.2 Eye accessing movements for a right-handed person

Pause for thought

1. Can you identify any preferences in your thinking and language?

2. Try out the eye accessing model on a friend by asking questions such as: 'What did you have for dinner last night?' A right-handed person should look right according to the model as they are remembering a past event.

3. Try: 'What will you be doing in five years?' This should produce a look to the left as they try to imagine the scene.

4. Does it work?

and Mathison point out (2003:361), 'there is little academic work to date on this innovative field of practice'. Critics charge NLP with being ill-conceived and lacking in academic rigour. This gap between academics and practitioners is as wide now as it ever has been and there is little sense of any rapprochement between the two groups. It is true that Bandler and Grinder were more interested in the practical application of their investigations rather than elucidating on the theoretical underpinning aspects. Consider this statement from their 1979 book, *Frogs into Princes*: 'We have no idea about the real nature of things and we're not particularly interested in what's true. The function of modelling is to arrive at descriptions which are useful' (1979:7). Devilly (2005) makes the point that NLP is certainly less popular now than it was in its heyday of the 1970s and 1980s. Glasner-Edwards and Rawson (2010:94) go much further and describe NLP as 'certainly discredited'. However, it is important to bear in mind these critics are writing from a particular perspective, in that they are examining NLP from a clinical perspective rather than as a leadership tool. Anecdotal evidence from NLP master practitioners is clear—there is real benefit to understanding how your mind works and how to use different approaches to different people.

Criticism of the psychodynamic approach

Critics of these various approaches begin by focusing on the underpinning assumptions and research that are the foundations for the models and ideas. For example, Freud and Jung's work in part looked at abnormalities and psychoses within a limited population. Extrapolating this to leadership models is simply a step too far—'Where are the empirical, scientific tests?' ask Zemke (1992) and Hunsley et al. (2004). In addition, the simple approach of explaining complex behavioural patterns in terms of four functions, themselves manifestations of primitive biological drivers, is regarded by many as a reductionist approach. This means it ignores the wider complexities of the human condition, aspects of the environment, or organizational context in which the individual operates and reduces them to simplistic levels. These critics point to the MBTI model comprising only 16 different types and suggest that, surely, there are more than 16 different 'personalities' in the world.

The approach is not a powerful tool for change in that it does not ask a person to change their behaviour or to operate in a different way. The idea is to offer insights, and hence understanding, rather than a new set of skills. It is true this approach may be seen as a positive but it can also lead to a suggestion that 'I am what I am—deal with it'. In other words, an individual may see their behaviour as being justified in some way by the models and use this as an excuse for continuing to behave in a certain manner. It is not a powerful change agent in this sense as the models seek to offer a metaphorical mirror to the individual who can chose to examine closely the reflected image or ignore the likeness if they feel it is too hideous.

Others would point to the 'hijacking' of tools from one scientific field for use in another. The danger being that none of the methods outlined above was ever intended to be used as instruments to aid leadership. Each tool was designed to be used in a different context and there are implications for using these ideas in an environment they were not designed for. Tools developed by psychoanalysts for use with disturbed or mentally ill individuals may have profound implications when deployed with 'normal', healthy people seeking an insight into what makes them and others 'tick'.

Summary

Regardless of environment, it is true the material gathered via one of these methods does require interpretation either via an 'expert' or by the individual concerned. This can lead to charges of bias on the part of the interpreter, which means the approach lacks objectivity. One reviewer may regard a set of results in one way with another coming to a different conclusion. The providers of these psychometric instruments would counter this by pointing to the need to be properly licensed, trained, and accredited in the delivery and feedback of information before being given free rein with these tools.

Regardless, Jon Ronson (2006) points out the success of such programmes—when the TV presenter, Paul McKenna, and his company offered a seven-day NLP course for 600 delegates it produced £1 million of revenue for him. Other presenters, such as Derren Brown, have forged a similarly successful career from producing such shows as *The Heist* (2006), which used a number of different tactics to persuade willing volunteers to steal money (although Brown is sceptical about the veracity of NLP; Brown 2006). In summary, these tools remain attractive with individuals and management trainers alike, even if the academic community remains unconvinced about the empirical status of the tools.

 Case study   Jawaharlal Nehru (1889–1964)

Nehru is a venerated figure in India, where he is widely regarded as the father of modern India. He was born in 1889 to a middle class Indian family. Following his education in England at Harrow School and then Trinity College, Cambridge, he followed his father in terms of profession by becoming a lawyer. As a child, he was said to be quiet, thoughtful, and observant with an aversion to conflict—a trait that continued to manifest itself throughout his adult life, as he championed pacifism and the role of the United Nations. After completing his studies and qualifying at the Inner Temple, he returned to India in 1912 and practised law for some years. In 1916, he married Kamala Kaul and the following year they had a daughter, Indira. However, after the massacre at Amritsar in 1919, when British troops shot and killed as many as a thousand unarmed civilians, he decided to become involved with the Indian National Congress Party, which was campaigning against British rule in India.

The Indian National Congress Party, at the time, was led by the iconic figure of Mahatma Ghandi, and he was to become a central figure in the development of Nehru's future. In 1921, Nehru was finally imprisoned by the British for anti-Government activities and over the next 20 years he spent roughly nine years in prison. In 1928, partly because of his ability and partly through the patronage of Ghandi, he was elected as president of the party and began to formulate his ideas on the shape of India once it had thrown off the yoke of British rule.

As the Second World War drew to a conclusion, recognized by now as the natural heir and successor to Ghandi, Nehru began to negotiate with the British Viceroy, Lord Louis Mountbatten. Finally, in 1947, he became the first prime minister of an independent India, and he raised the flag of independence on 15 August 1947. He was to hold this post through to his death in 1964.

He was elected with a mandate from India's masses and he began to implement a policy of moderate socialism. He recognized the values of an open democracy underpinning a parliamentary system, similar to the British approach. He also recognized the need to get the Indian economy moving and encouraged inward investment and tried to harness the entrepreneurial spirit of his kinsfolk. He implemented a somewhat centralized control over some parts of the economy with the creation of the Planning Commission of India and he drew up the first Five-Year Plan in 1951, which charted the government's investments in industries and agriculture.

He also believed in a united India but was mindful of the deep ethnic divisions and ancient caste lines that divided his society. He wanted to create a secular society that incorporated all religions, faiths, and creeds. However, as the British withdrawal from India started to become inevitable, the powerful regional leaders began to quarrel, because their common enemy no longer existed. The loudest and most vociferous dissention to the idea of a multi-cultural India came from the Muslim League led by Muhammad Ali Jinnah, who was demanding a separate Muslim state of Pakistan. Nehru opposed this idea and tried to create a government that incorporated Muslims, Christians, and Hindus. However, this plan failed and, under pressure from Mountbatten who wanted to finalize British involvement in the sub-continent, he reluctantly agreed to the partitioning of India on 3 June 1947.

Fighting against this parochialism, Nehru established programmes such as the National Book Trust and the National Literary Academy which promoted the translation of regional literatures between languages and he also organized the transfer of materials between regions. In pursuit of a single, unified India, Nehru warned his warring factions, 'integrate or perish'. However, war was not far away and Pakistan and India fought over the disputed territory of Kashmir. A United Nations negotiated settlement was put in place but, despite the best efforts, Kashmir remains an unstable place with regular border clashes between armed separatist groups and Indian forces.

Despite these setbacks, Nehru was able to move India forward and, during the Cold War, both the United States of America and the Soviet Union competed to have India as an ally. Nehru resisted their overtures and turned his attention to joining them both as a nuclear-armed superpower. In 1948, he initiated the nuclear development strategy led by the Atomic Energy Commission of India (AEC) and Dr Bhabha—India is now rumoured to have roughly 100 nuclear weapons.

In his declining years, he became increasingly frustrated and disillusioned with the bickering and arguing within his own party and Indian politics in general. However, he continued in office and began to assert Indian authority in the region. In 1961, he sent in the Indian Army to liberate Goa, which, at the time, was a Portuguese colony. Operation Vijay, as it was called, involved air, sea, and land strikes for more than 36 hours, and was a decisive victory for India, ending 451 years of Portuguese colonial rule. More than 60 men from both sides were killed and the conflict drew a mixture of worldwide praise and condemnation. In India, the action was seen as liberation of an historical Indian territory and was celebrated. Perhaps buoyed by this victory, Nehru began a series of expansionist moves in the disputed border between India and China. These actions, coupled with the decision to offer asylum to the Dalai Lama, led to the Sino-India War in which the Indian forces were roundly beaten.

(Continued...)

Following this defeat, Nehru's health started to decline and on 27 May 1964 he suffered a fatal heart attack and died. Nehru was cremated in accordance with Hindu rites at the Shantivana on the banks of the Yamuna River, witnessed by hundreds of thousands of mourners who had flocked into the streets of Delhi and the cremation grounds. He was succeeded by Lal Shastri, who, in turn, was succeeded by Nehru's daughter, Mrs Indira Gandhi, in 1966. She was assassinated on 31 October 1984. Her son, Rajiv, was prime minister of India from 1984 to 1989, but he too was assassinated.

Sources

http://bbc.co.uk/history/historic_figures/nehru_jawaharlal.shtml (accessed 5 August 2013).

http://timesofindia.indiatimes.com/topic/Jawaharlal-Nehru (accessed 5 August 2013).

Brecher, Michael (1959) *Nehru: A Political Biography*. London: Oxford University Press.

Guha, Ramachandra (2007) *India after Gandhi: The History of the World's Largest Democracy*. New York: Harper Collins.

Nehru, Jawaharlal (1936) *Toward Freedom: The Autobiography of Jawaharlal Nehru*. New York: John Day Company.

Nehru, Jawaharlal (edited by S. Gopal and Uma Iyengar) (2003) *The Essential Writings of Jawaharlal Nehru*. Oxford: Oxford University Press.

Questions

1. Can you make any observations about Nehru's 'type'?

2. What would help you to make such decisions?

3. Could Nehru be considered to be a visionary?

Assignment—3,000 words

Write a 3,000 word essay using the following title as your starting point:

To what extent does an understanding of 'self' assist or hinder a leader in terms of their ability to influence others?

Consider yourself; what evidence can you uncover that would initially challenge then support Type theory? Conclude with a view that justifies your position on Type theory.

Comment on the following statement: 'Psychodynamics—its all touchy-feely rubbish. I don't need to "know myself" in order to lead as long as I know others.'

Further reading

Kelly, George (1955) *A Theory of Personality; The Psychology of Personal Constructs* (New York: W.W. Norton & Co.) is an interesting read for those interested in the nature of how humans make sense of their surroundings. His approach is to suggest that a human's mental processes are so developed and channelled that he is able to anticipate events. This ability to predict outcomes makes him capable of shaping environment rather than merely responding to it.

Pedler, Mike, Burgoyne, John, and Boydell, Tom (1994) *A Manager's Guide of Self Development* (Maidenhead: McGraw-Hill) is designed to be a self-help guide to assist a person to complete a self-appraisal and to engage in a 'programme' of learning events. It is aimed at individuals who find themselves in managerial roles but are struggling to understand how they manage and lead themselves, so is designed to be a workbook style rather an academic text.

Bannister, D. and Fransella, F. (1971) *Inquiring Man: The Theory of Personal Constructs* (New York: Penguin) is a book written by two psychologists who argue that 'Man' is a self-inventing explorer of his world. They support Kelly's view and outline a technique called Repertory Grid Technique as a method for helping individuals to explore their own 'constructs' or models of the world. It is more of an academic read and needs to be read with an eye to the prevailing climate within the world of psychology at the time the book was written.

Emotional intelligence

11

After reading this chapter you will:

● Gain an overview of what emotional intelligence 'is'.

● Understand the implications for leaders.

● Be able to appraise the concept critically.

Introduction

Definitions of emotional intelligence (EI) abound. However, a useful starting point is Mayer et al. (2008:511): 'Emotional Intelligence concerns the ability to carry out accurate reasoning about emotions and the ability to use emotions and emotional knowledge to enhance thought.' EI is another concept that divides the world of academics and practitioners. It is roughly 15 years since Daniel Goleman, when working as a reporter for the *New York Times*, came across research on EI written by two psychologists, Peter Salovey and John Mayer (1990). Excited by what he read, he put his journalistic skills and training as a psychologist to good use and wrote his career defining book, *Emotional Intelligence, Why it Matters More Than IQ* (Goleman: 1996). The book spent over 18 months on the best seller list and moved Goleman into the world of consultancy and wealth. The proposition put forward by Goleman was that, by managing one's own emotions, and manipulating other people's emotions, a person could become successful. Goleman made the claim that EI was more important than intelligence quotient (IQ) in determining the chances of an individual becoming 'successful'. The reason for this was linked to the changing nature of work and leadership from being a command and control activity to one concerned with winning the hearts and minds of the workforce. The ability to manage emotions in this more liberal environment, it was asserted, was the key skill for aspiring leaders and possession of such talent became a key to determining the likely success of a potential leader.

Off the back of this claim, a whole industry sprang up with countless articles, workshops, and courses designed to teach the elusive skill to an audience eager for the answer to personal and organizational challenges. Soon, the seductive nature of the idea that individuals could improve their emotional health had metamorphosed into a mechanism for becoming a better parent, salesperson, 'person', and lover (Steiner 1997). The number of books, webinars, conferences, and tests mushroomed into a multimillion-pound business with trainers and life coaches using the hypothesis in their work.

However, the assertions made have been challenged (for example see: Matthews et al. 2003) as not much more than smoke and mirrors with writers and researchers unable to agree on a definition of exactly what EI is, with any number of different models using subtly different concepts. Themes such as self-motivation, optimism, trustworthiness, and conscientiousness all figure in definitions, themes that did not appear in the original work. Indeed, the very basis of Goleman's book, and the multitude of papers, seminars, workshops, and training courses that have sprung up around the theme, is that EI can be learned. However, questions remain unanswered as to whether EI is a skill or trait, whether it is just a relabelling of existing theory, and if it exists at all. The academic research is still inconclusive with some researchers, such as Sanchez and Villanueva (2007:349), declaring that, 'no significant relationship was found between trait EI and collective task efficacy', contrasting with Palmer et al. (2001:6) who found that, 'EI as measured by the ability to monitor and manage emotions within oneself and others may be an underlying competency of transformational leadership'. Before commenting further, it may be advisable to explore the underpinning ideas behind this controversial subject, so that a measured approach can be taken before drawing conclusions about the validity and importance of EI in determining a leader's task efficacy.

The architecture of the brain

To begin to understand the nature of emotions, it is necessary to first delve into the relatively new world of brain science so that a grasp can be made of the basic chemical and biological processes at work when a human experiences emotion. The human brain has several key units that are at the heart of what makes us such complex and convoluted beings. Within the brain sits an ancient structure situated just above the brainstem (see: Figure 11.1). This almond shaped area, of which there are two, one on each side of the brain, is called the

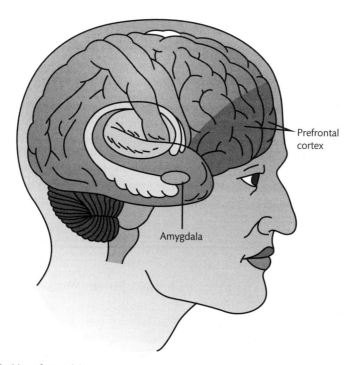

Figure 11.1 Position of amygdala

amygdale and research (Aggleton 1992) puts it at the heart of many of our deepest, most powerful, and uncontrollable urges.

The amygdala has a role to play in the storage of memories associated with emotional events and, in humans, is relatively larger than our nearest animal relatives, the great apes. Acting as a 'storehouse of emotional memory' (Goleman 1996:15), the presence of the amygdala gives life its richness and depth. Individuals without such a storehouse, either through surgery or through accident, are seen to be devoid of any recognition of emotion. They cannot connect with other humans, are unable to recognize emotion in others, and are not able to understand the impact of the environment on others.

Another part of the brain is the neocortex and hippocampus which is a much more sophisticated area nearer to the frontal lobes of the brain. This area also has a role to play in the broader **limbic system** as it takes stimuli from our various senses to enable us to make an informed response to what we interpret to be occurring before us. Researchers now believe the hippocampus recognizes and registers the 'facts' about a situation—for example, that we are watching a YouTube clip rather than experiencing 'reality', or that we are playing a computer game rather than storming the D-Day beaches ourselves. So, before an emotional response is generated to an external stimulus, the hippocampus regulates, interprets, and transmits information to the amygdala. The amygdala then sends appropriate signals to the rest of the body to cope with the situation such as blushing, laughing, or crying.

> **Limbic system:** This is a term first introduced by P. MacLean in 1952. He considered it to be the emotional centre of the brain. It is now thought of as a broad network drawing on various components within the brain that all contribute towards the management of emotions.

However, recent research by neuroscientists such as LeDoux (1996) has shown there is another pathway for electrical impulses to reach the amygdala in thousandths of a second. This near instantaneous response effectively bypasses the regulatory part of the brain. The short-circuit operates over 80,000 times quicker than the route via the hippocampus, which means stimulus can reach the amygdala before being assessed and regulated by the hippocampus. The reason for this is based on our days of living in caves among wild beasts. Survival in this harsh environment depended on the ability to think and act quicker than the bear or tiger that was confronting you. The choice in such situations, known colloquially as 'fight or flight', was not something to be considered carefully when faced by an angry predator as this delay would probably result in death. Instantaneous reaction without forethought was what was required in these

 Pause for thought

1. When were you last faced by a situation that required you to just react? What startled you? Did you 'jump'

2. What happened physically to you? Did you 'jump'?

3. Did your heart race and your muscles tense?

4. How did you feel once the situation had passed? Was 'jumping' the right response?

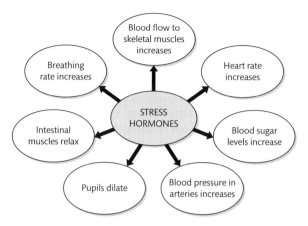

Figure 11.2 Physiological changes to stress

extreme situations and contributed to making homo sapiens the dominant species on Earth. The amygdala suddenly floods the body with a hormone called epinephrine (adrenaline) and other stress hormones, which cause various physiological changes in the body (see: Figure 11.2).

Whilst this response was quite useful in our early ancestors, and is still an important part of mammalian brains, it is rather limited and imprecise in that there are relatively few options available, you either 'fight' or run—essentially action precedes thought. The amygdala may not even wait for the full situation to unfold and will cause the body to react to early signs of a threatening situation. This means there is real danger of misinterpreting a situation or not choosing the right response. Fortunately, we no longer live in caves surrounded by any number of animals seeking lunch; however, the amygdala has not evolved sufficiently to take into account our move into high rise blocks and a world where the biggest threats lie in over-eating and a lack of exercise. When faced by an emotionally demanding situation, our less evolved brain can still short-circuit our more rational brain, severing the link between a rational, considered response and our environment.

Consider, for a moment, the last time you were the victim of someone pushing into a queue ahead of you. Perhaps you were in your car and had patiently waited in line at a set of road works getting frustrated as the traffic slowly dribbled forward. You begin to approach the set of cones marking the start of the work. Then, suddenly, a black BMW car hammers past and dives in front of you. How do you react? An angry blast on the horn? A raised fist? Or perhaps worse—the incidents of 'road rage' are increasing with more than 70 per cent of drivers admitting they have committed an aggressive act. But what if the driver was on the way to an emergency? What if their husband or wife was in mortal danger? And, if we are honest, how long did the extra car delay us? A few seconds at most. The chances are neither of these mitigating questions even entered your mind as you cursed their very existence. In effect, your amygdala has taken control of your mind and body creating a response that, whilst appropriate for facing a charging rhino, is far from fitting for our modern world. In such circumstances, our modern, rational brain and reactions have been swamped by our older, less evolved brain. There is no opportunity for our brain to weigh up the situation correctly, to consider a number of different options, and to select rationally the option most likely to result in a positive outcome. Salovey and Mayer (1990) considered EI to be the ability to manage the whole limbic system actively so that individuals could react having fully considered the nature of the situation facing them, rather than relying on ancient memories that may produce an undesirable outcome. They define EI as:

> the capacity to reason about emotions, and of emotions to enhance thinking. It includes the abilities to accurately perceive emotions, to access and generate emotions so as to assist thought, to understand emotions and emotional knowledge, and to reflectively regulate emotions so as to promote emotional and intellectual growth.

> (Mayer et al. 2004:197)

The implication being that by understanding, recognizing, and managing these urges, a person could hope to respond in a more sophisticated and considered manner to their immediate surroundings. The further implication being that this more thoughtful tactic would result in outcomes that are more beneficial.

 Pause for thought

1. When was the last time you suddenly experienced anger?
2. What did you do when the 'red mist' descended?
3. If you reflect on this event, was uncontrolled anger the most appropriate response?
4. Would 'counting to 10' have produced a different outcome for you?

The nature of intelligence

At this point it would be useful to take a step back and consider the wider issue of intelligence and the importance of the work of Howard Gardner (1943–). Gardner has an academic background that ranges from history to psychology. Studying at Harvard University, he became interested and yet frustrated by studies into psychology. He remarks thus:

> My mind was really opened when I went to Harvard College and had the opportunity to study under individuals—such as psychoanalyst Erik Erikson, sociologist David Riesman, and cognitive psychologist Jerome Bruner—who were creating knowledge about human beings. That helped set me on the course of investigating human nature, particularly how human beings think.

> (Howard Gardner quoted in Scherer 1999)

Gardner's journey helped to change the way in which psychologists and other professionals conceptualized human thought and intelligence.

Traditionally, schools and broader society recognized and rewarded individuals who were considered to be 'smart' as measured by a single attribute of their cognitive ability. This attribute tended to be a reflection of their linguistic and logical abilities as reflected in their reading and writing skills. This attribute has become known as a person's IQ. The roots of modern tests can be traced back as far as Imperial China and nineteenth-century France but most systems used today have some link to Charles Springer (see: Kaufman 2009) whose general intelligence theory became the dominant model for more than 30 years. Along with the theory, a number of tests were developed including John Raven's **progressive matrices**, which claimed to be able to measure a person's IQ. A 'normal' person was expected to score 100 on such tests with 95 per cent of the population sitting between 70 and 130. This became the broadly accepted benchmark for a whole series of judgements made about the 'worth' of any given individual. Their life chances broadly seemed to correlate to these measures and an individual's chances of success largely depended on their score with a person's health, wealth, and social standing being related to their IQ.

Progressive matrices: John Raven's matrices are a series of non-verbal items that ask a person to identify the next pattern given a series of black on white diagrams. The higher number a person is able to identify correlates to their IQ. (See: Raven, J. C. (1938). *Progressive Matrices: A Perceptual Test of Intelligence.* London: H.K. Lewis.)

Gardner (1983) made several claims that included a view that, just because an individual finds a particular task relatively 'easy', they may not be more 'intelligent' than someone who finds it harder. It may be that the former has managed to 'learn' the skill in a different way that appeals to their own cognitive abilities. Second, he proposed that, as well as the already established intelligences of literacy and numeracy, there were a number of other 'intelligences' that could be displayed by an individual. These two assertions meant that not only could psychologists, educators, and individuals consider 'intelligence' as relating to the gift of dance or the ability to play an instrument, but this 'intelligence' could be treated as being as important and prestigious as reading or numeracy. He suggested there were seven (later up to nine) different areas he considered met his criteria for being an 'intelligence'. Table 11.1 shows the different themes he proposed and the capability each bestowed on the individual.

One of the implications of this new approach to 'intelligence' was to consider an individual such as the footballer, David Beckham, as being on the same 'level' as the musician, John Lennon, and the physicist, Albert Einstein. Naturally, the liberal wing of education seized upon this notion as a justification for broadening and explaining the different behaviours and achievements in the classroom. Intuitively, the model could also help to explain why some incredibly successful academics struggle to make relationships with other people (they may have limited interpersonal intelligence perhaps). Or, indeed, the opposite, where individuals

Table 11.1 Gardner's multiple intelligences

Intelligence type	Capability and perception
Linguistic	words and language
Logical-mathematical	logic and numbers
Musical	music, sound, rhythm
Bodily-kinaesthetic	body movement control
Spatial-visual	images and space
Interpersonal	other people's feelings
Intrapersonal	self-awareness

Source: Adapted from Gardner (1999:41–43).

who were relatively unsuccessful at school have gone on to build highly successful careers and businesses—for example, Sir Richard Branson's dyslexia contributed to him leaving school with few formal qualifications but he soon developed the hugely successful Virgin brand.

However, Gardner's work has been attacked for lacking empirical support and for being both tautological and 'unfalsifiable' (for example see: Klein 1998). Gardner himself seems to recognize the concerns about his ideas, which, although to him felt intuitively right, lacked real scientific evidence. He puts the problem thus:

> I once thought it possible to create a set of tests of each intelligence—an intelligence-fair version to be sure—and then simply to determine the correlation between the scores on the several tests. I now believe that this can only be accomplished if someone developed several measures for each intelligence and then made sure that people were comfortable in dealing with the materials and methods used to measure each intelligence.

(Gardner 1999: 98)

However, what this research did achieve was to broaden out, in the public's perception, the idea that individuals could be intelligent in more ways than simply being good at mathematics or reading. This paved the way for the subsequent development of EI as an ability to be ranked alongside other, more traditional abilities.

 Pause for thought

1. What do you think about footballers being considered 'intelligent'?

2. Is this an excuse to label every 'ability' as an 'intelligence'?

3. Do you think this theory has any implications for schools and universities?

 Case study   Edward Saatchi

Edward Saatchi is the 26-year-old joint founder of NationalField (NF) (see: http://nationalfield.com (accessed 6 August 2013)) which is a social networking programme for private companies. Mr Saatchi is also the son of the writer, Josephine Hart, and the well-known advertising guru, Maurice Saatchi. Edward graduated from Oxford with a degree in literature before moving to the Sorbonne in France to read philosophy and economics. He is a self-confessed 'Obama Nut' and, in 2008, volunteered to help with Barack Obama's presidential election campaign. Whilst engaged as a volunteer on the Obama road show, he met two technology experts, Justin Lewis and Aharon Wasserman, who had developed an internal social network to save time on the endless meetings to report back on campaign calls and fundraising. Edward recognized the possibilities of the software which looks unashamedly like Facebook (a senior Facebook director is on the board). He makes the point that most companies have an intranet but that these are often out of date and used as a top down tool. Email is another problem with information overload and 'copied in' emails swamping inboxes with often hundreds of snippets of information. Edward wanted a system that created more of a community feel and a place for employees to ask questions, solve puzzles, and to float new ideas. He dismisses the notion of the flat hierarchy, which runs against conventional wisdom that 'flat is better'. He insists that a hierarchy can actually help people, as information can then be funnelled to the correct place. He feels that, apart from his mobile phone, what gets him up in the morning is the belief he is making working life that bit more tolerable. He points to the depressing life of an office worker,

> who genuinely feels that they are going to work nine to five and that their life starts when they leave the office. I've always thought that that was just terrible. I think that you can use technology to make that person's life more interesting and more fun.

His ideas are fast catching on, with the organization turning over US$1 million last year and a Europe launch planned for 2012. His unfailing confidence in his product is best summed up by his remarks, 'the power of social media has brought down dictators'. He sees this power of community being harnessed by forward thinking companies as a way of capturing ideas and enthusiasm from across the business.

Sources

McAndrew, D. (2012) 'McAndrew Meets ... Edward Saatchi'. *Professional Manager*, (February/March): 20–23.

Moulds, J. (2011) 'Edward Saatchi's Private Social Network Aims to Make Businesses More Democratic'. *Daily Telegraph*, 1 October 2011.

Urwin, R. (2011) 'Son of Saatchi: Edward, the British Mark Zuckerberg'. *The Evening Standard*, 19 October 2011.

Questions

1. Can you think of any reasons why individuals like Saatchi and Facebook's Zuckerberg are successful?

2. What do you think of his idea to make companies more 'social and community-like'?

3. Do you think evangelical zeal as demonstrated by such characters as Saatchi is an aspect of EI or simply evidence of an enthusiastic person?

What is EI?

Having examined the concepts of intelligence and emotion, the way is now clearer to combine these ideas into 'EI'. The idea that some individuals had the ability to cope better than others in everyday life was not a new one when Salovey and Mayer's paper (1990) was published. As far back as the early 1950s, for example, David Wechsler defined intelligence as, 'the aggregate or global capacity of the individual to act purposefully, to think rationally, and to deal effectively with his environment' (Wechsler 1958:7). Within this definition, he included a number of social and personal factors and suggested these were a key indicator of a person's ability to succeed in life. Even earlier, Thorndike and Stein talked about 'social intelligence' as the 'ability to understand and manage people' (1937:275). Indeed, Chapter 7, covering charisma and Transformational leadership, has the ability to master the emotions of others as well as oneself at its heart. So perhaps it should not have come as a surprise that material focused exclusively and explicitly on emotional manipulation should be as successful as it was.

With Gardner's work attracting attention, the way was clear for psychologists to investigate other areas of human abilities for potential benefit. Mayer and Salovey basically challenged the view that emotions hindered decision making. It was fashionable, and some would argue still is, to suggest that business logic demands a task-focused approach in which emotion has no part. Fineman (1996:291) puts it thus:

> Deeply rooted in Western (especially male) cultural beliefs about the expression of emotion is the belief that organizational order and manager/worker efficiency are matters of the rational, that is non-emotional, activity. Cool strategic thinking is not to be sullied by messy feelings. Efficient thought and behaviour tame emotion. Accordingly good organizations are places where feelings are managed, designed out or removed.

Mayer and Salovey begged to differ and contended that experiencing and expressing positive and negative emotions was necessary for personal growth and could make individuals better decision makers if they could recognize and harness emotions. They suggested that, by understanding more about our emotions, we could take more effective control of our bodies, which, in turn, would produce better outcomes when dealing with others and ourselves.

 Pause for thought

Consider for a moment this view of the role of emotion in decision making. Do you think emotions have any part to play or should a business seek to take a rational approach to decision making?

How about an individual? Should individuals recognize emotional elements to their own decisions?

For example, when making a decision about which car to buy, the price is only one factor considered. You may want to think about how you would feel in a particular car. A prestigious brand, such as Mercedes or Alfa Romeo, trade on the feeling that owning such a car offers an owner. Similarly, when making a decision about which wedding ring to buy, would a groom think about how his prospective bride will feel about presenting her with a cheap looking band?

In both cases, any car will achieve its purpose of moving you from A to B. Likewise, the wedding band is a symbolic gesture. So why not chose the cheapest runabout or marry with a piece of bent wire?

Their 'ability' model (Mayer and Salovey 1997) has evolved into four 'branches' (see: Figure 11.3) with each of the branches tied into an individual's other psychological attributes and overall personality. These abilities suggest the following attributes:

1. Perceiving emotion: This examines the extent to which an individual has the ability to recognize emotion in others by examining their face, voice, and other non-verbal signals, such as their posture. This may be harder than it appears and requires an individual to be able to distinguish minute subtleties in the tilt of the head, the smile, or the tone of voice.

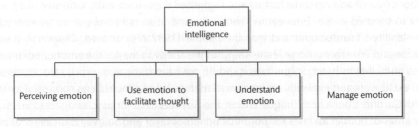

Figure 11.3 Four-branch model of emotional intelligence

For example, think about the difference between tears of joy running down a face and tears of sorrow. What clues would you look for so you could determine which of these you were observing? In a leadership sense, this could mean looking for signs of stress or confusion in a follower when faced with a challenging task.

2. Use of emotion: This is about using emotion to help with decision making rather than accepting that emotion clouds judgement. For example, some tasks or activities may be helped by using a type of mood. A task that needs focus and attention to detail may benefit from having a composed and a calm approach. Think about a goal kicker in rugby facing the howls and catcalls of the crowd as he steadies himself for the match winning conversion. He will have to slow his heart rate, clear his mind, and focus his entire being on the contact point of the ball. Alternatively, a rock guitarist just about to step onto the stage will be getting excited and 'up' for the performance. For leaders, this means ensuring you are in the right frame of mind for a particular task. For example, a calm, considered approach may be the best approach when disciplining an errant team member.

3. Understand emotion: Grasping the development and evolution of emotional states in others is a key to being able to manage relationships. This is about being able to understand what emotions are being seen, how these interact with each other, and how emotions change over a period of time. This ability is said to increase in line with a person's language skills and ability for predictive thought, both of which develop over time. An example might be a young child making breakfast for her mother in order to please her on Mother's Day. The child may even consider asking for a treat in return for her behaviour! Leaders may want to think through the consequences of their actions. For a leader, this may mean thinking through the reaction of the team to the news they will have to work over the weekend—again.

4. Manage emotions: This is where most individuals not familiar with the full implications of this approach see EI as being located. This branch requires the individual to be able to either suppress or generate a different behavioural response to a given situation than that which they would 'normally' do. So, for example, on becoming exasperated with a customer or frustrated by the lack of progress during a call centre conversation, the emotional response may be to scream or experience growing anger. Regulating and managing emotion in this sense means perhaps counting to 10 or smiling sweetly to an annoying client.

These four areas combine to offer the individual 'the ability to monitor one's own and others' feelings and emotions, to discriminate among them, and to use this information to guide one's thinking and actions' (Salovey and Mayer 1990:189)

Goleman's approach

Goleman took these ideas and refined them into a set of simple, easy to grasp stages. In addition, Mayer, Salovey, and Caruso developed a 'test' to measure the level of an individual's EI (see: MSCEIT V2.0; Mayer et al. 2003). This meant that the broader population could be introduced to these ideas and measure themselves in a 'scientific' way. Essentially, Goleman's approach was to combine Salovey's view of EI as a set of abilities into a more 'mixed' model that uses abilities, attributes, and other properties of an individual (Aslan and Erkus 2008)

1. Self-awareness: Goleman considers this first stage to be about 'mindfulness'. He talks about recognizing emotions in ourselves as the emotion begins to happen. He considers this to be the cornerstone of EI and makes the assertion that 'people with greater certainty about their feelings are better pilots of their lives' (1996:43). Other terms that coincide with this initial stage could be self-observation, or the ability to hover over one's self and 'see' the emotion developing. Put simply, it is about knowing what mood you are in at any given time. However, the challenge remains as to what extent individuals can either recognize their own emotions correctly or be honest enough to accept the emotion they feel at any given point. Major D. S. Gilbert-Smith, the decorated army officer and ex-Scottish Rugby Union player, says, 'leadership starts with oneself, learning to know and control oneself first, so that then and only then can one control and lead others' (2003:10).

2. Managing emotions: Here the emphasis in Goleman's early work seems to focus on the ability to control negative, powerful emotions that threaten to sweep us away with their force. For example, in his book he mentions 'The Rage Rush' (1996:60) and he sees this as further enabling individuals to cope better with life's challenges and as the next step towards control over one's emotions. Again, the individual's tendency towards neuroticism is worth considering as this may predispose some to this area more than others. The skills needed here are quite extensive, as the leader may need to control carefully not only language but also the non-verbal signals so important in convincing others as to the 'true' meaning of words.

 Pause for thought

Consider for a moment the time you geared yourself up for a fight with a shop whose product you bought that did not live up to expectations. You set your mind that you are going to tear a strip off the first shop assistant you meet. You begin with getting clear in your mind what you are going to say, you charge in brandishing the offending article and ask to 'see the manager'. What happens, as you demand a replacement and your money back, when the person facing you smiles and says, 'yes of course, here you go'? Does your mood change? Do you smile back, say thank you, and feel happier?

---

3. Motivating oneself: This step refers to the skill or ability to use emotions to motivate oneself towards a given goal. It also covers recognizing the dangers of emotions that can hamper progress or even stop a person from functioning correctly. Anxiety felt before your driving test is one example and the 'trick', according to Goleman, is to use this to help improve performance rather than allow it to take over and control our minds. Stage fright and the growing sense of panic as we attempt a difficult exam are more examples where emotion hampers rather than helps our performance.

These first three abilities combine to produce what Salovey said was at the core of EI, namely 'the ability to process emotion-laden information competently and to use it to guide cognitive activities like problem-solving and to focus energy on required behaviours' (Salovey et al. 2002:159). Goleman then moves the argument in to the social environment:

4. Recognizing emotion in others: Essentially this involves being able to read the subtle changes in facial expression, body language, and tone of voice in others correctly so

that you can understand what they are feeling. Empathy or the ability to 'read' people has been discussed in the context of charismatic leaders in Chapter 7. Those lacking this ability, alexithymia (Taylor and Taylor 1997), have great difficulty in describing their own emotions or identifying emotions in others. This gives them great difficulty in forming relationships with other people as they cannot gauge their impact on others or alter their approach to suit a partner's thoughts. However, a leader with this ability can choose to influence followers by building trust because the follower may feel the leader understands their perspective.

5. Handling relationships: This final ability moves somewhat away from the individual to the dyadic or group relations. Here, Goleman is possibly concerned with social intelligence which he sees as the ability to operate with others in group and social settings that we encounter daily. In his later books (Goleman et al. 2002; Goleman 2006), Goleman seems to focus more on this ability with a further assertion that it is the secret of many successful leaders. Albrecht (2005) supports this view by claiming that social intelligence is a form of social radar that helps a person understand the needs of others.

It is by combining these skills that a person may master EI and, hence, according to Goleman, become more successful in terms of managing their relationships with others, providing all parties with an increased sense of achievement and fulfilment. Essentially, the proposition is that noticing, understanding, and manipulating one's own and others' emotions can have a positive effect on the outcome of any given task.

 Case study   Mo Farah

Mohammed (Mo) Farah, along with Jessica Ennis, was one of the poster faces for the London Olympic Games of 2012. He was born in 1983 in Mogadishu, Somalia, and came to Great Britain aged eight, barely able to speak a word of English. In 2013 he became the 'double double' 5,000 metres and 10,000 metres Olympic and World Champion.. As well as holding numerous titles and records, Mo is married to Tania, has a daughter called Rhianna, and spends most of his year training in the USA with a number of high profile African athletes. Mo puts his success down to being inspired by Paula Ratcliffe, herself a highly successful athlete who runs the longer distance of the marathon. He has said that her words to him, 'Go out and be brave—just believe in yourself', just before his World Championship run, helped him overcome a series of negative thoughts crowding his mind as he approached the finish line with one of his competitors closing rapidly.

He is also clear about his faith and often has some difficult decisions to make about the competing demands of being a world-class athlete, and its attendant disciplines, and being a practicing Muslim. For example, he says: 'I'm a Muslim, so I observe the five pillars of Islam. During Ramadan, fasting isn't always the easiest thing for a sportsman. It's quite difficult to fit it in with your training. But that's what you have to do. You learn self-control.'

Looking forward to his home city of London's Olympic Games, where he was one of the gold medal favourites, he said this: 'I get really excited thinking about the London Olympics, but as an athlete I need to take one race at a time. What's most important for me now is that I stay focused.' He completed an unbelievable double by winning both the 5,000 metres and the 10,000 metres races.

On 25 March 2012, he supported the Sport Relief Mile, a charity event aimed at raising funds for disadvantaged people. He says this: 'A mile really isn't very far, which is why everyone should get involved. I'm not asking you to sprint the whole way or break any records, I'm just asking you to be

(Continued...)

there, ready and willing to show support for those who need it. London is gearing up for a fantastic year of sport and what better way to start it than with the Sport Relief Mile.'

Sources

Broadbent, Rick (2012)' Inspired by Paula and Ali, Clock is Ticking on Quest to Go Full Distance'. *The Times*, 13 January 2012.

John, Emma (2010) 'This much I know: Mo Farah'. *The Observer*, 10 October 2010.

Milmo, Cahal (2010) 'How Britain's Athletics Hero Escaped the Chaos of Somalia'. *The Independent*, 29 July 2010.

Randhawa, M Kiran (2012) 'Mo Farah races to support Standard's running campaign'. *London Evening Standard*, 7 March 2012.

www.mofarah.com (accessed 6 August 2013).

Questions

1. Do you think Mo Farah is emotionally intelligent?

2. What impact do you think emotions have on elite sportspeople?

3. Is there any correlation between how a sportsperson approaches a race and a leader trying to achieve a task?

Other perspectives

It would be naïve to consider Goleman's work as the sole contributor to the study of EI and, of course, although associated with the popularizing of the idea, he was not involved in any of the early theorizing of the concept. Cooper and Sawaf's model (1997) is based on four cornerstones:

1. Emotional literacy, or becoming familiar with your emotions.

2. Establishing an 'authentic' (see: Chapter 8) presence and building trust.

3. Having emotional depth, which means acting with integrity.

4. Emotional alchemy, which is a curious mix of intuition and the ability to spot opportunities.

Within this broad framework lie another 14 separate factors, which some (Cherniss 2000) feel overcomplicate the concept. Ashkanasy and Jordan (2008) present a five-level model of emotion in a much broader organizational context. So, their model ranges from 'within person EI', through interpersonal dimensions to groups, finally locating EI in organizational leadership. They feel that as the context changes so do the requirements and competencies associated with EI. Bar-On (1997, 2007) defines EI as 'an array of non-cognitive capabilities, competencies, and skills that influence one's ability to succeed in coping with environmental demands and pressures' (1997:14). His work has moved him to develop a measure for EI, the Bar-On Emotional Quotient Inventory™ (the EQ-i™), which is predicated on his claim that EI can be improved and developed by appropriate outside intervention. His model contains three distinct competences: understanding of self and others; being able to relate to others;

being able to adapt to environmental demand and changes. He shares Goleman's view that those with higher levels of EI, and hence having a higher Emotional Quotient (EQ), are able to manage stress better, solve problems, and so offer greater potential for success in life. Bar-On's EQ-i test is a self-report style questionnaire comprising 130 items that produce an individual 'score' across the five areas of his model. However, Day and Carroll (2008) were able to show it was possible for job applicants to 'fake' or manipulate the results of this test. For an overview of more 'tests', see the paper by Mayer et al. (2008).

 Case study   Tracey Emin

Tracey Emin (1963–) is an eminent British artist born in Croydon, London, but brought up in the seaside town of Margate in Kent. She is of mixed race with an English Romanichal mother and a Turkish Cypriot father (he was married to a woman other than her mother and divided his time between his two families). The family home was a hotel in Margate. Unfortunately, the business failed and this resulted in a period of hardship for the Emin family. Although regarded now as a 'grande dame' of the British art scene, Tracey has previously been thought of as a highly controversial figure.

Her early work does not survive as most was either destroyed by her or in the Momart warehouse fire of 2004. The work that brought her to the attention of the public and media was a blue tent covered with appliquéd names of individuals. The exhibit was titled *Everyone I Have Ever Slept with 1963–1995* and was shown in 1995 at the South London Gallery. The deliberately provocative title included reference to her sexual partners but also relatives she slept with as a child, such as her twin brother, and her two aborted children. The ambivalent nature of the piece was not, she said, about sex but about intimacy. She continued with this theme, and her 1999 Turner Prize shortlisted exhibit was called *My Bed*. This was an unmade bed with stained sheets and a number of dirty, used items such as knickers strewn around. Despite its notoriety, it was bought by Charles Saatchi for a reported £40,000. Tracey said the bed was in this state because she had stayed in it feeling suicidal. Other works by her have commanded fees at auction of over £130,000.

As her fame spread, she became more sought after by the Establishment and the tabloid press. In an interview with *The Independent* newspaper, she remarks about this increased attention: I feel like everything is going awry, like it's definitely not right. I feel the pressure again, and I hate it with all my soul. I feel the enormous pressure of failure. I feel like I am not at peace with my own mind, like I am being torn apart.

Given that two of her most famous pieces, along with more than 100 other 'Britart' works, were destroyed in the Momart warehouse fire of 2004, Emin is sanguine, commenting: 'The news comes between Iraqi weddings being bombed and people dying in the Dominican Republic in flash floods, so we have to get it into perspective.' However, she was less restrained when considering the general public's reaction to the fire, saying: 'The majority of the British public have no regard or no respect to what me and my peers do, to the point that they laugh at a disaster like a fire.' Adding for good measure: 'It is just not fair and it's not funny and it's not polite and it's bad manners. I would never laugh at a disaster like that—I just have some empathy and sympathy with people's loss.'

Tracey is well known for her charity work, either selling her own works or working as a 'celebrity auctioneer'. She designed a poster for the 2012 London Olympic Games, and she is currently the Professor of Drawing at the Royal Academy and a mentor for young British designers.

Sources

BBC (2004) 'Emin Anger Over Public "Sniggers"'. *BBC online*, 30 May 2004.

Emin, T. (2006) *Tracey Emin: Works 1963–2006*. London: Rizzoli.   (Continued...)

Emin, T. (2009) '"My Head and Face Became a Flash, My Body Strangely Sexy" My Life In A Column'. *The Independent*, 19 February 2009.

Meek, J. (2004) 'Art into Ashes'. *The Guardian*, 23 September 2004.

http://emininternational.com/ (accessed 6 August 2013).

Questions

1. Would you consider Emin to be a 'leader' in any sense?
2. What comments would you make about her 'intelligence'?
3. Could you consider her to be 'emotionally intelligent'?

The 'dark side' of EI

In a similar vein to the challenges posed by those who would use charisma to further their own desires rather than those of the wider community (see: Chapter 7), the use of EI can be used for anti, rather than pro, social reasons. Kilduff et al. (2010) suggest that, just as fiction points to characters such as Shakespeare's Iago and Machiavelli's Prince, who manipulate the emotions of others for their own devious ends, organizations must beware of individual managers who practice similar tactics. They suggest that, 'those high in EI, given competition for scarce resources typical in many organizations, are likely to use their skills to advance their own interests even at the expense of others in the workplace' (2010:130). The point being that, whilst having an ability in a certain area is one thing, the norms and values of the so-endowed individual need to be carefully considered because an individual may choose to use their talents differently from how proponents of EI suggest (e.g. Boyatzis and McKee 2005). The suggestion is that, if a person can correctly identify another's emotional state (e.g. sadness), they can incorporate this information into their own thinking and, by using appropriate words and gestures, manipulate the other person to their own ends. Those with strong EI abilities may, 'display emotions that are appropriate and conducive to achieving objectives, but their emotional presentation may differ from their inner feelings' (Kilduff et al. 2010:133).

The implication is that the use of EI as a tool is more likely when the individual is facing a situation with a high emotional content, such as an appraisal, job interview, or perhaps a contentious meeting. Furthermore, those with high EI are likely to focus on those individuals who are strategically important to them, which could mean subordinates looking for clues in their line manager and immediate colleagues, or managers looking for clues in their rivals and subordinates. An office worker, noticing her boss is feeling a little quieter than usual, may ask if everything is ok, thus moving closer in terms of relationship. This is not necessarily manipulative but it could have consequences when the manager is making decisions about who gets to participate in exciting new projects.

Another example may be a manager negotiating with another manager from a different department over the allocation of resources, such as the annual budget or production target. The high EI manager may be able to spot signs of stress or anxiety in their rival, which they could exploit to gain an advantage in the negotiations. This may enable them to gain additional resources or reduce a pressured target. Hogan and Holland, (2003), using the Holland Personality Inventory (HPI), examined occupationally successful individuals for their ability to identify signs that another individual was looking to collaborate or compete. They found a correlation between these two aspects.

In terms of the superior/subordinate relationship, a high EI manager may be able use these skills to manipulate a subordinate's lack of power or desire for power. For example, consider a project that requires the team to work late or over the weekend, a high EI manager may be able to persuade those seeking power that completion of the task would 'look good with the boss'; those lacking power may be browbeaten by such comments as, 'well if you don't do it I'm sure I can find someone who will', followed by a stony glare and silence.

In terms of managing emotions, this is not a revolutionary concept. Consider the example of the shop assistant faced with an angry customer: the shop assistant's training may be the *real* reason for the smile, which may override her authentic emotion, which could be to shout back at the aggressive customer. After all, she was not the one who bought the wrong sized dress! In this case, the smile is merely the means to an end, and carries no more significance in that it does not correlate to the individual's emotion, but it does convince the customer that she is being listened to. This ability to manage behaviour has links to impression management (for example see: Grant and Mayer 2009) and, as pointed out, 'because impression management can be mistaken for good citizenship, an individual who is acutely aware of the emotional climate in a particular situation and who is able to regulate self-emotion and manage the emotions of others, may be able to advance self-interest while gaining credit for good citizenship behaviour' (Kilduff et al. 2010:137; see also: Chapter 9).

Pillai (1996) goes further in suggesting that some high EI leaders can actively create situations that accentuate their strengths and make them appear to be charismatic. Recalling the suggestion in Chapter 7, whereby the social setting for the emergence of charismatic leaders was briefly discussed, the idea from Pillai is that high EI leaders may exploit a situation that generates emotional responses in others. They can either manipulate their own emotions to appear to be calm in a crisis or direct an individual's anger at a situation away from the leader towards their own performance.

All of this conjecture somewhat challenges the rosy world painted by Goleman and his acolytes who promote EI as a positive force capable of improving the lives of those who practice it. This view also suggests a somewhat ludicrous situation with two high EI individuals suspiciously eyeing each other trying to work out if any of their displayed emotions are 'real' or fake.

Criticisms of EI

Goleman's model of EI has been subjected to criticism in the research literature as being unsubstantiated by empirical research (Mayer et al. 2008). This theme is fairly consistent, for example Locke is unequivocal on the matter, stating that EI is 'invalid both because it is not a form of intelligence and because it is defined so broadly' (Locke 2005:425). Their complaint seems to focus on the idea that controlling emotions is not an 'intelligence' but a skill. Other psychologists also side with Locke, and Eysenck makes a broader attack by trying to undermine Gardner's work on multiple intelligences. He feels that labelling 'behaviour' as an 'intelligence' is fundamentally absurd (Eysenck 1998). Indeed it is this battle, between those who favour a more 'scientific' approach to the subject with strict definitions and empirical conclusions underpinned by statistical data, and those who simply want to 'use' the concept, that provides the most polemic debate in this area. Landy (2005) points this out and remarks on the vested interests of both camps with commercial operators keen to promote their books and courses, whilst academics are notoriously parochial with their results and data.

Another dispute lies in the nature of 'measurement' of EI, with Petrides et al. (2004) particularly concerned with the self-reporting nature of the majority of tests and tools used to this end. The difference between a perceived ability and the necessary actual wherewithal to demonstrate such a skill may be wide. A person may judge themself to be endowed with certain talents but may not be able to perform these in the field. The converse may also apply whereby a person has more talent in a given area than they actually believe. Most reasoned debate, though, centres on the belief that EI does give some insights into leadership, but there needs to be more intellectual rigour associated with the research if there is going to be some consensus achieved as to the link between levels of EQ and leadership efficacy.

Summary

Given the rather hyperbolic claims made by Goleman and others as to the efficacy of EI as a means to future health, wealth, and happiness, it is unsurprising that a vociferous, more sceptical counter-view has emerged. Inevitably, there will remain a disconnect between these two camps as, like so many concepts attached to leadership, it remains an ill-defined concept with many different layers and options. Walter et al. (2011:55), having reviewed a significant amount of evidence surrounding EI, summarizes the situation thus: 'evidence does suggest that EI has the potential to help scholars better understand leadership emergence, specific leadership behaviours and leader effectiveness. That said we also believe a lot remains to be accomplished.' Whilst emotions and the use of emotion has a role to play in understanding the methods and mechanisms associated with leadership, Goleman's five stages can only cast a light on part of that. Leadership is more than being able to decide whether to feel happy or sad at any given point.

 Case study   Elizabeth Tudor, Queen Elizabeth I

Elizabeth Tudor was the last of the Tudor monarchs of England, ruling from 1558 until her death in 1603. She was the daughter of Henry VIII and Anne Boleyn. However, her route to the monarchy was not a clear path; she eventually became queen upon the death of her half-sister, Queen Mary. News of Mary's death, on 17 November 1558, reached Elizabeth at Hatfield, England, where she was said to be in the park, resting under an oak tree. Hearing that she was queen, she quoted Psalm 118, line 23, in Latin: 'a Dominum factum est illud, et est mirabile in oculis notris' (it is the Lord's doing, and it is marvellous in our eyes). Her reign coincided with an upsurge in cultural and political development that is fondly remembered in Great Britain as the 'Elizabethan Age'. Elizabeth is now thought of as a charismatic orator and a deft political survivor, in an age when any government was rather chaotic with various real and imagined threats to the monarch.

On her ascension to the throne, Elizabeth inherited a weak and divided country that was regarded by the other European super-powers, Spain and France, as a cultural and political backwater. The economy was not strong, with a debt of over £250,000 owed to European banks charging 14 per cent interest. The country had lost its sense of identity and was riven by religious and political suspicion. However, by the end of her reign, her deft political skills and strong personal character had created a 'golden' age with England becoming a world super-power and the dominant political, military, and cultural force in the civilized world.

On 15 January 1559, Elizabeth was crowned by Owen Oglethorpe, Bishop of Carlisle, at Westminster Abbey, a little less than two months after the death of Mary I. The total cost of the celebrations, excluding the coronation banquet, was £16,741 (about £3.5 million today). In common with her predecessors (think about the wedding of Prince William and Catherine in April 2011), Elizabeth knew the importance of a good show, especially for a new monarch who needed to re-affirm her right to the crown. She clearly understood the power of the throne and how to use it to safeguard and enhance her position.

In an age when marriage was used as a political weapon, and despite pressure from her advisers, particularly her chief secretary, William Cecil, Lord Burghley, Elizabeth refused to marry. She had a close relationship with Robert Dudley, Earl of Leicester, and was not averse to using the promise of marriage for diplomatic purposes, but she asserted her independence until the end of her life. The situation came to head in 1588 after Elizabeth rejected a marriage proposal from Philip II of Spain. The indignant Spanish king, incensed by English piracy and forays into 'his' New World territories, sent his much-feared Armada to raid England. The Armada provided a 'Falklands' moment for Elizabeth that Mrs Thatcher would also benefit from some 400 years later. As the powerful fleet approached, Elizabeth's naval captains waited and, aided by inclement weather in the Channel, completely routed the Spanish.

Whilst she waited for news of the sea battle, Elizabeth travelled to Tilbury and addressed troops gathered ready for the predicted invasion. She delivered her most famous oratory, recounted thus:

> therefore I am come amongst you, as you see, at this time, not for my recreation and disport, but being resolved, in the midst and heat of the battle, to live and die amongst you all; to lay down for my God, and for my kingdom, and my people, my honour and my blood, even in the dust. I know I have the body but of a weak and feeble woman; but I have the heart and stomach of a king, and of a king of England too, and think foul scorn that Parma or Spain, or any prince of Europe, should dare to invade the borders of my realm ...

With the victory, the stage was clear for England to become the dominant naval and imperial power. Elizabeth recognized the opportunity and used her skill as a master of political science to manoeuvre her opponents and supporters to her will. She inherited her father's supremacist view of the monarchy, but showed great wisdom by refusing to antagonize Parliament directly. She acquired undying devotion from her advisers, who were constantly perplexed by her habit of waiting to the last minute to make decisions. She used this approach not as a method of procrastination but as a tactic to gain advantage. She manipulated the various factions (instead of being used by them), playing one off another until the exhausted combatants came to her for resolution of their grievances. Yet, she managed to enjoy almost unrivalled political power, whilst still maintaining the devotion of the whole of English society.

The later years of Elizabeth's reign are sometimes referred to as a Golden Age, with Shakespeare and Marlowe penning their life's work, the empire growing, and England slowly becoming richer. However, during this time, England and Elizabeth faced several major trials, including the growing threat of her cousin, Mary, Queen of Scots, who had a strong and legitimate (especially in the eyes of Catholics) claim to the throne of England. Elizabeth knew Mary was a threat and, eventually, Elizabeth signed her death warrant. Mary was executed in 1587, at Fotheringhay Castle.

Her legacy is one that is disputed by some whilst others remain convinced of her position as one of the founders of the modern Great Britain. Her expansionist agenda helped to lay the foundations for

(Continued...)

Victorian growth, and Elizabeth established an English church that helped shape a national identity that remains in place today. She died on 24 March 1603 at the ripe old age of 70, having ruled for 45 years. Her funeral was marked by the words of John Stow, a journalist of the time:

> Westminster was surcharged with multitudes of all sorts of people in their streets, houses, windows, leads and gutters, that came out to see the obsequy, and when they beheld her statue lying upon the coffin, there was such a general sighing, groaning and weeping as the like hath not been seen or known in the memory of man.

She was undoubtedly loved and revered by her subjects to the extent that her ascension to the throne on 17 November was marked and celebrated for some 200 years after her death. Even today, she is held as an iconic leader and symbol of national pride, venerated and celebrated in paintings, statues, and other cultural artefacts.

Sources

Collinson, Patrick (2007) *Elizabeth I*. Oxford: Oxford University Press.

Doran, Susan (2003) *Queen Elizabeth I*. London: British Library.

Howard, Newton H. (2007) *The Legacy of Queen Elizabeth I of England*. London: London University Press.

Loades, David (2003) *Elizabeth I: The Golden Reign of Gloriana*. London: The National Archives.

Weir, Alison (1999) *Elizabeth the Queen*. London: Pimlico.

Questions

1. To what extent would Elizabeth have recognized the term 'EI'?
2. Considering the 'dark side' of EI, what evidence is there that Elizabeth was not averse to manipulating emotions to her own ends?
3. Would Elizabeth have become as 'successful' if she had been born today and become a board director of a FTSE 100 company?

Assignment—3,000 words

Here are two alternative questions:
1. To what extent does the concept of EI explain why individuals who lack formal academic qualifications are able to inhabit leadership roles? Consider, for example, Richard Branson, Lord Alan Sugar, or Sarah Palin.
2. 'Women are more emotionally intelligent than men so they make better leaders.' What response would you give to this statement?

Further reading

Dann, Jill (2008) *Emotional Intelligence*. London, Hodder Education.
This is a very straightforward 'instant manager' book. It gives a quick overview of the subject but focuses most of the contents to applying the idea to the workplace. There are some practical and useful ideas but it does not have any critical debate around the subject. A useful overview but somewhat simplistic in terms of its academic analysis.

Hill, Dan (2007) *Emotionomics: Winning Hearts and Minds*. Edina, MN: Adams Business & Professional.
This book is written for anyone interested in why people make buying decisions and it proposes that emotion is at the heart of this decision. It is not an academic read but aimed at a 'practical' market interested in using emotions to help convince individuals. Given the debate about 'dark side' of EI, it is an instructive read.

Meyer, John P. and Allen, Natalie J. (1997) *Commitment in the Workplace: Theory, Research, and Application* (Advanced Topics in Organizational Behaviour). London: SAGE Publications.
Written at the height of the EI 'boom', the book makes some interesting links between employee commitment and the emotional attachment to an organization. The authors also discuss the idea of the 'over-committed' employee who blindly accepts the organization's will and does not question what is being asked. The depth of emotional commitment makes this step a dangerous one as it can make the organization blind to external threats.

Diversity and leadership

After reading this chapter you will:

● Explore some of the theoretical discussions underpinning diversity and discrimination.

● Consider the role of women and their influence on leadership development.

● Start to explore your own position on diversity, culture, and the implications for leaders in an increasingly complex and diverse workplace.

Introduction

This chapter is a no win chapter. This means there will be readers who will feel that, rather than being relegated to a chapter or text box, diversity in leadership should be incorporated into every single chapter, and for it to be placed as a discrete item almost says it all—'Here we go again! Diversity is a topic that sits outside the mainstream when it should be integral to everything we do.' Chin makes the point that 'some books devote one or two chapters to women and culture, allowing the remainder of the chapters to ignore diversity' (2010:150)—for example, Northouse (2010) chapter 13 is titled 'Women and Leadership'. On the other hand, there will be those who dispute this perspective and feel strongly that diversity has been ignored for so long that it needs 'special' and specific attention, (ironically Chin makes her comments in a 'Special Issue'). This chapter considers why these different positions exist and attempts to explore the underpinning social constructs that lie at the heart of 'diversity' as a phenomenon.

One of the reasons for this book being commissioned was to attempt to write a text that moved away from a North American perspective and to incorporate some more European and Eastern ideas on leadership. The case studies in the book have been chosen to illustrate the breadth of fields and characters that inhabit the leadership frame rather than presenting the 'great and the good'. This approach has been taken to enable readers to explore their own context of leadership and to make an attempt to move away from the heroic, Great Man vision of what leadership encompasses. As organizations become more complex, with links stretching around the globe, and more dependent upon their stakeholders for legitimacy to trade, as communities become ever more diverse and multi-cultural, the need to understand the implications for leadership has grown (for example see: Mumford et al. 2000)

However, there may be a darker, more sinister reason that sits behind the motivation to write a book that has more of a Eurocentric perspective—one that links closely to the theme of diversity. That reason is discrimination, and the motivation may be the author's perception that the North American view is in some way wrong, inadequate, or simply 'not the way we do things'. The chapter will explore some of these themes and offer a theoretical insight into how leadership, diversity, and discrimination occur and operate.

What is 'diversity'?

Diversity has many different associations. It can be attached to the theme of ecology and reflect the health of an ecosystem—often referred to as 'biodiversity'. In business, marketers will be familiar with the term when used in the context of developing a strategy that is intended to expand the organization into new markets and/or new products. Those with a financial bent will use the word when referring to a portfolio of investments that is spread wide to reduce risk. Diversity, in any of these contexts, suggests a positive move and one that should be encouraged. Similarly, we are going to examine the term when considering its impact on leadership, and how both diverse leaders and diverse followers present challenges for academics and practitioners by modifying some of the underpinning beliefs we have about the nature of leadership and of followers. However, diversity in leadership is also seen as a 'good thing'—a strategy to be encouraged—as, by being 'diverse', organizations can avoid some of the negative aspects of having a leadership paradigm that only reflects part of their stakeholders' values. Closely linked to this theme is the concept of discrimination which, to a degree, reflects the current cause for concern among the public, academics, and practitioners that something is 'wrong' with leadership and perhaps a lack of diversity is to blame for the series of poor decisions that have engulfed the world since 2008.

Implicit, and sometimes explicit, in the concern about how poor decisions are made by financial institutions, government agencies, and despotic leaders is the thought that it is down to men. It is the leadership style of men, often seen as fuelled by testosterone, that results in an aggressive, non-participative, selfish approach. This model excludes women from senior positions and the consequence is that leadership becomes seen as a 'male' occupation. Commentators, such as Eagly and Karau (2002), are concerned that organizations perceive women less favourably than men as potential occupants of leadership roles and evaluate behaviour that fulfils the prescriptions of a leader role less favourably when it is enacted by a woman. This means a self-fulfilling prophecy ensues of men with a stranglehold over leadership roles, which, in turn, means leadership becomes defined in male terms and a narrow view of what a 'successful leader' is becomes entrenched in organizational culture. This narrow view can lead to institutionalized prejudice about the qualities needed to be a leader, excluding those that do not have these attributes for such positions. Naturally, if being a 'man' is part of that view then women will be subtly ruled out of promotions and leadership roles. Whilst direct and indirect discrimination is illegal in the United Kingdom, it can be difficult to shift perceptions that have built up over many generations.

Discrimination, as defined by Allport (1954:51) when he cites the United Nations, is 'any conduct based on a distinction made on grounds of natural or social categories, which have no relation either to individual capacities or merits or to the concrete behaviour of the individual person'. In a legal sense, the Equality Act (2010) makes it illegal in England, Wales, and Scotland to discriminate on the grounds of age, religion, sex, sexual orientation, race, gender reassignment, disability, marital status, pregnancy, and maternity. One outcome of this is to potentially increase the range of individuals in leadership positions. However, the very fact we should need an Act of Parliament to guarantee something that most would agree is a vital part of any decent society, should begin to raise questions.

Pause for thought

1. How do you describe people like you?
2. Why do you think a mature, civilized society needs to legislate for fairness?
3. What could be some of the implications for leaders in modern organizations?

This Act was brought in to guarantee basic rights for almost every member of a modern, diverse society. However, in leadership terms, we should be thinking even broader than these attributes to consider fully the impact of leading in an age when organizations engage with a huge range of stakeholders. The National Council for Voluntary Organizations (NCVO) defines diversity in the context of organizations as, 'a successfully diverse workforce is one that contains people at all levels who have a range of different characteristics and who have been recruited on the basis of their abilities and competence to do the job' (NCVO 2012). In leadership terms, this can present the leader with many challenges as this means dealing with different people with different skills, needs, and wants consistently and fairly.

Social identity theory

One of the reasons behind the need for an Act of Parliament to guarantee fairness in our society can, perhaps, be explained by examining a theory drawn from the world of social psychology, called social identity theory. This theory also helps to explain the idea of the 'in-group' outlined in Chapter 9 when leader–member exchange theory was reviewed. This approach to leadership suggests leaders and followers form two different groups called the 'in-group' and the 'out-group'.

The idea of social identity theory, suggested by the Polish/British sociologist, Henri Tajfel, and his student, John Turner, takes the starting point that, in general, individuals are driven to develop a positive image of themselves and look for opportunities to build self-esteem. One way of doing this is to associate with other individuals to reinforce and build on this sense of 'self', possibly by affiliating one's self with a group. This association becomes a closed feedback loop which gathers strength by suggesting your group is 'better than the rest' and, because you are part of this group, you must also be 'better than the rest'. Of course, the natural extension of this is to develop further the idea of superiority by denigrating anyone not in your group—thus, in and out-groups emerge. As Tajfel puts it: 'the evaluation of one's own group is determined with reference to specific other groups through social comparison in terms of value laden attributes and characteristics. Positively discrepant comparisons between in-group and out-group produce high prestige, negatively discrepant comparisons between in-group and out-group result in low prestige' (Tajfel and Turner 1986:16).

This means, by showing favouritism to those perceived as being in your group, and by discriminating against those in the out-group, an individual builds self-esteem. This can be seen in any number of social situations—consider Manchester United and Manchester City football fans, supporters of Labour or Conservative parties, bankers and everybody else! Social experiments such as Jane Elliot's infamous 'blue eyes vs brown eyes' activities of the late 1960s or Zimbardo's prisoners/guards experiment at Stanford University in 1971 (Haney et al. 1973) also demonstrate this alarming tendency to create worlds where everybody is judged against membership of a particular group rather than their individual merits. This 'positive distinctiveness', as Mummendey (1995) calls it, leads to an 'us' vs 'them' situation via a three-stage process:

Stage 1. Categorization: Initially we group up objects and people to help us make sense of the world around us. These categories can be male/female; white/black; Scottish/Welsh, or almost any other taxonomy. Our brains are bombarded by millions of bytes of data every second. This process of classification helps to make sense of the complex world we live in. By simplifying and reducing the world to a set of groups, we can place unknown objects into a category and, hence, understand what that object or person is probably going to be like. So, for example, a person may have read that Yorkshire people are prudent with their money, so a Yorkshire man when encountered is likely to be thought of as 'tight-fisted' or reluctant to spend more than absolutely necessary because that is what Yorkshire men are like according to this ready-made mental map. Additionally, it may be the case that behaviours are interpreted as reinforcing this image and actions that challenge it are ignored.

Stage 2. Identification: Following on from this, we define ourselves in the context of these categories and adopt the behaviours and characteristics of the groups to which we wish to belong. This builds our sense of identity and enables us to function in our social world. We can belong to many different groups at once—for example, a student, a male, a footballer, and a human. As individuals, belonging to a group gives us a sense of perspective. We know who we are because we are in a group who are like us. Our sense of identity becomes bound up in the group and our self-esteem is closely linked to the fortunes of the group. So, when a supporter's football team does well, they feel good about themselves would be an example of this identification. Likewise, if their team loses on a Saturday, they might feel grumpy and deflated on Sunday.

In addition, group members are likely to adopt the behaviour and norms of the group they are closely identifying with. For example, a student may feel they 'have' to live in an untidy manner, not eat properly and spend most of their loan inappropriately because that is what students 'do'.

Stage 3. Comparison: The final part of the process can be the most dangerous and destructive. As part of the process of developing self-worth, building positive images in the group is one option. However, another route is to denigrate others not in your group thus amplifying the differences between your group and other people. Once this process begins it is difficult to arrest, and the opposing groups, if they wish to survive, will begin to complete for resources—such as other non-affiliated members. This means neutral individuals will be canvassed and enticed towards one or the other group. Groups will also compete for food, shelter, and jobs. There will be behavioural codes that mark out one group over another, perhaps clothing brands or other marks to differentiate each other. Remember that differences do not have to be real, just perceived as being different. Individual group members will define themselves by the differences between the groups as well as the similarity inside the group. Depersonalization and stereotyping follow along with any number of negative outcomes such as ostracization, violence, and war.

Pause for thought

Consider these statements:

> Some of my best friends are gay.
>
> On the whole, the educated, the upper classes, the emotionally mature, and the deeply religious are much less racist.
>
> I don't know why but I just don't like men with beards.

1. How do you feel about the sentiments expressed?
2. What insight does social identity theory provide into these opinions?

Whilst social identity theory is not without its critics, for example Huddy (2002) feels the theory oversimplifies group behaviour, it has made a significant impact in social sciences focusing on conflict and hostility between groups. In leadership terms, it can help us to understand why rivalry begins between groups—say the sales team and the accounts department. It can also help to identify the pressures to conform to a particular way of behaving, especially if the leader exhibits certain behaviours. If this behaviour is not congruent with corporate values, or inappropriate, it can be difficult to change without adjusting the whole culture of the group.

 Case study   Oscar Pistorius

Oscar Pistorius, aka 'The Blade Runner' is a South African athlete who, in 2012, became the first disabled athlete to compete alongside able bodied runners at the Olympic Games in London. Oscar was born in 1986 without fibulas, so not long after his birth he had both of his legs amputated just below the knee. In order to enable him to walk as normally as possible, he was fitted with a pair of leg extensions that he quickly mastered. When he was at school, he played many sports and was soon competing against and beating able-bodied people his own age. Eventually he qualified not only for the Para-Olympics of 2008 in Beijing but also for the full South African team. However, The International Association of Athletics Federations (IAAF), the governing body for athletics, ruled his artificial legs gave him an unfair advantage over other athletes and banned him from competing. Their reasoning at the time was that, 'any technical device that incorporates springs, wheels or any other element that provides a user with an advantage over another athlete not using such a device' was illegal. However, Oscar was not to be beaten and he appealed to the Court of Arbitration for Sport, which ruled in his favour. Oscar's mantra is: 'You're not disabled by the disabilities you have, you are able by the abilities you have.'

In February 2012, Pistorius was awarded the Laureus World Sports Award for 'Sportsperson of the Year with a Disability for 2012'. Laureus has previously recognised sporting icons such as Usain Bolt, Michael Schumacher, and Roger Federer with awards. This accolade firmly establishes Pistorius alongside these iconoclastic figures in terms of global fame. Then, in London in August 2012, Oscar progressed through to the semi-finals of the 400 metres event running 45.44sec, although he failed to make the cut for the final. However as he crossed the line in the semi-final, the winner, James Kirani of Grenada, rushed over to him and asked for his name tag pinned to his shirt. The two men exchanged their names with Kirani leading the applause for Oscar. 'Oscar is special,' said James, the world champion, 'It's a memorable moment for me to be out there competing with him.'

Of course, the tragic footnote to this story is that on the night of 13 February 2013 an incident occurred which resulted in the fatal shooting of his girlfriend, Reeva Steenkamp. Pistorius was subsequently charged with her murder, with the trial set for August 2013. Pistorius will contest the charges of premeditated murder, arguing he thought there was an intruder in his home.

Sources

Davies, Gareth A. (2007) 'My Sport: Oscar Pistorius'. *The Telegraph*, 9 May 2007.

Pistorius O. (2009) *Blade Runner* (trans. R. Servadio-Kenan). London: Virgin Books.

Steinberg, Jacob (2012) 'History Boy Oscar Pistorius Signs off with a Smile'. *The Guardian*, 5 August 2012.

Zirin, Dave (2012) 'Oscar Pistorius and "The Dignity of Risk"'. *The Nation*, 6 August 2012.

Questions

1. What does Oscar's story say about diversity and disability?

2. What do you make of Oscar's sporting mantra cited above?

3. Do you think Pistorius's journey has any relevance for leadership?

Leadership and gender

Although diversity is, as Chin (2010) points out, broader than gender differences, the respective merits of males and females as leadership role models is an interesting case study. Consider the early themes associated with trait theory studied in Chapter 2—Carlyle's model of a leader being a 'Great Man'—and link this right through to the disproportionate number of men in senior positions in FTSE companies—only 10 per cent had senior female directors according to Grant Thornton's (2012) review. This apparent lack of females in the literature and in leadership roles has been the subject of much debate, from Kanter (1977), through to the UK Office of National Statistics Report that shows for men, full-time earnings in 2011 averaged £539 per week, compared with £445 per week for women. So, despite years of legislation, and some changes in the public's perception of both men and women, women are still underrepresented in senior jobs and paid less than men, Schien (1976) best sums this up by saying, 'Think Manager—Think Male'.

It is not the case that women do not occupy leadership roles but some writers, such as Helgesen (1990), felt that leadership was being taught and championed as a 'male' career and the only approach for women was to act like men but in dresses and lipstick if they wanted to succeed. Role models for women in the 1980s tended to be either confrontational, aggressive women like Margaret Thatcher (see: Case study in Chapter 6) or overtly sexual women like the singer Madonna. Helgesen (1990) felt this approach was too narrow and, rather than focusing on what women lacked or needed to change in order to fit in, she moved to outline the positive contribution she believed women could make to an organization by being different from the existing paradigm.

 Pause for thought

The essential point of this argument is that 'leadership' is defined using words such as 'forceful', 'dominant', 'powerful', 'driving', 'assertive', and 'competitive'. These are words associated with 'maleness' and, as these are male traits, women cannot be leaders—ergo leaders are male.

Consider your early definition of leadership. What words did you use? Did you use words like these or others such as nurturing, collaborative, empathetic, and faithful? These words are more often associated with feminine traits.

However, the recent issues surrounding the world economy and political upheaval have moved some authors to claim that women actually make better leaders than men and it is only inbuilt institutionalized prejudice that prevents women from attaining senior positions. This view reached its zenith when Alice Sargent, author of *The Androgynous Manager* (1993), used the phrase 'glass ceiling' to describe in metaphorical terms, an invisible barrier that prevents women from attaining high level jobs. Since then, the term has entered the popular lexicon and is often quoted—as in *Women Still Face a Glass Ceiling* (Snowdon 2011) or *Women Can Break Through the Glass Ceiling* (Thompson 2012). Supporters of the claim that women are disadvantaged in the workplace are doubly frustrated as they claim that women actually make better managers and leaders than men. This view is often referred to as 'female advantage theory' (Eagly and Carli 2003). At the heart of this theory is the continuing search for what exactly a leader 'is' and how they achieve results. Supporters of women as leaders feel that women are intrinsically better suited to being a leader because their values, traits, and abilities enable them to influence, persuade, and inspire others in a more sustainable, transformational (see: Chapter 7) manner than men.

This approach quickly came to be seen by some as a panacea for the world's ills, and advocates (e.g. Eagly and Carli 2007a) cite the fact that more and more women are occupying leadership positions in corporate life, government organizations, and world politics. Consider, for example, the German Chancellor, Angela Merkel (see: Case study in Chapter 5), the Malaysian leader, Aung San Suu Kyi (see: Case study in Chapter 7), the British Home Secretary, Teresa May, the American Secretary of State, Hillary Clinton, and the 'face' of the 2012 London Olympics, Jessica Ennis. Adler (1996) likes to use the term, 'feminization' to describe this process. By this she means that previous 'masculine' environments such as banks and other financial institutions, characterized by aggressive sales techniques, long hours, and hard drinking, have become more open to 'female' values such as cooperation and tolerance. This has been caused by the influx of women into previously male-dominated careers. The slow but steady increase of women into high profile roles has attracted the attention of the academic community, who appear to be caught in two minds over the visible practice and a theoretical construct to explain the reality of organizational life. For example, Dobbin and Platz (1986:125) found little conclusive evidence in their meta-survey to 'support the proposition that leader's sex exerts a significant influence on leader behaviour or subordinate satisfaction'.

Supporters of feminine leadership advantage, such as Book (2000), claim that it is women, not men, who have the better skills for dealing with leadership challenges in the twenty-first century. This claim is based on the changing nature of leadership—not the changing nature of women. Traditionally, leadership was based on who was the strongest and best fighter or, as the Industrial Revolution swung forward, as a result of access to technology, capital, or both. This meant men formed the cadre of leaders and leadership became associated with the behaviour and values of those that had the attributes necessary to gain control of the aforementioned resources. Leadership meant getting the job done. The definition of 'successful manager' was a person who demonstrated stereotypical male qualities such as risk taking, assertiveness, and competiveness (for example see: Koenig et al. 2011). This meant that any women who entered the 'profession' were often judged against these attributes. Very often, this produced an exaggerated manifestation of these male behaviours in women along with artefacts to enhance their masculinity such as huge shoulder pads which altered their silhouette to look more like a man.

> **Sex** and **gender** are often terms used interchangeably. However, sociologists influenced by the feminist literature draw a finer distinction between the two. For them, 'sex' refers to biological differences whereas 'gender' is a concept defined by society. Vecchio makes the point (2002:644) that, often, discussions will focus on the measurement of sex—male/female—but discuss gender issues such as masculinity or femininity. For more on this theme, see: Kark and Waismel-Manor (2005) who discuss the themes of masculinity, femininity, and androgyny.

The contention is that leadership has changed as organizations have changed. There is a much greater need to form collaborative partnerships in modern organizations than has previously been the case. Consider, for example, the complex web of relationships that exist among the world's car makers. Volkswagen own Porsche, Volkswagen, Audi, Skoda, SEAT, Daimler, and Ducati—the Italian motorcycle manufacturer—whereas Fiat own Alfa Romeo, Ferrari, Fiat, Maserati, Lancia, and the truck maker, Iveco—this is without considering their joint ventures with Ford, Tata, and Citroen. On top of this is the need to communicate with a progressively more sophisticated workforce and an increasingly sceptical public. This means leaders have to demonstrate the ability to empathize, engage, persuade, and motivate their followers. It is suggested by advocates of female leadership advantage that these are female characteristics and because these values are coming to the fore, 'the gradual erosion of female disadvantage' (Eagly and Carli 2003:810) is now underway—put another way, the age of men and masculine values as the dominant leadership paradigm are coming to an end. The powerful effects of Transformational leadership explored in Chapter 7 and the key components—idealized influence, inspirational motivation, intellectual stimulation, and individualized consideration—are all behaviours that Eagly and her compatriots (Eagly et al. 2003) suggest women exhibit more consistently than men.

However, the path for women to occupy leadership roles consistently across more than traditional 'female' occupations, such as nursing and teaching, at all levels of organizational life is still not a clear route. According to Eagly and Carli (2007b), although there are indeed more women in management positions, women are still under represented in what they refer to as the 'C Suite' (2007b:63). By this they mean that women are generally doing well in terms of representation at lower hierarchical levels but those with real power and influence at a strategic level are still largely men. They put this down not to the 'glass ceiling' but to what they call the 'labyrinth' (2007b:64) of leadership. This metaphor, they claim, is a better allegorical model for the path facing women who attempt to achieve leadership roles because of two barriers placed before them which conspire together to create a societal structure almost impossible for women to navigate through.

Their contention is that women face two social constructs. The first is the general view that women are communal in nature. This means they are seen by society as compassionate, concerned for the well-being of others, gentle, and kind. Men, on the other hand, are seen as 'agentic' and display characteristics such as assertiveness, control, and dominance—precisely the attributes (so popular myth would have it) a leader needs. This means women are 'caught between a rock and a hard place' because, in trying to achieve a leadership position, they are faced with the dilemma of how to behave in order to achieve this. If they act with 'agentic' qualities, they risk being seen as the antithesis of what it means to be a woman, and, recalling the demands of authenticity in Chapter 8, could be regarded as 'false'. If they act communally, the accusation will be they simply do not have the backbone and moral fibre necessary to become a leader.

It is this 'role incongruity' that led Eagly and Karau (2002) to design a theory to explain why women did not fill many of the senior positions available. Their contention is that a group will be judged by society at large by the degree to which the group matches society's broad expectations for them. This means women will be viewed unfavourably as potential leaders because their communal attributes do not align with the 'agentic' requirements of leadership.

However Vecchio (2002) disputes this assertion. He says that neither sex has an inbuilt advantage in terms of leadership and that 'claims of masculine or feminine advantage do not have the data to support them' (2002:655). He asks if males and leaders do actually behave differently when in leadership roles, if males and females differ in terms of their effectiveness as leaders, what their follower behaviour is like, and where research in this area is heading. Having reviewed the claims of the gender advantage that underpins female leader advantage theory, he has suggested there was little conclusive data to support the claims that women make better leaders than men. He goes on to conclude that any evidence that pointed to this was 'highly equivocal' (2002:651).

Eagly and Carli (2003) in turn responded to Vecchio by claiming he was mistaken in how he had analysed the available data. They reintroduced the idea developed by Goldberg (1968) that women are culturally undervalued by both men and women, which leads to inbuilt bias in any empirical study. The debate swings back and forth with Rosette and Tost (2010) supporting the existence of a qualified female leadership advantage. Essentially, the debate still rages with the two opposing groups locked into discussions about research methodologies, the interpretation of data, and the impact of cultural pressures. However, a newer idea has emerged recently that offers an interesting 'third way' for managers of both sexes to consider when examining their own understanding of leadership.

Case study   Baroness Tanni Grey-Thompson DBE

On 26 July 1969, Carys Davina Grey was born. Her sister, Sian, called her 'Tiny'—mispronouncing the word as 'tanni'. The name stuck and we now know her as Baroness Tanni Grey-Thompson, Dame Commander of the Order of the British Empire (DBE), probably the greatest Para-Olympic athlete Great Britain has ever produced. Tanni was born with the congenital condition, spina bifida, which resulted in her having to use a wheelchair from the age of seven. However, despite this, she went on to win 16 medals, including six gold medals over the course of five Paralympic Games, and won the London Marathon six times between 1992 and 2002. Her autobiography is called, *Seize the Day: My Autobiography*. She retired from sport in 2007 moving seamlessly into a more public role where she speaks at events and chairs high profile committees, including acting as president of the 20:20 Commission.

The commission, emerging from an earlier review, was established in 2010 and has the purpose of researching and providing recommendations on what needs to be done to inspire and engage a new generation of civil society leaders. These recommendations are contained in a booklet called, *If not now, then when?*, and include a call to open up pathways into leadership to improve diversity among leaders, and for those who fund or commission the sector to include management and leadership development components in funding agreements.

Speaking at the launch event, Tanni said:

> It has never been more important to challenge civil society organisations, as well as Government and Business, to do more to engage and inspire future civil society leaders. They will be the leaders who will tackle the fall-out from today's challenges, as well as address the challenges of tomorrow. In a time when civil society organisations are faced with the biggest challenges in a generation, I am encouraged by the way these recommendations look to the future and offer a systemic solution to supporting emerging leaders.

Given the large-scale civil unrest experienced in London, Birmingham, and other British cities during the summer of 2011, the commission's analysis and action plan is well timed. Tanni will monitor the progress of the plan via a monitoring panel. The commission also supports a leadership development plan in partnership with Barclays (NCVO Barclays Leadership Programme 2012) which has the strapline: 'Leadership is a craft—you need to learn it.'

In addition, in the year the Olympics were held in London, she launched a new £8 million fund called 'Inclusive Sport' will help to tackle the opportunity gap that sees just one in six disabled adults playing sport regularly, compared to one in three non-disabled adults.

Sources

Davies, G. A. (2012) 'London 2012 Olympics: Tanni Grey-Thompson Supports New Fund to help Promote Sport For Disabled People'. *The Telegraph*, 21 May 2012.

Grey-Thompson, T. (2002) *Seize the Day: My Autobiography*. London: Coronet Books.

Leadership 20:20 - National Council for Voluntary Organizations. http://ncvo-vol.org.uk/ (accessed 8 August 2013).

http://tanni.co.uk/ (accessed 8 August 2013).

Questions

1. How has Baroness Grey-Thompson managed to use her attributes so they are maximized?

2. What difference does it make to have a person, such as Tanni, championing a cause?

3. What does this case study say about the meaning of 'leadership'?

Androgyny

If you consider some of the earlier theories reviewed, especially the Ohio State and situational leadership reviewed in Chapters 4 and 5, these models offer a dichotomous view of leadership with a leader being either task/structure oriented or relational/people oriented. In a similar way, gender and sex have been viewed as either male or female. What is interesting to observe is the evolution of ideas around gender alongside leadership constructs because, just as a view of gender being flexible has emerged in sociology, so too has the idea that leadership is more complex than a simple 'either/or' dichotomy. Maier (1992) was particularly critical of this approach and suggested that the models, by focusing on either tasks or people, falsify reality by making these mutually incompatible constructs, i.e. it is impossible to do both. Hence, a model emerged that attempted to place task/people on a sliding scale which enabled the leader to move between the different approaches.

> The etymology of **androgyny** is based on the Greek *'androgunos'* which is made from their words *'aner (ανōρ)'* meaning man and *'gune (γυνή)'* meaning woman. The word has come to describe a person of ambiguous sexual identity capable of exhibiting both male and female characteristics. Famous examples from popular culture include pop stars, David Bowie and Boy George, the movie star, Marlene Dietrich, and the fashion of the 1920s known as 'flapper girls'.

Similarly, ideas about the gender (not sex) of a manager have started to emerge which place masculinity and femininity, not in a dichotomous model, but on a sliding scale that enables individuals to choose an approach depending on the demands facing them at the time. The idea of **androgyny** in leadership terms is not particularly new; for example, Korabik (1990) cites Bolton and Humphreys (1977) who examined how the concept of ambiguous sexuality plays across leadership paradigms. Her observations led her to conclude that men and women exhibit both agentic traits associated with masculine leadership and communal behaviour associated with females. She also concluded that, 'research in the area of leadership often has been contaminated by a masculinity bias in which the task leadership function is viewed as more important than the social-emotional function' (1990:289).

More recent research, Rosette and Tost (2010) and Kark et al. (2012), has pointed towards the idea that effective leaders are not necessarily men or women but individuals who can exhibit masculine and feminine behaviours. This means men can be emotional and women can be harsh and driven—the key lies in selecting the most appropriate mode given the situation. This links back to some of the ideas raised in Chapters 5 and 6 with the research of Kark et al. suggesting 'that managers drawing on a combination of both agentic and communal characteristics are likely to have an advantage' (2012:636). In addition, the move to a more balanced set of behaviours, in terms of agentic and communal, may assist females in trying to escape the dilemma posed by role incongruity. In that, females can legitimately display both masculine and feminine behaviours in order to achieve the transformational aspects of leadership. Kark et al. (2012) conclude that the need for women to display androgynous behaviours is more important for them than for men, but that men should attempt this behaviour when working in mixed-sex groups, as women will identify more closely with such behaviour.

Part of this move to a more flexible approach towards what society understands or considers 'good' leadership to be, lies in the changing concept about the skills demanded in a complex world struggling with debt, ecological pressures, and an ever diminishing set of natural resources. Some countries, such as Iceland (see: Case study at the end of this chapter) have moved to bring in women instead of men to their key social roles as a reflection of the changes in their interpretation of what leadership means. For these countries, as well as researchers such as Gartzia and van Engen (2012), leadership is more about communal behaviour, but there is still a task to be accomplished and this better suits individuals who understand the need to deliver across a much broader range of behaviours than either merely shouting at subordinates or consoling with a cup of tea and a handkerchief.

The implications for leaders are that they need to assess carefully the nature of the learnt heuristic constructs that largely still define 'leadership'. It would seem that a swing towards a more female interpretation of the role is underway, and yet this may prove to be as counter-productive as the masculine construction in place for the majority of the past 100 years. The recent research, cited above, points to a blended approach that combines the stereotypical approach of men and women to produce a model that uses agentic and communal behaviour in a transformative manner.

Diversity and culture

As organizations have been able to expand their influence globally, there has been an increase in the level of interest in the impact national cultures may have on leadership style. Geert Hofstede's (1980) work is well documented, and researchers have pondered on the impact different national identities, values, and customs have on leadership in terms of a leader choosing an appropriate style. Mills (2005) and Arvonen and Ekvall (1991), among others, have carried out some interesting studies into this area. Mills suggests that American leaders use one of five different styles—directive, participative, empowering, charismatic, or celebrity—whereas he suggests Asian companies are often run on a patriarchal basis with power being handed down through generations. He sees this situation changing slowly as Asian organizations seek more 'professional' managers. It is also worth briefly considering the very nature of 'leadership' with the Western (some would say, American—see: Alvesson 2011) view of a leader as a strong, masculine individual. However, Alvesson (2011:152) points out that 'other societies, e.g. Scandinavians, may be less individualistic or masculine and favour more an egalitarian relationship'. Underpinning most of this work is the deterministic assumption that leaders and followers are not only influenced by a national culture, but also that they should be cognizant of it should they find themselves on an expatriate assignment. The series of 'Culture Shock' books (e.g. Kolanad 2009) are designed to assist the casual reader to avoid cultural faux-pas by illustrating certain customs and rites that should be observed so as not to cause offence, or worse, when operating in a foreign country.

Bringing this work more up-to-date has been the GLOBE project. This is an on-going project led by an American research group with the aim of determining the extent to which the practices and values of business leadership are universal (i.e. are similar globally), and the extent to which they are specific to just a few societies. A team of 160 scholars have worked

Table 12.1 Hofstede and GLOBE dimensions

Hofstede	GLOBE
Power distance	Power distance
	Uncertainty avoidance
Collectivism	Collectivism (1)
	Collectivism (2)
Long term orientation	Humane orientation
	Assertiveness
Uncertainty avoidance	Gender egalitarianism
	Long term orientation
Masculinity	Performance orientation

Source: Adapted from House et al. (2004).

together since 1994 to study societal culture, organizational culture, and attributes of effective leadership in 62 different cultures and countries. The ultimate question addressed by the GLOBE team concerned the extent to which the values and practices associated with leadership are either universal (worldwide) or specific to just a few societies. This quantitative research sparked a series of sharp exchanges between those who supported the work and those who sought to undermine it by attacking its methodology and underpinning philosophy (for example see: Jepson 2009). Nevertheless, the GLOBE team have published a series of books and articles (House et al. 2004) which have sought to update Hofstede's five domain model with a more complex nine domain approach (see: Table 12.1).

The next stage was to develop six 'global leadership behaviours' (House et al. 2002:8) based on Lord and Maher's (1991) 'Implicit Leadership Theory' which the team suggested were:

- Charismatic/Value-based: This captures a leader's ability to inspire, motivate, and to expect high performance outcomes on the basis of his/her firmly held core values. Charisma in this sense was taken to mean to inspire devotion to group goals via a leader's aura, dynamism, and persuasiveness.

- Team oriented: This describes emphasizing effective team-building and implementation of a common purpose or goal among team members.

- Participative: This reflects the degree to which managers involve others in making and implementing decisions. It was the opposite of 'autocratic' and 'non-participative'.

- Humane oriented: This reflects supportive and considerate leadership, but also includes compassion and generosity.

- Self-protective: It reflects the degree to which the leader seeks to preserve the integrity and power of the group. House et al. refer to it as 'being status- and class-conscious, evasive, ritualistic, procedural, normative, secretive, indirect, self-centred, and asocial' (2002:94).

- Autonomous: This reflects a leader who operates independently and is seen by others as being unique and autonomous.

Pause for thought

Reflect on this set of behaviours and the ideas presented in Chapter 4, especially the Tannenbaum and Schmidt (1958) model.

1. Can you see any similarities or challenges between the two ideas?

Using this model and their statistical analysis, they sought to identify national cultures with leadership styles—in other words, to answer the question as to which leadership style is likely to be successful in which country. The team believed they had achieved this and produced 10 different country-based clusters, each of which had a different 'perfect leader' profile. They also went on to describe what they saw as a set of 22 universal attributes that would be recognized worldwide as positive indicators of 'successful' leadership, and eight corresponding negative items that would inhibit effective leadership.

Summary

The message for leaders does not make for particularly comfortable reading because the relatively simple and straightforward world of the 'Great Man', if it ever did exist, has gone forever. Leaders have to be capable of managing in a complex and dynamic landscape that is made up of many different facets and many different tensions that arise from the web of interconnections. The most complex problem is being able to deal with both leaders and followers that comprise an ever-expanding number of nationalities, abilities, and demands. Being able to lead and/or follow when faced with this degree of heterogeneity, and stay within a legal framework that can present its own demands, requires managers to be flexible in their approach to the task/people. A quick search for 'illegal discrimination' will show how frequently companies and individuals get this aspect of their organizational life wrong. The better news is that, as leaders, there is a vital role to play in ensuring leadership is inclusive and draws on the skills and attributes of all rather than a chosen few. If the case studies in this chapter do nothing else, they do show that disabilities are no longer a barrier to a successful career. Leaders need to ensure they take cognizance of the fact that being different does not make someone 'wrong' or 'difficult'.

 Case study   Iceland

Iceland has a relatively small population of around 300,000 people, and yet almost all of the senior positions within the Althing (Iceland's parliament) are filled by women. The reason for this dramatic profile can be found in the dark days of early 2008 when the country almost went bust. In 2001, banks in Iceland were deregulated. This prompted a massive change in their approach to debt, risk, and profit, which eventually led to the near bankruptcy of the entire economy and a seismic shift in the balance of the sexes at the top of Icelandic society.

Iceland has a relatively small domestic economy of around US$10 billion, so, to expand further, the banks started to borrow money from abroad and aggressively marketed their savings rates to overseas organizations, investors, and the general public. Television advertising and full-page promotions appeared in many British newspapers during the early 2000s. Their interest rates hovered around 12 per

(Continued...)

cent whereas UK banks were offering around 4 per cent. Foreign money poured into the country, and in less than 10 years, the Icelandic stock market (ICEX) grew by 900 per cent. In thrall to this expansion, households began to borrow money, which fuelled inflation, and Icelandic businessmen, known as 'Vikings', began to buy up well-known British brands like Woolworths and West Ham United Football Club. Kaupthing, Landsbanki, and Glitner, the three biggest banks, grew to eight times the nation's gross domestic product. This meant that, when the banking crisis of 2008 hit as a result of Lehmann Brothers going under, the Icelandic currency (Krona) collapsed in value, losing almost 80 per cent against the Euro. The banks, now unable to make repayments of their debts, tried to pull back assets from abroad but overseas governments froze their assets which exacerbated the speed of the collapse. The government had to renationalize the banks and go to the International Monetary Fund for a USD $2 Billion bailout; the first country for nearly 30 years to do so. Unemployment jumped from 1.2 per cent to over 10 per cent and on 14 October 2008 the ICEX plunged by over 76 per cent. The result was that parts of the British public sector, including many charities, lost around £200 million.

One of the reasons suggested for this situation was the small cabal of men at the heart of Icelandic society that occupied many of the senior government and regulatory posts. For example, David Oddson held both the positions of prime minister and Central Bank chairman. As Carlin put it, 'the ruling party was overwhelmingly male, the bankers were practically all male and the rash, absurdly over-ambitious impulses that led a small nation of fishermen to believe they would all be swimming in champagne for the rest of their lives were clearly, categorically, exclusively male'. This meant the situation was ripe for exploitation and possible fraud. In April 2012, Geir Haarde, who was prime minister at the time of the crash, was found guilty by an Icelandic court of not doing enough to protect the country. In March 2011, Robert and Vincent Tchenguiz, who were part of the Viking group of high profile businessmen, were arrested in London by the UK's Serious Fraud Office as part of their investigation in conjunction with Iceland's Special Prosecutor's Office into the collapse of Icelandic bank, Kaupthing. The Icelandic public agreed with this analysis and they have voted into office women leaders. 'Iceland's women are blaming men for the financial crisis that has brought the country to its knees,' Manfred Ertel (2009), a German journalist, wrote, 'They are now looking for a female solution to clean up the mess.'

In 2009, Johanna Sigurdardottir was elected prime minister. In 2010, she made history by marrying her partner, Jonina Leosdottir, to make her not only the world's first openly gay leader, but also the first gay leader to get married. Her government has now banned strip clubs and paying for nudity in restaurants. For the last two years it has topped the World Economic Forum's report on equality between the sexes and, in 2012, *Newsweek* named it the best place in the world for women. Women hold the posts of Minister for Finance, Health, Environment and Industry, Social Affairs, and Justice. Forelle (2012) remarks that Iceland is now seen as a model for recovery with unemployment down, government bonds stable, and membership of the EU being actively pursued by the government. When asked how this turnaround has been possible, Halls Tomasdottir, head of a new financial organization in Reykjavik, said: 'We've brought greater female values into the financial world. The company isn't interested in investments that quickly generate high yields.' She goes on, 'The crisis is man-made, it's always the same guys.' 'Ninety-nine per cent went to the same school, they drive the same cars, they wear the same suits and they have the same attitudes. They got us into this situation—and they had a lot of fun doing it.'

Katrin Jakobsdottir, one of Iceland's new ruling women, sums up this new approach within Iceland thus:

In 2009 the word was, 'We need less of this macho thinking; we need pragmatic, strategically minded women in charge now'. What we have learnt since then is that if we want to stay out of crisis and build, we all know now we have to think in terms, not of the immediate future, but of the next 10 or 20 years. That is not the way a male-dominated government would be thinking; that is a female way of thinking.

Sources

Alexander, H. (2009) 'Iceland: Women end "Age of Testosterone"'. *The Telegraph*, 7 February 2009.

Carlin, J. (2012) 'A Nordic Revolution: The Heroines of Reykjavik'. *The Independent*, 21 April 2012.

Cochrane, K. (2011) 'Is Iceland the best country for women?'. *The Guardian*, 3 October 2011.

Ertel M. (2009) 'Iceland's Women Reach for Power'. *Der Spiegel*, 22 April 2009.

Forelle, C. (2012) 'In European Crisis, Iceland Emerges as an Island of Recovery'. *The Wall Street Journal*, 21 May 2012.

O'Brien, D., (2010) 'The Icelandic Banking Crisis: Causes, effects & implications'. *Social & Political Review*, 20(XX): 125–129.

Questions

1. To what extent do you agree that the crisis in Iceland was literally 'man-made'?
2. What difference do you think having women lead the recovery has made?
3. To what extent do you agree with Jakobsdottir's final analysis?

Assignment—3,000 words

1. 'Male Leaders have had their chance and they blew it.' Comment on the assumptions underpinning this statement. Outline whether you agree or disagree with these sentiments.
2. 'Followers are diverse so leaders must be diverse.' What benefits, challenges, and outcomes do you think could arise for an organization that follows the ethos expressed in this statement?

Further reading

Morrison, A. (1996) *The New Leaders; Leadership Diversity in America.* **San Francisco, CA: Jossey-Bass.**

Ann Morrison is an American author who writes widely on the theme of diversity in organizations. Her book gave organizations a number of practical steps to ensure white women and black men were able to be part of the leadership cohort. The interesting thing is, the book was first published in 1996 so is now over 15 years old. It is interesting to look back at some of the ideas to see how they have been received by organizations.

Chin, Jean Lau, Lott, Bernice, Rice, Joy K., and Sanchez-Hucles, Janis (eds) (2007) *Women And Leadership: Transforming Visions and Diverse Voices.* **Malden: Blackwell Publishing.**

The book from Chin et al. is written from a feminist perspective and covers leadership from this position. It defines feminist leadership and deals with many of the concerns surrounding feminist principles, barriers to organizational success, and feminist leadership styles. It broadly considers how feminist theory plays across leadership models and tries to appraise the literature surrounding feminist leadership. The foreword is written by Alice Eagly, who features heavily in this area of research.

From 2006 to 2011 the UK government sponsored a think-tank called the 'Cultural Leadership Programme'. Although it has now closed, the reports it supported are still available at http://culturalleadership.org.uk (accessed 8 August 2013). There is a wealth of statistics, qualitative data, and other really useful sources of information here. It is well worth downloading some of the reports if you want to study some of the outcomes of their research projects.

Power, influence, and authority

After reading this chapter you will:

- Begin to explore the implications of these terms for leaders.
- Understand more about your own thoughts on power.
- Be able to assess critically the different theorists' perspectives on the use, sources, and techniques associated with power.

Introduction

This chapter reviews the themes of power, influence, and conflict. As with many of the themes already explored in this book, the term 'power' has many different meanings and associated themes, such as control and authority. The purpose of the chapter is to outline some of the different perspectives so that you are able to begin your own assessment of the diverse ideas surrounding an essential element in the study of leaders and leadership. The chapter also explores the meaning of terms associated with power, such as influence, and moves through to consider some theoretical ideas concerned with sources of power. One challenge to confront immediately is your own understanding of power as it has a number of negative associations that we tend to be wary of in everyday discussions. Whilst we may secretly wish to be 'powerful', to openly admit such a thing is to invite looks of surprise and perhaps suspicion. The reason for this is that 'power' may suggest some kind of curtailment of freedom and liberties associated with a free choice. Impersonal institutions, such as governments, can be described as 'powerful'. Implied is a sense of hierarchy and of having to bend to the will of others—something we tend to fight against. History is also full of tales of megalomaniac villains corrupted by their power against which a heroic underdog emerges to right wrongs and return power to 'the people'. These underdogs usually emerge with great credit, and are feted as heroes, whilst the villains skulk off to purgatory. Kanter sums up this ambivalence thus, 'it is easier to talk about money and much easier to talk about sex, than it is to talk about power' (1979:65).

However, most of us live in societies that are governed by rules, regulations, and laws that, for the greater collective good, compel us to act and behave in a certain way. For Michelson (2001:193) power obviously is a pervasive reality in the life process of all modern-day organizations'. Many will be members of clubs, societies, or groups that have a codified set of standards that must adhered to in order to remain members of that cohort. Organizations are based around power and the structure of organizations explicitly denotes a power structure via its hierarchy. We experience 'power' in many different manifestations daily; from the family to the workplace; from our friends to our enemies. Power is unavoidable in our modern society and we need to grasp its implications as individuals as well as in our role as leaders so that we can avoid Lord Acton's (1907) oft-quoted suggestion that, 'power tends to corrupt, absolute power corrupts absolutely'. As Handy (1985:118) puts it, 'only the solitary artist or poet, the tramp or the hippie can enjoy that luxury'.

 Pause for thought

1. Do you consider yourself to be 'powerful'?

2. In what circumstances might your judgement change?

3. Try to define 'power'. Start with 'Power is...'.

What is 'power'?

The term 'power', if we were studying physics, would be relatively clear to understand and grasp. For a physicist it means 'the rate of transfer of energy', and it is measured in joules per second (J/S). It can be calculated by using the formula:

$$\text{Power} = \frac{\text{energy transferred}}{\text{time taken}}$$

We also have a reasonable handle on how power in this sense manifests itself. We think of a Formula 1 car as 'powerful'. We can also describe a 'powerful' wind as we see the direct effects of this in the bending of trees and the difficulty in walking against it. We might also discuss 'powerful' emotions and talk about how overjoyed we were at the birth of a child or death of an elderly relative. However, we are now beginning to explore the depths of the term because what is powerful for you may not be powerful at all for another person. Consider for example if Manchester United won the Champion's League—a fan may be ecstatic, or despondent if they are from a rival team. Others may be completely non-plussed by the whole affair having no idea what the Champion's League even is. However, what links these different themes is the sense that we 'feel' power when it (whatever 'it' is) arises. We can experience power in many ways and we often talk of feeling in the presence of power but what exactly is happening may be unclear. However, what physics does tell us is that power is a force, which is why we can feel it and use it.

In a leadership sense, there is a link between power and leaders as we have already thought about 'powerful leaders'—individuals who could strike terror into the minds of foes and love in the hearts of friends. In biblical terms, we discuss the 'power' of our God and how this power can influence our lives. However, we should begin to clarify what is meant by some of the terms being used here, because power and influence are two different, albeit linked, phenomena.

Academic definitions are common enough, for example Yukl (2010:199) defines power thus: 'the absolute capacity of an individual agent to influence the behaviour or attitudes of one or more designated target persons at a given point in time'. Whilst Northouse (2010:7) is more succinct: 'power is the capacity or potential to influence'. Picking up the negative themes is Pfeffer's (1992:2) view that 'power is the ability to get people to do things they otherwise would not have done'. This threatening undercurrent also comes across in Morgenthau's

(1985:11) allusion that, power may comprise anything that establishes and maintains the control of man over man'.

Whilst these definitions vary in their complexity, what they have in common is the link between power and influence. The two concepts are not the same and, as Handy (1985) is clear on, it is dangerous to conflate the two. These are different ideas and power is usually seen as the force behind the ability to influence. So, to have influence over or to be able to influence others requires you to have power. Defined in these terms, power is a noun whilst influence is a verb that suggests a dynamic, active process. If we accept that influencing is a fundamental aspect of leadership, we also have to accept that the acquisition and deployment of power is part of this process. In summary, Bass's (2008:265) thought that 'power is the potential to influence' best draws the themes together.

 Pause for thought

Machiavelli, in his book, *The Prince*, suggests: Power is the sole purpose of leadership.

1. What is your reaction to this declaration?

2. Do you agree or disagree with Machiavelli?

Machiavelli, N. (1952) *The Prince* (L. Ricci, Trans.). New York: Penguin Books (Original work published 1537).

Dimensions of power

As hinted at in the last section, power has some interesting variable dimensions. There are also a number of 'technical' terms that occur in the literature surrounding power. The first is the use of the word 'agent'. This refers to the body (person/organization) attempting to exert influence. The second idea is that of 'target'. This is the focus of the agent's influence. This influence can be explicit or implied, so power does not have to be used to be influential. As Gardner (1986:5) illustrates, consider a bank robber threatening a cashier with a gun. The robber only has to suggest violence—the target (literally in this case) does not know if the gun is real or if the intention to fire is genuine. Nevertheless, the robber can be said to be exerting power. Power can be relative as well as absolute, as in the case above. For example, a lecturer may have power as far as his students are concerned but relatively less power than the director of studies or the college principal. This power will also ebb and flow as time and circumstances change. After graduation, the same lecturer has little power over the same group of students. This is not to say the students will not respect the tutor but there is little for them to worry about in terms of assessment.

Diagrammatically, power and influence, and targets and agents can be represented as in Figure 13.1.

Within the agent's sphere of control lies the source of power which enables 'influence'. This is focused on the target causing action and an associated outcome (Line A). Before considering the outcomes, it is pertinent to start at the beginning of the process and examine some interesting dimensions of power. Some writers, such as Gardner (1986), view power as a social exchange rather than a one-way street (Line B). This means that followers have a choice of whether to follow the leader's command or to reject it, albeit they must live with the

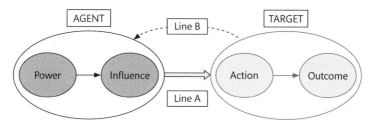

Figure 13.1 Power and influence, agent and target

consequences of their choice. For power to 'work', both the follower and leader must agree to work within a psychological contract—if the follower decides not to, there is little the leader can do. The more deterministic view of power may reject this perspective and argue that it is impossible or impractical to view followers as having this kind of choice but ultimately, Gardner (1986) suggests, it is the value of the exchange that drives the process. If there is no value in the exchange then the capacity to exert influence is gone. It is, according to Kouzes and Posner (1994:1), 'a reciprocal relationship between those who choose to lead and those who decide to follow'—with 'decide' being the key word. In the film, *The Great Escape*, Steve McQueen's laconic character repeatedly attempts escape only to be recaptured and placed in 'the cooler' or solitary confinement. He simply accepts this as part of the 'game', using the time to develop his throwing and catching skills. He does not accept confinement as a punishment but more a badge of honour. In a similar way, anti-social behaviour orders (ASBOs) were originally designed to act as a threat and deterrent to anti-social behaviour in the UK. However, as Brown (2011) points out, these orders soon acquired a 'must have' status among the under-classes in Britain, thus undermining the power structure behind them. In the same way, an employee could walk out if they decide to reject a legitimate instruction from their boss. Admittedly, they would have to face the consequences but for the leader to have 'power' via influence, the worker must acquiesce to the normative structure of the organization in question.

If we accept the situation whereby a follower acquiesces to the organizational norms, it is worth considering the possible options available to the worker. Broadly, the worker can do as they are bid willingly and enthusiastically, do as they are bid but with a degree of resentment, or appear to do as they are bid whilst actively conspiring to avoid the request. Technically, these three choices are:

1. Commitment: recalling previous thoughts relating to charismatic leadership and followership, this option requires the follower to have internalized the request from the superior. The follower will do their best to ensure the task is completed, demonstrating enthusiasm and pride in their work.

2. Compliance: here the follower will do as they have been instructed because they recognize the legitimacy of the command. They will comply with the terms of their employment contract to ensure they follow the letter if not the spirit of the demand. They will not stray outside the narrow confines of the task and will apply the minimal amount of effort to ensure the task passes muster but no more.

3. Resistance: in this case, the follower does not actually agree with the instruction and rejects the order. They may try delaying tactics, dispute the need for the request, or even try to

enlist third party support, say from their union, to ensure the task is not completed. As hinted at earlier, this reaction is not uncommon. For Guttridge (1992:1), disobedience is a defining characteristic of human behaviour: 'It is not surprising that in the Garden of Eden story the first utterance directed at humanity is a divine injunction and disobedience the almost immediate response.'

Again all of these choices operate dynamically and may change over time. A task initially rejected once attempted by the follower might become a favourite job. A different manager may elicit a different response given the same task. This leads onto the next challenge, which is identifying the source of a leader's power.

Sources of power

In broad terms, power is said to arise from two different sources; that of 'position' and 'person' or via an emergent property arising as a combination of the two. This means a person could hold power over another because of the nature of their role relationship—say, a manager to a subordinate. Alternatively, a person may have power because of the nature of their perceived personality—for example, their charisma (Chapter 7 covers this idea). However, within this framework lies a degree of complexity that has been explored by many authors over the years.

Toffler, an American 'futurist', produced a series of books culminating in *Powershift* (1990). In it he argues there are three main types of power: violence, wealth, and knowledge. He sees violence as a negative form of power as it can only be used to punish, wealth can be used to reward as well as to punish, whilst knowledge has the additional attribute of being used to transform or to change a situation (for example, Tim Berners-Lee sharing the programming language for the World Wide Web). In addition, Toffler argues that power is shifting from the use of violence to knowledge—something Handy and his 'knowledge worker' would agree with. Still, it would be naive at best to ignore violence in a world dominated by conflict in the Middle East, between the USA and terrorist groups, and the unrest in Europe caused by the Euro crisis of 2012.

However, the classic study into the source of different types of power is that of John French and Bertram Raven, two American psychologists. In the 1950s, they conducted a series of experiments from which they concluded that an individual's power stemmed from one of five possible sources (1959).

1. Legitimate power. This form of power is associated with a role and perceived authority. A follower, for an example an employee in an organization, will have acknowledged the hierarchy of the organization and will be expecting their line manager to issue instructions. As long as these instructions fall within the norms expected for the position occupied by the employee, then the employee will feel an obligation to, at least, comply with the instructions. The boss can issue orders and the subordinates, by and large, will accept them as legitimate and follow them. Any hierarchical organization, such as an army or civil service, will have legitimate power and the manifestations of this present throughout the organization. For example, a nurse graded as a 'level 7' would have legitimate power when working with another

nurse graded at 'level 5'. However, the level 7 nurse would be subservient in legitimate power terms to a doctor or consultant.

It is important to note two aspects related to legitimate power. The first is the scope of the power associated with the role. If the instruction received is perceived by the follower as being outside the scope of the leader's role, the instruction is unlikely to be seen as legitimate and may be resisted or ignored as a result. For example, if a manager asked one of the accounts team to clean her car. Secondly, because the power stems from the role and not the 'person', if the person loses or changes role, then their legitimate power evaporates too. The recent Arab Spring had a number of high profile incidents illustrating this switch. Colonel Gaddafi of Libya and President Mubarak of Egypt had to face the wrath of people who would have been cowed by their presence in the weeks leading up to their demise. However, as their role became unsustainable so too their power became illegitimate and, hence, evaporated. For leaders this is an important point, for if they lose their hierarchical position—they change jobs, are made redundant, or have to report upwards in the hierarchy—then they lose their legitimate power.

2. Coercive power. In this case, the wielder of such power is capable of either punishing or withholding benefits from the follower. Or at least the follower must perceive this to be the case—remember power does not have to be exercised to be influential. This form corresponds roughly to Galbraith's 'condign' power which effects 'submission by inflicting or threatening appropriately adverse consequences' (1983: 5). Leaders who use this type of power will effectively punish followers for not adhering to the standards, goals, rules, and procedures laid down either by them or by a higher authority to which the manager owes allegiance. As Yavas (1998) makes clear, coercive power is used by governments both with their own people and against other countries. The recent wars in Iraq and Afghanistan are all the evidence needed to demonstrate this point, with Locke (1952) providing the justification by claiming the use of coercive power as the only appropriate response to another's illegitimate use of coercive power. Parents, though, may also use this approach when attempting to discipline an unruly toddler. 'You will go to bed without watching television' is the same threat as 'if you do not pay your taxes you will go to jail'. However, it is worth noting that coercive power does not always manifest itself in these kind of overt and threatening statements. Richard Wright's emotional autobiography of growing up in southern USA details his experiences of hearing about lynchings and punishments meted out by racist white people:

> The things that influenced my conduct as a Negro did not have to happen to me directly; I needed but to hear of them to feel their full effects in the deepest layers of my consciousness. Indeed the white brutality that I had not seen was a more effective control of my behaviour than that which I knew.
>
> (cited in Wood 2009:1)

It is often hearsay and rumour that is sufficient for coercive power to be effective. Implicit in most of these examples is the existence of physical domination. However, in an organizational sense this is not often the case, unless unlawful bullying is present. Coercive power is most likely to be experienced in the form of less favourable reviews, withholding of company benefits, like pay awards, or disciplinary action after a period of real or perceived poor performance. In other types of organization, such as a prison, coercive power is almost a necessity of the system within which the participants operate. The Victorian panopticon is a visual representation of coercive power whereby the guards can watch over the prisoners.

For those who do deploy coercive power, there are some considerations that need to be borne in mind. The first is to consider the nature of the threat. This needs to be in terms the target fears, or at least views as an undesirable outcome should they continue on their current path or not comply with the instruction issued by the agent. In addition, the target must believe the agent has the capacity and will to carry out the threat. Hence, the mother's repeated exclamation, 'stop that or I'll smack you!' is not likely to have any effect on a misbehaving child if this has never happened before or the mother simply keeps repeating the phrase with no action. Next is to consider the effect on the target in terms of compliance, commitment, or resistance. As Yukl (2010:206) makes clear, 'coercion often arouses anger or resentment and may result in retaliation'. It is not likely to result in commitment on the part of the target. The miners' strike in England in 1984 was partly as a result of the forced closure of mines by the Thatcher government; similarly the poll tax riots of 1990 were a reaction to an imposed tax regime. These examples also make clear that coercive power can backfire on the agent, especially when the target either rejects the hierarchy that underpins the position of the agent or simply says 'I've had enough' and decides to fight back.

Nevertheless, coercive power, when used in a fair, non-discriminatory manner, underpins many of our democratic institutions and has a place in modern organizations. In the same way that a caring parent may use coercive power to stop their child from running onto the road after a football, a manager can use coercive power to reinforce rules, admonish lazy workers, and maintain discipline in crisis situations.

3. Reward power. At almost the opposite end of the scale is reward power—or resource power (Handy 1985). Here, the agent will have the perceived ability to control a resource valued by the target. It is used by an agent to reinforce a desired behaviour or to change a course of action towards something wanted by the agent. This means that, if the target agrees to the agent's request, they will be granted access to that resource which may be as varied as money, love, or freedom. As with coercive power, the target must believe the agent has the capacity and willingness to carry through their promise. In addition, the action required by the agent must be achievable by the target and worth the reward if completed. This type of reward is effectively an exchange of favour. The implicit agreement is, 'if you do this for me, I'll do that for you'. God's promise that a good life on earth will be followed by an eternity in heaven is one such example: 'Behold, the Lord God will come with strong hand, and his arm shall rule for him: behold, his reward is with him, and his work before him' (Isaiah 40:10). Similarly, graduates rely on the promise that, as a result of their hard work and cash spent gaining a degree, they will attain a better paid job.

There are many studies (e.g. O'Neil and McKeogh 2010) that point to the benefits of reward power over coercive power as reward power seems to generate compliance to the task instruction and, hence, an improved outcome for the agent. In leadership terms, this means offering pep talks to followers, praising their efforts, and thanks for a job well done. Whilst this may be within the gift of the manager, many organizations are constrained in their distribution of other, more material rewards. For example, schools and other public sector organizations in England are governed by a set of pay and promotion scales that cannot be circumvented by the leadership. This means reward power may be curtailed in some circumstances.

It is also worth considering some other challenges to any agent using this approach. The first is the nature of the reward. This must be valued by the target not necessarily by the agent. A manager may feel a financial incentive would help a worker to perform harder. However, if the worker is a harassed single mother trying to get back home in time for her son's return from school, a more appropriate reward would be a flexible work schedule. Secondly, rewards may be viewed as a bribe or possibly given with a hidden agenda. Most individuals are reasonably ethical and do not like to think they are prostituting themselves—a feeling they are 'being bought' is likely to result in resentment rather than commitment.

Finally, reward may result in the agent being viewed by the follower in simple economic terms and the law of diminishing returns is likely to apply. Consider the following scenario: A parent has an important dinner party at home. Their six-year-old son is misbehaving as the party approaches. The parent offers the child a chocolate bar if they go to bed with no more fuss. The child accepts and is good. The following month, the same scenario emerges. This time the parent offers a chocolate bar and a new toy. Should the same situation arise again when the parent wants the child to behave, what is the child likely to request? A chocolate bar, new toy, AND extra pocket money? The power relationship is somewhat reversed, with the child being able to demand, coercively, rewards from the parent now trapped by their own generosity. This can be seen, in an organizational sense, with unions expecting rewards at times when the management need them to respond positively to a request. The London Olympics in 2012 was one such example, where transport workers across London's network of tubes, buses, and rail were all sequentially successful in extracting additional pay from their employers.

If the above three sources of power are largely related to the *position* of the agent, whether that be a manager, parent, or prison guard, the next set relate more to the attributes of the person.

4. Expert power. Many will be familiar with the expression 'scientia est potentia' or its English translation of 'knowledge is power'. This maxim, often attributed to the English nobleman, Sir Francis Bacon, is at the heart of expert power, for it deals with the knowledge aspects of power. It operates successfully when the target believes the agent has access to knowledge, inaccessible to them, which will solve a problem. So, a householder may employ a builder or plumber to fix a problem they do not have the skill to attempt. Similarly, an office worker may need to call the IT helpdesk when their computer malfunctions.

In both of these scenarios, the target must believe the agent to be credible and trustworthy. Their problem must also matter to them sufficiently to warrant the cost of exchange that takes place as the price for accessing the information. This may be of monetary value but could also be more of a 'favour', placing an obligation on the target to be redeemed at some point in the future. As Green (1999) points out, the solution proposed must also appear rational to the target at the time. This may be a function of the agent's persuasiveness but also the urgency of the need for a solution. It is this credibility/persuasiveness issue that often presents problems for the target, especially if there are competing agents—for example, in a criminal trial where both the prosecution and defence lawyers will call different 'expert witnesses'.

In terms of using it, the challenge is often in retaining the knowledge advantage the agent has over the target. For example, a university lecturer in delivering lectures is sharing expert knowledge. Once this has been acquired by the students, the amount of expert power available to the lecturer has been diminished. In terms of maintaining expert knowledge, the agent should be engaged in continual learning to ensure the subject knowledge is current and relevant.

 Case study   Sally Clark

In November 1999, a young trainee solicitor called Sally Clark was convicted of the heinous crime of murdering two of her young infant sons. A key part of the evidence against her was provided by Sir Roy Meadow, who, at the time, was considered to be the leading expert in cases of cot death. Meadow believed the majority of infant cot deaths, where the baby dies overnight for no apparent reason, was on account of abuse by the parent and not from natural causes. He is attributed with the statement, 'one sudden infant death is a tragedy, two is suspicious and three is murder, until proved otherwise' (aka Meadow's Law). In Mrs Clark's trial, he offered a statistic that suggested that two cot deaths in a family was a 1 in 73 million chance and likely to occur once every 100 years. Meadow likened this to betting year after year on a horse at odds of 100 to 1 winning the Grand National, a picture the jury found compelling. Mrs Clark's firstborn son had died of cot death in 1996, the second died in 1998. The jury convicted her by a majority verdict and she was vilified as a heartless murderess.

However, her husband and supporters continued to fight to overturn the decision, believing her protestations of innocence. Slowly but surely the case against her began to unravel as Meadow's cited research and evidence began to fall apart. First, the statistic he quoted was declared invalid by the Royal Statistical Society. Following that, another expert (Professor Ray Hill) concluded that after one cot death another was more, not less, likely to happen. Next was the discovery that one of the boys may have died of natural causes after contracting a bacterial infection. Finally, after a second appeal, on 29 January 2003, Sally Clark was freed by the Court of Appeal.

Subsequently, Meadows was struck off the Medical Register by the General Medical Council (GMC) for serious professional misconduct, albeit this was later overturned by the High Court. Another expert, Alan Williams, the pathologist in the Clark case, was found guilty of 'serious professional misconduct' by the GMC. The law was changed so that a person could no longer be convicted based on expert testimony alone, and the immunity from prosecution enjoyed by expert witnesses was removed.

As a sad footnote to this tragedy, Sally Clark was found dead at her home on 16 March 2007, aged 42. Her husband said she never fully recovered from losing her two sons.

Sources

Batt, J. (2004) *Stolen Innocence: The Sally Clark Story - A Mother's Fight for Justice*. London: Ebury Press.

Meadow, Roy (May 1997) *ABC of Child Abuse*. London: BMJ books. pp100.

Moreton, C. (2007) 'A Broken Woman Who Was Haunted to an Early Grave', *The Independent*, 18 March 2007.

Questions

1. Why did the jury choose to believe Sir Roy Meadow initially?

2. In this case, who do you think was the 'agent' and who were the 'targets'?

3. How does this leave you feeling about expert power?

5. Referent power. This form of power correlates closely to the theme of charisma explored in Chapter 7. It arises from individuals seeking to please others they feel attracted to so that they feel, by doing something for them, they will get something in return. This exchange is not of money, as may be the case of reward power, but more of a psychological nature. It may be for the purpose of being able to claim to be close to the person or be seen by others as having similar traits. It is why David Beckham, Bollywood star and former Miss World, Aishwarya Bachchan, and Jessica Ennis are used to endorse products and are held as 'role models'. In general, people want to be like these characters, and by doing something 'for them' (e.g. buying their branded perfume or drinking their endorsed sport drink), they will inherit some of their hero's characteristics—be seen to be 'cool', for example. This imitation could also extend to bad behaviour too, which is why some criminal gang members are heavily influenced by a more senior member who may offer the promise of protection or patronage if a certain act is committed—often under the disguise of demonstrating loyalty. This kind of promise is also used by husbands and wives too—'you would do this if you really loved me' is typical of this kind of exchange.

There are many academic (e.g. Gaski 1986) as well as practitioner (e.g. Stewart 1989) studies that have sought to champion this form of power by identifying the degree of commitment referent power elicits from the target. The evidence is supportive of the claim that respected, trusted, and liked leaders are more likely to have committed followers than those who rely on coercion or another 'positional' power to achieve results.

However, as with the other forms of individual power, referent power does have its limitations. If a leader chooses to use this approach, there must be synergy between the spoken word and the act of exchange. In other words, if a leader promises inclusion and the chance, for example, to associate with the 'in-crowd' (see: Chapter 9 for more on this), this must be delivered. A leader that does not deliver against this promise will almost instantly lose referent power and be seen as manipulative and untrustworthy. Similarly, there is only so much a leader can ask of a follower based on their referent power. However, this will vary from leader to leader as their referent power is likely to be different for different groups. David Beckham's choice of underwear is not likely to have much sway with a non-footballing man, for example. Beckham has no referent power here. Kate Moss briefly lost some of her power when, in 2005, she was photographed allegedly snorting cocaine, albeit there have been those who have argued this was in fact a publicity stunt designed to increase her profile.

This final point indicates a danger of referent power in that it can come and go with the changing of fashion. So, a well-known pop star will quickly lose referent power when they cease to achieve hit records. Some leaders also misguidedly think the loyalty of their followers is down to their referent power and not the legitimate power acquired through their rank. Rather painfully, they discover the truth when they move or lose their jobs and their previously loyal subordinates do not want to have anything to do with them.

French and Raven's approach has been both criticized and developed since their first piece of research. Bass (2008) points out the lack of clarity between the different types, the different weights followers may attach to each one, and the correlation between the positional and personal groups. Eyuboglu and Atac (1991) point towards 'informational' power, which they classify as being able to control access to information required by the target. Google could be regarded as a 'powerful' organization because it can control what individuals have access to.

The World Wide Web could be considered 'powerful' too but what makes this case interesting is trying to decide on the agent/target status.

Clayton (2010) has suggested two more refinements; connection and resource power.

1. Connection power. This emerges from the agent controlling access to other people and resources via networking. Perhaps this is similar to expert power—after all, networking is a skill that can be developed. Nevertheless, this ability to make connections is considered a vital part of the modern manager's skill set and is recognized by Castells (2011)—he suggests this is why the World Wide Web is considered a 'powerful' tool, because it enables connections to be made quickly and easily. Perhaps this is the reason behind Facebook's power—it connects people.

2. Resource power. This is the ability to control access to an organizational asset. This manifests itself most clearly in the lowly clerk who controls access to the company's stationery cupboard. If a manager needs a new pen, paper clip, or envelope, they will first have to negotiate with the junior colleague with little legitimate power but a great deal of resource power. Without first circumventing this hurdle, the manager is helpless and will not be able to complete a relatively trivial task. So, although this is a form of legitimate power, it can be disproportionate to the relative hierarchy of the agent/target.

 Case study Joan of Arc

In the early part of the fifteenth century, France was a divided nation with the English controlling vast tracts of northern France, including the cities of Rouen and Paris. The 14-year-old French king, Charles VII, was uncrowned and living in Chinon among a population still recovering from the effects of the Black Death. The mood among the French was gloomy and cowed as they had not won a significant military victory against the English for years. In the spring of 1429, things looked as if they were about to go from bad to worse as the English now lay siege to Orleans which, if seized, would open up the remainder of France to the invader.

However, legend has it that on to the scene arrived one of the most remarkable and iconic figures in French history, Jehanne d'Arc from Domrémy—or Joan of Arc as she is more commonly known. Joan was an uneducated 19-year-old girl from a farming family living in what is now the Lorraine (northeast France). She had visions of various saints, from when she was about 12 years old, which implored her to strike back against the English and restore the Dauphin (the name for an uncrowned French king) to the throne.

Her first attempts to convince her largely male elders of her God-given mission were unsuccessful, but at last she managed to meet with Charles in Chinon, where an army was preparing to leave for the besieged Orleans. After listening to her, and gaining confirmation as to her chastity, a desperate Charles allowed her to join the army. Approaching the city of Orleans, she forsook the normal conservative tactics employed by the French and vigorously attacked the English, who were taken aback by the sight of a young girl dressed in full armour. The siege was broken in eight days as fortress after fortress fell. The final assault on the main English stronghold was led by Joan, where she was subsequently wounded. Despite her successes, she was again shunned by veteran army commanders but eventually they bent to her will. Her final battle led to a complete rout of the English at Patay. Here, her bold approach allowed the French to catch the English unprepared and, as a result, most of the enemy commanders were either killed or captured. This allowed Charles VII to enter Riems and to be finally crowned King of France.

However, in 1430 Joan's luck turned, as she was captured at Margny and handed over the English. In a politically motivated trial, she was accused and convicted of heresy. Throughout her trial, she conducted herself with skill and dignity, frequently astounding the court with her wisdom and intelligence. Nevertheless, on 30 May 1431, she was burned at the stake in Rouen and her ashes were scattered.

History has clouded her actual role, and some dispute the legend, but regardless of which account is believed the effect cannot be disputed. Charles remained as King of France and, after another 20 years, the English eventually left France. Joan was found innocent at subsequent retrials, and she was canonized by Pope Benedict XV in 1920.

Sources

DeVries, Kelly (1999) *Joan of Arc: A Military Leader*. Stroud, Gloucestershire: Sutton Publishing.

Fraioli, Deborah (2002) *Joan of Arc: The Early Debate*. London: Boydell Press.

Pernoud, Régine and Clin, Marie-Véronique (1998) *Joan of Arc: Her Story* (trans. Jeremy duQuesnay Adams). New York: St Martin's Press.

Taylor, Larissa Juliet (2010) *The Virgin Warrior: The Life and Death of Joan of Arc*. New Haven: Yale University Press.

Questions

1. Why was Joan able to convince others as to her mission?

2. Use French and Raven's typology to analyse different types of power used by Joan.

3. What relevance has Joan for modern leaders?

The dark side of power

Just as Luke Skywalker experienced in the *Star Wars* films, power can be a corrupting force. Perhaps the most famous manifestation of how the effects of power can work to move normally inscrutable men to extraordinarily cruel acts, are illustrated by the highly controversial experiments carried out by Stanley Milgram in 1960s America. Milgram was a Jewish professor at Yale and became interested in the trial of the Nazi war criminal, Adolf Eichmann. He was puzzled as to why seemingly normal, well-adjusted men could be made to perform acts that challenged their own personal values; for example, many of the guards at the Nazi death camps had proffered the defence that they were only following orders when inflicting pain and suffering on the camp inmates. He was struck by Hannah Arendt's (1963) phrase the 'banality of evil', which she had coined in her book, *Eichmann in Jerusalem*, which suggested that most Nazis were quite ordinary men. Milgram asked his colleagues and students how they would react and the vast majority maintained they would not commit such evil acts even under duress.

Milgram decided to carry out an experiment that remains controversial to this day. It was partly copied by the British showman, Derren Brown, in January 2006 and broadcast as *The Heist* on Channel 4. Initially, Milgram advertised for volunteers to take part in an experiment on memory and learning (see: Figure 13.2) for which participants would be paid $4.00.

When the participants arrived, they were split into pairs and asked to choose between two slips of paper. The individual with the word 'teacher' written on the slip was to assume this role and title throughout the experiment, likewise for the individual with the slip of paper with 'learner' on. The experimenter explained to the two individuals how the experiment was to be conducted. The teacher was to read to the learner a set of word pairs. The learner was to memorize these word pairs so that, when the teacher asked only one of the words, the learner was to

Public Announcement

WE WILL PAY YOU $4.00 FOR
ONE HOUR OF YOUR TIME

Persons Needed for a Study of Memory

*We will pay five hundred New Haven men to help us complete a scientific study of memory and learning. The study is being done at Yale University.

*Each person who participates will be paid $4.00 (plus 50c carfare) for approximatey 1 hour's time. We need you for only one hour: there are no further obligations. Your may choose the time you would like to come (evenings, weekdays, or weekends).

No special training, education, or experience is needed. We want:

Factory workers	Businessmen	Construction workers
City employees	Clerks	Salespeople
Laborers	Professional people	White-collar workers
Barbers	Telephone workers	Others

All persons must be between the ages of 20 and 50. High school and college students cannot be used.

*If you meet these qualifications, fill out the coupon below and mail it now to Professor Stanley Milgram, Department of Psychology, Yale University, New Haven. You will be notified later of the specific time and place of the study. We reserve the right to decline any application.

*You will be paid $4.00 (plus 50c carfare) as soon as you arrive at the laboratory.

- -

TO:
PROF. STANLEY MILGRAM, DEPARTMENT OF PSYCHOLOGY, YALE UNIVERSITY, NEW HAVEN, CONN. I want to take part in this study of memory and learning. I am between the ages of 20 and 50. I will be paid $4.00 (plus 50c carfare) if I participate.

NAME (Please Print) ....

ADDRESS ....

TELEPHONE NO .... Best time to call you...................................

AGE .... OCCUPATION .... SEX.......................

CAN YOU COME:

WEEKDAYS .... EVENINGS .... WEEKENDS ....

Figure 13.2 Milgram's advertisement

identify the missing word from four alternatives. If the learner was correct there would be no action from the teacher. However, if the learner was incorrect in their answer, the teacher was to deliver an electric shock to the learner. The purpose of this, explained the experimenter, was to investigate the relationship between memory, learning, and punishment with the hypothesis that being punished aided learning. The shock was to increase by 15V each time the learner delivered an incorrect answer. Starting from an initial 15V, the shock generator to be used by the teacher could deliver over 450V. Bearing in mind the standard voltage delivered by a UK domestic house socket is 240V, and is highly likely to kill anyone who is unfortunate enough to touch a bare wire, 450V is almost certainly fatal. The teacher was given a 45V shock, which

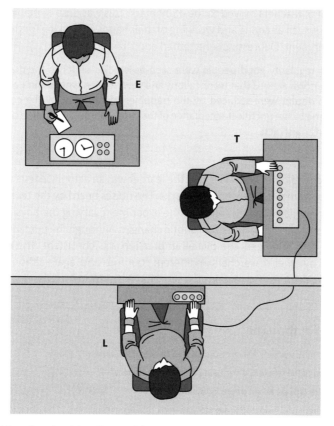

Figure 13.3 Position of teacher (T) and learner (L) in Milgram's experiment

is painful, to show what would happen to the learner. The learner was taken and placed into a chair and strapped in after being connected to the shock generator. The teacher was the led to an adjacent room in which they could hear the learner but not see them (see: Figure 13.3).

On the command of the experimenter, who was often sitting in the same room as the teacher, the teacher was told to begin the experiment. As time progressed, the learner began to get questions wrong and so the teacher increased the voltage. After passing 135V, the learner began to beg for the experiment to stop, often banging on the wall and screaming in pain. Assured by the experimenter, the teacher was urged to continue.

 Pause for thought

1. If you were the teacher, what would you do now?

Remember you have been paid $4.00 to be there and the experimenter asks you to continue.

If the teacher hesitated or questioned the experiment, the experimenter would say to them, 'the experiment requires you to continue' followed by the more forceful, 'you have no choice, you must go on'. Milgram observed that all of the teachers moved to 300V and more than 60 per cent of teachers moved to the 450V mark. This was despite many of them showing signs of stress, such as crying and wringing of their hands and asking for the experimenter to stop the experiment. Depressingly, he remarked:

> with numbing regularity good people were seen to knuckle under to the demands of authority and perform actions that were callous and severe. Men who are in everyday life responsible and decent were seduced by the trappings of authority, by the control of their perceptions, and by the uncritical acceptance of the experimenter's definition of the situation into performing harsh acts.
>
> (Milgram 1974:123)

What the teacher did not know was that the learner was an actor in league with the experimenter and they were not receiving any shocks. The noises heard by the teacher were delivered by a tape recorder. Milgram repeated the experiment varying the physical proximity of the learner and teacher along with other subtle changes. Although the percentage of teachers who moved to 450V changed, the overall impression was consistent. The experiment has been replicated by other researchers in different countries and, again although the percentages shift slightly, the message remains the same as Milgram's original work.

 Pause for thought

1. Why do you think teachers felt so compelled to torture the learner?
2. Can you identify the type of power being demonstrated here?
3. What does this tell you about power and influence?
4. If the experiment was repeated today, do you think the same results would be obtained?

Note: This type of experiment is now banned because of the unethical approach by the experimenter.

Summary

The chapter covered some of the important differences between power, influence, and authority. Power is a capacity to exert control over others; influence is the process through which this control is exerted; and authority stems from the leader's position in a normative power structure, such as those in governments or companies. Whilst for many power is a binding force that cannot be resisted, some researchers view the process as an exchange which needs both parties to agree upon. For these writers (such as Gardner), for power to be used both the leader and follower must agree to the implied social 'contract' that exists between the two. If this is not the case, the exchange between the agent and target will not take place.

If power is to be exerted by an individual manager, there are a number of different bases for that power. These bases can be either positional or personal or a combination of the two. Positional power is described as legitimate, coercive, or reward-based. Personal power can be referential or expert. Studies have shown that successful leaders use personal power, as this is a more effective in obtaining commitment, as opposed to compliance or resistance from followers and targets.

The obvious danger for managers is to ensure their power is used wisely. History is full of examples of powerful leaders becoming seduced by their own power and abusing the influence this brings. Whereas democracies have the opportunity to remove those who use their power to their own ends rather than the broader social 'good', organizations are not so fortunate. However, what is clear is that the recent world economic crisis has left many shareholders and stakeholders unhappy with senior directors and other wealthy individuals using their power to become richer. Whether this mood translates to continued pressure on the powerful, to ensure their power is used to benefit a broader group, will be an interesting process to observe.

 Case study Enron and 'The Natwest Three'

During the 1990s, the American company, Enron, grew from being a small, relatively insignificant company to the seventh largest company in America, worth around $60 billion with its shares worth around $90 each. The company traded in the energy market and employed around 20,000 people across 40 countries. It won awards for being America's Most Admired Company; but in December 2001 the company filed for bankruptcy, at the time the largest the world had seen. The company closed with its shares worthless which resulted in mass redundancies, its employees losing almost all of their pensions, and its senior executives jailed. The auditor of the company's accounts, Arthur Andersen, at the time one of the world's largest auditors, also collapsed and closed.

The reason for the sudden decent was down to the entire wealth of the company being an elaborate scam, with the company's true value being hidden behind complex accounting techniques and other financial instruments. Senior executives at the organization, including Ken Lay, the chairman, Jeff Skilling, the president, and Andy Fastow, the chief financial officer, were all jailed by the American courts for their part in the scandal.

In Britain, the affair embroiled the government and three former NatWest bankers, Giles Darby, David Bermingham, and Gary Mulgrew. These three were controversially extradited the USA, where they were tried and convicted of fraud after admitting their part in a scam which netted them around $7 million. At their trial, Mulgrew said that he had shown a 'lack of integrity' and 'exercised poor judgement', concluding that 'I have no one to blame but myself'. Darby admitted that he was 'wrong', and said 'I deeply regret my involvement in this whole affair'. Darby's lawyer stated that 'Andy Fastow and the culture of greed at Enron corrupted everybody and everything it came in contact with'. They served prison terms in the US and were freed in 2010.

Other casualties from the affair include Neil Coulbeck, an RBS employee, and an FBI prosecution witness who was found dead in July 2006. He had committed suicide by cutting his wrists. It has been alleged by his wife that after providing a statement to the FBI he was harassed and felt personally disturbed by his part in their extradition. The House of Commons discussed the case and it attracted mass media coverage.

Sources

Bermingham D. (2012) *A Price To Pay: The Inside Story of the NatWest Three*. London: Gibson Square Books Ltd.

Fox, Loren (2004) *Enron: The Rise and Fall*. Hoboken, NJ: J. Wiley & Sons.

Mulgrew, G. (2012) *Gang of One: How I Survived Extradition and Life in a Texas Prison*. London: Hodder & Stoughton.

Murphy, Kate (2008) 'NatWest 3' Sentenced to 37 Months Each'. *International Herald Tribune*, 22 February 2008.

US Federal Records Statement of Facts (Exhibit A to Plea Agreement, United States vs David Bermingham, Giles Darby and Gary Mulgrew). See: http://upload.wikimedia.org/wikipedia/commons/c/c9/NatWest_Three_David_Bermingham_Plea_Agr.pdf

(Continued...)

Questions

1. What is your reaction to the story?

2. Does this example support Lord Acton's hypothesis: 'power tends to corrupt, absolute power corrupts absolutely'?

3. Do you think it is inevitable that large organizations will use their power to bend the rules to ensure their shareholders benefit?

Assignment—3,000 words

1. Consider any formal relationship you have experienced, such as being at school, working in a company, or running a club. Analyse the power relationships you practised or received and identify why these episodes were successful or unsuccessful.

2. Why do you think the term 'power' has so many undesirable word associations?

3. Attempt to answer the question as to whether Milgram's experiments, repeated today, would achieve the same results as the original set.

Further reading

If you are interested in exploring the philosophical side of the debate in terms of power then try: Flyvbjerg, B. (1998) *Rationality and Power: Democracy in Practice*. Chicago: The University of Chicago Press.

This book, authored by Professor Bent Flyvbjerg of Oxford University, examines the history of power and democratic government. He examines some classical scholars, such as Thucydides, as well as more modern philosophers, such as Nietzsche and Max Weber. The book also explores the world of Machiavelli and how the thinking in *The Prince* is still relevant today.

For Machiavelli's *The Prince*, try Dent, J. (1995) *The Prince and Other Political Writings*, London: Everyman. It is a relatively short book written in the sixteenth century. In his book, Machiavelli describes how a 'Prince' could achieve power and dominance. However, Machiavelli's outline contains a whole host of scheming and devious acts in order to achieve this end. The book has been credited with introducing the word, 'Machiavellian' into our language when wanting to describe someone as sly, underhand, and generally morally bankrupt. Supporters of Machiavelli would claim that 'the end justifies the means'.

Finally, if you are interested in a broader political debate around power, why not have a look at the theme of cultural hegemony championed by the Italian, Marxist Antonio Gramsci (1891–1937). This is a view that suggests a ruling elite use a number of overt and covert strategies to ensure their views on what society considers to be 'right' become accepted as 'common sense truth'. A couple of different texts are a good beginning point. Nick Abercrombie and Bryan Turner (June 1978) 'The Dominant Ideology Thesis', in *The British Journal of Sociology*, 29 (2): 149–170 (The London School of Economics and Political Science: Wiley-Blackwell); or Lenny Flank (2007) *Hegemony and Counter-Hegemony: Marxism, Capitalism, and Their Relation to Sexism, Racism, Nationalism, and Authoritarianism*. St Petersburg, FL: Red and Black Publishers.

Leadership and teams

14

After reading this chapter you will:

- Be able to appraise critically the different theoretical models used to explain how teams operate.
- Have gained insight into your own approach to working in a team.
- Understand some of the advantages and dangers of working collaboratively in a team.

Introduction

This chapter will explore leadership in the context of teams. To say that teams have been the focus of almost countless articles, books, and other discourse is almost a given point (e.g. Guzzo and Shea 1993; Hackman 1987); an internet search using the term will produce in excess of four billion entries. Teams have received an increasing amount of attention, particularly over the past few decades, as organizations have come to rely on team-based arrangements to increase and improve quality, productivity, and customer service (e.g. Swezey and Salas 1992; Tannenbaum et al. 1996). Senge points out that teams are increasingly being seen as the cornerstone of organizational development. He describes a team as 'the fundamental learning unit of an organisation' (1990:10). Groups, rather than individuals, often make strategic decisions and organizations are spending ever more resources in developing team skills in individuals in the hope that this will transfer through to organizational capital. As organizations have moved towards decentralization, empowerment, and the use of outside agencies to deliver non-core activity, teams have become increasingly important in making critical decisions essential to organizational survival (Guzzo and Salas 1995). However, this plethora of comment has often clouded the investigation into how teams operate, as the definitions of the terms 'team' and 'team work' are still argued over by researchers.

In this chapter we explore the term 'team' and look at a number of different approaches to how teamwork can be explained and developed. In addition, some of the potential dangers of team working are discussed and contextualized. Given the diversity of the term and the number of different models, organizations, and theoretical approaches, the chapter can only focus on a limited number of ideas. However, these concepts are sufficient to enable the reader to explore further and to begin to shape their own ideas of how they might construct leadership 'in' and 'of' teams.

The broader historical aspects and the evolution of the organization

Organizations have identified a range of techniques and potential solutions to the question of how to make best use of limited resources, ranging from slaves, to chain gangs, to piece-work, to self-managing autonomous key workers (Duarte and Snyder 2001). As a first step, the changing theoretical hypothesizing of the nature of an organization gives a clue to how the thinking relating to such issues has evolved. When examining the early writing of organizational thinkers, such as Fayol (1949) and Taylor (1911), a view of the organization develops which has order and control as the dominant features of management and organizations. Fayol sets out 'Principles of Management' in which he identifies division of work, authority, and discipline as the cornerstone of a successful organization—no mention here of such terms as 'empowerment' or 'self-management' so familiar to the worker in a twenty-first-century company. The literature reflects a mechanistic approach to organizing where the emphasis was on processes and efficient production of products. The means to this end were through breaking production down into small parts which could be completed by individuals operating as part of a larger 'machine'.

This view is still present as a metaphor in many of today's organizations, especially those with a technical core dedicated to the manufacture of components, which are modelled on the teachings of Max Weber (1947) and Taylorism. Both of these were themselves based on eighteenth and early nineteenth-century concepts. The highly stable and efficient structures produced by this dogma achieved unprecedented success for the owners of capital. The 'bureaucracy' that evolved gave rise to a new breed of professional managers and administrators whose job it was to maintain the structure and to ensure the flow of inputs through to outputs. Mintzberg (1979) and, more recently, Whittington (2000) have made the link between 'machine bureaucracies' and past success. According to Procter and Mueller (2000) the key feature of the organization of labour during this period (Taylorism) was that it was mainly focused on the breaking of power that individuals working in groups were able to exercise. The rise of trade unionism in this period is a clue to the struggle for power between management and worker (Mathias 1983) as individuals began to react to the exercising of 'legitimate authority' (Weber 1947 and Chapter 13) by the owners of capital.

So, teams, in the modern sense of the word, were of little interest to managers in this epoch. The organization took care of the processes needed for production. Hierarchy and structure were used by organizations to direct resources towards goals. Individuals in this environment were used as units of production with little regard paid to sociological or psychological needs. The bureaucracy and organizations modelled on this premise were, at best, efficient—that is, they did things right. General Motors under Alfred Sloan, which became a model for the production of standardized goods, is a classical interpretation of the bureaucratic model, albeit even Sloan's organization had a degree of flexibility in that it contained self-managing departments with a core dedicated to coherence and the allocation of capital. However, the centralized and hierarchical organizational structure had at its heart a critical vulnerability that has threatened its continued existence. As the world has evolved new types of technology, this has given rise to new forms of organization and knowledge and, as a consequence, new types of workers have emerged to take advantage of these changes.

The changing environment

This vulnerability relates to three different social trends. The first is the rise of the 'knowledge worker', first named by Drucker (1969), and Atkinson's (1984) 'peripheral staff'. These individuals, on account of their skill set, own the means of production as companies move from manufacture to '**mentofacture**' (Burgoyne and Roe 2007). This means they can manage their own control systems and networks, hence undermining the structures generated by organizations designed to control and guide a workforce (for example see Arm Ltd. www.arm.com).

> **Mentofacture:** a term coined to describe organizations that focus on learning, human development, and technology to add value rather than manufacturing using raw natural materials.

Second, the arrival of relatively cheap information technology systems has presented organizations with a dual challenge and opportunity—to manage information and knowledge effectively and efficiently whilst ensuring the workforce remain committed to the central philosophy of the organization (Buchanan and Boddy 1983; Walton and Susman 1987; Zuboff 1988). This has meant that workers no longer need to be housed in expensive real estate or occupy capital resources, such as computer systems and desks. The attendant support staff, such as human resource managers and call centres, can be remote from the headquarters. Workers can operate remotely using text, video, and telephonic links. Of course, the disadvantage of such networks is the reduction in control and influence over such distant workers experienced by organizations using these systems (Symons, 2003).

Third, the consumer and marketplace have become increasingly competitive and better informed. Although there is often a suggestion that this is a theme repeated by successive generations, the majority of social commentators, such as Handy (1984), point out that the drive to produce goods and services with a much closer customer focus has become critical to a company's ability to survive. Echoing this, Atkinson and Meager (1986) make note of the 'Flexible Firm' during the 1980s, based on Japanese management techniques, which began to undermine the Sloanist model. The world of Henry Ford and 'any colour as long as it is black' has gone forever.

These three trends have combined to produce an environment where new kinds of organization are beginning to, or already have, emerged. The neo-Darwinian evolutionary period of Hannan and Freeman (1989) finally allowed the emergence of Miles and Snow's (1978) 'Prospectors' whilst encouraging the Sloanist 'Defenders' to die. The characteristics of these new organizations need discussion, but the new organizational forms suggested have, as a core competence, the systems in place to create sustainable competitive advantage by the ability to use knowledge, people, machines, and technology intelligently. Collaboration, teams, and teamwork seem to be an increasingly popular response to these environmental pressures.

 Pause for thought

1. Do you recognize any of these themes in the world around you?

2. Do you think 'knowledge' has become more important?

3. Why are you studying?

Academic research—different perspectives

As organizations have evolved in their use of team-based solutions, so too has the academic research into what a team 'is' and also what the nature is of the processes occurring between individuals operating in such structures. Whilst the aim of these descriptions and models is to provide clarity and insight into a complex area of human activity, frustratingly, as Salas and Cannon-Bowers (2001) highlight, efforts to understand and improve team performance have been on-going for more than 50 years, yet relatively little is known about some of the multifarious processes occurring within teams or even what is meant by teams and teamwork.

Conceptually, a team can be viewed as a socially constructed phenomenon or linking mechanism that integrates individuals and organizations (Hovath et al. 1996) and this chapter seeks to explore these internal processes. For example, Dyer (1984), in his review of the literature existing at the time, considered a team as having two or more people with a common goal, specific role assignments, and interdependence. Guzzo and Dickson recognize that teams often exist within a larger organizational context and see a team as:

> made up of individuals who see themselves and who are seen by others as a social entity, who are interdependent because of the tasks they perform as members of a group, who are embedded in one or more larger social systems (e.g. community, organisation), and who perform tasks that affect others (such as customers or co-workers).
>
> (Guzzo and Dickson 1996:308–309)

This theme of psychological recognition is picked up by Schein in his definition of a team as 'any number of people who interact with one another, are psychologically aware of one another, and perceive themselves to be a group' (Schein 1994:145) and McFletcher's (1996) view of 'a group of individuals who share work activities and the responsibility for specific outcomes'. Alternatively, Lewis (1993) rather loosely defines a team as 'a group of people who are committed to the attainment of a common objective, who work well together and enjoy doing so, and who produce high quality results'.

Salas et al. try to define this 'group boundary' by stating a team is:

> a distinguishable set of two or more people who interact dynamically, interdependently and adaptively towards a common and valued goal, who have each been assigned specific roles or functions to perform, and who have a limited life-span of membership.
>
> (Salas et al. 1992:4)

Within management and organizational domains, Shonk's (1992) view has been well received. According to him, a team is two or more people who must coordinate their activities to accomplish a common goal—it is the common goal and associated coordination that make the individuals a team. This aspect of accountability clearly appeals to organizations, and Katzenbach and Smith's (1993) definition of a team as, 'a small number of people with complementary skills who are committed to a common purpose, set of performance goals, and approach for which they hold themselves mutually accountable', has been widely adopted.

Pause for thought

1. Think about a time when you have worked or played in a team. How would you define a team?
2. Which of the various definitions outlined above appeal to you? Why?

Complexity strikes

The range of comment strikes one immediately when considering the expression 'team'. The variety of forms the construct can take and the range of organizational environments teams operate within give researchers problems when attempting to focus on a particular aspect of organizational behaviour. This seems especially true now as we move further away from Taylor's factory, Sloan's divisions, and a world built on strict hierarchies. Indeed, one could speculate that another of Foucault's 'epistemes' is dawning as we move to a society dominated by technology, uncertainty, and change—Handy's (1989) *The Age of Unreason* and Hock's (1999) *The Chaordic Age*—both suggested a new world order and a new way of organizing work which may now be upon us.

Another problem lies in defining the boundaries of the 'team'. Who is 'in' and who is 'out' are difficult questions to resolve, especially if the group operates at arm's length across different spacio-temporal dimensions. Indeed, an individual may have several different groups calling on their loyalty and industry. The task facing researchers has been to identify a model or approach that enables participants, observers, and organizations to first understand what is the 'best' way of creating a team and then to ensure the team 'performs' to organizational requirements.

An initial review of the literature in this area seems to reflect the same sense of frustration voiced above. Paris et al. (2000:1053), make the point that 'team researchers have struggled to identify those critical skills or traits that enable teams to coordinate, communicate, strategise, adapt and synchronise task relevant information'. In addition, Drucker, the doyen of management writers, puts his point across with characteristic bluntness when he remarks that although 'team building has become a buzzword in American business, the results are not overly impressive' (2002:1). He goes on to identify 'management' as having yet to learn how to make teams work effectively whilst recognizing, as do Ramesh and Dennis (2003), that teams are now embedded into modern, global organizations.

'When is a team not a team?'

What is clear is that this plethora of different definitions and comments makes understanding and analysis difficult, and opens the door to critics of a team-based approach. Perhaps, as Sinclair (1992) warns and as Michael Schrage (1995:xi) states, 'the word team has become so politicised, so ensnared in the pathology of the organisation that we don't really know what it means anymore'. Picking up on these themes, Nahavandi and Aranda (1994) discovered that many employees believed that working in a team environment was a waste of productive time because too much time is spent on the unproductive routine of building trust

Table 14.1 Differentiating groups and teams

Groups	Teams
Strong, clearly focused leader	Shared leadership roles
Individual accountability	Individual and mutual accountability
The group's purpose is the same as the broader organizational mission	Specific team purpose that the team itself delivers
Individual work products	Collective work products
Run efficient meetings	Encourage open-ended discussion and active problem-solving meetings
Measure its effectiveness indirectly by its influence on others (e.g. financial performance of the business)	Measure performance directly by assessing collective work products
Discuss, decide, and delegate	Discuss, decide, and do real work together

Source: Adapted from Katzenbach and Smith (1991).

and agreement. Whilst effort spent 'team building' is commendable, Allender (1993) showed it does not always translate into higher productivity or increased creativity. These concerns, which seek to build on Casey and Critchley's (1984) argument that a team may not be the most effective construct to solve certain organizational issues, cast doubt on the panacea promised by using teams to solve organizational woes. Katzenbach and Smith (1993) do make the point that groups do not become a 'team' just because someone labels them a team. In seeking to explain this concept further, they seek to differentiate between groups and teams (see: Table 14.1). Their point being that, whilst organizations may use the word 'team' as it has a number of positive associations, the reality may not reflect Katzenbach and Smith's requirements for 'true' team work.

This may leave the study of teams and the associated leadership in a difficult place as there seems to be little agreement over what a team is and how organizations label these work-groups. However, a number of different ideas have emerged which purport to aid under-standing of this fascinating area.

 Case study Volvo

In 1974, Volvo built a new car production facility at Kalmar. The Kalmar plant dispensed with the production line system used in car manufacturing since Henry Ford revolutionized the way in which products were made. In a production line, each worker has a very small specialized role and once a task is completed the job is passed along to the next operative until the whole unit is assembled. Workers carry out the same task and work at a speed set by the machinery. In Volvo's new plant, there was a different physical arrangement, with large open rooms and windows. Along with the new environment, the existing job roles were dispensed with, so all workers became multi-skilled and able to carry out each other's role. Instead of doing a small specialized role, each room was occupied by a team of 15 to

25 workers who were made jointly responsible for performing, in a specified time, a broadly defined task, such as the electrical wiring, door assembly, fitting upholstery, or installing the exhaust system. The individual teams were free to decide on who did what and when. One immediate benefit was the reduction in shop floor management and the need for supervisors quickly became redundant. Once the task was done, the semi-finished car would move on to the next team, via a computer-controlled trolley.

The reasoning behind this revolutionary approach was to give the workforce a sense of ownership and a greater responsibility. Volvo also hoped for an improvement in morale along with the associated benefits of a healthier, more engaged workforce. It is not surprising that the Kalmar plant soon had a steady stream of visitors from other manufacturers and academics keen to experience this new Utopia. However, the reaction was less than positive, with other car manufacturers particularly scathing about the likely outcomes of the experiment. A Peugeot representative is reported to have said: 'There is no chance whatsoever that the experiment will be emulated. Kalmar's operating costs are 30% higher than those at a conventional plant in France.' Whilst General Motors added: 'We have no desire to copy this—our Ohio plant can produce 400,000 cars per year; Kalmar 30,000.' Perhaps more surprising were comments from other car workers who felt this was not a good idea: 'Team work requires constant attention. On the assembly line, I can do a routine job and daydream which blocks out the drudgery of work.'

Initially, Volvo's experiment paid off and, in 1987, they constructed another plant at Uddevalla. In this plant, a team would be responsible for building a complete car. However, eventually the teams became embroiled in endless internal debates and friction arose between individual workers. Sadly, both plants closed amid rising costs as efficiency fell and, by 1995, Volvo was producing cars at Gothenburg using a highly automated traditional assembly line. Rather ironically, Volvo are now owned by the American car giant, Ford.

Sources

Barker, J. R. (1999) *The Discipline of Teamwork: Participation and Concertive Control*, London: SAGE Publications.

Kohler, Heinz (1997) *Economic Systems and Human Welfare: A Global Survey*, Cincinnati, OH: South-Western, 278–279 and 411–413.

Van Hootegem, Geert, Huys, Rik, and Delarue, Anne (2004) 'The Sustainability of Teamwork Under Changing Circumstances: The Case of Volvo-Ghent'. *International Journal of Operations & Production Management*, 24(8): 773–786.

http://volvogroup.com (accessed 12 August 2013).

Questions

1. What do you think about Volvo's idea?

2. Was it doomed to failure from the beginning?

3. Could the experiment be repeated today with greater chance of success?

Team models theories

Despite an extensive review of the literature concerning small groups and team research covering the period 1955 to 1980, Dyer (1984) asserted there was a lack of adequate theory that could be applied to teams. The questions that he could not find satisfactory answers to included: What are the unique features of teams? What are the characteristics of good teams? What factors influence team performance? Since Dyer's review there have been other researchers examining team dynamics who have produced an inordinate number of models, such as Hackman's (1987) normative model of group effectiveness, and entire texts dedicated to working with groups and teams (see: Dyer 1984; Schein and Bennis 1965). What follows is a review of some of the myriad views on teams ranging from norm-based models to role, phase, and, finally, a shared mental approach. This should enable the reader to begin to understand the various different methods for viewing their own position within the team.

Normative team models

Normative team models, such as Hackman (1983) and Clutterbuck (1999), are models that try to identify group-level outcomes expected to emerge as a result of individuals adhering to a set of agreed behavioural norms.

Normative models seek to base themselves on explanatory theory and Clutterbuck (1999), among others, has paid particular attention to the processes and values that need to be managed if a team is to achieve its goals (see: Figure 14.1). He identified a range of characteristics a team would need to possess, almost regardless of the task being attempted. These characteristics were found by his research to be fundamental to the achievement of the team goals and included such ephemeral values as 'trust' and 'fun'. Critics of this approach point to the difficulty of measuring these values and of attempting to agree on what is meant by trust and fun. Each individual will have different ideas as to what is meant by these terms and agreeing on their meaning is likely to take considerable effort.

Figure 14.1 Clutterbuck's norm team model

Source: Adapted from Clutterbuck (1999).

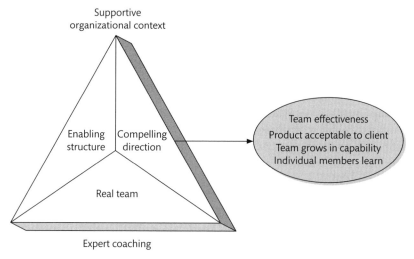

Figure 14.2 Hackman's team model

Source: Adapted from Hackman (2002).

Hackman (2002) uses three criteria to describe 'effectiveness' in terms of being able to judge whether a team has 'performed' well or not so well. These are: the production of a product acceptable to clients; growth in team capability; and a group experience meaningful and satisfying for group members. A version of Hackman's 'model' is shown in Figure 14.2, which illustrates the various components linking together in a dynamic framework. However, as he points out, having defined a 'clean, reliable performance measure in the laboratory that effectiveness criteria are not so straightforward for teams that perform work in organizational settings' (2002:23), meaning that, whilst this may look good under controlled conditions, out in the work place things may not be so clear.

Descriptive team models

These 'input-output' models are designed to explore the implications of work group effectiveness and posit that various 'input' factors affect 'output'. The underlying paradigm being that group interactions mediate between the input–output performance relationship. The key shared by most of the descriptive models is that interaction between people affects the team's output. These frameworks can be further codified into two different sub-sets: those that describe the individual team members, and those that focus on the team as a whole.

Individual role models—Belbin's approach

Despite early work by Benne and Sheats (1948), who identified three team roles: group task roles, group building and maintenance roles, and individual roles, Belbin's (1981) model is probably the best known of this genre (Jones 1993). The purpose of the model is to describe a range of roles that should be filled within any team that hopes to achieve its goals. The model is based on work carried out over a nine-year period by Belbin at Henley, and later in Cambridge. He observed students studying for their MBA who played a computer-based business simulation game similar to Monopoly. He was puzzled by why so-called Apollo (high performing) teams emerged from apparently random groupings. In addition, he wondered why teams with a membership of high IQ individuals often failed to perform as well as other groups. Using Cattell's (1946) Personality Inventory (16PF), he devised a model that allocated characteristics to certain roles observed in the Apollo teams. He initially identified eight team roles that people prefer to adopt when working in a group, and he gave these roles different names: Plant, Resource Investigator, Shaper, Completer Finisher, Monitor Evaluator, Team Worker, Company Worker, and Chairperson (Belbin 1981). However, he later (Belbin 1993) added the Specialist role and slightly revised the labels given to the roles (see: Figure 14.3). According to Belbin's theory, all successful teams contain a full complement of these team roles. Using a Jungian-based approach, he developed an instrument to ascertain an individual's preferred role. This was completed using a Self-Perception Inventory (SPI) and an 'independent' assessment, the Observation Assessment (OA).

As well as the strength or contribution they provided, each team role was also found to have what was called an 'allowable weakness'. This is a characteristic of the behaviours that may hinder the team, but are accepted by the team as a natural consequence of that individual's type. For example, the unorthodox Plant could be forgetful or scatty, or the Resource Investigator might forget to follow up on a lead. Whereas Shapers may, when faced with time pressure to complete a task, become aggressive and bad-humoured.

Whilst this model has been used for many years it does have certain limitations, which critics such as Furnham et al. (1993) highlight. For example, the questionnaire used to determine 'role preference' is of the self-assessed type with an ipsative scoring mechanism. This raises a whole series of questions surrounding the issue of self-awareness. As well as this, there is very little linkage through to competence within the role. In other words, although the respondent may believe they carry out a role well and assess themselves as 'competent', they may not be particularly skilled at the tasks required by the role. Broucek and Randall (1996) raised further concerns when they identified construct validity issues between the two forms used—the SPI and OA. Whilst Belbin's colleague, Dulewicz (1995), was able to go some way to refuting the claims of Broucek and Randall, his results are difficult to generalize across wider organizational contexts. In addition, Belbin makes no comment on the dynamic processes which drive a team towards its conclusion—usually the completion of a certain task or goal. Bannister and Fransella (1971) are particularly critical of this approach, arguing that use of the 16PF instrument, based as it is on trait-based psychology, does not consider the 'whole' person and as such ignores consequential aspects of an individual's belief system and associated motivation.

 Pause for thought

1. Having thought about your behaviour in a team, can you identify with any of the descriptions in Belbin's model?

2. What do you think about the idea of 'allowable weakness'?

BELBIN

Team Role Summary Descriptions

Team Role	Contribution	Allowable Weakness
Plant 	Creative, imaginative, unorthodox. Solves difficult problems.	Ignores incidentals. Too pre-occupied to communicate effectively.
Resource Investigator 	Extrovert, enthusiastic, communicative. Explores opportunities. Develops contacts.	Over-optimistic. Loses interest once initial enthusiasm has passed.
Coordinator 	Mature, confident, a good chairperson. Clarifies goals, promotes decision making, delegates well.	Can be seen as manipulative. Offloads personal work.
Shaper 	Challenging, dynamic, thrives on pressure. Has the drive and courage to overcome obstacles.	Prone to provocation. Offends people's feelings.
Monitor Evaluator 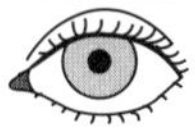	Sober, strategic and discerning. Sees all options. Judges accurately.	Lacks drive and ability to inspire others.
Teamworker 	Co-operative, mild, perceptive and diplomatic. Listens, builds, averts friction.	Indecisive in crunch situations.
Implementer 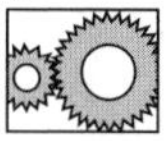	Disciplined, reliable, conservative and efficient. Turns ideas into practical actions	Somewhat inflexible. Slow to respond to new possibilities.
Completer Finisher 	Painstaking, conscientious, anxious. Searches out errors and omissions. Polishes and perfects.	Inclined to worry unduly. Reluctant to delegate.
Specialist 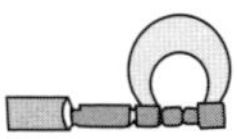	Single-minded, self-starting, dedicated. Provides knowledge and skills in rare supply.	Contributes on only a narrow front. Dwells on technicalities.

Figure 14.3 Belbin team roles

Source: Reproduced with kind permission of Belbin Associates.

Margerison–McCann team management wheel

Despite these concerns, role profiles are still popular, with Obeng (1994) developing a framework using five different 'stereotypes' aimed at project management, and Margerison et al. (1986), who developed a similar model to Belbin's in that it uses Jungian theory (see: Chapter 10) to identify which type of team role an individual prefers to work in. The team roles they identify are: Reporter Adviser, Creator Innovator, Explorer Promoter, Assessor Developer, Thruster Organizer, Concluder Producer, Controller Inspector, and Upholder Maintainer (see: Figure 14.4).

Team roles are identified through the individual completing a 60-item, forced choice index, called the Team Management Index (TMI). Preferred roles and related roles are based on the respondent's answers factored onto four scales pertaining to how the individual relates to others, how information is used, how this information is used to make decisions, and how individuals organize themselves and other people.

The TMI approach is based on first understanding the activities that need to be carried out in order for a team to complete a task successfully. Their research suggested there were nine different types of work (see: Table 14.2) needing to be addressed for a team to perform their task well.

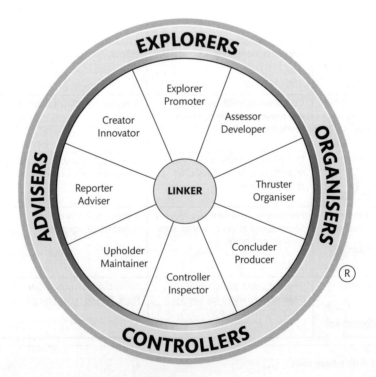

Figure 14.4 Margerison–McCann team management wheel

Source: Margerison and McCann. Reproduced with permission.

Table 14.2 The types of work model

Activity	Purpose
Advising	Obtaining and disseminating information
Innovating	Creating and experimenting with ideas
Promoting	Searching out new opportunities
Developing	Assessing and testing new approaches
Organizing	Implementing ways of making things work
Producing	Operating systems on a regular basis
Inspecting	Checking and auditing systems
Maintaining	Ensuring standards are upheld
Linking	Coordinating and integrating the team

Source: Margerison and McCann (2000). Reproduced with permission.

The next stage was to identify which activities individual team members felt most comfortable with and performed well. This was achieved by interviewing team members about their experiences and their own motivation. Moving forward, Margerison and McCann (1990) wanted to be able to predict which roles individuals would be most suited to, and they devised their Team Management Profile Questionnaire, which suggested a particular 'major' role and two 'related' roles as being most suitable for a given individual. Each of these roles has a set of characteristics and, similarly to Belbin, has positive and weaker aspects when considering their contribution to the team (see: Table 14.3).

The research, based on five years of study, has echoes of the Myers–Briggs Type Inventory (see: Chapter 10) and as such is well supported by psychometric data. However, as Bartram (1995) points out, the ipsative nature of the instrument creates certain problems when trying to obtain psychometric data—for example, around scale inter-correlations and the factor structure. Despite these criticisms, role-based theory models have become almost ubiquitous in many team-based training courses and management development programmes (Partington and Harris 1999).

 Pause for thought

1. What do you think of the TMI model?
2. Do you recognize any of the behaviours in yourself?
3. In your opinion, how does it compare to Belbin's approach?

Table 14.3 Team management profiles

Margerison-McCann role	Behavioural characteristics	Belbin equivalent
Reporter Adviser	This is an advisory role whereby they gather information and present it to others so it can be easily understood. They are methodical and careful. They do not enjoy conflict and will move to diffuse a situation or move away from its direct effects.	Monitor Evaluator
Creator Innovator	Future orientated and they enjoy thinking up new ideas. Independently minded, they challenge the status quo. They can be unstructured and often like working alone or in small teams.	Plant
Explorer Promoter	Good networkers and both entrepreneurial and persuasive. They take ideas to others and bring back contacts. They often have a 'big picture' approach but can miss detail and operational matters.	Resource Investigator
Assessor Developer	With their good analytical approach, they are a bridge between ideas and action. They like organizing new activities but can move on once the initial thrust is complete rather than see things through.	Coordinator
Thruster Organizers	They like making things happen and set objectives and deadlines for others. Structured and disciplined in their approach, their task focused mind-set can make them blind to relational issues.	Shaper
Concluder Producer	Practical and enduring, their ability lies in seeing things through to the end. They enjoy routine and are dependable. Change needs to be convincing for them to embrace it, otherwise it will be seen as change for change's sake.	Completer Finisher
Controller Inspector	Really careful and meticulous, they enjoy facts, figures, and rules and checking output against a set of predefined criteria. They may be seen as inflexible and dogmatic if there is deviation from norms.	Implementer
Upholder Maintainer	Guided by their strong sense of right and wrong, they can be dedicated to a cause that matches these beliefs. They weld the team together with quiet understated emotion. They can be stubborn and resistant if actions compromise their values.	Team Worker

Source: Adapted from *TMS Handbook* (2000) TMS Development International Ltd. with permission.

 Case study   HMS *Brilliant's* control room

A Royal Navy ship's control room sits at the heart of its ability to defend itself against attack and to carry out its broader functions. The control room houses the systems that coordinate the ship's weapon systems, communication, and command functions. There are a number of highly sophisticated computer systems, including radar to provide a tactical view of the battle zone, a computer that is capable of tracking incoming threats and allocating an appropriate weapon to deal with the threat, and digital links to every part of the ship including the engine room, bridge, and upper deck. The room itself is deep inside the ship with no portholes offering a view outside. However, the key to the ship's survival is not the weapons systems but the behaviour of highly trained women and men that operate the control room. Each system is under the control of a senior rate who listens to the input from a team of operators. The senior rate feeds this information to an officer called the Principal Warfare Officer

(PWO). This officer is responsible for the tactical response of the ship to attack rather than the Captain. If the ship is damaged in the attack, the responsibility for dealing with the damage is immediately passed to the Damage Control teams who, distributed in key locations around the ship, will rush to fight fires or plug holes in the hull. Each of these commands is issued in seconds as different situations emerge, and the lives of the ship's crew will literally depend on each person within the team reacting correctly and quickly. To ensure that this smooth teamwork has the greatest chance of success, the ship's crew will have been trained under conditions as close to 'real' as possible before being allowed to proceed on their mission. Unless the Captain and his crew can convince a team of assessors based at the Navy's Training School in Portland that they are capable of dealing with almost any perceived threat, they will not be allowed to put to sea. It is this rigour, training, and commitment to a common goal that will save lives when an emergency occurs.

Source

Author's own experience.

Questions

1. Imagine yourself in a darkened Operations Room with the battle about the start, how are you feeling?
2. What behaviours do you hope to see in your colleagues?
3. How could a model such as the TMI help to train the crew?

Time or phase-based models

A different approach examines the development of certain emotions and activities as experienced by individual team members as their relationships with others in the team evolve over time. In 1965, Bruce Tuckman synthesized pre-existing literature to suggest a model (see: Figure 14.5) still widely quoted today. In 1977, Tuckman and Jensen updated the model to add

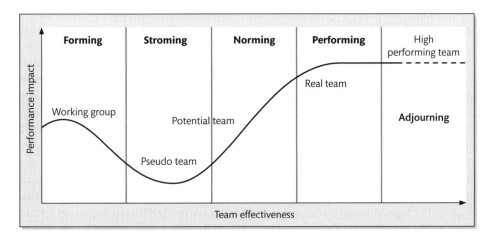

Figure 14.5 Tuckman and Jensen's phase-based model
Source: Adapted from Tuckman and Jensen (1977).

Table 14.4 Comparative phase-based approaches

Bass and Ryterband (1979)	Woodcock (1979)	Tuckman and Jensen (1977)	Glass (1996)
Developing mutual trust	Undeveloped team	Forming	Birth
Communications and decision making	Experimenting team	Storming	Childhood
Motivation and productivity	Consolidating	Norming	Adolescence
Control and organize	Mature	Performing (adjourn)	Maturity

'adjourning' to reflect the end phase of a team's life cycle. This approach involves describing the team as evolving through a series of steps or phases as time progresses. It implies the team begins at a fixed point in time (formation), moves to exploration of individual member expectations (storm), this leads to the development of team 'rules' (norms), which in turn allows the group to perform the required task.

Bass and Ryterband (1979) also use four stages, as do Woodcock (1979) and Glass (1996). Table 14.4 shows how the different models use slightly differentiated terms to describe the activities being experienced by team members at any particular point.

Whilst this approach captures some of the dynamic energy and relationships within teams possibly not encompassed in Belbin's world, there are several flaws inherent within this typology. For example, the model implies the team members begin 'forming' in the same space–time continuum. In today's flexible and ever-changing world, this rarely happens. Individuals join teams at different points and leave often at inconvenient (from the task perspective) times. This means individuals may not have 'stormed' or 'normed' with their colleagues and, hence, there is the possibility of a schism in the team dynamics. The development of remote working, partnerships between organizations across the world, and home working mean that the space–time dimension is also being eroded with consequences for the phase development. This issue of remoteness, with the associated issue of time zone mismatch, raises another concern with this model in that the metaphorical construct of a clock implies equidistance between the phases, and of equitable domain space within the phase boundaries—that is, the same amount of time is spent storming as performing. Gersick (1988) does attempt to recognize this issue by suggesting that time and space through the various phases is variable, but her results are still largely experimentally based and have not been replicated in other environments. As Gersick points out, 'researchers have typically worked with groups with short life-spans, usually minutes or hours, and studied them in a laboratory as they performed a limited task of solving a specific problem' (1988:10).

The challenge usually proffered when faced with this type of model is to attack the paradigm of 'group development as an inevitable progression' (Gersick 1988:11). In these examples, the group cannot move to phases three and four without having achieved a satisfactory 'result' in phases one and two. Although some (Scheidel and Crowell 1964) have suggested an iterative cycle rather than linear process, Poole (1981, 1983a, 1983b) raised serious challenges to this type of model by demonstrating there were many different sequences through which teams can develop. This approach says little about the mechanisms for change between phases, and only offers a relatively limited insight to group behaviour at a very specific point in time. The triggers for change between phases, and why such changes take place, are largely left unexplored. Gersick (1988) tries to rectify this by drawing on a concept established in the field of natural history—that of 'punctuated equilibrium' (1988:16). Using this concept, she describes a set of observations in which teams were seen to alternate between inertia (i.e. a steady state) and sudden revolutionary changes in behaviour. Again, despite challenges, these models are still highly popular with practitioners.

Team mental model

An alternative approach, designed to help understand why some work-based teams per-formed differently from others despite using such frameworks as described by Belbin (1981), Tuckman (1965), and Clutterbuck (1999), is known as team **mental model theory**. This rela-tively new model suggests that teams which share a common understanding of certain key issues relating to the task, the environment, their own processes, and values, and have an understanding of how each individual member thinks, perform better than groups with het-erogeneous understanding. This concept has become known as 'shared team mental model' theory (Cannon-Bowers and Salas 1990; Cannon-Bowers et al. 1993; Roe 2004) and is based on the work of Kelly (1955). This approach has been tested in various laboratory experiments and in command and control teams, such as those in military settings, or highly time-pressured environments, such as those in A&E operating theatres. However, critics of this approach point to a lack of 'real world' testing and a lack of intellectual rigour in defining the concept.

> **Mental model theory** is a theory for considering how individuals think and reason (see Kelly (1955) or any of Fay Fransella's work). The idea that individuals use mental models can be traced back to Ken Craik (1943) and his assertion that the mind constructs 'small scale models of reality' and that 'one of the most fundamental properties of thought is its power of predicting events' (1943:21).

Examining thoughts generated by David Casey's (1985) paper, 'When is a Team not a Team?', social psychologists considered the question posed in Casey's mind as what are teams 'constructing' when engaged in team building? Casey, although challenging the whole 'team building' construct, began to generate various ideas to explain what was happening when individuals make statements like this:

> We are a very tight group, a very humble group I like to think. But within the camp we have a lot of faith in each other. I look around the huddle before a game and I think 'I'm glad he's on our side'. That goes for every player. I've got a lot of faith in the guys around me and I've got that faith because I see the way they work day in, day out.
>
> Tom Wood, England Rugby Player, ahead of Grand Slam match April 2013.

The approach begins by challenging this kind of statement and by trying to understand what happens when teams are formed by organizations. The starting point for an explanation began with prior exposure to the concept of the 'Learning Organization'. Whilst this term has been derided for a lack of operational rigour, at least intellectually, the model proposed by Senge (1990) and Burgoyne et al. (1994), among others, makes some interesting challenges to how organizations are conceptualized. Among these perspectives is the view proffered by Senge that teams can learn, and when they do the intelligence of the team exceeds that of the individual members. Senge was influenced by the thinking of the distinguished physicist, David Bohm (1917–1992), who suggested that a new kind of mind was emerging based around collaborative group behaviour, and the Chilean biologists, Humberto Maturana and Francisco Varella (1987), who drew on biological analogies to explain organizational behaviour. Bohm and Peat (1989) speculated that people participate in a pool of common meaning that was not accessible individually. Drawing on broad analogies between the world of quantum physics and organizations, his approach was one of the *whole* organizing the *parts*, in contrast to the generally accepted proposition that individual components work together and 'generate' an organization (Leavitt 1983). Using this as a starting point, researchers began by exploring the general idea of the team as a cohesive biomass to ascertain if theories applied to individual cognition could be applied to teams. As a consequence, perhaps if teams could learn then they could be 'trained' to become more effective and efficient and hence 'perform' (to borrow from Tuckman).

In essence, whilst a 'group mind' is still based on the perceptions of individual members, it is more than the sum of such individual properties (Cooke 2002)—it is a group-level phenomenon (Klimoski and Mohammed 1994). Of course, individual belief structures play a pivotal role in developing socially shared cognition (Resnick 1991) but a group-level model is more than an aggregation of individual hopes, dreams, predictions, and expectations. To accept and adopt this approach, we need to consider 'the team' as a single organism or network somewhat recursively partitioned in time and space (especially if we want to look at the virtual world, see: Bohm and Peat 1989). This will mean considering the psychological space, that Kelly (1955) suggests individuals use as a place for classifying experiences, as also existing in a 'team' so there is a 'team space'. In addition, this space can exist in cyberspace (Hine 2000) when teams operate using remote communication methods and/or operate in an asynchronous manner. Roe (2004) suggests team mental models emerge from the interplay of individual team member cognition and team process behaviour, which combine to produce a shared understanding among team members.

Early researchers in this field, such as Rouse et al. (1992), Cooke (2002), and Klimoski and Mohammed (1994), focused their research on highly structured teams operating in fast paced environments, such as military command teams, driven by the general thesis 'that team effectiveness will improve if team members have an adequate shared understanding of the task, team, equipment and situation' (Mohammed and Dumville 2001:89). An often-quoted example is the performance of high-paced hospital emergency room operations. These environments are characterized by individuals operating in an environment where thought almost becomes automatic, as the task demands are immediate and urgent. Individuals will have spent many hours training together to enable them to deal with a range of reasonably well defined, albeit stressful, situations. It was speculated that, in order to cope with the demands placed on the team facing these types of environments, a shared mental model was present which enabled team members to anticipate each other's actions in a given situation. This anticipation meant that communication was non-verbal and implicit as the task progressed. Individual actions formed part of a well-worn and practised 'routine' that largely governed the actions of the individual actors. In this particular example, the individual team members, the lifesaving equipment, the routines governing the use of the equipment, and the patient could be considered to be one network whereby the components operate as a coherent whole displaying a common shared understanding of who does what, when, why, and how.

The next significant step came with the work of Orasanu and Salas (1993) and Weick and Roberts (1993) who began to apply this concept of a shared understanding of group norms to a limited number of quasi-military settings, such as the flight deck of an aircraft carrier. Weick and Roberts describe the concept of a collective mind as a 'pattern of heedful interrelationships of actions in a social system' (1993:357). They describe the wonderfully complex arena of a modern aircraft carrier and wonder why such environments do not produce accidents and disasters more often than is generally the case. They examined how a pilot lands his aircraft on the shifting deck of the carrier and conclude that this is 'not a solitary act' (1993:362) but a set of interrelated activities that conclude with the 'recovery' of the aircraft and pilot. This, they hypothesize, points to a collective mind, and they proposed a simple two by two matrix to show whether the group was developed or undeveloped, drawing on Tuckman's (1965) model, and whether the collective mind was developed or undeveloped.

It was this work, and related 'experiments' (e.g. Cannon-Bowers and Salas 1990; Cannon-Bowers et al. 1993), that eventually prompted Klimoski and Mohammed (1994) to attempt to draw together these disparate threads and to criticize research in this domain as having little conceptual basis or empirical rigour. They began by questioning the form, function, antecedents, and consequences of 'team mental models' (1994:403), effectively coining the phrase for the first time in academic circles. They concluded their review of the literature available at the time by stating that a 'shared team mental model goes beyond influencing the predictability of others... It sets up a chain of effects influencing multiple determinants of team effectiveness' (1994:425).

The next major investment in this area came from a set of researchers based in the United States' Naval Air Warfare Centre, in Florida. Beth Blickensderfer and her associates (Blickensderfer et al. 1997) carried out a whole series of cognitive experiments based around complex information-rich systems. These experiments sought to apply team mental model theories to the wider picture of team decision making, and focused attention on US Naval personnel completing a set of computer-based simulations. Roe (2004), developing the idea further, suggested that a team mental model was formed of different components as illustrated in Figure 14.6. So, a team, to be successful, needs to have a shared mental model around the themes of understanding their task, how they are going to operate collectively (team), some empathy with each other (type), and a grasp of the resources they have available (tools).

In summary, shared team mental model theory suggests that a team operates like a biological organism and 'learns' about its environment. For a team to be successful, the individuals within the team contribute to and share ideas, knowledge, and decisions about how to thrive in their shared environment.

 Pause for thought

1. What do you think about this idea, that individuals can create and share knowledge?

2. Do you think it is necessary for everyone to 'share common knowledge' for a team to be successful?

3. If you have worked in a team have you experienced anything like this?

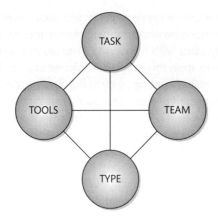

Figure 14.6 A shared team mental model

Source: Roe (2004) Model © Kevin Roe.

The downside of teams

Each particular approach has its own strengths and weaknesses—either the approach reflects the dynamic flow of energies within a group, or it captures the particular skills brought to bear by the individual members. However, no one model appears to harness the essential dynamics of a team, whilst offering leaders and team members a simple tool to aid analysis and understanding of their team. It is easy to argue, given the current vogue for work-based teams, the focus on organizations requiring and recruiting 'team players', and the vast sums of money spent by organizations on developing management teams, that team skills and the understanding of teams is still a key topic of interest for organizations worldwide.

In addition, all of the above discourse presupposes the need for a team to achieve a given end. Casey and Critchley (1984) and Sinclair (1992) are right to point out the potential difficulties to be found in the view of the team being the panacea for organizational task achievement. Whilst neither of these papers suggests teams have no place in decision making, they do point out that teams can sometimes be more of a hindrance than a help in some circumstances. Casey (1985) goes on to highlight the need for much higher-level cognitive skills and the need for a level of openness and sharing among team members that may be beyond either their capability or their willingness.

Further eroding the 'teams fix all' mentality comes McGregor (1960) who highlights the emotions likely to be experienced within an effective team as those of a relaxed, friendly, and cohesive atmosphere where discussion is free and open, but these are seldom found in practice. Kandola (1995) points out the potential for this nirvana to be the case but indicates that teams often fail to generate such harmonious environments. Brooks (2003) suggests this to be because individuals within the team have their own agenda and own reasons for doing things, which are outside the main 'task' set for the team. This leads, he suggests, to rumour, supposition, and innuendo—the group can generate 'negativity which can live on when it might have naturally subsided in individuals' (2003:111). In an attack on the claim that groups are more 'creative' than individuals, Asch (1951) pointed out the impact of peer group pressure on the willingness of individuals to contradict statements and decisions made by colleagues, and Diehl and Stroebe (1987) suggested that individuals working alone produced better quality ideas than groups.

Janis (1972:9), after studying famous cases in recent history, coined the phrase '**groupthink**' to describe the quality of decisions made by groups. He felt that, although groups believe they have both perfect knowledge and perfect rationality when making decisions, in fact they have neither. In examining a number of different cases, such as the decision in 1961 by President Kennedy to authorize the Bay of Pigs invasion, and, more recently, the 1986 *Challenger* Shuttle disaster (Hirokawa et al. 1988), he surmised that groups often curtailed discussion, reached false consensus, and considered only a very limited range of alternatives before making a decision and acting on that judgement. They do this for a number of reasons, such as the pressure to conform and a desire to please. The atmosphere produced by groupthink creates the following characteristics (Janis 1972):

- Illusion of invulnerability.
- Belief in the superiority of the group.
- Disparaging the opposition.
- Group consensus must be maintained.
- Illusion of unanimity.
- Creation of 'mind guards' around leader.

> **Groupthink** is: 'A mode of thinking that people engage in when they are deeply involved in a cohesive group, when the members' strivings for unanimity override their motivation to realistically appraise alternative courses of action' (Janis 1972:8)

More recently, Badie has used the idea to plot President Bush's decision for the USA to invade Iraq. She concluded that the 'post 9/11 mission was pathologically driven by groupthink, which caused a shift in the administration's view of Saddam from a troubling dictator to an existential threat to US security' (Badie 2010:1).

Summary

Given the above discourse and range of conceptual frameworks described, all of which, to varying degrees, seek to have identified 'the truth' about teamwork, there would appear to be little agreement as to what a team is and how it works. The very heterogeneity of organizational contexts that such constructs are located in may make this difficult—if not impossible. However, what may be more useful is to identify the themes and concepts at the heart of each of these models. In studying the various frameworks outlined above, key concepts do suggest themselves. Teamwork can be notoriously difficult to 'get right' and is frustrating for some people. Different personalities and different agendas can make working collaboratively a pointless exercise. The different contexts in which teams operate also make defining a generalized leadership approach rather difficult. The various academic models reviewed also offer a complex range of options that seek to champion a particular aspect of team dynamics. In terms of leading teams, perhaps we leave the last word to Drucker (1990:14):

> The leaders who work most effectively, it seems to me, never say 'I.' And that's not because they have trained themselves not to say 'I.' They don't think 'I.' They think 'we'; they think 'team.' They understand their job to be to make the team function. They accept responsibility and don't sidestep it, but 'we' gets the credit... This is what creates trust, what enables you to get the task done.

Teamwork can indeed be frustrating but also enormously rewarding if the leader recognizes the demands and deals with them appropriately. Successful leaders will have to lead teams and it is probably a core meta-competence required by leaders in the coming years.

 Case study Accident and emergency department

It is a worrying fact but most of us will at some point in our lives visit an accident and emergency department (A&E)—either as a patient or to visit someone who is a patient. The processes that operate in this high stress, critical care environment are designed to work so that an individual entering the department has the best chance of survival. However, there are also pressures from external factors, such as government targets, that affect these processes and it is interesting to consider how teamwork, leadership, and systems interact to produce a positive outcome—i.e. a patient survives. A&E carries certain kudos within the National Health Service (NHS) and nurses who operate in this environment go through an extended period of training that, as a minimum, lasts two years after initial qualification as a nurse. A&E produces moments of high drama, and health workers operate under extreme pressure whilst making decisions that can result in life or death for the patients in their care.

A patient may arrive in A&E via several different routes. These routes have names associated with the severity of the suspected injury or condition of the patient; for example, minor and major. It is down to a nurse or paramedic to decide on this 'rating'. The initial assessment affects how the patient is passed through the system and requires the individual carer to make a decision based on feedback received from the patient, possibly an ambulance crew or the patient's doctor (GP).

In many cases this is a simple operation as the patient may walk in to the A&E department, describe their condition—say a fall or a cut—and be easily dealt with; this is known as 'minor'. However, the situation becomes more complicated when 'majors' are about to happen. A 'major' occurs when there is a serious incident, such as a car crash or heart attack. A patient will be transported to A&E via ambulance and the first point of contact is a rapid assessment nurse (otherwise known as a RAT nurse). This person makes a decision when faced with the patient which could be immediate resuscitation, a move to a major care nurse, or perhaps for minor treatment if the injury is not thought to be life threatening.

The warning for an imminent major comes via a telephone in the nurse station—this is colloquially known as the 'Bat Phone'. If this rings, the nearest person picks it up and deals with the instructions coming down the phone. This will mean taking details of the patient, their vital signs, and the estimated time of arrival of the ambulance. Once this information is gathered, the shift coordinator takes over. This person is a Band 7 nurse which is roughly equivalent to a ward manager (most nurses are level 5, with a ward sister at level 6). It is the shift supervisor who coordinates the 12-hour shift and allocating roles and tasks to the team. At the beginning of the shift, the supervisor will give a briefing to the team and receive a brief from the preceding shift so that patients are handed over smoothly. The supervisor will not know who is on the team until the beginning of the shift. There may be 'regular' nurses who have worked together before as well as staff from outside agencies that will be covering for sickness, holiday, or other absence. The supervisor may know some of the preferences of the team—such as who is a good RAT nurse—but, effectively, will allocate people to roles without prior knowledge. Once this is complete, the team will move to position and begin their patient care.

One of the competing responsibilities for the supervisor, as well as keeping people alive, is to meet the government's target for a patient's time spent in A&E of four hours. This means that a patient, once they enter A&E, must be either discharged or admitted to the hospital within four hours. For a hospital to have achieved this target, this must be the case for 98 per cent of patients. If there is a 'breach' (the target is missed) the shift supervisor must account for the reasons for this to the oncoming shift supervisor, and ultimately to the hospital management. If the target is missed, it may result in the hospital being fined and receiving adverse publicity. There are various external factors that can affect the ability of the shift to meet this target, not least the number of cases they have to see, but also other reasons such as the availability of a certain specialist doctor. This is because an A&E doctor cannot admit a patient to hospital. This can only be done by a specialist, such as a paediatric consultant. If no such specialist is available, the patient will not be discharged. Canny shift supervisors will have a back-up plan that involves a short-stay admissions ward. This ward, usually with only a few beds, is outside the main hospital admittance procedure and may be used to place patients who are no longer in danger but cannot be discharged until they have been seen by the relevant expert.

Working in A&E needs a nurse to understand how the whole system works as, well as their individual role, as they may need to take on a position at any time as the situation changes rapidly around them. For example, if an incident deemed to be sufficiently serious occurs, the incoming ambulance crew may decide it needs a Trauma team available at A&E when they arrive. Although this is a rare event and has strict criteria attached, this involves bringing together a multi-disciplinary team of surgeons, anaesthetists, nurses, and senior A&E consultants. This team will be ready when the ambulances arrive to take over the immediate care of the patients. The significance of this is that relatively junior nurses can command instant responses from doctors, consultants, and other colleagues.

The atmosphere and culture within A&E is often one of 'work hard, play hard'. The pressures of the workload, coupled with the target times, require a certain kind of character to be able to cope with the stresses. There is a strong ethos of support for nurses, who may experience an extreme range of emotions as lives are literally fought for and yet may be lost. The teamwork required is vital, and the interaction between doctors, nurses, and other care professionals has been likened to more of a partnership than is apparent in other parts of the NHS, where a more formal hierarchy exists.

Source

Interview with experienced A&E nurse, 21 May 2012.

Questions

1. How could you use any of the different ideas discussed in this chapter to explore the teamwork present in an A&E department? For example, would a shared mental model assist the team to perform their task? Or how does the team go through Tuckman's phases?

2. What impact would an autocratic shift leader have on the performance of the department? Compare this with the behaviours you may see if the shift leader was democratic.

3. What significance, if any, is there in the 'Bat Phone' having no one person allocated to answering it?

Assignment and discussion questions—3,000 words

Here are some alternative suggestions to form the basis of a 3,000 word assignment:

Using an appropriate model, analyse the performance of a team of your choice. This could be drawn from any field such as business, sport, or the arts. Present your findings, along with a set of recommendations based on your analysis, to improve the performance of your chosen team.

Are teams always the solution to organizational challenges? Discuss this using examples drawn from two different organizational spheres, such as engineering or tourism.

Consider a recent poor decision made by a collective. This could be, for example, a political decision made by a government, an investment decision made by an organization, or a tactical decision made by a sports team. Ask yourself to what extent was 'groupthink' a factor in the decision?

Why do you think many organizations, when recruiting, have a criterion that assesses the applicants' suitability based on their performance as a 'team player'? What are the implications for individuals who are not such people?

Further reading

The Battle of Thermopylae is a good account of teamwork succeeding against mighty odds (Matthews, Rupert (2006) *The Battle of Thermopylae: A Campaign in Context*. Stroud: Tempus Publishing). It gives a narrative account of how the army of King Leonidas of Sparta, composed of roughly 7,000 men, held off a horde of over 100,000 Persians led by King Xerxes.

Evans, Ben (2007) *Space Shuttle Challenger: Ten Journeys into the Unknown*. New York: Springer Praxis Books. This sad book retells the disaster that befell Space Shuttle *Challenger* in 1986. It is instructive because subsequent speculation as to the reasons behind the disaster pointed to groupthink as a primary cause of the highly-educated and risk-adverse engineers allowing the shuttle to be launched. BBC2 commissioned a film in 2013 called *The Challenger*, staring William Hurt as the scientist, Richard Feynman, which gives an insight to the inquiry after the disaster.

There are many books that look at teams in a sporting context. One of the more recent is Stewart Cotterill's (2012) *Team Psychology in Sport* (Hove: Routledge). The book examines the role of the sport psychologist, and how understanding the individual is key to developing the collective. Given the success of the British Team at the Olympics in 2012, it makes for an interesting read. He attempts to incorporate practical themes, such as conflict management and how to plan and run meetings, so it does cover a great deal of ground.

Leadership and change

After reading this chapter you will:

- Understand how to generate a vision for change.
- Critically explore the process of change.
- Explore some of the reasons why change can be difficult to implement.

Introduction

This chapter is somewhat different from the preceding ones in that this section starts to focus on the 'what' aspects of leadership rather than the 'why' and 'how'. This is because creating change, managing change, implementing change, or clearing up the mess after a period of change are some of the most common themes a modern leader will encounter. In broad terms, the chapter adopts a systems view of the organization, which places the organization in a broad 'evolutionary' position. This is because, to a large extent, organizations, the individuals, and systems within them change because they are part of an open system (Rakotobe-Joel et al. 2002). That is, they receive input from their external environment, such as products and raw materials, and transform these inputs via series of internal processes into outputs (Grant 1991) that re-enter the system. However, as the external system changes, the inputs to an organization change, and so do the internal processes as a result of these new inputs. In addition, organizations experience internal change, such as the churn of employees joining and leaving, which can affect their performance. Examination of any relatively straightforward business planning model, such as Michael Porter's (2008) 5-Forces Model, can show the pressures on an organization—for example, the forces affecting new entrants into any particular business sector. This, in turn, can also affect the business and force it to alter its policies and process—for example, to ensure compliance with a piece of employment legislation. This means modern organizations, on account of the interconnections within the global world economy, are subject to constant change.

It is also fair to note that the literature surrounding change and change management is huge, so this chapter will focus on three elements of change: creating a vision, exploring the process of change, and the politics of change with recommendations for further reading should this be required. These three areas have been selected as they offer a broad insight into the main challenges facing managers as they seek to cope with change.

History of change

As H. G. Wells (1922) put it, 'adapt or perish, now as ever, is Nature's inexorable imperative'. By this, he is referring, of course, to the theory of evolution, which supports the view that organisms that change and adapt to suit their environment are those that will survive. Extending this idea to organizations (Morgan 2006) suggests that organizations too must adapt or perish in the same way the dinosaurs did. And the Greek philosopher, Heraclitus, is credited with the observation that 'nothing endures but change' over 2,500 years ago. It is a moot point to suggest change is a constant feature of human existence.

In leadership terms, change and the processes associated with change, such as the correct analysis of the circumstances surrounding the change, the generation of options and ideas to cope with the change, and the successful implementation of the selected plan, have always been present but often not articulated particularly well. It is also pertinent to consider the false assumption that, to some degree, leadership is about the first two and 'management' is concerned with the third. As discussed in the Introduction, the view that leadership and management are somehow two separate, albeit related, roles does not reflect the reality of most modern organizations where managers lead projects. What is more certain is the recent focus on 'change management' (should that be 'change leadership'?) as a key indicator of both successful organizations and successful individuals. Arvonen and Ekvall (1999) have suggested the dichotomous view of leadership as being either 'universal' (i.e. a particular approach will be effective in any situation) or 'contingent' (i.e. context sensitive) is a flawed model. Their research has introduced the concept of a third idea whereby a manager could be assessed against a 'change/development' scale as opposed to being simply orientated on a task/relations basis. They think, 'the new business environment will require new management abilities concerning development, creativity and radical innovation' (1999:244)—attributes they associate closely with change and the management of this activity (see: Figure 15.1).

 Pause for thought

Review your understanding of Blake and Mouton's approach as outlined in Chapter 3. This approach is what Arvonen and Ekvall (1999) consider to be 'universal' (they mean the model pays little attention to the situation facing the leader). Review your understanding of situational approaches in Chapter 5 (that is, leadership is influenced by external factors—context sensitive leadership).

1. Do you think change/development is a 'new' ability?
2. Could this mean leaders can be assessed across three different scales?

If the quotes from Wells and Heraclitus taken from an earlier age are true, then change has been around and part of the human race from the time man first walked on two legs—quite a profound change in itself. Whilst change is something of a constant—turning on the television or opening a newspaper will convince you of that point—it is false to suspect that

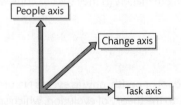

Figure 15.1 Three axis model of leadership

changes being experienced now are any more profound than other changes experienced by our forefathers. Radical change, such as the 'accelerating and unprecedented technological change' (Mokyr 1985:82) experienced during the Industrial Revolution of the eighteenth and nineteenth centuries, or the invention of the printing press by Guttenberg in 1436, have each created deep-seated shifts in our understanding of our cosmos and altered permanently our relationship with each other. Each epoch of human existence is marked by radical additions to technology, culture, and knowledge. The impact experienced in each of these periods is just as far-reaching as those we are currently experiencing as the digital, virtual world continues to shape our lives. The implication is that each revolutionary change has needed 'leadership' in order for organizations and societies to take advantage of them. The first stage in this is to consider how the new opportunities available to the organization can best be harnessed. This means having a clear idea of what the new, changed future might look and feel like.

 Pause for thought

1. Do you agree or disagree with the assertion that changes now are more far-reaching and fundamental than changes experienced in the past? Try to think of yourself as a 'citizen of the time' when thinking about these items:

   a. The realization the Earth moved around the Sun and not the other way around.

   b. That humans were apparently direct descendants of monkeys.

2. Could you cope without your mobile phone?

Vision

As we have already discussed in Chapter 7, transformational leaders have the ability to create and communicate to their followers the idea of a different future. Hayes (2010:159) makes the point that 'a strong vision can make a valuable contribution to the success of a change initiative'. Warren Bennis (1984) and Paton and McCalman (2008) concur and make the point that any successful change process begins with the understanding of what the new 'state' of the organization will look and feel like. So, whilst the need for leaders to have a clear idea of what the 'new' state will be is largely uncontested, what is unclear is how this step is completed by a leader. The difficult part is grasping how to articulate an ephemeral idea into terms that will be meaningful to a range of individuals, some of whom are likely to be hostile to any change. As Machiavelli suggests, (1515:24) 'nothing is so difficult to take in hand, more perilous to conduct, or more uncertain in its success, than to take the lead in the introduction of a new order of things'. By this, he is suggesting that change is a difficult process to implement and success is by no means guaranteed. The first issue to consider is exactly what is meant by a 'vision'. Joan of Arc (see the Case study in Chapter 13) had a vision when three saints appeared before her. However, a similar declaration is unlikely to persuade a sceptical workforce. The challenge is that the word 'vision' has so many connotations; from encompassing a number of 'values' to covering strategic objectives, having a natty 'strap line', or articulating a 'mission statement'.

Perhaps one of the best known models of exactly what a vision 'is' and how to construct one is Kotter's (1996) criterion drawn from his broad change 'framework' of eight stages, outlined later in this chapter (see: Models of the change process). His study and subsequent books have used this approach for underpinning a successful attempt at implementing change. Kotter studied more than 100 different organizations, both large and small, and analysed why change failed in these companies. He identified eight areas in common and developed a process map which suggests that, in order to be a successful leader in terms of implementing change, each stage needs to be addressed carefully and thoroughly before moving to the next. Peters and Waterman (1982) and Kanter (1989) have also identified a number of phases or elements to be put into place and examination of these different ideas suggests a number of overlapping areas when trying to create a unifying vision.

1. Imaginable: This means creating a 'picture', usually with metaphors and tropes of what the new future will look like. This can either be a new idea or hark back to some kind of golden halcyon days of yore. Winston Churchill, the British Prime Minister during the Second World War, often used the latter in his speeches asking the public to remain faithful to the idea of the British Empire. Martin Luther King, the American civil rights activist, used a picture of an America in the future in his iconic 'I have a dream' speech.

2. Desirable: The new future needs to be appealing to all of the stakeholders who have an interest in the organization. This can be challenging if this group is diverse, but essential if the leader is to create a sense of belonging within the broader community.

3. Feasible: Although the new vision needs to be inspirational, it must not be so fantastic as to appear unobtainable. The leader must articulate it in such a manner as to seem achievable with a degree of effort within the control of the stakeholders.

4. Focused: The vision should help individuals to make decisions when faced with uncertainty. The vision will give them a clear path so they can decide on a course of action when faced with a dilemma or choice.

5. Flexible: The vision, whilst clear in its appeal, should also be sufficiently malleable to allow both the leader and the followers to adapt should circumstances change for the better or worse.

6. Communicable: The best visions have a simple, straightforward message that can sum up the overall grand scheme, and can be grasped quickly by individuals. Here, leaders often look for a memorable phrase or mantra that can be repeated quickly. President Obama's first election victory in 2008 had the line, 'Yes we can', whilst Carlsberg lager has 'Probably the best lager in the world'.

 Pause for thought

Vision statements are not just for massive organizations. You can use Kotter's ideas when thinking about a project or dissertation. Imagine you are getting into a lift on the ground floor of a 10-storey building. A colleague gets in at the same time, the doors close and she asks you what your project is about. By the time the doors open on the top floor, some 30 seconds later, you need to have told her. Use the check list above to test your 'pitch'.

Here are some examples of vision statements from various sources illustrating the points above:

Amazon, the online retailer: 'Our vision is to be earth's most customer centric company; to build a place where people can come to find and discover anything they might want to buy online.'

Toys R Us, the toy company: 'Our Vision is to put joy in kids' hearts and a smile on parents' faces.'

Tata, the India conglomerate with interests in many different industrial sectors: 'We will spread our wings far beyond India, that we will become a global group, operating in many countries, an Indian business conglomerate that is at home in the world, carrying the same sense of trust that we do today.'

 Pause for thought

1. What do you make of these statements?

2. Can you get a feel for the organization from the statements?

3. How do they make you feel?

Different approaches to change

Many prominent 'change' authors, such as Kanter (1983), Lewin (1951), and Kotter (1996), conceptualize change as a 'journey' passing through stages as part of a process. Others view it as a singular event, such as when a law is changed, whilst Senge (1990) thinks of change as part of an on-going continual evolution. Whichever view is subscribed to, one thing in common is the need for action because change is about being different from before. Change is dynamic—that is, by definition, something has to happen and leaders need to focus on what needs to be done as well as ensuring the right things are delivered. Modern organizations do not have the luxury of stopping whilst a new computer system is installed or a new production process is implemented. Business has to continue as changes are made and this can be a very stressful time for both individuals and organizations alike. It is during these periods of intense upheaval that leaders really earn their rewards as they need to keep the various components of the organization functioning effectively as new modes of work are introduced and tested. In broad terms, there are two different models in use when considering what actions need to be taken: hard systems methodology and soft systems methodology.

Hard systems methodology (HSM)

This approach finds parallels with Rittel and Webber's (1973) older '**tame** and **wicked**' problems with tame problems being solved by using a HSM approach. Broadly, this approach starts with the question of 'How?' For example: 'How can we change this production process to be more efficient?', or 'How can we win this race?' In general, the approach, to be successful, needs a problem that can be well defined and contained. In terms of analysis, it involves a clear beginning and end—it is just the process in between that needs to be solved.

The distinction between **tame** and **wicked** problems is an idea that helps in understanding the nature of sociological problems. Tame problems can be hard to solve but tend to have a defined beginning and end, like a game of chess. They can be solved by applying previous solutions. Wicked problems are unique with no previous solution. They are symptoms of something else and, when solved, unintended consequences emerge which create another problem. Climate change is one such example.

In terms of outlining a process, Senior (2002) uses a model that has three distinct stages:

1. Description: This involves recognizing a problem and being able to articulate exactly what the problem is. This will involve diagnostics and the development of objectives and associated performance measures so the change can be assessed for efficiency. An example of this would be: 'How do we make this engine more powerful?'

2. Options: Here, the possible solutions to the problem can be developed, considered, and then prioritized in terms of the likelihood of them achieving the desired outcomes. So, extending the problem of how to make an engine more powerful, we could possibly increase the capacity of the engine, add fuel injection, add a supercharger, perhaps reduce the weight, or change the exhaust system. All of these will make a difference to the horsepower of the engine.

3. Implementation: In this final stage, the preferred option will be selected and the manager will allocate responsibilities and tasks, and monitor progress towards the end goal. There are roughly three different options to be considered in this stage. The first is to test out the ideas and to run pilot studies which can help with the final change; second, there could be a period where both the old and new systems are run in parallel as is often the case when companies implement new accounting systems; third, there is the 'Big Bang' approach—just do it!

There are many different models that use this HSM type of approach, such as Waterman et al. (1980) '7 S Framework'. This model, along with others, identifies components of a business linked together in an overall framework. The idea being that, by reducing an organization to a limited number of parts and connections, analysis and problem solving become much easier. These approaches do tend to work best where the problem can be easily recognized and a solution already exists somewhere. It relies on circumstances being similar to past experiences so that any proposed ideas about change can be delivered using an existing 'map'. Using this 'explorer' theme, if a person is lost, a map can help them to find their way. However, the problem with this approach is that there may be no map, the map may be wrong, and the person may not know where they are let alone where they are going. When this is the case, HSM gives way to soft systems methodology where ambiguity and vagueness are handled differently.

 Case study   Sweden: A 'Big Bang' approach to change

The majority of countries in the world, including most of continental Europe, drive on the right-hand side of the road. The United Kingdom, along with Australia, Japan, and some of the old Commonwealth countries such as India, still drive on the left, as did Sweden until 1967. However, at 04.50 a.m. on 3 September 1967 the entire country changed over to driving on the right from driving on the left. This was a dramatic example of the 'Big Bang' approach to change when everything had to happen immediately or death and chaos would have ensued.

In the years leading up to Dagen H (H day), or to use the Swedish 'Högertrafikomläggningen' (traffic change day), there had been vigorous campaigning for a change to driving on the right side of the road. The push for this was prompted by the fact that most of Sweden's neighbours already drove on the right and the long land border made changing over tiresome at best, dangerous at worst. However, the other issue was that most of Sweden's cars, lorries, and buses were already left-hand-drive vehicles—that is, made for driving on the right-hand side of the road so the driver can see clearly ahead. This meant that overtaking and other traffic manoeuvres were difficult and downright dangerous as the driver struggles to see what is coming. Despite this, more than 80 per cent of the population voted in a referendum to keep driving on the left. However, the change went ahead after the Swedish parliament, the Riksdag, voted, in 1963, to make the switch and overturn 200 years of practice.

The process began in the early hours on Sunday 3 September with all non-essential traffic being banned from roads from 01.00 a.m. until 06.00 a.m. Then at 04.50 a.m. all remaining traffic had to stop, and 10 minutes later at 05.00 a.m. they had to move across to the other side of the road. In addition, several changes were made to buses and bus stops, cars had new headlights fitted to avoid dazzling on-coming traffic, and new traffic signs were ready. After the change, the number of accidents fell from nearly 200 the previous week to 125. Critics put this down to an associated drop in the legal speed limit and, after a couple of years, the accident rate had risen back to its old level.

One of the interesting elements of this change is the development of a logo to publicize the change. The letter 'H' used stands for högertrafik or 'right-hand traffic'. The symbol was used in many different places, including adult underwear, to remind everyone of the impending change.

Sources

The Volvo Owners Club.

http://volvo.com—3 September 1967—'40 Years of Driving on the Right Side in Sweden'.

Hysell, P. (2009) 'Sweden finally began driving on the right side of the road in 1967'. Available at: http://www.examiner.com/article/sweden-finally-began-driving-on-the-right-side-of-the-road-1967 (accessed 16 August 2013).

Questions

1. What do you make of the decision to go ahead despite the majority not wanting to change?

2. What do you make of the use of a symbol? Are there any other examples you can think of?

3. Could a similar 'Big Bang' change happen in your country?

Soft systems methodology (SSM)

This approach, pioneered by Checkland (1981) and taken forward in the work of Senge (1990) and Burgoyne et al. (1994), takes a fundamentally different approach to change. However, what needs to be borne in mind is that SSM is not merely associated with 'soft and wicked' problems but can also be used with 'hard and tame' problems too. What is different is the way in which systems, such as organizations, societies, and other human groupings, are considered. HSM largely views humans as rational beasts that make reasoned and considered decisions (Johnson 1990), and it emerged as a way of simplifying complexity and helping to make sense of a connected world. In the HSM approach, systems are seen as 'real' and discrete. This means that a computer system, for example, can be physically seen to be the box of wires and circuit boards sitting in a room. The room itself is part of a bigger building in which the organization sits. There is a physical reality to these constructs and by understanding the parts we can make sense of the whole along with any 'problems' there happen to be within the collective system. The system will have a defined aim—to make a car, in the case of Ford, or to govern a state, in the case of a parliament. So, to improve productivity, say, an organization may decide to move the production line closer to the goods-in section of the factory because a time and motion study has highlighted it takes time to move raw materials from the factory gates to where they are used. HSM uses measurement and reasoned analysis in order to come up with a solution to a defined problem.

However, SSM takes a different approach and suggests that most, if not all, of the constructs above are nothing without humans. A computer is a box of inert components without software and an operator. The implication is that, by adding humans, we introduce a unique property and that is that each person can perceive a situation differently and, as a consequence, act differently. So, one person may view a car as a thing of beauty, something to be cherished and treasured, whereas another person may view a car as a symbol of pollution and selfishness. In a similar way, an organization can be viewed as a profit-making activity (as an economist such as Milton Freidman suggests), or as a vehicle for employment (as a worker may do), or as a mechanism for changing raw materials to finished goods (as a marketer may see it). In other words, the same physical entities can take on different meaning depending on the viewer's perspective. This may mean that solving one problem for one particular set of stakeholders may generate a problem for another group. One implication is that the 'rational actor' suggested by HSM could be seen to be somewhat of an over-simplification. This does not mean that people to not act 'rationally'—they do—but one person's rational behaviour is another person's bloody-mindedness or myopia. Checkland suggests this means that problems may be difficult to isolate and problematic in terms of understanding and defining the 'how' question, which is the starting point of HSM (see: Table 15.1).

Those leaders who subscribe to this less well defined definition of what and how systems and processes operate, are less likely to be concerned with 'how', but more with understanding 'why' things are done that way at all. In HSM, there is usually broad agreement about what needs to change. The disagreement lies in the 'how' this change is to be created. SSM, on the other hand, seeks to understand the purpose of the activity and the interconnectedness of causes, effects, and consequences.

Table 15.1 Differences between HSM and SSM

Hard systems methodology	Soft systems methodology
Problem is well defined	Problem can be undefined
System is clearly bounded	System is fuzzy-edged
Problem is separable from system	What is the problem?
Who ought to be involved is clear	Not sure who ought to be involved
Data to solve the problem is known and available	Unsure what information is needed
Know what the solution would look like	Not sure what the solution would look like
Test of success is established	Not sure how to measure success
End point is clear	Often no end

In order to help individuals use the approach with a degree of rigour, Checkland and Poulter (2006) developed a process, which is supported by a useful mnemonic system called CATWOE.

- Customers: The leader should think initially about who wins or loses from the change. How are these groups or individuals likely to react when the changes are announced?

- Actors: Who are the groups who will implement any change? How might they react and how will they view any change?

- Transformation: Exactly what changes are being proposed and how do they interlink? Consider the beginning of any process and the end— is this path easily defined? Whilst it may be relatively easy to identify a state that is unsatisfactory, what is harder is to define is the end point. Examine the 'vision' as this should articulate the end point.

- Weltanschauung: This is a German word for 'worldview'. It means consider the big picture, or how the situation being examined fits into the view of 'reality' of the chosen stakeholders. The difficulty here arises if there are different opinions as to the point and purpose of the system.

- Owners: This question directs you to consider who runs the systems or parts of the system you are seeking to change. This can help you identify whom you need to influence in order for the change to be delivered. A leader may need to consider what would make these people follow the instructions and what would be likely to make these groups resist the change.

- Environmental constraints: Here the leader should consider any external factors that may help or hinder progress. For example, what legislation is in place or what financial constraints are there?

This analysis will often lead to a 'systems map' where the different elements of the problem are shown as interconnected 'bubbles'. An example (see: Figure 15.2) of a SSM diagram shows

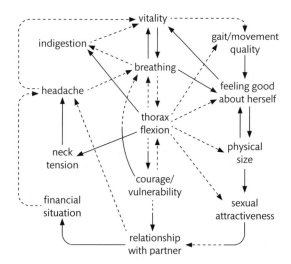

Figure 15.2 Example of SSM map of doctor's diagnosis

how a doctor may think about a patient with a stiff neck. Checkland, and advocates of SSM, maintain that by asking these kinds of questions, it is possible to approach change from a much more informed view. By considering the wider implications of any change process, a leader is likely to have a higher chance of success.

 Case study   The Greek Euro crisis 2012

In 2001, Greece joined the European Union (EU) and abandoned the Drachma for the Euro—this was despite being turned down for membership in 1999 because the country could not meet the economic conditions laid down by the EU. Part of the conditions for joining the Eurozone had been a reduction in government debt and a set of austerity measures—often referred to as the Maastricht Conditions. Nevertheless, Greece was welcomed into the Eurozone and introduced the Euro a year later, in 2002, to wide public support with around 80 per cent of the population supporting the move. The president of the European Central Bank, Wim Duisenberg, warned that Greece still had a lot of work to do to improve its economy and bring inflation under control. It was pointed out by many international investors at the time that Greece had one of the highest inflation rates in Europe. Public sector borrowing was also much higher than would be permitted normally under the EU rules governing entry to the project.

However, since 2008 the Greek economy has been faced with an almost perfect storm of financial conditions which has pushed the country and the Eurozone to the brink of meltdown, prompted resignations from politicians, seen mass public unrest, and calls for the country to be kicked out of the Euro. The first problem to be uncovered was the misreporting of government debt by the Greek government, which slowly but surely began to rise to 130 per cent of GDP—effectively meaning that the government owed more than the country earned. After the world economic crisis of 2008, the main Greek industries of tourism and shipping took a major downturn and this, together with mass tax evasion, increased government spending, and panicking investors, pushed the cost of Greek borrowing to an unprecedented high of nearly 35 per cent.

The Greek government had invested heavily in major public sector projects such as the 2004 Olympic Games, and public sector pay during this period also increased much faster than other countries. In short, the country was spending far more than it was capable of raising. Eventually, the government effectively ran out of cash to pay for its debts, at which point it appealed to its Eurozone neighbours for a bailout. Although there is a temptation to draw parallels between individual debt and a country in debt, there are important differences. If Greece was a person who had over-reached on their credit card, they could either work harder to earn extra cash or cut back on non-essential items. Greece tried both but was too far in debt for this to make a difference. The ultimate sanction for a person is to be declared bankrupt which, whilst uncomfortable for the individual concerned, will not affect that person's next-door neighbours or people living down the street. A country could 'default' on its debt—i.e. not pay. However, the problem for Europe is that Greece's debt is owed to many banks and other financial institutions in Germany (€6 billion), France (€40 billion), and United Kingdom (€8.5 billion)—in total, Greece owes around €300 billion. This means that, if Greece is allowed to default on its debts, there is a real risk of 'contamination' whereby the economies in these countries and, as a consequence, the whole of Europe could be severely damaged.

To avoid this doomsday scenario, the heads of Europe, led by the German Chancellor, Angela Merkel (see: Case study in Chapter 5), agreed a multibillion Euro bailout for Greece. This bailout has several different components, including an agreement to cut the debt owed, as a result of the hikes in interest rates, by €50 billion, a bailout fund of €270 billion, and an agreement by the Greek government to make massive reforms to public spending. The retirement age has been increased from 65 to 67 and most public sector employees have had their salaries cut—in total around €20 billion of cuts. This has provoked fury among the Greek population with mass riots and calls for Greece to leave the Euro and return to the Drachma. Unemployment has soared to 25 per cent, the debt mountain is forecast to continue to rise until 2015, and the economy is shrinking by 5 per cent per year.

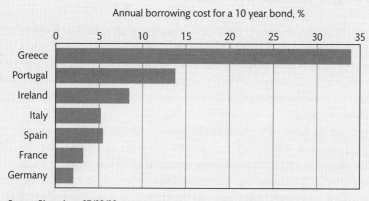

Annual borrowing cost for a 10 year bond, %

Source: Bloomberg 07/02/12.

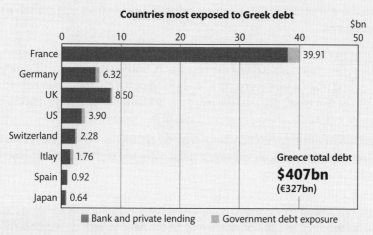

Countries most exposed to Greek debt

Source: BIS July 2012, Elstat.

The Greek Euro crisis 2012

Sources

'Eurozone Crisis Explained', bbc.co.uk, 27 November 2012.

Elliott, Larry (2011) 'A Simple Guide to the Greek Debt Crisis'. *The Guardian*, 21 July 2011.

'Greece's Sovereign-debt Crisis: Still in a Spin'. *The Economist*, 15 April 2010.

Wills, Andrew (2010) 'Rehn: No Other State Will Need a Bail-out'. *EU Observer*, 5 May 2010.

Questions

1. Use HSM and SSM to analyse the case study. What do you notice about using the different approaches?

2. To what extent is the crisis about 'leadership' as opposed to 'circumstance'?

3. What actions should the leaders of Europe take to avoid this situation happening again?

Models of the change process

If change is about action, to answer the thorny question of what leaders need to 'do' to enact change two models from Lewin (1951), Kotter (1995) are still used to help leaders to establish, maintain, and evaluate change. Whilst these models are useful, what needs to be borne in mind is the difficulty, as SSM reminds us, of seeing change as a discrete one-off event. Nevertheless, these two ideas can help a manager to identify key themes that must be addressed if change is to be successful.

Kurt Lewin was an American psychologist born in Germany who developed a number of ideas to explain how individuals and groups operated in social situations. His model (1951) of the phases linked to change draw on a metaphorical block of ice as inspiration, which Schein (1996:59) describes as 'fundamentally necessary in trying to explain various phenomena I have observed'. Lewin suggests the change process has three phases: unfreezing, change, and refreezing. The implication for leaders is that they need to consider the actions necessary to ensure the group they are leading moves from stage to stage to ensure a successful change.

1. Unfreezing: In this first stage, it is necessary to prepare individuals and the organization for change. This means articulating the new vision, breaking down the old structures and processes, and making sure everyone is ready to leave the old status quo behind. It is in this first stage that Lewin suggests the real 'pain' of change occurs, with individuals who are strongly attached to the old position likely to feel discomfort.

2. Change: Once the first stage is complete, the new systems, processes, and positions can be introduced. Individuals will take time to make sense of their new situation and adjustments may be needed.

3. Refreezing: The changes begun in stage 2, to move the organization to its new state, need to be embedded and confirmed. It is important here, as Senior (2002:309) makes clear, to avoid 'backsliding'; in addition, there may be the need to 'include recruitment of new staff who are untainted by the old habits'.

Lewin's model has its supporters and critics, alike. Supporters like the elegant simplicity of the model whilst critics dislike the final stage of refreezing. They suggest this does not reflect the modern organization's need for continuous change. From a leadership perspective, it, like most metaphorical models, has a use in that it can help to make sense of a complex organizational environment. However, it should not be adhered to without recognition of this complexity and an understanding that organizations are not blocks of ice waiting to be shaped—they may already be melting, i.e. in a state of flux.

Kotter's model (1995) again uses a process perspective and provides a detailed 'checklist' for leaders engaged in change. His model has eight stages rather than the three from Lewin.

1. Establish a sense of urgency: In the first instance, individuals need to recognize the need for change. They need to be ready to let go of the old ways and be dissatisfied with how the situation is at the moment. Achieving this can be difficult as organizational inertia and individual complacency are often forces that resist change.

2. Form a powerful coalition: This means getting together a team of like-minded supporters who have the expertise, power, and influence to make sure the change happens.

3. Create a vision: This area has already been discussed, but it remains the cornerstone of any successful change. Individuals need to understand where the change process is leading them and this new future must be more attractive than the one they are being asked to leave behind.

4. Communicate the vision: Whilst this may seem an obvious step, Kotter suggests organizations fail to address this adequately and he proposes that any leader scales the communication upwards by a factor of 10 to ensure the message is received by the followers.

5. Empower others: This means removing barriers to action such as restrictive practices or organizational rules that limit action. Transformational leaders will give their followers power and authority to act on the vision and enable those affected by the change to feel in control.

6. Create short term success: With many change processes taking months or even years to implement, Kotter argues that creating short term milestones and successes can help to keep individuals motivated and on track. For leaders this means celebrating achievements and recognizing when individuals have reached a target.

7. Consolidate and use success to generate more change: Here, he is arguing that, by using the momentum gained from the early wins, more changes can be introduced that will move the organization still further forward. Kotter's word of warning here is to make sure individuals see any success as not the end of the change but as a staging point towards the future.

8. Institutionalize the change: In a similar manner to Lewin's 'refreeze' stage, Kotter points out the need to ensure the new ways of working and thinking are firmly embedded in the organization. The benefits of the new systems need to be lauded and individuals working to the new processes need to be held as role models.

Again, critics point to the rather contrived feel to the overall process and point out the more 'random' manner of many change programmes. However, it does serve as a useful checklist if nothing else, and users report being able to check that they have carried out certain tasks whilst involved in the day-to-day issues that emerge as change programmes unfold.

Individual reaction to change

Turning attention now to how an individual may react to change, it is worth considering a number of themes. such as resistance and politicking. Elisabeth Kübler-Ross was a Swiss-born psychiatrist who was struggling to come to terms with the death of both parents. The culture surrounding her at the time was a mixture of 'stiff upper lip' and 'sweep it under the carpet' as a way of dealing with loss. She proposed a new hypothesis (Kübler-Ross 1969) that suggested individuals experiencing trauma or loss go through a whole series of emotions as part of a grieving process. This process, known as the Transition Curve (see: Figure 15.3), has been adapted and developed by researchers studying change and it has been suggested by some

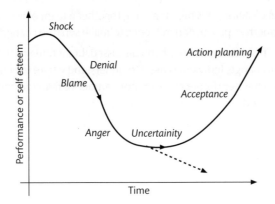

Figure 15.3 The transition curve

Source: Adapted from Kübler-Ross (1969).

authors, such as Hayes (2010) and Stuart (1995), that this process can be applied to individuals experiencing organizational change.

Stage 1. Shock and denial: In this first stage, individuals, especially those who have not experienced major change before, will react to news of change with confusion and a loss of direction. There may be a response that simply chooses to ignore any change and a view that could be summed up with, 'if I keep my head down everything will go away'. The overriding emotions at this stage can be fear, rejection, and a sense of being threatened.

Stage 2. Blame and anger: After the initial shock a second, more destructive, phase sets in with the individual experiencing anger and despair. Individuals may also enter into a blame game—'why me?'—and a bargaining phase—'If I work harder will you just let me be?' Their self-esteem is likely to dip and any performance indicators used will likely show a drop in work performance. Pessimism and a desire to fight back are likely to dominate at this point. However, for individuals who are able to move on, the next stage offers more hope.

Stage 3. Exploration: After a period of uncertainty, when the mood is likely to be dark and morale low, the individual is going to focus less on what is lost and more towards what may be gained in the new order. They are likely to begin testing out the new arrangements—perhaps with tentative enquires about how to do certain tasks or agreeing to discuss options and possibilities for new projects.

Stage 4. Acceptance: Finally, individuals may reach a point where they are able to make sense of the new systems and their place in the new order. There is also a chance their self-esteem and performance will be higher than it was at the beginning of the process. Many individuals report that, having gone through a period of change, they feel stronger as a result and better able to cope with life.

Whilst the model is not particularly well supported by empirical evidence, there is a significant group of psychiatrists who do feel it may help individuals to understand their own

Pause for thought

1. Think about a major change you have gone through, such as starting university or a new job. Can you identify any of these stages?
2. How, as a leader, could you use this idea when working with your team?

state of mind when faced with change. The implications of this idea for leaders are to ensure there is sufficient support for workers and colleagues going through a period of change. In addition, the need for an adequate communication process, and an indication of where and when to introduce more changes, can be taken if the leader is aware of the emotional 'state' of the team.

Politics of change

The extension of the quote from Machiavelli given in the Vision section reveals his reasons for suggesting change is difficult. The full line reads thus:

> There is nothing more difficult to take in hand, more perilous to conduct, or more uncertain in its success, than to take the lead in the introduction of a new order of things. For the re-former has enemies in all those who profit by the old order, and only lukewarm defenders in all those who would profit by the new order.

It is to these 'enemies who profit by the old order' that we now turn our attention. Organizational politics has a bad press as it is invariably associated with devious, sly, and underhand tactics. However, McCalman (2001) and Hardy (1996) are among an increasing number of researchers who are moved to suggest that organizational politics is unavoidable but, if understood, can be a force for good when leading change. Paton and McCalman (2008:254) say that 'politics may be defined as the use of power through influencing techniques and tactics (sanctioned or unsanctioned) aimed at accomplishing personal and/or organizational goals'. The basis for this is that very few organizations benefit from being an entirely unitarist nirvana where there is a universal 'all for one and one for all' attitude. Modern organizations are more pluralist in nature, with a number of different agendas, and leaders need to be able to understand this arena. The Chartered Management Institute commissioned a study which concluded that:

> Greater priority needs to be given to developing leaders with the capacity to manage the political dimension. They need an ability to see and communicate the big picture, make connections, be credible with different groups and broker relevant political and strategic relationships.

> (Charlesworth et al. 2003:7)

Individuals are likely to indulge in office politics for a wide number of reasons such as the need to preserve status, to undermine rivals, to secure scarce resources, or to block changes considered a disadvantage to a particular agenda. There are a number of different studies into this area, such as Buchanan and Badham (1999), Mintzberg (1983), and Meltzer (2003), which make the link between lies, politicking, and other covert behaviour designed to achieve personal, as opposed to organizational, goals.

Tactics used, according to Buchanan and Badham (1999), include the following activities:

- Controlling access to information.
- Cultivating a favourable impression.
- Developing a base of support.
- Blaming and attacking others.
- Aligning oneself with more powerful others.
- Playing political games.

A key tactic for any individual involved in these areas can be the ability to use information selectively or to twist a version of events to suit a particular agenda. Meltzer's study of office politics (2003) identified different types of lies that are intended to advantage the liar and/or disadvantage others:

- Self enhancement: This means over-emphasizing personal achievement.
- Ingratiation: Here, the player will make friends with powerful individuals, perhaps laughing at jokes, losing contests, and generally 'toadying' up to superiors.
- Fraudulent achievement: A more serious step as this involving deliberately falsifying data and records.
- The 'noble' lie: Plato describes this type of lie as an attempt to maintain a false hierarchy by claiming that some groups are simply not intelligent enough to grasp the full implications of a particular situation. An example might be: 'Well I can't tell you what is going on because you just wouldn't understand.'
- Permissible exploitive lies: What some may call 'white lies'. These are often minor distortions designed to hide truths from others.

The link between these ideas and office politics has been made by many different researchers, such as Yukl and Falbe (1990), who identified eight different tactics, Henry Mintzberg (1983), who looked at 13 'games', and Buchanan and Badham's (2008) 10 Turf Games. This third model is interesting as they suggest that playing these games can help managers to establish a position from which they can seek to influence the change agenda within the organization. It may also assist a more strategic leader by helping them to identify subordinates who are attempting to subvert the change process by creating a false position.

1. Image building: This may be simply dressing the part and looking confident. This is about establishing credibility and appearing competent.
2. Information manipulation: This can take the form of either withholding vital data from others, releasing selective figures, or even dumping massive amounts of statistics on others to overwhelm them.
3. Scapegoating: A favourite of politicians as this involves blaming someone else for the problem.

4.   Alliances: Sometimes done surreptitiously where an individual or group will link with others in order to create a critical mass to defeat an opponent. Sometimes this can lead to subsequent problems as the alliance breaks down; for example, consider the Russian/American/British alliance at the end of the Second World War.

5.   Networking: Turning up at meetings or informal events, like the boss's golf day, can offer opportunities to push an agenda.

6.   Compromise: This is where one party will agree to support the other in return for a favour the next time. The coalition government in the United Kingdom, formed in 2010, is an example of this.

7.   Bureaucracy: By using the organization's rules, processes, and procedures, an individual can frustrate opponents by requiring certain documents to be completed or forms to be filled in.

8.   Position: This means choosing projects that enhance the individual's visibility and avoiding projects that may fail. It could also involve hedging one's position and creating ambiguity so that each side believes they are being supported.

9.   Spin doctor: This suggests a process of altering messages and information to suit a particular person or audience. Telling people what they want to hear is one such approach—the point being that bearers of good news are usually made welcome. Unfortunately, the opposite is also true—the bearer of bad news can be tainted by association.

10. Dirty tricks: At the extreme end of behaviour, as this may involve blackmail, gossip, and spying.

The implications for leaders are that, despite their best efforts, there may be individuals within the organization who seek to defend their existing position perceiving the new future will in some way disadvantage them. It is best for the leader in these circumstances to be aware of the possibility there may be those who will seek to undermine their authority by the use of Machiavellian tactics. As the saying goes: 'Forewarned is Forearmed!'

 Pause for thought

1.   Have you ever encountered 'office politics'?
2.   Have you ever used any of the techniques above to protect your position?

Summary

At the beginning of the chapter three areas, key to understanding and leading change, were outlined. These areas were to appreciate the need to be clear on where any change outcome is likely to lead—establish a vision; second, to be aware of the complexity of change and the need to consider the 'connectedness' of organizations; third, to appreciate that not everyone is going to be inspired by the new future and may want to hang on to the present. In addition, a number of different themes were introduced to show how change is a constant part of human and, by extension, organizational life. It is an inescapable part of most managers' portfolio and can rate among the most stressful yet rewarding aspects. Change is not to be feared but it is to be recognized and treated with respect.

 Pause for thought

Consider your own journey to this point in your life. Think about the changes you have embraced. Perhaps you are sitting for a new qualification or you got a new job recently. In a wider sense, think about when you left home for the first time or when you passed your driving test. These are all changes that will have affected your life. You have coped with them and moved to a new future.

 Case study   The Church of England

In November 2012, the Church of England, a Protestant church headed by the Archbishop of Canterbury (Bishop Justin Welby), voted to continue with their ban on women becoming bishops. This is despite the Church allowing female priests since 1994 and other Anglican churches having female bishops, including churches in the USA, Cuba, and Swaziland. This news, which stunned the Church's hierarchy and made headlines as far away as the *The Jakarta Post*, was seen as a disaster for the outgoing head, Dr Rowan Williams, who had hoped to put this internecine dispute to bed. The move to consecrate women into the office of bishop has been a highly divisive and emotive subject for decades within the Anglican movement, as the role and position of women sits at the heart of any interpretation of the Bible. On this occasion, there had been much work carried out over the preceding 12 years behind the scenes trying to agree on terms that would suit the reformers and reactionaries, and it was felt a compromise had been reached.

In the Church of England there are three 'houses', Bishops, Clergy, and Laity (laity are ordinary members of the Church but they are not priests—so, typically, they are musicians, administrators, and sextons) and when these three are combined they form the General Synod. For a motion to be passed there needs to be a two-thirds majority in favour in each of the three houses. On the day of the vote (20 November 2012) there were impassioned speeches from the Archbishop of York, Dr John Sentamu, and a whole host of other senior bishops imploring the delegates to support the motion, but to no avail. On this occasion, the bishops voted in favour by 44 to 3, the clergy by 148 to 45, but among the laity, 132 voted for women but 74 voted against which meant the two-thirds majority of 138 had not been reached, thus the motion was not carried by six votes.

The Rt Rev. Christopher Lowson said after the vote, 'this is a very sad day indeed', whilst Rev. Rachel Weir said, 'we're absolutely devastated'. Given that 42 out of 44 dioceses in England supported women bishops, many individual members of the Church were left wondering where this left the Church, whose Supreme Governor is H.M. Queen Elizabeth II. However, before considering the future it is worth examining why a significant minority of laity felt compelled to vote against a measure that seems to reflect both modern society and common sense.

At the heart of the argument against women bishops lies the phrase 'headship' which means to those who accept it, such as the 'Reform' movement, that a man cannot be subservient to a woman. From their position, this means, if women became bishops, both men and women would have to accept the primacy of women in this case, which, theologically, they cannot accept. This perspective originates from certain passages in the Bible such as, 'for the husband is the head of the wife as Christ is the head of the Church, His body, of which he is the Saviour' (Ephesians 5:23) and St Paul's 'I do not permit a woman to teach or have authority over a man' (1 Timothy 2:12). To accommodate these objections, the reformers, led by Rev. Janet Appleby, had drafted an amendment that allowed parishes who objected to female bishops to ask for a male bishop to be appointed to deliver services in line with their theological wishes. However, this compromise failed to win approval from either side, with reformers saying this would just entrench views whilst opponents said it did not get around their fundamental objection that women simply cannot be bishops. As Rev. Prebendary Rod Thomas, who chairs the conservative evangelical group, Reform, said, 'we are being required to accept something that we don't believe the Bible teaches. The legislation requires us conservative evangelicals to accept women as bishops when the Bible says they should not be in that position'.

Where this leaves the Church is unclear, with a revised proposal unlikely to be tabled until 2015. Prime Minister David Cameron condemned the rejection, saying women bishops should have been allowed 'a long time ago'. The Archdeacon of Norwich, the Ven. Jan McFarlane, tweeted: 'took off clerical collar before walking back to hotel. Ashamed to be associated with the CofE [Church of England] tonight.'

Sources

Barr, R. (2012) 'Church of England says No to Female Bishops'. *The Jakarta Post*, 21 November 2012.

Burkill, M. (2012) 'Why are There Objections to Women being Bishops in the Church of England?'. http://reform.org.uk/resources (accessed 21 November 2012).

Goddard, M. (2012) 'Evangelical Opponents of Women Bishops; What is Sought and Required?' (accessed at http://fulcrum-anglican.org.uk/5470).

'Women Bishops' http://churchofengland.org (accessed 21 November 2012).

Questions

1. What does this tell you about the challenges facing leaders trying to enact change?

2. Do you think enacting changes in democratic organizations is any different from organizations with a more traditional hierarchy, such as a commercial company? Why?

3. Can you think of any strategy or actions the reformers could take to satisfy the laity?

Assignment—3,000 words

Critically analyse a change project in a company that you are familiar with. Consider the causes, desired outcomes, and actual outcomes of the process. Make some recommendations to the organization based on your analysis.

Comment on the following statement: 'Why do workers always hate change? Don't they know that unless the company moves forward we could all be out of a job?' What models could you use to explain to the manager who said this why this is the case?

'Change, Politics, and Conflict are an inevitable part of Organizational life.' Discuss this statement using appropriate theoretical ideas. Conclude with a perspective that agrees or disagrees with the statement.

Further reading

The literature surrounding change is huge but here are a few thoughts:

Barbara Senior's book *Organizational Change* (now in its fourth revision with Stephen Swailes) is a fairly straightforward introduction to the broader themes in terms of leading change in organizations. It covers the organizational setting and strategies for managing change by deploying hard or soft systems methodology.

Senior, B. and Swailes, S. (2010) *Organizational Change*. Harlow: Pearson.

Patrick Castel and Erhard Friedberg have written up an interesting case study of a successful organizational change. Many texts tend to focus on the failures—for example, Kotter's original work looked at the common factors in failed change projects. This example, from the French healthcare sector, suggests the change process resulted in a better process.

Castel, P. and Friedberg, E. (2010) 'Institutional Change as an Interactive Process: The Case of the Modernization of the French Cancer Centres'. *Organization Science*, 21 (2): 311–330.

Finally, Tamra Mercieca's book (2012) is a study of personal change and how she overcame depression. There are a number of case studies and self-help guides. This version is also available as a Kindle download so you can develop yourself whilst riding on the bus.

Mercieca, T. (2012) *The Upside of Down: A Personal Journey and Toolkit to Overcome Depression.* Bloomington, Australia: Balboa Press.

16 Leadership development

After reading this chapter you will:

- Understand some of the challenges surrounding the development of leaders.
- Begin to understand the context in which leadership development needs to be placed.
- Explore some of the alternative approaches used by organizations.

Introduction

This chapter will cover the broad strategic organizational context for developing leaders and some of the tactical methods used to achieve this goal. Given the level of concern surrounding the role 'leadership'—or the lack of it—has played in some of the challenges facing the world, it is important to understand why organizations invest in this activity and why different organizations view the development of their leaders from different perspectives. The case studies are organizationally focused to give an insight into how modern businesses are facing the challenges of ensuring their leaders are 'fit for purpose' in the twenty-first century. It will examine the business case for leadership development and the link between strategy and leadership development. Also reviewed are the changes over time—in terms of how leaders have been developed—the tools, and the techniques employed such as the use of 'competency frameworks'.

What is leadership development?

On the face of it this is an easy question to answer: the development of leaders. But pause for a moment and consider the implications here. Remember the challenges faced in defining 'leadership' experienced in the early part of the book. Your response to the question, 'what is leadership?', is likely, by extension, to affect your response to 'what is leadership development?'. For example, if you view leadership as some kind of inherent characteristic (a trait), you will be seeking a different developmental path from a person who considers leadership to be a complex social process (such as leader-member exchange (LMX)) because these two concepts have fundamental differences in terms of how leadership manifests itself in social contexts. However, not to complicate further, the main challenge if distilled would seem to be the challenge of 'born' or 'made'. That is, are leaders born with the abilities, attitude, and application to lead organizations or do they need to be trained and taught how to do this? Organizations faced with this question have evolved a series of different responses to ensure they harness 'leadership'.

Pause for thought

Revisit your thoughts on exactly what is meant by 'leadership'.

1. What are the implications for developing leaders if you hold a particular perspective?

2. Why, for example, are you reading this book? Do you hope it will somehow make you a more 'effective' leader? How do you think this will happen?

Burgoyne (2010:43) says that leadership development 'in the widest sense involves the acquisition, development and utilization of leadership capability or the potential for it'. This means, to a certain extent, it does not matter which particular definition of leadership an organization favours, as long as it is consistent in terms of accepting the limitations of the particular paradigm; the organization can refine its leaders by identifying leadership capacity in its current or prospective workforce. Most modern organizations with a workforce of 50 or more employees will have an explicit leadership development strategy which codifies their approach to how this activity is embedded into the organization. Even those smaller organizations without such an explicit definition will have an implicit approach—even if 'development' is based on the owner's whim. Recently, there has been a revitalized interest in this area, with management schools proliferating (try finding a UK-based university that does not have one), and chartered bodies, such as the Chartered Management Institute, and think-tanks, such as the British Academy of Management, all focusing on the development of leaders and leadership. Leadership books by the thousand inhabit libraries, and television schedules are full of 'leaders' offering advice and guidance through such programmes as *Dragons' Den*, *The Apprentice*, and *The Hotel Inspector*. Given this interest, it is worth considering why this is the case and why organizations invest so heavily in this aspect of their business.

Why bother?

Leadership development is big business. Estimates put the spend, on managerial and leadership books alone, at £30 million in 2011. MBA programmes in the UK cost anything from £13,000 to £60,000. The question is, why do organizations commit to these sums when Bones (2011) claims that leadership has failed? Deming (1982), the doyen of modern quality standards, suggested that teaching and implementing 'leadership' was one of the key components of a successful organization, placing leadership at the heart of any business. He felt that leadership underpinned organizational development and the associated systems for improving quality. It is this view that has been largely accepted by organizations with aspirations to become world class—that successful organizations need successful leaders (Fulmer and Wagner 1999). For these businesses, there is a clear and causal link between the efficacy of leadership and measurable organizational success. Mabey and Salaman (1995) expand on this perspective and look to a wider agenda to uncover an organization's willingness to invest money and resources in developing their leaders. They point to a number of different themes that may help to explain why businesses are often willing to spend thousands on the development of an individual.

- Functional performance: In line with Deming, they feel an organization will make the assumption there is a direct link between learning, individual performance, and organizational performance. This means organizations will seek to recruit and train their managers based on the view that leadership and managerial skills can be both taught and learnt. This knowledge will be transposed to a manager deemed to have 'potential' with the view that they are capable of becoming a higher performing individual, who, in turn, will make the organization more competitive and profitable.

- Political reinforcement: A more subtle, and probably implicit, agenda is that based on the assumption that current leadership practice within the organization is 'right'. This notion is then reinforced by leadership development that reiterates this paradigm. The skills, language, attitude, and behaviour of senior managers are relayed and copied by junior managers so the culture of the business remains stable.

- Reward: Leadership development schemes can be seen as recognition of good performance by managers. Being designated as a 'high potential' manager adds kudos and status to an individual, who may seek this label as either a rite of passage or as a badge of honour. Many of today's graduates expect to be on some kind of leadership development programmes as part of their psychological contract with their employer. This makes such programmes a virtual necessity for any organization seeking to recruit graduates into its workforce.

- Psychic defence: This theme, linked to the previous idea, suggests that leadership development offers a mechanism for managers to establish themselves in the organization's pecking order. Being sent on external or internal 'courses'—maybe an MBA or some other accredited programme—the manager can gain a competitive advantage for themselves when measured against their peer group. This helps them feel more secure and valued by the organization.

Essentially, as Carmichael et al. (2011:87) point out, 'the main purpose of management development is to enhance effective management behaviour'. There are, according to Mumford (1991), three different aspects of 'development' that need to be addressed by organizations. The first is to have a working definition of what the organization considers to be 'effective leadership'. This is likely to be influenced by a whole range of factors wrapped up in the organization's identity and culture. The second is to have a strategic developmental process that enables a prospective manager to travel a path that enables them to absorb the necessary skills, attitudes, and knowledge that will make them effective. Finally, is a sound tactical grip on the particular activities that an individual could undertake to ensure any learning is effective.

Burgoyne's (1988:40) model suggests this set of drivers results in organizations having a leadership development 'strategy' that has differing degrees of robustness in terms of how it links to, and adds value to, the host organization. His model has seven different layers or rungs according to the degree of integration between individual career development of the prospective leader and the host organization's strategic aims. These rungs represent organizational leadership development plans ranging from those that have almost no link between the individual and the organization to those where there is active discussion between the two parties to ensure there is synergy between them. This more unitarist perspective aims to ensure that as the organization evolves so does the manager, and vice versa.

1. No systemic management development: Although this suggests an organization with no leadership development programme, this must be viewed cautiously. Organizations in this first stage often do have such a programme but it is based either on informal learning, where the individual managers learn from each other in a casual, unstructured manner, or it is ad hoc. Often, events will be arranged in reaction to crises such as succession planning—typically, the organization is suddenly left without a key leader and will need someone to take over very quickly. Organizations such as this are likely to be reactive and to have a leadership cohort that is relatively immature but with significant 'elder statesmen' in place. Health and safety training as a result of an accident or 'diversity' training as a result of a legal issue are both examples of this type of development. So, development is not planned or evaluated for impact on either the individual or the organization.

2. Isolated tactical management development: Organizations residing here do have management development activities as part of their broad organizational development strategy but these are uncoordinated and lack any real linkage to the needs of the business or the individual. Individuals do demand development and are likely to be committed to any programme they undertake. The problem is that these activities may have no real impact on the organization as there is a disconnect between the other systems that relate to individual development, such as the performance appraisal system.

3. Integrated and coordinated structural and development tactics: Here, the requirements of the manager's immediate and future career aspirations are considered when deciding on an appropriate training and development route. There is often a much clearer link between the systems relating to leadership development, with efficient administration and resources to support this function. Indeed efficiency is the key word here but the challenge not yet considered is whether this process is effective in delivering improved performance and organizational benefits.

4. Management development that implements corporate policy: This means using management development tactics to deliver the organization's key aims and objectives. The circumstances for this to happen demand a clear understanding of where the organization wishes to be and having the wherewithal to link the ambitions of the organization to achievable management development activities. However, the danger is that future organizational plans at a strategic level are stymied by a failure to grasp the operational implications. The unintended consequence may be completely unfeasible plans being attempted with little chance of success.

5. Management development strategy input to corporate policy formation: The danger outlined in Stage 4—of a gap between strategic intention and tactical reality—can be overcome by moving to Stage 5 on the hierarchy. This means having a reciprocal, open feedback channel between the hopes, dreams, and aspirations of the organization and the practical reality of leadership capacity and capability. Organizations will need to have a system of checks and balances in place to ensure there is a realistic chance of delivering the corporate plan in the short, medium, and long term by accurately assessing the ability of the leadership cohort to deliver against these demands.

6. Strategic development of the management of corporate policy: Burgoyne's final 'rung' does not require any radically new system or process. He believes it is more a 'state of mind' requiring the feedback loop outlined above to include managerial development becoming an explicit input to strategic planning. This has echoes of Senge's (2006) 'Learning Organisation' as it involves a flow of ideas and input from various levels and layers within the organization.

Burgoyne (1988:40) explicitly defines a hierarchy of 'effectiveness', with organizations occupying a space higher up the ladder having a greater chance of capturing the benefits of 'good' leadership practice than those further down the ladder. The empirical evidence available, such as the Chartered Management Institute (CMI) joint report with Penna (McBain et al. 2012), or the Worrall and Cooper (2012) survey, would support this explicit link between leadership development and organizational success.

 Case study   Chartered Management Institute

The CMI is the only chartered body representing professional managers in the UK. Originally formed in 1947 as the British Institute of Management, it has a membership of 90,000 individuals drawn from the private, public, and third sectors. Its role is to 'increase the number and standard of professionally qualified managers and leaders'.

Its current chief executive, Ann Francke, who draws on experience of boardrooms in FTSE quoted companies such as Procter and Gamble, is a passionate advocate of effective leadership development, seeing this as key to restoring the bond of trust between individuals and organizations. It is this breakdown between society and businesses that she sees as one major legacy of the deepest recession the modern world has ever experienced, with inadequate leadership being one reason behind the decay.

Citing two independent research papers, she points to the impact effective leadership can have on an organization. The first, by Worrall and Cooper (2012), paints a disturbing picture of a management cohort under considerable pressure to produce short-term results against a background of cost-cutting. This has accompanied an increase in leadership styles associated with authoritarian and bureaucratic behaviour. Far from helping businesses develop, there is evidence to suggest this is counterproductive in terms of employee well-being and organizational productivity. The second report, produced in partnership with Penna (2012), suggests that nearly half (43 per cent) of the managerial cohort in England is considered to be ineffective. The link between high performing organizations and high performing managers is also clear, with 80 per cent reporting a positive correlation between the two. On the downside, in low performing organizations only 39 per cent agree their managers are effective. The bald conclusion reached by the reports is that high performing organizations have high performing leaders and their investment in leadership development is repaid in terms of financial results, employee engagement, and well-being.

When asked why she believes organizations, despite this evidence, continue to make little effective investment in their leadership cohort, she believes many people still cling mistakenly to the belief that managers are born and not made. She points to many organizations that promote a functional expert, based on their competence at a technical role, and expect them to muddle through when occupying a leadership role. This puzzles her because these very same organizations would not dream of employing an accountant, for example, and not training that person in the required techniques in the organization; whereas newly appointed leaders are given little to no training on how to lead and

(Continued...)

manage. For her, leadership can be both taught and learnt and she sees 'competences' as part of this process.

The Institute's flagship award is the status of Chartered Manager. This award has four components which, when combined, demonstrate the ability of an individual to perform as an effective manager. First, the award requires an academic qualification at degree level; second, it needs the individual to demonstrate a positive, quantifiable impact on the business; third, ethical conduct is also required via adherence to a code of conduct; and, finally, the individual must demonstrate continuous professional development (CPD). Ann calls it a 'practical MBA'—albeit at considerably less cost than an academic one.

Her forthcoming book, *FT Guide to Management*, due for publication in late 2013, will reinforce her message that modern leaders must reconnect with their broader stakeholders, including 'society', and quickly rediscover an ethical base for the decisions they take. She feels that organizations have lost sight of their raison d'être and points to the beginning of the financial crisis as an example of how an organization can lose its path by forgetting to pay attention to the basics of sound management. Part of an organization's role must be to add value to its broad stakeholder community, not just its shareholders, as, without this link, an organization will 'float' away from its connection to its original purpose much like an untethered boat slowly drifting out to sea.

In terms of the future, she feels a greater diversity among the boardrooms of major organizations is long overdue. She does have sympathy for the view that women can and should be making a much more visible contribution to the development and evolution of leadership in organizations because of their ability to use multiple 'lenses', such as the role of mother, wife, and business person, when considering the 'right' path for their business. She feels too many boardrooms are still places where men, power, and the fear of failure dominate; whereas, females with a more collegiate and collaborative mind-set have had to make a decision as to whether they accept this culture in order to progress or reject it and risk being ostracized by the organization. In the past, she feels women have only had these two choices but now, citing the changes made in Rwanda post genocide, where women make up over half the parliament, as evidence the world is changing, she hopes women can make a stronger contribution to top boardrooms. In addition, she would like to see Chartered Manager status existing alongside other chartered occupations as the mark of excellence. She is also pursuing other professional bodies with a view to embedding Chartered Manager within their awards so that an ethical approach to business becomes much more mainstream. She would also hope to see business schools modifying their formal programmes, such as MBAs, to incorporate more practical people management skills, and for these skills to be given as much emphasis as learning the difference between a brand management strategy and a debt reconstruction agenda.

Source

Interview with Ms Ann Francke, 12 October 2012.

Francke, A. (forthcoming) *FT Guide to Management: The Definitive Guide to Being an Effective Manager* (Financial Times Series).

Questions

1. To what extent do you agree with the CMI's analysis of organizations being part of society and, as such, having a responsibility to operate with this duty in mind?

2. What is your analysis of Ann's view on leaders being made *not* born?

3. Can you envisage a development scheme where men are taught how to 'think female'?

Organizational factors

It is worth positioning the theme of leadership development within the broader concept of organizational development. This will enable you to explore how and why different organizations approach the topic of 'development' sometimes using completely opposing methods, curricula, and strategies.

Historical development

We have already explored some of the difficulties with defining 'leadership' as well as the associated debate between what constitutes leadership and what management is. Organizations facing this type of argument have responded by developing a number of different models based on what leadership paradigm was seen to be functional at the time. So, this means that an organization operating when trait theory ruled the roost looked for certain inherited characteristics in its leaders and managers. This often meant selecting individuals from a small cohort or dynasty as it was believed that 'great' families spawned 'great' individuals. Evidence of this can be seen in any visit to a historic castle or country mansion where centuries of famous individuals drawn from the same family adorn the walls. Similarly, as the debate around what constituted effective leadership moved to behaviours, contingency and transformational, organizations shifted their own diversity, recruitment, and development agenda to suit. This led to some of the issues explored in Chapter 12 where the behaviour of successful leaders was defined by those already in such positions. This left companies dangerously incestuous and lacking in the necessary diversity to cope with changes in their environment. However, as the debate has moved towards a more integrated definition of leadership and management, where both roles are seen as essential to any successful organization and mastery of both the more 'relational' leadership and 'task' management activities are desirable, organizations have migrated to a similar approach.

Organizational identity, culture, and strategy

The leadership development strategy of an organization is a sub-set of the wider organizational culture. An organization's culture is a reflection of many interacting elements found within a business. Culture is probably best summed up by the McKinsey Organisation's oft-copied words, 'the way we do things around here' (Bower 2003). There are many different models that examine this aspect of organizational life. One of the most frequently cited is the Johnson et al. (2005) 'Cultural Web', which aims to draw on the complex network of factors that combine to shape the culture of an organization. Combined with, and often as a consequence of, this corporate identity comes the organization's strategy. Whittington's (1993) typology (see: Figure 16.1) offers a simple model designed to assist with the analysis and understanding of strategy. His four-fold model suggests that an organization's strategy largely depends on two independent variables: the purpose of the organization's activities, and the internal activities designed to enable the organization to function. In his model, the desired outcomes can either be directed to making profits or have a wider, more pluralist bent. The internal processes can be either very deliberate and considered or reactionary and 'on the hoof'. This generates four types of organization, and with this will come the need for a different leadership model that fits with these broad ideals. As Thorngate (1976) suggests, to us it is implausible to have a general, simple, and accurate model for social behaviour, however, this approach can help with our framing of a problem and to illustrate a certain idea.

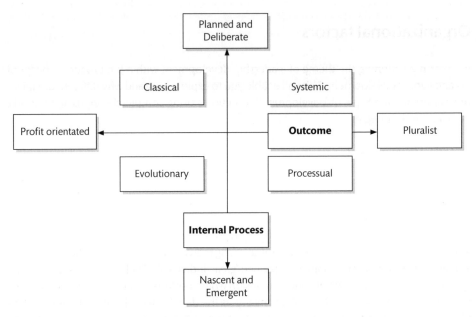

Figure 16.1 Formulation of organizational strategy

Source: Adapted from Whittington, R. (1993) *What is Strategy and Does it Matter?* London: Routledge.

Using this approach we can consider each of the four types and the possible link to how leadership and leadership development manifests itself within each of the four different categories of organization.

1. Systemic: In this first model, the strategy of the organization is the result of an agenda that seeks to engage with the organization's stakeholders whilst having a set of internal processes that are quite formal and designed. The leadership paradigm here could be one where context is important along with understanding how the organization operates in a much broader environment than simply having 'shareholders'. Leaders will have to manage a number of complex internal and external relationships.

2. Classical: The drive in this kind of organization is to achieve profits. It will probably be led by a powerful individual or a small cadre of like-minded individuals who see the ends as justifying the means. The management will respond well to those who have a similar outlook to their own and will probably have a fairly clear and unequivocal view of what leadership means.

3. Evolutionary: This kind of organization is also profit focused but has a much more dynamic feel to it. It is receptive to changes in its environment and can adapt in order to survive in a Darwinian model where survival is based on an ability to thrive in a changing environment. Leaders here will need to be capable of moving quickly to react to any environmental change and will need a strong network of followers who can make decisions based on their judgement of what is best for the organization.

4. Processual: This kind of organization has a broad view of what it is trying to achieve and may have different parts of the organization moving in different directions. Debate and

discussion abound as different themes are picked up from the external stakeholders. Strategy will vary among managers and it may be the case that some individuals do not comply with the declared strategy.

 Pause for thought

1. Can you identify any organizations that fit with these broad themes? For example, what type of organization do you think a university is? Where would you place McDonald's or BMW?

2. Can you think of any of the broad leadership approaches in the first part of this book that may 'fit' with a particular strategic approach?

3. Could you see a case for suggesting a large bureaucracy such as the civil service is 'Systemic' with leaders who may need to consider the broad context of their decisions?

Leadership and competencies

The most common model that organizations operate is to codify their interpretation of what 'excellence' in any role means, so that in the context of their business they develop a set of 'competencies'. Broadly, this approach is based on McClelland's (1973) work that defines what an individual needs to be able to master in order to perform according to the organizational demands. Defined as 'an underlying characteristic of an individual that is causally related to effective or superior performance in a job' (Boyatzis 1982:21), the idea is to establish what smaller activities an individual needs to be able to complete in order to be able to perform a larger task. For example, to be an 'excellent' hairdresser, a person would need to be able to demonstrate their ability at the physical tasks of cutting hair, applying colour and tint, washing and drying hair. However, they would also need to be skilled at the more subtle art of designing new hairstyles and ensuring their client had a hair style that matched their broader physical and emotional attributes. This breakdown of a larger, more complex task into smaller activities is, in most competency models, referred to as 'units' and 'elements'.

The exact format of competency frameworks differs from company to company, yet the underpinning rationalist philosophy is fairly consistent. The view is that, by identifying the behaviour, skills, and attitude of the individual worker, codifying these into a format that has descriptors, indicators, and examples, the organization and the individual can judge accurately how well the observed person is progressing towards a set ideal. Where there is an identified gap between the observed set of skills and behaviour, the organization and the individual can implement a corrective plan designed to ensure the individual changes their current position towards one more in line with the expectations of the company. Implicit in this approach are a number of key assumptions that must be considered when examining this methodology. The first is that, by examining 'successful' individuals in their role, another person who replicates this behaviour will also be successful. Brownell (2006) suggests this is probably a false assumption and goes on to question if such behaviour can actually be learnt and demonstrated by another person—as an aside, it is worth considering the implications here for authentic leadership as reviewed in Chapter 8. There is also the rather curious view that, in order to improve a person's role achievement, the only course of action is to focus on their weak competencies or those they display but not to the required organizational level. There is often little attention given to further developing those areas considered to be 'strengths'.

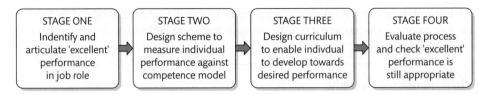

STAGE ONE	STAGE TWO	STAGE THREE	STAGE FOUR
Indentify and articulate 'excellent' performance in job role	Design scheme to measure individual performance against competence model	Design curriculum to enable indivdual to develop towards desired performance	Evaluate process and check 'excellent' performance is still appropriate

Figure 16.2 Competency framework design

Competencies can be used in almost any job role from astronaut to grave digger. As long as the process outlined in Figure 16.2 is followed, there is little to suggest a framework cannot be developed that will result in a set of defined occupational standards for this activity. In England, the Management Standards Centre is the body responsible for defining, updating, and monitoring the competencies or standards for managers in the UK. This body was originally called the Management Charter Initiative and was born out of the government's desire to see a more 'professional' approach to leadership and management in the UK. This organization has as its mission statement, 'to fulfil the needs of employers by developing a skilled management workforce through promoting our nationally recognized set of standards and qualifications which have full employer relevance and ownership'. Their model, originally developed in 2004 and updated in 2008, is 'based on extensive consultation with genuine managers doing real management jobs' (see: http://www.management-standards. org (accessed 14 August 2013)) and is now referred to as the Management and Leadership National Occupational Standards (NOS), see: Table 16.1.

Table 16.1 shows the activities of a manager broken down into six distinct areas in a similar manner to the ideas explored in Chapter 3. In each of the main areas there are up to 19 separate indicators a manager should be able to demonstrate. For example, within 'Working with people', a manager should be able to 'develop productive relationships with colleagues' through to 'help team members address problems affecting their performance'. The point of this is that, if used by an organization, this effectively defines leadership and management in the context of that organization. So, in conjunction with a number of other processes, such as annual appraisals, a manager can constantly improve by analysing their behaviour and performance against these standards. Where there is a gap between the expected level of performance in a particular category, say 'Working with people', the individual can choose to access appropriate career development initiatives.

Competency models, although popular in organizations, are not without their critics. Bolden and Gosling, based at the University of Exeter's Centre for Leadership Studies, draw their criticisms into five areas (Bolden and Gosling 2006).

1. Reductionist: They mean here that, by breaking management down into 'Standards' and 'Units', this reduces a complex social activity into chunks which do not reflect the holistic

Table 16.1 National Occupational Standards leadership competencies

Managing self and personal skills	Providing direction
Facilitating change	Working with people
Using resources	Achieving results

nature of the role. They feel leadership is an integrated activity that needs to be seen as an interwoven set of relationships rather than a discrete number of actions. For them mastery of a few units of behaviour in no way demonstrates the complexity of leadership.

2. Context: Given the standards are the 'National Occupational Standards', this means the role of the manager has the same components regardless of where the manager is operating or within what industry. This means a Royal Naval Officer would be expected to achieve competency across the same framework as a manager in a call centre. The particular context the leaders and followers occupy, as we have seen in Chapters 5 and 6, can be an important aspect to be considered and ignoring this may remove a relevant dynamic. Although Mintzberg (1973) suggested that managerial roles did have many common elements, Bolden and Gosling are sceptical that a model that 'assumes a common set of capabilities no matter what the nature of the situation, individuals or task' (2006:150) can be accurate.

3. Historical: Competencies are usually developed from empirically derived evidence—perhaps from direct observation of individuals carrying out the role, from diaries kept by practitioners, or from surveys across a particular cohort. The approach prior to gathering this data is to select a group of individuals who are somehow seen to be excellent at the role—whether this is the case could be questioned. However, from this point the information is distilled into the units that make up a full role. The criticism levelled here is that this process represents an historical record of what *was* needed to be excellent in a role not what *will* be needed in the future.

4. Assessment: The cliché uttered by many organizations seeking to improve processes is, 'what gets measured gets managed'. This means that, in order to monitor and improve a process, it is necessary to be able to quantify it. This results in targets and percentage improvement scales such as those within the **Six Sigma** Quality Improvement process. The question with a social process such as leadership is whether this model, derived from manufacturing processes, can be applied in the same way. Is it possible to place a figure on the subtle human nuances that go to make up a smile or a frown that accompany any interaction between two people? Using competences requires the organization to agree to this methodology, as a manager will often be graded on their achievement of units based on a nominal scale.

> **Six Sigma is** a process improvement tool first introduced by Motorola in 1986 and widely used in General Electric under Jack Welch during the 1990s. It aims to improve quality in a process by removing the variations in that process. It uses a number of statistical methods and aims to achieve a level of 'perfection' whereby there are less than 3.4 defects per million parts.

5. Curriculum: As in the process outlined above—that of measuring achievement against a set ideal—the result is a map of the 'gap' between actual performance and desired performance. This usually means the individual concerned is asked to develop a plan to close the gap via a series of planned interventions, such as attending a training course. So, for example, if a manager is seen as not reaching the required standard in 'working with people' because their leadership approach is deemed to be 'autocratic' then they may be asked to attend a short course on 'Developing your Leadership Style'. It has been suggested that this model results in a prescriptive and poorly tailored approach to the development of the individual concerned. There is little attention paid to the specific needs of the individual manager in terms of how they may best acquire the 'missing' competencies or to the connection between their

development and their job role. In addition, it could be suggested that, by breaking down leadership into a series of training events, this further erodes the holistic nature of leadership.

Despite these criticisms, competencies remain popular with organizations across many different sectors, not just leadership. Competencies help both individuals and organizations understand some of the areas needed to be mastered by prospective leaders. However, as Gill (2011) points out, competencies need to be defined in the context of the organization with particular care being focused upon those concerned with handling uncertainty, unpredict-ability, and direction. One way of dealing with this is to think of leadership competencies as meta-competencies, that is, to identify the ones that enable leaders to diagnose the need for, develop, and utilize the operational competencies that are needed in specific situations and for specific periods. Three of these were established in research by Burgoyne and Stuart as applied intelligence, balanced learning habits, and emotional resilience (1976). These, and the model of which they are part, are the basis for *A Manager's Guide to Self-Development*, the sixth edition of which is now in production (Pedler et al. 2007).

 Case study   Competencies in action

The Future Leaders Trust is an education charity set up in 2006 'to address educational disadvantage by transforming outstanding current or former teachers into effective, inspirational school leaders for challenging schools'. This activity is principally aimed at schools that have the biggest challenge in terms of attracting and retaining leaders. These schools are often those with the lowest position on school league tables, and suffering from low morale and high incidents of poor student achievement. Part of the process of developing a good teacher into an outstanding leader involves using a competency framework based on two distinct areas considered to be vital if a school teacher is to make the successful transition into a very demanding leadership role. This approach seeks to combine elements of how a person thinks and behaves with clarity around what is being implemented and delivered across the school.

The behavioural element has three components underpinned by a series of sub-skills:

1. Thinking
   a. Analytical thinking
   b. Conceptual thinking
   c. Curiosity and eagerness to learn.
2. Being
   a. Self-swareness
   b. Integrity
   c. Personal drive
   d. Resilience and emotional maturity.
3. Leading
   a. Impact and influence
   b. Inspiring others
   c. Holding to account
   d. Relating to others
   e. Developing others
   f. Collaboration.

This sits alongside the Skills and Experience Framework

- Leading, teaching, and learning
- Leading school culture
- Leading the organization
- Leading people.

So, this means an individual could demonstrate competence in terms of the behavioural elements but not have the necessary skill set, and vice versa. Within this broad philosophy, individuals are encouraged to self-assess themselves using a grading scale (see: Table 16.2).

Table 16.2 Example of using the self-assessment levels

Knowledge and understanding			Involvement / expertise			Whole school leadership and demonstrating impact	
1c	1b	1a	2c	2b	2a	3b	3a
Limited / no knowledge	Some understanding and knowledge	Depth of understanding undertaken Additional reading / visits etc.	Practical individual expertise in this topic	Practical Involvement working with others in this topic	Practical development of others in this topic	Implementing and leading this topic across a school	Developed and adapted strategy across a school in this topic and demonstrated impact

Once this process has been completed, Future Leaders develops a bespoke development programme comprising intensive formal sessions, coaching from experienced head teachers, and action learning sets.

Since the programme started, the organization has trained more than 350 teachers, who now occupy head and senior management positions at more than 200 different schools. Future Leaders claim to be able to show that schools which have employed a future leader for at least two years since the programme began have improved their results at a faster rate (4.57 per cent) than the national average (2.35 per cent).

Sources

Interview with Catrina Plastow, Director of Training and Development, The Future Leaders Trust.

The Future Leaders Trust, *Demonstrating Impact Report*, May 2011.

http://future-leaders.org.uk (accessed 14 August 2013).

Questions

1. What do you make of the dual competency approach—behavioural and task? Can you see any links to other leadership models that also used this approach?

2. What might be the strengths and weaknesses of the self-assessment framework?

3. What challenges might a prospective leader face in making the transition from teacher to head?

How are leaders developed?

Having explored some of the reasons why organizations may wish to develop their leaders, and one of the major strategic approaches to this activity, it is worth exploring some of the ideas that underpin the more tactical activities of learning and development. The first point to make is that 'learning and development' as a broad theme is often considered to be a specialist field. For example, the Chartered Institute of Personnel and Development (see: http://www.cipd.co.uk/ (accessed 14 August 2013)) have a dedicated career path and qualification base for individuals considering this option. So, within this chapter the broad themes will be outlined along with recommendations for further research and reading if this particular theme requires a more in-depth analysis.

In terms of the techniques used to develop individuals, there is a multitude of approaches used by organizations. These can range from long, accredited programmes such as MBAs, which take anything from one to three years to complete, to short workshops designed to last a few hours. The settings for these can also vary enormously from prestigious business schools, such as Ashridge and Henley, both based in England, to in-house provision or 'corporate universities', such as the ones run by large organizations (Jarvis 2001) like British Airways. The content of these courses are usually tailored to a particular organizational need such as programmes aimed at developing a particular skill—for instance, 'dealing with difficult employees' or 'managing negotiations'. Others will have an emphasis on a particular leadership idea, such as Fielder and Chemers' LPC model reviewed in Chapter 6. Within each of the broad programmes come any number of different techniques with lectures, role playing, group activities, outdoor pursuits, tests, and assessments all figuring in leadership training schemes.

Business games

These activities are based on participants being asked to engage in an activity designed to replicate the effect of leadership decisions on a fictitious organization. Often, these games are computer based with decisions being inputted into a software suite that analyses the outcomes based on a complex set of algorithms. Participants can see the effect of their decisions quickly and begin to learn how their decision affects an organization. The basic premise is that, by participating in these metaphorical simulations, individuals can see how their decision affects a business without having to wait for months or years and so can modify their choices should the effect be adverse. The degree to which this actually happens is unclear with little research available. Naish and Birdi's (2001) study looked at some elements, but more recently Tao et al. (2012) have explored this area and it remains a popular activity for organizations.

Case studies

Here, individuals or, more likely, small groups are given real-world examples of activities within organizations. The situation and likely outcomes are discussed within the group, sometimes with input and guidance from trained facilitators who will guide the group through the process, seeking recommendations from the group as to what they would have done in similar situations. Alongside written case studies, which describe past events, role playing can also be employed. This entails the participants exploring a situation with either another participant or facilitator using a predefined outline script. Common examples of this type of activity involve helping a manager deal with performance reviews or disciplinary meetings where a difficult or potentially confrontational event can be explored safely.

Competency-based workshops

This involves the manager attending a short, formal programme, often over a day or less, with the intention of studying a particular aspect of their development needs—such as how to understand management reports or employment law. Formal training events can be held on-site as part of a bespoke package, or off-site as part of an open access course. Each approach has advantages—a bespoke programme can pick up particular organizational nuances, but may become staid and risk being old fashioned. External programmes can be more innovative and varied, but may lack any real connection to the sponsoring business's environment. What they have in common is that these interventions are designed to address a very specific shortcoming identified in a leader's competency. An example of this would be SELEX's programme outlined in the case study at the end of this chapter.

Outdoor pursuits

Participants explore different problems and physical challenges in outdoor settings. The purpose of such activities is to develop self-confidence and team spirit. Typically, groups will be presented with a problem, such as crossing a lake without a boat, just a collection of barrels, ropes, and planks. From these items, the group are expected to work out how to build a suitable raft and to cross the lake. Again, research on how these activities translate into organizational benefits is sparse and there is a risk these activities can be dominated by a physically stronger person to the exclusion of the physically impaired. Shivers-Blackwell (2004) carried out a review of this area when examining the effect on prospective MBA students and found limited impact on their behaviour.

Psychometric assessment

Chapter 10 has explored some of the tools available and the ideology that surrounds these instruments. However, it is the case that organizations do deploy a number of different tools, such as the MBTI, OPQ32, and 16PF, to assess an individual's personality. When coupled with coaching, it is thought this assists individuals to gain reflective insight into their own character and to understand how their own behaviour can influence a third party's perception of them.

Coaching

This activity has become increasingly in vogue as a method of helping individuals to focus on aspects of their behaviour that may be causing a concern to the organization, or areas needing to be developed such as 'dealing with difficult people' (Kearns 2006). A coach can be either internal or external to the company but there are several areas in common. The first is the need to establish a positive, open, and professional relationship between the coach and coachee. Next, is the need to set the boundaries and scope of the intervention, and, finally, how the individual coachee will be able to 'measure' their own progress. Annette Fillery-Travis and David Lane (2006) feel many organizations establish coaching sessions based on an incorrect assumption and do not make best use of what can be an expensive and time-consuming activity.

Mentoring

This option differs from coaching in that is almost exclusively managed in-house. It usually involves a more experienced manager taking a younger, less experienced manager under their wing to help them with their development in the organization. Often, the mentor will be from a different part of the business and can assist the mentee with some of the political issues encountered in some larger organizations.

Action-based learning and job rotation

These activities are common on many graduate development schemes. Individuals using this approach will be tasked with undertaking small-scale projects within different departments. The complexity and risk factors associated with the projects are likely to be small initially, but will involve active feedback from senior management on completion. If the individual undertaking the project is deemed to be 'successful', it is likely they will be moved to a different area with a more complex and challenging assignment to complete. O'Neil and Marsick's (2007) book gives some good advice on how to set up and manage these types of scheme.

Summary

Leadership develop activities and the broader framework varies enormously from organization to organization. The evidence from some reports, such as Mabey (2006) and Worrall and Cooper (2012), makes it clear that investment in leadership provides clear benefits to the organization. However, take-up is patchy across the UK with only 1 in 5 managers having any formal qualification in this field (McBain et al. 2012). Newer initiatives, such as the Chartered Manager status offered by the CMI, are making some slow but sustained progress towards offering sceptical organizations more concrete evidence that to be a world class organization you need world class leaders. The methods for delivering this agenda are also numerous with the number of organizations claiming to offer leadership development increasing almost daily. Nevertheless, leadership development does remain, for some organizations at least, central to their organizational development and, as such, will become more important as they face continuing uncertainty in terms of finance, globalization, and competition. For individuals, the challenge is to remain competitive in what is sure to become an increasingly complex arena and to make the right choices when it comes to designing a leadership career ladder. Formal qualifications may help in this process but, as the various organizational case studies show, there is more to being a successful leader than having a qualification that has 'leadership' or 'management' in the title.

Case study SELEX Galileo

SELEX Galileo is large international electronics company specializing in the defence sector. It employs more than 7,000 people in various countries around the world and turns over €1,796 million. It is part of the larger Italian group, Finnmeccanica, based in Rome. SELEX Galileo can trace its history back to being part of BAE Systems and beyond to the original Marconi Company. They undertake research and development as well as manufacturing highly sophisticated sensors, such as radar, and they are a major supplier to the Eurofighter 'Typhoon' aircraft.

Two key challenges demanded a new approach to leadership development in the organization, and to seriously consider a new model. The first challenge was their amalgamation into the larger Finnmeccanica Group. The two organizations had very different cultures; beyond the obvious differences between Italian and British cultures, these extended to the operating environment. To compound the cultural distance between the two organizations was the physical reality of being located in different countries, which made the development of a joint vision, in terms of leadership, much harder to design and communicate.

The second challenge arose from the external environment, with increased competition and the decline of traditional markets. For a long period, SELEX Galileo had been able to rest on the expertise and skill of its engineering prowess; however, suddenly it needed to make its engineers aware of this 'new' world and to encourage them to think much more about 'clients' than elegant engineering solutions. The new Director of Human Resources and Organization, Riccardo Meloni, asked Evan Jones (then the Head of Learning and Development) to provide a solution.

The result of these challenges was the development of three key 'principles' that now underpin the leadership development approach across SELEX Galileo.

1. Visible commitment from senior management: Any programme must be seen to be supported by the senior management team. This is taken to mean that senior managers must be physically present and 'in the room' when more junior members are embarking on their development programme.

2. Customer participation: Participants are encouraged to engage with their customers and to see the impact of their work. As an example of this sought connection, the organization conducts joint training with the customer community and customers routinely speak at leadership development events. These experiences connect people to the importance of their work, where they are often developing systems that protect the lives of service men and women. One particularly poignant (and un-scheduled) experience was when graduate engineers visiting RAF Lyneham observed rehearsals for the removal of coffins of those killed in Afghanistan from a transport plane, a theatre where SELEX equipment is being used.

3. Develop internal networks and friendships: Wherever possible, delegates are chosen to reflect the multi-cultural and multi-discipline environment in which they work. Follow-on activities and networks are encouraged to maintain the bonds that are created, encourage innovation and sharing of ideas, and to pursue 'real work'.

With Riccardo Meloni's vision and support, and with these broad principles in place, Evan and his team could now move to 'operationalize' a broad international development framework—'pyramid'—which worked at all levels within the business. This structure ensures there is a real link between leadership development and measurable, tangible outputs for the business. Alan Beesley, the current VP Education and Knowledge Management, is quite clear that, as the organization has a strong engineering culture, it is important for this aspect of 'measurability' to be present as this ensures a high degree of engagement by the senior managers. He puts it thus:

> We do want to make sure that there is a benefit from the programmes—this is not so much the old 'cost benefit analysis' argument, but more to do with motivation. If the delegates can see a clear connection

(Continued...)

between the programme and their day-to-day work, they are much more inclined to take it seriously, and the improvements follow as a matter of course. One such example was the work done as part of the Senior Leadership Programme—this programme consists of a series of workshops on the theme of the company strategy, where we asked them to consider some growth options, but without being specific—we did not know the answer! The programme was a combination of strong external speakers and internal testimonials, and individual and group coaching (with MBTI), and the delegates were organized into IPTs (Integrated Project Teams) and it lasted about 9 months (probably about 10 working days during this period). The proposals were presented to Company Management and one of these was assigned several hundred pounds investment to develop the business case. In fact four proposals were taken forward during the first year, and there is now a supporting implementation team at working level. The connection between the programme and its business benefit is clear.

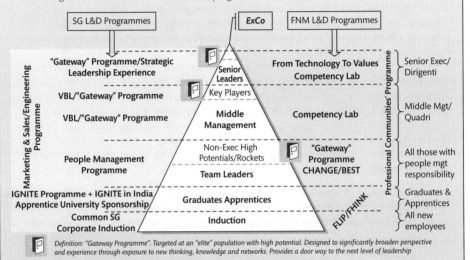

Definition: "Gateway Programme". Targeted at an "elite" population with high potential. Designed to significantly broaden perspective and experience through exposure to new thinking, knowledge and networks. Provides a door way to the next level of leadership

Reproduced with permission of Selex Galileo

The important point here is the empowering nature of the development programme. Alan is quite clear—the organization's hierarchy do not have all of the answers—he calls it 'leadership with ambiguity'. It is incumbent on the managers on the development programme to take real ownership of their ideas. If the senior executives can be convinced of the viability of an idea, then funds are dedicated to the development of that theme. This means managers must have faith in their own ability to deliver as suddenly they may be tasked with designing a whole new machine. For example, one idea proposed by a group on the programme was to develop a medical application. This is completely outside the current core product range of SELEX Galileo. However, the proposing team thought differently—they pondered on the expertise in the organization, such as robotics and control systems, considered their client's needs and the nature of their client's environment (a battle ground), and thought SELEX Galileo could make a viable contribution. After presenting the idea to the senior executives (ExCo), funding has been released to drive this project forward.

Both Alan and Evan think it is this connection between ideas, leadership development, and corporate strategy that makes the programme so powerful. The pyramid structure ensures this ethos flows up and down the business so more junior project managers get involved with senior programme directors. This helps to reinforce the understanding that development is linked to corporate strategy and junior individuals can see how their development is a planned element of a broader organizational development strategy.

Source

Interview with Mr Alan Beesley and Mr Evan Jones, SELEX Galileo offices, London, 23 November 2012.

Questions

1. Alan Beesley has an engineering background whilst Evan is more a 'traditional' leadership development expert. How significant do you think this combination has been in creating the SELEX Galileo model?

2. What do you think about the three key 'principles' that underpin the SELEX Galileo approach?

3. Do you think it is important for an organization to have a leadership development strategy that is inclusive? Or, do you think such a programme should be reserved for the brightest few so resources can be focused and targeted?

Assignment—3,000 words

Ideas for a 3,000 word assignment:

1. Using any organization that you are familiar with, analyse their leadership development strategy and make recommendations for improving this strategy.
2. Comment on the following statement: 'There's no competency framework for a good leader. You either are or are not capable of leading'. What paradigm would support the statement and how would you argue against this position?
3. Why do some organizations not bother with any formal leadership development when there is evidence to suggest leadership is key to an organization's success?

Further reading

Rosemary Ryan's book, *Leadership Development* (2008, Oxford: Butterworth Heinemann) is written from a practical perspective but comes at the topic from a human resources professional angle rather than a leadership one. This means the author deals with the detail of 'how' rather than 'why'. Nevertheless, if you are looking for a hands-on guide, this type of book can be quite useful.

On a slightly different track, you might try Warren Bennis's updated *On Becoming a Leader* (2009, New York: Basic Books). This deals with the more 'personal' side of leadership development so makes the point that the best systems and processes are useless without some kind of raw material and willingness. There are obvious links back to the themes of authenticity explored in this book in Chapter 8 as he considers the idea of 'knowing yourself' in his book in Chapter 3.

Finally, never one to miss out on a theme author, John Adair's book, *How to Grow Leaders* (2009, London: Kogan Page) identifies what he considers to be seven key principles. These are a mixture of organizational and individual and the text ranges between him suggesting organizational development alongside ideas more suitable for individuals to pursue. Like most of his books, it is an entertaining read full of anecdotes and 'real-world' examples.

Strategic leadership

After reading this chapter you will:

- Be in a position to understand what a strategic leader 'is'.
- Be able to grasp the significance of a strategic leader.
- Be able to identify key functional skills associated with strategic leadership.

Introduction

In a similar vein to Chapter 15, this chapter is more about what a leader 'does' than considering a theoretic frame concerned with identifying how a leader or leadership may be contextualized. If the other chapters were concerned with leadership 'inside' an organization, this chapter considers leadership 'of' an organization (Boal and Hooijberg 2001). The chapter seeks to explore how 'strategic' leadership is any different from other forms of leadership experienced within organizations. We also examine some of the key themes associated with strategic leadership, such as the need for a much more holistic, systems view of the organization. In keeping with this idea of the strategic leader being embedded in a web of information and complexity, the relationship between the person at the top and their environment is reviewed. It is also fair to say that leadership as displayed by those individuals at the top of organizations has come under increasing scrutiny and, at times justified, criticism. The Enron scandal of 2000 (Chapter 13 case study), the more recent RBS/UBS/Barclay's London interbank offered rate (LIBOR) rigging scandal, and the general mayhem caused by the financial crisis of 2008 have caused some (e.g. Bones 2011) to question if strategic leadership, if not capable of making correct decisions, is actually needed at all. The chapter explores some of these ideas and one of the key attributes of strategic leaders—the ability to learn.

What is 'strategic leadership'?

In common with many other themes in this field, defining exactly what is meant by 'strategic leadership' brings with it many different views and opinions. Different organizations will have different terms for 'the person at the top'; such as the American term chief executive officer (CEO), where the UK version is managing director (MD), and the German version is Geschäftsführer. These words can conjure up an image of a large office on the top floor of an impressive skyscraper, an imposing oak desk, and a door jealously guarded by a personal assistant. However, the reality is often very different, with organizations keen to ensure their senior people, whilst remunerated appropriately, are seen to be delivering value-for-money as well as adhering to a complex and changing set of values. Adair (1990) has the role made up of three overlapping activities: giving the business direction, building a successful team, and being creative in terms of solving complex problems. Gill (2011:227) has it as 'showing the way through strategies, informed by shared values, in the pursuit of a vision and purpose'. Hambrick (1989:6) recognizing the problem definitions bring—both having them and a lack thereof—uses 'the people who have overall responsibility for an organization—the characteristics of those people, what they do and how they do it'. This means strategic leadership in this chapter is concerned with exploring and understanding the nature of leadership when experienced by those who are responsible for guiding the organization towards a vision (see: Chapter 15). So, whilst the early part of this book was concerned with exploring conceptual models surrounding leadership and how the term has evolved, this chapter looks much more closely at the end result of a leader's output. Both Rickards (2012) and Grint (2010) are quite clear that without such leaders we cannot hope to organize anything beyond small networks, so successful strategic leadership remains a key theme for many of the world's organizations. Ireland and Hitt (2004:63) were also convinced that 'without effective strategic leadership, the probability that a firm can achieve superior or even satisfactory performance when confronting the challenges of the global economy will be greatly reduced'.

Do we need strategic leaders?

Recent debate on the impact of strategic leaders on their organizations has moved between two competing views. One, pioneered by Hambrick and Mason (1984), suggests the direction and nature of organizations are a direct function of the values, experiences, and cognitive abilities of those at the top of the organization. This is because, they suggest, a complex and unknown world is interpreted differently by different people. The consequence being, strategic leaders will make judgements about the nature of our world based on their past experiences and use this interpretation to create competitive organizational strategies for their organizations. They put it thus: 'the manager's eventual perception of the situation combines with his/her values to provide the basis for strategic choice' (Hambrick and Mason 1984:195). This idea, referred to as 'upper echelon theory', places the senior leadership of the organization in a position from which they create the organization's strategy based on their own biases and perception of the 'right' thing to do. There is evidence (Yan and Tan 2013) to suggest companies that 'match' their strategic leader's attributes to their corporate plan perform better when compared with those who have a mismatch; however, the case is far from proven.

The other view, a more deterministic perspective, is led by the giants of strategic writing familiar to any MBA graduate, authors such as Igor Ansoff (1965), Peter Drucker (1955), and Michael Porter (1985). All of these writers make various claims to have invented the discipline of corporate strategy and have their own favourite model and framework. Their techniques, such as SWOT analysis, the 5-Forces Model, or PESTLE analysis, suggest that anyone with access to this type of training could implement a strategy. Mintzberg and Waters (1985) along with Whittington (1993) contributed to the debate with their discussion on how organizations 'made' strategy. They examined the difference between 'planned' strategy and 'emergent' strategy, concluding that emergent strategies imply a degree of planned chaos that may in fact be more effective in a turbulent world than a planned strategy. The point being that different schools put different emphasis on the ability of a senior leader to create, implement, and manage a strategic approach to their organizations' environment—but the way to do this is via rigorous, detached, rational analysis.

Pause for thought

1. What do you make of these two different ideas? The upper echelon theory suggests that, to understand organizations, you need to understand the values of the top leaders; whilst determinants suggest that strategic planners use objective analysis to create a rational response to the environment.

2. What do you think about the idea that organizations are made in the image of their leaders? Or do
you think organizations are simply a reflection of their environment?

3. Would Apple Computers be any different if a different leader was at the helm? Steve Jobs was the
original leader but what if, say, Richard Reed (see: Chapter 8 case study for Innocent Drinks) owned
the business?

More lately, Hambrick (2007) has introduced the idea of a leader's discretion in terms of how
much freedom the top leaders have to create and implement strategies. For him this bridged
the gap between the two models: where one suggested top leaders were the creative power-
houses behind every successful company, to the other suggesting the environment and the
analysis of that environment drove strategy. This later view suggests that senior leaders may face
internal constraints when trying to shift policy towards their own design. These constraints may
be in the form of a board of directors or shareholders that may wish to limit any alterations.

 Case study   Frances O'Grady

The Trades Union Congress (TUC) is an umbrella organization in the United Kingdom formed in 1868
to act as a champion for trade unions and their members. Based in London, it is managed by a General
Secretary and it boasts more than six million members in 54 different unions. Until recently, the General
Secretary of the TUC was always a man. However, in January 2013, the General Council, made up of 56
members, elected Ms Frances O'Grady as their next General Secretary thereby sweeping away one of
last bastions of male primacy in British employment. Or, as the Left-wing website, Socialist Unity, put it,
'shifting the "male, pale and stale" stereotype to a profile that better fits a six million plus membership
that is now 50:50 men and women'.

O'Grady was born in Oxford to a family already steeped in trade unionism. Her father was a trade
union official at the Leyland car manufacturing plant at Cowley, Oxford. After doing well at school, she
moved to Manchester to read Politics and Modern History. Those who knew her as a student noticed
how she became increasingly aware of the social and economic divisions within British society. She
graduated and began her long-term career within the trade union movement by starting work as a
researcher in The Transport and General Workers Union (TGWU), focusing on issues of equality.

From here she moved to leadership roles within the movement, finally taking the top job in early
2013. In her new job she has been described as 'ordinary, campaigning, committed to justice—a
combination that in some might come across as a bit pious, but not in Frances O'Grady' (Maguire 2012).
O'Grady, herself, says, 'I worry that some politicians still think we are living in the 1950s where the man is
the main breadwinner and the woman works for pin money. Actually, most families where there are two
parents depend on two incomes to get by. It really sticks in the throat of a lot of women, the idea that
they're easier to pick on and their money is somehow less important'.

Looking ahead to the challenges facing her, she says she 'hopes to use her role at the head of the TUC
to nail some myths about the trade union movement being male-dominated'. It is this campaigning
zeal, combined with a calm and down to earth approach, that have earned her immediate respect

in politics. Bolderson (2012) says, 'I suspect if someone met her and didn't know her, they wouldn't immediately say she was a campaigner because she will just introduce subjects in a way that relates to people's lives instead of preaching from a pulpit'. And Chorley (2012) says, 'She's just a human being—a really normal person'.

Sources

Bolderson, C. (2012) 'Profile: Frances O'Grady, the new TUC General Secretary'. BBC Radio 4, 18 August 2012.

Chorley, M. (2012) 'Frances O'Grady: "Women are feeling hard done by"'. *The Independent*, 9 September 2012.

Maguire, K. (2012) 'A Single Mum and the First Female Face of Trade Unionism—Meet Frances O'Grady, Queen of the TUC'. *The Mirror*, 16 July 2012.

http://socialistunity.com/frances-ogrady-to-be-tuc-general-secretary (accessed 21 January 2013).

Questions

1. What challenges face Frances in her new role?

2. What difference do you think she can make to her organization? Consider your response in the light of upper echelon theory and determinism.

3. What do you make of the comments about her personality and any possible strategic changes she makes?

The modern environment

It is worth considering the nature of the environment facing leaders today so that the extent to which the current challenges facing strategic leaders can be assessed. In Chapter 15, it was suggested that change has been a constant feature of business environments. However, there may be other elements that make today's world different from previous eras, such as the influence of technology or differing pressures from society. In broad terms, Castells (1996) gazed into the future and considered the effect of a number of trends that he saw as influencing individual decision making. He thinks both individuals and organizations have a fundamental need to find sense in their environment and this creates a powerful drive for identity and meaning. However, he believes this has been undermined by elemental changes to the social, political, and economic landscape of the world. These changes, Castells argues, have made societies powerless to influence their destiny and have given rise to an acceptance of individualism where individuals focus on defending their own interests rather than considering the impact on their immediate neighbours. He sees political cynicism caused by a de-legitimization of institutions as they become more isolated from the people they serve (perhaps illustrated by the rise of the United Kingdom Independence Party (or UKIP) as a reaction to the feeling that European laws override British law); social scepticism caused by the fading away of major social movements such as religion (perhaps replaced by fundamentalism in the shape of Al-Qaeda and the religious Right); and intellectual nihilism arising from mass media intrusion (perhaps making fame seem the 'new' faith) as the major factors influencing the restructuring of society and organizations. All of these combine to produce a set of global conditions that create a complex and complicated environment for a senior leader to contend with.

Alongside these broad themes, the rise of technology as a major influence on our daily lives has been extensively mapped. It is the effect of this technology that is of most interest as Smith and Marx (1994) argue strongly that technology does not determine society but rather technology embodies society, and neither does society determine technological innovation, it uses it. Clearly the 'Age of the Smart Machine' (Zuboff 1988) is upon us and has moved beyond simple automation where manual tasks, previously carried out by workers, were made quicker, better, and cheaper by machines, to a world of 'informating' (1988:9) where information and data is available at the click of a mouse button. This has had three significant impacts on the way in which humans operate (Burgoyne 2012). First, our working patterns have changed with many individuals and organizations operating from remote settings capable of communicating instantly with their colleagues regardless of distance or time; second, the relationship between workers/machines/other workers has altered to become more of a virtual world, where relationships are conducted via an intermediary computer terminal meaning asynchronous working is now the norm; and, third, the relationship between a customer and company has moved from a physical exchange to one based in a virtual environment. This has caused seismic shifts in the way organizations conduct their business, as witnessed by many UK-based retailers (e.g. Comet, HMV, Jessops) who went into receivership in early 2013 unable to compete with internet-based rivals such as Amazon.

These changes have combined to create an external environment very different from those experienced by some of the iconic strategic leadership figures from past decades. Jack Welch of General Electric, Alfred Sloan of General Motors, and Soichiro Honda, who founded his eponymous organization, would have probably created very different organizations if they had been around in today's business environment. Just consider the nature of today's powerful organizations, such as Google, Facebook, and Apple—almost their entire 'entity' is a virtual one located in a complex environment managing to be simultaneously remote and immediate. As Kelly (1995:25) speculated when looking forward 20 years: 'the atom is the past. The symbol of science for the next century is the dynamic net.'

As well as the external pressures from technology and society, there are several other trends worth considering that influence today's strategic leaders. The first is the purpose of the strategic leader. As Bass (2008:682) points out, the drive for CEOs during the later part of the twentieth century was simply about defeating the competition. This meant increasing market share with the ultimate aim of becoming the sole supplier in any given market even if this meant damaging returns to investors and profitability. Survival was the Darwinian force driving decision making. Alongside this, almost imperceptibly at first, a force grew into a tsunami of greed with the world plunging into a deep recession as a result of financial institutions entering into a disastrous cycle of risk and reward that burst in 2008. As a result of this, there has been a move to realign the ethical practices underpinning corporate behaviour. For example, Antony Jenkins, the CEO of Barclays Bank PLC, who was appointed in the wake of the interbank rate fixing scandal in 2011, has told his staff either to sign up to a new ethical policy or leave the organization. Strategic leaders in modern organizations have no doubt both inherited and created a very complex world where the definition of 'success' is changing from one where profit, market share, and return on investment are becoming increasingly anachronistic. A chief executive in any contemporary organization is as likely to have to report and manage 'goodwill', ethical values, and public perception in addition to more traditional measures. Ireland and Hitt (2004:64) sum the situation up thus: 'There is virtually uniform agreement that the complexity, turbulence and extraordinary changes during the 1980s and 1990s are contributing to the rapid development of an ultracompetitive global economy'—and remember, this was written before the global crash of 2008.

What does a strategic leader 'do'?

In terms of activities, Finkelstein et al. (2007) have produced a model that has four distinct elements that attempt to summarize the complexity that exists at the head of a modern organization—strategic definition, strategic thinking, strategic alignment, and strategic enactment—which, combined with a 'transformational' approach (see: Chapter 7), produce strategic leadership. It is this model that provides a useful framework for exploring strategic leadership and some of the challenges that underpin this vital activity.

Strategic definition

In Chapter 15 we discussed the need to develop a vision for an organization capable of harnessing the hopes and dreams of the entire organization. Additionally, as well as acting in this sense, this idea is also linked to a 'value proposition'. This term relates to the added-value or distinctiveness of the organization. A strategic leader needs to be able to answer the question: 'What is it that makes our company better than a competitor?' Ireland and Hitt (2004:63) make it clear that creating a distinctive proposition is at the heart of a strategic leader's role because, 'when strategic leadership processes are difficult for competitors to understand, and hence imitate, the firm has created a competitive advantage'. Even with not-for-profit organizations, there is need to create a sense of uniqueness about the business so that sponsors, donors, and the wider stakeholder network understands what their commitment to the business 'means' for them. This proposition should address the following issues:

- Price: What is the overall approach to pricing of the product/service? Is it to be premium priced or more at the lower end of the scale? Consider the difference between Ryanair, the low cost airline, and, say, British Airways as an example.

- Features: Are the features of the goods or service to be basic or is the product to be packed with technology? Look at examples of some modern television sets—some are packed with features such as 3D, surround sound, and internet connectivity whilst others are relatively simple with a limited number of free channels.

- Quality: Whilst no service can be positioned as poor in terms of quality, consider the difference between a luxury car such as a Mercedes and a relatively modest one made by Kia or Dacia.

- Support: Again, the customer can be offered a choice here between a service that offers unrivalled levels of support and those that do not. For example, Virgin Airlines offers its top paying customers a chauffeur driven limousine to collect them from their home to take them to the airport, whilst other service providers charge extra for even booking a ticket using the 'wrong' type of credit card.

- Availability: This relates to how your product or service reaches its intended market—the 'route to market'. Is the product going to be made available in every corner of the globe using a wide range of shops, suppliers, dealers, or franchisees, or is it going to be heavily restricted, perhaps in a particular area or via a certain exclusive outlet. Here you can think about certain designer clothes that can only be bought at chic boutiques through to the ubiquitous Tesco or McDonald's present in most high streets.

- Reputation: This is closely associated with the values of the brand itself. This can be highly prestigious through to purely functional. Supermarkets can be a good example here, with Waitrose, Marks and Spencer, and Selfridges occupying the prestigious end of the market, and discounters, such as Aldi, Makro, and Lidl, at the functional end.

Essentially, this formula should make it clear to employees, customers, and competitors exactly what the organization is in existence for and what it is willing and not willing to do in order to achieve that goal.

Once this focus has been established, the leader can move on to designing competencies for the organization (see: Chapter 16). However, more than being a focus on job-specific capabilities, the leader needs to understand what the organization needs to be good at—or at least better at than competitors. For example, if a strategic leader wants to create an organization that has a vision of being 'the fastest to market', they will have to be skilled at packaging, distribution, warehousing, and transport. If a company sees itself as 'the highest quality', they will need to be good at quality processes such as Kaizen or Six Sigma, and so on. These 'core competencies' (Prahalad and Hamel 1990) are the 'collective learning in the organization' (1990:82) and are what makes one company different from another. The interesting development in this area of organizational development is the move towards these competencies being located in the minds of the workforce rather than in some piece of machinery or access to a particular raw material. So, it is the ideas and innovation that increasingly mark out successful organizations from others. And, unlike raw materials, core competencies located in the minds of the workforce do not become depleted over time, but may decide to walk out of the door—which makes the task of looking after the workforce another key theme for the strategic leader. This feature links to the ability to learn and adapt covered later in this chapter.

 Pause for thought

1. What do you think are the 'core competencies' of these organizations:

    a. Apple

    b. McDonald's

    c. Toyota

    d. Tata Motors of India.

2. What makes these companies different from their competitors?

3. Why are they able to sustain this 'difference'?

Strategic thinking

'**Systems thinking** is that required to produce the synergies that are more than the sum of the individual parts of the organization' (Bass 2008:682). This means developing a wider perspective than the purely functional role occupied by many managers within the organization. Not only is it necessary to examine the immediate environmental landscape facing the organization, and make judgements about how best to engage with the conditions, but the strategic leader must also be capable of looking into the future to see what opportunities and threats are likely to face the organization. The extent to which a leader can manipulate that environment, in the way Steve Jobs of Apple or Bill Gates of Microsoft were able to, is open to debate. However, what is certain is that strategic leaders need to articulate the vision for their business, as discussed in Chapter 15.

> **Systems thinking** and system science is a diverse form of analysis that argues to understand complex social and biological problems—you need to understand the holistic nature of the network surrounding the nucleus of the issue. Perhaps best summed up by the phrase, 'the whole is more than the sum of the parts', it was championed by Peter Checkland in the 1980s. It argues against reductionism and asks users to consider the relationship between elements of a system as well as the workings of the whole system (Checkland 1981).

Having a systems perspective simply means seeking an understanding of how the complex world works rather than only looking inward at problems and challenges. A strategic leader must be able to understand the implications of policy directives or new technological breakthroughs. By keeping a wider perspective, the strategic leader can adjust the organization to take advantage of changes in the environment or avoid the worst effects of any challenges. Some organizations even use a 'test' to check their senior leaders for this 'helicopter vision', such as the LSQ developed by Peter Honey (2006). This 'environmental scanning' was identified by Senge et al. (1999) as a key attribute of a strategic leader.

Senge and the 'learning organization' school (Senge 1990) have been keen to establish a link between the ability of the organization to learn and its chances of survival and growth. Although an agreed definition of such an entity is still subject to debate (Garvin 2000), the essence of the argument seems to be that, for an organization located in the 'knowledge economy', the ability to learn remains a key competence. Senge's ideas resulted in the *Fifth Discipline* book, and his subsequent tomes selling in their millions, and his being named 'Strategist of the Century' by the *Journal of Business Strategy*. According to Senge (1990: 3), learning organizations are:

> Organizations where people continually expand their capacity to create the results they truly desire, where new and expansive patterns of thinking are nurtured, where collective aspiration is set free, and where people are continually learning to see the whole together.

Whilst individuals may have the capacity to learn, what was new about his ideas was the suggestion that not all organizations were in a position to harness this creative zeal. Their internal systems and culture could be restricting the innovative potential and making the organization vulnerable to collapse. He argued for mastery of five 'disciplines' (competencies): Systems thinking, personal mastery, mental models, building shared vision, and team learning. At the heart of this new type of organization is the need to master 'system thinking' and 'system maps' that show how different parts of a system relate to each other.

It would follow, if upper echelon theory is adopted, that a strategic leader should embody this attribute and be seen to be a 'learner'. However, this term does seem somewhat ambiguous, especially as Senge also sees the leader as a teacher. Boal and Hooijberg (2001) have attempted to expand on this notion of learning by identifying what they consider to be three essential facets of learning: absorptive capacity, adaptive capacity, and managerial wisdom.

1. Absorptive capacity: This is 'the dynamic capacity that allows firms to create value and to gain and sustain a competitive advantage through the management of the external knowledge' (Camisón and Forés 2010). This involves some kind of active strategy for gathering information and data about the external environment, distilling it into useful knowledge, and using this for competitive advantage. Whilst this activity may seem to be the domain of a research and development department, to be successful the activity needs to be much wider than a focus on new products or services. A strategic leader needs to understand subtle shifts in government policy, changing consumer habits, new cultural norms, and other alterations in socioeconomic conditions. Not only must the leader be able to recognize these shifts, but they must also be able to grasp how to exploit them for the benefit of the organization and stakeholders.

2. Adaptive capacity: Linked to strategic flexibility, this is defined as 'a set of abilities that enable firms to lead or respond to change' (Combe et al. 2012). We addressed some of the themes surrounding change in Chapter 15, but here the additional emphasis is on capacity to adapt to change. This means change becomes an embedded principle rather than a one-off event to be 'managed'. This requires strategic leaders to be capable of constantly addressing new ideas, innovation, and future trends.

3. Managerial wisdom: This is a more complex concept as two different themes are combined. The first is concerned with 'seizing the day' or spotting the right time to make a decision. Boal and Hooijberg cite the ancient Greek word, *Kairos*, meaning 'the supreme moment', to suggest that strategic leaders need to understand when the conditions, both inside and outside their organization, are right for exploitation. The second theme is an area already reviewed in Chapter 11 about emotional intelligence. The link here is to suggest that it is not sufficient just to know when to take action but, because the strategic leader needs to work through others, it is also necessary to know how others will react to the decision to act.

This is a useful addition to the established need for strategic leaders to 'learn' as it develops the idea of what they need to learn about and the cognitive abilities necessary to facilitate this activity.

 Pause for thought

Although this 'systems thinking' and 'helicopter vision' sound relatively straightforward, they can be difficult to maintain in the face of crisis. Consider this expression often seen in American offices:

When you are up to your neck in alligators, it is difficult to remind yourself that your initial objective was to drain the swamp.

1. What do you think it means, and what are the implications for strategic leaders?

Strategic alignment

This element is about ensuring the organization is in a fit and ready state to engage with their chosen market. The systems, procedures, and processes necessary to ensure products can reach the customer, that customers can access the 'value proposition' defined earlier, and that all of this is done in accordance with the organizational culture and values, form a vital part of the strategic leader's remit. Some, such as Adair (1990), would argue that this is purely an operational role not worthy of a senior leader's attention. However, there are many stories of organizations failing because there is a gap between strategy and tactics (Bowman 1995). Any organization that creates an impression in a customer's mind and then neglects to deliver on this is bound to fail. Similarly, an organization that does not have the correct mechanism for ensuring its product, however revolutionary and exciting, can get into the hands of paying customers is also going to struggle to survive.

Included in this element is the creation and maintenance of the company's culture. The workforce will need a context in which to set their work and will need a framework to guide their decision making. It is the culture of the organization that determines this perspective. Again, there is a dilemma for the strategic leader to be carefully considered here—that of history versus 'the future'. The core competencies referred to above may have been acquired over many years—for example, consider the prestigious British car maker, Rolls Royce, which began in 1906—and form part of the culture of the business. The question a strategic leader will have to answer though is if this culture, 'the way we do things around here', is appropriate for the future—remember the implications of the vision for the organization discussed earlier.

A necessary and difficult part of this alignment/culture theme is the question of control. That is, to what extent employees have freedom to operate, against the degree to which the organization seeks to regulate their activities. Recently, the issue of control, or lack of it, has produced some spectacular business crashes. In 2012, Kweku Adoboli, a UBS trader, was jailed for seven years by the British courts for swindling £1.2 billion from the bank, at the time the largest banking fraud ever committed. In his defence he said that he had acted in the best interest of the bank and that traders were encouraged to take risks and if it went wrong there would be nothing more than a mild reprimand. He was able, by concealing his activities, to exceed his authorized trading limit by a factor of 10. At one point, in mid-2011, he had gambled over £12 billion of the bank's money. This situation arose despite the similar case of Jérôme Kerviel in 2008. He was an employee of the French bank, Société Générale, based in Paris. He managed to lose €4.9 billion for the bank and was convicted in 2010. What is remarkable about the two cases is that neither man was said to have profited personally from the fraud and both were easily able to circumvent the controls put in place by the banks following the collapse of Barings Bank in 1994—caused by Nick Leeson, another rogue trader.

However, the need to control employees' activities can be a difficult balance to get right. Companies need to be careful, as it has been shown that restriction on autonomy can de-motivate employees. Christ et al. (2012:28) say, 'formal controls that are perceived to restrict employees' autonomy (such as preventive controls) reduce employees' intrinsic motivation'. Whilst organizations have a legitimate interest in the activities of their employees, and a legal obligation to ensure actions carried out in their name are safe, there is a real risk of stifling creativity and innovation if there is too close a watch held over their behaviour. Employees need to feel trusted and a draconian micromanagement approach is unlikely to foster a feeling of mutual respect between employees and managers. A strategic leader has to set the tone for this balance by gaining an understanding of how the business operates, its key interdependencies, and its responsibilities.

 Pause for thought

Review the earlier chapters on situational leadership and contingency theory.

1. What factors may influence the degree to which a leader seeks to control employees as opposed to allowing a wide amount of discretion when making decisions?

2. Why do you think the examples of massive fraud emerge from the banking sector? Why are traders allowed to gamble with significant amounts of capital?

Strategic enactment

Here, the strategic leader is connecting the overall strategy with the necessary business tactics. Change management is a key skill to be deployed, for as the strategy evolves so too will different parts of the organization. Creating this flexible, yet anchored organization is a difficult balancing act as there will be those who will gain as parts of the business grow and others that lose as the emphasis switches. Keeping the tactical organization working as strategy evolves can be one of the most demanding elements. Shareholders are notoriously impatient in requiring a return on their investment and will not tolerate for long an organization that does not offer a reasonable return on investment. This means the strategic leaders have to ensure a constant flow of outputs despite an uncertain set of inputs.

Earlier, under the theme of 'strategic definition', the need to manage effectively the development of the workforce was introduced. It is under the theme of 'strategic enactment' that this requirement is formally located. Today's workers are becoming increasingly well educated and self-aware. The old concept of a 'job for life' has long gone and workers are now far more aware of the need to ensure they are expanding their knowledge base and capable of adding value to the organization via their minds rather than their muscles. However, the quid pro quo for organizations is the demand to ensure this workforce has access to developmental opportunities. Tata Industries of India has its own Management Training Centre located in Pune with a strategic link to Harvard Business School, whilst Toyota spent nearly US$9 billion on research and development in 2010, which equates to nearly US$1 million per hour. Kyläheiko et al. (2011) are unequivocal over the need to ensure knowledge in organizations is the new critical resource for organizations. They say: 'It is now clear that fundamental changes in the economy have shifted the sources of competitive advantage from the external sources, like monopoly power based on entry barriers and tangible assets, to intangible assets like knowledge and intellectual property rights' (2011:273). Aspara et al. (2011), when examining the turnaround of fortunes at Nokia, the Finnish technology company, attributed the success in part to recognizing the value of tacit knowledge available inside the company. Both the Chartered Institute for Personnel and Development (CIPD) and the Chartered Management Institute (CMI), two bodies purporting to support the management and leadership cohort in the United Kingdom, have well-developed learning and development programmes. In addition, they both require any member to be able to progress their 'continuous professional development' (CPD) as a condition of membership.

A related theme to this is the challenge of managing not only a well-educated workforce, that demands learning opportunities as part of the psychological contract with employers, but also the nature of an increasingly diverse global workforce. This means strategic leaders will need to be sensitive to different cultural norms, be able to harness the ideas born from different social environments, and recognize that different markets demand a different response. Given these demands, a strategic leader will have to make the choice between four different human resource strategies (HRS) (Aswathapa and Dash 2008). An ethnocentric approach involves using the same HRS as used in the host's country. So, an American multinational, if expanding into India, would use American policies, would probably use American managers in key positions, and would reward its employees using an individually focused system because this is the approach used in the USA. Whilst this has the benefit of exposing the host's managers to different cultures, this 'may be counter-productive' (Aswathapa and Dash 2008:274) as the home employees react against a perceived block on their own development. An alternative is to recruit local managers who may be more culturally sensitive in a model known as polycentric. Whilst this may be a cheaper alternative, it runs the risk of exposing managers to levels of expectation they are not comfortable with. In addition, the outlet will use local employment policies which can be very different from the host's—for example, around equal opportunities or health and safety. Allied to this model is a related concept of 'regio-centric' where a blend of both host managers and managers drawn from the region is deployed. So, a French manager may be used in a German subsidiary or an Indian in a Pakistani company. Again, the potential issues this can cause speak for themselves. The final model is a geocentric approach where the best person for the role is selected regardless of their ethnicity. This requires culturally sensitive recruitment techniques but can produce an integrated model offering a wide range of opportunities and benefits to a global workforce (Sims 2007).

As hinted at earlier, the additional factor facing strategic leaders is the need to ensure a broad ethical framework is in place to guide business decisions. Whilst cynics of this notion may point to such themes as 'corporate social responsibility', 'triple bottom line reporting', and 'balanced score card' as ideas that claimed to have addressed the need to consider the wider impact of business decisions, it is clear that organizations are under pressure as never before to ensure they operate ethically. Brenkert (2010) points out how business ethics are very much a 'hot topic' around the boardrooms of the world. This means ensuring that business decisions are taken having been evaluated through the lens of the corporate values. Openness, honesty, and trust cannot hope to flourish in a business that does not have these as normative values within the senior leadership. Therefore, it is down to the strategic leader to make it explicit about how the organization will operate. Whilst the strategic leader is rightfully concerned with ensuring the organization survives in a turbulent world, stakeholders will be watching to ensure this is done in a way that ensures social concerns are considered fully.

In summary, a strategic leader needs to know what the business is trying to achieve (strategic definition), understand how the internal and external environments affect and are likely to affect the organization (strategic thinking), ensure the business is ready to meet the promise made in the vision (strategic alignment), and, finally, be capable of bringing all of the parts of the business together in one coherent socio-technical system (strategic enactment).

Case study   Mahendra Singh Dhoni

Mahendra Singh Dhoni is the Indian cricket captain worth, according to *Forbes* magazine, US$26.5 million making him the thirty-first richest sportsman in the world. In addition, *Time* magazine added him to its 'Time 100' list of the 100 most influential people of 2011. His profile in India puts him ahead of more globally well-known sportsmen, such as David Beckham, Tiger Woods, and Sebastian Vettel. Better known as MS Dhoni or 'Mahi', he has his own dedicated website and he is lauded by crowds wherever he goes.

If leadership is about 'results', as Grint (2005) suggests, then Dhoni's record as the leader of the team is impressive. Under his guidance, India won the World 20:20 Cup in 2007, achieved number one status in the International Cricket Council (ICC) Test rankings, and, perhaps most impressively, won the 2011 World Cup. In the final of this tournament, India were playing Sri Lanka in Delhi. At the beginning of the game, the crowd noise was so deafening the umpire could not even hear the Sri Lankan captain call heads or tails at the initial coin-toss, which had to be redone. Sri Lanka batted first and scored an impressive 275 runs off their allocation of 50 overs, including a century from Jayewardene, leaving India with the highest run chase ever faced in a World Cup final. India started their innings poorly and were soon reduced to 31 runs for 2 wickets inside 7 overs including that of their talismanic batsman, Sachin Tendulkar. Following a slight recovery, another Indian wicket fell and Sri Lanka looked like the favourites for the crown.

It was at this point that Dhoni made his move. He promoted himself in the batting order and strode out to the wicket in an all or nothing gamble. India needed more than six runs an over to win the game. With his partner, Gambhir, Dhoni began to fight back against the rampant Sri Lankan attack. The game neared its climax, with India still needing 15 runs off the last 17 balls. Dhoni, with the crowd in a state of frenzy, smashed a huge six far over the bowler's head to win the match. He finished with an unbeaten 91 runs off only 79 balls, the Man-of-the-Match award, and the World Cup.

Tendulkar, the world's best batsman, heaped praise on Dhoni, claiming him to be the best captain he has played under. Tendulkar pointed to Dhoni's calm influence that was rubbing off on all his teammates and the way, even under such extreme pressure from every corner, Dhoni handles it, marking him out as a remarkable man.

Sources

'India Crowned Champions After A Pulsating Contest'. *The Hindu* (India), 25 September 2007.

'India lands 2011 World Cup final'. BBC Sport, 8 July 2006.

Schwartz, Peter J. and Smith, Chris (2011) 'Dhoni Forbes' Top Earning Cricketer'. *Time*, 26 July 2012. Available at: http://forbes.com/sites/chrissmith/2012/07/26/ms-dhoni-sachin-tendulkar-lead-the-worlds-highest-paid-cricketers/ (accessed 16 August 2013).

http://espncricinfo.com (accessed 15 August 2013).

Questions

1. What do you think was going through Dhoni's mind as he considered the strategic options facing him as the third Indian wicket fell?

2. Evaluate Dhoni's performance as a strategic leader using the elements of strategic definition, thinking, alignment, and enactment.

3. What significance is there in Tendulkar's remarks?

Summary

In this chapter we examined some of the debates surrounding strategic leadership and how the activity differs from other forms of leadership. The role was defined as being focused on the activities of those who have overall command of an organization and have to enact a strategic vision for the organization. The notion of 'upper echelon theory'—seeing organizations as a reflection of their leaders—was introduced alongside the more deterministic view whereby leaders use analysis to decipher their environment objectively. The challenge of the case studies was to consider if a different outcome could be envisaged if a different stance was taken on the primacy of a strategic leader. The activities of a strategic leader were placed into four main themes: strategic definition (linked to the creation of a vision), strategic thinking (systems thinking), strategic alignment (culture and control), and strategic enactment (HRM and ethics). It is clear that, despite the recent concern about the quality of strategic leaders, and their ability to guide the world's organizations through a turbulent time, this activity will become increasingly important in a time of complexity, uncertainty, and conflict.

 Case study   The state of retailing in Britain

In January 2013, the British high street took a severe knock when three well established brand names filed for insolvency. Jessops, the camera retailer, Blockbuster, a DVD rental store, and, perhaps the largest, HMV, a record store established in 1930, all called in the receiver following a difficult trading period. At HMV, more than 4,300 employees were at risk of losing their jobs unless a buyer could be found for a business owing £176 million. They joined Comet, Clinton Cards, Peacocks, and JJB Sports as the latest casualties of the long recession. The question being asked is whether this marks the beginning of the end for a retail-based high street.

The doom-mongers suggest the internet and web-based retailers, such as Amazon, are effectively driving traditional retailers out of business. This is a fashionable attack given that Amazon were accused of evading tax due to the British government by using a series of accounting tricks. Their profits in the UK in 2011 were declared as £3.3 billion on which they paid £1.8 million tax—a sum roughly equating to 5 per cent when they should have been paying closer to 20 per cent. They were able to do this by claiming their British operation is a subsidiary of the Luxembourg-based head office. Taxes are then paid at the Luxembourg rate which is substantially lower than the UK rate. Amazon are not alone in doing this as Starbucks and Google have also been caught up in the scandal. Campaigners claim it is these 'morally bankrupt' practices, coupled with lower overheads, that have contributed towards irreparably damaging the traditional high street. The story is repeated in other European countries. For example, in France, FNAC, a large record chain, is under severe financial pressure and Schlecker, in Germany, has already closed.

However, looking for a single cause of all of these closures is probably a simplistic approach and there may be a number of different reasons worth exploring. The first is to examine the strategic leadership of these retailers to see if there are any common themes. There is a great deal of angst and existential woe caused by the HMV demise because many people grew up with the brand and it represents part of a nostalgic past where young people would while away hours flicking through records. However, this type of behaviour and buying pattern has disappeared completely with new ways to access music, DVDs, and other retail goods. iTunes and other digital stores have revolutionized how individuals access music,

(Continued...)

films, and other entertainment. Companies such as LOVEFiLM and Netflix can provide instant access to new and recent film releases whilst Amazon seems to stock everything from aerials to xylophones. As Jon Copestake, retail analyst at The Economist Intelligence Unit, explains: 'A theme is beginning to emerge on the high street as sellers of obsolete products using outmoded channels see their creditors waiting until after Christmas to call in debts.' The claim is that these companies were simply bad companies poorly managed and led by individuals out-of-touch with the demands of twenty-first-century shoppers.

But Phil Wrigley, Chair of Majestic Wine and LXB Retail Properties, when addressing Oxford University students, said: 'The UK high street was in a death spiral. The combined powers of supermarkets, shopping malls and the internet are squeezing the life out of it.' However, counting against this perspective is the fact that only 10 per cent of all consumer spending is done on the web. Georgina Whyatt, an academic at Oxford Brookes University, suggests that individuals are seeking a social experience when they shop and those stores and high streets that offer this are the ones that are thriving and surviving. She points to the number of coffee shops inside department stores, shopping malls with 'food halls' and easy access to other entertainment venues, such as cinemas, as examples of the blended experience demanded.

In 2011, Mary Portas, a retail entrepreneur, published a report that suggested a five-point plan to protect the high street. She said:

1. Ensure landlords (often large financial institutions) do not leave property vacant.

2. Give local communities a say in what they want in their high street.

3. Town centres should be run like a business, so management is a vital component.

4. A reduction in red tape, a cheaper set of business rates, and affordable car parking were a necessity.

5. Ensure large retailers and councils support the high street with an appropriate planning regime.

A total of 27 towns were selected as an experiment and they were offered £100,000 to kick start a rejuvenation of their high street, with the results being mixed. However, one outcome has been a 'Distressed Retail Property Taskforce' designed to address the issue of disused shops and boarded up properties.

Sources

Carey, S. (2012) 'Is the UK High Street Facing an Inevitable "Death Spiral"?'. *The Guardian*, 13 February 2012.

Hiscott, B. (2013) 'Plan B or Bust: George Osborne Warned High Street Will Die Unless Tories Act'. *Mirror*, 16 January 2013.

Jeffries, S. (2013) HMV and the death of the British high street: why do we care? *The Guardian*, 15 January 2013.

Pickard, J. (2012) 'The Portas Review: One Year On'. *Financial Times*, 29 October 2012.

Simpson, E. (2012) 'High Street Taskforce Aims to Rejuvenate Retail'. BBC News, 29 October 2012.

Questions

1. What is your analysis of the situation facing high street shops?

2. What do the different perspectives of upper echelon theory and determinism offer as tools to understand why Amazon and the like have risen so fast whilst traditional shops have struggled?

3. What do you make of Portas's plan?

Assignment—3,000 words

Here are some ideas for a 3,000 word assignment:

1. Identify two different companies—one that has flourished and one that has failed. Analyse the leadership of these examples to see if there could have been a different outcome if the organization had been led differently.
2. What do you understand by the term 'strategic leadership'? How is it different from 'leadership' as a more general concept?
3. Identify a person you consider to be a successful strategic leader. Use the ideas in this chapter to analyse the success of this individual and make some recommendations for other leaders based on your analysis.

Further reading

The 'Investors in People' award is a UK-based people management standard. Its focus is to change business performance through an active people development policy. A third of the UK's businesses use Investors in People because they believe benefits will arise as a result of implementing the standard. Within the award is a section that deals with strategic leadership as the keystone to developing the business. You can explore the model further at their website: http://www.investorsinpeople.co.uk/Home/index.html.

Again in the UK, the Institute of Directors has a professional development scheme for aspiring and existing directors. This is a competency-based approach that requires the candidate to achieve several different criteria. It is interesting to see how the criteria developed by this body compare with other, similar organizations across the globe and if the model really does prepare a leader for a strategic role.

On a more academic note, the *Harvard Business Review* (Jan/Feb 2013) carries an article by Paul Schoemaker, Steve Krupp, and Samantha Howland entitled 'Strategic Leadership: The Essential Skills'. These skills are the abilities to anticipate, challenge, interpret, decide, align, and learn. In the article, they describe the six skills in detail and include a self-assessment to enable the reader to identify the skills that need most attention. The article goes on to suggest that a leader needs to be proficient in all to be effective. You may wish to contrast this article with Steven Covey's material.

Covey, S. (1989) *The Seven Habits of Highly Effective People*. New York: Simon & Schuster;

Covey. S. (2012) *The Wisdom and Teachings of Stephen R. Covey*. New York: Free Press.

Bibliography

Chapter 1

Arnott, D. H. (1995) 'The Five Lenses of Leadership'. *The Journal of Leadership Studies*, 2: 137–141.

Avolio, B. J. and Gardner, W. L. (2005) 'Authentic Leadership Development: Getting to the root of positive forms of Leadership'. *The Leadership Quarterly*, 16(3): 315–338.

Barbuto, J. E., Fritz, S. M., Matkin, G. S., and Marx, D. B. (2007) 'Effects of Gender, Education, and Age upon Leaders' Use of Influence Tactics and Full Range Leadership Behaviours'. *Sex Roles*, 56(1–2): 71–83.

Bass, B. (2008) *The Bass Handbook of Leadership* (4th edn). New York: Free Press.

Bass, B. M. and Avolio, B. J. (1997) *Revised Manual for the Multifactor Leadership Questionnaire*. Redwood City, CA: Mind Garden.

Bass, B. M. and Riggio, R. E. (2006) *Transformational Leadership* (2nd edn). New Jersey: Lawrence Erlbaum Associates.

Bingham, W. V. (1927) 'Leadership'. In Metcalf, H. C. *The Psychological Foundations of Management*. New York: Shaw.

Blair, T. (2003) 'Speech to House of Commons'. *Hansard, 18 Mar 2003: Column 760*. London: The Stationery Office.

Blair, T. (2010) *A Journey*. London: Random House.

Bones, C. (2011) *The Cult of the Leader*. Chichester: J. Wiley & Sons.

Bowden, A. O. (1926) 'A Study of the Personality of Student Leaders in the United States'. *Journal of Abnormal and Social Psychology*, 46: 521–528.

Covey, S. (2004) *The 7 Habits of Highly Effective People*. London: Simon & Schuster Ltd.

Fayol, H. (1916) *General and Industrial Management*. London: Pitman.

Fiedler, F. E., Chemers, M. M. and Mahar, L. (1976) *Improving Leadership Effectiveness: The Leader Match Concept*. New York: J. Wiley & Sons.

Forrest, J. (2005) *The Space Shuttle Challenger Disaster: A Failure in Decision Support System and Human Factors Management*. Originally prepared 26 November 1996, published 7 October 2005. DSSResources.com. Available at: http://dssresources.com/cases/spaceshuttlechallenger/ (accessed 24 July 2013).

Gardner, J. W. (1986) *The Tasks of Leadership* (Leadership Paper No.2). Washington, DC: Independent Sector.

Grint, K. (2005) *Leadership: Limits and Possibilities*. Basingstoke: Palgrave Macmillan.

Grint, K. (2010) *Leadership: A Very Short Introduction*. Oxford: Oxford University Press.

Grint, K. (2011) 'A History of Leadership'. In Bryman, A., Collinson, D., Grint, K., Jackson, B., and Uhl-Bien, M. (eds) *The Sage Handbook of Leadership*. London: SAGE Publications.

Grove, A. S. (1986) 'Tapping into the Leader Who Lies Within Us'. *Wall Street Journal*, 7 April: 22.

Janis, I. (1972) *Victims of Groupthink*. Boston: Houghton Mifflin.

Judson, H. F. (1986) 'The Legend of Rosalind Franklin'. *Science Digest*, 94: 56–66.

Kirkbride, P. (2006) 'Developing Transformational Leaders: The Full Range Leadership Model in Action'. *Industrial and Commercial Training*, 38(1): 23–32.

Kotter, J. P. (1990) *A Force for Change: How Leadership Differs from Management*. New York: Free Press.

Lewin, K., Lippit, R., and White, R. K. (1939) 'Patterns of Aggressive Behaviour in Experimentally Created Social Climates'. *Journal of Social Psychology*, 10: 271–301.

Likert, R. (1979) 'From Production and Employee Centeredness to Systems 1–4'. *Journal of Management*, 5(2): 147–156.

Mintzberg, H. (2009) *Managing*. Harlow: Pearson.

Montor, K. (1998) *Naval Leadership: Voices of Experience* (2nd revised edn). Annapolis, MD: Naval Institute Press.

Northouse, P. G. (2010) *Leadership: Theory and Practice*. London: SAGE Publications.

Rickards, T. (2012) *Dilemmas of Leadership* (2nd edn). Abingdon: Routledge.

Sawyer, R. D. (2005) *The Essential Art of War*. New York: Basic Books.

Strom, K. J. and Eyerman, J. (2008) 'Interagency Coordination: A Case Study of the 2005 London Train Bombings'. *National Institute of Justice Journal*, 260(July): 8–11.

Sugar, A. (2011) *The Way I See It: Rants, Revelations And Rules For Life*. Basingstoke: Macmillan.

Taylor, F. W. (1911) *The Principles of Scientific Management*. London: Harper & Brothers.

Terry, L. D. (1995) 'The Leadership Management Distinction: The Domination and Displacement of Mechanical and Organismic Theories'. *Leadership Quarterly*, 6: 515–527.

Tolstoy, L. (1993) *War and Peace (Wordsworth Classics)*. Ware: Wordsworth Editions Ltd.

Vinkenburg, C. J., van Engen, M. L., Eagly, A. H., and Johannesen-Schmid, M. C. (2011) 'An Exploration of Stereotypical Beliefs about Leadership Styles: Is Transformational Leadership a Route to Women's Promotion?'. *The Leadership Quarterly*, 22(1): 10–21.

Yukl, G. (2010) *Leadership in Organisations* (7th edn). Upper Saddle River, NJ: Pearson Prentice Hall.

Zaleznik, A. (1977) 'Managers and Leaders: Are They Different?'. *Harvard Business Review*, 55: 67–68.

Chapter 2

Allport, G. W. (1937) *Personality: A Psychological Interpretation*. New York: Henry Holt & Co.

Allport, G. (1950) *The Nature of Personality: Selected Papers*. (1950; 1975). Westport, CN: Greenwood Press.

Ayman, R. and Korabik, K. (2010) 'Leadership – Why Gender and Culture Matter'. *American Psychologist*, 64(3): 157–170.

Behan, R. (2007) 'Why on Earth Would Anyone Want to Work for Sir Alan Sugar?'. *The Daily Mail*, 13 June 2007.

Bennis, W. (1997) *Managing People is like Herding Cats*. New York: Executive Excellence Publishing.

Bingham, W. V. (1927) 'Leadership'. In Metcalf, H. C. (ed.) *The Psychological Foundations of Management*. New York: Shaw.

Bird, C. (1940) *Social Psychology*. New York: Appleton-Century.

Blake, R. and William Roger, L. (eds) (1992) *Churchill: A Major New Reassessment of His Life in Peace and War*. Oxford: Oxford University Press.

Boyce, L. A., Zaccaro, S. J., and Zazanis Wisecarver, M. (2010) 'Propensity for Self-Development of Leadership Attributes: Understanding, Predicting, and Supporting Performance of Leader Self-Development'. *The Leadership Quarterly*, 21(1): 159–178.

Carlyle, T. (1849) *On Heroes, Hero Worship and the Heroic in History*. Boston: Houghton-Mifflin.

Cattell, R. (1965) *The Scientific Analysis of Personality*. London: Penguin.

Chapple, E. D. and Donald, G., Jr, (1946) 'A Method of Evaluating Supervisory Personnel'. *Harvard Business Review*, 24: 197–234.

Digman, J. M. (1990) 'Personality Structure: Emergence of the Five-Factor Model'. *Annual Review of Psychology*, 41: 417–440.

Eysenck, H. (1991) 'Dimensions of Personality: 16: 5 or 3? Criteria for a Taxonomic Paradigm'. *Personality and Individual Differences*, 12: 773–790.

Fielder, F. E. (1964) 'A Contingency Model of Leadership Effectiveness'. In Berkowitz, L. (ed.) *Advances in Experimental Social Psychology* (vol. 1: 149–190). New York: Academic Press.

Flemming, E. G. (1933) 'The Pleasing Personality of High-School Girls as Related to Other Traits and Measures'. *Journal of Educational Sociology*, 6(7): 401–409.

Galton, F. (1869) *Hereditary Genius*. New York: Appleton.

Gardner, J. (1989) *On Leadership*. New York: Free Press.

Gladwell, M. (2008) *Outliers: The Story of Success*. New York: Little, Brown & Co.

Grint, K. (2005) *Leadership: Limits and Possibilities*. Basingstoke: Palgrave Macmillan.

Hogan, R. T. and Fernandez, J. E. (2002) 'Syndromes of Mismanagement'. *The Journal for Quality and Participation*, [1040–9602] 25(3): 28–31.

Hogan Development Survey. Available online at: http://hoganassessments.com/assessments-hogan-development-survey (accessed 25 July 2013).

International Personality Item Pool (IPIP). Available online at: http://personal.psu.edu/j5j/IPIP/ (accessed 25 July 2013).

Jenkins, W. O. (1947) 'A Review of Leadership Studies with Particular Reference to Military Problems'. *Psychological Bulletin*, 44: 54–79.

Judge, T. A. and Bono, J. E. (2000) 'Five-Factor Model of Personality and Transformational Leadership'. *Journal of Applied Psychology*, 85(5): 751–765.

Judge, T. A., Bono, J. E., Ilies, R., and Gerhardt, M. W. (2002) 'Personality and Leadership: A Qualitative and Quantitative Review'. *Journal of Applied Psychology*, 87: 765–780.

Jung, C. G. (1 August 1971) 'Psychological Types'. *Collected Works of C. G. Jung* (Volume 6). Princeton: Princeton University Press.

Kassin, S. (2003) *Psychology*. USA: Prentice-Hall, Inc.

Lord, R. G., Brown, D. J., Harvey, J. L., and Hall, R. J. (2001) 'Contextual Constraints on Prototype Generation and Their Multilevel Consequences for Leadership Perceptions'. *The Leadership Quarterly*, 12: 311–338.

Lord, R. G., De Vader, C. L., and Alliger, G. M. (1986) 'A Meta-Analysis of the Relation Between Personality Traits and Leadership Perceptions: An Application of Validity Generalization Procedures'. *Journal of Applied Psychology*, 71: 402–410.

Mann, R. D. (1959) 'A Review of the Relationship Between Personality and Performance in Small Groups'. *Psychological Bulletin*, 66(4): 241–270.

McCall, M. W. and Lombardo, M. M. (1983) *Off the Track: Why and How Successful Executives Get Derailed*. Greensboro, NC: Centre for Creative Leadership.

McClelland, D. C. and Boyatzis, R. E. (1982) 'Leadership Motive Pattern and Long-Term Success in Management'. *Journal of Applied Psychology*, 67: 737–743.

Munson, E. W. (1921) *The Management of Men*. New York: Holt.

Mushonga, S. M. and Torrance, C. G. (2008) 'Assessing the Relationship Between Followership and the Big Five Factor Model of Personality'. *Review of Business Research*, 8(6): 179–187.

Myers, I. B. (1962) *The Myers–Briggs Type Indicator*. Palo Alto, CA: Consulting Psychologists Press.

Northouse, P. G. (2010) *Leadership: Theory and Practice*. London: SAGE Publications.

Pedler, M., Burgoyne, J., and Boydell, T. (2007) *A Manager's Guide to Leadership*. Maidenhead: McGraw Hill.

Roberts-McCabe, G. (2010) 'Why Ambitious Leaders Derail'. *Canadian Manager*, Spring(2): 5–9.

Rosener, J. (1990) 'Ways Women Lead'. *Harvard Business Review*, Nov/Dec: 119–125.

Stogdill, R. M. (1948) 'Personal Factors Associated with Leadership. A Survey of the Literature'. *Journal of Psychology*, 25: 35–71.

Stogdill, R. M. (1974) *Handbook of Leadership: A Survey of Theory and Research*. New York: Free Press.

Tupes, E. C. and Cristal, R. E. (1961) 'Recurrent Personality Factors Based on Trait Ratings'. *Technical Report ASD-TR-61-97*. Lackland Air Force Base, TX: Personnel Laboratory, Air Force Systems Command.

Van Velsor, E. and Leslie, J. B. (1995) 'Why Executives Derail: Perspectives Across Time and Cultures'. *Academy of Management Executive*, 9(4): 62–72.

Yukl, G. (2006) *Leadership in Organisations* (6th edn). New Jersey: Prentice Hall.

Yukl, G. (2010) *Leadership in Organisations* (7th edn). Upper Saddle River, NJ: Pearson Prentice Hall.

Zaccaro, S. J. (2007) 'Trait Based Perspectives of Leadership'. *American Psychologist*, 62: 6–16.

Chapter 3

Adair, J. (1973) *Action Centered Leadership*. Aldershot: Gower.

Adair, J. (2009) *How to Grow Leaders: The Seven Key Principles of Effective Leadership Development*. London: Kogan Page.

Blake, R. and Mouton, J. (1964) *The Managerial Grid: The Key to Leadership Excellence*. Houston: Gulf Publishing Co.

Blake, R. and Mouton, J. (1982) 'Management by Grid Principles or Situationalism; Which?'. *Group and Organisation Studies*, 7: 207–210.

Covey, S. (1989) *The Seven Habits of Highly Effective People: Restoring the Character Ethic*. London: Simon & Schuster.

Domjan, Michael (ed.) (2003) *The Principles of Learning and Behaviour* (5th edn). Belmont, CA: Thomson/ Wadsworth.

Fayol, H. (1916) *Administration Industrielle et Générale; Prévoyance, Organisation, Commandement, Coordination, Controle* (in French). Paris: H. Dunod et E. Pina.

Fayol, Henri (1949) *General and Industrial Administration* (Transl. of 1916 work). London: Sir Isaac Pitman & Sons Ltd.

Gulick, L. H. (1936) 'Notes on the Theory of Organization'. Gulick, L. and Urwick, L. (eds) *Papers on the Science of Administration*. New York: Institute of Public Administration.

Katz, R. (1955) 'Skills of an Effective Administrator', *Harvard Business Review*, 33(1): 33–42.

Kouzes, J. M. and Posner, B. Z. (2007) *The Leadership Challenge* (4th edn). San Francisco, CA: Jossey-Bass.

McGregor, D. (1960) 'The Human Side of Enterprise'. *The Management Review*, 46(11): 22–57.

Mintzberg, H. (1973) *The Nature of Managerial Work*. New York: Harper & Row.

Mumford, M., Zaccaro, S., Harding, F., Jacobs, T. O., and Fleishman, E. (2000) 'Leadership Skills For A Changing World: Solving Complex Social Problems'. *Leadership Quarterly*, 11(1): 11–35.

O'Connor, J., Mumford, M. D., Clifton, T. C., Gessner, T. E., and Connelly, M. S. (1995) 'Charismatic Leaders and Destructiveness: A Historiometric Study'. *Leadership Quarterly*, 6(4): 529–555.

Pavlov, I. P. (1927/1960) *Conditional Reflexes*. New York: Dover Publications (The 1960 edition is an unaltered republication of the 1927 translation by Oxford University Press.)

Pedler, M., Burgoyne, J., and Boydell, T. (2007) *A Manager's Guide to Self Development* (7th edn). Maidenhead: McGraw-Hill.

Pollitt, D. (2010) 'Rubicon Directors Give Lessons In Leadership'. *Human Resource Management International Digest*, 18(5): 25–26.

Skinner, B. F. (1953) *Science and Human Behaviour*. Oxford, UK: Macmillan.

Stenmark, C., Shipman, A., and Mumford, M. (2011) 'Managing the Innovative Process: The Dynamic Role of Leaders'. *Psychology of Aesthetics, Creativity, and the Arts*, 5(1): 67–80.

Thorndike, E. L. (1901) 'Animal Intelligence: An Experimental Study of the Associative Processes in Animals'. *Psychological Review Monograph Supplement*, 2: 1–109.

Watson, J. B. (1930) *Behaviourism* (revised edition). Chicago: University of Chicago Press.

Chapter 4

Argyris, C. (2001) 'Breakthrough Leadership'. *Harvard Business Review*, 79(11): 29–29.

Arvonen, J. and Ekvall, G. (1991) 'Change Centred Leadership: An Extension of the Two Dimensional Model', *Scandinavian Journal of Management*, 7(1): 17–26.

Deal, T. E. and Kennedy, A. A. (1982) *Corporate Cultures: The Rites and Rituals of Corporate Life*. Harmondsworth: Penguin Books.

Effrat, A. (1968) 'Review: Democratizing and Producing'. *Science*, 162(3859): 1260–1261.

Gordon, R. (2011) 'Leadership and Power'. In Bryman, A., Collinson, D., Grint, K., Jackson, B., and Uhl-Bien, M. (eds) *The Sage Handbook of Leadership*. London: SAGE Publications.

Johnson, G. and Scholes, K. (2001) *Exploring Corporate Strategy*. Harlow, UK: Pearson.

Kent, E. (2010) 'Jobsworth Makes My Blood Boil'. *Times Educational Supplement*, 30 April 2010: 36.

Likert, R. (1961) *New Patterns of Management*. New York: McGraw-Hill.

Lussier, R. N. and Achua, C. F. (2004) *Leadership: Theory, Application, Skill Development* (2nd edn). Eagan, MN: Thomson-West.

Maier, N. (1968) 'The Subordinate's Role in the Delegation Process'. *Personnel Psychology*, 21(2): 179–191.

Mills, D. Q. 'Asian and American Leadership Styles: How Are They Unique?'. *HBS Working Knowledge*, 27 June 2005. (Also published in *Asian Diversity* magazine, December 2005.)

Myers, I. (1980) *Gifts Differing*. Palo Alto, CA: Consulting Psychologists Press.

Northouse, P. G. (2010) *Leadership; Theory and Practice* (5th edn). Thousand Oaks, CA: SAGE Publications.

Stogdill, R. M. (1948) 'Personal Factors Associated with Leadership: A Survey of the Literature'. *Journal of Psychology*, 25(January 1948): 35–71.

Stogdill, R. M. and Coons, A. E. (eds) (1957) *Leader behaviour: Its Description and Measurement*. Columbus, OH: Bureau of Business Research, Ohio State University.

Tannenbaum, R. and Schmidt, W. H. (1958) 'How to Choose a Leadership Pattern'. *Harvard Business Review*, 36(March–April): 95–101.

Vroom, V. H. and Jago, A. G. (1988) *The New Leadership: Managing Participation in Organizations*. Englewood Cliffs, NJ: Prentice-Hall.

Vroom, V. H. and Yetton, P. W. (1973) *Leadership and Decision-making*. Pittsburgh: University of Pittsburgh Press.

Yukl, G. (2006) *Leadership in Organisations* (6th edn). New Jersey: Prentice Hall.

Chapter 5

Blanchard, K. and Johnson, S. (1982) *The One Minute Manager*. New York: Harper Collins.

Blanchard, K., Zigarmi, P. and Zigarmi, D. (1985) *Leadership and the One Minute Manager: Increasing Effectiveness through Situational Leadership*. New York: William Morrow.

Byrne, J. A. (1986) 'Business Fads: What's In and Out'. *Business Week*, 20 January: 40–47.

Duarte, L. and Snyder, N. T. (2006) *Mastering Virtual Teams: Strategies, Tools, and Techniques that Succeed*. New York: J. Wiley & Sons.

Fiedler, F. E. (1967) *A Theory of Leadership Effectiveness*. New York: McGraw-Hill.

Fleishman, E. A. and Peters, D. (1962) 'Interpersonal Values, Leadership Attitudes and Managerial Success'. *Personnel Psychology*, 15(2): 127–143.

Gordon, R. F. (1994) 'Substitutes for Leadership'. *Supervision*, 55(7): 17–21.

Graeff, C. L. (1983) 'The Situational Leadership Theory: A Critical View'. *Academy of Management Review*, 8(2): 285–291.

Graeff, C. L. (1997) 'Evolution of Situational Leadership Theory: A Critical Review'. *Leadership Quarterly*, 8(2): 153–171.

Hersey, P. (1984) *The Situational Leader*, Escondido, CA: Centre for Leadership Studies.

Hersey, P. and Blanchard, K. H. (1969) 'Life Cycle Theory of Leadership'. *Training and Development Journal*, 23(2): 26–34.

Hersey, P. and Blanchard, K. H. (1977) *Management of Organization Behaviour: Utilizing Human Resources* (3rd edn). Englewood Cliffs, NJ: Prentice-Hall.

Hersey, P., Angelini, A. L., and Carakushansky, S. (1982) 'The Impact of Situational Leadership and Classroom

Structure on Learning Effectiveness'. *Group and Organization Studies*, 7(2): 216–224.

Hersey, P., Blanchard, K. H., and Johnson, D. E. (2001) *Management of Organization Behaviour: Leading Human Resources* (8th edn). Englewood Cliffs, NJ: Prentice-Hall.

Howell, J. P. (1997) 'Substitutes for Leadership: Their Meaning and Measurement–An Historical Assessment.' *Leadership Quarterly*, 8(2): 113–116

Howell, J. P., Bowen, D. E., Dorfman, P. W., Kerr, S., and Podsakoff, P. M. (1990) 'Substitutes for Leadership: Effective Alternatives to Ineffective Leadership'. *Organisational Dynamics*, Summer: 40–55.

Howell, J. P., Dorfman, P., Dorfman, W., and Kerr, S. (1986) 'Moderator Variables in Leadership Research'. *Academy of Management Review*, 11(1): 88–102.

Kerr, S. and Jermier, J. M. (1978) 'Substitutes for Leadership: Their Meaning and Measurement'. *Organisational Behaviour and Human Performance*, 22(3): 375–403.

Kilmann, R. H. (1984) *Beyond the Quick-Fix*. San Francisco, CA: Jossey-Bass.

Kunzle, B. (2010) 'Substitutes For Leadership in Anaesthesia Teams and Their Impact on Leadership Effectiveness'. *European Journal of Work & Organizational Psychology*, 19(5): 505–531.

Manz, C. C. and Simms, H. P. (1987) 'Leading Workers to Lead Themselves: The External Leadership of Self Managing Work Teams'. *Administrative Science Quarterly*, 32(1): 106–128.

McGregor, D. (1960) *The Human Side of Enterprise*, New York: McGraw-Hill.

Mills, C. W. (2007) *Angela Merkel* (Modern World Leaders). New York: Chelsea House Publishers.

Podsakoff, P. M., Todor, W. D., and Schüler, R. S. (1983) 'Leader Expertise as a Moderator of the Effects of Instrumental and Supportive Leader Behaviour'. *Journal of Management*, 9: 176–185.

Reddin, W. J. (1967) 'The 3-D Management Style Theory'. *Training & Development Journal*, 21(4): 8–17.

Rollinson, D. (2002) *Organisational Behaviour and Analysis: An Integrated Approach* (2nd edn). Harlow: Pearson Education Ltd.

Van Maurik, J. (2001) *Writers on Leadership*. Harmondsworth, UK: Penguin.

Vecchio, R. (1987) 'Situational Leadership Theory: An Examination of a Prescriptive Theory'. *Journal of Applied Psychology*, 72(3): 444–451.

Wu, Y. (2010) 'An Exploration of Substitutes for Leadership: Problems and Prospects'. *Social Behaviour and Personality*, 38(5): 583–596.

Chapter 6

Bryman, A., Collinson, D., Grint, K., Jackson, B., and Uhl-Bien, M. (2011) *The Sage Handbook of Leadership*. London: SAGE Publications.

Burns, T. and Stalker, G. M. (1961) *The Management of Innovation*. London: Tavistock.

Evans, M. G. (1970) 'The Effects of Supervisory Behaviour on the Path–Goal Relationship'. *Organisational Behaviour and Human Performance*, 5: 277–298.

Evans, M. G. (1996) 'R. J. House's "A Path-Goal Theory of Leader Effectiveness"'. *Leadership Quarterly*, 7(3): 305–309.

Fiedler, F. E. (1965) 'Engineering the job to fit the Manager'. *Harvard Business Review*, 43(5): 115–122.

Fiedler, F. E. (1967) *A Theory of Leadership Effectiveness*. New York: McGraw-Hill.

Fiedler, F. E. (1993) 'The Leadership Situation and the Black Box in Contingency Theories'. In Chemers, M. M. and Ayman, R. (eds) *Leadership Theory and Research: Perspectives and Directions*. New York: Academic Press.

Fiedler, F. E. (1996) 'Research on Leadership Selection and Training: One View of the Future'. *Administrative Science Quarterly*, 41(2): 241–250.

Fiedler, F. E. and Chemers, M. M. (1984) *Improving Leadership Effectiveness: The Leader Match Concept* (2nd edn). New York: J. Wiley & Sons.

Fiedler, F. E., Chemers, M. M. and Mahar, L. (1976) *Improving Leadership Effectiveness: The Leader Match Concept*. New York: J. Wiley & Sons.

Fiedler, F. E. and Garcia, J. E. (1987) *New Approaches to Effective Leadership: Cognitive Resources and Organisational Performance*. New York: J. Wiley & Sons.

Fiedler, F. E. and Mahar, L. (1979) 'The Effectiveness of Contingency Model Training: A Review of the Validation of Leader Match'. *Personnel Psychology*, 32: 45–62.

Grean, G. B., Orris, J. B., and Alvares, K. (1971) 'The Contingency Model of Leadership Effectiveness: Some Experimental Results'. *Journal of Applied Psychology*, 55(1): 196–201.

House, R. J. (1971) 'A Path-Goal Theory of Leader Effectiveness'. *Administrative Science Quarterly*, 16: 321–339.

House, R. J. (1996) 'Path-goal Theory of Leadership: Lessons, legacy, and a Reformulated Theory'. *Leadership Quarterly*, 7(3): 323–352.

Hunt, J. G. (1991) 'A Theory of Leadership Effectiveness' (Book Review). *Journal of Management*, 17(2): 504.

Jermier, J. M. (1996) 'The Path-Goal Theory of Leadership: A Sub-textual Analysis'. *Leadership Quarterly*, 7(3): 311–316.

Kabanoff, B. (1981) 'A Critique of Leader Match and its Implications for Leadership Research' *Personnel Psychology*, 34: 749–764.

McGrath, J. E. (1984) *Groups: Interaction and Performance*. Englewood Cliffs, NJ: Prentice Hall.

Mockler, R. J. (1971) 'Situational Theory of Management'. *Harvard Business Review*, May: 146–155.

Morgan, G. (1986) *Images of Organisations*. London: SAGE Publications.

Rollinson, D. (2002) *Organisational Behaviour and Analysis* (2nd edn). Harlow, Essex: Pearson.

Shaw, M. E. (1963) *Scaling Group Tasks: A Method of Dimensional Analysis* (Tech. Rep. No. 1). Gainesville: University of Florida.

Strube, M. J. and Garcia, J. E. (1981) 'A Meta-analytic Investigation of Fiedler's Contingency Model of Leadership Effectiveness'. *Psychological Bulletin*, 90: 307–321.

Taylor, F. W. (1911) *The Principles of Scientific Management*. New York and London: Harper & Brothers.

Utecht, R. E. and Heier, W. D. (1976) 'The Contingency Model and Successful Military Leadership'. *Academy of Management Journal*, 19(4): 606–618.

Vroom, V. H. (1964) *Work and Motivation*. New York: J. Wiley & Sons.

Woodward, J. (1958) *Management and Technology*. London: HMSO.

Yukl, G. (1981) *Leadership in Organisations*. Englewood Cliffs, NJ: Prentice Hall.

Yukl, G. (1989) *Leadership in Organisations* (2nd edn). Englewood Cliffs, NJ: Prentice Hall.

Yukl, G. (2006) *Leadership in Organisations* (6th edn). Englewood Cliffs, NJ: Prentice Hall.

Chapter 7

Bandura, A. (1977) *Social Learning Theory*. Englewood Cliffs, NJ: Prentice Hall.

Bandura, A. (1986) *Social Foundations of Thought and Action: A Social Cognitive Theory*. Englewood Cliffs, NJ: Prentice-Hall.

Bass, B. M. (1985) *Leadership and Performance Beyond Expectations*. New York: Free Press.

Bass, B. M. (1998) *Transformational Leadership: Industry, Military, and Educational Impact*. Mahwah, NJ: Erlbaum.

Bass, B. M. (2008) *The Bass Handbook of Leadership: Theory, Research and Managerial Applications* (4th edn). New York: Free Press.

Bass, B. M. and Avolio, B. J. (1990) 'The Implications of Transactional and Transformational Leadership for Individual, Team and Organisational Development'.

Research in Organisational Change and Development, 4: 231–272.

Bass, B. M. and Avolio, B. J. (1993) 'Transformational Leadership: A Response to Critiques'. In Chemers, M. M. and Ayman, R. (eds) *Leadership Theory and Research: Perspectives and Direction*. San Diego, CA: Academic Press.

Bass, B. M. and Avolio, B. J. (1995) *The Multifactor Leadership Questionnaire*. Redwood City, CA: Mind Garden.

Bass, B. M. and Avolio, B. J. (1997) *Revised Manual for the Multifactor Leadership Questionnaire*. Redwood City, CA: Mind Garden.

Bass, B. M. and Riggio, R. E. (2006) *Transformational Leadership* (2nd edn). New Jersey: Lawrence Erlbaum Associates.

Bennett, J. (2008) 'The Television Personality System: Televisual Stardom Revisited After Film Theory'. *Screen*, 49(1): 32–50.

Bennis, W. (2003) *On Becoming a Leader*. Philadelphia: Basic Books.

Blair, T. (2003) *Opening Speech to House of Commons Tuesday 18 March 2003*. London: HMSO.

Bones, C. (2011) *The Cult of the Leader*. Chichester: J. Wiley & Sons.

Brown, S. and O'Donnell, E. (2011) 'Proactive Personality and Goal Orientation: A Model of Directed Effort'. *Journal of Organizational Culture, Communications and Conflict*, 15(1): 103–119.

Bryman, A. (1992) *Charisma and Leadership in Organisations*. London: SAGE Publications.

Burns, J. M. (1978) *Leadership*. New York: Harper & Row.

Conger, J. A. (1989) *The Charismatic Leader: Beyond The Mystique of Exceptional Leadership*. San Francisco: Jossey-Bass.

Conger, J. A. (2011) 'Charismatic Leadership'. In Bryman, A., Collinson, D., Grint, K., Jackson, B., and Uhl-Bien, M. *The Sage Handbook of Leadership*. London: SAGE Publications.

Conger, J. A. and Kanungo, R. N. (1987) 'Towards a Behavioural Theory of Charismatic Leadership in Organisational Settings'. *Academy of Management Review*, 12(4): 637–674.

Conger, J. A. and Kanungo, R. N. (1998) *Charismatic Leadership in Organisations*. Thousand Oaks, CA: SAGE Publications.

Conger, J. A., Kanungo, R. N., and Menon, S. T. (2000) 'Charismatic Leadership and Follower Effects'. *Journal of Organisational Behaviour*, 21: 747–767.

Crant, J. M. and Bateman, T. S. (2000) 'Charismatic Leadership Viewed From Above: The Impact of

Proactive Leadership'. *Journal of Organizational Behaviour*, 21(1): 63–75.

Diaz-Saenz, H. R. (2011) 'Transformational Leadership'. In Bryman, A., Collinson, D., Grint, K., Jackson, B., and Uhl-Bien, M. (2011) *The Sage Handbook of Leadership*. London: SAGE Publications.

Downton, J. (1973) *Rebel Leadership: Commitment and Charisma in the Revolutionary Process*. New York: Free Press.

Friedman, H. S., Prince, L. M., Riggio, R. E., and DiMatteo, M. R. (1980) 'Understanding and Assessing Nonverbal Expressiveness: The Affective Communication Test'. *Journal of Personality and Social Psychology*, 39: 331–351.

Friedrich, C. J. (1961) 'Political Leadership and the Problem of the Charismatic Power'. *Journal of Politics*, 23: 3–24.

Grix, J. and Parker, A. (2011) 'Towards an Explanation for the Decline in UK Athletics: A Case Study of Male Distance Running'. *Sport in Society*, 14(5): 612–628.

Handy, C. (1989) *The Age of Unreason*, London: Hutchinson.

Heider, F. (1958) *The Psychology of Interpersonal Relations*. New York: J. Wiley & Sons.

House, R. J. (1976) 'A Theory of Charismatic Leadership'. In Hunt, J. G. and Larson, I. L. (eds) *Leadership: The Cutting Edge*. Carbondale, IL: Southern Illinois University Press.

House, R. J. and Howell, J. M. (1992) 'Personality and Charismatic Leadership'. *Leadership Quarterly*, 3: 81–108.

Humphreys, J. (2001) 'Transformational and Transactional Leader Behaviour' [Electronic version]. *Journal of Management Research*, 1: 149–159.

Javidan, M. (2004) 'East Meets West: A Cross-Cultural Comparison of Charismatic Leadership Among Canadian and Iranian Executives'. *Journal of Management Studies*, 41(4): 665–692.

Kets de Vries, M. (2001) *The Leadership Mystique: An Owner's Manual*. London: Financial Times/Prentice Hall.

Lowenstein, K. (1966) *Max Weber's Political Ideas in the Perspective of Our Time*. Amherst, MA: University of Massachusetts Press.

Maslow, A. H. (1943) 'A Theory of Human Motivation'. *Psychological Review*, 50(4): 370–396.

Meindl, J. R., Ehrlich, S. R., and Dukerich, J. M. (1987) 'The Romance of Leadership and the Evaluation of Organisational Performance'. *Academy of Management Review*, 12(1): 91–109.

Mintzberg, H. (1983) *Power In and Around Organisations*. Englewood Cliffs, NJ: Prentice Hall.

Perinbanayagam, R. S. (1971) 'The Dialectics of Charisma'. *The Sociological Quarterly*, 12(3): 387–402.

Pfeffer, J. (1977) 'The Ambiguity of Leadership'. *Academy of Management Review*, 2(1): 104–112.

Potts, J. (2009) *A History of Charisma*. Basingstoke: Palgrave Macmillan.

Reich, R. (1985) 'The Executive's New Clothes'. *The New Republic*, 13(1): 23–28.

Seibert, S. E., Kraimer, M. I., and Crant, J. M. (2001) 'What Do Proactive People Do? A Longitudinal Model Linking Proactive Personality and Career Development'. *Personnel Psychology*, 54(4): 845–874.

Selznick, P. (1957) *Leadership in Administration: A Sociological Interpretation*. New York: Harper & Row.

Shamir, B., House, R. J., and Arthur, M. B. (1993) 'The Motivational Effects of Charismatic Leadership: A Self-Concept Based Theory'. *Organisation Science*, 4(4): 577–594.

Sohm, R. (1892) *Kirchenrecht*. Leipzig: Duncher & Humblot.

Tourish, D. and Vatcha, N. (2005) 'Charismatic Leadership and Corporate Cultism at Enron: The Elimination of Dissent, the Promotion of Conformity and Organizational Collapse'. *Leadership*, 1: 455–480.

Trice, H. M. and Beyer, J. M. (1993) *The Cultures of Work Organisations*. Englewood Cliffs, NJ: Prentice Hall.

Weber, M. (1947) *The Theory of Social and Economic Organisations* (trans. Talcott Parsons). New York: Free Press (original published in 1924).

Whisker, D. (2012) 'Apocalyptic Rhetoric on the Religious Right: Quasi-charisma and Anti-charisma'. *Max Weber Studies*, 12(2): 159–184.

White, Deborah (21 October 2008). 'Five Reasons Why Obama Won the '08 Election —Steady Leadership, Calm Temperament'. About.com. (Retrieved 10 August 2013).

Yammarino, F. J. (1993) 'Transforming Leadership Studies: Bernard Bass' Leadership and Performance Beyond Expectations'. *Leadership Quarterly*, 4(3): 379–382.

Yukl, G. (1999) 'An Evaluation of Conceptual Weaknesses in Transformational and Charismatic Leadership Theories'. *Leadership Quarterly*, 10(2): 285–305.

Yukl, G. (2006) *Leadership in Organisations* (6th edn). Englewood Cliffs, NJ: Prentice Hall.

Chapter 8

Adam, J. (1916) *Platonis Apologia Socratis*. Cambridge,UK: Cambridge University Press.

Arbinger Institute (2010) *Leadership and Self-Deception: Getting Out of the Box* (2nd edn). San Francisco, CA: Berrett-Koehler Publishers.

Avolio, B. J. and Gardner, W. L. (2005) 'Authentic Leadership Development: Getting to the root of positive forms of Leadership'. *The Leadership Quarterly*, 16(3): 315–338.

Avolio, B. J., Luthans, F., and Walumbwa, F. O. (2004) 'Authentic Leadership: Theory-building for Veritable Sustained Performance'. Working Paper, Gallup Leadership Institute, University of Nebraska-Lincoln.

Barnard, C. I. (1938) *The Functions of the Executive*. Cambridge, MA: Harvard University Press.

Bass, B. M. (1990) *Bass and Stogdill's Handbook of Leadership: Theory, Research, and Managerial Applications* (3rd edn). New York: Free Press.

Bass, B. M. and Avolio, B. J. (1997) 'Full Range of Leadership Development'. *Manual for the Multi-factor Leadership Questionnaire*. California: Mind Garden.

Bennis, W. and Thomas, R. J. (2002) *Geeks and Geezers: How Era, Values and Defining Moments Shape Leaders*. Watertown, MA: Harvard Business Press.

Burgoyne, J., Beech, D., and Roe, K. (2013) *What is Wrong with Leadership*, in print.

Caza, A. and Jackson, B. (2011) 'Authentic Leadership'. In Bryman, A., Collinson, D., Grint, K., Jackson, B., and Uhl-Bien, M. (eds) *The Sage Handbook of Leadership*. London: SAGE Publications.

Chan, A., Hannah, S. T., and Gardner, W. L. (2005) 'Veritable Authentic Leadership: Emergence, Functioning and Impacts'. In Gardner, W. L., Avolio, B. J., and Walumbwa, F. O. (eds) *Authentic Leadership Theory and Practice: Origins, Effects and Development*. Oxford: Elsevier Science.

Collingwood, S. (1898) *The Life and Letters of Lewis Carroll*. London: Fisher Unwin.

Collins, J. C. (2001a) *Good to Great: Why Some Companies Make the Leap ... And Others Don't*. New York: Harper Collins.

Collins, J. C. (2001b) 'Level 5 Leadership: The Triumph of Humility and Fierce Resolve'. *Harvard Business Review*, 79(1): 67–76.

Cooper, C. D., Scandura, T. A., and Schriesheim, C. A. (2005) 'Looking Forward But Learning From Our Past: Potential Challenges to Developing Authentic Leadership Theory and Authentic Leaders'. *The Leadership Quarterly*, 16: 475–493.

Criswell, C. and Campbell, D. (2008) *Building an Authentic Leadership Image*. Greensboro, NC: The Centre for Creative Leadership.

Franklin, B. (1740) 'Poor Richard's Almanac'. In Leo Lemay, J. A. (ed.) *Benjamin Franklin: Autobiography, Poor Richard: Autobiography, Poor Richard, and Later Writings*. New York: Library of America.

Gardner, W. L. (1992) 'Lessons in Organizational Dramaturgy: The Art of Impression Management'. *Organizational Dynamics*, Summer 92, 21(1): 33–46.

Gardner, W. L. (2003) 'Perceptions of Leader Charisma, Effectiveness and Integrity: Effects of Exemplification, Delivery and Ethical Reputation'. *Academy of Management Review*, 23: 32–58.

Gardner, W. L., Avolio, B. J., Luthans, F., May, D. R., and Walumbwa, F. O. (2005a) 'Can You See The Real Me?: A Self-Based Model of Authentic Leader and Follower Development'. *The Leadership Quarterly*, 16(3): 343–372.

Gardner, W. L., Avolio, B. J., Walumbwa, F. O. (2005b) 'Authentic Leadership Development: Emergent Trends and Future Directions'. In Gardner, W. L., Avolio, B. J., and Walumbwa, F. O. (eds) *Authentic Leadership Theory and Practice: Origins, Effects and Development*. Oxford: Elsevier Science.

Garger, J. (2008) 'Developing Authentic Leadership in Organisations: Some Insights and Observations'. *Development and Learning in Organisations*, 22(1): 14–16.

George, W. (2003) *Authentic Leadership, Rediscovering the Secrets to Creating Lasting Value*. San Francisco, CA: Jossey-Bass.

George, W. and Sims, P. (2007) *True North: Discover your Authentic Leadership*. San Francisco, CA: Jossey-Bass.

Gilbert, D. T. and Jones, E. E. (1986) 'Exemplification: The Self-presentation of Moral Character'. *Journal of Personality*, 54: 593–615.

Handy, C. (1994) *The Empty Raincoat: Making Sense of the Future*. London: Arrow Books.

Harter, S. (2002) 'Authenticity'. In Snyder, C. R. and Lopez, S. J. (eds) *Handbook of Positive Psychology*. New York: Oxford University Press.

Howell, J. M. and House, R. J. (1992) 'Personality & Charismatic Leadership'. *Leadership Quarterly*, 3(1): 81–108.

Illies, R., Morgeson, F. P., and Nahrgang, J. D. (2005) 'Authentic Leadership and Eudaemonic Well-being: Understanding Leader-Follower Outcomes'. *The Leadership Quarterly*, 16(3): 373–394.

Kernis, M. H. (2003) 'Towards a Conceptualisation of Optimal Self-Esteem'. *Psychological Enquiry*, 14(1): 1–26.

Leach, K. (1999) *In the Shadow of the Dreamchild*. London: Peter Owen Ltd.

Lowe, K. B., Kroeck, K. G., and Sivasubramaniam, N. (1996) 'Effectiveness Correlates of Transformational and Transactional Leadership: A Meta-Analytic Review of the MLQ Literature'. *The Leadership Quarterly*, 3: 385–425.

Luthens, F. and Avolio, B. J. (2003) 'Authentic Leadership Development'. In Cameron, K. S., Dutton, J. E., and Quinn, R. E. (eds) *Positive Organisational Scholarship: Foundations of a New Discipline*. San Francisco, CA: Berrett-Koehler Publishers.

Luthens, F. and Avolio, B. J. (2009) 'The 'Point' of Positive Organisational Behaviour'. *Journal of Organisational Behaviour*, 30(2): 291–307.

May, D., Chan, A., Hodges, T., and Avolio, B. (2003) 'Developing the Moral Component of Authentic Leadership'. *Organisational Dynamics*, 32: 247–260.

Philips, A. (1994) *On Flirtation*. Cambridge, MA: Harvard University Press.

Rayment, J. and Smith, J. (2011) *Misleadership: Prevalence, Causes and Consequences*. Farnham: Gower.

Shamir, B. and Eilam, G. (2005) 'What's your Story? A Life Histories Approach to Authentic Leadership Development'. *The Leadership Quarterly*, 16(3): 395–417.

Terry, R. W. (1993) *Authentic Leadership: Courage in Action*. San Francisco, CA: Jossey-Bass.

Walumbwa, F. O., Avolio, B. J., Gardner, W. L., Wernsing, T. S., and Peterson, S. J. (2008) 'Authentic Leadership: Development and Validation of a Theory Based Measure'. *Journal of Management*, 34(1): 89–126.

Winnicott, D. W. (1965) 'Ego Distortion in Terms of True and False Self'. In *The Maturational Process and the Facilitating Environment: Studies in the Theory of Emotional Development*. New York: International UP Inc.

Yammarino, F. J., Dionne, S. D., Schriesheim, C. A., and Dansereau, F. (2008) 'Authentic Leadership and Positive Organisational Behaviour: A Meso, Multi-Level Perspective'. *The Leadership Quarterly*, 19(6): 693–707.

Chapter 9

Baker, S. D. (2007) 'Followership: The Theoretical Foundation of a Contemporary Construct'. *Journal of Leadership & Organizational Studies*, 14(1): 50–60.

Bjugstad, K., Thach, E. C., Thompson, K. J., and Morris, A. (2006) 'A Fresh Look at Followership: A Model for Matching Followership & Leadership Styles'. *Journal of Behavioural and Applied Management*, 7: 304–319.

Bligh, M. C. (2011) 'Followership and Follower-Centred Approaches'. In Bryman, A., Collinson, D., Grint, K., Jackson, B., and Uhl-Bien, M. (eds) *The Sage Handbook of Leadership*. London: SAGE Publications.

Bones, C. (2011) *The Cult of the Leader*. Chichester: J. Wiley & Sons.

Burns, J. M. (1978) *Leadership*. New York: Harper & Row.

Chaleff, I. (1995) *The Courageous Follower*. San Francisco, CA: Berrett-Koehler.

Crant, J. M. and Bateman, T. (1993) 'Assignment of Credit and Blame For Performance Outcomes'. *Academy of Management Journal*, 36(1): 7–27.

Dansereau, F., Graen, G. B., and Haga, W. (1975) 'A Vertical Dyad Linkage Approach to Leadership in Formal Organisations'. *Organisational Behaviour and Human Performance*, 13: 46–78.

Deluga, R. J. (1992) 'The Relationship of Leader-Member Exchanges with Laissez-Faire, Transactional and Transformational Leadership in the Naval Environment'. In Clark, K. E., Clark, M. B., and Campbell, D. P. (eds) *Impact of Leadership*. Greensboro, NC: Centre for Creative Leadership.

Follett, M. P. (1949) *The Essentials of Leadership*. London: Management Publications Trust Ltd.

Graen, G. and Scandura, T. A. (1987) 'Towards a Psychology of Dyadic Organising'. *Research in Organisational Behaviour*, 3: 395–420.

Graen, G. and Uhl-Bien, M. (1991) 'The Transformation of Professionals into Self-Managing and Partially Self-Designing Contributors: Towards a Theory of Leadership Making'. *Journal of Management Systems*, 3: 25–39.

Green, S. G., Mitchell, T. R., and Wood, R. E. (1981) 'An Attributional Model of Leadership and the Poor Performing Subordinate: Development and Validation'. *Research in Organizational Behaviour*, 3: 197–235.

Green, S. G. and Mitchell, T. R. (1979) 'Attributional Processes of Leaders in Leader-Member Exchanges'. *Organisational Behaviour and Human Performance*, 23: 429–458.

Greenberg, J. (1982) 'Approaching Equity and Avoiding Inequality in Groups and Organisations'. In Greenberg, J. and Cohen, R. L. (eds) *Equity & Justice in Social Behaviour*. New York: Academic Press.

Grint, K. (2010) *Leadership: A Very Short Introduction*. Oxford: Oxford University Press.

Hall, R. (2012) '2011: The Year Leadership Died'. *Marketing Solutions: ABA Bank Marketing* (January–February): 12–13.

Hannah, Sean T., Avolio, Bruce J., Luthans, F., and Harms, P. D. (2008) 'Leadership Efficacy: Review And Future Directions'. *The Leadership Quarterly*, 19(6): 669–692.

Harris, K. J., Wheeler, A. R., and Kaemar, K. M. (2009) 'Leader-Member Exchange and Empowerment: Direct and Interactive effects on Job Satisfaction, Turnover and Intentions, and Performance'. *Leadership Quarterly*, 20: 371–382.

Heider, F. (1958) *The Psychology of Interpersonal Relations*. New York: J. Wiley & Sons.

Hersey, P. and Blanchard, K. H. (1988) *Management of Organization Behaviour: Utilizing Human Resources* (5th edn). Englewood Cliffs, NJ: Prentice Hall.

Hersey, P. and Blanchard, K. H. (1993) *Management Of Organization Behaviour: Utilizing Human Resources* (6th edn). Englewood Cliffs, NJ: Prentice Hall.

Kelley, R. E. (1988) 'In Praise of Followers'. *Harvard Business Review*, 66(6): 142–148.

Kelley, R. E. (2008) 'Rethinking Followership'. In Riggio, R. E., Chaleff, I., and Lipman-Blumen, J. (eds) *The Art Of Followership: How Great Followers Create Great Leaders and Organisations*. San Francisco, CA: Jossey-Bass.

Leary, M. R. and Kowalski, R. M. (1990) 'Impression Management: A Literature Review and two-Component Model'. *Psychological Bulletin*, 107(1): 34–47.

Linden, R. C. and Maslyn, J. M. (1998) 'Multidimensionality of Leader-Member Exchange: An Empirical Assessment through Scale Development'. *Journal of Management*, 24(1): 43–72.

Lord, R. G. and Maher, K. J. (1991) *Leadership and Information Processing: Linking Perceptions and Performance*. Boston: Unwin-Hyman.

Manske, F. (1988) *Secrets of Effective Leadership—A Practical Guide to Success*. New York: Leadership Education & Development.

Meindl, J. R. (1990) 'On Leadership: An Alternative to the Conventional Wisdom'. *Research in Organisational Behaviour*, 12: 159–203.

Meindl, J. R. (1998) 'The Romance of Leadership as a Follower-centric Theory: A Social Construction Approach'. In Dansereau, F. and Yammarino, F. J. (eds) *Leadership: The Multiple-Level Approaches – Part B: Contempoary and Alternative*. Stamford: JAI Press.

Miller, R. L., Butler, J., and Cosentino, C. J. (2004) 'Followership Effectiveness: An Extension of Fiedler's Contingency Model', *Leadership & Organization Development Journal*, 25(4): 362–368.

Mitchell, T. R. (1979) 'Attributional Processes of Leaders in Leader-Member Interactions'. *Organizational Behavior and Human Performance*, 23(3): 429–458.

Rost, J. (2008) 'Followership: An Outmoded Concept'. In Riggio, R. E., Chaleff, I., and Lipman-Blumen, J. (eds) *The Art Of Followership: How Great Followers Create Great Leaders and Organisations*. San Francisco, CA: Jossey-Bass.

Senge, P. (1990) *The Fifth Discipline: The Art and Practice of the Learning Organization*. New York: Doubleday.

Shamir, B., Pillai, R., Bligh, M. C., and Uhl-Bien, M. (2007) *Follower-Centered Perspectives on Leadership: A Tribute to the Memory of James R. Meindl*. Charlotte, NC: Information Age Publishing.

Sparrowe, R. T. and Liden, R. C. (1997) 'Process and Structure in Leader Member Exchange'. *Academy of Management Review*, 22: 522–552.

Stacey, R. (2012) *Tools and Techniques of Leadership and Management: Meeting the Challenge of Complexity*. London: Routledge.

Subramaniam, A., Othman, R., and Sambasivan, M. (2010) 'Implicit Leadership Theory Among Malaysian Managers: Impact of the Leadership Expectation Gap On Leader-Member Exchange Quality'. *Leadership & Organization Development Journal*, 31(4): 351–371.

Wayne, S. J., Shore, L. M., and Liden, R. C. (1997) 'Perceived Organisational Support and Leader-Member Exchange: A Social Perspective'. *The Academy of Management*, 40(1): 82–111.

Chapter 10

Bandler, R. and Grinder, J. (1975) *The Structure of Magic I: A Book About Language and Therapy*. Palo Alto, CA: Science and Behavior Books.

Bandler, R. and Grinder, J. (1979) *Frogs into Princes: Neuro Linguistic Programming*. Moab, UT: Real People Press.

Brown, D. (2006) *Tricks of the Mind*, (Specifically Part Four: Hypnosis and Suggestibility, Section Neuro Linguistic Programming, Sub section, The eyes have it (some of the time). London: Transworld Publishers.

Brown, D. (2008) 'The Heist Interview', Channel 4, 18 November 2008.

Corballis, M. C. (1999) 'Are we in our right minds?'. In Salas, S. (ed.) *Mind Myths: Exploring Popular Assumptions About the Mind and Brain*. Chichester: J. Wiley & Sons.

Devilly, G. J. (2005) 'Power Therapies And Possible Threats To The Science Of Psychology And Psychiatry'. *Australian and New Zealand Journal of Psychiatry*, 39(9): 437–45.

Dilts, R., Grinder, J., Bandler, R., and DeLozier, J. (1980) *Neuro-Linguistic Programming: Volume 1, The Study Of The Structure Of Subjective Experience*. California: Meta Publications.

Ellerton, R. (2005) *Live Your Dreams... Let Reality Catch Up: NLP and Common Sense for Coaches, Managers and You*. Oxford: Trafford Publishing.

Freud, S. (1938) *The Basic Writings of Sigmund Freud* (ed. A. A. Brill). New York: Modern Library.

Glasner-Edwards, S. and Rawson, R. (2010) 'Evidence-Based Practices in Addiction Treatment: Review and Recommendations for Public Policy'. *Health Policy*, 97(2–3): 93–104.

Hirsh, S. K. and Kummerow, J. M. (1998) *Introduction to Type in Organisations* (2nd edn). Palo Alto, CA: Consulting Psychologists Press.

Hunsley, J., Lee, C. M., and Wood, J. M. (2004) 'Controversial and Questionable Assessment Techniques'. In Lilienfeld, S. O., Lohr, J. M., and Lynn, S. J. (eds) *Science and Pseudoscience in Clinical Psychology*. New York: Guilford.

Jung, C. G. (1923) *Psychological Types*. New York: Harcourt, Brace.

Jung, C. G. (1961) *Memories, Dreams, Reflections*. New York: Vantage Books.

Korzybski, A. (1933) *Science and Sanity*. New York: Institute of General Semantics.

Myers, I. B. (1980) *Gifts Differing*. Palo Alto, CA: Consulting Psychologists Press.

Myers, I. B. (2000) *Introduction to Type*. Mountain View, CA: CPP Inc.

Myers, I. B. and McCaulley, M. H. (1985) *A Guide to the Development and Use of the Myers-Briggs Type Indicator*. Palo Alto, CA: Consulting Psychologists Press.

O'Connor, J. and Seymour, J. (1993) *Introducing Neuro-Linguistic Programming: Psychological Skills for Understanding and Influencing People*. London: Thorsons.

Ronson, J. (2006) 'Don't Worry, Get Therapy'. *The Guardian*, 20 May 2006.

Shapiro, M. (2007) *Neuro Linguistic Programming*. London: Hodder.

Tosey, P. and Mathison, J. (2003) 'Neuro-Linguistic Programming and Learning Theory: A Response'. *The Curriculum Journal*, 14(3): 361–378.

Zemke, R. (1992) 'Second Thoughts about MBTI'. *Training*, 5(4): 43–47.

Chapter 11

Aggleton, J. P. (ed.) (1992) *The Amygdala*. New York: Wiley-Liss.

Albrecht, K. (2005) *Social Intelligence: The New Science of Success*. San Francisco, CA: J. Wiley & Sons.

Ashkanasy, N. M. and Jordan, P. J. (2008) 'A Multi-level View of Leadership and Emotion'. In Humphrey, R. H. (ed.) *Affect and Emotion: New Directions in Management Theory and Research*. Charlotte, NC: Information Age Publishing.

Aslan, S. and Erkus, A. (2008) 'Measurement of Emotional Intelligence: Validity and Reliability Studies of Two Scales'. *World Applied Sciences Journal*, 4(3): 430–438.

Bar-On, R. (1997) *The Bar-On Emotional Quotient Inventory™ (EQ-i™): A Test of Emotional Intelligence*. Toronto, Canada: Multi-Health Systems.

Bar-On, R. (2007) 'The Bar-On Model of Emotional Intelligence: A Valid, Robust and Applicable EI Model'. *Organisations and People*, 14: 27–34.

Boyatzis, R. E. and McKee, A. (2005) *Resonant Leadership: Renewing Yourself And Connecting With Others Through Mindfulness, Hope And Compassion*. Boston: HBS Press.

Cherniss, C. (2000) 'Emotional Intelligence: What it is and Why it matters'. The Annual Meeting of the Society for Industrial and Organisational Psychology, New Orleans, LA, 15 April 2000.

Cooper, R. and Sawaf, A. (1997) *Executive EQ. Emotional Intelligence in Business*. London: Putnam.

Day, A. L. and Carroll, S. L. (2008) 'Faking Emotional Intelligence (EI): Comparing Response Distortion on Ability and Trait-based EI Measures'. *Journal of Organizational Behaviour*, 29(6): 761–784.

Eysenck, H. E. (1998) *Intelligence: A New Look*. New Brunswick: Transaction Publishers.

Fineman, S. (1996) 'Emotion and Organising'. In Clegg, S. R., Hardy, C., and Nord, W. R. (eds) *Handbook of Organisational Studies*. London: SAGE Publications.

Gardner, H. (1983) *Frames of Mind*. New York: Basic Books.

Gardner, H. (1999) *Intelligence Reframed. Multiple Intelligences for the 21st Century*. New York: Basic Books.

Gilbert-Smith, D. (2003) *Winning Hearts and Minds*. London: Pen Press.

Goleman, D. (1996) *Emotional Intelligence: Why It Can Matter More Than IQ*. London: Bloomsbury Publishing Ltd.

Goleman, Daniel (2006) *Social Intelligence: The New Science of Human Relationships*. New York: Bantam Books.

Goleman, D., Boyatzis, R., and McKee, A. (2002) *Primal Leadership: Realising the Power of Emotional Intelligence*. Boston, MA: Harvard Business School Press.

Grant, A. M., and Mayer, D. M. (2009) 'Good Soldiers And Good Actors: Prosocial And Impression Management Motives As Interactive Predictors Of Affiliative Citizenship Behaviours'. *Journal of Applied Psychology*, 94: 900–912.

Hogan, J. and Holland, B. (2003) 'Using Theory To Evaluate Personality And Job Performance Relations: A Socioanalytic Perspective'. *Journal of Applied Psychology*, 88: 100–112.

Kaufman, A. S. (2009) *IQ Testing 101*. New York: Springer Publishing Company.

Kilduff, M., Chiaburu, D. S., and Menges, J. I. (2010) 'Strategic Use of Emotional Intelligence in Organizational Settings: Exploring the Dark Side'. *Research in Organizational Behaviour*, 30: 129–152.

Klein, P. D. (1998) 'A Response to Howard Gardner: Falsifiability, Empirical Evidence, and Pedagogical

Usefulness in Educational Psychologies'. *Canadian Journal of Education*, 23(1): 103–112.

Landy, F. J. (2005) 'Some Historical And Scientific Issues Related To Research On Emotional Intelligence'. *Journal of Organisational Behaviour*, 26: 411–424.

LeDoux, J. E. (1996) *The Emotional Brain: The Mysterious Underpinnings of Emotional Life*. New York: Simon & Schuster.

Locke, E. A. (2005) 'Why Emotional Intelligence is an Invalid Concept'. *Journal of Organisational Behaviour*, 26: 425–431.

Matthews, G., Zeidner, M., and Roberts, R. (2003) *Emotional Intelligence: Science & Myth*. New York: Bradford Books.

Mayer, J., Roberts, R., and Barsade, S. G. (2008) 'Human Abilities: Emotional Intelligence.' *Annual Review of Psychology*, 59: 507–536.

Mayer, J. D. and Salovey, P. (1997) 'What is Emotional Intelligence?'. In Salovey, P. and Sluyter, D. (eds) *Emotional Development and Emotional Intelligence: Implications for Educators*. New York: Basic Books.

Mayer, J. D., Salovey, P., and Caruso, D. R. (2004) 'Emotional Intelligence: Theory, Findings and Implications'. *Psychological Enquiry*, 15(3): 197–215.

Mayer, J. D., Salovey, P., Caruso, D. R., and Sitarenios, G. (2003) 'Measuring Emotional Intelligence with the MSCEI V2.0'. *Emotion*, 3: 97–105.

Palmer, B., Walls, M., Burgess, Z., and Stough, C. (2001) 'Emotional Intelligence and Effective Leadership'. *Leadership & Organisation Development Journal*, 22(1): 5–10.

Petrides, K. V., Furnham, A., and Frederickson, N. (2004) 'Emotional Intelligence'. *The Psychologist*, 17(10): 574–577.

Pillai, R. (1996) 'Crisis and the Emergence of Charismatic Leadership In Groups: An Experimental Investigation'. *Journal of Applied Social Psychology*, 26: 543–562.

Salovey, P. and Mayer, J. D. (1990) 'Emotional Intelligence'. *Imagination, Cognition, and Personality*, 9: 185–211.

Salovey, P., Mayer, J. D., and Caruso, D. (2002) 'The Positive Psychology of Emotional Intelligence'. In Snyder, C. R. and Lopez, S. J. (eds) *Handbook of Positive Psychology*. New York: Oxford University Press.

Sanchez, J. C. and Villanueva, J. J. (2007) 'Trait Emotional Intelligence and Leadership Self-Efficacy: Their Relationship with Collective Efficacy'. *Spanish Journal of Psychology*, 10(2): 349–358.

Scherer, M. (1999) 'The Understanding Pathway: A Conversation with Howard Gardner'. *Educational Leadership*, 57(3): 12–16.

Steiner, C. (1997) *Achieving Emotional Literacy. A Personal Program to Improve your Emotional Intelligence*. New York: Avon Books.

Taylor, G. J. and Taylor, H. S. (1997) 'Alexithymia'. In McCallum, M. and Piper, W. E. (eds) *Psychological Mindedness: A Contemporary Understanding*. Munich: Lawrence Erlbaum Associates.

Thorndike, R. L. and Stein, S. (1937) 'An Evaluation of the Attempts to Measure Social Intelligence'. *Psychological Bulletin*, 34: 275–284.

Walter, F., Cole, M. S., and Humphrey, R. H. (2011) 'Emotional Intelligence: sine qua non of Leadership or Folderol?'. *Academy of Management Perspectives*, February: 45–59.

Wechsler, D. (1958) *The Measurement and Appraisal of Adult Intelligence* (4th edn). Baltimore, MD: The Williams & Wilkins Company.

Chapter 12

Adler, N. J. (1996) 'Global Women Political Leaders: An Invisible History, An Increasingly Important Future'. *Leadership Quarterly*, 7: 133–161.

Allport, G. W. (1954) *The Nature of Prejudice*. Reading, MA: Addison-Wesley.

Alvesson, M. (2011) 'Leadership and Organisational Culture'. In Bryman, A., Collinson, D., Grint, K., Jackson, B., and Uhl-Bien, M. (eds) *The Sage Handbook of Leadership*. London: SAGE Publications.

Arvonen, J. and Ekvall, G. (1991) 'Change Centred Leadership: An Extension of the Two Dimensional Model'. *Scandinavian Journal of Management*, 7(1): 17–26.

Bolton, E. B. and Humphreys, L. W. (1977) 'A Training Model for Women ? An Androgynous Approach'. *Personnel Journal*, 56: 230–234.

Book, E. W. (2000) *Why The Best Man For The Job Is A Woman: The Unique Female Qualities Of Leadership*. New York: Harper.

Chin, J. L. (2010) 'Introduction to the Special Issue on Diversity and Leadership'. *American Psychologist*, 65(3): 150–156.

Dobbin, G. H. and Platz, S. J. (1986) 'Sex Differences in Leadership: How Real Are They?'. *Academy of Management Review*, 11: 118–127.

Eagly, A. H. and Carli, L. L. (2003) 'The Female Leadership Advantage: An Evaluation Of The Evidence'. *The Leadership Quarterly*, 14: 807–834.

Eagly, A. H. and Carli, L. L. (2007a) *Through The Labyrinth: The Truth About How Women Become Leaders*. Boston, MA: Harvard Business School Press.

Eagly, A. H. and Carli, L. L. (2007b) 'Women and the Labyrinth of Leadership'. *Harvard Business Review*, September: 63–71.

Eagly, A. H., Johannesen-Schmidt, M. C., and van Engen, M. (2003) 'Transformational, Transactional and Laissez-Faire Leadership Styles: A Meta-Analysis Comparing Women And Men'. *Psychological Bulletin*, 129: 569–591.

Eagly, A. H. and Karau, S. J. (2002) 'Role Congruity Theory of Prejudice Toward Female Leaders'. *Psychological Review*, 109(3): 573–659.

Gartzia, L. and van Engen, M. (2012) 'Are (Male) Leaders "Feminine" Enough? Gendered Traits of Identity as Mediators of Sex Differences in Leadership Styles'. *Gender in Management*, 27(5): 292–310.

Goldberg, P. (1968) 'Are Women Prejudiced Against Women?'. *Transaction*, 5: 316–322.

Grant Thornton (2012) 'Women in Senior Management: Still Not Enough'. *Grant Thornton International Business Report 2012*. London: Grant Thornton.

Haney, C., Banks, W. C., and Zimbardo, P. G. (1973) 'Study of Prisoners and Guards in a Simulated Prison'. *Naval Research Reviews*, 9: 1–17. Washington, DC: Office of Naval Research.

Helgesen, S. (1990) *The Female Advantage: Women's Ways of Leadership*. New York: Doubleday.

Hofstede, G. (1980) *Culture's Consequences, International Differences in Work-Related Values (Cross Cultural Research and Methodology)*. Newbury Park, CA: SAGE Publications.

House, R. J., Hanges, R. J., Javidan, M., Dorfman, P. W., and Gupta, V. (eds) (2004) *Culture, Leadership, and Organizations: The GLOBE Study of 62 Societies*. Thousand Oaks, CA: SAGE Publications.

House, R., Javidan, M., Hanges, P., and Dorfman, P. (2002) 'Understanding Cultures and Implicit Leadership Theories Across The Globe: An Introduction to Project GLOBE'. *Journal of World Business*, 37(1 Spring): 3–10.

Huddy, L. (2002) 'From Social to Political Identity: A Critical Examination of Social Identity Theory'. *Political Psychology*, 22(1): 127–156.

Jepson, D. (2009) 'Studying Leadership at Cross-Country Level: A Critical Analysis'. *Leadership*, 5(1): 61–80.

Kanter, R. (1977) *Men and Women of the Corporation*. New York: Basic Books.

Kark, R. and Waismel-Manor, R. (2005) 'Organisational Citizenship Behaviour: What's Gender got to do with it?'. *Organization*, 12: 889–917.

Kark, R., Waismel-Manor, R., and Shamir, B. (2012) 'Does Valuing Androgyny and Femininity Lead to a Female Advantage? The Relationship Between Gender-Role,

Transformational Leadership and Identification'. *The Leadership Quarterly*, 23(3): 620–640.

Koenig, A. M., Eagly, A. H., Mitchell, A. A., and Ristikari, T. (2011) 'Are Leader Stereotypes Masculine? A Meta-Analysis of Three Research Paradigms'. *Psychological Bulletin*, 137: 616–642.

Kolanad, G. (2009) *India (Culture Shock!): A Survival Guide to Customs and Etiquette*. London: Marshall Cavendish.

Korabik, K. (1990) 'Androgyny and Leadership Style'. *Journal of Business Ethics*, 9(4/5 Perspectives on Women in Management Research): 283–292.

Lord, R. and Maher, K. L. (1991) *Leadership and Information Processing: Linking Perceptions and Performance*. Boston: Unwin-Everyman.

Maier, M. (1992) 'Evolving Paradigms of Management in Organizations: A Gendered Analysis'. *Journal of Management Studies*, 4: 29–45.

Mills, D. Q. (2005) 'Asian and American Leadership Styles: How Are They Unique?'. *HBS Working Knowledge* (27 June). (Also published in *Asian Diversity Magazine*, December 2005.)

Mumford, M. D., Zaccaro, S. J., Harding, S. J., Jacobs, T. O., and Fleishman, E. A. (2000) 'Leadership Skills for a Changing World: Solving Complex Social Problems'. *The Leadership Quarterly*, 11(1, Spring): 11–35.

Mummendey, A. (1995) 'Positive Distinctiveness and Social Discrimination: An Old Couple Living in Divorce'. *European Journal of Social Psychology*, 25: 657–670.

NCVO website (2012) http://www.ncvo-vol.org.uk (accessed 8 August 2013).

Northouse, P. G. (2010) *Leadership: Theory and Practice*. London: SAGE Publications.

Office for National Statistics (2011) *2011 Annual Survey of Hours and Earnings: Key Findings*. London: ONS.

Rosette, A. S. and Tost, L. P. (2010) 'Agentic Women and Communal Leadership: How Role Prescriptions Confer Advantage to Top Women Leaders'. *Journal of Applied Psychology*, March(2): 221–235.

Sargent, A. G. (1993) *The Androgynous Manager*. New York: AMACOM.

Schien, E. (1976) 'Think Manager, Think Male'. *The Atlanta Economic Review*, March–April: 21–24.

Snowdon, G. (2011) 'Women Still Face a Glass Ceiling'. *The Guardian*, 21 February 2011.

Tajfel, H. and Turner, J. C. (1986) 'The Social Identity Theory of Intergroup Behaviour'. In Worchel, S. and Austin, W. G. (eds) *Psychology Of Intergroup Relations*. Chicago, IL: Nelson-Hall.

Tannenbaum, R. and Schmidt, W. H. (1958) 'How to Choose a Leadership Pattern'. *Harvard Business Review*, 36(March–April 1958): 95–101.

Thompson, M. (2012) 'Women Can Break Through the Glass Ceiling'. *The Independent*, 12 April 2012.

Vecchio, R. P. (2002) 'Leadership and Gender Advantage'. *The Leadership Quarterly*, 13: 643–671.

Chapter 13

Acton, Lord John (1907) 'Letter to Bishop Mandell Creighton, 5 April 1887'. In Figgis, J. N. and Laurence, R. V. (eds) *Historical Essays and Studies*. London: Macmillan.

Anon (2007) 'Book of Isaiah 40:10'. *The Holy Bible, New Living Translation*. Carol Stream, Illinois: Tyndale House Publishers, Inc.

Arendt, H. (1963) *Eichmann in Jerusalem: A Report on the Banality of Evil*. New York: Penguin.

Bass, B. (2008) *The Bass Handbook of Leadership*. New York: Free Press.

Brown, K. (2011) 'Beyond 2Badges of Honour": Young People's Perceptions of Their Anti -Social Behaviour Orders'. *People, Place & Policy Online*, 5(1): 12–24.

Castells, M. (2011) 'A Network Theory of Power'. *International Journal of Communication*, 5: 773–787.

Clayton, M. (2010) *Brilliant Influence: What the Most Influential People Know, Do and Say*. Upper Saddle River, NJ: Prentice Hall.

Eyuboglu, N. and Atac, O. A. (1991) 'Informational Power: A Means For Increased Control In Channels Of Distribution'. Psychol. Mark, 8(doi: 10.1002/mar): 197–213.

French, J. R. P. and Raven, B. (1959) 'The Bases of Social Power'. In Cartwright, D. and Zander, A. *Group Dynamics*. New York: Harper & Row.

Galbraith, J. K. (1983) *The Anatomy of Power*. Boston: Houghton Mifflin.

Gardner, J. W. (1986) *The Nature of Leadership: Introductory Considerations* (Leadership Paper 1). Washington, DC: Independent Sector.

Gaski, J. F. (1986) 'Interrelations Among a Channel Entity's Power Sources: Impact of the Exercise of Reward and Coercion on Expert, Referent, and Legitimate Power Sources'. *Journal of Marketing Research*, 23(1): 62–77.

Green, R. D. (1999) 'Leadership as a Function of Power'. *Proposal Management*, Fall: 54–56.

Guttridge, L. F. (1992) *Mutiny: A History of Naval Insurrection*. Annapolis: Naval Institute Press.

Handy, C. (1985) *Understanding Organisations*. London: Penguin Group.

Kanter, R. M. (1979) 'Power Failure in Management Circuits'. *Harvard Business Review*, 57(4): 65–75.

Kouzes, J. M. and Posner, B. Z. (1994) *The Leadership Challenge*. San Francisco, CA: Jossey-Bass.

Locke, J. (1952) *The Second Treatise on Government*. New York: Macmillan.

Michelson, B. J. (2001) 'Leadership and Power Base Development: Using Power Effectively to Manage Diversity and Job-Related Interdependence in Complex Organizations'. In Lester, R. I. (ed.) *AU24 Concepts for Air Force Leadership*. Alabama: Air University Press of Alabama.

Milgram, S. (1974) *Obedience to Authority; An Experimental View*. New York: Harper Collins.

Morgenthau, H. J. (1985) *Politics Among Nations: The Struggle for Power and Peace* (6th edn). New York: Alfred A. Knopf.

Northouse, P. G. (2010) *Leadership: Theory and Practice* (5th edn). Thousand Oaks, CA: SAGE Publications.

O'Neil, A. and McKeogh, S. (2010) 'Harnessing The Power of Reward and Recognition'. *Funworld*, 26(11): 148–150.

Pfeffer, J. (1992) 'Understanding Power in Organisations'. *California Management Review*, 34(2): 29–50.

Stewart, T. A. (1989) 'New Ways To Exercise Power; There Are Five Kinds Of Power, The Experts Say, And Chief Executives Have All Of Them At Their Disposal. But Nowadays The Best Bosses Mostly Use Just Two'. *Fortune*, 120.11(Nov. 6, 1989): 52. http://money.cnn.com/magazines/fortune/fortune_archive/1989/11/06/72713/index.htm (accessed 16 August 2013).

Toffler, A. (1990) *Powershift: Knowledge, Wealth and Violence at the Edge of the 21st Century*. New York: Random House.

Wood, A. L. (2009) *Lynching and Spectacle: Witnessing Racial Violence in America, 1890–1940*. Chapel Hill, NC: University of North Carolina Press.

Yavas, U. (1998) 'The Bases of Power in International Channels'. *International Marketing Review*, 15(2–3): 140–150.

Yukl, G. (2010) *Leadership in Organisations*. San Francisco, CA: Pearson.

Chapter 14

Allender, H. D. (1993) 'Self-Directed Work Teams: How Far is Too Far?'. *Industrial Management*, 35(5): 13–15.

Asch, S. (1951) 'Effects of Group Pressure on the Modification and Distortion of Judgements'. In Guetzkow, H. (ed.) *Groups, Leadership and Men*. New York: Carnegie Press.

Atkinson, J. (1984) *Flexibility, Uncertainty and Manpower Management*, IMS Report No. 89. Brighton, UK: Institute of Manpower Studies.

Atkinson, J. and Meager, N. (1986) *Changing Working Patterns: How Companies Achieve Flexibility to Meet New Needs*. London: Institute of Manpower Studies, National Economic Development Office.

Badie, D. (2010) 'Groupthink, Iraq, and the War on Terror: Explaining US Policy Shift toward Iraq'. *Foreign Policy Analysis*, 6(4): 277–296.

Bannister, D. and Fransella, F. (1971) *Inquiring Man*. London: Penguin.

Bartram, D. (ed.) (1995) *Review of Personality Assessment Instruments (Level B) for Use in Occupational Settings*. Leicester, UK: British Psychological Society.

Bass, B. M. and Ryterband, E. C. (1979) *Organisational Psychology* (2nd edn). London: Allyn & Bacon.

Belbin, R. M. (1981) *Management Teams: Why They Succeed Or Fail*. Oxford: Butterworth-Heinemann.

Belbin, M. (1993) *Team Roles at Work*. Oxford: Butterworth-Heinemann.

Benne, K. D. and Sheats, P. (1948) 'Functional Roles of Group Members'. *Journal of Social Issues*, 4(2): 41–48.

Blickensderfer, E., Cannon-Bowers, J. A., and Salas, E. (1997) 'Theoretical Bases for Team Self-Correction'. *Advances in Interdisciplinary Studies of Work Teams*, 4: 249–279.

Bohm, D. and Peat, F. D. (1989) *Science, Order and Creativity*. London: Routledge.

Brooks, I. (2003) *Organisational Behaviour: Individuals, Groups and Organisations* (2nd edn). Harlow: Prentice Hall.

Broucek, W. G. and Randall, G. (1996) 'An Assessment of the Construct Validity of the Belbin Self Perception Inventory and Observers Assessment from the Perspective of the 5 Factor Model'. *Journal of Occupational and Organisational Psychology*, 69: 389–405.

Buchanan, D. A. and Boddy, D. (1983) *Organisations in the Computer Age*. Aldershot: Gower.

Burgoyne, J. and Roe, K. (2007) 'Organisational Archaeology'. *Business Leadership Review* IV(III): 1–8.

Burgoyne, J., Pedler, M., and Boydell, T. (1994) *Towards the Learning Company – Concepts and Practices*. UK: McGraw-Hill.

Cannon-Bowers, J. A. and Salas, E. (1990) *Cognitive Psychology and Team Training: Shared Mental Models in Complex Systems*. Miami, FL: Society for Industrial and Organisational Psychology.

Cannon-Bowers, J. A., Salas, E., and Converse, S. (1993) 'Shared Mental Models in Expert Team Decision

Making. In Castellan Jr, N. J. (ed.) *Individual and Group Decision Makin*. Hillsdale, NJ: Erlbaum.

Casey, D. (1985) 'When is Team not a Team?'. *Personnel Management*, 17(1): 26–29.

Casey, B. and Critchley, B. (1984) 'Second Thoughts on Team Building'. *Management Education and Development*, 15(2): 163–175.

Cattell, R. B. (1946) *The Description and Measurement of Personality*. New York: World Books.

Clutterbuck, D. (1999) 'Raising the Ante on Team Learning'. *Organisations and People*, 6(4): 2–8.

Cooke, N. J. (2002) 'Team Cognition'. Online Conference available at: http://cs.bham.ac.uk/~whe/Cooke_Teams.ppt (accessed 16 August 2013).

Craik, K. (1943) *The Nature of Explanation*. Cambridge, UK: Cambridge University Press.

Diehl, M. and Stroebe, W. (1987) 'Productivity Loss in Brainstorming Groups: Towards the Solution of a Riddle'. *Journal of Personality and Social Psychology*, 53: 497–509.

Drucker, P. F. (1969) *The Age of Discontinuity*. New Jersey: Harper Row.

Drucker, P. F. (1990) *Managing the Non-Profit Organisation*. Oxford: Reed.

Drucker, P. F. (2002) *Managing in the Next Society*. New York: St Martin's Press.

Duarte, D. and Snyder, N. (2001) *Mastering Virtual Teams: Strategies, Tools and Techniques that Succeed*. California: Jossey-Bass.

Dulewicz, V. (1995) 'A Validation of Belbin's Team Roles from 16PF and OPQ Using Bosses Ratings of Competence'. *Journal of Occupational and Organisational Psychology*, (68): 81–99.

Dyer, J. L. (1984) 'Team Research & Team Training: A State-of-the-art Review'. *Human Factors Review*, 8: 285–319.

Fayol, H. (1949) *General Principles of Management* (Chapter 4 translation). Pitman, USA: Constance Storrs. (French original published 1916.)

Furnham, A., Steele, H., and Pendleton, D. (1993) 'A Psychometric Assessment of the Belbin Team Role Self-Perception Inventory'. *Journal of Occupational and Organisational Psychology*, 66: 245–257.

Gersick, C. J. (1988) 'Time and Transition in Work Teams: Towards a New Model of Group Development'. *Academy of Management Journal*, 31(1): 9–41.

Glass, N. (1996) *Management Masterclass: A Practical Guide to the New Realities of Business*. London: Nicholas Brealey.

Guzzo, R. A. and Dickson, Markus W. (1996) 'Teams in Organisations: Recent Research on Performance

& Effectiveness'. *Annual Review of Psychology*, 47: 331–338.

Guzzo, R. A. and Salas, E. S. (1995) *Team Effectiveness and Decision Making in Organisations*. San Francisco, CA: Jossey-Bass.

Guzzo, R. A. and Shea, G. P. (1993) 'Group Performance and Intergroup Relations in Organisations'. In Dunnette, M. D. and Hough, L. M. (eds) *Handbook of Industrial and Organisational Psychology* (2nd edn vol. 3). Palo Alto, CA: Consulting Psychologists Press.

Hackman, J. R. (1983) *A Normative Model of Work Team Effectiveness*. New Haven: Yale University Press.

Hackman, J. R. (1987) 'The Design of Work Teams'. In Lorsch, J. W. (ed.) *Handbook of Organisational Behaviour*. New York: Prentice Hall.

Hackman, J. R. (2002) *Leading Teams: Setting the Stage for Great Performances*. Boston: Harvard.

Handy, Charles (1984) *The Future of Work*. Oxford: Blackwell.

Handy, C. (1989) *The Age of Unreason*. London: Business Books.

Hannan, M. T. and Freeman, J. (1989) *Organizational Ecology*. Cambridge, MA: Harvard University Press.

Hine, C. (2000) *Virtual Ethnography*. London: SAGE Publications.

Hirokawa, R., Gouran, D., and Martz, A. (1988) 'Understanding the Sources of Faulty Group Decision Making: A Lesson from the Challenger Disaster'. *Small Group Behaviour*, 19: 411–433.

Hock, D. (1999) *Birth of the Chaordic Age*. San Francisco, CA: Berrett-Koehler.

Hovath, L., Callahan, J. L., Croswell, C., and Mukri, G. (1996) 'Team Sensemaking: An Imperative for Individual and Organisational Learning'. In Holton, E. F. (ed.) *Proceedings of the Academy of Human Resource Development* Minneapolis, MN, 29 February–3 March 1996.

Janis, I. (1972) *Victims of Groupthink*. Boston: Houghton Mifflin.

Jones, S. (1993) *Psychological Testing for Managers*. London: Piatkus.

Kandola, R. (1995) 'Managing Diversity: New Broom or Old Hat?'. *International Review of Industrial and Organisational Psychology*, 10: 131–167.

Katzenbach, J. R. and Smith, D. K. (1991) 'The Discipline of Teams'. *Harvard Business Review*, March/April: 111–120.

Katzenbach, J. R. and Smith, D. K. (1993) *The Wisdom of Teams: Creating the High Performance Organisation*. Cambridge, MA: Harvard University Press.

Kelly, G. A. (1955) *The Psychology of Personal Constructs*. New York: Norton.

Klimoski, R. and Mohammed, S. (1994) 'Team Mental Model, Construct or Metaphor'. *Journal of Management*, 20(2): 403–437.

Leavitt, H. J. (1983) 'Suppose We Took Groups Seriously...'. In Hackman, J. R., Lawler, E. E., and Porter, L. (eds) *Perspectives on Behaviour in Organisations*. New York: McGraw-Hill.

Lewis, J. P. (1993) *How to Build and Manage a Winning Project Team*. New York: American Management Association.

Margerison, C. J. and McCann, D. J. (1990) *Team Management: Practical new Approaches*. Mercury: London.

Margerison, C. J. and McCann, D. J. (2000) *The Handbook of TMS Accreditation*. York, UK: TMS Development International Ltd.

Margerison, C., McCann, D., and Davies, R. (1986) 'The Margerison-McCann Team Management Resource—Theory and Applications'. *International Journal of Manpower*, 7 I(2): 2–32.

Mathias, P. (1983) *The First Industrial Nation* (2nd edn). London: Methuen.

Maturana, H. and Varella, F. (1987) *The Tree of Knowledge: Biological Roots of Human Understanding*. Boston, MA: Shambala Publications.

McFletcher, D. (1996) *Teaming by Design: Real Teams for Real People*. Chicago, IL: Irwin.

McGregor, D. (1960) *The Human Side of Enterprise*. New York: McGraw-Hill.

Miles, R. E. and Snow, C. C. (1978) *Organizational Strategy, Structure, and Process*. Stanford: Stanford University Press.

Mintzberg, H. (1979) 'An Emerging Strategy of "Direct" Research'. In van Maanen, J. (ed.) *Qualitative Methodology*. Beverly Hills, CA: SAGE Publications.

Mohammed, S. and Dumville, B. (2001) 'Team Mental Models in a Team Knowledge Framework: Expanding Theory and Measurement Across Disciplinary Boundaries'. *Journal of Organisational Behaviour*, 22: 89–106.

Nahavandi, A. and Aranda, E. (1994) 'Restructuring Teams for the Re-Engineered Organisation'. *Academy of Management Executive*, 8(4): 58–68.

Obeng, E. D. A. (1994) *All Change*. London: Pitman Publishing.

Orasanu, J. and Salas, E. (1993) 'Team Decision Making in Complex Environments'. In Klein, G. A., Orasanu, J., Calderwood, R., and Zsambok, C. E. (eds) *Decision Making in Action: Models and Methods*. New York: Ablex.

Paris, C., Salas, E., and Cannon-Bowers, J. A. (2000) 'Teamwork in Multi-person Systems: A Review and Analysis'. *Ergonomics*, 43(8): 1052–1075.

Partington, D. and Harris, H. (1999) 'Team Role Balance and Team Performance: An Empirical Study'. *The Journal of Management Development*, 18(8): 694–706.

Poole, M. S. (1981) 'Decision Development in Small Groups 1: A Comparison of Two Models'. *Communication Monographs*, 48: 1–24.

Poole, M. S. (1983a) 'Decision Development in Small Groups 2: A Study of Multiple Sequences of Decision Making'. *Communication Monographs*, 50: 206–232.

Poole, M. S. (1983b) 'Decision Development in Small Groups 3: A Study of Multiple Sequences of Decision Making'. *Communication Monographs*, 50: 321–341.

Procter, S. and Mueller, F. (2000) *Teamworking*. London: Macmillan.

Ramesh, V. and Dennis, A. R. (2003) *Coordination and Communication in Global Virtual Teams: The Integrated Team and the Object-Orientated Team*. Unpublished paper presented to HICSS.

Resnick, L. B. (1991) 'Shared Cognition: Thinking as Social Practice'. In Resnick, L. B., Levine, J. M., and Teasley, S. D. (eds) *Perspectives on Socially Shared Cognition*. USA: APA.

Roe, K. (2004) *A Shared Team Mental Model*. Working Paper. Lancaster, UK: Lancaster University.

Rouse, W. B., Cannon-Bowers, J. A., and Salas, E. (1992) 'The Role of Mental Models in Team Performance in Complex Systems, IEEE Transactions on Systems'. *Man and Cybernetics*, 22: 1296–1308.

Salas, E. and Cannon-Bowers, J. (2001) 'Special Issue Preface'. *Journal of Organisational Behaviour*, 22: 87–88.

Salas, E., Dickinson, T. L., Converse, S. A., and Tannenbaum, S. I. (1992) 'Towards an Understanding of Team Performance and Training'. In Swezey, R. W. and Salas, E. (eds) *Teams: Their Training & Performance*. New Jersey: Ablex.

Scheidel, T. and Crowell, L. (1964) 'Idea Development in Small Group Discussion Groups'. *Quarterly Journal of Speech*, 50: 140–145.

Schein, E. H. (1994) *Organisational Psychology*. New Jersey: Prentice Hall.

Schein, E. H. and Bennis, W. (1965) *Personal and Organisational Change*. Chichester: J. Wiley & Sons.

Schrage, M. (1995) *No More Teams!: Mastering the Dynamics of Creative Collaborative*. New York: Doubleday.

Senge, P. M. (1990) *The Fifth Discipline: The Art and Practice of the Learning Organisation*. New York: Doubleday.

Shonk, J. H. (1992) *Team Based Organisations: Developing a Successful Team Environment*. USA: Irwin.

Sinclair, A. (1992) 'The Tyranny of a Team Ideology'. *Organisational Studies*, 13(4): 611–626.

Swezey, R. W. and Salas, E. (1992) *Teams: Their Training & Performance*. New York: Ablex.

Symons, J. (2003) 'Taking Virtual Team Control'. *Professional Manager*, March 2003: 25–29.

Tannenbaum, S. I., Salas, E., and Cannon-Bowers, J. A. (1996) 'Promoting Team Effectiveness'. In West, M. A. (ed.) *Handbook of Workgroup Psychology*. Chichester: J. Wiley & Sons.

Taylor, F. W. (1911) *Principles of Scientific Management*. London: Harper & Brothers.

TMS International Ltd. (2000) *TMS Handbook*. York: TMS International Ltd.

Tuckman, B. W. (1965) 'Developmental Sequence in Small Groups'. *Psychological Bulletin*, 63(6): 384–399.

Tuckman, B. W. and Jensen, M. (1977) 'Stages of Small Group Development'. *Group and Organisational Studies*, 2: 419–427.

Walton, R. E. and Susman, G. I. (1987) 'People Policies for the New Machines'. *Harvard Business Review*, March/April: 98–106.

Weber, M. (1947) *The Theory of Social and Economic Organisation* (Translated and edited by A. M. Henderson and T. Parsons). New York: Free Press.

Weick, K. E. and Roberts, K. H. (1993) 'Collective Mind in Organisations: Heedful Interrelating on Flight Decks'. *Administrative Science Quarterly*, 38: 357–381.

Whittington, R. (2000) *What is Strategy and Does it Matter?* (2nd edn). London: Cengage Learning.

Woodcock, M. (1979) *Team Development Manual*. Aldershot: Gower.

Zuboff, S. (1988) *In the Age of the Smart Machine: The Future of Work & Power*. Oxford: Heinemann.

Chapter 15

Arvonen, J. and Ekvall, G. (1999) 'Effective Leadership Style: Both Universal and Contingent?', *Creativity & Innovation Management*, 8(4): 242–250.

Bennis, W. (1984) 'The Four Competencies of Leadership'. *Training & Development Journal*, 38: 144–149.

Buchanan, D. and Badham, R. (1999) 'Politics and Organizational Change: The Lived Experience'. *Human Relations*, 52(5): 609–629.

Buchanan, D. and Badham, R. (2008) *Power, Politics and Organisational Change: Winning the Turf Game*. London: SAGE Publications.

Burgoyne, J., Pedler, M., and Boydell, T. (1994) *Towards the Learning Company: Concepts and Practices*. UK: McGraw-Hill.

Charlesworth, K., Cook, P., and Crozier, G. (2003) *'Leading Change in the Public Sector: Making the Difference'*. London: CMI Advisory Panel chaired by Sir Michael Bichard.

Checkland, P. (1981) *Systems Thinking, Systems Practice*. Chichester: J. Wiley & Sons.

Checkland, P. B. and Poulter, J. (2006) *Learning for Action: A Short Definitive Account of Soft Systems Methodology and its use for Practitioners, Teachers and Students*. Chichester: J. Wiley & Sons.

Grant, R. M. (1991) 'The Resource-Based Theory of Competitive Advantage: Implications for Strategy Formulation'. *California Management Review*, 33(3): 114–135.

Hardy, C. (1996) 'Understanding Power: Bringing about Strategic Change'. *British Journal of Management*, 7 (Special Issue): 3–16.

Hayes, J. (2010) *The Theory and Practice of Change Management* (3rd edn). Basingstoke: Palgrave Macmillan.

Johnson, G. (1990) 'Managing Strategic Change; The Role of Symbolic Action'. *British Journal of Management*, 1: 183–200.

Kanter, R. M. (1983) *The Change Masters: Corporate Entrepreneurs at Work*. New York: Thomson Business Publishing.

Kotter, J. P. (1995) 'Leading Change: Why Transformation Efforts Fail'. *Harvard Business Review*, 73(2): 59–67.

Kotter, J. P. (1996) *Leading Change*. Boston: Harvard Business School Press.

Kübler-Ross, E. (1969) *On Death and Dying*. London: Routledge.

Lewin, K. (1951) *Field Theory in Social Science*, New York: Harper & Row.

Machiavelli, N. (1515) *The Prince* (Translated by George Bull). London: Penguin Books.

McCalman, J. (2001) '"But I did it for the Company!" The Ethics of Organisational Politics During Times of Change'. *Reason in Practice, The Journal of Philosophy of Management*, 1(3): 57–66.

Meltzer, B. N. (2003) 'Lying: Deception in Human Affairs'. *International Journal of Sociology and Social Policy*, 23(6/7): 61–79.

Mintzberg, H. (1983) *Power in and Around Organizations*. Englewood Cliffs, NJ: Prentice Hall.

Mokyr, J. (1985) *The Lever of Riches: Technological Creativity & Economic Progress*. Oxford: Oxford University Press.

Morgan, G. (2006) *Images of Organisations*. Thousand Oaks, CA: SAGE Publications.

Paton, R. A. and McCalman, J. (2008) *Change Management: A Guide to Effective Implementation* (3rd edn). London: SAGE Publications.

Peters, T. J. and Waterman, R. H. (1982) *In Search of Excellence*. New York: Harper & Row.

Porter, M. E. (2008) 'The Five Competitive Forces that Shape Strategy'. *Harvard Business Review*, 86(1): 86–104.

Rakotobe-Joel, T., McCarthy, I. P., and Tranfield, D. (2002) 'Structural and Evolutionary Approach to Change Management'. *Computational & Mathematical Organization Theory*, 8: 337–364.

Rittel, H. and Webber, M. (1973) 'Dilemmas in a General Theory of Planning'. *Policy Sciences*, 4: 155–169. [Reprinted in Cross, N. (ed.) (1984) *Developments in Design Methodology*. Chichester: J. Wiley & Sons.]

Schein, E. H. (1996) 'Kurt Lewin's Change Theory in the Field and in the Classroom: Notes Toward a Model of Managed Learning'. *Systems Practice*, 9(1): 27–47.

Senge, P. (1990) *The Fifth Discipline: The Art and Practice of the Learning Organisation*. New York: Doubleday.

Senior, B. (2002) *Organisational Change*. Harlow: Pearson.

Stuart, R. (1995) 'Experiencing Organisational Change: Triggers, Processes and Outcomes of Change Journeys'. *Personnel Review*, 24(2): 1–87.

Waterman, R., Peters, T. and Phillips, J. (1980) 'Structure is Not Organization'. *Business Horizons*, 23(3 Jun): 14–26.

Wells, H. G. (1922) *A Short History of the World*. New York: Macmillan.

Yukl, G. and Falbe, C. M. (1990) 'Influence Tactics in Upward, Downward and Lateral Influence Attempts'. *Journal of Applied Psychology*, 75: 416–423.

Chapter 16

Bolden, R. and Gosling, J. (2006) 'Leadership Competencies: Time to Change the Tune?'. *Leadership*, 2: 147–163.

Bones, C. (2011) *The Cult of the Leader*. Chichester: J. Wiley & Sons.

Bower, M. (2003) 'Company Philosophy: "The Way We Do Things Around Here"'. *The McKinsey Quarterly*, 2: 110–117.

Boyatzis, R. E. (1982) *The Competent Manager*. New York: J. Wiley & Sons.

Brownell, J. (2006) 'Meeting the Competency Needs of Global Leaders: A Partnership Approach'. *Human Resource Management*, 45(3): 309–336.

Burgoyne, J. (1988) 'Management Development for the Individual and Organisation'. *Personnel Management*, June: 40–44.

Burgoyne, J. (2010) 'Crafting a Leadership and Management Development Strategy'. In Gold, J., Thorpe, R., and Mumford, A. (eds) *Gower Handbook of Leadership and Management Development*. Farnham: Gower.

Burgoyne, J. G. and Stuart, R. (1976) 'The Nature, Use and Acquisition of Managerial Skills and Other Attributes'. *Personnel Review*, 5(4): 19–29.

Carmichael, J., Collins, C., Emsell, P., and Haydon, J. (2011) *Leadership and Management Development*. Oxford: Oxford University Press.

Deming, W. E. (1982) *Out of the Crisis*. Cambridge, MA: MIT Press.

Fillery-Travis, A. and Lane, D. (2006) 'Does Coaching Work or Are We Asking the Wrong Question?'. *International Coaching Psychology Review*, 1(1): 23–36.

Fulmer, R. M. and Wagner, S. (1999) 'The Evolving Paradigm of Leadership Development'. *Organisational Dynamics*, 25(4): 59–72.

Gill, R. (2011) *Theory and Practice of Leadership*. London: SAGE Publications.

Jarvis, P. (2001) *Universities and Corporate Universities: The Higher Learning Industry in Global Society*. Stirling, VA: Stylus Publishing.

Johnson, G., Scholes, K., and Whittington, R. (2005) *Exploring Corporate Strategy* (7th edn). Harlow: Pearson Education.

Kearns, P. (2006) 'Does Coaching Work?'. *Training Journal*, May: 41–44.

Mabey, C. (2006) 'Management Development Works. The Evidence'. *Achieving Management Excellence Research Series 1996–2005*. London: CMI.

Mabey, C. and Salaman, G. (1995) *Strategic Human Resource Management*. Oxford: Basil Blackwell.

McBain, R., Ghobadian, A., Switzer, J., Wilton, P., Woodman, P., and Pearson, G. (2012) *The Business Benefits of Management and Leadership Development*. London: Chartered Management Institute in conjunction with Penna Consulting.

McClelland, D. C. (1973) 'Testing for Competence Rather Than for Intelligence'. *American Psychologist*, 28: 1–14.

Mintzberg, H. (1973) *The Nature of Managerial Work*. New York: Harper & Row.

Mumford, A. (1991) *The Gower Handbook of Management Development*. Farnham: Ashgate Publishing.

Naish, R. and Birdi, K. (2001) 'Evaluation of the Effects of a Management Development Centre Program on Development, Retention and Business Performance'. *Book of Proceedings*. The British Psychological Society 4–5 January 2001 Occupational Psychology Annual Conference, Winchester.

O'Neil, J. and Marsick, V. J. (2007) *Understanding Action Learning*. New York: American Management Association.

Pedler, M., Burgoyne, J. G., and Boydell, T. (2007) *A Manager's Guide to Self-Development* (5th edn). Maidenhead: McGraw-Hill.

Senge, P. (2006) *The Fifth Discipline: The Art and Practice of the Learning Organisation* (2nd edn). London: Random House.

Shivers-Blackwell, S. L. (2004) 'Reactions to Outdoor Teambuilding Initiatives in MBA Education'. *Journal of Management Development*, 23(7): 614–630.

Tao, Yu-Hui, Rosa, C., and Hung, Y. K. C. (2012) 'Effects of the Heterogeneity of Game Complexity and User Population in Learning Performance of Business Simulation Games'. *Computers & Education*, 59(4): 1350–1360.

Thorngate, W. (1976) 'Possible Limits on a Science of Social Behaviour'. In Aboud, F. E., Gergen, K. J., and Strickland, L. H. (eds) *Social Psychology in Transition*. New York, NY: Plenum Press.

Worrall, L. and Cooper, C. (2012) *The Quality of Working Life. Managers' Wellbeing, Motivation and Productivity*. London: CMI.

Whittington, R. (1993) *What is Strategy and Does it Matter?* London: Routledge.

Chapter 17

Adair, J. (1990) *Great Leaders*. Guildford: Talbot Adair Press.

Ansoff, H. I. (1965) *Corporate Strategy*. New York: McGraw-Hill.

Aspara, J., Lamberg, J.-A., Laukia, A., and Tikkanen, H. (2011) 'Strategic Management of Business Model Transformation: Lessons from Nokia'. *Management Decision*, 49(4): 622–647.

Aswathapa, K. and Dash, S. (2008) *International Human Resource Management*. Delhi: Tata McGraw-Hill.

Bass (2008) *The Bass Handbook of Leadership; Theory, Research and Managerial Applications* (4th edn). New York: Free Press.

Boal, K. and Hooijberg, R. (2001) 'Strategic Leadership Research: Moving On'. *The Leadership Quarterly*, 11(4): 519–549.

Bones, C. (2011) *The Cult of the Leader*. Chichester: J. Wiley & Sons.

Bowman, C. (1995) 'Strategy Workshops and Top Team Commitment to Strategic Change'. *Journal of Managerial Psychology*, 10(8): 4–12.

Brenkert, G. (2010) 'The Limits and Prospects of Business Ethics'. *Business Ethics Quarterly*, 20(4): 703–709.

Burgoyne, J. (2012) 'Beyond Leadership? Is it approaching its sell-by date?'. *The Grove Journal*, 1(1): 6–14.

Camisón, C. and Forés, B. (2010) 'Knowledge Absorptive Capacity: New insights for its conceptualization and measurement'. *Journal of Business Research*, 6(7): 707–715.

Castells, M. (1996) *The Rise of the Network Society*. Oxford: Blackwell.

Checkland, P. (1981) *Systems Thinking, Systems Practice*. New York: J. Wiley & Sons.

Christ, M. H., Emett, S., Summers, S. L., and Wood, D. A. (2012) 'The Effects of Preventive and Detective Controls on Employee Performance and Motivation'. *Contemporary Accounting Research*, 29(2): 432–452.

Combe, I. A., Rudd, J. M., Leeflang, P., and Greenley, G. E. (2012) 'Antecedents to Strategic Flexibility: Management cognition, firm resources and strategic options'. *European Journal of Marketing*, 46(10): 1320–1339.

Drucker, P. F. (1955) *The Practice of Management*. London: Heinemann.

Finkelstein, S., Harvey, C., and Lawton, T. (2007) *Breakout Strategy: Meeting the Challenge of Double-Digit Growth*. New York: McGraw-Hill.

Garvin, D. A. (2000) *Learning In Action. A Guide To Putting The Learning Organization To Work*. Boston, MA: Harvard Business School Press.

Gill, R. (2011) *Theory and Practice of Leadership*. London: SAGE Publications.

Grint, K. (2005) *Leadership: Limits and Possibilities*. Basingstoke: Palgrave Macmillan.

Grint, K. (2010) *Leadership; A Very Short Introduction*. Oxford: Oxford University Press.

Hambrick, D. C. (1989) 'Putting Top Managers Back in the Strategy Picture'. *Strategic Management Journal*, 10: 5–15.

Hambrick, D. C. (2007) 'Upper Echelons Theory: An Update'. *Academy of Management Review*, 32(2): 334–343.

Hambrick, D. C. and Mason, P. A. (1984) 'Upper Echelons: The Organization as a Reflection of Its Top Managers'. *Academy of Management Review*, 9: 193–206.

Honey, P. (2006) *Learning Style Questionnaire*. London: Pearson.

Ireland, R. D. and Hitt, M. (2004) 'Achieving and Maintaining Strategic Competitiveness in the 21st Century: The Role of Strategic Leadership'. *Academy of Management*, 19(4): 63–77.

Kelly, K. (1995) *Out of Control: The Rise of Neo-Biological Civilisation*. California: Addison-Wesley.

Kyläheiko, K., Jantunen, A., Puumalainen, K., and Luukka, P. (2011) 'Value of Knowledge: Technology Strategies In Different Knowledge Regimes'. *International Journal of Production Economics*, 131(1): 273–287.

Mintzberg, H. and Waters, J. A. (1985) 'Of Strategies, Deliberate and Emergent'. *Strategic Management Journal*, 6(3): 257–272.

Porter, M. E. (1985) *Competitive Advantage: Creating and Sustaining Superior Performance*. New York: Free Press.

Prahalad, C. K. and Hamel, G. (1990) 'The Core Competence of the Corporation'. *Harvard Business Review*, 68(3): 79–91.

Rickards, T. (2012) *Dilemmas of Leadership*. London: Routledge.

Senge, P. (1990) *The Fifth Discipline*. London: Century.

Senge, P., Kleiner, A., Roberts, C., Ross, R., Roth, G., and Smith, B. (1999) *The Dance of Change: The Challenges of Sustaining Momentum in Learning Organisations*. New York: Doubleday/Currency.

Sims, R. (2007) *Human Resource Management: Contemporary Issues, Challenges And Opportunities*. Charlotte, NC: IAP.

Smith, M. R. and Marx, L. (eds) (1994) *Does Technology Drive History? The Dilemma of Technological Determinism*. Cambridge, MA: MIT Press.

Whittington, R. (1993) *What is Strategy and Does it Matter?* London: Routledge.

Yan, L. and Tan, C. (2013) 'Matching Business Strategy and CIO Characteristics: The Impact on Organizational Performance'. *Journal of Business Research*, 66(2): 248–260.

Zuboff, S. (1988) *In the Age of the Smart Machine: The Future of Work and Power*. New York: Basic Books.

Index